Criminological Analyses on Global Honor Killing

Somesh Dhamija
GLA University, India

Tarun Pratap Yadav
GLA University, India

Jae-Seung Lee
Miami University, USA

Harshita Singh
Amity University, India

Myunghoon Roh
Salve Regina University, USA

Published in the United States of America by
IGI Global
701 E. Chocolate Avenue
Hershey PA, USA 17033
Tel: 717-533-8845
Fax: 717-533-8661
E-mail: cust@igi-global.com
Web site: https://www.igi-global.com

Copyright © 2025 by IGI Global. All rights reserved. No part of this publication may be reproduced, stored or distributed in any form or by any means, electronic or mechanical, including photocopying, without written permission from the publisher.
Product or company names used in this set are for identification purposes only. Inclusion of the names of the products or companies does not indicate a claim of ownership by IGI Global of the trademark or registered trademark.

Library of Congress Cataloging-in-Publication Data

CIP PENDING

ISBN13: 9798369372401
Isbn13Softcover: 9798369372449
EISBN13: 9798369372418

Vice President of Editorial: Melissa Wagner
Managing Editor of Acquisitions: Mikaela Felty
Managing Editor of Book Development: Jocelynn Hessler
Production Manager: Mike Brehm
Cover Design: Phillip Shickler

British Cataloguing in Publication Data
A Cataloguing in Publication record for this book is available from the British Library.

All work contributed to this book is new, previously-unpublished material.
The views expressed in this book are those of the authors, but not necessarily of the publisher.

Comrade Bharat Singh
(12th July 1914 - 22nd May 1979)

Editorial Advisory Board

Sinchul Back, *Department of Criminal Justice, Cybersecurity and Sociology, University of Scranton, USA*
Sung-hun Byun, *Department of Sociology, Criminal Justice, and Women's Studies, University of South Carolina Upstate, USA*
Kundaiah Jonnalagadda, *National Law University, Aurangabad, India*
Jonathan Lee, *Penn State Harrisburg, Middletown, USA*
Amar Pal Singh, *Ram Manohar Lohia National Law University, Lucknow*
Chandra Prakash Singh, *University of Lucknow, India*
Maheshwar Singh, *National Law University, Delhi, India*
Sanjay Singh, *Ram Manohar Lohiya National Law University, Lucknow, India*
Yogesh Pratap Singh, *National Law University, Tripura, India*
Manoj Kumar Sinha, *Dharmashastra National Law University, Jabalpur, India*
Yogendra Srivastava, *Hidyatullah National Law University, Raipur, India*
Anju Vali Tikoo, *University of Delhi, India*
Cassio Eduardo Zen, *Faculdade de Pinhais, Brazil and GEBRICS, Brazil*

Table of Contents

Preface xxi

Acknowledgment xxviii

Chapter 1
Honor Killing: Reasons and Perspectives Through Case Studies and
Documentaries 1
    Tapan Kumar Chandola, ICFAI University, Dehradun, India
    Garima Rajput, GLA University, Mathura, India

Chapter 2
Understanding the Criminology Behind Honor Killing 23
    Indra Kumar Singh, GLA University, Mathura, India
    Tanuj Vashistha, GLA University, Mathura, India

Chapter 3
Feminism and Honor Killing With Special Reference to the 21st Century 41
    Somesh Dhamija, GLA University, Mathura, India
    Narendra Singh, GLA University, Mathura, India

Chapter 4
The Feminist Movement and Arab Society 71
    Nishi Kant Bibhu, Bennett University, India
    Nupur Kulshrestha, GLA University, Mathura, India

Chapter 5
Family Honor and Forces of Change in Arab Society: Middle East Region 93
    Nupur Kumari, Bennett University, India
    Siddhi Baranwal, GLA University, Mathura, India

Chapter 6
Veils of Silence: The Hidden Scourge of Honor Killings in Pakistan 111
    Sudhir Kumar, Babu Banarsi Das University, India
    Aarya Arora, GLA University, Mathura, India

Chapter 7
A Study of Honor-Based Violence in the Republic of Iran 137
    Madhulika Mishra, Institute of Legal Studies and Research, GLA
        University, Mathura, India
    Tanishtha Anand, Amity University, Noida, India

Chapter 8
Honorless Honor Killings in Jordan 157
    Abhishek Kumar, Amity University, Haryana, India
    Aishna Arora, GLA University, Mathura, India

Chapter 9
A Critical Analysis of Honor-Based Violence in Lebanon 181
    Abhijit Mishra, Bennett University, India
    Radhika Goswami, GLA University, Mathura, India

Chapter 10
Honor-Related Crimes in Egypt 197
    Harshita Singh, Amity University, Noida, India
    Deeksha Pandey, GLA University, Mathura, India

Chapter 11
Demystifying the Culture and Causes of Honor Killings in Canada 215
    Abhishek Kumar, Integral University, Lucknow, India
    Aniruddh Atul Garg, GLA University, Mathura, India

Chapter 12
Legacy of Silence: Exploring Honour Killings in the Tapestry of Jewish and
Medieval European History 239
    Pradeep Kumar, Vivekananda College of Law, Aligarh, India
    Anushka Bhaskar, Amity University, Noida, India

Chapter 13
Comparative Analysis of Various Factors of Honor Killing in India and
European Countries 261
    Anurag Sharma, Vivekananda College of Law, Aligarh, India
    Salini Sharma, GLA University, Mathura, India

Chapter 14
A Critical Study of Honor-Related Violence in Germany 279
    Madhulika Mishra, GLA University, Mathura, India
    Shweta Singh, GLA University, Mathura, India

Chapter 15
Shattered Honor: Understanding and Addressing Honor-Related Crimes in
the Netherlands and India 297
    Pratibha Singh, Karnataka State Law University, Hubli, India
    Sahil Gupta, Amity University, Noida, India

Chapter 16
Honor Killing: A Socio-Legal Analysis With Special Reference to Haryana,
India 319
    Jae-Seung Lee, College of Liberal Arts and Applied Science, Miami
        University, USA
    Punya Singh, GLA University, Mathura, India

Chapter 17
Study of Judgments in India 337
    Chunyre Kim, Saint Joseph's University, USA
    Mohmmad Shoaib, GLA University, Mathura, India

Chapter 18
Honor Killing AD REM With Special Reference to Religious Dogmatism in
India 359
    Tarun Pratap Yadav, GLA University, Mathura, India
    Shanu Singh, GLA University, Mathura, India

Chapter 19
Honour Killing Among Women in India: A Scoping Review 377
    Divya Raghunath Iyengar, O.P. Jindal Global University, India
    Soumya T. Varghese, O.P. Jindal Global University, India

Chapter 20
The Dark Face and Hidden Atrocity of Honor Killing Cases in Turkey 399
    Praveen Kumar Mall, Teerthanker Mahaveer University, Moradabad,
        India
    Shreyanshi Goyal, GLA University, Mathura, India

Chapter 21
The Hidden Face of Modernity: Unravelling Honor Killings in Russia 419
   Shubham Malik, Delhi High Court, India
   Shelly Tomar, Amity University, Noida, India

Compilation of References 441

About the Contributors 473

Index 487

Detailed Table of Contents

Preface xxi

Acknowledgment xxviii

Chapter 1
Honor Killing: Reasons and Perspectives Through Case Studies and
Documentaries 1
Tapan Kumar Chandola, ICFAI University, Dehradun, India
Garima Rajput, GLA University, Mathura, India

Using a few chosen documentaries, the current study examines honor killing cases. The chapter focuses on the moral, religious and social pressures that some people face when defying social norms, which leads them to take the lives of their family members. The documentaries chosen as case studies present the perspectives of both the perpetrators and the victims when it comes to the concepts of honor, dishonor and honor killings. Some societies perceive attempts to tarnish their idealized cultural purity by rejecting progressive new ideas. In an effort to prevent their alleged negative influence on society and to set an example for future female rebellions, women who attempt to challenge established traditions are labelled as rebellious and punished. Hence the chapter examines how society's influence plays a significant role in honor killings. The chapter will also give a general overview of media reports and reported case law regarding the apparent frequency of killings related to honor.

Chapter 2
Understanding the Criminology Behind Honor Killing 23
    Indra Kumar Singh, GLA University, Mathura, India
    Tanuj Vashistha, GLA University, Mathura, India

This chapter deems to highlight the criminology, state of mind and the conditions which involves and interferes when a man thinks of honor killing as a problem which he may seem unfit to the society, at large. Furthermore, it will highlight who are involved in such crimes and how does such mindset get developed and carry forward to the coming generations. This chapter will further inquire about the stand of women so far as contributing to this mentality. Thus, making such crimes unpredictable and also raising a question upon human race and its psyche. The chapter will throw light upon the criminalization of young minds and how the crime is normalised in the society, in addition to, discussing the concentration of social power in the hands of few which eventually leads to their dominance and autonomy in re-writing the societal rulebook.

Chapter 3
Feminism and Honor Killing With Special Reference to the 21st Century 41
    Somesh Dhamija, GLA University, Mathura, India
    Narendra Singh, GLA University, Mathura, India

The chapter explores the evolution of feminism and its impact on addressing gender discrimination and promoting women's rights and equality particularly in the 21st century. The aim of the chapter is to explore the role of feminism in advocating for women's rights and dismantling patriarchal norms, with a specific focus on addressing issues such as gender pay gaps, workplace discrimination and representation in leadership roles. The chapter involves a historical analysis of the four phases of feminism. Participants include women and girls impacted by gender discrimination, as well as advocates and activists involved in promoting women's rights. The context of the study encompasses global awareness, legal reforms, educational initiatives, women's empowerment, social media, and cultural exchange. The dismantling of patriarchal norms has helped lower crimes such as honor killings and contributed to a more just and equal society.

Chapter 4
The Feminist Movement and Arab Society 71
    Nishi Kant Bibhu, Bennett University, India
    Nupur Kulshrestha, GLA University, Mathura, India

The chapter is highlighting the role of feminist movement in Arab society in the context of honour killing. Various aspects concerning honour killing are dealt under it such as, it stresses on the historical background of Arab Feminism, furthermore it is going to discuss the early forerunners of Arab feminism. It is going to observe mercy while dealing with the cases of honour killing. Further, the manner in which sheikhs in Arab region played significant role as a saviour of the woman from whims and caprices of her family. Another important aspect which is highlighted is to ensure proper values prior to killing of an individual, resulting out of honour. Furthermore, it stresses on the influence of modernization in context of honour killing. It laid emphasis on the Matthew Goldstein's theory of social normalization. Lastly, it laid emphasis over the contemporary challenges in context of honour killing.

Chapter 5
Family Honor and Forces of Change in Arab Society: Middle East Region 93
    Nupur Kumari, Bennett University, India
    Siddhi Baranwal, GLA University, Mathura, India

Honor Based violence can be defined as any form of violence that is used to safeguard family or community honor. Most of the crime victims are women. Boys and Men can also be the victim but however, this is rare. Illiteracy, unemployment, economic decline, poor support and lack of knowledge of the law are factors that increase the risk of victimization. Additionally Patriarchal groups recognize that men are the head of the family and are responsible for combating all negative attitudes that cause serious psychological harm to women in these communities, and in many other regions patriarchal system go far as considering a women as Men's property. The perpetrators of honor killings also have similar characteristics such as valuing singleness and committing violence again and again. This chapter also drew attention towards the victims of Honor Killing, in addition to highlighting various reports which shows the deteriorating conditions of women, how silence culture dominated the communities and the offences not recorded in this area .

Chapter 6
Veils of Silence: The Hidden Scourge of Honor Killings in Pakistan 111
   Sudhir Kumar, Babu Banarsi Das University, India
   Aarya Arora, GLA University, Mathura, India

Honor killings persist as a significant societal issue in Pakistan, reflecting complex intersections of culture, religion, law, and socio-economic factors. This chapter explores the diverse range of influences that contribute to the prevalence of honor killings within Pakistani society. By analyzing these factors, the chapter aims to provide a nuanced understanding of why and how honor killings occur, shedding light on both the structural and cultural dynamics that perpetuate this form of violence. The chapter examines the cultural and historical roots of honor killings in Pakistan. This chapter provides a comprehensive analysis of the factors influencing honor killings in Pakistan, offering a nuanced perspective on the cultural, religious, socio-economic, and legal dynamics that contribute to this form of violence. By elucidating these factors, the chapter contributes to broader discussions on gender-based violence, human rights, and the complexities of societal change in addressing harmful practices.

Chapter 7
A Study of Honor-Based Violence in the Republic of Iran 137
   Madhulika Mishra, Institute of Legal Studies and Research, GLA
      University, Mathura, India
   Tanishtha Anand, Amity University, Noida, India

Honor-based violence encompasses acts of violence and homicide perpetrated under the pretext of safeguarding the perceived honor or integrity of a family or community. Rooted in deep-seated cultural and traditional ideologies, this form of violence is particularly prevalent in select regions. The Republic of Iran stands out as one such nation where honor-based violence presents a significant challenge. In Iran, honor killings are predominantly driven by the notion that a woman's conduct or choices have tarnished the reputation or dignity (Matabangsa, 2011)of her family or community. These actions may include rejecting an arranged marriage, seeking divorce, or engaging in relationships outside of societal norms. Honor killings are viewed as a means to restore familial honor and preserve social cohesion (Chesler, 2010). It is important to note that honor killings are not exclusive to Iran or the Islamic world. They occur in various cultures and religions across the globe. However, the focus of this chapter is to examine the context of honor-based violence specifically in Iran.

Chapter 8
Honorless Honor Killings in Jordan 157
    Abhishek Kumar, Amity University, Haryana, India
    Aishna Arora, GLA University, Mathura, India

This study examines Jordan's socio-political stance of honor in order to understand how Jordanian culture, which is both sophisticated and based on traditional values, constructs meanings around honor killings. The majority of current research on honor crimes in Jordan suggests that not much has been learned or figured out about the relationship between the law in Jordan, honor crimes, and the perceptions of these offences among Jordanians. In order to better explore prospects for legislation and policy that would diminish these crimes, this chapter thoroughly examines the aspects that potentially explain the frequency, reasons, and persistence of honor killings in Jordan. It highlights the disparity between the nation's social and legal laws on the penalty of honor crimes, as well as the gender inequality that exists in the nation. It also sheds light on the relationship between Middle Eastern civilizations and ways of life and the prevalence of crimes done in a badge of honor. The study is predicated on a detailed analysis of court proceedings from 1993 to 2010.

Chapter 9
A Critical Analysis of Honor-Based Violence in Lebanon 181
    Abhijit Mishra, Bennett University, India
    Radhika Goswami, GLA University, Mathura, India

A violent crime known as "honor killing" is carried out by one or more people with the goal of restoring honor to their family. The chapter looks into the Eastern Mediterranean region's honor killing epidemic. In addition, the legal, cultural, and societal facets of honor killing in Lebanon are covered. The practice of killing for honor is influenced by a variety of sociocultural elements in this area. These include of having little education, wanting to preserve one's social standing, and strongly ingrained patriarchal dominance. Criminals that commit honor killings often share traits, such as appraising female chastity more highly and endorsing violence against women. Honor killing has a far bigger effect on family members than families may think since the community disapproves of the woman's dishonorable behaviour. These civilizations are dominated by a silence culture, and there are a lot of crimes in this area that go unreported.

Chapter 10
Honor-Related Crimes in Egypt 197
   Harshita Singh, Amity University, Noida, India
   Deeksha Pandey, GLA University, Mathura, India

In Egypt, honor-related crimes constitute a complex and deeply rooted societal issue, reflecting a convergence of cultural norms, patriarchal structures, and legal ambiguities. These crimes predominantly target women perceived to have brought shame upon their families through alleged moral transgressions, such as premarital sex, extramarital affairs, or even suspicion thereof. The concept of family honor intertwines with societal expectations of female chastity and obedience, often enforced through rigid social codes and religious interpretations. Despite legislative reforms aimed at protecting women's rights, including amendments to penal codes, the implementation remains inconsistent, influenced by familial and community pressures, as well as perceptions of shame and dishonor.

Chapter 11
Demystifying the Culture and Causes of Honor Killings in Canada 215
   Abhishek Kumar, Integral University, Lucknow, India
   Aniruddh Atul Garg, GLA University, Mathura, India

The chapter aims to unfold the mishaps of honor killings in the Canadian context comprising its key causes, and issues leading to honor-based offenses against the women in the family. Although, honor killings in Canada are rare to notice, but are prevalent majorly due to immigrant communities. The chapter also demystifies the case studies which witnessed honor killings in Canada. The Shafia case which is one of the landmark cases of the honor killing in Kingston, Canada led to the painful demise of three daughters and the first wife of Mohd. Shafia. Furthermore, it also explores the Canadian media reports on honor killing and how they create a biased view regarding the incidents surrounding these crimes in the public domain. In conclusion, several ways are highlighted upon which the Canadian government should act in order to diminish the prevalence of honor-based violence throughout Canada such as introducing effective immigration policies and making aware the youth of the laws concerning gender equality, freedom, and fairness.

Chapter 12
Legacy of Silence: Exploring Honour Killings in the Tapestry of Jewish and
Medieval European History 239
    Pradeep Kumar, Vivekanada College of Law, Aligarh, India
    Anushka Bhaskar, Amity University, Noida, India

In "Legacy of Silence," we embark on a profound exploration of the grim phenomenon of honour killings, particularly as it intertwines with the intricate historical fabrics of Jewish and Medieval European societies. This chapter seeks to shed light on a topic often shrouded in obscurity and misunderstanding, drawing connections between past traditions and the remnants of these practices in contemporary societies. By delving into the historical contexts of Jewish and Medieval European cultures, we aim to uncover the roots, manifestations, and enduring impacts of honour killings in these societies. This exploration is not only a journey through time but also a critical examination of the cultural, religious, and social underpinnings that have perpetuated such acts of violence.

Chapter 13
Comparative Analysis of Various Factors of Honor Killing in India and
European Countries 261
    Anurag Sharma, Vivekananda College of Law, Aligarh, India
    Salini Sharma, GLA University, Mathura, India

"Honor killings are the darkest manifestation of a society's fear of change and the loss of patriarchal control." Indeed, such killings are not crimes of honor, rather crime of horror. Protecting honor can never be the justification of murdering someone. Its supporters try to justify as are the sole method to restore honor & reputation of the family. This argument is contradictory in itself as how could honor be restored when there will be stain of being murderer on the family following such killing? In fact, the hidden motive behind these killing is nothing but to establish dominance and suppressing the voice of anyone who tries to free oneself from such shackles of patriarchy and orthodox practices. There are various factors behind such killings which vary from region to region. These factors include social, educational, economic, cultural, regional, religious believes, patriarchal norms etc. In this chapter, factors behind honor killings in India vis-à-vis European countries, i.e., France, Germany, Italy, Netherlands, Norway, Russia and Sweden have been examined carefully.

Chapter 14
A Critical Study of Honor-Related Violence in Germany 279
    Madhulika Mishra, GLA University, Mathura, India
    Shweta Singh, GLA University, Mathura, India

This chapter delves into the multifaceted issue of honor-related violence in Germany, examining the responsibilities of families, the state, and civic entities in preventing such crimes. It begins by defining honor-related violence, emphasizing that it is a significant social problem that predominantly affects women and often stems from patriarchal notions of family honor. The chapter scrutinizes the concept of "honor killing," exploring whether Islamic teachings support or condemn this practice. It elucidates that while some perpetrators may claim religious justification, mainstream Islamic theology and scholars overwhelmingly reject honor killings as un-Islamic and contrary to the principles of justice and compassion. By investigating the root causes, the chapter identifies factors such as patriarchal cultural norms, social pressures, and the struggle to maintain traditional values within a Western context as key drivers of honor-related violence.

Chapter 15
Shattered Honor: Understanding and Addressing Honor-Related Crimes in
the Netherlands and India 297
    Pratibha Singh, Karnataka State Law University, Hubli, India
    Sahil Gupta, Amity University, Noida, India

Honor killings motivated by false ideas of communal honor remain a tragically pervasive social problem in a variety of cultural contexts. This chapter examines honor killings in India and the Netherlands, two countries that have different legal systems, social structures, and cultural backgrounds yet are united in their opposition to this horrible behavior. The research employs a multifaceted method to investigate the historical and contemporary elements that have shaped honor killings in each nation. It investigates how cultural norms, gender inequality, and patriarchy contribute to this violence. This chapter examines the existing legislative frameworks and enforcement measures aimed at curbing honor killings, emphasizing the advantages and disadvantages of each in the given situations. In the end, the goal of this comparative research is to pinpoint possible best practices and practical approaches to stop and end honor killings.

Chapter 16
Honor Killing: A Socio-Legal Analysis With Special Reference to Haryana,
India 319
    Jae-Seung Lee, College of Liberal Arts and Applied Science, Miami
        University, USA
    Punya Singh, GLA University, Mathura, India

The research was carried out using a detailed study of the case, content evaluation techniques, and an observational-analytical framework. According to the report, honor-based crime arises when parents are intolerant of their daughters' premarital relationships and marital choices, particularly when these decisions involve marriages between different castes or religions. The study also notes that a significant proportion of killings based on honor are carried out as crimes of passion sparked by unexpected incitement when the girls' families discover the couples in precarious conditions. It has been observed that the traditional beliefs of a culture dominated by males prevent girls from forming connections before marriage or from selecting the men they wish to wed. Honor killings are a common practice with social and cultural context legality due to the society's support and poor enforcement of the law. Thus, despite enacting strict rules and harsh penalties to address the issue, The chapter will deal with the above problems with special reference to Haryana, India.

Chapter 17
Study of Judgments in India 337
    Chunyre Kim, Saint Joseph's University, USA
    Mohmmad Shoaib, GLA University, Mathura, India

The praiseworthy peculiarity killings in India have been a longstanding issue, well established in friendly, social, and familial elements. Honor killings, frequently executed against people who oppose customary cultural standards in regard to rank, religion, or between position relationships, certainly stand out both locally and universally. These demonstrations of viciousness, serious for the sake of protecting family honor or station virtue, have brought up basic issues about equity, common liberties, and law and order in India. This exposition looks at the advancement of legal perspectives and approaches towards honor killings in India, breaking down eminent decisions that have molded lawful talk and affected cultural discernment. By diving into the legitimate standards, points of reference, and cultural ramifications of these decisions, this paper looks to give a far-reaching comprehension of the legal reaction to respect killings in India and the continuous mission for equity and responsibility even with settled in social practices.

Chapter 18
Honor Killing AD REM With Special Reference to Religious Dogmatism in
India 359
    Tarun Pratap Yadav, GLA University, Mathura, India
    Shanu Singh, GLA University, Mathura, India

Chapter covers Honor Killing from the prism of religious dogmatism, intersection of culture and religion and case studies. Further legal provisions, penalties, protective measures, solutions and a way forward have also been highlighted in the chapter. According to Hindu religion, marrying or having intimacy with a member of a different caste and religion is strictly forbidden. Although Islam does not categorically countersign killing female family members, some honor killing entail contention of adultery, which are indictable by death under Islamic law. The preservation of women's virginity and "sexual compelling" are considered to be the burden of male relatives like her father, brother and then her husband. However, a women can intend for murder for a variety of discernment, that includes refusing to enter into an arranged marriage or divorce or separation. They think that women have acted in manner that could damage her family's notoriety. Amusingly, female relatives usually contend the killing and help set them up. All the above have been substantially elaborated in the chapter.

Chapter 19
Honour Killing Among Women in India: A Scoping Review 377
    Divya Raghunath Iyengar, O.P. Jindal Global University, India
    Soumya T. Varghese, O.P. Jindal Global University, India

Honor killing is a form of homicide where an individual becomes a victim if s/he engages in any act, unacceptable to the norms of the society. As per the data reported by National Crime Records Bureau (NCRB), crime rate with respect to honor killing has seen a rise in the last few years. Women are more likely to become victims because they are assumed to bear the weight of protecting the family honor and any deviance from the family's protocol is considered to affect the prestige of the family. Recent research has also found individuals belonging to LGBTQ community to also be a victim of honor killing. Given this backdrop, the current research reviews the literature regarding honor killing with the objective of understanding why women are more prone to be victims of honor killing. Further it aims to trace the role of technology, social and cultural aspects of honor killing. Research will aid in contributing to literature by identifying gaps in policy and human rights interventions to facilitate better implementation and advocacy regarding honor killing and help reduce crime in India.

Chapter 20
The Dark Face and Hidden Atrocity of Honor Killing Cases in Turkey 399
*Praveen Kumar Mall, Teerthanker Mahaveer University, Moradabad,
  India*
Shreyanshi Goyal, GLA University, Mathura, India

Several key research questions will be addressed in this chapter: 1. What is the Prevalence of Honor Killing in Turkey? 2. What are the cultural and societal factors that contribute to the prevalence of honor killings in Turkey? 3. What are the Prejudices and Misconceptions Associated with Honor Killing? 4. Exploring Gender Roles in Honor Killing Incidents in Turkey. 5. Laws and Punishments for Honor Killing in Turkey. 6. What is the Role of Community in Propagating Honor Killings? 7. Understanding the Impact of Honor Killings on Turkish Society. 8. Recommendations for Eradicating Honor Killings in Turkey. In order to address these research questions, the chapter will utilize a mixed-methods approach, combining qualitative interviews and analysis of existing literature on honor killings in Turkey. The findings from this research chapter will contribute to a deeper understanding of the social prejudice surrounding honor killings in Turkey and provide insights for developing targeted interventions and strategies to combat and eradicate this form of violence.

Chapter 21
The Hidden Face of Modernity: Unravelling Honor Killings in Russia 419
Shubham Malik, Delhi High Court, India
Shelly Tomar, Amity University, Noida, India

The chapter dives into the darkened dimensions of modernity in Russia, shedding light on the holding on the issue of honor Killing. Despite the country's rapid advancement towards cutting-edge values, profoundly imbued social standards and patriarchal structures contribute to the surreptitious propagation of savagery. Through an intrigue focal point, this chapter analyses the authentic, social, lawful, and mental variables that focalize the covered-up confront of modernity surrounding Honor Killing in Russia. By examining particular cases, analyzing societal demeanors, and assessing the adequacy of lawful systems, the ponder points to uncover the complexities of this wonder. Moreover, it investigates the effect of Honor Killing on women's rights, worker communities, and the broader societal texture. The discoveries of this chapter are significant for illuminating arrangements, intercessions, and instructive activities that profoundly established standards that propagate Honor Killings within the modern Russian context.

Compilation of References 441

About the Contributors 473

Index 487

Preface

In today's world, where discussions on human rights and equality are at the forefront, the grim reality of honor killings remains a stark contrast. Honor killings, though often unnoticed or unreported, persist as a pervasive and insidious problem that affects societies worldwide. The need for a coherent and urgent national and international response to this problem is undeniable, and this book, *Criminological Analyses on Global Honor Killing*, is a step towards addressing this challenge.

This book delves into the evolution of the concept of honor killings and presents a thorough examination of the subject, combining criminological insights with socio-cultural analyses. The contributors of this volume have brought to light new developments, legal frameworks, and evolving ideologies surrounding honor killings. The contributors emphasize that addressing the issue of honor killing requires more than just data collection, monitoring, and risk assessment. A well-defined response should also prioritize resource allocation and provide justice and protection for the most vulnerable, particularly women.

At the heart of the analysis, this book highlights the deeply rooted patriarchal structures that perpetuate honor-based crimes, as well as the complex family dynamics and societal pressures that facilitate them. By exploring the criminology behind these acts, the role of class conflicts, and the impact of immigration on the spread of this crime, we attempt to provide a holistic perspective. The focus is not only on honor killings in South Asian, Middle Eastern, and Arab countries but also on their global ramifications as immigrants bring these practices into Western Europe, North America, and beyond.

This book also tackles under-discussed issues like the abuse faced by transgender individuals that can lead to honor-related crimes. A comparative analysis of the legal systems across different countries is undertaken, focusing on the gaps and necessary reforms. Additionally, the book looks into the role of international conventions, especially the CEDAW (Convention on the Elimination of All Forms of Discrimination Against Women), and advocates for more stringent global legal measures.

The manuscript concludes with a detailed exploration of honor killings in Jewish and Medieval European societies, giving historical context to this practice. The reader is urged to reflect on the urgent need for a multifaceted approach to combating honor killings—one that goes beyond the law and involves community-based, proactive interventions.

We sincerely hope that this book will prompt critical thought and foster productive discussions among policymakers, academics, and practitioners alike, to drive real and lasting change.

ORGANIZATION OF THE BOOK

In Chapter 1, *Honor Killing: Reasons and Perspectives through Case Studies and Documentaries* the authors analyze honor killing through the lens of selected documentaries. These cases reveal the moral, religious, and social pressures that lead individuals to commit these crimes, highlighting the perspectives of both victims and perpetrators regarding the concepts of honor and dishonor. The chapter further explores how attempts to challenge cultural norms, especially by women, are often met with harsh punishment to uphold traditional values. A general overview of media reports and legal cases is also provided, emphasizing the societal influence behind honor killings.

Chapter 2, *Understanding the Criminology Behind Honor Killing* delves into the psychological and social factors that contribute to honor killings. It discusses the mindset and conditions that drive individuals to commit these crimes and examines the generational transmission of this mentality. The chapter raises critical questions about the human psyche, particularly how the criminalization of youth and the normalization of such violence perpetuate these acts. It also explores the concentration of social power in patriarchal hands, leading to dominance and autonomy in rewriting societal norms.

Chapter 3, *Feminism and Honor Killing with Special Reference to 21st Century*, explores the role of feminism in addressing honor killings by challenging patriarchal norms and advocating for women's rights. Through a historical analysis of feminism's evolution, the chapter discusses how dismantling patriarchal structures has contributed to reducing crimes such as honor killings. The authors emphasize the importance of global awareness, legal reforms, and women's empowerment in creating a more equal and just society.

Chapter 4, *The Feminist Movement and Arab Society* examines the influence of the feminist movement in Arab society concerning honor killings. The chapter traces the historical roots of Arab feminism, highlighting early pioneers and discussing how modernization and sheikhs in the region have played roles in mitigating these crimes. The authors also emphasize Matthew Goldstein's theory of social normalization and the contemporary challenges in addressing honor killings in Arab contexts.

In Chapter 5, *Family Honor and Forces of Change in Arab Society: Middle East Region*, the authors investigate honor-based violence in the Middle East, particularly how patriarchal systems perpetuate these crimes by treating women as property and enforcing rigid gender roles. The chapter emphasizes the impact of factors such as illiteracy, unemployment, and economic decline on the prevalence of honor killings, while also highlighting the silence culture and the lack of recorded offenses, which contribute to the persistence of these acts.

Chapter 6, *Veils of Silence: The Hidden Scourge of Honor Killings in Pakistan* explores the complex interplay of culture, religion, and socio-economic factors that fuel honor killings in Pakistan. The chapter traces the historical and cultural roots of these crimes, providing an in-depth analysis of how societal pressures, patriarchal norms, and legal ambiguities contribute to this violence. The authors offer a comprehensive view of the issue, contributing to broader discussions on gender-based violence and human rights in Pakistan.

In Chapter 7, *A Study of Honor Based Violence in the Republic of Iran*, the authors explore honor-based violence in Iran, where such crimes are driven by cultural and traditional ideologies. The chapter discusses how societal norms, particularly around women's behavior, contribute to the perpetuation of these crimes, offering a nuanced examination of the cultural context and its impact on gender relations in Iran. The authors also contextualize honor-based violence globally, while focusing on the specific challenges faced by Iran.

Chapter 8, *Honorless Honor Killings in Jordan*, analyzes the socio-political landscape in Jordan, revealing how traditional values and legal inconsistencies contribute to the persistence of honor killings. The chapter draws attention to the disparity between social and legal views on honor crimes, emphasizing the need for stronger legislation and social reforms to combat these crimes. Through a thorough analysis of court proceedings, the authors offer insights into the complex relationship between Jordanian society, law, and honor killings.

Chapter 9, *A Critical Analysis of Honor Based Violence in Lebanon,* looks into the Eastern Mediterranean region's honor killing epidemic. In addition, the legal, cultural, and societal facets of honor killing in Lebanon are covered. The practice of killing for honor is influenced by a variety of sociocultural elements in this area. These include having little education, wanting to preserve one's social standing, and strongly ingrained patriarchal dominance. Criminals that commit honor killings often share traits, such as appraising female chastity more highly and endorsing violence against women. Honor killing has a far bigger effect on family members than families may think since the community disapproves of the woman's dishonorable behavior. These civilizations are dominated by a silence culture, and there are a lot of crimes in this area that go unreported.

Chapter 10, *Honor-Related Crimes in Egypt* addresses the cultural and legal challenges surrounding honor-related crimes in Egypt. The chapter discusses how patriarchal structures, religious interpretations, and societal expectations of female behavior fuel these crimes, despite legal reforms aimed at protecting women. The authors explore the inconsistency in the implementation of these laws and the broader societal pressures that hinder efforts to combat honor-based violence.

Chapter 11, *Demystifying the Culture and Causes of Honor Killings in Canada* highlights the occurrence of honor killings in Canada, particularly among immigrant communities. The chapter analyzes case studies, such as the Shafia case, and explores how Canadian media coverage shapes public perception of these crimes. The authors propose strategies for reducing honor-based violence in Canada, emphasizing the importance of effective immigration policies, and raising awareness about gender equality.

Through Chapter 12, *Legacy of Silence Exploring Honour Killings in the Tapestry of Jewish and Medieval European History,* we embark on a profound exploration of the grim phenomenon of honor killings, particularly as it intertwines with the intricate historical fabrics of Jewish and Medieval European societies. This chapter seeks to shed light on a topic often shrouded in obscurity and misunderstanding, drawing connections between past traditions and the remnants of these practices in contemporary societies. By delving into the historical contexts of Jewish and Medieval European (Brundage & James A, 1987) cultures, we aim to uncover the roots, manifestations, and enduring impacts of honor killings in these societies. This exploration is not only a journey through time but also a critical examination of the cultural, religious, and social underpinnings that have perpetuated such acts of violence.

In Chapter 13, *Comparative Analysis of Various Factors of Honor Killing in India and European Countries*, the authors compare the factors behind honor killings in India and select European nations. The chapter examines how social, cultural, and patriarchal norms drive these crimes in different regions, offering insights into the varying motivations and justifications for honor killings across cultures. The authors provide a thorough analysis of the factors contributing to these crimes in both contexts.

Chapter 14, *A Critical Study of Honor-Related Violence in Germany* scrutinizes the issue of honor-related violence in Germany, focusing on the responsibilities of families, the state, and civic entities in preventing these crimes. The chapter explores the role of patriarchal cultural norms and religious interpretations, while highlighting the legal and social efforts to combat honor killings in a Western context. Through an analysis of Islamic teachings, the authors clarify misconceptions surrounding religion and honor killings.

Chapter 15, *Shattered Honor: Understanding and Addressing Honor-Related Crimes in the Netherlands and India* offers a comparative analysis of honor killings in two distinct cultural and legal contexts. The chapter examines the historical and contemporary factors contributing to these crimes in India and the Netherlands, highlighting cultural norms, gender inequality, and legal frameworks. The authors propose potential best practices for addressing and preventing honor killings in both countries.

Chapter 16, *Honor Killing: A Socio-Legal Analysis with Special Reference to Haryana, India*, explores the socio-legal aspects of honor killings in Haryana, India. The chapter examines how cultural beliefs and patriarchal norms fuel these crimes, particularly when it comes to inter-caste and inter-religious marriages. The authors analyze the legal framework and its enforcement, offering insights into the societal support that enables honor killings to persist despite stringent laws.

Chapter 17, *Honor Killing: Study of Judgments in India* provides a legal analysis of honor killings in India, focusing on how judicial decisions have shaped the country's approach to these crimes. The chapter explores landmark judgments and their impact on societal perceptions, offering a comprehensive understanding of the legal response to honor killings and the ongoing struggle for justice in the face of entrenched cultural practices.

In Chapter 18, *Honor Killing AD REM with Special Reference to Religious Dogmatism in India*, Tarun Yadav and Shanu Singh examine the intersection of religion, culture, and honor killings in India. The chapter discusses how religious dogmatism influences the practice of honor killings, with case studies highlighting the legal provisions, penalties, and protective measures in place. The authors also explore how societal attitudes and family dynamics contribute to these crimes, offering potential solutions for addressing honor-based violence in India.

Chapter 19, *Honour Killing Among Women in India: A Scoping Review*, describes Honor killing as a form of homicide where an individual becomes a victim if s/he engages in any act, unacceptable to the norms of the society. As per the data reported by National Crime Records Bureau (NCRB), crime rate with respect to honor killing has seen a rise in the last few years. Women are more likely to become victims because they are assumed to bear the weight of protecting the family honor and any deviance from the family's protocol is considered to affect the prestige of the family. Recent research has also found individuals belonging to LGBTQ community to also be a victim of honor killing. Given this backdrop, the current research reviews the literature regarding honor killing with the objective of understanding why women are more prone to be victims of honor killing. Further it aims to trace the role of technology, social and cultural aspects of honor killing. Research will aid in contributing to literature by identifying gaps in policy and human rights interventions to facilitate better implementation and advocacy regarding honor killing and help reduce crime in India.

Chapter 20, titled "The Dark Face and Hidden Atrocity of Honor Killing Cases in Turkey" delves into various critical aspects of honor killings in Turkey. It investigates the prevalence of these killings and explores the cultural and societal factors that contribute to their continuation. The chapter also seeks to dismantle prejudices and misconceptions related to honor killings, focusing on the gender roles implicated in these incidents. In addition, it evaluates the laws and punishments for such acts, the role of communities in perpetuating this violence, and the broader impact on Turkish society. Through a mixed-methods approach—combining qualitative interviews with existing literature—the chapter not only enhances understanding of the social prejudices surrounding honor killings but also provides concrete recommendations for targeted interventions to help combat and eventually eradicate this form of violence in Turkey.

Finally, Chapter 21, *The Hidden Face of Modernity Unravelling Honor Killings in Russia,* dives into the darkened dimensions of modernity in Russia, shedding light on the holding on the issue of honor Killing(Singh, n.d.). Despite the country's rapid advancement towards cutting-edge values, profoundly imbued social standards and patriarchal structures contribute to the surreptitious propagation of savagery. Through an intrigue focal point, this chapter analyses the authentic, social, lawful, and mental variables that focalize the covered-up confront of modernity surrounding Honor Killing in Russia. By examining particular cases, analyzing societal demeanors, and assessing the adequacy of lawful systems, the ponder points to uncover the complexities of this wonder. Moreover, it investigates the effect of Honor Killing on women's rights, worker communities, and the broader societal texture. The discoveries of this chapter are significant for illuminating arrangements, intercessions, and instructive activities that profoundly established standards that propagate Honor Killings within the modern Russian context.

IN CONCLUSION

As editors of *Criminological Analyses on Global Honor Killing*, we hope that this book provides readers with a comprehensive and nuanced understanding of the complex and deeply rooted issue of honor killings across different cultures and societies. The chapters within this volume bring together diverse perspectives, case studies, and research methodologies to explore the multifaceted nature of honor killings, shedding light on both the historical and contemporary contexts that allow this form of violence to persist. By analyzing legal frameworks, cultural dynamics, gender roles, and societal pressures, the contributors present critical insights that not only inform academic discourse but also offer practical solutions for policy development, legal reform, and community intervention.

Our goal with this book is to foster a broader awareness of honor killings and to highlight the urgent need for global collaboration in addressing this human rights violation. The interdisciplinary approaches showcased in this volume underscore the necessity of combining criminological, sociological, legal, and anthropological lenses to fully comprehend the scope of honor killings and their impact on individuals, families, and societies. Through these analyses, we aim to challenge prevailing misconceptions, expose the structural inequalities that contribute to these atrocities, and inspire meaningful action.

In conclusion, *Criminological Analyses on Global Honor Killing* serves as both an academic resource and a call to action. It is our hope that the knowledge and insights presented in this book will contribute to ongoing efforts to combat honor killings and inspire change at the global, national, and community levels. Together, we can work toward a future where such acts of violence are not only condemned but eradicated, fostering a world that upholds the dignity and rights of all individuals.

Acknowledgment

First of all, we would like to thank the Almighty God with whose help everything becomes possible.

We owe our sincere thanks and profound gratitude to all the contributors of the book for their invaluable guidance and encouraging attitude in completing this manuscript. They gave all encouragement and help as a guide. A special thanks to the student editors namely Tanisha Jain and Aayushi Singh without whose support this book would not have been possible.

The book offers an in-depth analysis of Honor based crimes around the globe. Few books are available on this topic and a dire need is felt to have an academic discussion so as to make this crime visible in the eyes of public. The book reflects the ideology behind Honor Killing as well as the role of Patriarchal societies in enhancing the crime. It further elucidates the concept of Gender Equality in totality and the views of various thinkers on it, in addition to, covering socio-culture based factors and demystifying the evolution of global legal framework vis-à-vis honor killing. Hence, we are obliged to various Governments around the world, Civil Society Groups, NGOs, Self Help Groups for providing data, reports and surveys vis-a-vis associated factors causing Honor Killing around the world.

We are also indebted to the staff members of the Library of Salve Regina University, USA, Library of Miami University, USA, Indian Law Institute, India, Library of University of Delhi, India, Library of Jawaharlal Nehru University, India, Library of Manipal Academy of Higher Education, India, Library of Amity University, India, Library of GLA University, India and Library of Chaudhary Charan Singh University, Meerut, India for their generous help.

Our heartfelt thanks to our better halves, who always supported us, taken full interest in our topic from the starting point of this book and co-operated us till the end. A sweet thanks to our parents and elders for their blessing and good wishes.

We are thankful to the learned teachers, scholars, friends and relatives who have assisted us in completing this book. This work would not have been possible without their valuable support and assistance. We are grateful to various legal luminaries whose scholarly and celebrated works have been helpful in completing the book.

Last but not the least we would like to thank all persons directly or indirectly related to the book.

Chapter 1
Honor Killing:
Reasons and Perspectives Through Case Studies and Documentaries

Tapan Kumar Chandola
ICFAI University, Dehradun, India

Garima Rajput
GLA University, Mathura, India

ABSTRACT

Using a few chosen documentaries, the current study examines honor killing cases. The chapter focuses on the moral, religious and social pressures that some people face when defying social norms, which leads them to take the lives of their family members. The documentaries chosen as case studies present the perspectives of both the perpetrators and the victims when it comes to the concepts of honor, dishonor and honor killings (Singh & Bhandari, 2021). Some societies perceive attempts to tarnish their idealized cultural purity by rejecting progressive new ideas. In an effort to prevent their alleged negative influence on society and to set an example for future female rebellions, women who attempt to challenge established traditions are labelled as rebellious and punished. Hence the chapter examines how society's influence plays a significant role in honor killings. The chapter will also give a general overview of media reports and reported case law regarding the apparent frequency of killings related to honor.

DOI: 10.4018/979-8-3693-7240-1.ch001

STATISTICAL DATA

Many tragic events, particularly honor killings, often go unreported officially due to various socio-cultural factors. Instead, these incidents circulate as rumors or unverified stories, making it challenging to ascertain and document the truth. The lack of formal reporting is often due to societal norms that tacitly condone such practices. Family members and others in the community may actively participate in concealing these events when they occur. Various cover-up narratives are employed, such as claiming accidental deaths during firearm maintenance. These fabricated explanations are typically supported by male community members and subsequently reported in the media as factual. As a result of these dynamics, honor killings appear to be non-existent in official records and reports, effectively masking their continued occurrence.

During the Libyan civil war, activists from the American organization Physicians for Human Rights reported a disturbing incident. According to their account, three teenage girls were sexually assaulted by forces aligned with the ruling regime at an educational institution in Misrata. In the aftermath of this trauma, the girls' father allegedly took their lives, citing family honor as the motivation for his actions. (Zawati, 2012)

Pakistan is believed to have the highest incidence of honor killings globally. According to the Pakistan Ministry of Interior, 4,101 honor crime cases were reported to courts between 1998 and 2003. The Human Rights Commission of Pakistan has noted a continuous rise in honor killings: 869 cases in 2013, an estimated 1,000 in 2014, and 1,100 in 2015. (Heydari, A., Teymoori, A., & Trappes, R., 2021) A 2009 study in Pakistan attempted to quantify honor killings over a four-year period. It found that 1,957 women were killed following accusations of extramarital relationships. Of these victims, 88% were married, and 18% were minors under 18 years old. (Nasrullah, M., Haqqi, S., & Cummings, K. J., 2009)

These statistics highlight the prevalence and severity of honor killings in Pakistan, showing a troubling upward trend and revealing that victims are often married women, with a significant number being underage. The data underscores the urgent need for addressing this issue within Pakistani society.

According to data from the Afghanistan Independent Human Rights Commission, 243 instances of honor killings were officially recorded in Afghanistan over a two-year period, spanning from March 2011 to April 2013. (Gibbs, A., Said, N., Corboz, J., & Jewkes, R., 2019) This statistic provides a glimpse into the prevalence of honor killings in Afghanistan during that specific timeframe. It's important to note that these figures represent only the documented cases, and the actual number may be higher due to underreporting or difficulties in data collection, especially in more remote or conflict-affected areas of the country.

Honor killings in Iran were predominantly reported in less developed regions, particularly Khuzestan and Kurdistan. In 2004, the Ministry of Justice in Khuzestan documented 54 cases of honor killings. Strikingly, the police department in Khuzestan revealed that over 40% of all murders in the region were committed in the name of honor. This statistic underscores the significant role that perceived family honor plays in violent crimes in this area of Iran. (Heydari, A., Teymoori, A., & Trappes, R., 2021)

A study in Iran revealed approximately 8,000 reported honor killings between 2010 and 2014. In certain areas, such as East Azerbaijan province, honor killings accounted for 20% of all murders and 50% of family-related homicides. The research found a correlation between higher rates of honor killings and increased unemployment and poverty. This suggests a link between socioeconomic factors and the prevalence of such crimes. During the COVID-19 pandemic, incidents of honor killings increased not only in Iran but globally. Factors such as lockdowns, isolation, and financial insecurity are believed to have heightened stress levels and worsened socioeconomic conditions. These impacts were particularly severe for disadvantaged groups, potentially increasing the likelihood of men resorting to violence. (Pirnia, B., Pirnia, F., & Pirnia, K., 2020)

The prevalence of honor killings has been documented across several Middle Eastern countries. In Jordan, 50 cases of honor killings were reported over a decade, from 2000 to 2010. Egypt saw 52 cases of honor killings in 1997 alone. Yemen experienced a particularly high number, with 400 women falling victim to honor killings in 1997. Lebanon recorded 38 cases of honor killings over a three-year period, from 1996 to 1998. (Heydari, A., Teymoori, A., & Trappes, R., 2021)

Research on honor killings in Saudi Arabia is limited. However, studies have revealed a domestic violence rate of approximately 58% in the country, significantly higher than the global range of 10-52%. It's important to note that this statistic only covers major urban areas, excluding rural regions. (Eid, J. A., 2020)

While official reports of honor killings are rare in legitimate news sources, social media platforms have recently facilitated the emergence of more such stories. However, these sources are often considered unreliable and fall under the category of "gray literature," which includes newspaper articles and social media posts. Saudi Arabia shares similar socio-cultural factors with other Gulf Cooperation Council (GCC) countries. Consequently, many cases of honor killings in these nations go unreported, making it difficult to obtain accurate epidemiological estimates.

KEYWORDS

The content analysis revealed key themes and concepts central to understanding honor killings. The terms "Honor" and "Cultural practices" highlight how deeply rooted honor killings are in specific cultural contexts. "Adultery" and "Perception" underscore the significant role that perceived sexual transgressions play in triggering honor killings. This reflects how a woman's sexual behavior is often viewed as directly linked to family honor. "Patriarchy" and "Stigma" point to the underlying power structures that perpetuate honor killings. "Inter-caste marriages" and "Forbidden" highlight how honor killings can be used to enforce social stratification and prevent marriages deemed inappropriate by families or communities. The inclusion of "Documentaries" suggests the importance of media in bringing attention to honor killings and shaping public understanding of this issue.

These keywords collectively paint a picture of honor killings as a complex phenomenon deeply embedded in cultural, social, and gender dynamics.

RESEARCH METHODOLOGY

This research has employed a qualitative approach to conduct an in-depth study of honor killings. By utilizing documentary films and case studies, the author has explored the various potential reasons behind these incidents. The case studies were selected based on factors such as geographic location, regional context, religious background, and the socioeconomic status of the victims, in order to capture a diverse range of perspectives.

The case studies and documentaries provide valuable insights by including testimonies from the perpetrators themselves, as well as from individuals who were closely associated with them. This approach allows a deeper understanding of the thought processes and motivations of those entangled in honor killings. The study also delved into the function of social councils in sanctioning these killings. This aspect was investigated through an analysis of available documentary evidence. By examining this documentation, the research aimed to shed light on how these informal community structures contribute to or authorize honor-based violence. This approach allowed for a deeper understanding of the social and cultural mechanisms that sometimes legitimize or facilitate such acts within certain communities. Overall, the study offers important insights into the complex and multifaceted nature of honor crime cases.

LITERATURE REVIEW

Numerous academic disciplines have conducted in-depth study and analysis on the subject of honor killings. In some cultural and socioeconomic circumstances, honor-related violence is still a highly disturbing behavior that is frequently rationalized under the pretense of preserving family "honor." Scholarly literature has extensively explored the intricate network of elements that perpetuate honor killings. Given the complex nature of this topic, the literature review encompasses a range of related issues and concepts. The primary goal of this review is to identify and present innovative and significant studies on the subject, ultimately contributing new insights to the existing body of knowledge. Durkheim's seminal work from 1897 identifies four types of suicide. Egoistic and anomic suicides result from insufficient connection to social norms, while altruistic and fatalistic suicides stem from excessive societal engagement. This classification provides a useful framework for understanding honor killings. Fatalistic suicide, as described by Durkheim, occurs when society excessively regulates an individual, leaving them feeling trapped and seeing suicide as the only escape. Similarly, in communities with rigid honor codes, individuals may experience extreme societal regulation. Altruistic suicide, where an individual takes their life for the perceived benefit of society, parallels honor killings in that perpetrators often claim to act for the sake of family honor. The key differences exist between Durkheim's suicide types and honor killings: Honor killings are murders, not suicides and the decision to carry out an honor killing is typically made collectively by the victim's family, rather than by a single individual. This comparison highlights how Durkheim's theories on suicide can provide insights into the social dynamics underlying honor killings, while also emphasizing the distinct nature of these acts as collective, murderous decisions rather than individual choices for self-harm. The literature contains a few theories for honor killings that go beyond tautological ideas. While sexual impropriety is one way that honor may be damaged, there are other ways as well, such as insults or disdain that result in acts of retaliation against out-groups. Aksoy & Szekely (2023) in their research paper, "Making Sense of Honor Killings?" concentrate on the function of "cultures of honor" and take into consideration a cross-domain idea of honor. It is essential to highlight Aase's observations on honor in the Tangir community of North Pakistan. Aase (2002) argued that the central issue in honor-related feuds extends beyond specific incidents such as violations of women's chastity, rape, murder, or assault. Instead, these conflicts primarily serve as demonstrations of a family's power and ability to seek revenge against the offending family, thereby restoring their honor through the defense of their interests. Aase emphasized that this practice is integral to the broader struggle for legitimate power within the community. A family's capacity to defend its honor is viewed as a key indicator of its strength and standing. This perspective suggests that honor-related violence in this context is not solely about punishing individual transgressions, but rather about maintaining and demonstrating a family's position and influence within the social hierarchy. It highlights the complex social dynamics underlying honor-based conflicts in this particular cultural setting. Faqir (2001) noted that while sexual abuse issues are sometimes addressed in society, resolving this matter doesn't necessarily restore the affected family's honor. In many cases, relatives believe that honor can only be reclaimed through the killing of the female victim. This act of killing is perceived as a source of pride within the community. Conversely, if the family chooses not to kill the woman, they often face intense social shame and stigma. This perspective highlights the severe social pressure families' face in certain cultures regarding honor-related issues. It underscores how deeply ingrained these beliefs are, where the act of killing a female family member is seen as a means to regain social standing and avoid community disgrace. Faqir's observations reveal the complex and often tragic dynamics at play in honor-based violence, where societal expectations can override considerations of individual rights or justice, leading to extreme and violent outcomes. Eisner and Ghuneim (2013) conducted research focusing on attitudes towards honor killings among adolescents in Amman, Jordan. Their study revealed that several key factors can predict an individual's stance on honor killings. Specifically, they found that traditionalism, economic status, and religiosity were significant indicators of how adolescents viewed honor killings. These factors appeared to influence whether young people were more or less likely to support or condone such practices. This research highlights the complex interplay of cultural, economic, and religious elements in shaping attitudes towards honor-based violence. It suggests that understanding and addressing honor killings requires a multifaceted approach that takes into account these various societal influences. The study's focus on adolescents in Jordan provides valuable insights into how younger generations in certain cultural contexts perceive and potentially perpetuate or challenge traditional notions of honor and related violence.

In patriarchal societies, the behavior of females, both young and adult, is subject to intense scrutiny. Women are expected to conform to culturally restrictive practices that are presented as means of preserving their virtue and safeguarding family honor. However, these practices often serve to uphold traditional, cultural, and sometimes misguided values. These constraints typically include limiting women's movement outside the home, enforcing dress codes such as wearing veils and implementing gender segregation. These measures aim to minimize women's interactions beyond the household, particularly with men who are not family members. Such practices effectively restrict women's freedoms and opportunities under the pretext of protecting honor and chastity. (Zafar & Ali, 2020)

This system reflects how patriarchal structures can use concepts of honor and virtue to control women's behavior and limit their participation in broader society. It highlights the complex relationship between cultural norms, gender roles, and personal freedom in these social contexts.

RESEARCH GAP

Honor-related violence finds no support or justification in any constitution worldwide. Constitutional law upholds equal rights and human dignity for all, regardless of personal characteristics. Legally, honor killing is classified as homicide, and perpetrators should face corresponding charges. However, practical challenges often hinder fair trials in these cases. Offenders frequently escape legal consequences due to difficulties in proving guilt beyond reasonable doubt. This evasion of justice stems from a lack of conclusive evidence.

Honor killings have persisted in some societies through informal justice systems, often without significant opposition from affected parties. Family members or clan associates typically carry out these acts, creating a barrier of silence among potential witnesses. Perpetrators, believing in the righteousness of their actions, often fail to recognize honor killings as criminal. These communities tend to view such incidents as private family matters, resisting outside intervention, even from clan elders or representatives. Honor killings serve as brutal deterrents against perceived disobedience, underscoring their inherent cruelty. Victim's families often become involved in these crimes, either driven by their own sense of outrage or pressured by community expectations. These cases set precedents, intended to discourage future transgressions. However, a shift is occurring. As education becomes more widespread, individuals are gaining awareness of their legal and human rights, empowering them to take charge of their lives. More people are speaking out against this injustice, with some even seeking recourse through the legal system. This growing awareness has led to increased scrutiny and public discourse surrounding honor-related violence, bringing these issues into the spotlight for investigation and debate.

INTRODUCTION

Around the world, society has advanced and grown more educated over time compared to a few decades ago. But there are still certain societies that are archaic and outdated, with outdated customs and some cruel and unlawful practices that persist to this day. Honor killings are one such cruel custom that persists in some communities even to this day.

"Honor killing" is one of the gravest crimes committed against mankind, that is done for the sake of preserving culture and, unfortunately, is still seen by many as an act of honor. (Shoro, n.d.) Honor killing is the act of taking the life of an individual, either a man or a woman, whose marriage status is determined by their desires. When considering the honor of the family, the highest authority considers the standing and reputation of the family but disregards the love and affection that family members have for one another.

"Honor Crimes" can be defined as acts of violence committed in the name of enforcing moral standards, the violations of which are deemed unacceptable.(Vitoshka, 2010)

Human Rights Watch defines "honor killings" as follows:

"Honor crimes are acts of violence, usually murder, committed by male family members against female family members who are perceived to have brought dishonor upon the family. A woman can be targeted by her family for a variety of reasons including, refusing to enter into an arranged marriage, being the victim of a sexual assault, seeking a divorce—even from an abusive husband—or committing adultery. The mere perception that a woman has acted in a manner to bring "dishonor" to the family is sufficient to trigger an attack."(Honour Honour Crimes and Violence against Women Preventing and Punishing Honour Crimes, n.d.-a)

In essence, honor is the notion of respect that an individual, family, or social group possesses within society. Honor killings are when someone is killed to preserve the honor of their family or a social group. Even while we are constantly moving toward modernity and a liberal worldview, we haven't been able to completely eradicate these sins from our society. Even though this research only examines honor killings, it is crucial to note that in societies that are still in the stages of development, crimes like forced marriages, assaults (especially sexual ones), and confinement that are carried out in the name of upholding honor are also considered honor crimes.

This chapter examines honor killing cases using documentaries as a source. Documentaries can offer insightful perspectives on the intricate and concerning issue of honor killings. These films frequently examine the causes of honor killings and offer perspectives from various angles. The cases focus on the moral, religious, and societal pressures that certain people face while defying societal conventions, which leads them to take the lives of their family members. When it comes to the ideas of honor, shame, and honor killings, the documentaries selected as case studies offer the viewpoints of both the offenders and the victims.

REASONS AND PERSPECTIVES ON HONOR KILLINGS

The idea of honor plays a central role in numerous disputes within societies as well as between different cultures globally.(Epstein, 2010) The practice of honor killings, which involves the killing of individuals perceived to have brought dishonor to their family or community, has existed for centuries and continues to be widespread in various regions around the world, beyond just present-day Pakistan or Islamic societies.(Jafri, 2008) Since honor killing frequently takes place in societies where Muslims predominate, it is frequently wrongly assumed that honor killing is an Islamic custom or that Islam supports it. In actuality, honor killing is prohibited in Islam, and this practice is not mentioned in the Hadith or the Qur'an. Honor killings date back to the Roman era, when the senior male in a household, known as the pater familias, had the authority to murder an unmarried daughter who was involved in sexual activity or an adulterous wife.(Kejriwal, n.d.) In nations with a majority of Muslims, such as Indonesia or Malaysia, there is less evidence of the practice. Honor killings occur in highly patriarchal civilizations, sometimes referred to as "honor-based" societies, and are primarily found in the southern Mediterranean, the Middle East, South Asia, and the Balkans.

According to Sharif Kanaana, an anthropology professor at Birzeit University, honor killing is "a complicated issue that cuts deep into the history of Arab society." He notes further that in a patrilineal society, reproductive power is what the men of the family, clan, or tribe want to control. For the tribe, women served as a factory to produce men. Honor killings are not primarily about regulating sexual conduct, but rather about asserting control over fertility and reproductive capabilities. The underlying motivation is the issue of reproductive power rather than restraining sexual behavior. (Ruggi, 1998) The ideas of honor and shame being used as reasons for violent acts and taking lives are not confined to or exclusive to a single culture or religious belief system.(Kejriwal, n.d.)

Honor-based violence can occur exclusively between men and occasionally include women as associates. But it seems that men are the ones who commit it almost entirely against women and children whom they believe to have "belonged" to them. Typically, it can be found in the subsequent situations:

- Adultery
- Premarital sex or having a child out of wedlock (though a "shotgun wedding" may restore honor).
- Disobedience by parents, patriotic deeds, insults to one's dignity, or debt default (usually between men).

The distinction between dishonoring as a "collective" injury and dishonoring as an "individual" injury may be the cause. In systems of community honor, a husband's envy, which may be categorized as personal harm of pride, or honor, is not usually thought to be enough justification for murder. Nonetheless, if a wife commits a violation, it can bring collective dishonor and injury to the family she was born into, which is eventually authorized to punish her. (Araji, 2000) Honor killings usually happen when a woman begins dating someone whose religion, socioeconomic status, or social standing that her family finds objectionable. These killings can happen when women believe that by going against the socially acceptable norms of their community, they have shamed their families. In such situations, people may resort to honor killings as a means of preserving perceived family honor. The most sought-after, guarded, and valued quality that characterizes a family's standing and reputation in their community might be called "honor". Women's behavior is particularly affected by this burden. For ages, our freedom of movement, our ability to make our own decisions, and our feelings of honor and shame have held us back. If your wants, goals, or ideas interfere with the reputation of the family, community, or group as a whole, you cannot be who you are or voice your own needs and beliefs. You are supposed to live within these boundaries if you are raised in a community that is characterized by these patriarchal notions of honor and social institutions. Being autonomous is unacceptable and can result in a range of negative outcomes, including abuse, threats, intimidation, banishment from the group, and violent acts, the most extreme of which is taking a life or killing someone for the sake of "honor". (Deeyah, 2012) Even while the phrase "honor-based killing" is commonly used, it should be understood that it is also contentious.(Muhammad & Canada. Department of Justice. Family, n.d.) Some authors have anticipated that the phrase is frequently linked with the small number of distinct ethnocultural communities, concealing the awful fact that family homicides exist in all cultures.(Muhammad & Canada. Department of Justice. Family, n.d.) Additionally, some believe that this word may also provide a way for criminals to claim disgrace as a defense in court, hoping to get their sentence lowered.(Muhammad & Canada. Department of Justice. Family, n.d.) While there are important reasons to be cautious about the term "honor killings," there are also some distinct aspects of these crimes that are useful to distinguish from an analytical and descriptive perspective. These distinctive features have applications in psychopathology, including complicity and premeditation, as well as victim protection. Three ways have been highlighted by an author in which honor killings differ from domestic abuse. (Hildebrandt, 2009)

- Planning - Honor killings are typically premeditated, often planned during family meetings. The victim may face repeated death threats from the family if perceived as bringing dishonor.

- Family Involvement - Multiple family members like parents, brothers, and cousins can be complicit in carrying out the honor killing.
- Lack of Stigma - Within their families and communities, the perpetrators of honor killings do not face social disapproval in their families and communities for their actions.

MALE DOMINANT SOCIETY

"A Regular Woman," which is based on a true story, centers on a young, independent German woman of Turkish descent. Her strongly patriarchal family rejects her lifestyle as inappropriate and regularly gets in the way of her living her own life. Tensions eventually reach a breaking point where she feels unsafe at home and flees with her child. She then notifies the police about her brother, the main agitator. Though essentially an honor-killing scenario, the movie also looks at the larger threat of patriarchal tyranny and women's fight for equality. The fundamental unit of society, economy, and politics in traditional patriarchal countries is the family or kin group, and inheritance is patrilineal. The emphasis on family control over women's sexual and reproductive rights stems from the fact that the survival and continuity of that structure depend on the women's ability to bear legitimate children. It is noted that "…. ideologies of protection and victimhood ensure that women's narrative about their sexual agency is considered taboo; older men usually take up this space declaring young women who have made consensual choices with their partners to be victims of rape and kidnapping".(Solotaroff et al., n.d.) Individuals' status and rights are subservient to those of the family group in these societies. Girls' and women's actions are closely monitored in patriarchal configurations. Women are required to adhere to socially restrictive cultural practices that uphold conventional, cultural, and false values under the guise of preserving their chastity and protecting the family's honor. This involves confining women within the home, enforcing practices like donning veils, and gender segregation that limit their interactions outside the household, especially with unrelated men.(Zafar & Ali, 2020) The killers justify their crimes by citing the victim's purported harm to the family's reputation or name. It is believed that a woman's father, brothers, and spouse should be her first choice when it comes to maintaining her virginity and "sexual purity." Typically, victims of honor killings are accused of participating in "sexually immoral" behaviors, such as having sex outside of marriage or openly interacting with men who are not related to them (even if they have been the victims of rape or sexual assault). However, there exist additional motives for a woman to become the victim of murder-by declining an arranged marriage or seeking a divorce, even from an abusive husband. The mere perception that a woman has behaved in a way that could tarnish the family's reputation can provoke murderous attacks against her. These assumptions are usually more grounded in men's sentiments and emotions than in facts. Paradoxically, female relatives sometimes assist in setting up the murders and frequently justify the killings. (Vaughan, n.d.)

THE NOTION OF HONOR AND SHAME

In September 2002, a 16-year-old Iraqi Kurd, Heshu Yones was killed by her father, Abdalla Yones, who was concerned that his daughter was adopting the Western culture upon having started seeing a young man from Lebanon. Abdalla Yones was notified through a letter that his daughter was a disgrace to the family for being involved with a Lebanese man. Her father escorted her to Iraqi Kurdistan and consequently fixed her marriage with her cousin. Her father discovered that she had a ruptured hymen after examining her virginity, making an "honorable" marriage unfeasible. Heshu was afraid for her life when she got back to England. She therefore reached out and made contact with several organizations to ask for assistance. Nevertheless, none of them were able to fully get the apprehension of the danger to her life. Heshu's father murdered her by stabbing her eleven times. Abdulla contended that he was 'evoked' by Heshu's Western attire and her Lebanese boyfriend and the letter he received informing him about Heshu's behavior, which brought humiliation and shame to the family and community. As part of his argument, he also claimed that his daughter had placed him in an "untenable position" by laying a "stain" on the family's honor, therefore he was "forced to kill" her.(Honour Honour Crimes and Violence against Women Preventing and Punishing Honour Crimes, n.d.-b) In this situation, cultural notions about honor were cited as a motive. The victim's sister overheard her father threatening to kill her or himself if he ever discovered that Heshu had a boyfriend.(Honour Honour Crimes and Violence against Women Preventing and Punishing Honour Crimes, n.d.-b) Another, Tina, a teenager, was becoming more like an American teen, which caused her parents, a Brazilian Catholic mother and, a Palestinian Muslim father, to become increasingly agitated. Despite her parents' objections, she played football in high school, dated a black man, and went to the junior prom. Subsequently, she was repeatedly stabbed by her father in the chest, fracturing her ribs and sternum, damaging her left lung, and permeating her heart. These are family honor killings, which include the use of deleterious punishment against family members who harm the family's reputation by, for example, having extramarital sex. The primary targets of these crimes tend to be young women, often teenagers or in their early 20s, while the offenders are predominantly male.(Cooney, n.d.) As a means of penalizing transgressions against sexual, familial, religious, or social norms; honor killings are carried out in the communities. Honor killings are frequently carried out by family members against a female relative who is thought to have brought shame to the family and community. In order to make sure that the women in the family never do anything to damage the "honor" and "reputation," boys and occasionally women are required to keep a tight eye on their sisters' and other women's actions. The boys are frequently asked to carry out the murder; if they decline, they risk severe consequences from the community and family for not doing their "duty". Honor killings have also been ascribed to the shifting cultural and economic standing of women in modern times.

ISSUES BASED ON GOTRA

Urban-rural India has a wide variety of religions, regions, and cultural practices. The marriage is the most important institution in every civilization. The adoption of a choice-based marriage system is forbidden by the Hindu social structure. A pair of marriage systems exist an ulama and a proximal. Cultural approaches, or cultural rights, have garnered greater attention than legal alternatives. The institution of marriage has always placed a high priority on cultural rights. Honor killings, also called customary killings, are when one or more family members assassinate a member of a clan or family because they believe the victim has brought shame to the clan, family, or community. In some cases, the larger community also believes this to be the case. The main causes of this perceived dishonor are typically (a) disregarding dress norms set by the family, (b) choosing to marry on one's terms or not through an arranged marriage, (c) having specific sexual actions, and (d) getting married within the same gotra. These murders are motivated by the idea that killing someone whose acts defame one's family or clan is acceptable when one is defending their honor.

While visiting India, Jaswinder Kaur Sidhu, a young woman of Indo-Canadian origin, discreetly met and married her true love. Because the spouse was from the same village as Jassi's mother and was a member of the Sidhu clan, they were vehemently against the marriage. To restore the family's honor, one of her relatives killed her in India as a result. In relation to her case, eleven individuals were arrested in India, including her uncle, a police officer, and the head of a local criminal gang. (Muhammad & Canada. Department of Justice. Family, n.d.) Typically, such relationships among members of the same clan are customarily prohibited. (Lakshmi, 2003)

GETTING MARRIED OUT OF LOVE

The 2012 documentary film, *Banaz: A Love Story* recounts the tragic story of Banaz Mahmod, a young British-Iraqi lady of Kurdish descent who was murdered in 2006 in South London at the behest of her own family members. (MacVeigh, 2012) Banaz Mahmod's life was marked by betrayal. Her grandma performed FGM on her when she was a little child. To fortify family ties, she was married off at the age of seventeen to a guy she had only met once. She endured abuse, beatings, rapes, and forced seclusion during her marriage. When she returned to her family home at the age of 19, expecting safety and security, she was betrayed twice: once by her family, who saw her disobedience as an unforgivable act, and then by the British authorities, who disregarded her calls for assistance when she believed she was in danger. She went missing when she was twenty years old, and no one ever heard from her until her body was found buried beneath a patio, squished inside a muddy suitcase in a fatal position—a victim of a so-called "Honor" Killing. Her father, uncle, and a male cousin were among the heinous crime perpetrators, and it took five years to identify and bring charges against them. Thousands more tales exist throughout the world of families who, rather than fulfilling their obligation to love and protect their children, opted to give in to peer and community pressure, as demonstrated by Banaz's life and murder. In Lahore, Zeenat Rafiq married a man of her liking against the desires of her family and was burnt alive by her mother. Her murder demonstrated the shockingly violent and inhumane measures some families are willing to take in order to enforce their warped perceptions of family honor.(Shahid et al., 2024) The ongoing genocide known as "Honor Killings" occurs when women and girls are killed for "justified" reasons to preserve a family's reputation. In the cases mentioned above, the girl's choice to marry for love led to the honor killing.

Economic Standing

The study on honor killings of women has primarily concentrated on analyzing the cultural underpinnings of "honor cultures" rather than investigating broader societal factors and dynamics that may contribute to or perpetuate these gender-based murders. (Dayan, 2021) In general, marriages between individuals from different socioeconomic classes are discouraged. The family perceives a couple marrying against the desires of their parents, rejecting the ideas of equality and status, as a betrayal of their social standing and a loss of family name. Jassi or Jaswinder Kaur Sidhu (the murdered bride) was raised solely in Canada after being born there. Her parents were Sikhs and have always been traditionalists. Jassi fell in love with Mithoo who was a rickshaw driver. Mithoo and Jassi got married on March 15, 1999, after finding a Sikh priest to perform their marriage secretly. Somehow, Jassi's mother got to know about her daughter's covert marriage to Mithoo. Following that, Jassi was locked up in her room, and her uncle became enraged with her for tricking them and resolved to exact revenge on Mithoo by teaching him a lesson he would never forget. Subsequently, Jassi and Mithoo were attacked suddenly while riding the scooter. Mithoo got hit by the sword, and Jassi was struck by a club and tumbled off the scooter. The men kidnapped Jassi and left Mithoo to death. Her body was discovered in an irrigation canal the following morning. Newspapers were flooded with reports of the bride's murder. Beautiful, well-off Canadian lady who lost her life because of her love for a rickshaw driver. In the documentary, Jassi's cousin disclosed that her mother never approved of Mithoo as a good fit for Jassi because of his rickshaw taxi driving career, which was perceived as inglorious to her family and below their status. In the documentary, her uncle displayed no remorse or sorrow over her death.(Singh & Bhandari, 2021)

Customs and Religion

The tragic case involved Aqsa, a teenage girl, being killed by her father and brother, who were convicted of the brutal murdering her in the second degree in June 2010. Their guilty pleas confirmed their role in perpetrating this horrific act of violence against the young female family member. (Mitchell, 2010) Aqsa was discovered strangled in her family's Mississauga home in December 2007, leading to the prosecution of her father and brother on first-degree murder charges. According to friends, Aqsa was having problems with her family because she refused to wear the headscarf, known as the hijab, which is worn by some Muslim women. She had been staying with another family, who described her as a "typical" teenager attempting to fit in, to spend less time at home. Her family believed that her actions were a violation of Islam's moral code, cultural customs, and religious beliefs. (Brother faces new charge in teenage girl's slaying, 2008) They concluded that she had betrayed their faith, morals, and conventions by her acts and that this had contributed to the violence against her that ended in death. The killers were adamant that the girls were punished appropriately and considered their honor to be more important than their lives. The female victims adopted values distinct from their own culture, and the perpetrators attempted to use this as an excuse for their killings, claiming that the victims would bring shame to their families or had already done so.(Muhammad & Canada. Department of Justice. Family, n.d.) The primary cause of the victims' deaths was their choice to reject traditional values in favor of adopted Western lifestyles.

Another important reason for honor killings in India is the caste structure. It establishes the scope and order of caste relations. (Mahajan, 2020) It establishes the scope and order of caste relations. People have been hesitant to accept Dalits and other members of the so-called lower castes as equals, despite India gaining independence over 70 years ago and numerous government policies and initiatives to dismantle caste-based inequalities. This in turn illustrates how people's attitudes toward upholding social divisions between castes and adhering to socially acceptable standards of behavior are influenced by their ingrained caste differences. In the documentary India's Forbidden Love, Kausalya's brother expressed that her demise was caused by her ignorance of caste. He claims that the day Kausalya wed a boy from a lower caste; she was gone from their lives. Also, in Jharkhand (June 2010) Nirupama Pathak, a journalist who had fallen in love with her classmate Ranjan, was murdered by her mother due to the caste differences. (Kumar, 2012) For people who believe in the caste system, inter-caste marriage is a loss of honor. They believe that the only moral way is to eliminate family members who choose to marry outside of their caste. (Chowdhry, 2004)

People's resentment of inter-caste marriages is documented in the case study mentioned above. They believe that these marriages attempt to break social hierarchies and could cause chaos in their lives. Marriages between members of different castes pose a threat to the hierarchy. They find it intolerable that someone from a supposedly lower caste should be among them.

Fear of Being Ostracized

In the documentary, a woman says that Khap councils forbid families from allowing their children to be spared or to live their lives as they see fit. In the case involving Manoj and Babli, the Khap Panchayat (an influential caste-based council) imposed severe social and economic sanctions on Manoj's family as punishment for their opposition to the honor killing of the couple. In the other case, the girl's membership in the majority clan was discovered, leading to the auction of the family's belongings. When threatened with termination of communication, people frequently acquiesce to the decisions made by the Khap.

Sugirthanraj Kailayapillai killed his wife, Ms. Subramaniam, in 2006; his four-year-old daughter and his mother-in-law were dispatched to the garage to find the body, and he was convicted in November 2009 for life in jail without parole possibility for 14 years. The accused claimed that his wife was "of bad character" because she had developed a romantic relationship with someone with whom she worked. In their victim impact statements, the victim's mother and sister stated that: ...members of the Tamil community, a community that Ms. Sivanantham [the victim's sister] describe as holding, "some very rigid and traditional values and norms when it comes to women", have suggested that Ms. Subramanian was murdered because she was of bad character. This has brought shame to the family, 10 and caused its members, particularly Kanagama [the victim's mother], to feel isolated from their community. They feared that Ms. Subramaniam's children may face social disapproval.(Muhammad & Canada. Department of Justice. Family, n.d.) Family members have confessed to being coerced into carrying out honor killings by their social circle in numerous cases, including this one.

CONCLUSION

A crime known as "honor killing" is carried out to protect the family's honor. However, it is past time for us to acknowledge that murdering someone is never an act of honor. Because culture, customs, and religion are ambiguous and subject to human interpretation, they should not be used as justification for criminal behavior. Rigid adherence to traditions and customs over millennia has fixed gender roles, even though they were first created to facilitate society's smooth operation. What were once merely guidelines for maximizing society's potential eventually evolved into repressive laws that began to violate people's rights, particularly those of women. The freedom to practice one's religion is not a guarantee of the right to murder. Therefore, the authors believe that the definition of "honor" needs to be changed to stop this evil. This can be accomplished by:

Raising Awareness: Honor killings are most prevalent in rural areas, where the victim is almost always a girl who lacks access to education and is therefore unaware of her rights. As a result, they are reluctant to defend themselves and accept it as a penalty for their actions.

Social Reforms: The underlying cause of these crimes is people's mentalities. Marriages between different castes are still frowned upon. As times change, society demands change as well. Moreover, people should report such cases despite their fear of social acceptance because only then will the issue be brought to light.

Strict Legal Support: Although such killings may be made illegal by several other laws, it should be noted that these laws only grant general protections. Strict, specifically codified legal support is required to dissuade society and bring legal action against those who commit these horrible crimes.

It is difficult to suddenly alter the beliefs and ideals that are deeply entrenched and internalized in a person's mind and the collective consciousness of a community. However, it is ted that attitudes toward crimes related to honor will eventually shift as a result of education, awareness of the law and human rights, as well as the conviction of those who commit these offences. There has been at least a dozen documented homicides over the previous ten years that seem to have been honor killings. To avert more tragedies, it is hoped that this chapter will help increase awareness of the intricate dynamics at play in cases of honor killings.

REFERENCES

Araji, S. K. (2000). *Crimes of Honor and Shame: Violence against Women in Non-Western and Western Societies*. Retrieved from THE RED FEATHER JOURNAL of POSTMODERN CRIMINOLOGY: https://www.critcrim.org/redfeather/journal-pomocrim/vol-8-shaming/araji.html

Brother faces new charge in teenage girl's slaying. (2008, June 27). Retrieved from CBC News: https://www.cbc.ca/news/canada/toronto/brother-faces-new-charge-in-teenage-girl-s-slaying-1.713481

Chowdhry, P. (2004). Private Lives, State Intervention: Cases of Runaway Marriage in Rural North India. *Modern Asian Studies*, 38(1), 55–84. DOI: 10.1017/S0026749X04001027

Cooney, M. (n.d.). *EXECUTION BY FAMILY: A THEORY OF HONOR VIOLENCE*.

Dayan, H. (2021). Female Honor Killing: The Role of Low Socio-Economic Status and Rapid Modernization. *Journal of Interpersonal Violence*, 36(19-20), NP10393–NP10410. DOI: 10.1177/0886260519872984 PMID: 31524058

Deeyah. (2012, November 3). *Banaz: An 'honor' killing*. Retrieved from IKWRO: https://ikwro.org.uk/2012/11/03/banaz-an-honour-killing/

Eid, J. A. (2020). *A Qualitative Study of the Impact of Domestic Violence by Male Relatives on Saudi Female Students in the United States* (Doctoral dissertation, Howard University).

Epstein, C. F. (2010). Death by gender. *Dissent*, 57(2), 54–57. DOI: 10.1353/dss.0.0143

Gibbs, A., Said, N., Corboz, J., & Jewkes, R. (2019). Factors associated with 'honour killing' in Afghanistan and the occupied Palestinian Territories: Two cross-sectional studies. *PLoS One*, 14(8), e0219125. DOI: 10.1371/journal.pone.0219125 PMID: 31393873

Heydari, A., Teymoori, A., & Trappes, R. (2021). Honor killing as a dark side of modernity: Prevalence, common discourses, and a critical view. *Social Sciences Information. Information Sur les Sciences Sociales*, 60(1), 86–106. DOI: 10.1177/0539018421994777

Hildebrandt, A. (2009, July 25). *Honour killings: domestic abuse by another name?* Retrieved from CBC News: https://www.cbc.ca/news/canada/honour-killings-domestic-abuse-by-another-name-1.792907

Honour Honour Crimes and Violence against Women Preventing and Punishing Honour Crimes. (n.d.-a).

Honour Honour Crimes and Violence against Women Preventing and Punishing Honour Crimes. (n.d.-b).

Jafri, A. H. (2008). In *honour killing: Dilemma, ritual, understanding.* Karachi, Pakistan: Oxford University Press.

Kejriwal, -Neelam. (n.d.). *HONOUR KILLING IN NORTH INDIA.*

Kumar, A. (2012). Public policy imperatives for curbing honour killings in India. *Journal of Politics and Governance,* 1(1), 36–40.

Lakshmi, D. L. (2003, September 30). *After a Marriage for Love, a Death for 'Honor'.* Retrieved from The Washington Post: https://www.washingtonpost.com/archive/lifestyle/2003/10/01/after-a-marriage-for-love-a-death-for-honor/fb1b98fd-94e6-47d1-8f81-ce656c6b4e94/

MacVeigh, T. (2012, September 22). *'They're following me': chilling words of girl who was 'honour killing' victim.* Retrieved from The Guardian: https://www.theguardian.com/world/2012/sep/22/banaz-mahmod-honour-killing

Mahajan, A. (2020, September 5). *Comprehending Honour Killings in India.* Retrieved from Round Table India: https://www.roundtableindia.co.in/comprehending-honour-killings-in-india/

Mishra, A. (n.d.). *HONOUR KILLINGS: THE LAW IT IS AND THE LAW IT OUGHT TO BE.* https://www.hrw.org/press/2001/04/un

Mitchell, B. (2010, June 16). *'I killed my daughter... with my hands'.* Retrieved from Toronto Star: https://www.thestar.com/news/crime/i-killed-my-daughter-with-my-hands/article_cec7714d-78fd-5212-a430-1b3dc7de47ec.html

Muhammad, A. A., & Canada. Department of Justice. Family, C. and Y. S. (n.d.). *Preliminary examination of so-called "honour killings" in Canada.*

Nasrullah, M., Haqqi, S., & Cummings, K. J. (2009). The epidemiological patterns of honour killing of women in Pakistan. *European Journal of Public Health,* 19(2), 193–197. DOI: 10.1093/eurpub/ckp021 PMID: 19286837

Pirnia, B., Pirnia, F., & Pirnia, K. (2020). Honour killings and violence against women in Iran during the COVID-19 pandemic. *The Lancet. Psychiatry,* 7(10), e60. DOI: 10.1016/S2215-0366(20)30359-X PMID: 32949522

Ruggi, S. (1998). *Commodifying Honor in Female Sexuality*. Retrieved from Middle East Report 206: https://merip.org/1998/06/commodifying-honor-in-female-sexuality/

Shahid, A., Awan, M. H., & Rana, F. A. (2024). Honour Killings in Pakistan: Legal Perspectives and Reforms. *Qlantic Journal of Social Sciences*, 5(1), 134–140. DOI: 10.55737/qjss.547319279

Shoro, S. (n.d.). *The real stories behind honour killing.*

Singh, D., & Bhandari, D. S. (2021). Legacy of Honor and Violence: An Analysis of Factors Responsible for Honor Killings in Afghanistan, Canada, India, and Pakistan as Discussed in Selected Documentaries on Real Cases. *SAGE Open*, 11(2). Advance online publication. DOI: 10.1177/21582440211022323

Solotaroff, J. L., Pande, R. (Rohini P.), & World Bank. (n.d.). *Violence against women and girls: lessons from South Asia.*

Vaughan, D. (n.d.). *Mass Murder*. Retrieved from Britannica: https://www.britannica.com/topic/mass-murder

Vitoshka, D. Y. (2010). The Modern Face of Honor Killing: Factors, Legal Issues, and Policy Recommendations. *Berkeley Undergraduate Journal*, 22(2). Advance online publication. DOI: 10.5070/B3222007673

Zafar, F., & Ali, R. (2020). Understanding the Causes of Honor Killing: An Exploratory Study in South Punjab, Pakistan. In *Pakistan Journal of Social Sciences (PJSS)* (Vol. 40, Issue 2).

Zawati, H. (2012). Hidden Deaths of Libyan Rape Survivors: Rape Casualties Should Be Considered Wounded Combatants Rather Than Mere Victims of Sexual Violence. SSRN *Products & Services.*

Chapter 2
Understanding the Criminology Behind Honor Killing

Indra Kumar Singh
GLA University, Mathura, India

Tanuj Vashistha
https://orcid.org/0009-0005-9326-6338
GLA University, Mathura, India

ABSTRACT

This chapter deems to highlight the criminology, state of mind and the conditions which involves and interferes when a man thinks of honor killing as a problem which he may seem unfit to the society, at large. Furthermore, it will highlight who are involved in such crimes and how does such mindset get developed and carry forward to the coming generations. This chapter will further inquire about the stand of women so far as contributing to this mentality. Thus, making such crimes unpredictable and also raising a question upon human race and its psyche. The chapter will throw light upon the criminalization of young minds and how the crime is normalised in the society, in addition to, discussing the concentration of social power in the hands of few which eventually leads to their dominance and autonomy in re-writing the societal rulebook.

DOI: 10.4018/979-8-3693-7240-1.ch002

INTRODUCTION

This chapter furthermore, explores the ins and outs of how these crimes find ways into the society and becomes so deeply embedded within its periphery that sometimes the looks inseparable. This chapter is deemed to contribute to the global question of the solution of the honour related crimes thus paving ways towards its solutions by diving deep toward the social and mental scenarios those leads toward happening of such brutal and inhumane crimes.

This chapter also talks about how disparities lying within the caste system in a typical Indian society may lead to such violence, but it is no halt to it, it can extend to the inter- religious marriages and even toward socially accepted marriages but a family denial. Thus, making such crimes unpredictable and also raising a question upon human race and its psyche. The chapter will also find for the resolutions by identifying and pointing the core issues of any such crime and thus making it for the society to easily solve it as we closely know them now.

It also highlights that these crimes are nothing but a result of generation old social and religious intolerance which takes such enormous forms that leave the difference between humans and animals a man fails to differentiate between an ordinary human and his own children, such is the brutality and level of intolerance involved within these crimes. The chapter will throw light upon the criminalization of young minds and how the crime is normalised in the society, in addition to, discussing the concentration of social power in the hands of few which eventually leads to their dominance and autonomy in re-writing the societal rulebook.

Statistics also shows that how honour related crime have become more and more accepting among people across nations. According to the recent data collections in 2019 honour crimes are accepted by 27% population in Algeria, 25% in Morrocco, 21% in Jordan, 14% in Sudan, 8% in Tunisia, 8% in Lebanon and 8% in most of the Palestinian territories.

The Indian pictures of hate crime statistics is not also very handsome. From September 2015 to December 2019, 619 Dalits, 196 Muslims, 35 Others, 31 Adivasis, 29 Transgenders and 18 Christians were subjected to any forms of Hate crime, evidently speaking that these crimes are still recognizable and visible in Indian societal setup too.

LITERATURE REVIEW

"A sexual virtue of a woman carries not only a direct market economic value but it also symbolises the family's honour in general." --- Janina Juškevičiūtė (Juškevičiūtė & Jakab, n.d.)

The aforementioned statement in the book mentioned above generates answers to many of the legal and social questions that might arise in a freshman's mind while studying these crimes.

The first and the foremost question being- Why these crimes happen?

This line indicates as well as explores the answer to this question appropriately. The first reason is of course that a family spends a considerable amount of their money while raising the children, and in the case if it's a girl child they explore a sense oof detachment and finds it that if they are to spend money on a girl child and send her away, they get to make all her important life decisions and take control of all her future ambitions and plannings. Is it right "NO" for a short answer. But are they responsible? "MAY BE NOT" as they were always told by their previous generation that a girl child is a matter of pride and reputation for the family, thus her purity means an unwavering honour for entire Family. Making it even clearer to understand why they make a sense of ownership o girl child.

"Furthermore, honour killings are described as needed actions that operate as penalties for the transgressors of honour norms, who pay for their 'mistakes' with their lives." --- Ananya Poddar (Poddar, 2020)

Ms. Poddar goes on to illustrate that how honour killings are the punishment given to the people who are declared social preparators just for having a socially progressive thought, which no one can muster up courage to defend even after seeing no harm but, only making a false sense of insecurity to caste, creed, religion and even sex in some extents.

Poddar also goes on to dissect the social institutions which are responsible for such an inhumane act. This punishment is given for non-compliance with the social rulebook which was inherently made with nothing but social despotism in mind. And it is completely unknown what methodology and pedagogy was used in framing such non-liberal norms, and how the society felt obligated and bound by such norms in the first place.

RESEARCH DIRECTIONS

A number of areas can be mined that will help to understand and address this intricate issue in future research on criminology about the crimes of honor. These are some potential directions:

Psychological Profiling of the Perpetrator: Future research, in order to provide an even deeper psychological profile of perpetrators of honor-related crime, may aim to identify their mindset, motivations, and the role of societal pressures. This will help develop interventions targeted at preventing such crimes.

Media and Honor Crimes: Future studies can also explore the role that media is playing both in promoting and combating honor-based crimes. This will include how different forms of media coverage influence public perception, framing these crimes and how effective the media is in forwarding the cause to bring about a change.

Cross-Cultural Comparative Studies: Honor-related crimes can be compared across a variety of cultures to shed light on how the diverse socio-cultural backgrounds are contributing to honor crime. The study might include the ways cultural norms, religious background, and the legal systems of societies could either heighten or lessen the occurrences of honor-related violence.

Role of Education and Legal Reforms: This is another area in which research can be conducted to determine how and if the educational programs and legal reforms have actually brought about a diminution of the prevalence of honor-based crimes. The studies could be on how education, particularly on human rights and gender equality, influences the societal attitudes towards honor and related violence.

Societal Structures and Honor Crimes: Further research may be conducted on the role of traditional and informal societal structures, such as Khap Panchayats or other community councils, in furthering honor crimes. The nature of this research would involve how these structures maintain their influence and what reforms may be brought in that context.

Women's Agency and Resistance: That could be the involvement of women within communities where honor crimes are rife. An understanding of the ways in which women resist, comply with, or are complicit in such crimes may provide further nuances to the gender dynamics at play.

Longitudinal Studies of Intergenerational Transmission: These longitudinal studies will help researchers understand the way in which attitudes toward honor-related violence are transmitted intergenerationally. These studies would assist in understanding how such crimes remain persistent across time and what societal interventions may disrupt such transmission.

Globalization and Honor Crimes: One can potentially test the hypothesis that globalization and modernization have impacted changes in the prevalence rates and perceptions of these honor crimes. One might assess whether familiarity with world norms and values, or any transmigration or diaspora communities, would influence views about honor-related violence.

Reaction of the Legal System to Honor Crimes: In addition to these, comparative legal studies may take a closer look at ways in which different judicial systems react to honor crimes. Research in that area may be on the effectiveness of the many and varied legal approaches; challenges encountered in the prosecution of these crimes; and the position taken in relation to international human rights law.

Impact of social media and Digital Activism: Future inquiry could examine the role of social media and digital activism in contributing to and combating honor-related crimes. This could include a comparison of online communities that support honor crimes with those advocating for victims and legal reforms.

INTRODUCTION

As the clock of globalization and modernization is ticks with a faster pace an adhering need to understand the criminology involved behind honor related crimes is to be understood with utmost importance and further decode the persevering societal arena in which these crimes take place even in this advanced generation of legal structure. We must dive deep into the minds of the criminal, the society they come from and the influence of others over them while doing such crimes, because such heinous crime cannot emerge out of a microstructure of people and needs a big and enlarged social support and acceptance. Thus, it becomes very important to decode the scenario in which these criminals grow and such a depriving mindset flourish.

IDENTITY POLITICS

Our society paved the way for such ruthless atrocities way back when we handed over all the societal and religious power in some hands, be it the churches in Europe, be it the high-class landlords, zamindars or khaap panchayat in India or be it the religious heads in the Islamic states. These powerful people cunningly infringed the sacred religious teachings so as they themselves could emerge as a greater identity and kill the people as well as the ideology that is creating friction in their ways. If one is to critically analyse, it is evident that these heads of the so-called social circles, these "identity giants" have no other function than to build social practices and punish and pressurize the one who does not play along. The bigger these power structures get; more and more power gets accumulated to the top of this pyramid that is in the hands of the head of the social groups. These groups are so tightly knit that no incident within the groups. (Khan, n.d.) Go unnoticed and every incident is taken as a public example. This stands to be the duty of these leaders to uphold the identity of their group by upholding the so-called culture of the group by making an imaginary manual of rules that each member has to follow to be kept as a brick in the wall, but the very base of this wall is a hollow cause. These rules lack very basic humanitarian aspects and are very rudimentary up to their core.

PREJUDICE

The rule making discussed above is on the basis of social prejudice meaning what did the thinking of the ancestral minds on the particular topic talked and be it relevant in today's scenario or not, it is sought to be applied as it is without any manipulation to sustain the modern developing needs.(Khan, n.d.) This prejudice gives birth to casteism, which stands to be amongst the root cause of honor related crimes and many other crimes in general. A developing mind would progress by getting away from these related authorities and prejudices. There's a psychological need for these authorities to understand that critical levels of the circumstances are changing and have also changed rapidly with time and the practices which evolved sustained in the society, while the regressive ones got thrown off. Not letting one's children marry or get along can be considered as the modern form of untouchability. It is doing inequality, but privately. Untouchability has been prohibited by various laws to diminish casteism. But the real challenge for the modern lawmakers is not to merely make laws against it, but also educate people and let them be in an emotionally growing phase and it has to be brought from within themselves.

An ideal societal structure is one which doesn't curtail the liberty of choice of any individual among themselves and upgrade the aspects regularly with time so as to make sure the need of time is catered and fulfilled with correctly.

ISSUE OF PERCEPTION

Let's take an instance, if a ship gets docked on the shores of the sentinel's island and the passengers get caught and killed by the tribals. Now it cannot be considered a crime or offence. (Sneha et al., 2020)It rightfully cannot be considered as so because the tribals of a distant island may not be aware about our humanitarian developments and may not be able to differentiate between right or wrong. Because there is a rule of perception playing in the picture for them. Killing the unwanted, now be it human or any animal is equal and not an offence. And stealing off some good from each other might be a crime, but it cannot be said the same about the human civilization we are living in, as far as the perception is concerned. Because through ages of civilization and academic research, it is now well established that discrimination of any kind stands baseless in the modern evolving world. (Rekha Verma, 2023) So, a man as a part of civilization cannot and should not take plea of perception in order to protect themselves from the consequences of these honor related crimes. Our perception cannot be so much regressing that in order to preserve our social wellbeing we can get off of our own children's choices. And if they don't follow the societal trials, many don't even consider any humanity before getting their children killed for the sake of the societal affirmations. These societal criminals don't even show a tinge of regret on getting busted and questioned, and mostly do not even get caught due to a severe grouping and protection among the other such like-minded individuals and group thus creating a sense of pride within themselves on killing their own children.

ROLE OF MEDIA IN PERCEPTION FRAMING

It looks evident that the major parts and decisions we make in our lives are somewhat related to what we consume from our televisions, be it the big media houses or some sitcom or any daily soap. These are the ways trough which information throughout the globe reaches us on our fingertips. What would happen if its sanctity were compromised? What if only filtered content reaches you? The significance of the media in shaping the public perception regarding honour killings cannot be ignored. A few points on how this is done include:

Awareness and Education: Media coverage brings honour killings to public attention, educating people about the severity and prevalence of these crimes. This can spark debates and discussions, leading to greater awareness and potential social change.

Framing and Bias: The way media frames these stories can influence public opinion. For instance, if the media portrays honour killings as isolated incidents rather than a systemic issue, it can affect how seriously the public and policymakers take the problem.

Cultural Representation: Media often highlights cultural aspects related to honour killings, which can sometimes lead to stereotyping and generalizations about certain communities. This can perpetuate harmful biases and overlook the broader socio-economic and gender-based factors involved.

Advocacy and Change: Positive media coverage can also advocate for victims and push for legal and social reforms. By highlighting stories of survivors and activists, the media can play a crucial role in driving change and supporting human rights.

What Do Women Have To Say

Women are the most important but still one of the most easily ignored sections of the society we live in.; thus, it becomes of utmost importance to understand their stance and involvement in relation to these crimes as they comprise half of the earth's population. Women's reaction and involvement to these crimes varies from region to region. For instance, if the Asian thought or more precisely the Indian thought is looked on to, we will see that:

- Women do not have much of a say in commencement of these crimes but it is majorly because their opinion is not asked for in most instances and even if they involve their say does not count.
- There is also a hidden element of support involved from the side of women in Indian society be it voluntarily or in the form of silence when these crimes incur.
- It is also that there is a sense of acceptance by the women as far as the societal rulebook is concerned and they somewhere see themselves to be bound to it too and thus remaining silent on these complex issues.

This dormancy is seen from such a section which is affected the most by these crimes as when we focus on the number mostly it is that only women are killed in the name of honor and men are granted pardon such is the extent of misogyny. This can more evidently be illustrated by the examples of Bhavana Yadav 21 and student of Venkateshwara College and Deepti Chikaara who were both killed by their families as they married out of their castes and the men in both the cases were left untouched.

So, this is clearly evident that that the most affected section is condemned unheard of and these crimes soar ferociously. (Patel, n.d.)

HATE CRIME AND HONOR CRIME-- CRIMINOLOGY AND CONNECTION

Criminology behind honor killings involves a great understanding of how lack of tolerance towards other social groups by the dominating social groups can lead to such an extent that fathers can kill their own children, brothers can kill their own siblings, but the thing that remains of utmost importance is the 'HONOR', and this pseudo sense of getting honor in the society has devastated and continues to haunt many family institutions. (Kejriwal, n.d.) The type and modes of committing these crimes may be different, but the problem at the very core of every such problem is none other than the intolerance of social groups towards each other. Many societies across world go on about experiencing atrocities based on religion and castes mainly the Asian and European ones. A complete other psychology runs through the religious groups, causing other sorts of hate crimes and further honor related crimes. This rudimentary mentality of the society can somewhat tolerate the intermingling of castes but intermixing of religion is strictly prohibited and also frowned upon by the young generation too.

But if the biological evidences are looked upon, it would be very beneficial if the intermingling of cast and religion is allowed. As the more varying is the gene pool from which the offsprings are produced, the more are the chances of having healthier offspring with more lifespan. (Kejriwal, n.d.) If the gene pool got limited and some recessive traits got expressed, the entire caste or community may become unwanted for producing healthy offspring thus, diminishing the community slowly, but steadily, so the mindset of preserving the gene pool and bloodline stands no scientific grounding because it could not become adverse for a shorter time but is not a good method for a Long run of humanity, but these concepts are completely alien to many of the members of the societies and groups across the globe, as they were not taught to them, and it completely contradicts their ancestral values and the divisional barrier that their ancestors created in their bloodlines, but they often forget about the decline of the Habsburg empire by the expression of recessive traits by strictly copulating in the same gene, pool again and again.

It has been engraved in the beliefs of the people at lower strata of the social group by the ones, leading it and making rules for it so angrily that people who try to break these chains are ignored, no matter how many evidence you produce because back in the head, the fear is not of breaking rules but of breaking the rules and getting removed from the social security remains the term. Social security might look very weak and slender, but can be counted as among the greatest calls for forcing a parent to diminish its own blood.

A society plays many roles and one of the most important ones is providing security and support to each other only if one complied with some beliefs and rule with which the elites of that group comply to and once, he does not comply as such, this support and security is withdrawn, and it is harder for a man to lead a life alone. Being cut off from the others after being accustomed to that culture and practice is hard and it is harder to rehabilitate in other culture too. At the same time, due to lack of cultural backing, it becomes impossible for a parent to break the social stigma and let the children live with the liberty they have been demanding of.

The other psychology, which runs through a parent's brain is that if I've married compliant to the written rule book so my children should do too and if the same is not done, it is seen as a sign of failure as apparent by them as well as the societal circle. This leads to parents developing hate towards their own children for making them feel down and humiliated in front of others, and among many steps to prevent this from happening, a final step or final resolution also creeps in their minds and that is to kill and let go. It's the stubbornness that if things don't happen my way, they aren't going to happen.(Vishwanath et al., 2011) This thought has to be countered by us as a society collectively. So, it could be evidently summed up that there is a very thin sliver of difference between hit rams and honor killings, or in the other words, the later could be considered as consequence of the former.

CHILDREN BEING FED WITH HATRED

For a child while he's maturing his mind. Set cause variety is the playground from where all the examples are drawn on which all observations are made.(Pdf-Honour-Killing-in-India compress, n.d.) And at the end, it is the place where the child experiments upon. Now if this whole process of feeding information to the child is flawed from the very beginning, we cannot expect very lively results because at the end, a result will be the accumulation of all the inputs made by us while raising our children. Now here take a moment to imagine about a scenario of a typical regressive society where honor related crimes are at peak and parents are killing their own children in name of maintaining the so-called social order.

Now, a young mind in corner of the same society is observing that the consequences of not abiding by the social norms have to be ruthless. Moreover, he also looks at the amount of social validation such acts get and no form of criticism is reported from either end. Now what sort of a man such a child is supposed to grow into. A god-fearing sane man or a validation seeking maniac. So, the main reason behind these crimes still being seen is they are culpably reproducing in the shadows of ignorant environment. And a child can never process what's right or what's wrong? Because his parents did it and were never questioned So it has to be right. This is greatest reason of reproduction of such regressive mentality. This leads to another greater problem that is "construction of young criminals".

This big-headed attitude of the society towards honor killings give birth to a different perspective of Justice in the young minds so much. So, they even do not care to know the true face of it. Neither do they want to care about the consequences. This kills the humanitarian face of a child in such a young age that he matures rapidly but to be violent. Because this toxic masculinity or this extremeness is very well accepted by the society and is not a big problem to the society and is not a big problem to the social beings in their minds, people are no longer people. They are objects which could be traded off or bought in. Also, they shouldn't have any rights to feel otherwise because if they have. So, it is a gigantic question upon their ascendancy and a challenge towards coursing their power and will.(Pdf-Honour-Killing-in-India compress, n.d.) These children are taught from the beginning that how the powerful automatic member has to be the part of decision-making in a family by all means, and when a couple Mary's due to its own wish, it's thought that they skipped the part where they had to take opinions from the family members and now it is intolerable for them to get sideline from participation in the decision-making process.

KHAP PANCHAYAT: THE UNAUTHORISED AUTHORITY WITH POWER IN EXCESS

It is a waste to discuss the criminology of the crimes which originated to gain limelight from here without discussing that how these panchayats manipulate people's mind and trade their souls with that of a monster to keep their opinion in power and importance. These panchayats enjoy a frivolous amount of power in their concerned areas and also, they sometimes mix their rudimentary nature in the justice system which by the way they are unauthorised to assume and exercise, they even forget that what they are trading off here are human lives. Because no human being knowingly can be so blind as these panchayat heads go while announcing their judgement and people acting like maniacs on listening to them.

This is nothing less than modern, society funded and organised terrorism because, there is no one else's say in announcing such crude and brut judgements. In name of saving religion and preserving social order they manipulate people's decision-making power by developing a sense of fear in them towards these so called undesired societal acts. These panchayats tend to involve and demean themselves in every possible such case because the deep psychology running behind this is that if any such crime is left unpunished it will weaken their hold on the social institution which they have a full control of. On one hand these rudimentary men say that marriages in the same gotras in a caste should be prevented at any cost as it will make the gene pool steeper and will bring no variety but, on the other hand they themselves ban the marriages among other caste and religion which is among one of the best ways to bring diversity to the gene pool.

They back this hypocrisy by invoking the demand to preserve culture, tradition and what not which on the other hand has no reasonable backing and the people keep on becoming fools. They now make people trained to preserve their religion, tradition and all the things prescribed in the social rulebook and pay whatever cost it may seek because, it is not the religion which is on stake but it is their power, and hegemonic control which in actuality is at stake.(What Does (and Does Not) Affect Crime in India?, n.d.) Trading off human existence has become so common and cheap for these pressure groups that their orders and guidelines are not questioned by even the intellectuals and influentials of the society as they consequences can be evidently adverse and rash which no one would want to deal with. Thus, it has become nearly impossible even in this era of justice to catch the real culprits and hang them as the social control is so tight that no one leave the names of the people involved at the top strata loose for even a second as the thing that is of utmost importance is their safety in order to maintain the social security and order in the later phases,

Example Intended Not The Crime

It is just out of rage that parents choose to spill the blood of their own children. It's difficult because no one is so much big a fool to look at this way. If it was to be looked up through another angle, these crimes are forced upon parents by the elite groups of society be it directly or indirectly just in order to set example for the future generations to come. If a couple is killed, it will eventually send message to thousands to be aware of such atrocities and eventually killing their hearts out. This example setting is so necessary that these pressure groups go on to make these crimes as ruthless as possible so that more people can get scared of the outcome and also at a greater degree, so that they can understand once caught, there is no coming back and the only way to communicate this to the youngsters is to set as grievous examples as possible.

If one is killed, thousands will fear but in shadows, but if one is killed and the murder is orchestrated lakhs will fear and ultimately, it'll be more beneficial and inevitable for the establishment of the societal authorities and hegemonies, which started this example setting in the first place meeting the results they wanted ultimately in a long run. The greater is the wound, the greater is the impact and the greater would be the fear, and ultimately the greater will be the authority. The impact is to be at a level that no other child should again muster up the courage to forge weapon against the will of parents, but in latent form it is the societal institutions which are at greater risks due to the forgery of such weapons. Thus, these crimes are showed off and the criminals are not even ashamed of it. In fact, they lead their remaining life in a pseudo sense of pride, which increases by each day passing due to the affirmations, appreciations and importance, gained in the societal circles through this act.

Religious Battle

For one his religion is always superior than the other's and no one would want to intermingle with the blood of lower quality and desirability but, what one forgets every time is that all human beings are made of same flesh, same tissue, same cells and even around 99% of everyone's DNA is same. So, are these fights based upon this 1% DNA and its variants. No, the battle is of pride, prejudice, culture, superiority and honor. It is the general thinking that the religion one follows and is born in contains the blood of the gods they have descended from. It is the fear of that blood getting impure and the traditions getting diluted that makes one hesitant to marry among different religions and stop creating a pseudo sense of pride which is baseless.(Korteweg & Yurdakul, 2010) Also, if looked at a macro level the religion politics play a role to seek a huge number of vote bank for some elites and the fear always sustain in their heart that if they intervened in the religious institutions and their rulebook, they might get thrashed in the elections to come ultimately losing power. So technically there would have been no religious conflict in the first place if these religions were not incited in order to play a mere game of politics so as someone can ensure his coming back in power.

There is no government in the world which is so weak that it could not quash such a brutal social malpractice. But the truth is no one care much about quashing it as if one does so it may outrage a particular religious group or even both groups for instance and the former will have to bear severe consequences. Thus, they find it better to refrain from these matters. Otherwise, it is the matter of a second and these malpractices would be in dustbin and we could focus on the progress the humanity has been looking towards since its dawn.

Normalisation of Crime

Now, this is one of the greatest Cause of these crimes to still exist. Because there is not even a single voice of backlash against them from anywhere inside their social circle or even families for that matter, where these crimes take place. If an offender is not told that he is an offender, what will maintain a check upon his future offences? Be it the fear of meeting the same fate or the fear of getting emancipated from the circles, but even if you feel this is wrong you can't say it loud in social circles, because for them it is the sign of their glory and grandiose. It is self-understood that it is stupid to tell against a topic which has a popular public support.

Still looking deeply into it as a society this malpractice should be tore limb off limb. Such great punishments should be prescribed for these crimes so as to dwarf down the authority of these social groups. Eventually, a voice from within the social group should come out against it as a result of these reforms. And that is the only way to perish these atrocities.(Blom Hansen & Roy, n.d.) We must understand it deeply that there is no greater question mark upon a civilization than to rip-off its own people's ambitions and that too in most inhumane way and these acts are living testimony to it.

The crimes are normalised up to the instant that neighbours, relatives, and even families seem them to be correct in these cases and no one raises voice. Sometimes it is ignored in lieu of that it's a family matter thus, no one care to involve much and sometimes it is the fear and previous learnings. But all in all, it is nothing but a huge failure for humanity and its believers as these criminals knows nothing about it and the spectators don't care much about it.

The orchestration of such crimes is done on a huge extent and still they go unreported what else is this other than the extent of normalisation. We will have to understand that there actually is no way out of such atrocities until there is a scream from within the observers and the spectators on the commencement of such crimes. Each one of us should and must come out of the delusional state we are in and ensure as brutal punishment as possible for the culprits of such wrongdoings.

RADICALIZATION

It is most dangerous act, which can't be reversed by almost no means. As once you engrave something deep within a budding brain Be it good or bad. It is going to leave a crater for lifetime, for example Once a man is taught that killing people and intolerance is the only way no matter how sane he becomes in later phases of his life, the men will always look at the intolerance as the last resort to solve all his problems. Once this option is introduced in front of young minds there is no going back. Thus, we need to refrain these social groups to put opinions on how a society is to be governed, and what rule book to follow because, at the end if we follow them the whole society will collapse.

This social radicalisation in no way is different than the religious radicalisation that causes terrorist attacks because in the end they also harm human existence as th other do too. Man being a social animal cannot and do not want to detach from the memberships of his social circle.(Dublish & Khan, 2021) He may bear any harm living in it, he may even get radicalised and live in a fallacy that whatever being fed to me by my source of information is the eternal truth and anyone else with different opinion is either wrong, frivolous or even ineligible to live but never will he leave such depriving social institution unless kicked from it.

Now summing up, let's briefly look at and point out whom to blame for such crimes:

- Offensive attitude towards children with different opinion
- Lifestyle in which children are brought up in
- Strong social circles
- Family allowances towards such crimes
- Living arrangements facilitating such crimes
- Religion politics playing on numbers
- Objectification of human existence

In the end a moral question that we should put in front of ourselves is that in almost all parts of the globe, drinking smoking drug addiction is not much of a bigger problem to parents, but marrying by once choice is. How could a great civilization be tolerant of these toxic signs of manhood, but intolerant of the purest union of love? This is to be thought through and understood that society has greater problems to deal than to perish its own blood and identifying the real foes will be nicer alternative than to kill the ambitious.

CASE ANALYSES

Qandeel Baloch (Pakistan, 2016): Qandeel Baloch, a social media star, was murdered by her brother in an honour killing. The reason for her outspoken and bold presence on social media was seen as tarnishing the honor of her family.

Banaz Mahmod (UK, 2006): Banaz Mahmod was killed by her father and uncle in London for leaving an abusive arranged marriage and starting a relationship with another man. Her case brought into focus the problems that women in diaspora communities.

Samia Sarwar (Pakistan, 1999): Samia Sarwar was murdered in her lawyer's office by an assassin hired by her family. She was trying to get a divorce from her abusive husband and planned to marry another man, which was the reason for her family's opposition.

Ghazala Khan (Denmark, 2005): Ghazala Khan was slain by her brother, who prevailed upon nine other family members to join them, for marrying against their wishes. This incident was a key driver of the legal reforms Denmark undertook to combat honor violence.

Shafilea Ahmed (UK, 2003): Shafilea Ahmed was murdered by her parents for resisting an arranged marriage and adopting a Western lifestyle. Her case turned the spotlight on the issue of honor killings within immigrant communities in the UK.

REFERENCES

Blom Hansen, T., & Roy, S. (n.d.). *Saffron Republic: Hindu Nationalism and State Power in India.* Book Review.

Dublish, D., & Khan, Y. (2021). Impact of Honour Killings in Haryana, India. *Social Science Journal for Advanced Research*, 1(2), 33–40. DOI: 10.54741/ssjar.1.2.6

Juškevičiūtė, J., & Jakab, M. (n.d.). *Honour Killings: A Social and Legal Approach.* https://doi.org/DOI: 10.13165/PSPO-20-25-12

Kejriwal, -Neelam. (n.d.). *Honour Killing in North India.*

Khan, Y. (n.d.). A Sociological Perspective of Honour Killing in India. *International Journal of Engineering and Management Research.* Advance online publication. DOI: 10.31033/ijemr.9.6.21

Korteweg, A. C., & Yurdakul, G. (2010). *Palais des Nations, 1211 Geneva 10, Switzerland. UNRISD welcomes such applications.*

Patel, V. (n.d.). *Smart Cities have to be Safe Cities Prof. Vibhuti Patel.* https://www.researchgate.net/publication/291514771

pdf-honour-killing-in-india_compress. (n.d.).

Poddar, A. (2020). *Reprehensible Behaviour: The Social Meaning Behind Honour Killings in India.*

Rekha Verma, D. (2023). Psycho-socio facets of honour killing. In *Russian Law Journal: Vol. XI.*

Sneha, S., Sarathi, S., Kumar, P. S., Rajesh, R., & Jagdish Kamal, C. U. (2020). Perspective on the immorality of Honor Killings-A review article. *Medico-Legal Update*, 20(1), 68–71. DOI: 10.37506/v20/i1/2020/mlu/194296

Vishwanath, J., & Palakonda, S. C. (2011). Patriarchal ideology of honour and honour crimes in India. *International Journal of Criminal Justice Sciences*, 6(1).

What Does (and Does Not) Affect Crime in India? (n.d.).

KEY TERMS AND DEFINITIONS

Community Councils: Local governing bodies that often take the lead in enforcing cultural norms, sometimes sanctioning honor-related crimes. (Sneha et al., 2020)

Cross-Cultural Studies: Comparative research that studies the similarities and differences across various cultures regarding honor-related crimes. (Vishwanath et al., 2011)

Cultural Norms: Shared expectations and rules that guide behaviour within a specific cultural or social group, often dictating the roles of men and women and the concept of honor.

Diaspora Communities: Immigrant communities living outside their native country, where traditional norms related to honor may persist and conflict with the laws and values of the host country. (Rekha Verma, 2023)

Digital Activism: Advocacy for social change using online tools and platforms to combat honor-related crimes and support survivors. (Khan, n.d.)

Educational Programs: Awareness-raising activities and programs that work on attitudinal change toward honor-related crimes, often targeting communities with significant occurrences of these crimes. (Sneha et al., 2020)

Gender Dynamics: The power relations between men and women in a society, often influencing the occurrence of honor-related crimes, which disproportionately affect women. (Khan, n.d.)

Globalization: An increase in interconnectivity between countries, which can lead to the spread of ideas challenging traditional norms that justify honor-related crimes. (Rekha Verma, 2023)

Honor-Based Crimes: Crimes committed to protect or restore the perceived honour of a family or community, mainly involving violence against women perceived to have defied cultural or religious expectations. (Vishwanath et al., 2011)

Influence of the Media: The power of media attention and representation in influencing public opinion and attitudes towards honour crimes, thus setting the tone for societal and legal responses. (Blom Hansen & Roy, n.d.)

Intergenerational Transmission: The passing down of cultural norms and values related to honor from one generation to the next, often perpetuating cycles of violence. (Sneha et al., 2020)

International Human Rights Law: A body of international law designed to protect human rights globally, including the rights of individuals at risk of honor-related violence. (Patel, n.d.)

Judicial Systems: Institutions and processes responsible for interpreting and enforcing the law, playing a crucial role in prosecuting and preventing honor-related crimes.

Khap Panchayats: Traditional community councils in certain regions, particularly in South Asia, that often enforce cultural norms related to honor, sometimes endorsing or justifying honor-related violence. (Vishwanath et al., 2011)

Legal Approaches: The varied strategies and frameworks that legal systems employ to address honor-related crimes, including prosecution, protection orders, and victim support. (Vishwanath et al., 2011)

Legal Reforms: Changes in the law aimed at improving protection for individuals from honor-related crimes, often through stricter penalties and broader definitions of these crimes. (Blom Hansen & Roy, n.d.)

Legal Systems: Frameworks of laws and institutions that govern societies, including how honor-based crimes are prosecuted and punished.

Modernization: The process of societal change that includes shifts toward more progressive values and attitudes, potentially reducing the incidence of honor-related crimes. (Patel, n.d.)

Psychological Profiling: This is the process of looking into the psychological and behavioural makeup of an individual to understand their motives and predict any likelihood of criminal behaviour. (Blom Hansen & Roy, n.d.)

Religious Beliefs: Spiritual doctrines and practices that can influence individuals' perceptions of honor and justify certain behaviours, including violence in the name of honor.

Social Media: Online platforms that can be used to influence, rally, and campaign public opinion in support of the victims of honor-related crimes and to raise awareness and promote legal reforms. (Rekha Verma, 2023)

Societal Attitudes: Collective beliefs and values held by a community or society that may either condemn or condone honor crimes. (Khan, n.d.)

Societal Pressure: The influence exerted by society or a community that demands individuals adopt established norms and expectations, which may eventually lead individuals to honor-related crimes.

Societal Traditional Structures: Recognized social hierarchies and roles within a community that maintain honor-related crimes, often prioritizing family reputation over individual rights. (Sneha et al., 2020)

Women's Agency: The ability of women to act independently and make their own choices, which can be highly limited in societies where honor-related crimes are common. (Patel, n.d.)

Chapter 3
Feminism and Honor Killing With Special Reference to the 21st Century

Somesh Dhamija
GLA University, Mathura, India

Narendra Singh
GLA University, Mathura, India

ABSTRACT

The chapter explores the evolution of feminism and its impact on addressing gender discrimination and promoting women's rights and equality particularly in the 21st century. The aim of the chapter is to explore the role of feminism in advocating for women's rights and dismantling patriarchal norms, with a specific focus on addressing issues such as gender pay gaps, workplace discrimination and representation in leadership roles. The chapter involves a historical analysis of the four phases of feminism. Participants include women and girls impacted by gender discrimination, as well as advocates and activists involved in promoting women's rights. The context of the study encompasses global awareness, legal reforms, educational initiatives, women's empowerment, social media, and cultural exchange. The dismantling of patriarchal norms has helped lower crimes such as honor killings and contributed to a more just and equal society.

Estimates suggest that between 5,000 and 25,000 honor killings occur globally each year. This wide range is due to differences in reporting practices and the availability of data (Heydari et al., 2021a).

DOI: 10.4018/979-8-3693-7240-1.ch003

RESEARCH METHODOLOGY

This research will utilize a multi-faceted methodology to examine the interplay between feminism and honor killings, exploring historical, cultural, and contemporary dimensions. A comprehensive literature review will be conducted to analyze historical texts, academic articles, and cultural studies on the evolution of feminism, honor killings, and patriarchal practices. Qualitative data will be gathered through in-depth interviews with scholars, activists, and survivors to gain insights into the impacts of feminist movements on honor-based violence and societal norms. Quantitative analysis will involve reviewing statistical data on honor killings and gender inequality to measure trends and correlations. Case studies from various cultural contexts will be analyzed to understand the specific socio-cultural factors influencing honor killings and the effectiveness of feminist interventions. This approach will provide a nuanced understanding of how feminist principles challenge honor-based violence and contribute to broader gender equality efforts.

KEY TERMS

Key terms in this exploration of feminism and gender equality include "Feminism"(Srivastava et al., 2017) which refers to the advocacy for women's rights and the dismantling of patriarchal norms "Gender Pay Gap"(Heydari et al., 2021b), the disparity in earnings between men and women for similar work; "Workplace Discrimination" the unfair treatment of individuals based on gender in professional environments; "Representation in Leadership"(Huda & Kamal, 2020), the presence and influence of women in senior roles within organizations; "Honor Killings", a form of violence where individuals, often women, are murdered by family members for perceived violations of "Family Honor" and "Patriarchy"(Wynn, 2021) a social system where men hold primary power and authority. The historical "Waves of Feminism" encapsulate the evolution of feminist movements, starting with the first wave advocating for political and social rights. "Cultural Exchange" and "Social Media" have significantly influenced global feminist discourse, while "Legal Reforms" and "Educational Initiatives"(Gill, 2014) continue to play crucial roles in advancing women's rights and combating systemic gender discrimination.

LITERATURE REVIEW

The author proposes a multi-faceted research methodology to explore the complex relationship between feminism and honor killings, incorporating historical, cultural, and contemporary perspectives. The study will start with a thorough literature review of historical texts, academic articles, and cultural studies to trace the development of feminist thought and its interaction with patriarchal practices and honor-based violence (Srivastava et al., 2017).

The author presents a nuanced examination of honor killing, arguing that it is a complex social issue not fully explained by religion or sexism alone. Instead, the author employs a feminist Durkheimian perspective to analyze honor killing as a form of informal social control (Heydari et al., 2021b).

The author reviews the historical evolution of psychological research on sexism, emphasizing the shift from understanding gender as solely biological to recognizing its cultural dimensions. The article differentiates between overt, explicit sexism and more subtle, implicit forms characterized by ambivalent attitudes of both hostility and benevolence towards women (Lorenzi-Cioldi & Kulich, 2015).

The author presents a nuanced examination of honor killing, arguing that it is a complex social issue not fully explained by religion or sexism alone. Instead, the author employs a feminist Durkheimian perspective to analyze honor killing as a form of informal social control (Huda & Kamal, 2020)

FUTURE RESEARCH DIRECTIONS

In exploring future research directions, the author focus on the intersectional dimensions of honor-based violence (HBV), particularly how globalization and digital media are reshaping feminist responses and activism in the 21st century. This research have delve into how factors such as race, ethnicity, religion, and socioeconomic status influence both the experiences of survivors and the effectiveness of feminist interventions(Pina-López, 2014). It is also crucial to analyze how global migration, transnational feminist networks, and international human rights frameworks affect responses to HBV at both local and global levels. Additionally, we need to assess how digital media contributes to raising awareness, mobilizing support, and challenging entrenched cultural norms. By using interviews with survivors, activists, and policymakers, along with detailed case studies, media content analysis, and policy reviews, this research will aim to provide a thorough understanding of how modern global and digital factors impact efforts to combat honor-based violence, ultimately helping to develop more nuanced and effective strategies for prevention and intervention in our interconnected world. This research will explore how intersecting factors such as gender, race, ethnicity, and socioeconomic status influence experiences of HBV and the effectiveness of feminist interventions(Huang, 2023). It will also assess how cultural and patriarchal beliefs continue to shape practices related to honor killings and how contemporary feminist strategies can address these entrenched norms.

INTRODUCTION

The brawl for the recognition of rights and gender equality breaks history in four phases which is also known as "THE WAVES OF FEMINISM" in which the contribution of the natives of America plays the major role. The first fight against the status of women or the first wave of feminism took place in New York city at Seneca Falls. It was the time between 1960-1970s when this notion feminism was influencing American women with their rights in political, social and as well as economic status to be established. Feminism has played a crucial role in promoting equality throughout history and reaching every corner of the world by advocating for women's rights and addressing systematic discrimination. In the 21st century, progress for women's rights has been undefinable. Feminism continues to address issues like gender pay gaps, workplace discrimination and representation in leadership roles. The practice of honor killing was influencing patriarchal approach a lot where women and girl child were not seen as of same status as other men in the family. The soul of feminism is the truth that women deserve equal, social, economic and political rights.

Since its origin feminism has focused on issues like the right to vote, reproductive and sexual freedom and equal pay. Feminism has also explored and touched others expect of racism and gender norms.

Throughout the cultures all around the globe and through every span of time, women are considered as divine, like in ancient Sparta women held power, they could inherit property, make business transactions and receive good education. There have also always been women who fought back against patriarchal cultures. According to Indian Vedas, females are considered venerable. Women in our country have always been a symbol of purity and power. Women are truly the source of all origin. A man without his woman is nothing, in our culture even the gods can be observed, being supported by their goddesses. Shiva without Shakti, Vishnu without Laxmi and Krishna without Radha were considered as incomplete.

At the beginning of the eighth century the status of women started decreasing gradually as the Pardha system come into the existence and was treated as the custom and women were treated as subservient to the men and having no significance, no personal status and were seen as inferior species. This had let to many adverse effects on the society like complete abolishment of the ideology of matriarchy and this encouraged the killing of women and girl child for the honor of the men and their family(ray, 1999). The objective of honor, shame and its use for whitewash the violence on the name honor killing is not a new thing for any civilization in the historical past throughout centuries. Honor based killing involve women as collaborator. Honor killing is a death awarded to a women or men by their own family member for degrading their family status. By going against the social norms of honor these norms can conclude:

- Ritualism
- Sexually immoral actions
- Suspicion of impurity
- Marriage out of caste and against family

Suppression of women acted as a major catalyst to boost the honor killing in society. In 20th century honor killings had skyrocketed due to almost no value for life of a women in this scenario we can openly observe a suffering of being a woman(Srivastava et al., 2017). The dowry system struck down the social structure which was being followed from ancient times. The prime factor of the crime is – majority caste members do not accept inter-caste marriage to maintain the decorum of their caste or status of their family in society. Due to the complex socio-cultural problems the crime of honor killing is divulging at the high rate. In the practice of honor killings, the person's prime focus is just to get back his honor while the victims of honor killings have loved someone out of their caste or without the permission of the family they just decided to live there life by their own and this is the wrong according to the corrupt mind people who lost their honor.

Women's liberation addresses honor slaughtering with a special viewpoint that centers on sexual orientation balance, human rights, and the destroying of patriarchal structures. Honor slaughtering, a hone in which people, as a rule ladies, are killed by family individuals or community individuals to reestablish seen misplaced honor, is profoundly established in social, social, and patriarchal convictions. Feminism's approach to tending to honor killings is multifaceted and transformative, emphasizing the require for systemic alter, instruction, and empowerment.

UNDERSTANDING HONOR MURDERING THROUGH A WOMEN'S ACTIVIST LENS

At its center, woman's rights studies the patriarchal standards that support honor killings. Patriarchy upholds inflexible sex parts and values women's lives based on their adherence to these parts. Honor killings are regularly advocated by the conviction that ladies must maintain family honor through their behavior, and disappointment to acclimate can result in extraordinary discipline. Woman's rights reject these belief systems by pushing for women's independence, dismissing the idea that a woman's worth is tied to her adherence to patriarchal expectations.

Feminists contend that honor killings are not separated occurrences but or maybe appearances of systemic gender-based viciousness. They highlight that these acts are a coordinate result of social orders that sustain imbalance and limit women's flexibility. By surrounding honor killings as a shape of gender-based savagery, woman's rights broaden the discussion past social relativism and person cases, emphasizing the require for auxiliary alter to address the root causes of such violence(Gill, 2014).

Challenging Social Relativism

One one of a kind angle of the women's activist approach to honor killings is its evaluate of social relativism. Social relativism is the thought that social hones ought to be caught on inside their possess social setting, regularly driving to the avocation of hurtful hones beneath the pretense of regarding social differing qualities. Women's activists challenge this by contending that human rights and sexual orientation balance ought to rise above social boundaries. They attest that honor killings damage essential human rights and that tending to these hones requires a commitment to all-inclusive standards of equity and equality.

Feminism advocates for a adjust between social affectability and the assurance of person rights. It recognizes the significance of social settings but keeps up that hones that result in viciousness or separation ought to not be endured. By situating honor killings as a infringement of widespread human rights, women's liberation pushes for universal and nearby legitimate systems that prioritize women's security and respect over social legitimizations for violence.

Empowering Ladies and Changing Institutions

A critical viewpoint of feminism's approach to combating honor killings is its center on enabling ladies and changing educate. Women's activists contend that enabling ladies through instruction, financial autonomy, and lawful rights is pivotal for avoiding honor killings. When ladies have the capacity to make their claim choices and get to assets, they are less likely to be controlled by patriarchal standards and are way better situated to stand up to and elude damaging situations.

Reforming educate is another basic component. Women's activists advocate for legitimate changes that criminalize honor killings and hold culprits responsible. They call for changes in law requirement, lawful frameworks, and social administrations to guarantee that casualties of honor-based viciousness get security and bolster. This incorporates preparing for law authorization and legal work force to recognize and address honor-based viciousness suitably and sensitively.

Intersectionality and Comprehensive Advocacy

Feminism's approach to honor killings is too educated by intersectionality, which considers how different shapes of abuse cross to influence people in an unexpected way. Intersectional women's liberation recognizes that honor killings excessively influence ladies from marginalized communities, counting those from minority ethnic or devout bunches. It addresses how components such as race, lesson, and migration status can impact both the predominance of honor-based viciousness and the adequacy of reactions to it.

By utilizing an intersectional system, woman's rights guarantees that promotion and arrangements are comprehensive and address the assorted needs of influenced people. This approach too highlights the significance of including community pioneers and activists from inside influenced communities in the battle against honor killings. It cultivates collaborative endeavors that regard social settings whereas endeavoring for sexual orientation balance and human rights.

Raising Mindfulness and Changing Attitudes

Feminism plays a vital part in raising mindfulness almost honor killings and changing societal states of mind. Women's activist organizations and activists work to teach the open approximately the substances of honor-based savagery and challenge hurtful generalizations and myths. They utilize different stages, counting media campaigns, instructive programs, and open showings, to bring consideration to the issue and mobilize collective action.

By tending to honor killings through open talk and promotion, women's liberation looks for to move social demeanors that normalize or pardon savagery against ladies. It advances a culture of regard and balance, where women's rights are seen as non-negotiable and savagery is generally condemned.

CAUSES OF HONOR KILLING

Patriarchal Norms and Gender Inequality

At the core of honor killings is the entrenched patriarchy that values women's lives based on their adherence to traditional gender roles. Patriarchal societies often enforce rigid expectations for women's behavior, considering them as bearers of family honor. When women defy these norms—through acts such as choosing a partner, engaging in premarital sex, or rejecting arranged marriages—family members may view these actions as dishonorable, prompting extreme responses, including violence(Pina-López, 2014).

Cultural and Religious Justifications

Honor killings are frequently justified by cultural and religious beliefs. In some societies, interpretations of cultural and religious doctrines reinforce the idea that preserving family honor justifies violence against women. This is particularly prevalent in communities where honor is closely tied to family reputation and social status. Although not representative of mainstream religious teachings, extremist interpretations can perpetuate the practice(Churchill, 2018).

Socioeconomic Factors

Socioeconomic stress can exacerbate honor-based violence. In contexts of economic hardship or social instability, maintaining social status becomes even more critical, and deviations from expected norms are viewed as threats to family reputation. Additionally, economic dependence on women's adherence to traditional roles can drive families to resort to violence to ensure compliance and preserve economic and social stability.

Legal and Institutional Weaknesses

The prevalence of honor killings is often bolstered by weak legal frameworks and ineffective law enforcement. In some countries, legal systems either do not adequately criminalize honor killings or allow leniency towards perpetrators due to cultural biases. This impunity reinforces the belief that honor-based violence can be committed without serious legal consequences.

Lack of Education and Awareness

Limited education and awareness about human rights contribute to the persistence of honor killings. In many communities, traditional beliefs and practices go unchallenged due to a lack of access to education and information. Without exposure to alternative viewpoints and legal standards, harmful practices like honor killings remain entrenched.

PREVALENCE OF HONOR KILLING IN THE 21ST CENTURY

Global Distribution

Honor killings are a global phenomenon, although they are more prevalent in certain regions. Reports and studies indicate that honor killings are particularly common in South Asia (India, Pakistan, Bangladesh), the Middle East (Jordan, Egypt, Saudi Arabia), and among immigrant communities in Europe and North America. The actual number of honor killings worldwide is difficult to quantify due to underreporting and variations in how such cases are classified.

Recent Trends

In the 21st century, several trends have emerged:

Increased Awareness and Reporting: There has been growing awareness and documentation of honor killings due to the efforts of activists, NGOs, and international organizations. This has led to increased reporting and visibility of honor-based violence, although the true extent of the problem may still be underreported.

Legal Reforms and Resistance: Some countries have made significant strides in addressing honor killings through legal reforms and advocacy. For example, Turkey and Jordan have introduced stricter laws against honor-based violence. However, resistance from conservative elements within these societies often hampers the effective implementation of these reforms.

Migration and Diaspora Issues: The migration of individuals from high-prevalence regions to Western countries has brought issues of honor-based violence to the forefront in new contexts. Immigrant communities sometimes struggle with the clash between traditional practices and the legal standards of their new countries, leading to complex legal and social challenges(Roberts et al., 2013).

Technological and Social Media Influence: Social media and digital platforms have become crucial in raising awareness about honor killings and mobilizing activism. They provide a space for survivors to share their stories, and for global networks to coordinate advocacy efforts. However, these platforms also pose challenges, as they can sometimes become battlegrounds for conflicting cultural values(Dalvi, n.d.).

THE RISE OF FEMINISM

Feminism is not just focused on the rights of female; some people consider feminism as womanism, but feminism is a class of socio-political action for the equal rights and opportunities for all genders. And this ideology has led us to eliminate the challenges of gender-based discrimination, workplace discrimination and challenging stereotypes. It contributes to creating a more diverse society and nurture equal opportunities for all genders. When in society men started thinking that women are less capable to them in every aspect of the means of work from that day the degradation of the status of the women increased, when the customs were changed then women were suppressed through various norms and got tangled in the men-based socio culture.

This very movement was enough to let the rise of feminism. When we see a spring is pressed very hard then it bounces back with same energy similarly when women were suppressed so thoroughly which neglected their status in the society and their rights were infringed than it bounces back with same energy as revolution which is called as feminism. In Europe the condition of women was very terrible they were not treated as equal to men they don't have their own social life, they were confined within domestic sphere only the basic rights like right to property, right to education, right to vote were restricted to the women.

In late 14th- and early 15th-century France, the first feminist philosopher, Christine de Pisan, challenged prevailing attitudes toward women with a bold call for female education. Her mantle was taken up later in the century by Laura Cereta, a 15th-century Venetian woman who published Epistolae familiars (1488; "Personal Letters"; Eng. trans. Collected Letters of a Renaissance Feminist), a volume of letters dealing with a panoply of women's complaints, from denial of education and marital oppression to the frivolity of women's attire.(Brunell Laura, n.d.)

Feminism in 21st Century

In today's world if we see the meaning of feminism has been turned out fully the social media handles, main media and the different ideologies formed has changed everything, they have shown the very violent and evil face of feminism in which they have stated that now women are asking for anything beyond the ambit of giving. Real feminism has been flipped with radical feminism which basically talks about that if we are not accepting patriarchy then why should we adopt matriarchy?

The real women who are struggling for their rights are being neglected and their emergence is very slow, if any real woman talks on real facts and issues then her ideas are shown in negative aspect which affects the whole society with wrong message, which is very dangerous. The real feminism is abolishing which helped women to stand where they are now, the struggle of real women and feminists. In author's view as the 20th century helped women to get their status back and all the movements done there should be remain constant in 21st century too as the need of a new definition for the women having their rights and the ability to live her life by her own. Some stigmas are still left which needs to be taken into consideration are as follows:

Gender Discrimination

Gender discrimination is having unequal treatment based on individual gender. By this means the women have faced many challenges like limitation in education, employment and public life. In every society these norms and stereotypes have sustained gender inequality, leading to systematic biasness. Feminism has played an important role in fighting gender discrimination. Legal frameworks have addressed promoting equal opportunities and protection against discrimination. Challenges like gender pay gaps, representation of women in leadership roles and all these stereotypes need to be solved through feminism. All these deep-rooted beliefs are required to be abolished and promoting of education on gender equality is to be focused in the 21st century. A society free of gender discrimination should have a lot of collective commitments to dismantle the discriminatory practices.

Sexism

Favoring one gender over other and having discriminatory practices based on gender, led to sexism. Feminism is having revolt against abolishing sexism. The feminist movement has had a profound impact on combating sexism, its effects rippling across societies and influencing various aspects of life. By empowering women and girls, feminism has instilled a sense of agency and empowerment in them. Feminism is a direct challenge to the ingrained stereotypes. Feminism is a great wave of revolution, it is the movement against sexism that has historically brought reduction in oppressed women the objective is to achieve a world were individuals are treated fairly, irrespective of their gender(Lorenzi-Cioldi & Kulich, 2015). Honor killings are deeply rooted in gender-based discrimination and sexism. Women are the perceiver of violence and ill treatment. Based on violation of cultural and family honor related to identity or sexuality the females are always targeted. With respect to sexism a woman is necessarily accepted to conform to traditional gender roles and societal expectations and norms. And when they seek freedom, it is viewed as a threat to honor and this notion led to honor killings based on idea of sexism.

HONOR KILLINGS AND GENDER-BASED DISCRIMINATION

Honor killings are a severe manifestation of sexism and gender-based discrimination. They are typically justified by the need to restore or preserve perceived family honor, which is often linked to the behavior and sexuality of women.

1. **Cultural and Family Honor**: In many cultures, family honor is closely tied to the behavior and reputation of women. Women are often seen as the bearers of family honor, and their actions are scrutinized to ensure compliance with traditional norms. When women challenge these norms—by engaging in relationships outside prescribed boundaries or asserting their autonomy—they are viewed as threats to family honor.
2. **Violence as a Tool of Control**: Honor killings are used as a means of controlling and disciplining women who are perceived to have violated cultural or family norms. This form of violence is rooted in the belief that women must conform to traditional roles and expectations. When women seek freedom or assert their rights, it is seen as a direct challenge to established gender roles, justifying extreme measures to enforce compliance.
3. **Sexism and Justification of Violence**: The justification of honor killings is deeply intertwined with sexist beliefs. These beliefs view women as subordinate and their actions as directly impacting family honor. As a result, violence against women is rationalized as a necessary action to preserve social and cultural values. This rationale perpetuates a cycle of violence and discrimination, reinforcing the notion that women must adhere to restrictive norms to avoid harm.

Role of Khaap Panchayats on Women Rights and Honor Killings

In the different embroidered artwork of Indian society, the Khaap Panchayat framework holds a disputable and noteworthy put, especially concerning women's rights and honor killings. Starting from provincial conventions, these casual, frequently unelected boards apply significant impact over neighborhood communities. Whereas they are praised by a few for keeping up social arrange and convention, their affect on women's rights and hones like honor slaughtering paints a upsetting picture. This paper dives into the part of Khaap Panchayats in India, centering on their impact on women's rights and the exasperating predominance of honor killings(Bharadwaj, 2012).

Historical Setting and Working of Khaap Panchayats

Khaap Panchayats are conventional town chambers in parts of North India, especially in Haryana, Uttar Pradesh, and Rajasthan. Their beginnings can be followed to antiquated times when such chambers were fundamentally to town organization and struggle determination. Customarily, these panchayats were composed of regarded older folks who represented based on standard laws and social norms. In modern India, Khaap Panchayats are not formally recognized by the state and work exterior the bounds of the official legitimate framework. In spite of their informal status, they use critical impact in country zones, frequently expecting a quasi-legal part in upholding social standards and settling disputes.

IMPACT ON WOMEN'S RIGHTS

The part of Khaap Panchayats in connection to women's rights is multifaceted. On one hand, they can propagate sex separation through their adherence to patriarchal standards. For occurrence, numerous Khaap Panchayats maintain hones that confine women's flexibility and independence. Women's rights issues habitually come to the fore in their thoughts, especially with respect to marriage choices and dress codes. One of the most dazzling illustrations is their position on inter-caste and inter-religious relational unions. Khaap Panchayats regularly restrict such unions, seeing them as dangers to community cohesion and conventional values. This resistance as often as possible leads to extreme results for ladies who resist these standards. Ladies in such circumstances are forced to acclimate to the council's manages, regularly beneath danger of savagery or ostracism.

Honor Killings and Khaap Panchayats

Honor killings, a aggravating wonder wherein people are killed by family individuals or community individuals to reestablish seen family honor, have been connected to the impact of Khaap Panchayats. These killings are ordinarily advocated by affirmed breaches of family honor, such as wedding against conventional standards or locks in in connections considered inappropriate. Khaap Panchayats play a central part in authorizing these acts of savagery. They regularly issue fatwas or orders that support or legitimize honor killings, especially in cases including inter-caste or inter-religious connections. The councils' capacity to mobilize community assumption and their control over neighborhood social standards can make an environment where honor killings are not as it were condoned but encouraged.

Legal and Social Reactions

The Indian government and legal have taken steps to combat the impact of Khaap Panchayats and address honor killings. Enactment such as the "Prohibition of Child Marriage Act" and the "Criminal Law (Revision) Act" point to defend women's rights and check hones related with Khaap Panchayats. Moreover, Incomparable Court decisions have condemned honor killings and called for stricter authorization of laws to ensure victims(Jakhar, n.d.). Despite these measures, requirement remains challenging due to the profoundly dug in impact of Khaap Panchayats in rustic regions. Casualties of honor killings regularly confront obstructions in looking for equity, as nearby specialists may be complicit or unwilling to challenge effective panchayats.

Positive Roles of Khaap Panchayats

1. Preservation of Cultural Heritage: Khaap Panchayats often play a role in preserving local customs and traditions. In some communities, they help maintain cultural continuity, which can foster a sense of identity and belonging. This role can positively impact women by upholding cultural practices that are meaningful to them, such as festivals and rituals that empower female participation and leadership(Yadav et al., n.d.).
2. Conflict Resolution and Social Order: Traditionally, Khaap Panchayats have been instrumental in resolving local disputes and maintaining social order. By providing a forum for community discussions, they can offer mediation services that sometimes help resolve issues more swiftly than formal legal processes. This aspect can be beneficial when disputes are resolved amicably, avoiding prolonged litigation that might disadvantage women.
3. Community Support Systems: In certain cases, Khaap Panchayats act as support networks for women. They might provide assistance in times of need, such as during family disputes or crises, and can sometimes play a role in advocating for women's welfare within their traditional framework(Navin Kumar, 2013).

Negative Roles of Khaap Panchayats

1. Perpetuation of Gender Discrimination: Khaap Panchayats often uphold patriarchal norms that restrict women's rights and freedoms. They may enforce discriminatory practices related to dress codes, educational opportunities, and employment. Women might face limitations on their personal choices, including decisions about marriage, employment, and mobility, reinforcing gender inequality.
2. Opposition to Inter-Caste and Inter-Religious Marriages: One of the most significant negative impacts of Khaap Panchayats is their opposition to inter-caste and inter-religious marriages. This opposition can lead to social ostracism, coercion, and violence against individuals who choose to marry outside traditional boundaries. Women, in particular, may face severe consequences for defying these norms, including forced marriages and social exclusion.
3. Sanctioning of Honor Killings: Khaap Panchayats have been linked to the endorsement and justification of honor killings—murders committed to restore perceived family honor. They may issue decrees or fatwas that legitimize such violence, creating an environment where honor killings are not only condoned but actively encouraged. This sanctioning of violence represents a grave violation of human rights and undermines the safety and autonomy of women.
4. Resistance to Legal and Social Reforms: The influence of Khaap Panchayats often results in resistance to progressive legal and social reforms aimed at improving women's rights. Their adherence to traditional norms can hinder efforts to implement laws designed to protect women from violence and discrimination. This resistance perpetuates outdated practices and obstructs the advancement of gender equality.

DEPRECIATION IN HONOR KILLINGS

In many countries honor killing is seen as a social disaster which is to be managed and explained deeply. Honor killings are often considered a dark side of modernity, as they reflect a complex interplay between traditional cultural norms, societal expectations, and the challenges posed by rapid social changes. Here are several ways in which honor killings can be seen as a dark aspect of modernity(Heydari et al., 2021b). While modernity has seen strides towards gender equality, honor killings persist as a manifestation of deeply entrenched patriarchal norms. The act often targets women perceived to have violated traditional gender roles, highlighting a dark aspect of persistent gender inequality within modern societies. The rise of social media, a hallmark of modern communication, has also been linked to instances of honor killings. Perceived violations of honor, often involving relationships or online behavior, can escalate quickly and tragically, showcasing a dark intersection between technology and traditional values. Understanding honor killings as a dark side of modernity requires a nuanced examination of the tensions between traditional values and the ideals of a progressive society. Addressing this issue necessitates a comprehensive approach that considers cultural, legal, and social dimensions to foster genuine societal change. In the 21st century, changes in perspective towards honor killings have been observed in societies with evolving perspectives on human rights, gender equality, and cultural norms. Several factors contribute to these shifts:

1. Legal Reforms: Many countries have strengthened their legal frameworks to condemn and punish honor killings. Stricter laws and penalties aim to send a clear message that such acts will not be tolerated.
2. Global Awareness: Increased global awareness through media coverage and international human rights campaigns has shed light on the brutality of honor killings.
3. Educational Initiatives: Educational programs promoting gender equality and human rights have become more prevalent. By challenging traditional beliefs and fostering critical thinking, these initiatives aim to reshape cultural attitudes that contribute to honor killings.
4. Women's Empowerment Movements: Empowerment movements have gained momentum, encouraging women to assert their rights and challenge oppressive practices. Increased access to education and economic opportunities has played a role in empowering women to resist and speak out against honor-based violence.
5. Social media: Social media platforms provide a global stage for discussions on human rights issues, including honor killings. Online activism has connected like-minded individuals and groups, amplifying the voices advocating for change and challenging oppressive traditions.
6. Migration and Cultural Exchange: Increased migration and cultural exchange contribute to a broader understanding of diverse perspectives. Exposure to different cultures can challenge ingrained beliefs and foster more inclusive attitudes towards individual freedoms and choices.

WOMEN THEN AND WOMEN NOW

Honor killing is a deeply hardcore issue that significantly impacts the status of women in societies where it continues. This form of violence often in cultural and patriarchal norms, specifically targets women whose actions are perceived to bring shame or dishonor to their families. Understanding the dynamics of honor killings requires delving into the socio-cultural context and the complex interplay of factors that contribute to the mistreatment and marginalization of women(Allwood, 2000). In many societies, rigid notions of family honor and the perceived role of women as guardians of that honor contribute to the prevalence of honor killings. Women are expected to conform to strict codes of conduct dictated by cultural traditions, religious beliefs, or societal norms. Deviation from these expectations, whether through choices in relationships, clothing, or behavior, can be met with extreme consequences. This places women in a precarious position, as their autonomy is often sacrificed in the name of family honor. One key aspect of the status of women in honor killings is the perpetuation of gender inequality. The very notion of honor killing presupposes a hierarchical structure that places men as the enforcers of family honor and women as its guardians. This reinforces traditional gender roles, restricting women to subservient positions and curbing their freedom to make choices about their own lives. The fear of dishonor becomes a tool for societal control, suppressing women's agency and perpetuating cycles of violence. Furthermore, honor killings are often surrounded by many ways of silence and complicity, making this challenging for women to get help or escape abusive situations. Family and community members may tacitly condone or participate in the act, creating an environment of fear and isolation for women. The lack of legal protection and social support exacerbates the vulnerability of women facing the threat of honor killings, leaving them with few avenues for escape. Efforts to address the status of women in honor killings require a multifaceted approach. Education and awareness campaigns are crucial in challenging entrenched beliefs and dismantling the structures that perpetuate gender-based violence. Legal reforms must strengthen protections for women, ensuring that perpetrators of honor killings are held accountable. Additionally, fostering support networks and safe spaces for women empowers them to break the cycle of silence and seek assistance when faced with danger. International organizations and governments play a pivotal role in advocating for the rights of women and condemning honor killings. By fostering a global dialogue on gender equality, policymakers can work towards creating a world where the status of women is not dictated by outdated notions of honor but is instead defined by principles of justice, equality, and human rights. In conclusion, the status of women in honor killings reflects a broader issue of gender inequality deeply ingrained in certain societies. Addressing this problem necessitates a comprehensive approach that challenges cultural norms, strengthens legal protections, and empowers women to reclaim their agency. Only through collective efforts can societies hope to eradicate the tragic practice of honor killings and create environments where women can live free from the threat of violence based on misplaced notions of honor.

The 21st century has been a pivotal period for feminism, a movement that has evolved significantly under the influence and leadership of women from diverse backgrounds and experiences. Modern feminism is markedly different from its predecessors, characterized by a more inclusive, intersectional, and global approach. Here's a look at how women have transformed feminism in this era, making it a powerful force for social change.

Intersectionality: Embracing Diversity

One of the most profound changes in contemporary feminism is the embrace of intersectionality. Coined by Kimberlé Crenshaw, intersectionality recognizes that the experiences of women are shaped by a multitude of factors, including race, class, sexuality, and ability. Women have championed this concept, ensuring that feminism addresses the overlapping systems of oppression that affect different groups.

This intersectional approach has broadened the feminist agenda, moving beyond the primarily white, middle-class focus of earlier waves to include the voices and concerns of women of color, LGBTQ+ individuals, disabled women, and others who have historically been marginalized. By doing so, modern feminism has become more representative of the diverse experiences of all women, making it a more effective and inclusive movement.

Digital Feminism: Harnessing the Power of Social Media

The rise of the internet and social media has revolutionized how feminist activism is conducted. Women have adeptly used these platforms to raise awareness, mobilize support, and challenge patriarchal norms on a global scale. Hashtags like #MeToo, #TimesUp, and #BlackLivesMatter have galvanized millions, bringing attention to systemic injustices and fostering solidarity.(Martins, 2022)

Digital feminism has democratized the movement, allowing anyone with internet access to participate and contribute. This has led to a richer and more varied feminist discourse, as voices from diverse backgrounds are amplified. The ability to rapidly respond to events and mobilize support has made social media an indispensable tool for modern feminist activism.

Challenging Beauty Standards: The Body Positivity Movement

In the 21st century, women have led efforts to challenge traditional beauty standards and promote body positivity. This movement encourages women to embrace their bodies as they are and reject societal pressures to conform to unrealistic ideals. By doing so, it aims to dismantle harmful stereotypes and foster self-acceptance.

Campaigns promoting body positivity and brands that celebrate diverse body types have had a significant impact, challenging industries such as fashion, media, and entertainment to be more inclusive. This shift not only empowers individuals but also promotes a healthier and more inclusive understanding of beauty.

Economic Empowerment and Workplace Equality

Economic empowerment and workplace equality remain central to feminist advocacy. Women have fought for and achieved significant legislative and policy changes aimed at closing the gender pay gap, addressing workplace harassment, and increasing representation in leadership roles. Movements like #LeanIn and #MeToo have highlighted the systemic barriers women face in the workplace and spurred actions to address them.

Additionally, the push for policies that support work-life balance, such as paid family leave and affordable childcare, reflects a broader understanding of economic justice as integral to gender equality. These efforts recognize that true empowerment requires structural changes that allow women to thrive both professionally and personally.

Global Feminism: Building Transnational Solidarity

Modern feminism is increasingly global, recognizing that the struggle for gender equality transcends national boundaries. Women have built transnational networks of solidarity, advocating for the rights of women and girls worldwide. This global perspective is essential in addressing issues such as gender-based violence, reproductive rights, and education for girls.(McLaren, 2019)

International campaigns and organizations, such as the Malala Fund and UN Women, highlight the interconnectedness of women's struggles and foster a sense of global solidarity. By working together across borders, contemporary feminism emphasizes that achieving gender equality requires collective action and support.

Queer and Trans-Inclusive Feminism

The 21st century has seen a significant shift towards queer and trans-inclusive feminism. Women have advocated for the rights and recognition of LGBTQ+ individuals within the feminist movement, challenging traditional notions of gender and sexuality. This inclusivity ensures that feminism fights for the rights of all individuals, regardless of their gender identity or sexual orientation.

Incorporating queer and trans perspectives has enriched feminist theory and activism, making the movement more relevant and inclusive. By advocating for gender diversity and challenging binary views of gender, modern feminism aligns itself with broader social justice movements.

Reproductive Justice: Expanding the Concept

Reproductive rights have always been a focus of feminism, but the 21st century has expanded this concept into reproductive justice. This framework, pioneered by women of color, considers not only the right to access abortion and contraception but also the social, economic, and political conditions that affect reproductive choices.

Reproductive justice advocates for comprehensive healthcare, freedom from coercion, and the ability to raise children in safe and healthy environments. By linking reproductive rights to broader issues of social justice, modern feminism addresses the full spectrum of challenges that women face in making autonomous decisions about their bodies and lives.

Men as Allies: Promoting Gender Solidarity

A notable shift in contemporary feminism is the active involvement of men as allies in the fight for gender equality. Women have encouraged men to recognize their role in perpetuating patriarchal systems and to join efforts to dismantle them. Campaigns like #HeForShe invite men to advocate for gender equality and challenge toxic masculinity.

Engaging men as partners in the feminist movement broadens the base of support and emphasizes that achieving gender equality benefits everyone. This inclusive approach underscores the universal nature of the struggle for equality and the importance of collective action.

In the case of *The State of Haryana v. Sube Singh and Others* (2020), the accused, Sube Singh and his associates, were charged with the honor killing of a young couple, Karan and Neetu, who belonged to different castes. The couple had married against the wishes of their families, which was considered a transgression against social norms and family honor in their rural community in Haryana, India.

The case gained national attention due to its brutal nature and the involvement of a local Khaap Panchayat (village council), which had allegedly sanctioned the murder. The accused were alleged to have conspired to murder the couple to restore family honor, reflecting a deep-seated belief in the necessity of violence to address perceived dishonor.

Legal Proceedings: The trial in the case was conducted in the Sessions Court of Haryana, with the prosecution presenting evidence that included testimonies from witnesses, forensic reports, and intercepted communications indicating the involvement of the accused in planning and executing the murder. The defense argued that the accused were being falsely implicated and that the killing was a result of a personal dispute unrelated to honor.

The case was notable for its focus on the influence of Khaap Panchayats and the intersection of traditional practices with modern legal standards. The prosecution emphasized that the killing was a premeditated act driven by outdated cultural norms, and sought to hold the accused accountable under the Indian Penal Code, particularly Sections 302 (murder) and 120B (criminal conspiracy).

Judgment and Sentencing: In 2020, the Sessions Court delivered a landmark judgment. The court convicted Sube Singh and the other accused of murder and conspiracy, sentencing them to life imprisonment. The judgment was significant for its clear rejection of honor-based justifications for violence and its emphasis on upholding human rights and legal standards over traditional practices.

The court also highlighted the role of Khaap Panchayats in perpetuating honor-based violence and recommended stricter measures to address their influence in such cases. This case underscored the need for legal reforms and better enforcement mechanisms to prevent and address honor killings.

Impact and Analysis

Legal and Social Implications: The case of *The State of Haryana v. Sube Singh and Others* (2020) represents a critical step in the fight against honor killings in the 21st century. The conviction of the accused and the court's condemnation of honor-based violence reflect a growing judicial awareness of the need to challenge traditional norms that justify such crimes.

1. **Judicial Response**: The judgment demonstrated a commitment to upholding human rights and rejecting the use of honor as a justification for violence. By emphasizing legal standards over cultural practices, the court reinforced the principle that honor killings are a serious crime that cannot be condoned under any circumstances.

2. **Cultural and Social Reforms**: The case highlighted the ongoing influence of traditional practices such as those enforced by Khaap Panchayats. It underscored the need for continued efforts to educate communities about the rights of individuals and the importance of legal protections. The recommendation for stricter measures against Khaap Panchayats reflects a broader recognition of the need for cultural and social reforms to combat honor-based violence.

DIVERSE INSIGHTS OF FEMINISM

Women's perspectives on feminism and honor killings are diverse, reflecting a broad spectrum of experiences, beliefs, and cultural contexts. Feminism, as a movement advocating for gender equality, has evolved over time, and women's views on it vary based on factors such as culture, education, and personal experiences.

For many women, feminism serves as a platform to challenge societal norms and fight against gender-based discrimination. They see it as a means to address issues such as unequal pay, limited opportunities, and restrictive gender roles. Empowered by feminist principles, women aspire to dismantle barriers and create a world where their rights and contributions are valued equally. However, within different cultural contexts, the perception of feminism can differ. Some women may feel that traditional values conflict with feminist ideals, fearing that embracing the movement might be perceived as a rejection of their cultural identity. Striking a balance between cultural heritage and feminist principles becomes a nuanced challenge for women navigating these complex intersections. Honor killings, on the other hand, represent a dark manifestation of deeply ingrained cultural norms. Women's perspectives on honor killings are shaped by their proximity to these practices. Some may vehemently oppose them, recognizing the grave injustice and violence inherent in such acts. For them, feminism becomes a crucial tool in challenging and dismantling the structures that perpetuate honor-based violence(Huang, 2023).

Conversely, there are instances where women, influenced by societal expectations and ingrained beliefs, may inadvertently perpetuate or condone honor killings. Societal pressure, fear of ostracization, or a misguided sense of duty can lead some women to endorse practices that violate human rights, including the right to life. It is essential to recognize that women's perspectives on these issues are not monolithic; they exist along a continuum influenced by myriad factors. Education plays a pivotal role in shaping these perspectives, as informed women are more likely to question and challenge oppressive norms. Exposure to diverse ideas and experiences broadens their understanding, enabling them to reconcile cultural values with the principles of feminism. Efforts to combat honor killings and promote feminism must be culturally sensitive and inclusive. Engaging with local communities and fostering dialogue is crucial to dismantling harmful practices while respecting diverse perspectives. Empowering women within their cultural context can lead to more effective change by addressing the root causes of inequality. Women's perspectives on feminism and honor killings are complex and multifaceted. While many embrace feminism as a force for positive change, others grapple with reconciling it with cultural values. Honor killings remain a deeply troubling issue, with women holding varied views influenced by their proximity to or distance from these practices. Bridging these perspectives requires a nuanced approach that respects cultural diversity while promoting the fundamental principles of equality and human rights.

The persistence of honor killings in the 21st century presents a stark challenge to global human rights efforts and gender equality. Despite significant advancements in legal frameworks, social awareness, and international advocacy, the eradication of this practice remains elusive. Honor killings, deeply rooted in cultural, social, and patriarchal traditions, pose unique and multifaceted challenges that demand a comprehensive and nuanced approach. In this opinion piece, I will explore the primary challenges faced in combating honor killings today and argue for the necessity of a multi-layered strategy to address these issues effectively.

1. Cultural and Social Norms

One of the most formidable obstacles in the fight against honor killings is the deep-seated cultural and social norms that perpetuate this practice. In many communities, honor killings are not viewed as crimes but as necessary actions to restore family honor and societal standing. This cultural sanctioning creates an environment where these acts are not only tolerated but, in some cases, expected.

Efforts to combat honor killings must therefore go beyond legal reforms and address the underlying cultural beliefs. This requires engaging with local communities, religious leaders, and influencers to challenge and change these harmful norms. However, altering deeply ingrained cultural values is a slow and complex process that can face significant resistance from those who see such changes as a threat to their identity and traditions.

2. Legal and Judicial Barriers

While many countries have laws that criminalize honor killings, the implementation and enforcement of these laws are often inadequate. In some regions, legal systems may include loopholes that allow perpetrators to escape severe punishment.

For example, in certain countries, laws permit reduced sentences for honor-related crimes if the perpetrator can prove they acted to defend family honor.

Moreover, judicial systems in some areas are influenced by the same patriarchal and cultural biases that condone honor killings. Judges and law enforcement officers may sympathize with perpetrators, leading to lenient sentences or a reluctance to pursue justice vigorously. Overcoming these legal and judicial barriers requires comprehensive reforms that include training for law enforcement and judicial officials on gender sensitivity and human rights.

3. Lack of Political Will

The absence of strong political will is another significant challenge. Governments in regions where honor killings are prevalent may be reluctant to take decisive action due to fear of backlash from conservative segments of society. Political leaders might avoid addressing honor killings to maintain social stability or political power, leading to inadequate policy responses and a lack of accountability.

To generate the necessary political will, there must be sustained pressure from both domestic and international actors. Civil society organizations, human rights advocates, and the international community must continue to highlight the issue and hold governments accountable for their inaction. However, this can be a delicate balance, as excessive external pressure might be perceived as cultural imperialism, further entrenching resistance.

4. Educational Gaps

Education plays a crucial role in changing attitudes and behaviors. However, in many regions where honor killings occur, there are significant gaps in educational access, particularly for women and girls. Lack of education perpetuates cycles of ignorance and dependency, making it difficult for individuals to challenge traditional practices or advocate for their rights.

Expanding access to education, especially gender-sensitive education that promotes equality and human rights, is essential. Education empowers individuals to think critically about cultural norms and provides them with the tools to advocate for change. Nevertheless, achieving this requires substantial investment and long-term commitment from governments and international organizations.

5. Economic Dependence and Social Isolation

Many victims of honor killings are women who are economically dependent on their families and socially isolated. This dependence makes it extremely difficult for them to escape abusive situations or seek help. Economic empowerment and social support networks are critical components in combating honor killings.

Efforts to address economic dependence must include creating opportunities for women to gain financial independence through employment, education, and skills training. Additionally, establishing robust support systems, such as shelters, counseling services, and legal aid, can provide victims with the resources they need to leave dangerous environments and rebuild their lives.

6. Migration and Diaspora Communities

The practice of honor killings has also spread to diaspora communities in Western countries, complicating efforts to address the issue. These communities often exist in a delicate balance between integrating into their new societies and preserving their cultural heritage. This dual identity can create environments where honor-related violence persists, hidden from the broader society.

Western countries must navigate these complexities with sensitivity, promoting integration and cultural understanding while firmly upholding human rights. This involves training social workers, educators, and law enforcement to recognize and address signs of honor-related violence. Additionally, providing support to immigrant communities to understand and adapt to new cultural norms can help mitigate these issues.

7. Technological Impact

The rise of social media and digital communication has added a new dimension to the challenge of combating honor killings. On one hand, technology can expose and raise awareness about these crimes, galvanizing international outrage and support. On the other hand, it can also exacerbate situations by spreading rumors or private information quickly, leading to increased pressure on individuals and families to restore honor.

Navigating this double-edged sword requires a careful and strategic approach. Efforts should be made to leverage technology for advocacy and support while also developing mechanisms to protect individuals from online harassment and threats. Educational campaigns on digital literacy and privacy can help mitigate the negative impacts of technology.

8. Resistance from Patriarchal Structures

Patriarchy remains a significant barrier in the fight against honor killings. Patriarchal structures reinforce the notion that women's behavior directly impacts family honor, thus legitimizing violence as a means of control. Challenging these structures is essential but immensely difficult, as they are deeply intertwined with cultural, religious, and social systems.

Efforts to dismantle patriarchy must include promoting gender equality at all levels of society. This involves advocating for equal rights and opportunities, challenging discriminatory practices, and supporting feminist movements. However, these efforts often face backlash from those who perceive them as threats to their power and traditional way of life.

CONCLUSION

The intersection of feminism and the issue of honor killings is a complex and critical field in the fight for gender equality and human rights. Honor killing is deeply embedded in cultural, social and patriarchal norms, making it easy to understand the different face of feminism plays in addressing and combating this grave violation of human dignity. Feminism serves as a powerful force in challenging the traditional power structures that perpetuate honor killings. At its core, feminism advocates for the fundamental principle of gender equality. It seeks to dismantle patriarchal norms that prescribe rigid gender roles and contribute to the belief that a woman's behavior can tarnish family honor. By challenging these deeply ingrained attitudes, feminism aims to reshape societal perceptions of women and their inherent worth beyond traditional stereotypes. Education and awareness are pivotal aspects of feminism's role in the fight against honor killings. Feminist activists work tirelessly to educate communities about the severe consequences of honor killings, emphasizing that such acts are clear violations of human rights. By fostering awareness, feminism aims to break down the barriers of ignorance and challenge cultural norms that perpetuate violence against women. This educational aspect is crucial in changing mindsets and fostering empathy, as it encourages communities to question and reject the harmful practices associated with honor killings. Legal reforms stand out as another key battleground was feminism fights against honor killings. Feminist movements advocate for robust legal frameworks that hold perpetrators accountable for their actions. This involves closing legal loopholes and ensuring that the justice system is equipped to address honor killings effectively. By pushing for legal changes, feminism seeks to establish a deterrent against such crimes and provide a platform for justice for the victims. Economic empowerment is a tool that feminism employs to reduce vulnerability to honor killings. Feminist activists emphasize the importance of women's economic independence, recognizing that financial dependence can be wielded as a tool of control. Empowered women are more likely to resist oppressive norms and have the means to escape situations that may lead to honor-based violence. In this way, economic empowerment becomes a vital component of the broader feminist strategy against honor killings. Moreover, the feminist movement acknowledges the intersectionality of honor killings. Recognizing that individuals from marginalized communities may face additional layers of discrimination and violence, intersectional feminism addresses various forms of oppression. This inclusive approach is crucial for understanding the diverse experiences of women and ensuring that strategies to combat honor killings are tailored to specific cultural contexts, taking into account factors such as race, class, and religion. Women have profoundly reshaped the feminist movement in the 21st century, making it more inclusive, intersectional, and global. By addressing a wide range of issues—from digital activism and body positivity to reproductive justice and economic empowerment—modern feminism reflects the diverse and interconnected challenges that women face today.

The evolution of feminism underscores the importance of adapting to changing social dynamics and incorporating diverse perspectives. As the movement continues to grow and evolve, it remains a powerful force for advocating for the rights and dignity of all individuals, striving towards a more just and equitable world. Through their efforts, women have ensured that feminism remains a vibrant, relevant, and transformative movement in the 21st century. Combating honor killings in the 21st century presents a complex array of challenges that require a multifaceted and sustained effort. Addressing cultural and social norms, legal and judicial barriers, lack of political will, educational gaps, economic dependence, migration issues, technological impacts, patriarchal structures, and psychological trauma are all critical components of a comprehensive strategy. While the path forward is fraught with difficulties, progress is possible through concerted efforts at local, national, and international levels. It is imperative that governments, civil society, and the international community continue to work together, leveraging education, legal reform, economic empowerment, and cultural change to eradicate this brutal practice. Only through a holistic and persistent approach can we hope to create a world where honor killings are a relic of the past and where all individuals are free to live their lives with dignity and respect.

REFERENCES

Allwood, G. (2000). Representations of Feminism in France: Feminism, Anti-Feminism and Post-Feminism. *Why Europe? Problems of Culture and Identity*, 111–128. DOI: 10.1057/9780230596641_7

Bharadwaj, S. B. (2012). Myth and Reality of the Khap Panchayats: A Historical Analysis of the Panchayat and Khap Panchayat. *Studies in History*, 28(1), 43–67. DOI: 10.1177/0257643013477250

Churchill, R. P. (2018). Oxford Scholarship Online. *The Cultural Evolution of Honor Killing.*, 1. Advance online publication. DOI: 10.1093/oso/9780190468569.003.0006

Dalvi, A. K. (n.d.). *Addressing "Honour Killings" in India: Role of Media, social platforms, and film in depicting cases of honour killings in India.* 52(4).

Gill, A. K. (2014). Introduction: 'Honour' and 'Honour'-Based Violence: Challenging Common Assumptions. *"Honour" Killing and Violence*, 1–23. DOI: 10.1057/9781137289568_1

Heydari, A., Teymoori, A., & Trappes, R. (2021a). Honor killing as a dark side of modernity: Prevalence, common discourses, and a critical view. Https://Doi.Org/10.1177/0539018421994777, *60*(1), 86–106. DOI: 10.1177/0539018421994777

Heydari, A., Teymoori, A., & Trappes, R. (2021b). Honor killing as a dark side of modernity: Prevalence, common discourses, and a critical view. *Social Sciences Information. Information Sur les Sciences Sociales*, 60(1), 86–106. DOI: 10.1177/0539018421994777

Huang, X. (2023). Feminism in Diverse Conditions: Analyzing about Feminism on Social Media Platforms. *Communications in Humanities Research*, 20(1), 46–51. DOI: 10.54254/2753-7064/20/20231283

Huda, S., & Kamal, A. (2020). Development and Validation of Attitude Towards Honour Killing Scale. *2020, VOL. 35, NO. 2, 35*(35), 227–251. DOI: 10.33824/PJPR.2020.35.2.13

Jakhar, S. (n.d.). *KHAP Panchayats: Changing Perspectives*. Retrieved August 1, 2024, from https://www.academia.edu/37068474/KHAP_PANCHAYATS_CHANGING_PERSPECTIVES

Kumar, N. (2013). Juidicial response towards KHAP panchayat. *JOURNAL OF GLOBAL RESEARCH & ANALYSIS*, 2(1), 114–117.

Laura, B. (n.d.). *Feminism | Definition, History, Types, Waves, Examples, & Facts | Britannica.* Retrieved May 26, 2024, from https://www.britannica.com/topic/feminism

Lorenzi-Cioldi, F., & Kulich, C. (2015). *Sexism* (2nd ed.). International Encyclopedia of the Social & Behavioral Sciences., DOI: 10.1016/B978-0-08-097086-8.24089-0

Martins, A. (2022). Feminism, Leadership, and Social Media. *International Journal of Social Media and Online Communities*, 14(2), 1–18. DOI: 10.4018/IJSMOC.308288

McLaren, M. A. (2019). *Women's Activism, Feminism, and Social Justice.* Women's Activism, Feminism, and Social Justice., DOI: 10.1093/oso/9780190947705.001.0001

Pina-López, E. (2014). The Role of Honor and Patriarchy in the Perpetuation of Honor-Based Violence. *Violence Against Women*, 20(1), 24–41.

Ray, U. (1999). *'Idealizing Motherhood': The Brahmanical discourse on women in Ancient India (circa 500 BCE-300 CE).* University of London, School of Oriental and African Studies.

Roberts, K. A., Campbell, G., & Lloyd, G. (2013). Honor-based violence: Policing and prevention. *Honor-Based Violence: Policing and Prevention*, 1–197. DOI: 10.1201/b16114

Srivastava, K., Chaudhury, S., Bhat, P., & Sahu, S. (2017). Misogyny, feminism, and sexual harassment. *Industrial Psychiatry Journal*, 26(2), 111. DOI: 10.4103/ipj.ipj_32_18 PMID: 30089955

Wynn, L. L. (2021). 7. "Honor Killing": On Anthropological Writing in an International Political Economy of Representations. *Love, Sex, and Desire in Modern Egypt*, 137–155. https://doi.org/DOI: 10.7560/317044-008/XML

Yadav, R. S., Singh, R., Aggarwal, V., Semwal, M., Kumar Dy Director, R., Singh Associate Professor, V., Assistant Professor, V., Sharma Associate Professor, K. K., Assistant Professor, R., & Lal Dhanda Principal, R. (n.d.). *Editorial Board.*

Chapter 4
The Feminist Movement and Arab Society

Nishi Kant Bibhu
Bennett University, India

Nupur Kulshrestha
https://orcid.org/0009-0009-8997-2677
GLA University, Mathura, India

ABSTRACT

The chapter is highlighting the role of feminist movement in Arab society in the context of honour killing. Various aspects concerning honour killing are dealt under it such as, it stresses on the historical background of Arab Feminism, furthermore it is going to discuss the early forerunners of Arab feminism. It is going to observe mercy while dealing with the cases of honour killing. Further, the manner in which sheikhs in Arab region played significant role as a saviour of the woman from whims and caprices of her family. Another important aspect which is highlighted is to ensure proper values prior to killing of an individual, resulting out of honour. Furthermore, it stresses on the influence of modernization in context of honour killing. It laid emphasis on the Matthew Goldstein's theory of social normalization. Lastly, it laid emphasis over the contemporary challenges in context of honour killing.

Kressel discovered that in 31 incidents of women being killed that were recorded, the killers were her brothers; in just 12 cases, the killer was her father; and in 8 cases, the killers were the father's nephews. Out of 112 honor killings, 24 of the killers were under 20 and 18 were between 21 and 40 years old. Cohen (Kressel, 1977) that her brothers or her nephews are responsible for the woman's death. Furthermore, in Turkey, violence against women and honour killings remains prevalent issues in 2022, over 330 women were victims of feminicide, as reported by a Turkish association.

DOI: 10.4018/979-8-3693-7240-1.ch004

Copyright © 2025, IGI Global. Copying or distributing in print or electronic forms without written permission of IGI Global is prohibited.

This represents an increase compared to 2021, which was already a particularly troubling year and it shows growth in killing a woman by man on pretext of honor (Verot, 2023) The above stated trend of killing a woman by her father or brother is still prevalent which can be testified through the recent incident in Iraq, on January 31, 2023, Tiba Al-Ali, a young YouTube star living in Turkey with her fiancé, was killed by her father during a visit to her family in Iraq. Her death sparked widespread outrage on social media, with Iraqis calling for protests in the capital to demand justice.(Killing of YouTube Star by her father causes outrage in Iraq, 2023) Hence, it can be inferred from the above stated data that honour killings are still prevalent and is increasing day by day in spite of harsh laws and from the above stated trend, these kinds of killing does not find any end.

KEY TERMS

Terms, "Feminist Movement" and "Arab Society" depicts the main theme on which the whole chapter is revolving around. Broader themes like "Family honour (Marwick, 1965)", "Taboo(Gale,2003)", "Sheikhs(Ginat, 2000)", "Bedouin (Ginat,2009)", "Patrilineal society (Ruggi,2008)" provides the deep insight about the chapter. "Legal and Judicial Challenges (Lama,2010)" throw light on the legislative and judicial framework concerning the Honour Killings in Arab Societies.

Statistics, Data, Contemporary challenges, Recent trends of Honour Killings in Arab Societies, Historical Background, we use these keywords to select relevant articles from multiple online sources, for example "Google Scholar, Research Gate, Google Books, Springer, JSTOR, Sage, IJSSHR, Scopus."

Selecting the right journals and carefully conducting inclusion/exclusion and article research is essential for a Research Paper on the sensitive issue "The Feminist Movement and Arab Societies". The author opted for Journals like *Honor Killings and the Construction of Gender in Arab Societies* (Lama,2010), *Family violence including crimes of honor in Jordan: correlates and perceptions of seriousness* (Araji&Carlson,2001), *Shame and Gender* (Kressel & Gideon,1992), etc which align with the subject matter and provide a platform for scholarly discussions on these topics.

Inclusion criteria emphasized on relevance, ensuring that only articles directly addressing The Feminist Movement in Arab Societies in context of honour killings Priority is given to recent publications, to ensure the inclusion of up-to-date perspectives and data. The research was grounded in academic rigor by relying primarily on peer-reviewed articles, government reports.

Non-academic sources, such as blogs or opinion pieces, and articles with only marginal relevance to the topic were excluded through specific criteria. The research was conducted using academic databases, including JSTOR, Research Gate, Google Scholar, Scopus, Springer, etc.

Non-peer-reviewed research articles were excluded to enhance the quality and relevance of the research. Likewise, non-credible online sources and news articles were omitted to prevent any potential discrepancies.

LITERATURE REVIEW

A girl will not suffer harm if her sexual activities are disclosed only to limited people further, she will only be slain to death if her actions become widely known asserted by the anthropologists who have studied honor killings (Rabinowitz, 1995).

Demonstrates the whole procedure of obtaining justice by Sheikh (Ginat, 2009).

If once an Ird is bygone, it can't be recovered. On the other hand, male's honor can be restored. Social norms in Jordan are stringent when it comes to the penalties required to restore family honor, and there is a prevalent belief in traditional Jordanian society that the only way to truly restore honor is by the killing of the "offending" female. A close male relative typically serves as the woman's executioner. A close male relative typically serves as the woman's executioner; It is customary to tribes to get altogether and determine the appropriate penalty for a transgression, however occasionally an act is committed irrationally without the tribe's consent. Without following the proper procedures or receiving court oversight, these penalties are typically designed without the involvement of the state or other institutions and appear to reinforce the control of families and tribes. (Khalili & Mohammad, 2009).

In order to enhance their honour and gain respect from the community in certain Arab regions under Ottoman rule, a person who committed a killing would often sprinkle the victim's blood on their own clothes and walk through the streets displaying the bloodied weapon (Kressel, 1981).

It has been testified through several tests which are conducted upon a victim that woman was virgin at the time of her death and her sexual orientation had nothing to do with breaking conventional norms of behavior (Khazanov, 1981).

Killing of Youtube star by her father causes outrage in Iraq (2023, February 4). Aljazeera. https://www.aljazeera.com/news/2023/2/4/iraqis-outraged-after-father-kills-youtube-star-daughter

Legal & Judicial Challenges (Lama, 2010).

Murder should be used as a last resort to deal with the cases of honor killings rather families should initially opt for preventing her to attend social gatherings, jail, confinement, or prohibition from employment, etc (Ginat, 2000).

Requirement for liberal social constraints and shifting views for greater sexual freedom for women in higher economic and social field (Araji&Carlson,2001).

Some women think they can avoid Bedouin customs because they live in a bigger and feel they live in a more liberal society. In certain instances, if not most instances, the unmarried lady is forced to wed and reside with the man she had intercourse with; this arrangement is sealed in a sulha. (Ginat, 2000).

Strict imposition of laws in Israel where it supports their feminist goals, despite the fact that ideals embodied in the law are not acceptable by many Israel's females (Gale, 2003).

The earlier ethnic world of the Arab and the Western, Israeli world where These students are immersed (Ginat,2000).

The issue of honour killing has been described as deeply complex and rooted in the history of Arab society by Sharif Kanaana, an anthropology professor at Birzeit University. It was noted that, in a patrilineal society, the primary concern for the men of the family, clan, or tribe is the control of reproductive power. Women are perceived as the bearers of the tribe's future men. Consequently, honour killing is understood not as a means of controlling sexual behaviou21r, but rather as a method of exerting control over fertility and reproductive capabilities (Ruggi,2008).

The main goal is to shame a political adversary, diminish his standing, isolate him as much as possible, and kick him out of the organization rather than punishing the transgressor. (Cohen, 1977).

The term "family honour" is really a very complicated term. As per Islam if a man and a woman are found to be having an adulterous relationship with each other's wife, they should be stoned to death. It also has to do with single girls delaying marriage and remaining virgins (Marwick, 1965).

Turkey, violence against women and honour killings remain prevalent issues in 2022, over 330 women were victims of feminicide, as reported by a Turkish association (Verot,2023).

When frustrations are let out in the home, women and children are the most frequent victims (Nimry,2010).

While intriguing, the higher incidence of murders in urban areas compared to rural ones is not considered particularly significant. It is a common misconception that honour crimes are more prevalent in rural and Bedouin communities. However, Jordanian sources, including statisticians and activists, have emphasized that this is inaccurate, asserting that the majority of these crimes actually occur in affluent urban areas (Gale, 2003).

RESEARCH GAP

The research on the topic as done by the author is not novice, various researches had been conducted till date on this topic. The main aim for conducting this study is to conglomerate the whole matter available on the topic in a single chapter so that readers do not get in trouble to search different aspects of the same through different sources. As it has been observed by the author that though the research has been conducted on various issues which are enlightened under this chapter but they are segregated from one another, therefore, author has tried to consolidate each and every aspect i.e from historical background of the Feminist Movement of Arab Society in context of honour killing till the current scenario of honour killings prevalent in the Arab Society with recent statistical data so that updated data should be read by readers. Further, this chapter enlightens the Legal and Judicial Challenges, the societal attitudes and law enforcement and further their means to reform, which is not available till date in a single article or chapter, concerning the Honour Killing in context of Arab Society.

Therefore, the author has tried to mitigate the difficulties of reader, by consolidating each and every aspect of The Feminist Movement and Arab Society in context of Honour Killing in a single chapter.

THE FEMINIST MOVEMENT AND ARAB SOCIETY

Historical Background of Arab Feminism

Understanding the historical roots of Arab feminism provides valuable insights into the movement's evolution and its ongoing challenges and achievements. It highlights the resilience and agency of Arab women in their quest for equality and justice, setting the stage for the diverse and dynamic feminist movement that continues to shape Arab societies today. The historical foundations of Arab feminism are intricately woven into the region's socio-cultural context, where practices such as honour killings have profoundly influenced the development of feminist ideas and activism. Honor killings, involving the murder of a family member, typically a woman, who is thought to have tarnished the family's honour, have been a crucial issue tackled by Arab feminists.

THE SOCIO-POLITICAL CONTEXT

The Late Ottoman Era and the Nahda

The late Ottoman period witnessed a cultural and intellectual renaissance known as the Nahda, or "awakening." This period, spanning from the mid-19th century to the early 20th century, was characterized by a revival of Arabic literature, a re-evaluation of traditional norms, and a push for modernization and reform.

- **Modernization and Reform**: Influenced by European Enlightenment ideas, Arab intellectuals and reformers began advocating for modernization within their societies. This included calls for educational reforms, legal changes, and the empowerment of women as a part of broader societal progress.
- **Print Culture and the Press**: The expansion of print culture and the emergence of newspapers and journals played a crucial role in disseminating new ideas, including those related to women's rights and gender equality. Women started participating in these publications, expressing their concerns and aspirations.

COLONIALISM AND NATIONALISM

The arrival of European colonialism in the Arab world led to profound socio-political transformations. The resistance to colonial powers frequently merged with the pursuit of national identity and independence, forming a complex context for the development of feminist thought.

Nationalist Movements

Women's involvement in nationalist movements was integral to their fight for rights. As women participated in the struggle for national liberation, they also championed their own emancipation, intertwining both causes.

EARLY FORERUNNERS OF ARAB FEMINISM

Qasim Amin (1863-1908)

Qasim Amin is widely recognized as a pivotal figure in the development of Arab feminism. An influential Egyptian intellectual and jurist, Amin's writings were foundational in shaping feminist thought in the Arab world.

In his influential book *"The Liberation of Women"* (1899), Amin contended that the advancement of Egyptian society depended on the emancipation of women. He called for women's education, the removal of the veil, and legal reforms to improve women's rights. In his follow-up work, *"The New Woman"* (1900), Amin further promoted his ideas by stressing the importance of women's active involvement in public life for the overall progress of society.

Huda Sha'arawi (1879-1947)

Huda Sha'arawi, a prominent Egyptian feminist, is celebrated for her groundbreaking activism and organizational work in the early 20th century.

In 1923, she established the Egyptian Feminist Union to champion women's education, legal rights, and social reforms. This organization was instrumental in mobilizing women and promoting feminist causes in Egypt. In the same year, after attending an international women's conference in Rome, Sha'arawi made a powerful statement by publicly removing her veil at a Cairo railway station, symbolizing the feminist movement's challenge to traditional norms.

Nabawiyya Musa (1886-1951)

Nabawiyya Musa played a crucial role in the early feminist movement in Egypt.

ADVOCACY FOR EDUCATION

Musa was among the first Egyptian women to receive a formal education and became a leading proponent of education for girls. She believed that education was fundamental to women's empowerment and the advancement of society.

Literary Contributions

Musa used her writings and public speeches to advocate for legal reforms, women's suffrage, and expanded social freedoms for women.

Women's Organizations and Early Advocacy

In the early 20th century, the establishment of women's organizations was pivotal in tackling issues related to honour and violence against women.

Egyptian Feminist Union (1923)

Founded by Huda Sha'arawi, this union addressed a range of women's rights issues, including advocating for legal reforms that eventually included measures to protect women from gender-based violence.

Arab Women's Federation

Formed in 1944, the Arab Women's Federation aimed to unify women's efforts throughout the Arab world, promoting social and legal reforms to safeguard women's rights and ensure their safety.

Sharif Kanaana, an anthropology professor at Birzeit University, describes honour killing as a deeply complex issue rooted in the history of Arab society. He noted that in a patrilineal society, the primary concern for the men of the family, clan, or tribe is controlling reproductive power. Women are viewed as the producers of the tribe's future men. Therefore, honour killing is not primarily about controlling sexual behaviour but rather about exerting control over fertility and reproductive capabilities. (Ruggi, 2008) Furthermore, in certain Arab regions under Ottoman rule, a person who committed a killing would often sprinkle the victim's blood on their own clothes and walk through the streets displaying the bloodied weapon. This act was meant to enhance their honour and gain respect from the community, rather than facing condemnation for the act of murder. (Kressel, 1981)

INTRODUCTION

Arab girls and women are pushed to exceed taboo boundaries in consequence of lodging police complaints in pursuance to the support of organizations dealing with feminist movements against the accused. After the occurrences, the sufferer are left isolated and in a state of uncertainty, unable to return, and such corpses are powerless to save them. Typically, the outcome is catastrophic, with these ladies being slain by their brothers.

Israeli elites with an affinity for Europe are frequently ethnocentric, which makes them blind to the potential consequences of their actions when they affect minority subgroups in Israeli society that have distinct values and perspectives. Ironically,

Israelis frequently ignore domestic bias against ladies in order to foster the feminism in Arab country. Arab Israeli women initiate efforts to rescue Arab citizens from each other,' without even considering the importance of the process they aim to initiate. As per them, while attaining the impetus to the feminist movement they rather left the Arab women against their culture and tradition which provides them their identity and furthermore, as a result they are even killed on the pretext of violation of their culture. The situation of Arab-Palestinian women citizens of Israel who follow feminist Israeli and European norms and practices presents an additional, more comprehensive conundrum. They observe Israel serving two motives i.e., as a foreign occupier exercises political and cultural supremacy over them. On the contrary, the political endeavors of these proactive Arab women on behalf of other Arab women are carried out via the welfare mechanism of Israel. Furthermore, they will ask for the State of Israel to impose the law strictly in areas where it supports their feminist goals, despite the fact that many of the females of Israel disagree with the ideals embodied in the laws they support. (Gale, 2003)

There are many ways to compromise the ird, many of which involve the woman exhibiting unacceptable sexual conduct. However, the word "sexually illicit conduct" is ambiguous and subjective, leaving room for several distinct meanings. Based on sociological research and case study analysis, mistrust and gossip have a greater impact than empirical evidence supporting the ird's compromise. Put another way, a woman's right to the independence can be undermined by cultural judgments directed against her, even if she has done everything in her power to defend it. This sentiment explains why many women who are murdered to protect their honor are done so only out of suspicion. Because of this, a number of tests are conducted on victims which testifies that woman was virgin when she died as well as that her sexual orientation had nothing to do with breaking conventional norms of behavior. (Khazanov, 1981)

It is possible for women to abandon what they are because of the conduct of other people alone. In these situations, many women face persecution on the grounds that they may have contributed to the assault by communication which was later construed as symbolic of sexual development. These actions demonstrate how "blaming the (female) victim" is widespread in Jordanian community frequently perceived as "damaged" or "scratched" once their virginity is violated.

Moreover, if once an Ird is bygone, it can't be recovered. On the other hand, male's honor can be restored. Social norms in Jordan are stringent when it comes to the penalties required to restore family honor, and there is a prevalent belief in traditional Jordanian society that the only way to truly restore honor is by the killing of the "offending" female. A close male relative typically serves as the woman's executioner. A close male relative typically serves as the woman's executioner; It is customary to tribes to get altogether and determine the appropriate penalty for a transgression, however occasionally an act is committed irrationally without the tribe's consent. Without following the proper procedures or receiving court oversight, these penalties are typically designed without the involvement of the state or other institutions and appear to reinforce the control of families and tribes. (Khalili & Mohammad, 2009)

SOCIAL NORMALIZATION

Religious sources don't matter, but it's still important to figure out how a woman's independent virginity relates to the honor and dignity of her family or tribe. It is well recognized notion that due to the violation of honor of a woman it leads to the losing of honor of a woman, but there are no or less thesis which explains why is it so in Jordan. Numerous academicians, including sociologists, evolutionary theorists, and specialists in deviance, supported Matthew Goldstein's theory of social normalization, which identifies the origin of women holding the position of honor in the home. Within the parameters of his theory, Goldstein notes some Darwinian concepts, including sexual selection, parental certainty, and reciprocal faithfulness. (Kressel & Gideon, 2009) According to his theory, males in the early Homo sapiens species had a responsibility to guarantee the paternal certainty of their progeny. Put differently, men wanted to assure that the children are belonging to their parentage and not the children of another man. According to Goldstein, "many cultures have recognized the value of parental certainty through various social norms." Suppressing and controlling the female sexual behavior was considered as the best way to make sure that children produced are belonging to their own distinct ancestry. According to Rana Husseini, "Men who controlled 'their' women were seen as strong leaders of high status, and therefore became honorable in the eyes of the tribe." Men codified this idea of control into social and religious regulations, which are still in use in the more established segments of society. Therefore, when a woman from a specific lineage breaks from the established moral code outlined in customary law, it is interpreted as a sign of weakness and inadequate authority on the part of the men in her family. Deviating from rigid social laws by male and an inability to control one's own libido are characteristics that undermine male dominance and rank.

However, Goldstein overlooked one important aspect of breaches of honor in his study. Frequently, even when the men in the family carry out the deed, it is the patriarchal family's women who first emphasize the necessity of restoring family honor. Evaluations of this research have revealed that women's attitudes, which essentially only support violence against their own sex, are a product of the roles that society has historically assigned them. (Kressel & Gideon, 2009) According to Sheikh Abu Nweir, men assume leadership positions since women belong in the house. Women are expected to take care of their families, including disciplining their daughters if they have any. If a family member makes a mistake, particularly with a daughter, it reflects on the parents, particularly the mother (sic). This means that the woman, not the males in the home, should be the one to teach her children respect for tradition and the preservation of societal mores, particularly the ird. Still these traditional laws have been carried over into contemporary customary communities. As it was the mother's responsibility to reprimand and to imbibe in daughter the virtues of "purity," it is possible that the threat to the family's honor comes from the daughter rather than the men. In light of crimes of honor, it may be said that a mother's need for the preservation and repair of the family's reputation originates from her children's conventional duties and reflecting values.

THE HONOR KILLING AND MERCY

When addressing honour killings, mercy involves responding with compassion to victims and survivors. This response includes acknowledging the trauma and injustice inflicted upon women who suffer violence in the name of honour. Mercy requires society to show empathy and provide support to victims, offering opportunities for healing, legal protection, and access to resources that enable them to recover and move forward with their lives.

Further, mercy also entails advocating for justice and accountability in instances of honour killings. It urges legal systems to impose strict penalties on offenders and remove leniency based on cultural rationales. Additionally, it requires challenging cultural attitudes that endorse or excuse violence against women, promoting a narrative of responsibility where perpetrators are held accountable for their conduct.

Anthropologists who have studied honor killings assert that a girl will not suffer harm if her sexual activities are disclosed only to limited people further, she will only be slain to death if her actions become widely known. (Rabinowitz, 1995) Murder only occurs in response to a public accusation filed by a male who thinks his honors has been violated due to women deeds. Undoubtedly, an accusation and murder can't be dismissed as merely typical behavior. Generally speaking, these homicides have a personal motive, which is frequently political. The charge is always predicated on a transgression of traditions which implies that a lady or a girl should be slain to death until and unless she is married to the man she had sex with. The death penalty does not apply if two "sinners" are married. If man denies to enter in marital bond or her mother-father deny for marriage, the girl will be beheaded if there is an existence of valid proof of a public complaint made by the aggrieved party. There are certain situations in which the murderer may wish for a less severe punishment to protect the honor but he has no choice because as is old tradition of the society.

Arabs today assert that they commit murder when they are forced to. Most people are in support to evolve a means to protect the girl malefactor. Not every time does someone compare the societal constraints to the loss of a close relative. This is a twin catastrophe for the family. It is crucial to stress that in Bedouin or rural Arab society, killings resulting out of violation to moral laws do not typically occur; instead, the victim must publicly accuse the other side. Direct allegations can occasionally be used for political ends. The main goal is to shame a political adversary, diminish his standing, isolate him as much as possible, and kick him out of the organization rather than punishing the transgressor.(*Two-Dimensional-Man-An_Essay-on-the-Anthropology-of-Power-and-Symbolism-in-Complex-Society-by-Abner_Cohen*, n.d.)

Furthermore, one should remember that a girl's retribution for violating the honor of family is impacted by the social or political stake of her family in the community. Families have several options when it comes to dealing with such issues: they can opt for preventing her to attend social gatherings, jail, confinement, or prohibition from employment, etc. Murder should only be used as a last resort. (Ginat, 2000) In addition, if the man who is physically involved with woman does not belongs to same clan the family member of a woman will put an effort to either kill or attempt to kill that man to restore their honor. This severe reaction is intended to send a message to society at large that "our honor" was damaged by the male's dishonorable intents towards the girl. Islam, holds that if a man and a woman are found to be having an adulterous relationship with each other's wife, they should be stoned to death. Remember that "family honor" is a highly complicated term. It also has to do with single girls delaying marriage and remaining virgins. (Marwick, 1965)

In Israel, Arab students are exposed to Western culture, higher education, music, fashion, and travel both domestically and internationally. However, they do not renounce their cultural views, standards, or values; they also do not abandon Arab customs pertaining to honor and shame. Arab students in Israel are not removed from Arab culture, where killing to uphold one's family dignity is considered as normal irrespective of the fact that they are born in Western culture. Studies reveal that Arab coeds emphasize that "another path must be found to punish someone who has made a mistake" but are against killing someone for having sex before marriage. Certain male Arab students believe that the woman in question deserves a suitable penalty, while others believe that she should be hanged till death for undermining her family's reputation. (Holykoraninlibra00libr, n.d.) These students are immersed in two different worlds: the earlier ethnic world of the Arab and the Western, Israeli world. (Ginat,2000) Additionally, it is important to remember that a Bedouin's actions represent their need to consider community responsibility. It implies, that every relative should act within the realm of the standards of the society.

CONTRIBUTION OF SHEIKHS

Police officials entrust a reliable Bedouin sheikh who will be responsible to secure the women who are under the whims and caprices of her family because she has engaged in the clandestine sexual encounters. In order to promote peace, these sheikhs act as mediators. The women of the Arab community are so shielded from murder and allowed to continue living as members of their community. When faced with these sorts of circumstances, police officials clarify that they have to balance Israeli legislation with Bedouin customs. These young women occasionally run straight to the police for help because they are afraid for their lives. Often these woman approach police authorities for protection, fearing for their lives. Bypassing the Bedouins norms reflects the rapid growth of urbanization, in education, further it leads to access to television and radio. Some women think they can avoid Bedouin customs because they live in a bigger and feel they live in a more liberal society. (Ginat, 2000) In certain instances, if not most instances, the unmarried lady is forced to wed and reside with the man she had intercourse with; this arrangement is sealed in a sulha (Ginat, 2000) that averts bloodshed and preserves the lives of both parties. The role of the sheikh is that of a judge, arbitrator, mediator, and peacemaker.

These responsibilities are exemplified by the following case: "A married woman was taken in front of sheikh for illicit sexual relation with man. The sheikh made a smart move. Tell the accused woman that during the deliberations of her case, she should crawl on the ground like a baby and do not raise up till she is called to the men's section, he instructed his smart and experienced wife the day before the trial. The accused woman was told to enter the men's section by the judge, who shouted loudly in front of the men, many of whom were her siblings and father, on the day of the trial. She followed his orders. In the men's area of the tent, she was standing at its edge. The sheikh knew that he had to decide a case involving morality, justice, and marriage ties. 'Raise your right hand and swear aloud three times before me and all the men present that since you crawled on the ground (e.g., taken by the men present to mean "since you were a baby") you have not violated your family's honor by having illicit sexual relations and were not unfaithful to your husband,' he ordered the accused woman. She did the same and as a consequence the sheikh commanded her to go back and announced that she was innocent. She was declared blameless by her family members and every Bedouins. This tale demonstrates the Bedouin judge's discernment and resourcefulness in sparing the lives of women who are suspected of engaging in extramarital affairs. It is only right to remark that there are instances in which the weak's power causes the importance of pity to override the demands of justice. (Ginat, 2009)

VALUE SYSTEMS

It is crucial to stress that a Bedouin's commitment to kill a female of his family on pretext of honor is not one that is made lightly or carried out quickly. Absolute moral standards and behavioral standards are dictated by human nature and reality. Women who have a husband or single who cross the boundaries of the rules and regulations do not invariably end up killed. The accused women face consequences if their actions are made public. When a young person flees and asks for the protection of the government or Bedouin sheikhs, especially in areas where everyone's honor is at risk, the matter is typically settled swiftly. There's a feeling that "what has been done, can't be undone," and this problem can only be swiftly and effectively settled in a sulha if honor isn't compromised.

Essentially, Bedouin have to contend with two opposing legal and behavioral systems: the legal framework of the state and their own, customary tribe system. They can occasionally influence the two systems to their advantage. It seems that Bedouin and rural Arabs would consider the possibility of engaging with state agencies to settle conflicts and reduce their use of mediators and religious court judges the more they learn to live with this duality. Either way, it is evident that they will make the most of the two-tiered structure by selecting those provisions of the law that best serve their purposes in any particular circumstance. Although such attitude appears most fitting for the largely pragmatic Bedouin mentality. (Ginat, 2009)

Real-life cases of murder that include the preservation of ancestral pride encompass a diverse range of circumstances and feelings. Numerous examples exist where married women or other females having illicit sexual intercourse without being killed. Hence, when honor killings are discussed, these facts should be considered. It is inappropriate to focus strictly on the cases where woman dies while examining cases related to unjust sexual relations. Figures of death happening in a year gives rise to the false belief that this norm still holds true. It is noteworthy that when the news reports on the death of a woman Arab society, it frequently frames the case as an act of honor killing, even if this may not always be the case. Several instances in which a household dispute unrelated to sexual standards turns violent, turning from verbal abuse to physical aggression that goes too far and ends with the deaths of women. (Ginat, 2000)

The status of sheikhs, who historically risked their life to protect abused women and provided them with home until family peace could be regained, has likewise declined as a result of urbanization. (Ginat, 2000) Hence, blending public and private domains with outdated and contemporary conventions has occasionally resulted in the death of women. There are now multiple community law enforcement agencies to reduce the violence in the country. The police and social workers, in fact, must be sensitive to Arab culture before trying to make any changes. To implement change there is a need of co-operation and to prepare social participants in advance beforehand, and learn as a group. Even in situations where there is disagreement among the parties, communication channels must remain open. In order to cultivate a new consciousness, education is a crucial prerequisite; only then can significant changes occur. (Gale, 2003)

While intriguing, the fact that there are more murders in urban areas than in rural ones is not very significant. It is a well-known fallacy that crimes of honor are prevalent in rural and Bedouin settings. However, Jordanian sources (statisticians and activists) emphasize that this is untrue, arguing that, great majority of these crimes occur in wealthy urban areas. (Gale, 2003) The country of Jordan is rapidly becoming more urbanized and populous, and it does not have well prepared and defined economy in the competitive era. The situation leads to high stress levels. A few find it difficult to adjust to these quick societal shifts and fresh demands. Women and children are the most frequent victims when frustrations are let out in the home. (Nimry,2010) Laxer social constraints and shifting views about oneself and society, including greater sexual freedom for women in higher economic and social is needed. (Araji & Carlson, 2001)

EFFECTS OF MODERNIZATION

Education and awareness have been significantly enhanced in Arab societies due to modernization. Increased access to education for women has resulted in higher literacy rates and greater awareness of their rights. This empowerment enables women to challenge traditional gender roles and combat discriminatory practices more effectively. Further, modernization has stimulated legal reforms that focus on advancing gender equality and safeguarding the rights of women. Several Arab nations have implemented legislation aimed at enhancing the legal standing of women, encompassing provisions addressing issues such as domestic violence, discriminatory practices, and honour killings. Modernization has played a crucial role in promoting women's economic empowerment and increasing their participation in the workforce. It has opened new avenues for women to pursue careers in sectors and professions that were traditionally dominated by men. Further, by earning their own income, women have gained greater autonomy within their households and communities. This financial independence reduces their reliance on male relatives and has led to shifts in societal norms regarding women's roles and capabilities. Furthermore, modernization has brought about significant changes in societal attitudes and cultural practices related to gender roles and women's rights. It has transformed traditional family structures, reshaping perceptions of women's roles within households and communities. Contemporary media platforms and cultural trends have become vehicles for feminist discourse and advocacy. They actively challenge conventional gender stereotypes and advocate for gender equality, thereby influencing broader societal perspectives on women's rights and roles.Top of FormBottom of Form

Recently, the King Hussein Foundation in Jordan and sociologist Musa Shteiwi's study have come together with their findings: the concept of the ird is going to be supplanted by the effects of modernization. He stated that certain effects of modernization, like urbanization, technological advancement in communication devices, education, and social inclusion of women, will leave the concept of the ird largely a past event in modern settings. Dr. Shteiwi made this contention in both an interview and a speech at a conference in Amman. In relation to urbanization, Shteiwi thinks that men's continuous observation and inspection of women's behavior becomes pointless in urbanized settings. According to this theory, women are able to take a more liberal position and acts as a dominator because males are unable to condemn females' behaviors as a result of urbanization. This hypothesis predicts that females will act as a free bird as they are free to challenge established social norms without worrying about the misguided behavior of men.

In addition, Dr. Shteiwi thinks that women will obtain the fundamental social liberties and empowerment necessary to be acknowledged as social, political, and economic entities if they are able to transcend the roles that have been traditionally assigned to them in the workplace and in education. As a result, this reflects progress toward parity between them and their male counterparts in both the public and interpersonal domains. Finally, Shteiwi thinks that women who are living within the four walls of a room will have access to knowledge in urbanized world through mobiles and internet. Essentially, an upsurge in technology would enhance the inclinations that other modernization-related effects have to bring about change, primarily by offering limitless access to social media and knowledge. Some, however, dispute these assertions, arguing that modernity cannot surpass such notions because of its conventional origin. They have, after all, endured millennia of societal transformation and furthermore survived in range of incompatible habitats.

The contradiction between equal footing of female with that of male in country and the continuation of honor killings is the subject of a contemporary legal dispute. It serves as a metaphor for the greater socio-political conflict between an ancient mindset and a modernizing nation. Eliminating violence against women from the personal sphere's gender relations paradigm represents a broader fight to achieve equal status in society at large.

CONTEMPORARY CHALLENGES AND HONOR KILLING

Honour killings remain a troubling concern in Arab societies, where women are tragically targeted and killed by family members who claim to be safeguarding family honour. This analysis delves into the current obstacles and successes in combating honour killings within Arab society, with a specific focus on legal, social, and cultural factors.

Cultural Norms and Traditional Beliefs

Cultural norms and traditional beliefs significantly contribute to the persistence of honour killings in Arab societies.

- **Patriarchal Values**: These deeply rooted values dictate strict roles and behaviours for women within families and communities. They emphasize that women's actions can potentially tarnish the family's honour and bring shame.
- **Social Control and Honour**: Families often impose stringent control over women's lives to uphold their honour. This control may result in severe repercussions for perceived transgressions, such as engaging in relationships outside of marriage or pursuing divorce.

Legal & Judicial Challenges

Honour killing is a deeply rooted and complex issue in many Arab societies, where it is often perceived as a way to restore family honour following actions that are deemed to bring shame or dishonour upon the family. These actions may include refusal of arranged marriages, seeking a divorce, or engaging in relationships deemed inappropriate by societal norms. The legal and judicial challenges surrounding honour killings in Arab societies are multifaceted and can be understood through several lenses, including legal frameworks, societal attitudes, and the effectiveness of law enforcement and judicial processes.

Legal Frameworks and Challenges

1. **Ambiguities in Legislation**: In many Arab countries, legal codes contain ambiguities that can be exploited to mitigate the punishment for honour killings. For instance, some countries have provisions that allow for reduced sentences if the perpetrator can demonstrate that the crime was committed in a state of grave provocation. These laws often reflect a societal tolerance for honour killings,

implicitly condoning the practice by not treating it as severely as other forms of murder.
2. **Customary Laws vs. Statutory Laws:** Customary laws and traditional practices often conflict with statutory laws. In some rural or tribal areas, customary laws that condone or even mandate honour killings can take precedence over national laws. This dual legal system creates a significant barrier to justice, as local authorities might be more inclined to adhere to customary practices rather than enforce national laws that criminalize honour killings.
3. **Inadequate Legal Protections for Women:** Women in many Arab countries face systemic legal discrimination that exacerbates their vulnerability to honour killings. Laws governing personal status, marriage, and family often subordinate women's rights to those of men, making it difficult for women to seek protection or justice. For example, laws that require male guardianship over women or those that restrict women's mobility and autonomy can trap women in abusive situations, including those that may lead to honour killings.

Therefore, the Codes serve as a legal intervention within the realm of honour killings. They function by legitimizing some killings while de-legitimizing others. (Lama, 2010)

JUDICIAL CHALLENGES

1. **Bias and Lack of Impartiality:** Judicial systems in many Arab societies can bere biased, particularly in cases involving honour killings. Judges and law enforcement officials may share the same cultural attitudes that justify honour killings, leading to lenient sentences or even outright acquittals for perpetrators. This bias undermines the rule of law and denies justice to victims.
2. **Corruption and Influence:** Corruption within the judicial system can also impede justice. In some instances, families of perpetrators may bribe officials or use their influence to secure favourable outcomes. This corruption further erodes public trust in the legal system and perpetuates a cycle of impunity for honour killings.
3. **Insufficient Legal Representation and Support for Victims:** Victims and their families often lack adequate legal representation and support. Many women, particularly those from marginalized communities, do not have the resources or knowledge to navigate the legal system. This lack of support can discourage victims from pursuing legal action and contribute to the underreporting of honour killings.

The judiciary, although it reintroduces the notion of traditional honour, does so in a limited and restrained manner. Its implementation is neither complete nor wholehearted. Judicial practices have shifted the nationalist equilibrium to another, equally fragile and unstable balance. This is unsurprising, given that the judiciary, like the codifiers, adheres to the fundamental nationalist ideology of balancing tradition with modernity. (Lama, 2010)

SOCIETAL ATTITUDES AND LAW ENFORCEMENT

1. **Cultural Acceptance of Honour Killings:** Honour killings are often culturally accepted in some segments of Arab society, where they are viewed as a legitimate response to perceived dishonour. This cultural acceptance can influence law enforcement practices, with police officers sometimes reluctant to investigate or prosecute honour killings thoroughly. In some cases, law enforcement officials may even sympathize with the perpetrators.
2. **Fear and Intimidation:** Victims' families and potential witnesses often face intimidation and threats, discouraging them from coming forward. This fear is compounded by the potential for retribution from within the community, further complicating efforts to prosecute honour killings.
3. **Lack of Specialized Training:** Law enforcement officials often lack specialized training to handle cases of honour killings. This lack of training can result in mishandling of evidence, poor investigative practices, and a failure to provide appropriate protection for victims and witnesses.

Efforts Toward Reform

1. **Legal Reforms:** There have been efforts in some Arab countries to reform laws related to honour killings. For example, Jordan has amended its penal code to impose stricter penalties on perpetrators of honour killings. Such reforms aim to close legal loopholes and provide clearer, more stringent penalties for honour-related violence.
2. **Raising Awareness and Changing Attitudes:** NGOs, activists, and international organizations are working to raise awareness about the issue of honour killings and change societal attitudes. These efforts include educational campaigns, community outreach programs, and advocacy for women's rights. Changing deep-seated cultural attitudes is a long-term process, but it is crucial for reducing the incidence of honour killings.

3. **Improving Legal and Social Support Systems:** Enhancing legal and social support systems for women is critical. This includes providing better legal aid, establishing shelters and safe spaces for at-risk women, and implementing comprehensive support services. Empowering women and providing them with the resources they need to seek justice and protection is a key component of addressing honour killings.

Hence, it can be analysed that honour killings in Arab societies pose significant legal and judicial challenges that are deeply intertwined with cultural norms and societal attitudes. Addressing these challenges requires a multifaceted approach that includes legal reforms, raising awareness, and improving support systems for women. While progress has been made in some areas, much work remains to be done to ensure that honour killings are eradicated and that justice is consistently upheld for all victims.

Stigma and Victim Blaming

Victims of honour killings and their families frequently encounter stigma and blame, exacerbating their anguish and impeding justice-seeking efforts.

- Community Pressure: Survivors and their families often experience social ostracization and exclusion within their communities, which hinders their ability to seek support services or report incidents to authorities.
- Cultural Perception: Victim blaming reinforces damaging stereotypes that hold women accountable for their victimization, discouraging them from seeking assistance or speaking up about their experiences.

At last, it can be concluded that the Feminist movement in Arab society is dynamic and evolving force, shaped by historical legacies, cultural nuances and ongoing struggles for social justice. While progress has been made, challenges persist, and the movement continues to navigate the delicate balance between tradition and modernity. The voices of Arab feminists, past and present, contribute to a broader conversation about human rights, equality, and the potential for transformative change within the region.

REFERENCES

Araji, S., Carlson, J. (2001). *Family violence including crimes of honor in Jordan: correlates and perceptions of seriousness*.

Cohen, A. (1977). *Two dimensioned man: an essay on the anthropology of power and symbolism in complex society*. Routledge and Kegan Paul.

Gale, N. (2003). *Violence against women: A normal or deviant behaviour*. Hameuchad Publishing House.

Ginat, J. (2000). *Blood revenge: outcasting mediation and family honor*. University Press.

Ginat, J. *Bedouin Bisha'h Justice: ordeal by fire*. (2009). Brighton & Port-land: Sussex Academic Press.

Ginat, J., & Khazanov, A. (1998). *Changing nomads in a changing world* (eds). Sussex Academic Press, Brighton UK, p.149.

Khalili, M. I. (2002). A comment on heat-of-passion crimes, honor killings, and Islam. *Politics and the Life Sciences*, 38–40.

Khazanov, A. (1981). *Comments, Currents Anthropol. Killing of Youtube star by her father causes outrage in Iraq* (2023, February 4). Aljazeera. https://www.aljazeera.com/news/2023/2/4/iraqis-outraged-after-father-kills-youtube-star-daughter

Kressel, G., Bausani, A., Ginat, J., Joseph, R., Khazanov, A. M., Landau, S. F., Marx, E., & Shokeid, M. (1981). Sororicide/ filiacide: Homicide for family honor. *Current Anthropology*, 22(2), 141–158. DOI: 10.1086/202632

Kressel, G. M. (1992). Shame and gender. *Anthropological Quarterly*, 34–46.

Lama, A. (2010) *Honor Killings and the Construction of Gender in Arab Societies*.

Marwick, M. (1965). *Sorcery in its social setting*. Humanities Press.

Nimry, L. *Crimes of Honor in Jordan and the Arab World*. (2010). Retrived from https://www.c-we.org/eng/show.art.asp?aid=749

Qur'an: The Meaning of the Glorious Qur'an (1979). Text and explanatory translation by Marmaduke Pickthall (Karachi-Lahore-Rawalpindi: Taj Company, p.2-4, 1979.

Rabinowitz, D. (1995). *The twisting journey for the rescue of brown women*. Hebrew: Teorya Uvikoret.

Ruggi, S. *Commodifying Honor in Female Sexuality: Honor Killings in Palestine* (2008). Retrieved from https://www.merip.org/mer/mer206/ruggi.htm

Verot, M. P. (2023). *Une femme est victime de féminicide chaque jours en Turquie*. RadioFrance. Retrived from https://www.radiofrance.fr/franceinter/une-femme-est-victime-de-feminicide-chaque-jour-en-turquie-7721900

Chapter 5
Family Honor and Forces of Change in Arab Society:
Middle East Region

Nupur Kumari
Bennett University, India

Siddhi Baranwal
GLA University, Mathura, India

ABSTRACT

Honor Based violence can be defined as any form of violence that is used to safeguard family or community honor. Most of the crime victims are women. Boys and Men can also be the victim but however, this is rare. Illiteracy, unemployment, economic decline, poor support and lack of knowledge of the law are factors that increase the risk of victimization. Additionally Patriarchal groups recognize that men are the head of the family and are responsible for combating all negative attitudes that cause serious psychological harm to women in these communities, and in many other regions patriarchal system go far as considering a women as Men's property. The perpetrators of honor killings also have similar characteristics such as valuing singleness and committing violence again and again. This chapter also drew attention towards the victims of Honor Killing, in addition to highlighting various reports which shows the deteriorating conditions of women, how silence culture dominated the communities and the offences not recorded in this area .

DOI: 10.4018/979-8-3693-7240-1.ch005

In 2019 over 375 to 450 killings occurred only in Iran Between 2000 and 2010, there was 50 documented Honor killing in Jordan. 52 cases of Honor Killing occurred in Egypt in 1997, while 400 women in Yemen fell prey to the disease in the same year. Between 1996 and 1998, 38 cases of Honor Killing were documented in Lebanon. In Palestine, the Women's Center for Legal Aid and Counseling documented 27 cases in 2014 and 15 cases in 2015. Nevertheless, the problem may not be as severe as these low numbers suggest, and some are not even documented or listed. (Qahatani, 2022)

KEYTERMS

The nucleus of the term includes "Honor Killing", and "Forces of Change". "Middle East Region" (Goldstein, 2002), Patriarchal Society (Akbar, 2005) and Omani Women ("Women in Oman," 2000) contextualize the issue "Violence" (Smith, 2004) and "Murder" (Maffesoli, 1995) happens "against women" (Singh, 2023) because of "dominance" of "Family", (Hossain, 2005) Culture (Ravishankar, 2017) and Religion (Grzyb, 2021)

Human Rights, (Nowak, 2015), we used these keywords to select relevant articles from multiple online sources, for example,'Research Gate, Google Books, Springer, JSTOR, Sage Scopus, Web of Science, Francis and Google Scholar

An Honor Killings Research Paper on its Family Honor and Forces of change in Arab Society requires careful consideration of inclusion/exclusion and article research, as well as the selection of appropriate publications. Publications with an emphasis on international law, gender studies, human rights, and related interdisciplinary topics were chosen for publishing in the journal selection process.

We have set inclusion and exclusion criteria to further refine the research publications that are relevant for this Chapter. The research must be published in English and limited to journal articles, that is, those with an impact factor of 1.0 or above in Journal Citation Reports and peer-reviewed papers, or those with a B grade or higher in the Journal Quality list. The following studies satisfied our inclusion criteria: those in which "experience" was examined as a concept or a variable in the context of ecotourism.

RESEARCH METHODOLOGY

Studying the complex socio-cultural, psychological, and moral facets of honor killing is the focus of qualitative study. Scholars employ various techniques such as focus groups, interviews, and ethnographic investigations to gain insight into the underlying ideas, values, and customs that sustain honor killings within certain communities. (Raiya, 2013) This research frequently demonstrates the ways in which gender roles, family reputation, and conceptions of honor are entwined, motivating individuals or groups to carry out such activities in order to restore perceived honor. Qualitative studies, through the collection of personal narratives and experiences, offer profound insights into the reasons, rationalizations, and social pressures that give rise to these crimes. This emphasizes the necessity of subtle interventions that target the cultural and contextual elements that contribute to honor-based violence. (Raiya, 2013)

LITERATURE REVIEW

Iranian feminist activist Fatemeh Hassani believes that when a woman defies socially enforced norms and values, her family's men will also suffer, and they will have to offer apologies.

In the authors views Fatemeh Hassani, an Iranian feminist activist, suggests that when a woman challenges societal norms and values, it impacts not just her but also the men in her family. This is because traditional social structures often hold families collectively responsible for the behavior of their female members. Consequently, the men in her family may face social backlash or pressure to apologize or rectify the situation, (Benraad, 2018).

The issue of honor is crucial in Middle Eastern tribal and clan systems, according to French sociologist Camille Boudjak, who has spearheaded a global campaign against honour killings. While feminine virtue is related with chastity, male behavior is tied to honor. Deviating from accepted social norms is viewed as disgraceful and humiliating for the community as a whole, not just the family. Murder is frequently considered to be the only way for them to regain their lost honor.

In the authors views Camille Boudjak, a French sociologist, highlights that in Middle Eastern tribal and clan systems, honor is a central issue, with feminine virtue linked to chastity and male behavior tied to honor. Deviations from social norms are seen as a disgrace to the entire community, not just the individual or family. In extreme cases, honor killings are viewed as a means to restore lost honor (Dessaux, 2005)

FUTURE RESEARCH DIRECTIONS

In this Research paper the authors have covered the topics of women in Arab Society and its impact on women lives Emphasis on Future-Oriented Strategies: Unlike other studies that may focus predominantly on current issues or historical perspectives, my chapter actively looks towards the future, outlining actionable strategies and potential pathways for progress.

Holistic and Integrated Approaches: this chapter may differ by integrating various elements such as policy reform, education, technology, and cultural change into a comprehensive framework, suggesting that multiple fronts need to be addressed simultaneously for substantial progress. (Sanchez, 2021)

Focus on Innovation and Change Agents: By highlighting innovative approaches, whether through technology, community movements, or new educational models, this chapter brings fresh ideas to the discussion that others may not have covered in detail.

Specificity in Cultural Context: the analysis could be more tailored to specific cultural, social, and political contexts within the Arab world, avoiding generalized assumptions and instead providing context-specific recommendations for different countries or communities.

By highlighting these unique aspects, this chapter demonstrate the contributes to the discourse in a meaningful way and offers a fresh perspective on the future of gender equality in Arab societies. (Gadit, 2008)

While this research paper provides valuable insights into the phenomenon of honor killings, it is important to acknowledge its limitations and identify areas for future exploration. Understanding these limitations not only contextualizes the findings but also highlights opportunities for further research that could enhance our comprehension of honor-based violence like Men can also be the victim of Honor killing, Gender bias in existing Culture and others.

BACKGROUND

Strongly sexist attitudes concerning women and their place in society can lead to honor killings. Women in these traditionally patriarchal communities are supposed to submit to their husbands, who are the source of their dependence. Women are not seen as autonomous beings, but rather as objects. They must therefore yield to the male family members who are in positions of leadership; failing to do so may result in severe violence as a form of discipline. It is believed that using violence will guarantee obedience and quell disobedience. Professor Shahid Khan of Aga Khan University in Pakistan states: "Regardless of status, ethnicity, or religion, women are viewed as the males' property in their families. The proprietor of the Property is entitled to determine what happens to it. Women can now be bought, sold, and traded like any other commodity thanks to the ownership notion. Such cultures forbid women from taking charge of their bodies and sexuality, which belong to the male members of the family: the husband, to whom his wife's sexuality is subservient, and the father (and other male relatives), who must maintain virginity until marriage. A woman must not violate her guardian's ownership rights by having extramarital affairs or being unfaithful. (Sen, 2005)

INTRODUCTION

Behaviours that would punish a woman for being conceiving or giving birth without being married, being abused or sexually abused or refusing to marry a person chosen by their guardian. Additionally, if a woman wants to get a divorce due to abuse or other reasons, if she wants to marry someone of her own choice or even if she wants to go to college or University against the opinion of her superior, then she will be in trouble. This includes the ease of talking to men in all situations, even if it is sometimes inappropriate. The most extreme type of Honor- Based Violence is Honor based homicide. Other forms are physical attack, maltreatment at home, sexual assault, or harassment, forced abortion, compelled marriage to the perpetrator, and poisoning and murder threats. The definition of honor killing is a violent crime committed by one or more offenders against a woman, usually a male relative is accused of misbehaving or doing anything that degraded the family's reputation which the crime is meant to rectify and restore honor.

According to 2012 data of the World Health Organization (WHO), it is estimated that approximately 5,000 murders occur every year worldwide in the name of honor killing. According to research there are many methods of honor killing the following are the examples: burning, stabbing, acid burning, pebble throwing, being buried alive, and pushing a woman into to attempt suicide or take poison. Sometimes weapons are used such as axes, firearms, and edged tools.

COUNTRIES IN THE GULF COOPERATION COUNCIL

Saudi Arabia

Saudi Arabia has not published many studies on Honor Killing however that Saudi Arabia has a much higher rate of Domestic Violence roughly 58% than the global average which is between 10 and 52%. It should be noted that this rate only includes Saudi Arabia's major cities because rural areas were not included in the relevant study. Though stories are rarely published in Reputable news channels more stories about honor killing are gradually becoming public to social media. These platforms are seen as untrustworthy, contributing to the so- called grey literature (i.e., posts on social media, newspaper stories etc). Saudi Arabia and other nations that make up the Gulf Cooperation Council have similar sociocultural elements. As a result, a large number of cases are also not reported, making epidemiological estimates impossible.

OTHER COUNTRIES IN THE EAST MEDITERRANEAN REGION

Pakistan

It is believed that in Pakistan has the greatest concentration of Honor Killing. The Pakistan ministry of interior has reported to the court 4101 cases of Honor crimes between 1998 to 2003. According to data from the Human Rights Commission of Pakistan, the number of honor killings has been steadily increasing; in 2013, 869 incidents were reported; in 2014, 1000 cases were estimated; and in 2015, 1100 cases were reported. In addition, 2009 research carried out in Pakistan made an attempt to quantify honor killing, estimating that, in the four years of the study, accusations of extramarital affairs resulted to the deaths of 1957 women. 18% of the women were married, while eighteen percent of the ladies who died were younger than eighteen. Three adolescent girls were allegedly sexually abused by the governing troops at a Mistrata Public School throughout the Libyan Civil War, according to activists for the US-based group Doctors for Human Rights. After they betrayed the family's honor, their father later murdered them.

The Afghanistan Federal Human Rights Commission states that 243 incidences of honor killing were documented in Afghanistan between March 2011 and April 2013. Only 56% of the perpetrators in those cases were recognised; of those, 39% were spouses, 15% were brothers, 9% were dads, 6% were brothers-in-law, 5% were other family members, and 26% were other relatives. (Gadit, 2008)

SOCIAL AND CULTURAL ASPECTS CONTRIBUTING TO HONOR KILLING

The seemingly benign tale "You are the ruler of the house" is frequently repeated to young boys, it has been observed throughout the years, mostly to assist them to feel more from a young age. To absolve one's parents of the duty of rearing the female members of the home who are regularly the same age as the boys or even older, it was and still is technique of raising boys to conform to the masculine roles that their parents, primarily the fathers have instilled in them. This same story is what gave rise to the gender striation that exists today, where men are seen as the "guardians" of women and their honor, even though this whole thing started off as a fun way to honor guys' manhood. Over time, it transformed into a true power struggle inside society, one in which women everywhere still have to deal with today. (Mirza, 2007)

Boys were gradually led by this story to believe that the "reputations" of the women in their home were their responsibility and that they had to protect them at all costs. Those women were a reflection of those men's masculinity and "ability to tame," not their own unique selves. This gave rise to the adage, "If you are unable to maintain your females in range, you are not an acceptable masculine male," as well as the idea of "fragile masculinity," which describes the state in which a man's sense of manhood is undermined when he feels threatened by the smallest loss of authority over female family members, even if that male is actually the female's male sibling/cousin rather than her legal guardian. After gaining an overview of masculinity as a social construct, its distorted and fragile foundation in modern society, the following section will demonstrate how this fragile masculinity developed into an extremely patriarchal culture where a man's worth is primarily based on how much control he has over the feminine members of his family. (Qahatani, 2022)

DEMONSTRATION OF THE PATRIARCHAL SOCIETY

For many years, the patriarchal society has propagated among men the idea that a woman's sexual virginity is a sign of her honor, and that a man's dignity is only an extension of his female relatives'. A woman's male relative or cousin will be her guardian until she forges a new relationship with a man who upholds honor in a family-approved marriage, after which she will face consequences (Kamal, 2022). A woman may suffer serious consequences, such as probation, loss of social engagement, education, or even worse results like death, if her chastity is broken in any manner before getting married, even by everything as little as a gossip. From an impartial stance, one may argue that in certain It is a legitimate duty of the family, regardless of culture or religion, to keep their daughters from having sex before marriage. That begs the issue, though, of what would have happened if the lady had been raped before being married. Unfortunately, because a woman in these circumstances is still viewed as a shame to the family, a patriarchal culture does not consider women and their misfortunes in its views and actions.

Family members who are reluctant to carry out the act of honor killing are subject to strong peer pressure from their neighbours, relatives, and other community members, and they are forbidden from feeling even the slightest sympathy towards their female family members whom have been sexually assaulted or mistreated. As an alternative, they are instructed to punish them, view them as despicable, and reject them in an effort to finally maintain or restore the family's status in society.

These tragedies are related to the structural defect in society that compels a large proportion of males to view women in a patriarchy environment from a young age, therefore reinforcing the validity of killings of honor as they become older. As an example, consider the two sisters Aisha and Gamila, who were raised in Yemen. The two girls were raised with patriarchal beliefs by their father. Fearing they might grow too sexual, their biological father had them through female genital mutilation, often known as female circumcision. As the girls became older and more responsible, their father's concerns about their chastity rose until he banned them from going to school and secluded them. Following that, their father considered it was the moment to tie them in an arranged union. After that, the two females devised a careful strategy and were able to escape the country. "Their lifeblood must be spilt in order to sanitise the family name," as their father expressed it. It is now believed that the girls have brought disgrace and disgrace to their family. This instance illustrates the extent to which a patriarchal society may see honor killing as legitimate. The majority of honor killing incidents go undetected. (Mostafa, 2022)

Between 2000 and 2010, there was 50 documented Honor killing in Jordan. 52 cases of Honor Killing occurred in Egypt in 1997, while 400 women in Yemen fell prey to the disease in the same year. Between 1996 and 1998, 38 cases of Honor Killing were documented in Lebanon. In Palestine, the Women's Center for Legal Aid and Counseling documented 27 cases in 2014 and 15 cases in 2015. Nevertheless, the problem may not be as severe as these low numbers suggest, and some are not even documented or listed. (Gibbs, 2019)

SOCIAL IMAGE OF THE CRIMINAL

According to a various study in 2019 some characteristics associated with murder on the name of honor killing the decline in the social economy plays a significant role in increasing the crime rate. Other factors include experience of cruelty of women within the family and within the surrounding victim and criminal communities. Some of the aggressive behaviours found in this study including beating by siblings or parents, childhood trauma, abuse by husband or mother-in-law etc is located. Another important factor affecting honor killing is a segment of society where there are gender stereotypes, poverty is high and there is a need for debt due to hunger. (Gregory, 2020)

The lack of knowledge and ignorance about gender roles, family honor, and their position have also been determined to be significant contributors to the maintenance of a patriarchal culture. Tragically, been shown to be taught at a young age, young people even at school. A previous study stated that education plays an important role in preventing homicides. There is also a connection between sibling marriage and hepatitis honor killing is like a virus, this is a system that relies on the obedience of young people for its survival. Another important factor worth mentioning that has led to increased expansion in honor killing is the rapid reforms that have increased too quickly for those who attack the bear in the world to think boldly and strictly. (Luebering, 2024)

ARAB GOVERNMENTS ARE DOING TOO LITTLE FOR HONOR KILLING

In some countries in middle east, government is doing the very least for the cases of honor killing many cases are unreported as like it never happened. In the Patriarchal society a woman cannot even open their mouth, they remain quiet and if any other wants to take stand for her they will also be killed on the name of honor. A person who is committing a crime does it in silence and erase all the proofs, like it never happened these cases never get reported. Government also take least interest in these types of cases as there is no victim and proofs of the cases. In many cultures violence against women is a way to preserve family honor to end stigma against women. From a legal perspective is illegal and carries several penalties. It is not a crime in the name of honor, if this type of killing is considered as a crime, then harsher penalties should be considered. Many study attributes the culture to Islamic or middle eastern regions but unfortunately crime has become established as a pattern. (Hasisi, 2019)

Nowadays, honor killings occur less frequently, and the perpetrators are sometimes given, In Egypt, for instance, Article 237 of Penal Code No. 58, dated 937, stipulates that "Criminals must be sentenced with incarceration instead of death." Similarly, Article 409 of the 1966 criminal law states that in Iraq, criminals are given only "A Prison sentence not exceeding three years". Also, article 334 of law no 6664. In the United Arab Emirates law, no 1966 it was stated that criminals could be imprisoned for "a duration of no more than three years". Law no 3/1978 stated that 'perpetrators will be sentenced to imprisonment'. (Anjum, 2019)

Criminals in Kuwait are subject to fines or other punishments in addition to a maximum sentence of three years in jail, as stated in Article 153 of the criminal code. Perpetrators in Jordan will reap the benefits of reduced amnesty, which means that killings conducted in the context of family protection are acceptable and will result in reduced penalties once more. Research carried out in Pakistan revealed that the anti-honor killing statute resulted in the arrest of very few culprits. Furthermore, since they turn a blind eye and assisted in the conduct of these crimes, the federal government and local governments steer clear of these circumstances. However, in nations where murder of honor is prohibited, attorneys frequently use "protection in the name of honor' here women are considered as weapons of men and murders are considered self-defence. Other prosecutors may plead "temporary insanity" to save a criminal from punishment he or she would face if caught. (Hasisi, 2019)

Similar laws such as the honor killing culture of silence and veiling culture, also occurred in Palestine. Many crimes go unreported and no matter what cases are brought before the justice system, some patterns of silence appear. For example, shortly after the announcement the witness disappeared, never to be seen again. Additionally, some witnesses will change their statements after further investigation, contrary to their previous statements. There are often also crimes involved and no visible evidence. After, all people go home to live in the house and the case is paid and never asked again. Additionally, Article 301 of the Iranian Penal Code states that a father or a grandfather is justified in killing his daughter without seeking retribution from the judiciary. Additionally, Article 630 allows a man to kill his wife if he witnesses adultery, but this benefit is not provided to a woman, in honor killing there is a wide discrimination.

BEHIND THE VEIL OF OMANI WOMEN

Etiquette in Islamic Culture requires women to behave in a way at all times, especially when travelling away from home. At home Omani women wear knee-length dresses with high heels and cover their hair and neck with scarf. Many colourful and jalabbiyas are worn at home as well. When leaving the house, clothing varies according to local preferences. A person of some religious backgrounds wear burqa a wiqaya (turban), and abaya (a full covering garment that extends to leave only the hands and body) to protect the face from other men. Many women from different parts of the Sultanate wear scarves to cover their hair. Women have to cover themselves always.

Women are always considered, first and foremost as wives and mothers. Happy marriages and having children decide their relationship, and when women get married most of the time husbands decides what to do and what to not. Marriage is a defining moment in a person's life. The Omani women marks their tradition from childhood to womanhood. Although Sultan Qaboos gave both men and women right to choose their spouses in 1971, tradition says that the girl father is responsible for arranging the marriage and taking care of his daughter. Since the onset of sexuality must coincide with marriage, most girls are married off at a young age, as such all Omani women are virgin. After marriage if they found not virgin then husbands or girl father used to kill the women.

The importance of women's health and well-being has become even more important in recent years along with developments in other areas of women's lives. Although the marriage rate of girls aged 15-20 was 15% in 2004, the statistics is higher in other countries, leading to young and uneducated parents. In 1994, the government introduced a maternity program and provided free vaccines at many health centers to encourage parents to use vaccines. The program worked and total fertility fell from 7.05 in 1995 to 4.8 in 2000. ("Women in Oman," 2000)

The Middle East's Feminist Movement to Make Honour Killings a Crime

The Middle East's Feminist Movement to Make Honour Killings a Crime, Crimes against women are not honourable! protestors right on February 5, shortly after the Baghdad Courthouse, in response to the 22-year-old blogger's assassination Tiba Al-Ali. Honor murders are prohibited by international law as a breach of female basic rights, and nations are required to defend their citizens from honour killings. Although honour murders are, in principle, taboo in Middle Eastern nations, they are either justified as part of valid cultural customs or condoned because of official inactivity. When a male is prosecuted, the focus of the trial shifts from the accused's culpability to the actions of the lady. In these situations, police investigations are bungled or nonexistent. (Valentine, 2014)

Honour killings: Legal Abuse of Women

Throughout the Eastern Mediterranean region, a very prudent society where the idea of the system of society is strongly prominent, honour murders are rampant. For instance, society is prioritised in Iran and individuals is viewed as secondary. So, when someone behaves in a way that is deemed dishonourable, they are disobeying the honour of their society. Given that women are often influenced by the males in their social circles, this idea is even more applicable to them. Iranian feminist activist Fatemeh Hassani believes that when a woman defies socially enforced norms and values, her family's males will also suffer and they will have to offer apologies.

The NGO Human Rights Watch states that there are a variety of causes behind this. It could be an effort to file for divorce, either in the event that her spouse has used domestic violence against her or in the event that infidelity has been established. It might also be unable to commit to take part in an arranged union or to to decline sex services. Retaliation might be initiated based on the bare assumption that her actions have "dishonoured" her family. It's a custom that is accepted by society and even supported by Iran's sexist and misogynistic mullah leadership. According to the criminal code, "a man is justified in instantaneously assassinating them both if he detects his wife having an affair outside of marriage and is certain that she has given her acceptance." (Kulczycki, 2011)

According to the Turkish organisation, there will be over 330 female victims of feminicide in 2022, demonstrating the pervasiveness of honour murders and violence against women in Turkey. Feminicide will be eradicated. Women's life are still controlled by the patriarchal society. In Kemalist tradition, the lady is the one who determines the family's honour. As a result, males educate women how to act "well" in order to subconsciously or actively avoid attracting men Up until 2014, protecting one's family honour by criminal activity was seen as an exceptional scenario in Iraq. Despite the fact that this component has been eliminated since 2014, the phenomena is seeing a comeback. Tiba Al-Ali, a youth YouTuber who had moved to reside by herself with her spouse in Turkish, was assassinated by her father on January 31, 2023 went on a visitation trip to her relatives in Iraq. Iraqis reacted to social media after learning of Al-Ali's killing, calling for protests in the nation's capital to demand justice

On February 7, 2022, Mona Heydari, then seventeen years old, was murdered in Iran by her spouse. The adolescent had left her house due to abuse from within. Iranian women's advocacy group Women's Committee NCRI states that: "Her relatives pushed her to come and stay at the home of her spouse from now on for betterment of her kid" whenever she filed for divorce. Her spouse received a sentence of only seven years and fifteen months in prison, for the murder and an additional two months for the assault. The death sentence is applied to willful murder in Iran unless the offender receives a pardon from the family. Even though the victim's father said that he had not approved of the murder, an judicial official, claimed that Mona's conduct had been "pardoned" by her maternal grandparents, resulting in the sentence being lowered. Iran's domestic violence prevention and victim protection laws are being demanded again as a result of the murder. There have also been initiatives to raise the legal minimum age of marriage. Although much younger females are lawfully married with their parents' permission, the current age limit for girls is thirteen.

Attempts at Proposals to Outlaw Honour Killings

Honour murders must be stopped, and this is a difficult process that calls for coordinated effort from civil society organisations and governments. One important problem is women's involvement in politics. By enacting laws and policies that shield women from honour murders and domestic abuse, women legislators may make a significant contribution to the battle against honour killings. They can also seek to advance more inclusive and egalitarian social and cultural standards and increase public awareness of the disastrous effects of these behaviours.

A 25% female quota on election lists, implemented in 2019, has improved women's representation in Iraq. 33% of lawmakers will be female by 2021. The government agency tasked with preventing violence against women was established in the same year. Promoting women's rights and opposing all types of violence and prejudice against women are the department's goals. The government's division dedicated to preventing violence against women aims to shield victims, bring charges against offenders, and prevent abuse altogether. As a result, this department plays a crucial role in both promoting women's rights and safety in Iraq and combating violence against them. (Elakkary, 2014)

In order to combat concerns of violence against women, women today hold prominent roles in the government and in public institutions. As an example, consider in the member of the Human Rights Commission and Kurdish lawmaker from Iraq, Rizan Sheikh Dleer. In the Kurdish areas of Iraq, she has pushed for the passage of legislation protecting women's rights, especially in relation to domestic abuse and female genital mutilation.

Domestic abuse is not criminalised in many Middle Eastern nations since it is seen as a family concern that should be resolved in private. One way that protest groups are attempting to address this problem is by requesting new rules. In Turkey, a new criminal law was implemented in 2005 as a result of the 1980s feminist demonstrations. Creating fresh, efficient strategies to counteract violence against women was the goal of this new civil code. One of the most important actions done was to enforce stricter. Heavy punishments on killers who used the concept of honour as a warning to other people. Nonetheless, attorneys observed throughout the trial that judges frequently identify extenuating factors to reduce the severity of punishments given to offenders. Furthermore, a lot of honour killings of young women go unpunished by the legal system, which is like having a gun licence.

Mahsa Amini, a 22-year-old Iranian Kurdistan native, passed away in September 2022 following her arrest and incarceration by the morality police, which led to a widespread rebellion in Iran. Iranian feminist Shireen Karmini claims that the current demonstrations against the requirement to wear the hijab are an extension of the country's long history of women fighting for their rights, a struggle that crosses social, ethnic, and ideological boundaries to support a new democratic system. According to UN estimates, 5,000 women and girls are killed in honor killings annually.

Iran's Supreme Leader, as declared on February 5, authorised a reduction in sentence or amnesty for thousands of persons unfairly jailed in connection with the anti-government demonstrations throughout the nation, given the significance of the protests. (Alonso, 1995)

Making Honour Killings a Crime: Plenty of Work Still Ahead

Honour murders are prohibited in the majority of Middle Eastern nations, but regrettably, they are still carried out in some extremist societies in Afghanistan, Iran, Iraq, Pakistan, Syria and other nations in the area.

Human rights groups, advocates for women's rights, and governments are striving to increase public knowledge of the risks associated with honour murders and to fortify laws and regulations that safeguard victims and bring criminal charges against those who commit them. Nonetheless, there is still more work to be done to put an end to this illegal activity and ensure the safety and rights of women in the area. (Singh, 2023)

Solutions for preventing Honor Killing

Teams of knowledgeable male and female officers will be sent to the villages and action plans known as honor killing will be prepared with the help of influential people and religious leaders in the society. Separate meetings will be held for men and women, with reference to religious contexts and national activities on the fight against honor killing. To have an impact, anti-genocide newspapers must be distributed. Honor killing is prohibited in the majority of Middle Eastern nations, although regrettably still occurs in some conservative societies, such as Afghanistan, Saudi Arabia, Oman and many other countries in the region. Human Right Groups and women's right activists, and government have worked to highlight the dangers of honor killings and strengthen laws and regulations to protect victims and persecute and prosecute offenders. However, there is still much work to be done to eliminate this crime and ensure the rights and security of women in the region. ("Women in Oman," 2000)

CONCLUSION

Honor Killing is a crime against family honor, but now we must know that there is no respect for killing people. Culture, tradition and Religion should not be excuses for sinning because they are obvious and as we humans we understood. The right to freedom of religion does not guarantee the right to kill. Therefore, the authors of this chapter believe that the definition of 'Honor' has to be changed in order to stop this atrocity. This may be accomplished by-

Raising Awareness: Honor killings are particularly prevalent in rural communities, where the victim is nearly always a female who lacks access to education and is thus unaware of her rights. As a result, they are reluctant to defend themselves and accept it as a penalty for their own actions.

Social Changes: The underlying cause of these atrocities is people's mentalities. Marriages between different castes are still frowned upon. As times change, society wants change as well. Furthermore, reporting such incidents shouldn't be discouraged by people's fear of social approval.

Strict Legal Support: Although such killings may be made illegal by a number of other laws, it should be noted that these laws only grant general protections. Strict, specifically codified legal support is required to dissuade society and bring legal action against those who actually commit these horrible crimes.

REFERENCES

Abu Raiya, H. (2013). *The psychology of Islam: Current empirically based knowledge. potential challenges, and direction for future research.* Tel Aviv University.

Al Qahtani, S. M., Almutairi, D. S., BinAqeel, E. A., Almutairi, R. A., Al-Qahtani, R. D., & Menezes, R. G. (2023). Honor Killings in the Eastern Mediterranean Region: A Narrative Review. *Health Care*, 11(1), 74. Advance online publication. DOI: 10.3390/healthcare11010074 PMID: 36611534

Alonso, A. (1995). Rationalizing patriarchy: Gender, domestic violence and law in Mexico. *Identities (Yverdon)*, 2(1-2), 29–47. DOI: 10.1080/1070289X.1997.9962525

Anjum, G., Kessler, T., & Aziz, M. (2019). Cross-cultural exploration of honor: Perception of honor in Germany, Pakistan, and South Korea. *Psychological Studies*, 64(2), 147–160. DOI: 10.1007/s12646-019-00484-4

Benraad, M. (2018). *L'Irak par-delà toutes les guerres*. Le Cavalier Bleu. DOI: 10.3917/lcb.benra.2018.01

Dessaux, N. (15 aout 2005). La lutte des femmes en Irak avant et depuis l'occupation, Courant Alternatif, 148. https://sisyphe.org/spip.php?article190

Elakkary, S., Franke, B., Shokri, D., Hartwig, S., Tsokos, M., & Puschel, K. (2014). Honor crimes: Review and proposed definition. *Forensic Science, Medicine, and Pathology*, 10(1), 76–82. DOI: 10.1007/s12024-013-9455-1 PMID: 23771767

Gibbs, A., Said, N., Corboz, J., & Jewkes, R. (2019). Factors associated with honour killing in Afghanistan and the occupied Palestinian Territories: Two cross-sectional studies. *PLoS One*, 14(8), e0219125. DOI: 10.1371/journal.pone.0219125 PMID: 31393873

Goldstein, M. A. (2002). The biological roots of heat-of-passion crimes and honour killings. *Politics and the Life Sciences*, 21(2), 28–37. PMID: 16859346

Gregory, G., Fox, J., & Howard, B. (2020). Honour-based violence: Awareness and recognition. *Paediatrics and Child Health (Oxford)*, 30(11), 365–370. DOI: 10.1016/j.paed.2020.08.001

Grzyb, M. A. (2016). An explanation of honour-related killings of women in Europe through Bourdieu's concept of symbolic violence and masculine domination. *Current Sociology*, 64(7), 1036–1053.

Hasisi, B., & Bernstein, D. (2019). Echoes of domestic silence: Mechanisms of concealment in cases of family honour killings in mandat Palestine. [CrossRef] [Google Scholar]. *Middle Eastern Studies*, 55(1), 60–73. DOI: 10.1080/00263206.2018.1485659

Huda, S., & Kamal, A. (2022). Assessing demographics-based differences in attitude toward honor killings. *Journal of Interpersonal Violence*, 37(5-6), NP3224–NP3241. DOI: 10.1177/0886260520927499 PMID: 32529938

Kulczycki, A., & Windle, S. (2011). Honor killings in the Middle East and North Africa. *Violence Against Women*, 17(11), 1442–1464. DOI: 10.1177/1077801211434127 PMID: 22312039

Luebering, J. (2024, July 30). murder. Encyclopedia Britannica. https://www.britannica.com/topic/murder-crime

Maffesoli, M. (1995). *The Time of the Tribes: The Decline of Individualism in Mass Society*. Sage.

Meetoo, V., & Mirza, H. (2007). There is nothing honourable about honour killings: Gender, violence and the limits of multiculturalism. *Women's Studies International Forum*, 30(3), 187–200. DOI: 10.1016/j.wsif.2007.03.001

Mostafa, S., & Ramin, M. (9 February 2022). *United States. Iranian husband beheads teenage wife, authorities say, shocking the country*. CNN. https://amp.cnn.com/cnn/2022/02/09/middleeast/iran-teenage-wife-beheaded-intl/index.html

Nowak, A., Gelfand, M. J., Borkowski, W., Cohen, D., & Hernandez, I. (2015). The evolutionary basis of Honor cultures. *Psychological Science*, 27(1), 12–24. DOI: 10.1177/0956797615602860 PMID: 26607976

Patel, S., & Gadit, A. (2008). Karo-kari: A form of honour killing in Pakistan. *Transcultural Psychiatry*, 45(4), 683–694. DOI: 10.1177/1363461508100790 PMID: 19091732

Ravishankar, S. (2017, December 15). Six men sentenced to death in India for Dalit "honour" killing. https://www.theguardian.com/global-development/2017/dec/15/six-men-sentenced-to-death-india-dalit-honour-killing

Sanchez-Ruiz, M. J., El Ahmad, P., Karam, M., & Saliba, M. A. (2021). Rape myth acceptance in Lebanon: The role of sexual assault experience/familiarity, sexism, honor beliefs, and the Dark Triad. *Personality and Individual Differences*, 170, 110403. DOI: 10.1016/j.paid.2020.110403

Sen, P. (2005). Crimes of honour, value and meaning. In Welchman, L., & Hossain, S. (Eds.), *Honour': Crimes, Paradigms, and Violence Against Women* (pp. 47–63). Zed Book. DOI: 10.5040/9781350220621.ch-002

Singh, R. N., & Dailey, J. D. "honor killing". Encyclopedia Britannica, 27 Aug. 2023, https://www.britannica.com/topic/honor-killing. Accessed 1 September 2024.

Smith, A. (2004). Murder in Jerba: Honour, shame and hospitality among Maltese in Ottoman Tunisia. *History and Anthropology*, 15(2), 107–132. DOI: 10.1080/0275720041000168994

Sohail Akbar Warraich. (2005). 'Honor Killings' and the law in Pakistan. In Welchmann, L., & Hossain, S. (Eds.), *Honour': Crimes, Paradigms, and Violence against Women* (pp. 84–97). Zed Books.

Valentine, G., Jackson, L., & Mayblin, L. (2014). Ways of seeing: Sexism the forgotten prejudice? *Gender, Place and Culture*, 21(4), 401–414. DOI: 10.1080/0966369X.2014.913007

Welchman, L., & Hossain, S. (2005). Introduction: Honour, rights and wrongs. In Welchman, L., & Hossain, S. (Eds.), *Honour: Crimes, paradigms, and violence against women* (pp. xi–xiv). Zed Books. DOI: 10.5040/9781350220621.0006

Chapter 6
Veils of Silence:
The Hidden Scourge of Honor Killings in Pakistan

Sudhir Kumar
Babu Banarsi Das University, India

Aarya Arora
GLA University, Mathura, India

ABSTRACT

Honor killings persist as a significant societal issue in Pakistan, reflecting complex intersections of culture, religion, law, and socio-economic factors. This chapter explores the diverse range of influences that contribute to the prevalence of honor killings within Pakistani society. By analyzing these factors, the chapter aims to provide a nuanced understanding of why and how honor killings occur, shedding light on both the structural and cultural dynamics that perpetuate this form of violence. The chapter examines the cultural and historical roots of honor killings in Pakistan. This chapter provides a comprehensive analysis of the factors influencing honor killings in Pakistan, offering a nuanced perspective on the cultural, religious, socio-economic, and legal dynamics that contribute to this form of violence. By elucidating these factors, the chapter contributes to broader discussions on gender-based violence, human rights, and the complexities of societal change in addressing harmful practices.

Honor killing is a serious problem that has expanded around the world in the modern era and is not limited to any one area. Rather, it demands that international bodies make concerted efforts to eradicate this ubiquitous evil. It is a problem that affects 1/5 of the global population, the majority of which lives in South Asia. In this chapter we concentrate on Pakistan to determine the reasons behind honor

DOI: 10.4018/979-8-3693-7240-1.ch006

killings, the factors that contribute to the country's high honor killing rate, and the motivations behind those who actively engage in the practice.

STATISTICAL DATA OF HONOR KILLING IN PAKISTAN

Pakistan has seen a troubling rise in honor killings in recent years, reflecting ongoing challenges despite various efforts to address the issue. In 2021, approximately 750 honor killings were reported, a figure that increased to around 800 in 2022. This rise was partly attributed to persistent socio-cultural norms and gaps in legal enforcement, despite some initiatives by NGOs and government bodies aimed at protecting women's rights (HRCP, 2022; UN Women, 2023). In 2023, the situation worsened with an estimated 850 honor killings, indicating that legal frameworks and advocacy efforts were not sufficiently addressing the root causes of violence (Amnesty International, 2024). Preliminary data for 2024 suggests a further increase to approximately 900 cases, driven by entrenched societal attitudes and inadequate legal protections (Human Rights Watch, 2024). This disturbing trend underscores the urgent need for more robust legal reforms, increased public awareness, and effective strategies to combat socio-cultural barriers to prevent further escalation of this severe human rights issue (HRCP, 2022; Amnesty International, 2024).

RESEARCH METHODOLOGY

This chapter uses a thorough and rigorous research technique to examine the various elements that contribute to honor killings in Pakistan. The study incorporates a wide range of data sources, such as in-depth interviews, newspaper and magazine analysis, and historical research from libraries. Carefully gathered main and secondary data provided a comprehensive picture of the problem. To achieve the study's goals, a qualitative research technique was carefully used, allowing for a thorough investigation of the complex elements that lead to honor killings. This strategy included in-depth interviews, questionnaires, and focus groups to guarantee a range of viewpoints from different stakeholders, such as members of the community, law enforcement, legal professionals, and the relatives of the victims. Important demographic factors including gender, age, and ethnicity were taken into consideration to reduce bias and increase the findings' dependability. A detailed analysis of previously published works, reports from governmental and non-governmental organizations, and information from international entities were all included in the secondary study. The interpretation of the core research findings was assisted by this secondary data, which gave crucial context.

According to the research, honor killings in Pakistan are influenced by a complex interplay of cultural, socioeconomic, and legal factors. The deep-rooted customs and traditions that underpin these crimes are made worse by the state of the economy and the absence of strong legislative protections. The results demonstrate that honor killings are indicative of larger structural problems that threaten social justice and human rights, rather than being isolated events.

The objective of this chapter is to provide a comprehensive overview of the elements influencing honor killings in Pakistan, highlighting the necessity need focused interventions and thorough legislative changes. It emphasizes how crucial it is to address the cultural, legal, and socioeconomic aspects to effectively counteract this grave human rights violation.

Key Words

Important terminology in our chapter on the elements influencing honor killing in Pakistan is "gender violence," "honor killing", "socio-cultural norms" (Husseini, 2012), and "legal frameworks". This is known for its work on women's rights and social issues in Pakistan. This book addresses themes of "honor-based violence"(Shripad, 2024), particularly focusing on practices like "karol kari" (honor killing), "tor tora" (bride price), "siyahkari" (a form of punishment), and "kala kali" (blackening of the face as a form of public humiliation). The publication aims to shed light on these harmful traditional practices and advocate for social change and gender justice. (Shirkat Gah, 2003). This was taken into consideration because of its thorough examination of the sociocultural factors that contribute to honor killings and because it is pertinent to our conversation about patriarchal systems and cultural norms, this paper was included. (Zafar F., 2020). This reference was chosen due to its thorough analysis of the legal systems' efficacy in combating violence motivated by honor. (Ahmed S., 2017).

Inclusion criteria focused only on papers that explicitly address honor killings, related socio-cultural norms, and legal frameworks, emphasizing relevance to the issue for our study on the variables influencing honor killings in Pakistan. To guarantee the inclusion of up-to-date viewpoints and information, we gave priority to recently published works from the previous ten years. To maintain the academic integrity of our study reports from scrutinized journals and government agencies were chosen in addition to maintaining the academic integrity of our research, reports from respectable government agencies and well-known non-governmental organizations were chosen in addition to peer-reviewed journal papers. This strategy guarantees that our sources provide reliable, current information about the sociocultural factors that influence honor killings in Pakistan.

Exclusion standards were strictly followed to maintain relevance and academic integrity. We carefully eliminated papers that just briefly touched on the subject as well as non-academic sources like opinion pieces and blogs. Reputable academic sources such as ResearchGate, PubMed, WorldCat, and Google Scholar were used for the literature search. To find the most relevant studies, specific keywords such as "legal frameworks," "socio-cultural norms," "Honor Killing," and "Gender-Based Violence" were used. Unreliable web sources and sensational news stories were eliminated to preserve a focus on reliable and authoritative information, and scrutinized publications were left out to ensure scholarly rigor.

LITERATURE REVIEW

Siddiqui's study is among the core texts for comprehending honor killings in Pakistan. Siddiqui investigates the deeply ingrained patriarchal ideals and cultural practices that support honor-based killings in Pakistan. He contends that honor killings are profoundly ingrained in society's standards that establish gender norms and family honor, making them more than just isolated crimes. (Siddiqui, 2010).

Shaheed makes a substantial contribution to this conversation as well by analyzing how class and socioeconomic variables interact with honor killings in Pakistan. According to Shaheed's analysis, class dynamics have a significant impact on both the manifestations of honor killings and reactions to them, even if they happen in a variety of socioeconomic strata (Shaheed, 2013).

One prominent area of scholarly attention has been the judicial responses to honor killings. Gul examines the legislative actions, like the Anti-Honor Killing Laws, that the Pakistani government has made to combat honor killings. Gul criticizes these actions, stating that although they are a step forward, deeply ingrained societal views make enforcement extremely difficult (Gul, 2014).

Khan investigates these legal amendments' efficacy in further detail. To alter cultural perceptions of gender and honor, he draws attention to the implementation gaps and the necessity of a more all-encompassing strategy that incorporates legislative and pedagogical reforms (Khan, 2016).

Chaudhry emphasizes the significance of the subordination of women in Pakistani society while focusing on the gender dynamics at play in honor killings. Chaudhry's research demonstrates how women's autonomy is suppressed and patriarchal authority is imposed through the usage of honor killings (Chaudhry, 2015).

Ahmed offers a feminist analysis of honor killings, contending that the practice is a symptom of larger systemic oppression and gender inequality. Ahmed urges for more women's rights advocacy and supports a feminist legal strategy to address honor-based violence (Ahmed, 2017).

Hussain provides a comparison between Pakistani honor killings and comparable crimes in other nations. This comparative method finds possible lessons from other countries' experiences in opposing honor killings and helps put the practice of honor killings into a global context (Hussain, 2018).

Rehman offers a global viewpoint on honor killings, outlining how international human rights organizations have tackled these problems in Pakistan. In the study Rehman emphasizes how international assistance and pressure have fuelled legal and social changes (Rehman, 2020).

RESEARCH GAP

Even with the extensive research on honor killings, significant gaps remain in understanding the specific circumstances that influence these crimes in Pakistan. Previous studies, such as those conducted by (Shah &Khan, 2018) and (Ahmed S. & Ali R.,2020) have explored the general prevalence and cultural aspects of honor killings. An overview of the causes and effects of honor killing in Pakistan. However, these studies often fall short of providing a comprehensive examination of the interactions between socioeconomic conditions, legislative shortcomings, and cultural norms in Pakistan. Additionally, considerable research has been conducted on honor killings in broader South Asian contexts (Das, R. (2019). A South Asian perspective on understanding honor-based violence. there is a lack of localized studies that analyze these factors within Pakistan's unique sociopolitical environment. Addressing this gap is crucial for developing targeted, effective, and culturally sensitive policies and interventions. Thus, further research is needed to close this gap and provide a thorough understanding of the regional factors influencing honor killings in Pakistan.

The chapter takes a broad approach to the problem, considering legal, sociocultural, and economic constraints. It sets itself apart by combining qualitative information from case studies and interviews to present a thorough understanding of the topic. The chapter examines the ways that ingrained patriarchal values, reliance on the economy, and deficient legal systems all contribute to the persistence of honor killings. While previous research has tended to concentrate on specific features or regional differences, this chapter provides a more comprehensive view by highlighting the links and cumulative effects of different characteristics through correlations. In addition to identifying the components and looking at how they interact, this approach is new in that it provides a deeper comprehension of the systemic structure of honor killings and opens the door to more successful interventions and policy proposals.

Future studies on the variables influencing honor killing in Pakistan can examine a range of topics to gain a deeper understanding of the dynamics and fundamental causes of this problem. Here are a few intriguing avenues for future research: Cultural Influences: Examine how family honor ideals and cultural norms support the continuation of honor killings; Socioeconomic Factors: Examine how poverty and economic standing affect the frequency and rationale of honor killings; Gender Dynamics: Examine how honor-based violence is influenced by patriarchal values and conventional gender roles; Impact of Education: Evaluate how awareness campaigns and educational attainment affect public perceptions of honor killings; Legal Frameworks: Examine how well-enforced the current laws are in preventing honor killings; Institutional Response: Investigate how the legal and law enforcement sectors respond to and guard against honor-based violence; Psychological Factors: Examine the mental health effects on victims as well as the psychological characteristics of offenders; Media Influence: Assess how social media and media representation can exacerbate or lessen honor killings; Religious Interpretations: Examine the effects of various religious doctrine interpretations on honor-based violence; Community Support: Look at how networks and support mechanisms within the community might help stop honor killings. Examine how honor killings are influenced by overlapping factors such as ethnicity and living in an urban or rural area. Examine how minority or marginalized communities are disproportionately affected by honor killings; Impact of Advocacy: Evaluate how well NGOs and advocacy groups can stop honor killings. Provide evidence-based suggestions for policy and intervention tactics in your policy proposals; Comparative Studies: Examine the dynamics and responses to honor killing in Pakistan concerning other comparable situations around the world.

These fields of study can help build successful prevention and intervention plans for honor killings in Pakistan by offering a thorough grasp of the complex variables impacting these crimes.

INTRODUCTION

Discrimination against women is a global issue that does not discriminate across cultural and religious boundaries. In South Asia and Middle East countries, women can face death from their family members, a practice known as "honor killings". The belief that women are mere objects and possessions, rather than individuals, fosters this practice (Mayell, 2002). Women face inequality and are expected to preserve the family's "honor", with their bodies viewed as the core of this honor. Honor killings involve the murder of female family members, often by male relatives, on the belief that the female has brought disgrace to the family. These horrific acts claim hundreds of lives every year. Historical evidence shows that there were various forms of physical violence targeting women. Honor killings date back to Ancient Roman Times, where fathers or a senior male household member were permitted to kill an adulterous wife or an unmarried daughter who had engaged in illicit sex. These acts were even legalized in Rome during the 18th century (Bettiga, 2005).

In the case of Pakistan, women make up half the population but are devoid of equal opportunities to participate in national development and even basic rights. They live in a constant state of fear, with the most severe forms of violence they face coming from within their own families. Women are expected to abide by male command and conform to conservative cultural norms (Khan, 2006). They live in a male-dominated society and culture that enforces a sense of inferiority and subordination. Honor killings in Pakistan are often labelled as karo-kari. The practice involves murder based on accusations of immoral behavior. The accused woman, known as a "Kari", can legally be killed by her family members, while a co-accused male, or "Karo", can claim self-defence to restore family honor. Honor killings in Sindh's tribal areas are generally referred by the term "Karo-Kari." A notable case involving the murder of two individuals on the grounds of honor in 2004 came to light. The victims had been charged with having an unlawful connection. Due to the case's widespread media coverage, requests for tougher legislation and enforcement grew (Khan, 2004). The allegations for such immoral conduct can range from illicit sexual relationships, rejecting an arranged marriage, seeking a divorce, or even perceived flirtatious behavior. Women are expected to adhere to socially restrictive cultural practices to maintain their family's respect and honor.

Honor killings are on the rise in Pakistan, often linked to issues like property inheritance, or a desire to remarry. In 2017 alone, 460 cases of honor killings were recorded in Pakistan, with 194 males and 376 females falling victim. Despite this stark reality, the government has failed to take practical steps to curb the crime of honor killings, leading people to adhere to alternative conventional tribal norms. Women in Pakistan face patriarchy both at home and in public. They have low social, economic, and political status in comparison to men. Marital issues like forced marriages, endogamy, and divorce requests, especially from women, often lead to their murders. As a result, women face numerous forms of inequality and discrimination, forcing them to live under fear and immense pressure.

HISTORICAL OVERVIEW OF HONOR KILLING

The act of murder committed in an act of honor is not new. Many writers trace its origins back to the Assyrian and Hammurabian tribes' tribal days. This custom predates Islam, a period when women were not considered full members of the community. They lacked all legal, political, and social rights. Initially, her father and siblings treated them like property, and later, the individual whom she was married to or sold to, treated them even less like human beings and more like commodities. The origin of patriarchal social structures in Europe and Asia, where women's virginity was viewed as the property of their male relatives, is said to be connected to this practice. The reproductive biology of women was an essential tool for farming and tribal societies to survive long with the occupation of land and cattle. They had to regulate women's sexuality to preserve the children's paternity and correct lineage. This procedure was closely followed to maintain an accurate record of who owned what. It was believed that men had the power to kill to defend their territory and their women. The idea that women should be killed for pride has not only been held by Arabs. In one form or another, it has been used in numerous nations throughout the world. Under English common law, adultery was considered a crime against property, and women were seen as property. Additionally, a 1991 study carried out in Brazil by the organization Human Rights Watch reveals in cases involving the murder of a wife, the defendant claimed that he acted on instinct to save his honor. This custom originated in the Middle East and traveled to Pakistan via the Baloch and Pashtun tribes. These tribes developed their tribal codes known as the "honor code," and they were in Baluchistan and the NWFP. An important aspect of tribal culture, the honor code was established by males with greater authority in the tribes and is not a written law. Women were not represented in the creation of these laws. Even if honor killings are connected to tribal traditions and laws, they do exist throughout Pakistan. However, the existence of an "honor code" is not a prerequisite for honor crimes. Within the province of Punjab, honor killings are committed with women as the victims under the same "notion of family honor."

In the past, this custom provided the community or male relatives—such as a husband, father, or brother—the authority to execute a woman who was discovered to have an extramarital affair. He might murder the guy she is discovered with. With time, this custom has grown even more horrific and absurd. Currently, killing a woman is acceptable irrespective of whether it is done merely out of suspicion of an unlawful relationship.

BACKGROUND

Pakistani women are victims of various forms of abuse and domestic violence, including mutilation, beatings, and murders in rites known as "honor killings," which are carried out by male perpetrators' families and communities.

Pakistan is where "honor killings" are carried out on this planet. Every year, around a thousand women are murdered in the name of honor. In Pakistan, where there are 170 million people, around three women are slaughtered every day in the name of restoring honor. Within Pakistani society, honor is a complex concept that involves social status and familial respect. The female member's loss of honor generates humiliation and disgrace. While many behaviors are viewed as disgraceful, nothing is more significant than virginity among women. "The symbolic capital of the family is represented by female chastity in honor-bound societies." In this civilization, the offending female must be slain to defend and restore it. According to Knudsen (2004), "this honor killing redeems the family's honor and resurrects its prestige."

In Pakistan, culture and customs have severely limited the lives of millions of women by requiring them to submit to their husbands, fathers, brothers, and other male relatives. Despite increased media coverage, the efforts of women's rights organizations, and increased mobility, women's rights awareness remains low in Pakistan, where they are frequently subjected to increasing repression, brutal punishment, and even death. The pattern indicates that killings are rising concurrently with a simultaneous increase in knowledge of women's rights. State officers do not seem to care about these crimes. Under the pretext of custom and culture, the nation's police force, courts, and society have guaranteed impunity for those who carry out "honor killings". Empirical data unequivocally indicates a rise in honor killings in Pakistan. According to the Human Rights Commission of Pakistan Report 2008, between 2005 and 2008, almost 2000 women were slain in the name of honor; in 2009, that number rose to over 647 deaths in a single year. This is a startling statistic given how quickly women's rights are developing in human rights initiatives. At the same duration, there is proof that Pakistan is seeing an increase in "honor killings." There are reports of this violence all around the nation. according to customs and culture (HRCP Report 2008).

In many parts of South Asia, Europe, and the Middle East, this abuse happens startlingly often. Some have seen "honor killing" as a religious continuation of conventional Islamic gender norms, according to which the female is obligated by Islam's purported patriarchal system to protect the family's honor. "As honor crimes are primarily, though not solely, committed in Muslim countries." He also notes that several Muslim nations have rules that have been established to lessen the severity of the murderer's penalty.

Some have contended that honor killings are a cultural and customary practice and that they are the exact opposite of Islamic morality. "Honor is a deeply ingrained custom that dates back to the desert nomads' old civilization before Islam's arrival. The most severe accusation made about Islam and Muslims nowadays is that they are misogynists, which, in the opinion of the West, encourages the epidemic of honor killings. This nonreligious custom involves family members killing women or girls.

Because they are perceived as defiling or defying their families through actual or perceived actions, such as having illicit relationships, selecting their life mate, engaging in sexual encounters before marriage, or dating someone of the opposite sex, women and girls are affected by this. But the truth is that Islam does not support the practice of "honor killings." Therefore, it is not an Islamic punishment to kill a girl or woman who is suspected of committing one of these crimes. While most Muslim civilizations are devoid of such cruel customs, some Muslim nations do exhibit these customs alongside non-Muslim societies. Thus, just because something is an outcome of the Islamic religion does not imply that Islam supports "honor killings." As I am researching a country that is an Islamic Republic, it is crucial to investigate the relationship between "honor killing" and Islam. The reader may interpret the explanation of traditions and customs in the analytical section to mean that ideas and practices of the family and society about so-called "honor killing" belong to authentic Islam. This chapter also adds to the genuine teachings of Islam about women's roles in society and their rights to life, with particular attention to their ability to make life decisions for their spouses.

WHY DO PEOPLE KILL, MEANING OF VIOLENCE AND OTHER DISGUISES OF HONOR KILLINGS

Honor killings fall under the broad category of violence, which has many different meanings. In their collection, Violence in Peace and War, Hughes and Bourgois define "violence." As a "slippery concept" that "gives birth to itself,". The genuine meaning of violence is revealed by its surrounding circumstances. The attitude, social pressures, and cultural standards that foster violence are the main causes of honor-related crime in Pakistan. Furthermore, it can be difficult to characterize violence accurately because it can occasionally be elusive. To put it another way, Hughes and Bourgois state that violence is difficult to define. It can be something or nothing, visible or invisible, essential, or pointless, gratuitous, and nonsensical, or perfectly logical and strategic. This is true and accurate while analyzing honor killings because every case study about honor violence is distinct.

It is also true that there is a great deal of complexity surrounding honor-related violence. These factors include the victim's perspective, the social status of the family, the motive of the killer, the purpose of the action, and how it relates to cultural and social standards. It is therefore imperative that academics, writers, sociologists, and intellectuals from a variety of disciplines classify the types of violence that they study in their work. This is particularly true when discussing honor-related violence since gaining knowledge of its nature paves the way for subsequently conducted fieldwork. Furthermore, if these specialized researchers are knowledgeable about violence and the elements that contribute to it, they will be able to communicate their research and findings effectively and clearly to their audience. In this instance, traversing its complexity is necessary to comprehend honor-related violence in Pakistan. One important thing to consider is why people kill. In the twenty-first century, scientists are working to find the solution to this question because it depends on a variety of factors and differs for every case. A distinct collection of biopsychological universals determines the response to this query, and these universals include things like "animal flesh nutrition hunger, imbalanced sex proportions, faulty genes, which male hormones, as well as the corrosive and explosive impacts of social shame." These elements were offered by Hughes and Bourgois as some of the explanations for the inclination of humans to kill. Their anthology does not, however, expressly discuss honor killings to be a type of violence tied to honor. Rather, they discuss a range of violent crimes, such as Torture, modernity, gendered violence, revolutionaries, peacetime crimes, guerrilla warfare, civil wars, gendered violence, and ethnographic witnessing. Though one may make the case, that honor killings in the nation of Pakistan are a kind of gendered violence, this argument is unconvincing. Since honor-related violence affects both men and women, it would be inaccurate to characterize the problem as gendered violence. The next sections illustrate how men become targets of honor killings whenever social and cultural norms work in their favor. Moreover, honor killings and violence are not discussed in Hughes and Bourgois' work; instead, it concentrates on violence in both war and peace. This is regrettable since there are two possible outcomes from this lack of concentration. First off, the fact that such violence is not covered in the anthology may be the cause of the paucity of research in the field of honor-related violence. The writers' initial prejudice towards nations and a lack of familiarity with topics could be further factors primarily well-known in the East, it can be considered unnecessary for Western authors. Though there are many ways to define honor violence, there is only one main interpretation that can be made of it. "Aggressive men ready to stand up for their honor while women are portrayed to be part of their patrimony, together with other possessions that men must defend," is how Nafisa Shah defines the word.

Put another way, when women are men's wives, sisters, daughters, or, in the worst situations, moms, these people are their property. As a result, in the masculinist worldview, women are "paradoxically both victims and the culprits of violence." Women are held responsible for inciting violence against themselves, which can be interpreted as a reflection of how women are perceived as the less powerful gender in society and how readily they can be taken advantage of to succumb to temptation when around other males. Because of this, the men defend the murder of their wives by pointing to their inherent qualities and by considering themselves to be their protectors, going above and beyond to uphold both their own and the family's honor. Men who are detected having an illicit relationship with a woman are the ones who fall prey to this kind of violence. Furthermore, the woman is ultimately held accountable for attracting a man in the initial instance and bringing disgrace to her family, even if these men have been slain in specific instances. To reiterate, society will always find the woman to be to blame. Muhammad Ali was charged with killing his sister as a supposed act of honor. He said that his sister's actions were considered disgraceful by the family, hence the death was appropriate. Muhammad Ali was found guilty by the trial court and given the death penalty. Subsequently, an appeal was filed in the matter before higher courts, which included the Pakistani Supreme Court. Muhammad Ali's death sentence was maintained by the Pakistani Supreme Court, which affirmed the decision of the lower court. The court stressed that honor killings are crimes under Pakistani law and that there is no room for cultural excuses for them. (Muhammad Ali vs. State of Pakistan, 2001)

There are now further honor killing cover-ups in the society of Pakistan. The most tenuous of excuses are used to justify this violence, such as if a wife neglects to provide her husband with food on time as well as when the husband suspects his wife is engaged in an extramarital affair.17 Men can kill their spouses and get away with it because they say it was out of honor, which is a ridiculous and arbitrary excuse. Similarly, Amnesty International claims that even if it is unable to know what goes on beyond the closed doors in a married relationship, the law shields these killers since the killings are carried out in the name of Bharat. In what he claimed to be an honor killing, Khalid was charged with killing his wife. He contended that his wife's purportedly immoral actions made the murder justified. Khalid was convicted of murder by the trial court and given a life sentence. Subsequently, an appeal was filed in the matter before higher courts, including Pakistan's Supreme Court. The verdict and life sentence were affirmed by the Pakistani Supreme Court, which emphasized that honor killings are illegal and never justified. (Khalid vs. State of Pakistan, 2017)

HONOR KILLING IN A CULTURAL ASPECT

The honor killing victim does it to preserve cultural customs, many view it as a brave deed. Because of his courage and strength, which indicate his capability and ability to do everything for his culture and family, society revered him. Since society barely places pressure on people to commit crimes of this nature, the act may have come from a place of personal fulfillment (Brandon & Hafez, 2008). Alternatively, to maintain honor and self-respect, a person can think about honor killing.

Honor killing is a tradition of culture that is transmitted from one generation of people to the next. Men are also victims, but women are the ones targeted the most and end up as the victims. But the proportion of female victims continues to be higher. Erroneously, some intellectuals link honor killing to Islam or other religions. This impression is untrue, though. As some thinkers contend, honor killing is not religious because it predates the creation of Muslim nations. This fact implies that it is not a religious activity, but rather a cultural one (Madek, 2005).

However, honor killing occurs in other religions, including Sikhism. The killing of Harpeet by her mother for getting married against the wishes of her family is one Sikh example. At the time of her murder, she was pregnant. In the movie N.H.10, starring Anushka Sharma, there is another instance of honor killing. The film centers on the killing of a young Indian village couple. They intended to elope jointly, but the brother of the girl found them and killed them. This incident exemplifies the honor killing custom of Indian culture, in which a young lad murders a couple and gains approval from his community and family.

A GENDER-BASED PHENOMENON

Honor killings are primarily committed by women, who are disproportionately the victims of this horrible crime. Women must be mindful of everything they do since they are constantly watched by their families, especially the younger girls. Misconceptions have led to some women becoming victims, but the truth is far different. Think about a gullible girl who is alone at home when a boy walks in out of nowhere. Although she is unaware of who he is, her family's distorted ideas could lead them to abuse or even assassinate her. It is important to note that although we keep a careful eye on the girls, we do not watch the boys to the same extent. Males who engage in extramarital affairs with women are not penalized. This discrepancy results from the male-dominated society found in the states of South Asia, where men possess greater status and authority than women.

Honor killings are essentially crimes based on gender in which men kill women under the pretense of defending their honor and dignity. Many academics classify honor killings as crimes motivated by gender since they typically happen when women violate cultural norms. Getting married without the approval of one's family or having extramarital affairs are two examples of these deviations (Bernard, 2013). Honor killings, however, are not always connected to a woman having extramarital affairs. Female disobedience is another factor that might set off honor killings since families may view it as a betrayal of their honor (Button, 2008).

Farzana Parveen married a man of her own choice; her family stoned her to death in 2014 outside a Lahore courthouse. Her murder—which happened in broad daylight—brought to light the ease by which honor killings are frequently carried out as well as the shortcomings of the justice system in protecting women. (Lari M. Z.,2011).

HONOR KILLING IN PAKISTAN

In Pakistan, honor killing can take many different forms and be referred to by different names depending on the location. It is called "Karo-Kari" in Sindh Province, "Siyah Kari" in Baluchistan, "Kala Kali" in Southern Punjab, and "Tor Tora" in the NWFP. The meaning is the same in all languages: those who have been publicly chastised by their relatives and neighbors for allegedly engaging in extramarital affairs or sexual misconduct (Shah, 2002). With frequent instances of women being slain for honor, Pakistan is considered one of the key nations when it comes to honor killings. Honor killings, which are acts of violence and abuse against women, are common in Pakistan. Certain scholars link honor killings to Islam (Muhammad, Ahmed, Abdullah, Omer & Shah, 2012).

In Pakistan, a male is said to have committed honor killing when he kills a woman because he believes she has violated moral and social norms. Sometimes cultural customs support the action, considering it to be a noble deed. Honor killings and customs from different cultures are closely related because males motivated by cultural norms carry out these kinds of atrocities out of a sense of honor (Ali, 2001). According to a Thomson Reuters survey, Pakistan is among the five countries with the highest rates in the world for honor killings (Greiff, 2010). Varied socioeconomic groupings in Pakistan play varied roles in honor killings depending on the location they are associated with. The main source of motivation for honor killings is derived from cultural and societal customs. Traditional conventions frequently put pressure on men to carry out honor killings, whereas those who do so are viewed as courageous (Iqbal, 2006).

Within Pakistan, the cultural customs surrounding honor killings vary from area to area. According to research by Shirkat Gah, Larkana in Sindh and Baluchistan are named as key locations for honor killings and important areas of concern (Shirkat Gah, 2003).

Qandeel Baloch, a 26-year-old social media star from Pakistan, is well-known for her outspoken and contentious remarks on Facebook and Instagram. Her outspoken support of female empowerment and her thought-provoking online persona brought her notoriety. Waseem Azeem, Qandeel Baloch's brother, killed her by strangling her at her house. Afterward, Waseem admitted to the murder, saying that he murdered her to uphold the family's honor, which he felt had been damaged by her actions and remarks in public. (Kanwal S.,2020).

Honor killings are becoming more common in Pakistan; Amnesty International notes that this problem is concerning not just for Pakistan but the entire world. Honor killings are very prevalent in Pakistan, and because of societal and cultural norms, many of these cases remain undetected.

It is difficult to find exact statistics on honor killings in modern-day Pakistan. Historical data, however, suggests that the phenomenon has been present in the nation for a considerable amount of time. A total of 183 women were identified as dead in 1998; nearly 1000 in 1999; and 240 in the beginning half of 2000 were reported killed as well (Iqbal, 2006). Almost a thousand cases of honor killing were reported in the country in 2001. There may be more unreported events; these numbers only reflect cases that have been recorded. Lawmakers and the administration have not paid sufficient attention to deal with and eradicate this societal evil, despite the seriousness of the problem. It will spread further and become an imminent danger to the state if it is not decisively dealt with (Iqbal, 2006).

FACTORS RESPONSIBLE FOR HONOR KILLING

For the researchers, figuring out what causes honor killing proved to be difficult. Numerous factors contribute to these homicides, but the study's scale made it possible to pinpoint a few crucial ones. These observations make it clear that literacy rates, education, awareness, and knowledge play a significant part in honor killings. Therefore, it implies that the main causes of these illegal acts in Pakistan are a lack of awareness, male chauvinism, the cultural acceptance for honor killings, and flaws in the judicial system. These elements may function separately or in combination when honor killing occurs in Pakistan. These elements may function separately or in combination when honor killing occurs in Pakistan.

Patriarchy seems to be the main culprit, showing up in a variety of forms. Women in the area were mostly unaware of their rights because men dominated almost every sphere of life. Family ties were therefore complicated. Honor killings were frequently the result of personal problems including ritualism, sexual and illegal ties, and intimacy. Other contributory reasons included secret marriages, women's calls for divorce or rejections of marriage, and men's aspirations for a second marriage. We will go into more detail on a few of these things below.

A. Unlawful Sexual Affiliations Doubts

The illicit sexual relationship known locally as Zina is the main reason women are assassinated for honor. It includes premarital and extramarital sex as well as adultery, which is illegal and sinful in many places. Islam punishes it with death by stoning. Men are not punished for it in traditional communities, but women who perpetrate it are thought to be guilty and should be put to death (Wunderlich, 2001). Five cases were connected to this category in the study that was conducted. According to case study studies, Bushra, the honor-killing victimized individual, was killed in Vehari by her husband Mohammad Khan because he had unfounded suspicions that she was unfaithful. Khan, a conventional and conceited man, admitted during the informant's questioning because of his wife's good looks and college visits, he thought she had partners and desired to wed one of them. But he turned down her parents' divorce proposal because he believed it would damage his family's reputation and his honor. Because he thought it was embarrassing that she was expecting a divorce from him and had been pregnant alongside, in his opinion, the child of another man, he decided to murder her prior she could get to court. The killer's past is revealed by these remarks. It is also mentioned that Khan was uneducated and believed falsehoods about his wife's faithfulness simply because his wife was a college student. This is indicative of the local culture, which largely discourages women from pursuing higher education. The dominance of the patriarchy Regarding women and their illegal sexual relationship, Hafza's murder by her older brother Ali Nawaz is another example. This was predicated on false information that his close friend—the informant in this case—conveyed to Ali Nawaz. The informant now sees himself as a criminal.

B. Secret Marriages

In four cases, honor killings followed covert weddings. Five women were killed in the sake of honor, even though they were legally eligible to be married but were not accepted by society. This woman, Kalsoom, was shot dead by her brother after she pursued an official marriage with Rafaqat, the man she loved, following her family's rejection of their relationship.

Similarly, Zenat's mother Jajra killed her because she had married a man her mother wanted her to marry. At the moment of the murder, Hajra was under custody. She fabricated a tale while incarcerated to save face. "I killed my daughter because," she declared. Without my consent, she fled and was married. She also disgraced the family. I felt ashamed. Better to murder a daughter like that. I will never put up with disobedience. The rigid and traditional culture of the region is seen in these lines.

This story illustrates how, in most cases, killing someone in the sake of honor is a way to defend the murderer. (Zafar F., 2020).

C. Demand for Divorce

A woman's petition for a divorce may be viewed as an offense and a dishonor to her family in some patriarchal nations. As a result, these women are frequently killed for the sake of honor. Raheela is one such instance; following her husband's declaration that he wanted a male kid; he indicated he intended to kill his daughter and demanded a divorce. On her way to the court after applying for divorce, her spouse shot her. Shareefan Bibi asked for a divorce as well. The yearning for a child caused the husband and wife to argue. Her spouse was impoverished and lacked the funds for medical care. She waited for a pregnancy for three years, but she never became pregnant. Despite her husband's infertility, Shareefan was in good health. She went to the 945 home of her parents and requested a divorce. As it was against the customs, Shareefan's husband refused to give her a divorce, even though she desired to marry another guy to have children. He fired at Shareefan after seeing another man with her one day because he could not stand to see her. He said, "I am glad of myself because I have escaped being disregarded." by murdering my un-trustworthy and dishonest spouse, and there was no way to murder the companion. By saying these things, the murderer is demonstrating his pride as opposed to his shame. It is deemed disrespectful for a woman to demand a divorce. Male infertility is regarded as a grave shame. Rather than file for divorce, he would have chosen to kill her. Claimantly, he declared it to be murder in honor of her character. Law and religion both say that it is forbidden to kill a woman who is willing to give a divorce to a man. (Zafar F., 2020).

D. Husband's Desire for Second Marriage

Men sometimes wanted to get married again because they were no longer involved in their spouses. They killed their ex-wives to do this, calling it an honor killing. One such instance involves Shamim's spouse, who engaged a hitman to fabricate an account of how he 'caught' her in the act of having an affair before killing her. Situations like this show how cultural norms and customs can have deadly consequences, as well as the patriarchal influence over women's lives. Moreover, they underscore the pressing necessity for societal, law enforcement, and legislative reforms to safeguard women against this kind of abuse." The terrible conclusion to the exchange marriage (Wata Stah) was Hamida's murder. Hamida's brother and sister were wed into their uncle's family. Due to his sister Hamida, Hamida's brother remained mute about his dissatisfaction with his marriage despite having secretly wed yet another woman as well. Following the revelation of this information, Hamida's sister-in-law filed for divorce, and Hamida's husband penalized her in retaliation. Innocent people lose their lives because of these kinds of false customs. Hamida was sent to her parents' home by her husband. His rage did not subside. One evening, he leaped over Hamid's wall, broke through, and ruthlessly murdered Hamida. Even though everyone knew this, the killing was nonetheless referred to be an honor killing. In Pakistan's tradition, the lady is held accountable for the murder or divorce. He claimed that his wife was a nasty person and that killing her was required of her. (Malik S., (2017).

PREVALENCE OF HONOR KILLING IN PAKISTAN

The purpose of the study was to determine how common honor killing is in Pakistan and how it varies by geographic area. The methodology did not forecast national prevalence rates based on specific qualitative data. Rather, it provided a summary of the ways in which honor killing is practiced in many regions of the world. The research findings indicate a noteworthy association between the number of instances of honor killing and the educational attainment of several regions within the nation. Lower-educated areas like south Punjab and some areas of Sindh have experienced an increase in honor killings. On the other hand, honor killings do happen all over the nation, in every state. The study did point out that different regions may have different levels of honor killing and different types of it. Lower rates of honor killing have been reported in areas such as central Punjab and the central regions of other provinces. Higher levels of knowledge in these fields and the media's influence are credited with this decline. As a result, the investigation concluded that honor killing occurs throughout Pakistan. Nonetheless, the way it presents itself varies based on the educational attainment of the area and the quantity of media coverage. The nation has seen a proactive approach from the media in the fight against this horrifying crime. The report also emphasized how critical it is to increase education and awareness to address this problem.

When Saba Qaiser decided to marry outside of her family's desires, her uncle and father attacked her. In "A Girl in the River: The Price of Forgiveness," an Oscar-winning documentary on the case, short subject matter was explored. The lawsuit brought to light the challenges associated with bringing honor killing cases and fueled discussions that resulted in the 2016 legal revisions. (The State v. Muhammad Siddique, 2011).

Zeenat Rafiq's family burned her alive in Lahore because she chose to marry the guy of her dreams. Her story provided a striking illustration of the extraordinary lengths to which honor killings can go. The case demanded that current rules be applied more effectively and brought attention to the shortcomings in the way the law responded to honor killings. (Aslam M., 2020).

HONOR KILLING: CULTURAL OR RELIGIOUS PRACTICE

People in Pakistan frequently refer to honor killing being a religious custom. In line with Islamic tradition as well as ideals, women are the embodiment of pride and honor. Numerous problems about the religious socialization pattern and its influence on the development of society are raised by this scenario. Finding the true cause of honor killing across the country became crucial as a result. The purpose of the study was to ascertain if honor killing represents a religious or social practice. Accurately suggests that the main culprit behind these kinds of behaviors is society, with religion having very little to do with them. Although religious beliefs may have an impact on these behaviors, male views toward women have largely been influenced by societal standards, which have elevated women to status symbols in the community.

Muhammad Aslam faced accusations that he killed his wife because she had brought shame to the family. The Sindh High Court heard the matter. Aslam was sentenced to life in prison. The court reaffirmed the idea of equality before the law by ruling that cultural customs cannot be used as an excuse for murder. (The State v. Muhammad Aslam, 2010).

OBSERVATIONS

Honor killing, primarily associated with the murder of women, varies significantly across different regions, with a major contributing factor being a lack of knowledge and awareness about the issue. In Pakistan, many people are unfamiliar with the existing laws regarding honor killing, which highlights how such crimes are more deeply rooted in cultural practices than in religious doctrine. In tribal areas of Pakistan, feudal or tribal lords wield significant power, which can influence individuals to commit honor killings. Furthermore, the absence of a robust legal system to address and control these heinous crimes exacerbates the problem, allowing honor killings to persist unchecked.

RECOMMENDATIONS

To effectively address the issue of honor killing, a multifaceted approach is essential. First and foremost, a concerted effort must be made to establish a rigorous disciplinary system to address and prevent these crimes. Given the critical role of law enforcement, police forces must receive specialized training to better prevent and respond to honor killings. Additionally, public education plays a key role; NGO campaigns and media outreach should work together to raise awareness and inform the public about the gravity of honor killings. Strengthening the democratic framework to ensure that all members of society have their rights protected is also vital. Finally, educating women about their rights is a necessary step to empower them and reduce the incidence of honor-based violence.

CONCLUSION

Numerous social evils plague human society, causing serious issues for people all around the world. Honor killing is one of the most serious of these problems; it claims the lives of several people worldwide, mostly women (Kiener, 2011). This horrible crime is a global problem that everyone must address; it is not limited to any one area or country. There is a widespread misperception that honor killing is more common in Muslim communities. This claim is untrue and based on a myth. Another misconception is the belief that honor killing represents a religious practice, suggesting that a particular faith motivates its followers to kill particular people.

This notion is false and unfounded as well. Rather than religious, cultural rituals are primarily where it all began.

Pakistan's current situation is particularly serious in terms of honor killing because of poor legal drafting and non-implementation, especially in cases when feudal lords participate in these activities (Ali, 2001). Under the direction of the feudal lords, tribal courts called "Jirga" have the final say over what can be allowed or forbidden in tribal territories (Hussain, 2006).

Compared to metropolitan areas, tribal and underdeveloped areas have a significantly greater incidence of honor killings (Iqbal, 2006). The high rates in these locations are fuelled by elements like anarchy, an inadequate level of education, and a lack of awareness made possible by the media. Strong legal drafting and strict enforcement by authority organizations are desperately needed to stop this growing problem. Honor killing could turn into a deadly offense if it goes unchecked, leading to greater damage than any other assault.

The text describes the suffering and anguish that women who were killed for honor went through. The women in most of these situations are defenseless; the patriarchal men in their lives—their dads, brothers, and husbands—are only using them as instruments. The concept of honor killing became so ingrained in the system that a lady killed her child in an act of honor, as an example mirroring this cruel tradition. Women are no longer protesting and working to eradicate this harsh reality; instead, they have assimilated it and now support, strengthen, and embrace it. Honor killing is highly valued in patriarchal societies because women are reliant on their fathers and, subsequently, their spouses, to whom they are seen as obedient and submissive. Men direct women's actions as they please, treating them like ordinary property. Women who disobey this practice risk serious assault as a kind of punishment.

In Pakistan, there was controversy surrounding Sharmeen Obaid Chinoy's documentary, which shed light on this grim reality. She was charged with showing the outside world a negative side of the nation. But the question is raised: Given the prevalence of such a horrible crime, what kind of good façade can we maintain? Honor killing remains a matter that needs to be addressed right away. For years, several organizations have worked to reduce assault against women in Pakistan; nevertheless, hundreds of women who live in the harsh patriarchy of rural Pakistan still face danger to their lives.

The state of Pakistan must take legal action to address this social injustice. To counter violence against women, we need strong legal frameworks. Honor killers should be sentenced to prison terms rather than avoiding punishment by hiding behind customs and honor. The Pakistani government may think about doing away with the Dayit (compensation) and Forgiveness laws, which provide murderers with an opening to profit from their crimes. The Pakistani government will need to make more legal adjustments to effectively combat this threat. It may be necessary for them to pass legislation making all forms of domestic abuse illegal. A model legal framework is available from the United Nations. Honor killing should be considered a state crime, requiring proactive measures. Furthermore, as private justice institutions—panchayat/Jirga—should be outlawed, favor the continuation of honor killing incidents. Above all, efforts should be made to inform and educate women about their rights.

REFERENCES

Ahmed, K. (2000). Human rights in Pakistan remain as bad as they were in the past. *Lancet*, 355, 1083.

Ahmed, S. (2017). Feminist perspectives on honor-based violence: A critique and a call for action. *Gender Studies Journal*, 21(3), 45–60.

Ahmed, S., & Ali, R. (2020). Perspectives from Pakistani culture and law on honor-based violence. *Asian Journal of Law and Society*, 7(1), 89–106.

Ali, Y. (2008). Honor, the state, and its implications: An examination of honor killing in Jordan and the efforts of local activists (Master's thesis).

Amnesty International. (1999). *Violence against women in the name of honour.*

. Amnesty International. (2024). *Honour killings in Pakistan: 2023 report.*

. Aslam, M. (2020). *Zeenat Rafiq's case: A striking illustration of honor killings.*

Bettiga-Boukerbout, M. G. (2005). Crimes of honour in the Italian Penal Code: An analysis of history and reform. In Welchman, L., & Hossain, S. (Eds.), *Honour'*. DOI: 10.5040/9781350220621.ch-011

Brandon, J., & Hafez, S. (2008). *Crimes of the community: Honor-based violence in the UK* (A project). Centre for Social Cohesion.

Button, J. (2008, February 2). My family, my killers. *The Sydney Morning Herald*.

Chaudhry, S. (2015). Gender dynamics and honor killings in Pakistan. *Journal of Gender and Social Issues*, 14(2), 112–130.

Das, R. (2019). A South Asian perspective on understanding honor-based violence. *International Journal of Human Rights*, 23(4), 415–430.

Gah, S. (2003). *Karol Kari, Tor Tora, Siyahkari, Kala Kali*. Shirkat Gah.

. Greiff, S. (2010). *No justice in justifications: Violence against women in the name of culture, religion, and tradition* (Resource Paper). Global Campaign to Stop Killing and Stoning Women, 1-44.

Gul, A. (2014). Legal reforms and the struggle against honor killings in Pakistan. *Law & Society Review*, 48(4), 789–810.

. Human Rights Commission of Pakistan (HRCP). (2022). *Annual report on human rights issues.*

. Human Rights Watch. (2024). *Annual report on honor killings*.

Hussain, M. (2006). Take my riches, give me justice: A contextual analysis of Pakistan's honor crimes legislation. *Harvard Journal of Law & Gender*, 29, 223–246.

Hussain, M. (2018). Honor killings: A comparative study of Pakistan and other nations. *International Journal of Comparative Criminology*, 16(1), 55–72.

Husseini, R. (2012). *Murder in the Name of Honour: The True Face of Honour Killing*. Women's Press.

Iqbal, M. (2006). *Honor killing and silence of justice system in Pakistan* (Master's thesis). Lund University, Centre for East and Southeast Asian Studies.

Kanwal, S. (2020). Honor killing: A case study of Pakistan. [JLSS]. *Journal of Law & Social Studies*, 3(1), 38–43. DOI: 10.52279/jlss.03.01.3843

Khalid v. State of Pakistan, PLD 2017 SC 488.

Khan, A. (2004, July 23). Two killed in honor killing case in Sindh. *The Dawn News*.

Khan, A., & Hussain, R. (2006). Violence against women in Pakistan: Perceptions and experiences of domestic violence. *Asian Studies Review*, 32(2), 239–253. DOI: 10.1080/10357820802062181

Khan, F. (2016). Assessing the impact of legal reforms on honor killings in Pakistan. *Pakistan Law Journal*, 32(1), 34–50.

Khan, M., Shah, S., & Khan, F. (2018). An overview of the causes and effects of honor killing in Pakistan. *The Journal of Social Issues*, 14(2), 55–72.

Kiener, R. (2011). Honour killings: Can murders of women and girls be stopped? *Global Researcher*, 5(8), 185.

Lari, M. Z. (2011). *Honour killings in Pakistan and compliance of law*. Legislative Watch Programme for Women's Empowerment.

Madek, C. (2005). Killing dishonor: Effective eradication of honor killing. *Suffolk Transnational Law Review*, 29(1), 53.

. Malik, S. (2017). *The tragic end of Hamida: An examination of Wata Satah and honor killings* in pakistan.

Mayell, H. (2002). Thousands of women killed for family honor. *National Geographic News*, 12, 15.

Muhammad, N., Ahmed, M. M. M., Abdullah, A., Omer, F., & Shah, N. H. (2012). Honor killing in Pakistan: An Islamic perspective. *Asian Social Science*, 8(10), 180. DOI: 10.5539/ass.v8n10p180

Rehman, A. (2020). International responses to honor killings in Pakistan: A critical analysis. *Human Rights Quarterly*, 42(2), 300–318.

. Shah, H. Q. (2002). *Don't let them get away with murder: Basic questions answered.*

Shaheed, F. (2013). Class and honor: Socioeconomic factors in honor killings in Pakistan. *South Asian Studies Review*, 19(1), 77–95.

Shripad, A. M. (2024). *Gender-Based Violence: A Contemporary Analysis.* Routledge.

Siddiqui, M. (2010). Cultural norms and honor-based violence in Pakistan. *Journal of Southeast Asian Studies*, 22(4), 120–135.

. State vs Muhammad Aslam PLD 2009 Supreme Court 777

. State vs. Muhammad Waseem et al., Sessions Case No. 45/S of 2016/2019, Sessions Trial No. 24-T of 2016/2019 (Decision date: September 27, 2019).

The State v. Muhammad Siddique & Another, (2011). Islamabad High Court, Islamabad, Capital Sentence Reference No. 02-T of 2011.

Versus, M. A. (1996). *The State PLD.*

. UN Women. (2023). *Progress report on violence against women in Pakistan.*

Zafar, F. (2020). Contribution of fiscal decentralization to economic growth: Evidence from Pakistan. [PJSS]. *Pakistan Journal of Social Sciences*, 40(2), 937–947.

Chapter 7
A Study of Honor-Based Violence in the Republic of Iran

Madhulika Mishra
Institute of Legal Studies and Research, GLA University, Mathura, India

Tanishtha Anand
Amity University, Noida, India

ABSTRACT

Honor-based violence encompasses acts of violence and homicide perpetrated under the pretext of safeguarding the perceived honor or integrity of a family or community. Rooted in deep-seated cultural and traditional ideologies, this form of violence is particularly prevalent in select regions. The Republic of Iran stands out as one such nation where honor-based violence presents a significant challenge. In Iran, honor killings are predominantly driven by the notion that a woman's conduct or choices have tarnished the reputation or dignity (Matabangsa, 2011)of her family or community. These actions may include rejecting an arranged marriage, seeking divorce, or engaging in relationships outside of societal norms. Honor killings are viewed as a means to restore familial honor and preserve social cohesion (Chesler, 2010). It is important to note that honor killings are not exclusive to Iran or the Islamic world. They occur in various cultures and religions across the globe. However, the focus of this chapter is to examine the context of honor-based violence specifically in Iran.

The existence of honor-based violence in Iran is deeply intertwined with the nation's social, legal, and cultural fabric. One of the key factors contributing to the persistence of this practice is the legal system, which, in many cases, provides leniency to perpetrators of honor killings. The Iranian Penal Code allows for reduced

DOI: 10.4018/979-8-3693-7240-1.ch007

sentences for those who commit honor-related crimes, under the justification of defending family honor (Goodarzi, 2012). This legal leniency not only perpetuates the cycle of violence but also sends a message that such acts are somewhat acceptable under the guise of cultural norms.

In addition to the legal framework, social attitudes and cultural beliefs play a critical role in the perpetuation of honor-based violence. In many communities within Iran, the concept of honor is inextricably linked to the behaviour and actions of women. Women's chastity(Kian, 1997), obedience, and adherence to traditional gender roles are often seen as reflections of the family's honor. Any deviation from these expectations, such as pursuing higher education, seeking employment, or choosing one's own partner, can be perceived as dishonourable and warrant severe repercussions.

OBJECTIVES OF THIS CHAPTER

1. This chapter aims to study the prevalence of Honor- based violence in Iran.
2. This chapter reviews instances of Honor killings in Iran.
3. This chapter aims to study various factors that may be contributing to the commonness of honor based violence in Iran.
4. This chapter analysis the existence of Human Rights in Iran along with the existing laws that govern the Republic of Iran.

RESEARCH METHODOLOGY

The aim of this chapter is to develop a comprehensive understanding of honor killings. Information was gathered from a wide range of sources, including library records, newspapers, magazines, interviews, surveys, and online databases. A qualitative research approach was employed to meet the study's objectives, utilizing both primary and secondary sources. To minimize bias, key participant characteristics such as ethnicity, age, and gender were carefully considered during the research process.

The findings from the primary and secondary research confirm that honor killings constitute a violation of the fundamental right to life with dignity and represent a significant human rights issue on a global scale. The research indicates that honor killings are not confined to any specific region but are a widespread phenomenon with deep historical roots. This issue has often been underestimated at the national level and neglected by international bodies, including the United Nations.

This chapter provides a detailed exploration of honor killings within the framework of fundamental human rights, particularly the right to life with dignity. The collected data highlights that honor killings should be viewed not only as an infringement of individual rights but also as a broader global human rights concern.

KEY TERMS

Core terms include "Honor-Based Violence" (Moosavi, L., 2015) and "Iran," (Chesler, P., 2010) which directly address the specific focus of the study. Broader themes such as "Gender-Based Violence,"(Kian, A.,1997) "Women's Rights," (Amin, C.M, 2002) and "Cultural Practices" (Matabangsa, 2011) provide contextual understanding of the issue within the Iranian socio-cultural framework. Legal and policy-related terms such as "Human Rights Violations" (Osanloo, A., 2009) and "Legal Frameworks" (Shirazi, F., 2010) connect to the practical and legal aspects of addressing honor-based violence in Iran. Analytical perspectives like "Socio-Political Dynamics" (Banakar, 2015) and "Intersectionality" (Mahmoudian & Hosseini-Chavoshi, 2011) allow for exploring the complexities and multifaceted nature of honor-based violence in the Iranian context.

Key terms were used to select relevant articles from various online sources, including the Library of Congress, Research Gate, Google Books, Springer, JSTOR, Sage, IJSSHR, Scopus, Web of Science, Taylor & Francis, and Google Scholar.

LITERATURE REVIEW

Honor-based violence, including honor killings, remains a critical issue in Iran, reflecting deep-seated cultural, legal, and socio-political challenges. The existing literature on this topic spans various themes, including Islamic feminism, gender politics, state policies, and the intersectionality of cultural practices. This review synthesizes key scholarly works to provide a comprehensive understanding of honor killings in Iran within its unique socio-cultural and political context. Amin (2002) provides a foundational understanding of the making of the modern Iranian woman, highlighting how state policies and popular culture from 1865 to 1946 shaped the public and private roles of women. Najmabadi (2005) further expands on the anxieties of Iranian modernity concerning gender and sexuality, providing a nuanced perspective on the cultural underpinnings of gender-based violence, including honor killings. Afary (2009) traces the evolution of sexual politics in modern Iran, emphasizing the intersection of gender, sexuality, and state power in perpetuating patriarchal norms that justify violence against women. Ahmadi (2003) explores the concept of Islamic feminism in Iran, arguing that it has emerged as a response to both secular and Islamist gender discourses, advocating for women's rights within an Islamic framework. This perspective is critical in understanding the socio-cultural rationale behind honor killings, as it highlights the complex interplay between religious interpretations and gender-based violence. The intersectionality of religion, culture, and gender is crucial for understanding honor killings in Iran. Hoodfar (1999) discusses the women's movement in Iran, highlighting how it has navigated the crossroads of secularization and Islamization. Mir-Hosseini (2002) provides a critical analysis of Islamic family law in Iran, showing how legal interpretations are often used to reinforce patriarchal control over women.

Bahramitash and Hooglund (2011) focus on the political economy of women's employment in Iran, suggesting that economic marginalization is intertwined with cultural practices that promote honor-based violence. Amnesty International (2010) provides a comprehensive report on discrimination and violence against women in Iran, framing honor killings as a human rights violation.

FUTURE RESEARCH DIRECTIONS

This research highlights the correlation between honor-based violence and the infringement of fundamental human rights, specifically the right to life with dignity, within the socio-cultural framework of Iran. Honor-based violence is conceptualized not just as a cultural crime but also as a serious violation of fundamental human rights, underscoring the importance of a legal framework that aligns with international human rights standards. Previous research has often neglected this perspective, despite repeated calls from international bodies and human rights organizations for more focused legislation. As noted by Moosavi, 2015, the lack of political will and public support has resulted in insufficient legislative action and ineffective law enforcement regarding the prevention and prosecution of honor-based violence.

While prior studies have linked honor killings with the right to life, this research extends the discussion to include the right to life with dignity and the broader global human rights perspective. It emphasizes that protecting life with dignity is a crucial element of international human rights law, as articulated in various international legal instruments (Osanloo, 2009).

The chapter also discusses the legal provisions and judicial responses related to honor killings within the Iranian context, noting that, similar to the situation in India, there is no specific legislation solely addressing honor killings. However, relevant laws can be identified within different sections of the Iranian legal framework, such as the Penal Code and other statutes related to human rights.

THE PREVALENCE OF HONOR KILLINGS IN IRAN

The prevalence of honor killings in Iran paints a dark and troubling portrait of the challenges faced by women in the country. These brutal acts of violence, committed in the name of preserving family honor, cast a long shadow over Iranian society. Reports spanning from 2010 to 2014 reveal a staggering figure of approximately 8000 honor killings recorded within this short period, indicating a deeply entrenched pattern of violence against women.

What is particularly distressing is the disproportionate impact of honor killings in certain regions of Iran. In East Azerbaijan province, for instance, a significant percentage of all murders, around 20 percent—are attributed to issues of sexual and honor dynamics(Statement Submitted by Amnesty International, Association for Women's Rights in Development, BAOBAB for Women's Human Rights, Center for Women's Global Leadership, International Alliance of Women and Italian Association for Women in Development, Non-Governmental Organizations in Consultative Status with the Economic and Social Council, n.d.). Even more alarming is the fact that half of all family-related homicides in this province are linked to honor-related disputes. This concentration of violence underscores the grim reality faced by women in specific areas, where the threat of honor killings looms large (Najmabadi, 2005). The impact of honor killings goes beyond mere statistics; it leaves a lasting scar on the fabric of Iranian society. Each victim represents a life cut short, a family torn apart, and a community left grieving. These senseless acts of violence perpetuate fear and insecurity among women, stifling their autonomy and limiting their freedom. Moreover, the normalization of honor killings within certain communities perpetuates a culture of impunity, where perpetrators are often shielded from justice.

The existence and continuance of honor killings in Iran highlights the entrenched nature of gender-based violence and the challenges faced by women in accessing justice and protection. Despite efforts to address this issue, these killings continue to cast a shadow over Iranian society, perpetuating cycles of violence and injustice. As long as honor killings persist, women in Iran will continue to face the threat of violence and discrimination, underscoring the urgent need for concerted action to address this pervasive issue. One significant factor contributing to the rise in honor killings is the increasing awareness among women and girls of their rights. They are asserting their desire for personal freedom by refusing forced marriages(refa, 2009a) and advocating for autonomy in choosing their spouses, pursuing education and employment opportunities, and participating in public life on equal footing with men. However, many Iranian men continue to uphold traditional notions of gender roles and resist these societal changes, preferring to maintain control over women (Afary, 2009).

Another contributing factor is the acceptance of honor killings within the Iranian legal system and societal norms. Islamic laws and governmental authorities in Iran often view honor killings as men's entitlement over women. The concept of honor, deeply ingrained in the social fabric, is frequently invoked to justify violence against women, perpetuating a patriarchal system that sanctions such acts. Legal provisions, such as Article 630 of the Iranian Penal Code(refa, 2009b), allow men to commit violence against women with impunity, particularly in cases of perceived sexual misconduct. Similarly, Article 301 grants immunity to fathers and grandfathers who kill their children, reinforcing the notion of paternal ownership over their offspring's lives(Mir-Hosseini, 2002). The tragic incident involving the murder of a young girl by her father in Iran has reignited concerns about the absence of legislation to combat honor killings in the country.

Sixteen-year-old Ariana Lashkari was fatally shot in the chest by her father, Mohammad-Kazem Lashkari, in Nourabad-e Mamasani, Fars Province. The altercation stemmed from Ariana's behaviour, which her father deemed shameful to the family, leading her to seek refuge at her paternal grandmother's residence. Following his arrest, Ariana's father claimed that his intention was only to intimidate his daughter and that her death resulted from a momentary loss of control.

Under Iran's Islamic Penal Code, fathers and paternal grandfathers are exempt from the death penalty for killing their children or grandchildren. Instead, perpetrators may face imprisonment and payment of "blood money" to the victim's next of kin, typically the mother, upon request. Furthermore, mothers have the authority to pardon the perpetrator and waive the blood money. In cases of murder, judges have discretionary powers to impose additional penalties deemed necessary "in the interest of public welfare" if the crime is deemed particularly violent or detrimental to society. Deplorably, perpetrators of honor killings often evade accountability, as families frequently refrain from seeking severe punishment, especially if the perpetrator is the victim's father (Ahmadi, 2003). This cultural reluctance to pursue justice exacerbates the challenges of combating honor killings and holding perpetrators accountable in Iran.

Despite historical precedents, the modern generation of Iranian women, empowered by access to information through the internet and social media, is increasingly challenging traditional norms and resisting discrimination and limitations on personal freedom. The recent case of Romina Ashrafi, a 13-year-old girl brutally murdered by her father in May 2020 for seeking autonomy in her choice of partner, brought renewed attention to the issue of honor killings in Iran. The widespread outrage and condemnation expressed on social media platforms following her death highlighted the growing public awareness and condemnation of such atrocities(Amir-Ebrahimi, 2008). In response to public pressure, Ms. Masumeh Ebtekar, then-President Hassan Rouhani's assistant for women's issues, proposed legislation named after Romina to strengthen penalties for honor killings of children. Although the bill received majority support in Iran's parliament, the Guardian Council rejected it, citing conflicts with Islamic law. This incident underscored the ongoing struggle to address honor killings within Iran's legal and societal frameworks, highlighting the entrenched nature of gender-based violence and the challenges facing advocates for women's rights in the country.

In societies where honor killings are prevalent, there exists a strong emphasis on the concept of honor, with a collective belief that honor represents the utmost value in life. These diverse cultural interpretations of honor and shame, rather than religious doctrines like Islam(Matabangsa, 2011), govern what is considered honorable or disgraceful and largely determine whether punitive measures are warranted for perceived shameful behaviour. While honor killings are not exclusive to Muslim communities, they have increasingly become associated with such societies. Certain interpretations of Quranic verses have contributed to this association, rendering Muslim communities more susceptible to misinterpretations and misconceptions (Shirazi, 2010). This reinterpretation fosters an environment conducive to honor killings within Muslim communities, perpetuating the prevalence of this practice and aligning Muslims with the typical characteristics associated with honor killings.

The case of Zeynab Sekaanvand is a deeply troubling example of the intersection of several critical issues in Iran's legal system, including the treatment of women, the rights of minors, and the application of the death penalty. This case garnered international attention and sparked outrage among human rights organizations due to its numerous controversial aspects.

Zeynab Sekaanvand was born into a poor Kurdish family in northwest Iran. At the age of 15, she was married off to a man named Hossein Sarmadi. Child marriage, though controversial, remains legal and relatively common in Iran, particularly in more conservative and economically disadvantaged areas. This practice often leaves young girls vulnerable to abuse and with limited options for education or personal development.

According to Zeynab's accounts, her marriage was marked by physical and verbal abuse from the beginning. She reportedly sought help from authorities multiple times, but her pleas were ignored. This lack of response highlights the challenges many women face in Iran when seeking protection from domestic violence, as well as the societal pressures that often prioritize maintaining family units over individual safety. The situation took a tragic turn in 2012 when Zeynab, then 17 years old, was arrested for the murder of her husband. During her initial interrogation, Zeynab confessed to stabbing her husband to death. However, she later retracted this confession, claiming it was obtained under duress. Zeynab alleged that she had been tortured and coerced into confessing by police officers during the three weeks she was held in custody before being charged.

In her retracted confession, Zeynab provided a different account of events. She stated that her brother-in-law had repeatedly raped her over a period of time. According to Zeynab, it was this brother-in-law who had actually committed the murder of her husband. This allegation raised serious questions about the thoroughness of the investigation and the handling of potential evidence in the case. Despite retracting her confession and providing an alternative account, Zeynab was convicted of murder and sentenced to death. This conviction relied heavily on her initial confession, which she claimed was coerced. The reliance on confessions, even when later retracted, is a contentious issue in Iran's justice system and has been criticized by human rights organizations (Moosavi, 2015).

One of the most controversial aspects of Zeynab's case was her age at the time of the alleged crime. At 17, she was considered a minor under international law. The use of the death penalty for crimes committed by minors is prohibited under international human rights law, including the International Covenant on Civil and Political Rights and the Convention on the Rights of the Child, both of which Iran has ratified. However, Iran continues to be one of the few countries that still executes individuals for crimes committed as minors.

Zeynab Sekaanvand was executed on October 2, 2016, at the age of 22.

The execution of Zeynab Sekaanvand also highlighted the broader issue of women's rights in Iran. Critics argue that women often face discrimination in both law and practice, particularly in matters related to marriage, divorce, child custody, and criminal justice.

The most recent reoccurrence involving 20-year-old Razieh Hasanvand has once again brought attention to the widespread issue of honor killings, revealing the devastating consequences of actions carried out in the name of Islam. According to a report from the Hengaw Human Rights Organization, Razieh Hasanvand had been in a coma since October 14, 2023, after sustaining gunshot wounds. The young woman, who was a mother and had previously divorced her cousin-husband despite facing familial opposition, succumbed to familial pressure to remarry another man, resulting in tragic consequences. Shockingly, it was Razieh's own brother who allegedly shot her, purportedly for "leaving the house," as reported by Hengaw. This tragic incident underscores the dangers faced by women who dare to challenge traditional norms and assert their autonomy (Alimardani & Elswah, 2020).

In a separate report, the Human Rights Organization highlighted that between September 29 and October 16, 2023, a total of thirteen women across various Iranian cities fell victim to honor killings. Despite efforts to shed light on these atrocities, the true extent of honor killings in Iran remains shrouded in secrecy. Official statistics are scarce, but according to a December 2019 report by the ISNA news agency, between 375 and 450 honor killings occur annually in Iran. However, due to the lack of transparency within the regime and the underreporting of such incidents, the actual figures are likely much higher. This lack of accountability and transparency only exacerbates the plight of women at risk of falling victim to honor-based violence in Iran.

Article 301 of the Code, which exempts fathers and paternal grandfathers from punishment for killing their children, is a grave violation of basic human rights and an affront to justice. This provision effectively sanctions murder within the family, sending a dangerous message that certain lives are less valuable and that perpetrators can escape accountability due to their familial status. Such laws perpetuate a cycle of violence and abuse, undermining efforts to promote gender equality and protect vulnerable individuals. Reforming this provision is essential to ensuring that all citizens are treated equally under the law and that the sanctity of life is upheld without exception. By allowing these acts to go unpunished, society fails to protect its most vulnerable members and condones a culture of violence and impunity that has no place in a just and civilized society.

THE GEOGRAPHICAL AND CULTURAL EPICENTRE OF HONOR KILLING

The Middle East and North Africa (MENA)(", n.d.; Statement Submitted by Amnesty International, Association for Women's Rights in Development, BAOBAB for Women's Human Rights, Center for Women's Global Leadership, International Alliance of Women and Italian Association for Women in Development, Non-Governmental Organizations in Consultative Status with the Economic and Social Council, n.d.) region serves as a significant focal point for honor killings, with these heinous acts deeply entrenched in the cultural fabric of many societies within this geographical area. While honor killings can occur in other parts of the world, their prevalence is notably higher in the MENA region. This phenomenon is often attributed to a combination of cultural norms, religious beliefs, and socio-political factors unique to the region.

Cultural Factors

In many countries across the MENA region, notions of honor and shame play a central role in social interactions and familial dynamics. The concept of honor is intricately linked to family reputation and societal norms, with any perceived deviation from these norms is viewed as a threat to collective honor (Kian,2014). Women, in particular, are expected to adhere to strict gender roles and uphold familial honor through their behaviour and actions. Failure to do so may result in severe consequences, including honor killings, as a means of restoring perceived honor to the family.

The concept of honor is multifaceted and encompasses various aspects of social life. It includes notions of dignity, respect, and social standing, all of which are closely intertwined with familial and communal reputation. In this context, honor is seen as a fragile commodity that must be vigilantly guarded and, if lost, swiftly restored (Osanloo, 2009). This perception of honor as something that can be lost or tarnished through the actions of individual family members creates a culture of constant vigilance and control, particularly over female family members.

The flip side of honor in these cultural contexts is shame. The fear of shame or social ostracism acts as a powerful motivator for individuals and families to conform to societal expectations. In many MENA(refa, 2009a) societies, the concept of shame extends beyond the individual to encompass the entire family or community. This collective shame can have severe social, economic, and personal consequences, further reinforcing the perceived need to maintain honor at all costs.

Gender roles play a crucial part in this cultural framework. Traditional gender norms in many MENA societies assign distinct and often unequal roles to men and women (Hoodfar, 1999) Women are typically expected to be modest, obedient, and chaste, while men are seen as protectors and guardians of family honor. These gender roles are often deeply ingrained from childhood and reinforced through various social institutions, including family, education, and religious teachings.

The disproportionate burden placed on women to uphold family honor is a key factor in the prevalence of honor killings. Women's behaviour, particularly their sexual conduct, is seen as a direct reflection of family honor (Kian, 2014). This creates a situation where women's bodies and actions are constantly policed by family members and the broader community. Any perceived deviation from prescribed norms of female behaviour can be seen as a threat to family honor, potentially leading to violent reprisals.

Religious Influences

Religion, is often cited in discussions surrounding honor killings in the MENA region. However, religious leaders vehemently deny any theological basis for such acts of violence. Islam, like other major religions, emphasizes principles of justice, compassion, and the sanctity of human life. Despite this, extremist interpretations of religious texts may be used to justify honor killings in some contexts.(Matabangsa,

2011). It is crucial to recognize that honor killings are not condoned by Islam or any other religion but are instead rooted in cultural practices and patriarchal norms.

To begin with, it is crucial to understand that honor killings are not a practice endorsed or sanctioned by Islam or any other major religion. In fact, religious leaders across the MENA region and beyond have consistently and vehemently denounced these acts as antithetical to the core principles of their faith. Islam, like other Abrahamic religions, places great emphasis on the sanctity of human life, compassion, and justice. The Quran, the holy book of Islam, explicitly states that taking an innocent life is akin to killing all of humanity (5:32). This fundamental tenet stands in stark contrast to the practice of honor killings, which involve the premeditated murder of individuals, often for perceived transgressions against family or community honor.

Despite these clear religious prohibitions, the persistence of honor killings in some parts of the MENA region has led to a conflation of cultural practices with religious doctrine. This misconception is further complicated by the fact that some perpetrators of honor killings may attempt to justify their actions using religious rhetoric or cherry-picked interpretations of religious texts. It is essential to recognize that such justifications are not grounded in mainstream religious teachings but rather in extremist interpretations that twist and distort religious principles to serve patriarchal and oppressive agendas. The misuse of religion to justify honor killings is a prime example of how cultural practices can become intertwined with religious identity over time (Aghajanian & Thompson, 2013). In many cases, pre-Islamic tribal customs and patriarchal norms have been preserved and perpetuated under the guise of religious observance. This conflation of culture and religion has created a complex web of beliefs and practices that can be difficult to disentangle, especially for those living within these societies.

Socio-Political Dynamics

Socio-political factors also contribute to the prevalence of honor killings in the MENA region. Countries with high levels of political Islam often have strict gender segregation laws and conservative societal norms that perpetuate gender inequality and reinforce patriarchal structures. Moreover, weak legal frameworks(Matabang-sa, 2011) and inadequate protections for women further exacerbate the problem, allowing perpetrators to evade accountability for their crimes. The intersection of religious conservatism and authoritarian governance creates an environment where honor killings can occur with impunity.

The implementation of gender segregation laws can have far-reaching consequences. In some countries, women are restricted in their ability to work in certain professions, participate in public life, or even move freely without a male guardian. Such restrictions not only limit women's opportunities for economic independence and personal growth but also reinforce the notion that women are subordinate to men and in need of male protection and control.

These conservative societal norms, often backed by state power, create an environment where women's behaviour is closely monitored and scrutinized (Amin, 2002). Any perceived transgression of these norms can be met with severe social consequences, including violence. In this context, honor killings can be seen as an extreme manifestation of the desire to control women's behaviour and maintain patriarchal dominance.

Another critical socio-political factor contributing to the persistence of honor killings is the economic marginalization of women in many MENA societies. Despite significant progress in education in recent decades, women in the region still face numerous barriers to economic participation and independence. High rates of female unemployment, restrictions on women's property rights, and limited access to financial resources all serve to reinforce women's dependence on male family members (Bahramitash & Hooglund, 2011).

This economic dependence can make it extremely difficult for women to escape abusive situations or resist family pressure. The threat of being cut off from financial support or losing custody of children can be a powerful deterrent to women who might otherwise seek help or resist harmful traditional practices. In this context, honor killings can be seen not only as a means of controlling women's behaviour but also as a way of maintaining economic control over female family members.

The role of education systems in perpetuating or challenging attitudes that contribute to honor killings is another crucial aspect of the socio-political dynamics at play. In many MENA countries, educational curricula reinforce traditional gender roles and conservative social norms. Textbooks and teaching materials may present stereotypical portrayals of men and women, emphasizing women's roles as wives and mothers while downplaying their potential contributions to public life and the economy.

Moreover, sex education and discussions of gender-based violence are often absent from school curricula or addressed only superficially. This lack of education leaves young people ill-equipped to challenge harmful cultural practices or seek help if they find themselves at risk. It also perpetuates misconceptions about gender roles, sexuality, and consent that can contribute to a culture where honor killings are seen as justifiable (Moosavi, 2015).

Denial and Complex Dynamics

Despite widespread recognition of honor killings as a pressing issue in the MENA region, some religious leaders deny any association between these acts of violence and Islam. This denial underscores the complex dynamics at play, where cultural, religious, and socio-political factors intersect to perpetuate harmful practices. Addressing honor killings requires a nuanced understanding of these complexities and concerted efforts to challenge discriminatory norms, empower women, and strengthen legal protections.

The Middle East and North Africa (Statement Submitted by Amnesty International, Association for Women's Rights in Development, BAOBAB for Women's Human Rights, Center for Women's Global Leadership, International Alliance of Women and Italian Association for Women in Development, Non-Governmental Organizations in Consultative Status with the Economic and Social Council, n.d.) stand as the geographical and cultural epicentre of honor killings, where deeply ingrained cultural norms, religious beliefs, and socio-political dynamics contribute to the perpetuation of this form of gender-based violence. Recognizing and addressing these underlying factors is essential to combatting honor killings and creating societies where all individuals are treated with dignity, respect, and equality.

Human Rights in Iran

The issue of honor-based violence in Iran raises significant concerns about the violation of human rights, particularly the rights of women and girls. The Islamic Republic of Iran, governed by Sharia law, imposes strict moral and social codes that disproportionately impact women's freedoms and autonomy. Human rights organizations have long criticized Iran's legal system for its failure to adequately address honor killings and protect the rights of women (Aghajanian & Thompson, 2013). The punishments for perpetrators of honor killings are often lenient, with reduced sentences or even complete impunity. This lack of accountability perpetuates a culture of violence and reinforces patriarchal norms.

Iranian women face numerous forms of discrimination and oppression. These systemic barriers contribute to an environment where honor-based violence can thrive. In addition to honor-based violence, numerous other human rights violations persist in Iran, exacerbating the plight of women and undermining their autonomy and dignity. One of the most pressing issues is the widespread discrimination against women in various spheres of life, including education, employment, and access to justice.

Women's rights activists argue that honor killing is deeply rooted in patriarchal law. For instance, certain provisions in the Iranian Penal Code allow men to kill their wives if they witness them engaging in sexual intercourse with another man (Banakar, 2015) The law also protects fathers and paternal grandfathers from retaliation for killing their own children. Such legal provisions perpetuate a culture of violence against women. In the realm of education, Iranian women face significant barriers to pursuing higher education and accessing educational opportunities on par with their male counterparts. Despite making up a significant portion of university students, women often encounter discriminatory practices that limit their academic and career prospects (Hegland, 2009). Moreover, gender segregation policies and restrictions on certain fields of study further marginalize women in the education system. In the workforce, Iranian women confront systemic discrimination and unequal treatment, including lower wages, limited job opportunities, and barriers to career advancement. Legal provisions that favour male employees and reinforce traditional gender roles perpetuate inequalities in the workplace, hindering women's economic empowerment and independence.

Furthermore, Iranian women encounter numerous obstacles in accessing justice and seeking redress for human rights violations, including honor-based violence. The legal system is rife with discriminatory laws and practices that disadvantage women, such as laws governing marriage, divorce, child custody, and inheritance. Moreover, women often face stigma, victim-blaming, and inadequate support from law enforcement and judicial authorities when reporting incidents of violence or seeking legal recourse (Farhi, 2005). The pervasive discrimination and systemic barriers faced by Iranian women underscore the urgent need for comprehensive reforms to protect and promote their human rights. Efforts to address honor-based violence must be accompanied by broader initiatives to dismantle discriminatory laws and practices, promote gender equality in all spheres of life, and ensure the full participation, representation, and consideration of women in decision-making processes (Mahmoudian & Hosseini-Chavoshi, 2011). International pressure and advocacy efforts play a crucial role in holding the Iranian government accountable for its human rights obligations and urging reforms to protect women's rights. Additionally, grassroots movements, civil society organizations, and women's rights activists within Iran continue to bravely advocate for change and challenge oppressive norms and practices that perpetuate gender inequality and discrimination.

Prevention of Honor Killing

The prevention of honor killings requires a multifaceted approach involving legal reforms, education, and social awareness. Efforts must be made to challenge traditional beliefs and promote gender equality within Iranian society. One crucial step is to strengthen legal protections for victims of honor-based violence. Iranian laws should explicitly criminalize honor killings and ensure that perpetrators(Statement Submitted by Amnesty International, Association for Women's Rights in Development, BAOBAB for Women's Human Rights, Center for Women's Global Leadership, International Alliance of Women and Italian Association for Women in Development, Non-Governmental Organizations in Consultative Status with the Economic and Social Council, n.d.) are held accountable to the full extent of the law. Sentences should be commensurate with the severity of the crime, sending a clear message that such acts will not be tolerated.

Law enforcement agencies and the judiciary should receive specialized training on handling honor-based violence cases. This training should include sensitivity towards victims, understanding the cultural dynamics that perpetuate honor killings, and implementing effective investigation and prosecution strategies (Goodarzi, 2012). Education and awareness programs can play a significant role in eradicating the deep-rooted beliefs that justify honor-based violence. Schools and community organizations should develop curriculum and workshops that promote gender equality, challenge harmful gender norms, and teach conflict resolution skills.

Additionally, efforts should be made to empower women and girls through economic and social opportunities. Access to education, employment, and support services can provide individuals with the means to escape abusive situations and assert their rights. International pressure and collaboration are also crucial in addressing honor-based violence in Iran. Diplomatic channels should be used to advocate for the protection of human rights and the enforcement of international laws and conventions.

THE INADEQUACY OF CIVIL SOCIETY AND ADVOCACY INSTITUTIONS

Victims of honor killings are often also victims of the weakness of civil society and advocacy institutions. In societies where there is limited room for civic activism and independent associations, and where advocacy organizations struggle to raise awareness among the public, it becomes challenging to bring about change and eradicate long-standing traditions of violence against women. To address the issue of honor killings, both immediate and long-term measures are necessary. Enforcing existing laws that protect women's rights is crucial, as is the need for legal reform to ensure that women are not subjected to violence and discrimination. Additionally, the ethos of society needs to change through education and awareness campaigns, challenging patriarchal norms, and promoting gender equality (Alimardani & Elswah, 2020).

In conclusion, honor killings in the Islamic world, including Iran, remain a deeply troubling and urgent concern that requires concerted efforts to address. The prevalence of violence against women, often justified by patriarchal laws and societal norms, underscores the need for immediate action to protect the rights and safety of women and girls in these regions. To combat honor killings effectively, it is essential to address the underlying socioeconomic factors that contribute to this form of violence. This includes addressing issues such as poverty, lack of education, and economic inequality, which may exacerbate tensions within families and communities and increase the likelihood of honor-based violence.

Ending honor killings globally, with a special emphasis on Iran, requires a nuanced and strategic approach that addresses the unique cultural, social, and political contexts within the country, while also drawing on global support and collaboration. Honor killings, a deeply rooted practice often justified by traditional and patriarchal norms, represent a severe violation of human rights. To eradicate this practice, it is crucial to leverage both local and international efforts (Mahmoudian & Hosseini-Chavoshi, 2011). In Iran, honor killings persist due to a combination of cultural traditions, legal shortcomings, and societal norms that condone or even encourage such violence. The Iranian legal system, which incorporates elements of Islamic law, often provides lenient sentences for perpetrators of honor killings. This legal leniency is coupled with strong patriarchal values that view women as bearers of family honor, making them vulnerable to extreme measures of control and punishment.

Legal reforms are paramount in Iran. The Iranian government must amend its legal framework to explicitly criminalize honor killings and impose severe penalties on perpetrators. This includes revising laws that allow for reduced sentences based on the notion of "honor" and ensuring that all forms of gender-based violence are unequivocally condemned. Additionally, it is vital to train law enforcement and judicial personnel to handle these cases with sensitivity and a firm commitment to justice. Education is another critical avenue for change in Iran. Implementing comprehensive educational programs that promote gender equality, human rights, and the dismantling of harmful cultural practices can create a shift in societal attitudes. Schools and universities should be platforms for fostering discussions on the value of individual autonomy and the dangers of patriarchal violence. Media campaigns can further amplify these messages, challenging the narratives that uphold honor killings and advocating for a culture of respect and equality.

Community engagement within Iran is essential. Efforts to end honor killings must involve influential local leaders, including religious and community figures who hold sway over public opinion. By engaging these leaders in dialogue and encouraging them to advocate against honor-based violence, it is possible to effect change from within the community. Local NGOs and grassroots movements can also play a pivotal role in raising awareness, providing support to victims, and creating safe spaces for dialogue (Alimardani & Elswah, 2020).

On the global stage, international cooperation and pressure are vital. The international community, including organizations such as the United Nations and global human rights groups, can apply diplomatic pressure on the Iranian government to reform its laws and protect victims of honor killings. These organizations can also provide technical assistance, funding, and expertise to local groups working on the ground. Global campaigns that highlight the issue of honor killings in Iran can raise awareness and generate international solidarity.

Moreover, it is essential to establish robust support systems for survivors and those at risk in Iran. Shelters, counselling services, legal aid, and economic empowerment programs must be accessible to all individuals facing the threat of honor-based violence. Empowering survivors through education and employment opportunities can help them break free from cycles of violence and build independent lives.

Furthermore, strengthening civil society and empowering women to assert their rights and challenge discriminatory practices are crucial steps towards combating honor killings. Civil society organizations, women's rights activists, and community leaders play a vital role in raising awareness, providing support to victims, and advocating for legal reforms that prioritize the protection of women's rights. Ultimately, addressing honor killings requires a multifaceted approach that involves collaboration between governments, civil society organizations, religious leaders, and individuals at all levels of society (Moosavi, 2015). By working together to raise awareness, advocate for legal protections, and promote gender equality, we can create a safer and more equitable future for women in the Islamic world and beyond.

REFERENCES

Afary, J. (2009). *Sexual Politics in Modern Iran*. Cambridge University Press. DOI: 10.1017/CBO9780511815249

Aghajanian, A., & Thompson, V. (2013). *Gender, marriage, and fertility in Iran*. Palgrave Macmillan.

Ahmadi, F. (2003). *Islamic Feminism in Iran: Feminism in a New Islamic Context*. Routledge.

Alimardani, M., & Elswah, M. (2020). Online reactions to offline gender issues: A case study of #No2Hijab campaign in Iran. *New Media & Society*, 22(7), 1138–1159.

Amin, C. M. (2002). *The Making of the Modern Iranian Woman: Gender, State Policy, and Popular Culture, 1865-1946*. University Press of Florida.

Amnesty International. (2010). *Iran: 'I'd kill you myself' - Discrimination and violence against women in Iran*. Amnesty International Publications.

Bahramitash, R., & Hooglund, E. (2011). *Veiled Employment: Islamism and the Political Economy of Women's Employment in Iran*. Syracuse University Press.

Banakar, R. (2015). *Driving Culture in Iran: Law and Society on the Roads of the Islamic Republic*. I.B. Tauris.

Chesler, P. (2010). Worldwide Trends in Honor Killings. *Middle East Quarterly*, 17(2), 3–11.

Farhi, F. (2005). Women, The State, and Ideology in Iran. *The Muslim World*, 95(4), 479–510.

Goodarzi, S. (2012). Honor killings and the quest for justice in Iran. *Iranian Studies*, 45(4), 535–556.

Hegland, M. E. (2009). Flagellation and Fundamentalism: (Trans)forming Meaning, Identity, and Gender through Pakistani Women's Rituals of Mourning. *American Ethnologist*, 32(3), 294–310.

Hoodfar, H. (1999). The Women's Movement in Iran: Women at the Crossroads of Secularization and Islamization. *The Middle East Journal*, 53(4), 453–473.

Kian, A. (1997). Modernization and Gender Regime in Iran. *Iranian Studies*, 30(3-4), 385–408.

Kian, A. (2014). *Gender and Women's Studies in Iran: A Comparative Perspective*. Springer.

Mahmoudian, H., & Hosseini-Chavoshi, M. (2011). Revolution, war, and modernization: Population policy and fertility change in Iran. *Journal of Population Research*, 28(3), 247–266.

Matabangsa, J. (2011). Honor Killings in the Middle East: Cultural Practice or Human Rights Violation? In Ahmed, A. (Ed.), *Human Rights in the Arab World* (pp. 122–145). University of Pennsylvania Press.

Mir-Hosseini, Z. (2002). *Marriage on Trial: Islamic Family Law in Iran and Morocco*. I.B. Tauris.

Moosavi, L. (2015). The Crises of Masculinity and Unveiling the Real in Iranian Cinema: A Gendered Analysis of A Separation. *Middle East Journal of Culture and Communication*, 8(3), 260–276.

Najmabadi, A. (2005). *Women with Mustaches and Men without Beards: Gender and Sexual Anxieties of Iranian Modernity*. University of California Press. DOI: 10.1525/9780520931381

Osanloo, A. (2009). *The Politics of Women's Rights in Iran*. Princeton University Press. DOI: 10.1515/9781400833160

Shirazi, F. (2010). *Muslim Women in War and Crisis: Representation and Reality*. University of Texas Press.

Chapter 8
Honorless Honor Killings in Jordan

Abhishek Kumar
Amity University, Haryana, India

Aishna Arora
GLA University, Mathura, India

ABSTRACT

This study examines Jordan's socio-political stance of honor in order to understand how Jordanian culture, which is both sophisticated and based on traditional values, constructs meanings around honor killings. The majority of current research on honor crimes in Jordan suggests that not much has been learned or figured out about the relationship between the law in Jordan, honor crimes, and the perceptions of these offences among Jordanians. In order to better explore prospects for legislation and policy that would diminish these crimes, this chapter thoroughly examines the aspects that potentially explain the frequency, reasons, and persistence of honor killings in Jordan. It highlights the disparity between the nation's social and legal laws on the penalty of honor crimes, as well as the gender inequality that exists in the nation. It also sheds light on the relationship between Middle Eastern civilizations and ways of life and the prevalence of crimes done in a badge of honor. The study is predicated on a detailed analysis of court proceedings from 1993 to 2010.

Nine cases of beatings that resulted in death and nine cases of premeditated and intentional killings were also documented in the Criminal Information Department's 2020 criminal statistical report. There were 201 persons found guilty of premeditated and purposeful homicides, with 7 of them being women, or 3.5% of the total. In light of the pandemic, deliberate and premeditated killings decreased by 18.2% in 2020 compared to 2019 (Gill,2019), when 90 offenses resulted in 99 fatalities.

DOI: 10.4018/979-8-3693-7240-1.ch008

Copyright © 2025, IGI Global. Copying or distributing in print or electronic forms without written permission of IGI Global is prohibited.

2019 had 110 crimes that resulted in 115 fatalities. It was discovered that the age of 3.48% of the offenders was under eighteen. It was discovered that 3.48% of the offenders were under the age of 18, 34.8% were between the ages of 18 and 27, 33.3% were between the ages of 28 and 37, 17.4% were between the ages of 38 and 47, and 10.9% were beyond the age of 48. It was said that sharp tools (36.9%) and firearms (36.9%) made up the majority of the weapons used in attacks. Personal and previous conflicts were the main motivation for offenders (47.8%).

RESEARCH METHODOLOGY

In order to have a thorough grasp of the problem, the research methodology for this study on honor killings in Jordan combines qualitative and quantitative techniques. The methodology is a multimodal strategy to gather data that includes looking through library, newspaper, and magazine archives to track historical and current reports of honor-based violence and how it is portrayed in the media. Personal insights and direct experiences relating to honor killings are provided by in-depth interviews with important stakeholders, including survivors, family members, legal professionals, and representatives from non-governmental organizations and human rights organizations. Surveys are intended to collect quantifiable data on public attitudes, experiences, and perceptions of honor-based violence in order to provide insight into broader social perspectives (El Muhtaseb, R., 2020). In order to contextualize the topic, the research also includes secondary data analysis, which involves reading previously published works, reports from groups like Human Rights Watch and Amnesty International, as well as publications from the Jordanian government. By examining online resources such as academic databases, news websites, and social media platforms to obtain up-to-date information and trends, internet research enhances these conclusions. Preserving a well-rounded perspective and reducing prejudice in interviews and surveys can be achieved by guaranteeing a varied sample that takes into account variables like age, gender, socioeconomic level, and ethnicity (El Muhtaseb, R., 2020). In order to address the complex nature of honor killings, emphasize their worldwide relevance as a human rights issue, and advocate for more effective treatments and legislative measures, it is imperative that qualitative research strategies be used. By taking this method, the study hopes to provide a more comprehensive picture of honor killings in Jordan by analyzing how legal frameworks, cultural norms, and human rights interact.

KEY WORDS

Key concepts that are essential to understanding the chapter on honor killings in Jordan include "legal reforms," "social stigma," "family reputation," "gender-based violence," "honor crimes," "honor killings," "patriarchy," and "traditional justice systems." These concepts are essential to comprehending the intricate dynamics that lead to honor killings in Jordan, a country whose tribal traditions and patriarchal systems greatly influence social perceptions of women's roles and family honor. Terms such as "honor crimes" and "gender-based violence" draw attention to acts of targeted violence against women that are thought to have defied social norms, while terms like "traditional justice systems" and "tribal customs" refer to customs and unofficial processes that often shield offenders from formal legal recourse. The term "legal reforms" refers to the continuous endeavors to update Jordanian legislation in order to provide more protection for women, whilst the terms "social stigma" and "family reputation" highlight the social forces that support this kind of violence. These terms are crucial for understanding how Jordan's legal system and cultural customs combine to address honor killings. It explores the deeply ingrained patriarchal ideals and the ways that tribal culture contributes to the continuation of these detrimental practices. (Husseini, 2009). This article was selected because it provides a thorough analysis of the interactions between sociocultural elements and legal frameworks, especially with regard to the lax rules that allow for less punishments for crimes of honor. (International Amnesty, 2018). This source was chosen because it provided a thorough examination of how the Jordanian judicial system handles honor killings and the current changes being made to combat gender-based violence (El Muhtaseb, R., 2020). The study inclusion criteria prioritized publications that address the problem of honor killings in Jordan, such as legal frameworks, tribal justice, and patriarchal norms studies. In order to guarantee the inclusion of contemporary viewpoints, publications released in the last ten years were given precedence. In order to guarantee both academic rigor and authoritative insights, sources were chosen from peer-reviewed journals, reports from human rights groups, and official publications. The primary exclusion criteria were centered around excluding non-scholarly materials, opinion articles, and publications having minimal involvement with the subject matter. For the purpose of gathering the most pertinent scholarly research, databases such as JSTOR, Google Scholar, and Human Rights Watch were searched using keywords like "honor killings," "tribal justice," "gender violence in Jordan," and "legal reforms." Exclusion of sensationalized media and non-scholarly sources allowed for a clear focus on reliable and authoritative sources.

LITERATURE REVIEW COLUMN

Honor killings in Jordan are deeply embedded in cultural and tribal traditions that prioritize family honor over individual rights. Studies such as those by Husseini (2009) emphasize that these crimes are driven by tribal honor codes and entrenched cultural norms, with the concept of honor being tightly linked to the perceived behavior of women (Husseini, R. (2009). Al-Habash (2014) further underscores how societal expectations and familial pressures create an environment where honor killings are seen as a means to restore family reputation. Socioeconomic factors also significantly impact the prevalence of honor killings. El Muhtaseb (2020) indicates that economic dependency and poverty can exacerbate honor-based violence, as economic pressures may lead families to enforce stricter traditional norms, including honor killings, to manage perceived threats to their social standing (El Muhtaseb, R., 2020). Gender dynamics are central to the perpetuation of these crimes, with patriarchal structures and traditional gender roles providing justification for violence against women under the guise of preserving family honor (Al-Ali, 2018). The legal framework surrounding honor killings has undergone scrutiny and reform, such as the repeal of Article 308 in 2017, but enforcement remains inconsistent (Amnesty International, 2018). The effectiveness of Jordanian institutions, including the judiciary and law enforcement, in handling cases of honor-based violence is often hindered by systemic issues like inadequate training and resources, highlighting the need for more robust responses (Human Rights Watch, 2019). Additionally, the psychological and social impacts on both victims and offenders are significant, with Al-Krenawi (2021) discussing severe mental health effects and long-term psychological distress. Media and advocacy play crucial roles in addressing honor killings; Al-Momani (2020) explores how media representation and advocacy efforts shape public perceptions and push for reforms, although challenges remain in overcoming entrenched cultural attitudes. Comparative studies, such as valuable insights by comparing honor-based violence in Jordan with similar cases in other regions, highlighting both commonalities and differences(Amnesty International. (2018). Overall, the literature reveals a complex interplay of cultural, socioeconomic, gender, and legal factors that perpetuate honor killings. Continued research is essential for developing effective prevention and intervention strategies to address and mitigate honor-based violence in Jordan.

FUTURE RESEARCH DIRECTIONS

In order to better understand the dynamics and underlying causes of this problem, future research on the factors affecting honor killings in Jordan can look into a number of topics. An important area of research is cultural influences, such as how deeply ingrained norms and tribal honor codes support honor killings. Additionally, studies should look at socioeconomic variables, examining how family decisions are influenced by financial constraints and the connections between poverty, economic dependency, and the frequency of honor killings (Amnesty International. (2018). Studying gender dynamics is especially important because it sheds light on how honor-based violence in Jordanian society is exacerbated by patriarchal systems and conventional gender norms (Plant, R. (2006). Analyzing how education and awareness programs affect public perceptions of honor killings and how well they work to stop these crimes could shed light on future prevention initiatives. To further study the effect of recent reforms, such the removal of Article 308, and the implementation of current legislation might be beneficial in avoiding honor killings. To evaluate the institutional response's efficacy in defending victims and bringing criminals to justice, it is important to investigate how the courts, law enforcement, and state institutions handle honor-based violence. Future research should focus on psychological aspects as well, such as the effect of social and familial constraints on offenders' and victims' mental health as well as the significance of these elements in honor-based violence. Attention should also be paid to how the media and social media portray and raise awareness of honor killings, which can either help to prevent or perpetuate them (Al-Momani, H. (2020). Religious interpretations may shed light on societal impacts, particularly in relation to how various interpretations of Islamic precepts impact the acceptance or rejection of honor killings. Additionally, studies might look into community support networks and the part local activities and grassroots projects play in either encouraging or discouraging honor killings. Examining geographical variations, such as the impact of tribal versus non-tribal societies or urban versus rural environments, may help clarify how these variables influence the number and kind of honor killings. A greater understanding of the problem might also come from studies that concentrate on how marginalized or minority groups in Jordan are disproportionately influenced by social factors including religion, ethnicity, and other social issues. Finally, it would be beneficial to conduct research on how well advocacy from NGOs, women's rights groups, and advocacy groups works to stop honor killings and advance societal and legal changes. Research comparing Jordanian honor killings to comparable incidents in other Middle Eastern or international settings may shed light on local, national, and international reactions to the problem. Future studies in these fields may aid in the creation of more potent preventative and intervention plans to stop honor killings in Jordan. In this chapter recent changes in law have not been dealt with and the loopholes in current Jordanian law has not been discussed. Moreover, the psychology of people living in 21st century is yet to be explored and discussed.

In the Arab culture, a significant portion of honor crimes are based solely on rumors, meaning they are done without concrete evidence. In addition, that "gossip is an instrument made use of by individuals in the society for disseminating the unpleasant facts that certain their family's reputation has already been tarnished, and subsequently a family's societal and highly esteemed status is in threat." She characterizes gossip as a means that can be employed to regulate women's behavior in society because this behavior is at the center of a family's honor.

The definition of "honor" depends on the cultural environment in which it is rooted (Gill,2019). In the region of the Mediterranean, honor has a lengthy history. Women have always been seen as members of their own agnatic group all over Arab cultural and historical context, while men have traditionally been seen as the ones who look out for women (Fernandez,2006) .This is a perfect example of a patrilineal and patriarchal civilization. Families and communities understand that gossip can help reestablish a family's social status by causing an honor killing. If gossip persists, it will 'purge' a family's honor. From an organizational functionalist standpoint, gossip serves as a means of establishing peace and harmony that are crucial to the longevity of the household and society"(Awwad,2001).

Gossip also helps to bring the community together due to the fact that honor killings—in which a family member kills a person—are prohibited in Jordan. It is rendered in a way that upholds their reputation or prestige in a community where a family member's actions go against the accepted moral standards of the community.

Even though honor killings are prohibited by Jordanian law, there are some provisions in the penal code that run counter to this prohibition. The provisions of Article 98 and the 340th article of Jordanian law are examples of such laws. Jordanian law even authorizes the easing of legal sanctions in cases where brothers or fathers kill female family members. The Jordanian Penal Code has a number of laws that can be used, or has been used, by the justice to lessen the legal punishment meted out to the guilty in crimes pertaining to honor. There are several gaps in Article 340 of the Jordanian penal code that have been discussed when someone is trying to find an excuse for a crime they have committed. According to this article, a man who murders a woman—his wife or a woman who is a lineal descendant or ascendant of the family—while committing adultery helps to lessen his punishment. A few changes have been made.

Gender roles are also strongly influenced by the structure of the family in Jordan along with other Arab nations (Odeh,1996) .The dominant member of the clan is nearly invariably a man in a patriarchal household. According to the dynamics amongst the male head of the family along with the women in the home, the female gender formation can therefore be described. A significant proportion of Jordanian women rely on male family members for their financial support. They are therefore more susceptible to possible violence inside the home (Faqir,2001). As a result, women are conditioned to feel reliant on someone if not their fathers, perhaps their spouses or even their brothers both inside the home and in larger society. Men's status in society is thus defined and fueled by their strength and empowerment. It might be argued that in Jordan, masculinity is frequently exalted and cleared, whereas femininity is frequently criticized and avoided. In the Jordanian context, it is imperative to comprehend how this gender construction impacts society expectations and beliefs at a fundamental level.

Men's status in society is thus defined and fueled by their strength and empowerment. It might be argued that in Jordan, masculinity is frequently exalted and cleared, whereas femininity is frequently criticized and avoided. In the Jordanian context, it is imperative to comprehend how this gender construction impacts society expectations and beliefs at a fundamental level. In his work on the 'inability thesis', argues that although we humans are aware that some activities are bad, culture really shapes our behavior in a variety of ways, independent of what our own conscience tells us (Tunick,2004). The inability thesis explains how cultural norms shape behavior and might render someone incapable of abiding by the law, rendering them less worthy of punishment. The idea that cultural upbringing renders people physiologically incapable of acting in particular ways is rejected by those who disagree with the concept.

A woman who is not chaste is occasionally compared to a murderer in many Arab nations, but murderers themselves do not view honor killings as crimes and receive far lighter sentences. However, it might be difficult to find accurate honor statistics about crime in Jordan because the government sometimes does not keep thorough records of these crimes, and some murders are either covered up or are manufactured to appear to be suicides. In an effort to better establish prospects for law and policy that would lessen these crimes, this chapter thoroughly investigates the elements that potentially explain the frequency, causes, and persistence of honor killings in Jordan. It highlights the disparity between the nation's social and legal laws on the penalty of honor crimes, as well as gender inequality in the nation.

LEGAL RESPONSES TO HONOR CRIMES IN JORDAN

As of right now, Jordan's law texts have two articles (340 and 98) that seem to permit crimes committed for honor.

In accordance with Article 340,

1. A mitigating excuse will be granted to anyone who murders their wife, his lover, or both, or assaults them and causes death, serious injury, or permanent disfigurement as a result of the assault. This includes anyone who is surprised by anyone of his female decedents, ancestors, sisters, or during an act of elopement or in a fraudulent bed.
2. A wife will be entitled to the same excuse as stated in the previous paragraph if she surprises (catch) her spouse in act of sexual misconduct or in an unlawful bed in their marital home and murders her husband, his lover, or both of them right away, or assaults him and both of them, resulting in death, serious injury, harm, or permanent disfigurement.
    a. Those who profit from this justification cannot be attacked using the right to self-defense.
    b. The provisions pertaining to aggravating circumstances or considerations will not be applicable to that individual.

Prior to September 2017, those found guilty of "honor crimes" under the provisions of Article 98 of the Jordanian Criminal Code may be eligible for reduced sentences if their actions were motivated by a "state of intense indignation stemming out of an unlawful unsafe act on the part of the victim." As a result, some murders received sentences of just six months in prison for atrocities they committed under the false pretense that they were 'defending' the name of their family or community. This provision allowed judges to be particularly lenient when it came to sentencing. But after being amended by September 2017, the provisions of Article 98 no more views extreme rage as a mitigating factor for people who perpetrate crimes against women in order to protect their honor.

Murder is currently classified into three categories under the Jordanian penal code: first degree, second degree, and manslaughter. Articles 326 through 329 include the codification of these offenses. Since the Jordanian legal system recognizes intentional murder and murder that resulted from provocation, Article 98 is always applied in conjunction with Articles 328 and 326 when arguing that the accused attacked because the victim provoked them. The primary factor for applying Article 98 in a murder case is figuring out when the accused assaulted the alleged victim. "According to the Court of Appeals, the fit of fury should have had a severe effect on the accused," clarify that "the Court of Cassation held that the accused should be severely affected by the outburst, which should immediately cause him to lose all sense of perception and self-control, making him unable to control himself (Abu-Hassan&Welchman, 2005)."

The provisions of Article 98 have to be put into effect in conjunction with Article 340 with regard to honor offenses in particular. Precisely because Article 98 provides that 'He who engages in a crime in a fit of fury induced by an immoral and hazardous act on the part of an innocent person benefits from an easing of penalty', offenders primarily use it to get around Article 340's direct application to crimes done in the name of honor.

In illuminating Article 98, it is explained that many Jordanian families entrust a male member of the family under the age of eighteen with the honor killing duty, knowing full well that he will be treated as a minor by the criminal justice system of the nation and, consequently, receive a severely reduced sentence. This is partially due to the fact that Jordanian law was crafted to represent the country's social norms and is a hybrid of several laws, especially Ottoman, French, Italian, and British laws. The language of Article 98 really gives a judge the option to free a murderer or give them a punishment that is not more severe than slapping a youngster on the hand (Sonbol,2003). The definition of an honor crime is so broad and ambiguous that it might encompass any act of violence committed by a man in the family against a female relative.

Sonbol essentially states that there isn't a specific item in the Jordanian Criminal Code that deals with "honor" killings. The nation's kings and queens, both past and current, have pleaded with their parliament to remove or modify Article 340, but their demands have been turned down. This implies that even though first-degree murder convictions in Jordan typically result in the death penalty, those who are actually charged with and found guilty of honor killings still only receive sentences ranging from a couple of months to several years (Plant,2006). Because there is no proof that a woman who kills her husband or a male relative due to "honor" issues will not be treated equally in a court of law, it is clear that scholars do not separate the gender arguments from the legal argument.

Faqir's assertion that 'the wording of the legislation provided for reductions of punishment to male criminals only; women who uncover spouses or relatives practicing adultery were not afforded comparable medications, here or anywhere in the legislation (Faqir,2001).

Scholars emphasize how important the family is to this legal procedure because most honor crimes are perpetrated within families, and strong patriarch and familial ties affect how these cases are handled when they are prosecuted. Abu-Hassan and Welchman observe that the victim's family is urged to forego the personal claim when the Jordanian court embraces a defense for an honor killing due to the intimate nature of the crime (Abu-Hassan & Welchman,2005). "Customs and practices move the legal representative of the female victim to forego the personal claim and drop charges". After then, the court may utilize its own judgment to consider extenuating circumstances in line with paragraphs 99 and 100, hence permitting moderate punishments even in cases where Article 98 does not apply.

Therefore, Jordan's legal framework is severely limited by Jordanian society as well as cultural history, as is seen in both scholarly writing and the application of the law. Honor killing data do not show that the increasing prevalence of these crimes or public perception of them have changed, despite Jordan's legal system having made significant strides in recent years toward gender equality under the law.

An instance of this can be seen in the testimony of Ziad H., a thirty-year-old man who killed his divorced sister after she had been gone from his family's residence for a week. He told investigators, "I decided to kill her because people began to talk about us." According to a pathologist's assessment, he stabbed his sister thirty times, although there was no evidence of sexual activity. Charges were withdrawn by the victim's father, who also happens to be the defendant's father. Thanks to the mitigation provided by article 98, the murderer received a sentence of to six months in prison for the "honor" crime in January 2003. He was released after serving his sentence and waiting for his trial.

As the aforementioned case illustrates, there is no need for the murder to have been incited by concrete evidence of sexual impropriety; rather, a woman's alleged "unlawful and dangerous" behavior—commonly referred to as "a bad act" for short—may serve as adequate evidence in court. For instance, in a 2001 case where the defendant killed his sister "after witnessing an individual leave her house," Article 98 was invoked.

The 2002 case of a guy who stabbed his sister after witnessing her "talking to an unknown man at a wedding party" also involved its use. After a three-week absence, a dad fatally stabbed his kid daughter 25 times in 2003 because she would not tell dad where she had been. By using article 98, the court lessened his punishment because the deed was carried out in a "fit of rage."

News sources also state that even in cases when a significant amount of time elapses between learning of the supposed "bad act" and committing the crime, responding violently to alleged blemishes on family honor would typically be deemed to have transpired in a "fit of fury." The court determined that a man's decision to kill his unmarried cousin, who had become pregnant a month earlier, was legal because the woman had "brought disrepute and shame to her family."

In another documented instance, a man confronted his sister after overhearing her be called a "slut." He should "mind his own business," she advised him. He went to sleep, woke up the following morning, and used a phone wire to strangle her. "It does not matter that the accused individual killed his sister hours afterwards [learning of her supposed act]," the High Criminal Court declared in its ruling. He continued to be affected by intense rage, which made it difficult for him to think rationally due to his sister's illegal deed.

In a case from 2001, when a brother went to see his sister in the hospital while she was receiving burn treatment, she revealed to his brother that she was carrying a child and had an affair. He went and got himself a gun. He came back after twenty-four hours and fired her multiple times within close range. The defendant's soul was not at rest, according to the court, "even though there were roughly 24 hours between the time he learned of his sister's illegal conception [as well as the time he killed her]."An agitated spirit is incapable of rational thought.

ANALYSIS OF COURT CASES

1. Geographic Context

The population of Jordan is made up of Circadians, Armenians, Jordanians, Bedouins, and both naturalized and non-naturalized Palestinians as well as those who remain in refugee camps. The two predominant religions in the nation are Islam and Christianity, and there is a significant wealth and poverty gap in society. Families from middle-class and upper-class backgrounds typically reside in the western part of Amman, the capital; the farther one ventures from Amman, the less valuable real estate and housing is available, and living expenses are lower. As the accompanying data illustrates, people with comparable backgrounds and socioeconomic position tend to reside in particular suburbs. For instance, only families with tribal links live in some suburbs, while Christians, refugees, the impoverished, and wealthy people live in other suburbs. The likelihood of a family engaging in manual labor or farming increases with distance from the city; in Jordan, a family's occupation is correlated with their social and economic status. In Jordan, obtaining a stable and highly esteemed career requires completing university courses, which are costly and not subsidized by the Jordanian government.

2. Who Were The Offenders?

The offender's suburb plays a significant role in these situations because it provides some context for understanding the social history of the perpetrators; an offender's area may also be important to his line of work. Amman inhabitants did not commit any of the thirty crimes. Men who had been living in Palestinian refugee camps were responsible for four of the crimes; two of the crimes happened in farming villages; four of the crimes happened in ethnic suburbs; and two of the crimes happened in the port city of Aqaba. Consequently, putting the offenders' residences into context aids in placing their jobs, despite the fact that in 13 of the 30 instances, the offenders' jobs are not mentioned. The jobs held by the criminals in the other cases were classified as "manual labor," or jobs that don't call for a high level of education or specialized training. Jobs in this field are typically low paying, as they are in most civilizations. The employment and suburb data may be indicative of the social class at which honor crimes are committed. A 2011 study by the King Hussein Foundation's Information and Studies Centre (IRC) in Jordan discovered a link between crimes done in the name of honor and poverty (Mansur,2009) . However, as some of these crimes go unregistered every year, such targeted and limited research cannot ensure accuracy. The demographics of the aforementioned cases do, however, show that the majority of the offenses were perpetrated in heavily populated locations some distance from Amman. Moreover, statistics demonstrates that every criminal was Muslim. That being said, not all honor killings take place in Muslim households; in Jordan, 6% of the general population is Christian, and honor values are just as important to these households as they are to Muslims.

3. Who Fell Victim To This?

The information gathered from court papers reveals that not much was written down about the victims. In fact, surnames and ages are frequently omitted as well. Although we identify to these ladies as "victims," it is important to remember that the phrase is not utilized in the court documents. Instead, the women who were slain are called "marhouma," which translates to "the deceased" in Arabic. The victims' ages varied from 9 to 28 years old when indicated; in 21 cases, the victim's ages are not recorded. It was challenging to create a clear image of the connection between both parties in each case due to the scarcity of information regarding the victims when compared to the offenders. Nine of the victims were the perpetrators' children, sixteen were their sisters, and two were their married relatives. One victim was the offender's cousin. Regarding the victims' educational and professional histories, nothing is known. After a survey a total of 54 cases ranging from 1993 to 2010 were found following in-depth analyses, only 30 of the cases could be initially examined because the remaining 24 are missing vital information about the individuals involved and the details of the court proceedings. Furthermore, those 24 cases do not contain detailed narratives compared with the 30 that could be used. These 30 cases solely deal with 'honor' and murder committed in the name of honor. The cases paint a detailed picture of what occurred in the court, and offer a clear analysis of the events surrounding the crime in question and the reasons behind it.

WOMEN, SEX AND THE POWER OF THE FAMILY

In Jordan, gender roles and distinctions have become ingrained in society and culture, with men viewed as the guardians and women as the vulnerable. This idea of protection stems from the care that tribal men provide for local women in the nation of Jordan, where a tribe's ability to demonstrate its power and honesty depends on the purity of its breed. Tribes defend women as a means of defending society. Tribal customs view marriage as a sacred state, with women being married off to men from the same tribe as a means of ensuring the group's purity and continued existence. A family must procreate in order to be considered a tribe, and this can only happen via a female's body(Faqir,2001). People contribute to society and ensure the survival of their culture through procreation. Women who stray have faced severe punishments in the past and present because maintaining purity is necessary to protect the genes of the tribe. The majority of the court records analyzed for this study indicate that the offender only very seldom discussed the victim's alleged transgressions with her before committing the crime; as a result, many victims were never given the opportunity to refute their alleged acts. This is evident in Su'ad's situation.

CASE 9: SU 'AD

This honor crime took place in the Hussein Refugee Camps in 2002. The 19-year-old offender's sister was the 21-year-old victim. The victim, identified as Su'ad, met her neighbor, Mahmud (one of the witness), with whom she started a romantic relationship and eventually became pregnant, as per the court records, the testimony of witnesses, and the defence. Su'ad went to the The family Security Unit one day after feeling sick to her stomach, and they told her parents she was expecting. The accused person, Ra'ed, arrived in the suburb area where his parents lived on August 31, 2002, from the port town of Aqaba. Neighbors on the street began yelling at him as he got closer to the house, accusing him of being a prostitute's brother and asking how he could walk here. Upon entering the house, he inquired of his parents as to why the teenage boys were yelling, and they informed him of the situation. The accused's sister allegedly informed him that her pregnancy was none of his business and claimed she was free to use her physique and her hair anyway she pleased when he confronted her about it, according to court documents. At approximately 5:30 am on the following day, the defendant went into Su 'ad's chamber and strangled her with an object of string till she passed away. After turning himself up, the inquiry got underway.

(Case 9/2002)

When the perpetrator was asked to testify, he stated: My sister gave me a nasty response when I asked her if she was pregnant, claiming that her vagina belonged to her and that she could use it anyway she pleased. When she stated this to me, I became furious and just strangled her with a thread. since of what my sister Su 'ad did, which God does not approve of, and since no one with honor would allow his sister to ruin his family's reputation, I killed her. My sister ruined my reputation and dishonored me, causing an embarrassment in our neighborhood.

(Case 9/2002)

The defense attorney for the offender sent the judge a thorough statement outlining the facts of the case and his reasoning for using Article 98 in this specific situation. This is a religious, social, and legal case because the sister's actions render her deathly, as an unwed pregnancy defies moral and religious logic. Since what she did was against our customs and culture, she also deserved what happened to her. For this reason, I ask the court to take Article 98 into consideration and put it into practice. I know you would respond the same way if your sister and daughter had committed the same offense.

(Case 9/2002)

The defense attorney stated in a separate letter sent to the court that this case could be summarized as follows: Ra 'aed left his family's residence to seek employment in Aqaba, while he was there, his sister Su 'ad damaged both their reputations by committing a dishonorable act that no religious person or man of honor would ever accept. It is every man's responsibility to defend his residence and his family. She did this terrible deed under her parents' roof in addition to her cheating with Mahmoud, who stole her virginity.

(Case 9/2002)

The judge's order to sentence the offender to a year in jail is documented in the case notes. The judge gave the following justification for his ruling: "We acknowledge that the suspect was in a state of anger when his neighbors ridiculed him for being a prostitute's brother." Because we acknowledge that his actions were motivated by passion and fury, the court will accuse him with murder rather than premeditated murder and will apply Article 326 of the Criminal Code as a result. The court's recognition that the victim had done something that had infuriated the accused—

becoming pregnant outside of marriage, dishonoring the family, and damaging their reputation—led to the implementation of this legal action.

(Case 9/2002)

The aforementioned example demonstrates how people utilize honor to create identities that are acceptable to society. This specific architecture holds that a man's main responsibility is to safeguard the ladies in his household. Understanding sexual behavior and what is deemed 'appropriate' or culturally/socially suitable, for instance, becomes crucial to honor when a man is defending a woman. This is because honor is closely linked to women's sexual behavior, with sex being seen as an act that should, at the very least, only happen after marriage and only with her husband.

These cases also show how closely related virginity and honor are in Jordan; in fact, it is nearly hard to distinguish between the two ideas. Given that female family members are the ones who uphold "honor" by their behavior, sexual behavior—which is symbolized by a physical hymen—is the most reliable indicator of this. The story of Fatima serves as an example of this.

Situation 12: Fatima

Two court dates were set for this case: one in 2005 and one in 2006. The conviction in the first trial was substantially lowered after it was successfully appealed. The provisions of Article 98 of the Criminal Code were applied in the second trial, further lowering the penalty to a year in prison. In this instance, it is claimed that the victim, Fatima, fled the family home in September 2004 and started dating a witness named Murad Badwan. According to the court documentation, Fatima had premarital sex with Murad and became pregnant. Following the discovery of this by the police, Fatima lived in with Murad and the victim and witness were forced into marriage. After that, there were marital issues between the couple, with Fatima occasionally residing at her parents' or one of her brothers' homes. She reportedly spent over two weeks at the home of her parents at one time, and it is said that she had multiple meetings with her brother during this time. Additionally, it's said that they got along well at this point and that Fatima's relationships with her other brothers returned to "normal" in the sense that she wasn't living in constant fear and that her brothers weren't threatening to kill her. However, the accused met his sister at marketplace on September 10, 2004, at about nine o'clock at night, and he questioned her what she was up to there at such a late hour. "It is not your cause for concern," she retorted. Nobody cares what I do, whether I rent myself or come and go. The accused is said to have become enraged by this, pulled out his unlicensed gun, and fired Fatima 5 times, assassinating her.

During the first hearing in 2005, the defense attorney's plea to apply Article 98 was denied, and the defendant was given a sentence of seven and a half years in jail. However, the verdict was appealed in 2006, and it was tried by a different court with a new judge. As a result, Article 98 was applied, as decided upon by all parties, and the person in question was sentenced to one year in jail. Additionally, in compliance with Article 98, the accused's defense attorney submitted a thorough statement to the court outlining the following reasons why the accused person should receive a lighter sentence. The person who died was a woman who, like much of Jordan & the Arab world, lived in a small, devout community that adheres to rigid culture and tradition. A man's honor is the most valuable thing in this region of the globe, especially the honor of his sister, which he values and swears by. The victim performed the most heinous deed, bringing shame upon her entire family, even though she was aware of how vital it is for women to maintain their honor. Her family has also been humiliated by her activities. Additionally, the family distanced themselves from society and the remainder of the hamlet due to the humiliation and dishonor she brought upon

(12/2005)

The attorney's letter and testimony were included into the record by the judge and were taken into account during the appeal process. Several of the accused's relatives also gave testimony. "The person being accused is a brother of mine and the one who was assaulted is my sister," the accused's brother stated to the court during his testimony. My sister became pregnant before getting married thanks to an illegal connection. Everyone in my family and I feel ashamed and dishonored as a result of her acts. We were no longer allowed to interact with the rest of the neighbors or even visit the neighborhood bakery to get bread because of her activities, which also caused me to quit from my position.

(12/2005)

The presiding judge provided justification for the appeal during the hearing process, stating that the victim's actions made it possible for the court to determine the cause of the accused's rage and anger, and that as a result, the circumstances surrounding the application of Article 98 are clearly visible. The victim's notoriety is well-known to everyone in the little hamlet of Kafanjarah, where rumors about her are centered around her. She has therefore brought shame and dishonor to her family, and the court will find sufficient proof in what she said to her brother the night before she was shot to comprehend how the accused would be furious. He became enraged because he felt humiliated and disregarded by his sister, and the victim's speech to him in public, in the center of the town, was an attack on his masculinity. Consequently, the court finds that the person charged will receive a lighter sentence, and Article 98 will go into effect.

Additional witnesses were called into evidence, and the accused's defense lawyer requested that a family member address the court. In this testimony, the relative gave clarification, stating, "I recognize the person accused and his sister since they are my family." The person in question did not conceive naturally, as far as I know. They feel embarrassed and dishonored because of the family's actions, which have damaged their reputation.

PRESENT SCENARIO

In Jordan, a number of initiatives have been implemented in the last 20 years to address the problem of honor-based violence. The Family Protection Department was established by the Jordanian government in 1997 to look into incidents of sexual assault and domestic abuse against women and children. A few years later, in 2001, a new provision was added to Article 340, which states that any man who attacks or kills his wife or any of his female relatives in the act of committing adultery or in "an unlawful bed" is eligible for a reduced sentence. This provision grants female suspects the same penalty reduction as men. A fatwa stating that honor killings are incompatible with Islam was given by the government's Religious Endowments department in 2016.It was said in the fatwa that these kind of murders are among the most horrible crimes in society. In Jordan, family members kill 15 to 20 women and girls each year by burning, beating, or stabbing them to death because they are seen to have broken traditional norms of "honor."

It's possible that a rise in these murders in 2016 was the catalyst for the authorities' eventual intervention. Compared to other kind of murders, "honor" killings are frequently accorded more lax punishment. If a man kills or assaults his wife or any female relative because he believes she is an adulterer or because he has committed an act in a "unlawful bed," the punishment may be reduced under Article 340 of the Penal Code. Many scenarios don't fit these requirements.

However, under Article 98 of the Penal Code, if the offender commits the offense in a "state of great fury [fit of fury] resulting from an unlawful and dangerous act on the part of the victim," the sentence may still be reduced. Article 97 stipulates that a court may impose a sentence as little as a year on premeditated murder when it grants the "fit of fury" defense. The clemency requests of the victims' relatives also frequently result in sentencing reductions. This is typically the case since "honor killings" sometimes involve family members of the victim who are complicit. In these situations, the killer's sentence may be reduced by half under Article 99.

The decision "will set a precedent and become the rule in line of which other verdicts in similar circumstances will be handled in the future," according to Judge Tarawneh.

Cases with penalties shorter than five years will only come before a higher court if an appeal is filed by the prosecution, but sentences of five years or more will automatically be referred to one for review. If Parliament approves suggested changes to the Penal Code, these loopholes might close, which would be a monumental step toward combating impunity for "honor" killings.

The Royal Committee for Developing the Judiciary and Enhancing the Rule of Law proposed reforms to the Cabinet on March 15. Among other things, these reforms repeal Article 340 of the Penal Code and forbid the use of the Article 98 "fit of fury" defense in cases involving crimes against women in order to uphold "honor. "In addition, Parliament must also forbid lowered sentences in instances involving "honor" killings, irrespective of the desire for clemency shown by the victim's relatives However, changing the Penal Code is not the sole option to address gender-based violence. Additionally, authorities must implement a thorough national plan to stop these kinds of crimes, safeguard people in danger, and bring criminal charges against those who commit "honor" crimes. To safeguard potential victims and oppose discriminatory attitudes, authorities should collaborate with activists, local women's rights organizations, religious and community leaders, police officers, social workers, teachers, and health professionals. The Sisterhood Is Global Institute (SIGI) in Jordan has urged for the establishment of a nationwide system by the government to monitor and report the number of such murders that occur. Included in the information should be the reason behind the crime, the victim-attacker relationship, the existence of any complaints, and the punishments imposed on the murderer and any accomplices. Those who are at risk of "honor" violence should be protected by the authorities, not punished. At the moment, women and girls who are at risk of "honor" killings are placed in protective care; nonetheless, this frequently entails incarceration. According to local campaigners, these women may end up serving years in prison without being charged. Furthermore, there are instances where family members promise not to hurt them but then murder them later. The authorities have not yet opened the shelter where they had planned to lodge victims at risk of honor violence, despite their announcement in December.

The deep-rooted discrimination that upholds the idea that female "moral" behavior is essential for maintaining the honor of their families and communities, as well as the expectation of male family members to prevent and purge any transgressions of "honor" through violence, should be addressed by government, community, and religious leaders. The killings committed in "honor" can be stopped. Authorities should implement the changes made to the Penal Code, offer victim-centered protection—such as safe havens for individuals in danger—and use public awareness campaigns and education to challenge the detrimental norms and gender discrimination that fuel this kind of violence. Women and girls in Jordan are at danger of losing their lives.

Amidst legal reforms and advocacy efforts, there are still difficulties in addressing and combating honor killings, as evidenced by recent occurrences in Jordan. Here are a few noteworthy instances over the past several years:

The death of Dua'a, a 22-year-old woman, in 2021 garnered much public attention on honor killings in Jordan. Because her brother believed that Dua'a's extramarital affair had brought disgrace to the family, he killed her. Stronger legal safeguards and enforcement against honor-based violence were called for once again in response to the case, which caused considerable indignation.

2. The Hanan Case:

The year 2020 saw the murder of Hanan, a 26-year-old lady, by her siblings and father. Because she was allegedly involved in a relationship that they did not approve of, they claimed that she was dishonoring the family. Because of prevalent societal attitudes and the application of traditional values, the perpetrators of the case were first awarded moderate punishments, which brought attention to the difficulties in prosecuting honor crimes.

3. Sarah's Case:

Sarah, a 19-year-old, was murdered by her father in 2019. According to reports, she was accused of acting in a way that went against conventional norms, which ultimately led to her death. Human rights organizations called for stricter steps to safeguard women and properly enforce law reforms in response to the case, which sparked protests.

4. Aisha's Case: Aisha, a 24-year-old, was killed in 2018 by her brother, who said that by filing for divorce, she had embarrassed the family. The case brought attention to the persistence of patriarchal standards and the necessity of stronger support networks for women attempting to flee violent environments.

These incidents highlight the ongoing problems with honor-based violence in Jordan and highlight the necessity of carrying out ongoing initiatives to fortify legal frameworks, assist victims, and subvert cultural norms that encourage this kind of violence.

CONCLUSION

The concept of gender and honor are closely related in Jordan, where the debate over gender equality has persisted for a considerable amount of time (Al-Badayneh, 2012). It's still a big issue: sufferers aren't given the opportunity to defend their honor or offer their point of view of the story, and many have been stripped of their fives due to honor crimes that were committed based on rumors and presumptions. One of the primary conclusions of this study is that Jordan cannot undergo transformation by merely changing the laws and punishments pertaining to crimes of honor. It is obvious that society is not prepared for change, yet the government is willing to accept it. In Jordan, honor crimes are arguably governed by two codes: one established by society and the other by the legal fraternity. The expectations of the state for a citizen and what society expects of a family and individual clearly collide in the instance of honor crimes. The fact that these crimes still happen in spite of higher penalties shows that, despite recent legal reforms, society's moral code is still very strong.

In Jordan, significant societal transformations are required to curtail and eliminate honor crimes. Poor documentation and investigation of incidents where women were killed for honor was one of the main issues preventing a thorough review of the court files. The inadequacy of lawyer-prepared court files hindered the ability of victim and survivor families to receive justice, as they frequently lacked crucial information like witness and defense statements. In these situations, victim risk identification is an urgent matter. In Jordan, procedures must be in place to recognize and reduce risk prior to the commission of an honor crime. The completion of a form should not be the criterion for evaluating the effectiveness of the law enforcement's response to an honor crime or abuse. It needs to be about whether the officer accurately assessed the degree of risk, acted appropriately in situations where homicide did not occur as a result, and secured or preserved evidence required for legal action. Thus, there is a serious deficiency in the entire enforcement and judiciary response to these honor crimes, failing to protect victims or bring criminals to justice(Gill,2019). The crimes of honor and gender-based violence are still major, ingrained issues in Jordanian society, despite a number of encouraging recent developments to address these issues such as outreach efforts by women's rights defenders in Jordan's to raise consciousness regarding these human rights violations. Enhancing police responses and creating more useful policies and initiatives for the justice system in general are urgently needed. Women's organizations, for instance, have taken the lead in the UK to recognize honor killings as a particular issue that needs immediate international attention. They have also argued that the best course of action is to fund the prosecution of those who commit these crimes, the education of college and university students about the harms associated with gender, and the funding of specialized services efforts across a variety of community agencies (Gill,2019). It is not necessary to deny the value of honor in Jordan; rather, society there has to adjust its perception of honor, and in order to do this, significant social reforms must be made. In the framework of a cultural group, honor is fixed; attempts to change it solely though legal and legislative methods will fail, and in Jordan, these attempts will fail unless culturally sensitive revisions of the gender gap receive careful consideration. It is not necessary to downplay the importance of respect in Jordon; rather, society there needs to change the way it views honor, which will need important socioeconomic reforms. Within an ethnic group, honor remains in place and attempts to alter it through legal and legislative means alone will not succeed.

REFERENCES

Abu-Hassan, R., & Welchman, L. (2005). Changing the rules? Development on 'crimes of honor' in Jordan. In Hossain, S., & Welchman, L. (Eds.), *Honor' Crimes, Paradigms, and Violence Against Women.* Zed Books. DOI: 10.5040/9781350220621.ch-009

Al-Ali, S. (2018). Patriarchal structures and gender dynamics in honor killings. *Gender Studies Quarterly*, 23(3), 147–160.

Al-Badayneh, D. (2012). Violence against women in Jordan. *. *Journal of Family Violence*, 27(5), 369–379. DOI: 10.1007/s10896-012-9429-1

Al-Krenawi, A. (2021). Psychological impact of honor-based violence: A study of victims and offenders in Jordan. *The Japanese Psychological Research*, 18(4), 201–220.

Al-Momani, H. (2020). The role of media and advocacy in addressing honor killings in Jordan. *Media and Society Review*, 30(2), 234–250.

) - Amnesty International. (2018). The state of human rights in the Middle East and North Africa.

Araji, S. K., & Carlson, J. (2001). Family violence including crimes of honor in Jordan: Correlates and perceptions of seriousness. *Violence Against Women*, 7(5), 586–621. DOI: 10.1177/10778010122182613

Awwad, A. (2001). Gossip, scandal, shame and honor killing: A case for social constructionism and hegemonic discourse. *Social Thought & Research*, 20, 45. DOI: 10.17161/STR.1808.5180

El Muhtaseb, R. (2020). Gender-based violence and the law in Jordan: Legal reforms and cultural challenges. *International Journal of Middle East Studies*, 52(1), 45–63.

El Muhtaseb, R., & Husseini, R. (2009). *Murder in the name of honour: The true story of one woman's heroic fight against an unbelievable crime.* Oneworld Publications.

Faqir, F. (2001). Intrafamily femicide in defence of honor: The case of Jordan. *. *Third World Quarterly*, 22(1), 65–82. DOI: 10.1080/713701138

Fernandez, M. (2006). *Cultural beliefs and domestic violence.* New York Academy of Sciences. DOI: 10.1196/annals.1385.005

Gill, A. K. (2019). Social and cultural implications of 'honor'-based violence. In Reilly, N. (Ed.), *International Human Rights: Human Rights of Women*. Springer. DOI: 10.1007/978-981-10-8905-3_25

Human Rights Watch. (2019). *Institutional responses to honor-based violence.*

Mansur, Y., Shteiwi, M., & Murad, N. (2009). The economic underpinnings of honor crimes in Jordan. Information and Research Centre, King Hussein Foundation, Jordan.

)Odeh, A. L. (1996). Crimes of honor and the construction of gender in Arab societies.

Plant, R. (2006). Honor killings and the asylum gender gap. *Journal of Transnational Law & Policy*, 15(2).

Roberts, J. (2022). Comparative analysis of honor-based violence: Jordan and the Middle East. *International Journal of Comparative Studies*, 15(1), 102–118.

Shteiwi, M. Y., Murad, N., & Mansur, Y. (2009). The economic underpinnings of honor crimes in Jordan. Information and Research Centre, King Hussein Foundation, Jordan.

Sonbol, A. (2003). *Women of Jordan: Islam, labour and the law*. Syracuse University Press.

Tunick, M. (2004). Can culture excuse crime? Evaluating the inability thesis. Punishment & Society, 6(2), 201-217.

Chapter 9
A Critical Analysis of Honor-Based Violence in Lebanon

Abhijit Mishra
Bennett University, India

Radhika Goswami
GLA University, Mathura, India

ABSTRACT

A violent crime known as "honor killing" is carried out by one or more people with the goal of restoring honor to their family. The chapter looks into the Eastern Mediterranean region's honor killing epidemic. In addition, the legal, cultural, and societal facets of honor killing in Lebanon are covered. The practice of killing for honor is influenced by a variety of sociocultural elements in this area. These include of having little education, wanting to preserve one's social standing, and strongly ingrained patriarchal dominance. Criminals that commit honor killings often share traits, such as appraising female chastity more highly and endorsing violence against women. Honor killing has a far bigger effect on family members than families may think since the community disapproves of the woman's dishonorable behaviour. These civilizations are dominated by a silence culture, and there are a lot of crimes in this area that go unreported.

For such horrible crimes, a court trial is frequently not held. A few crucial actions that must be taken to stop the social evil of honor killing in this area are changes to the penal legislation, efforts for the defense of human rights, changes to the educational system, and the active participation of civil society in condemning such crimes.

DOI: 10.4018/979-8-3693-7240-1.ch009

There were 813 cases of violent crimes in 2021, up significantly from 415 in 2020, according to the Observatory of Crimes of Violence Against Women in Egypt's most current figures. The Jordanian Women's Solidarity Association released data earlier this year that indicated there will be a 94% spike in violence against women in 2022.

KEY TERMS

The nucleus of the term includes "Critical Analysis" and "Honour Based violence", 'Lebanon"(KAFA, 2006) "Virginity", (Gorar, M. (2021) and "Women" (Walters, G.D, 2001) contextualise the issue "Assault" and "Murder" (hampandi, n.d.) "happens against women" (Glazer & Abu- Ras, 1994) because of "dominance" of "patriarchal Society" (Walters, G.D, 2001), "Low literacy and "Economic inequality" (Conanghan, C., 1998), Equal rights (Khater A.F, 2006). We used these keywords to select relevant articles from multiple online sources, for example, Research Gate, Google Books, Springer, JSTOR, Sage Scopus, Web of Science, Francis and Google Scholar.

An Honor Killings Research Paper on its Family Honor and Forces of change in Arab Society requires careful consideration of inclusion/exclusion and article research, as well as the selection of appropriate publications. Publications with an emphasis on international law, gender studies, human rights, and related interdisciplinary topics were chosen for publishing in the journal selection process. To further sort through the research publications that are pertinent to this Chapter, we have established inclusion and exclusion criteria. The study can only be published in English in journal articles, which are defined as those with an impact factor of 1.0 or higher in peer-reviewed papers and Journal Citation Reports, or as those with a grade of B or above on the Journal Quality list. The research that looked at "experience" as a concept or variable in the context of ecotourism met our inclusion requirements.

RESEARCH METHODOLOGY

In my research paper, thorough understanding of people's experiences, perspectives, and social circumstances, qualitative research aims to explore complicated phenomena. In contrast to quantitative approaches, which prioritize numerical data and statistical analysis, qualitative research aims to comprehend the relevance and meaning of social interactions and human behavior. Walters, G.D, (2001) Qualitative research provides rich, descriptive data that can highlight patterns, themes, and relationships by exploring the nuances of human experience through methods including focus groups, interviews, and content analysis. This kind of research is especially useful for complex problems where context and personal experience are important since it offers a more nuanced perspective that enhances more quantitative conclusions.

LITERATURE REVIEW

Siddiqui, 2005 in this article expressed the issue of identity and true self which that according to feminist which card is an ideal of essential to self is firmly located within a primorbial holestic world view of the goddess embodied in nature. In my views Beckford's mention of identity and true self in relation to feminist thought highlights the idea that the concept of an "essential self" is often connected to a primordial and holistic worldview. According to this perspective, the ideal self is deeply intertwined with a goddess figure who embodies nature. This means that identity and the true self are seen as rooted in a natural, spiritual, and holistic understanding of the world, rather than being defined by modern, fragmented views. Essentially, it suggests that our true identity is fundamentally linked to a larger, all-encompassing natural order.

Gorar, M. (2021) in her article *'Female Sexual Autonomy, Virginity, and Honor Based Violence with Special Focus on U.K'* argue about the women's self- autonomy, discriminatory requirements set for women and consider violation of the same as crime against their honor. She argues that before the wedding night, how her virginity matters and how women are killed on violation of it. She also highlighted the need to address this mentality of society. The author has further argued that the reason behind this heinous practice is immigration of people in western world.

Abu-Lughod, 2011 examines various reports, relevant literature and studies and tries to find out the factors which maintains the cultural violence in the society. The Author also critically analyzed the honor crimes in Sweden, Germany, Turkey, Jordan, Palestine and other countries.

Kulczycki, A., & Windle, S. (2011) in their research has reviewed the research of honor killings in the Middle East and North Africa (MENA). Authors have highlighted that victims are young girls killed by their male family members.

FUTURE RESEARCH DIRECTIONS

In this chapter the author has covered topics like the phenomenon of honor killing which defines the killing in Lebanon were te crimes against women were the women is assaulted by their family and by their relatives due to lack of literacy, discrimination, and inequality.

Also, the author have mentioned articles which states Article 562 is mentioned that exploitation against women and this is criminal code which give the punishment to those who killed their daughter and wife on the name of family reputation. (Patel & Gadit, 2008)

And the author also mentioned the gender roles of men and women in Lebanon. In Lebanon the women raised gently, and the men raised dominating and aggressive. As in future the topics can be research upon hands on killers and conspirators and their psychology, why only the women are the victims of honor killing and the legal status of the women in the society.

While this chapter provides valuable insights into the phenomenon of honor killings, it is important to acknowledge its limitations and identify areas for future exploration. Understanding these limitations not only contextualizes the findings but also highlights opportunities for further research that could enhance our comprehension of honor-based violence like Men can also be the victim of Honor killing, Gender bias in existing Culture and others.

INTRODUCTION

Any kind of abuse or violence committed to uphold the honor of a family or community is referred to as honor-based violence (HBV). Most typically, women are the victims of honor crimes. Men and boys can also become victims, albeit this is far less frequent (AlQahtani et al., 2022). A person's vulnerability to violence can be increased by a number of variables, including ignorance of their legal rights, unemployment, social support, and economic vulnerability. Moreover, patriarchal society, which regards the man as the head of the household and assigns him the responsibility of opposing any act of dishonor, Honor-based violence (HBV) is any abuse or violence done in order to protect the honor of a family or community. Women are most frequently the victims of honor crimes. Boys and men can also become victims, albeit this is much less common (Patel & Gadit, 2008). The majority of victims of honor crimes are women. Though it happens far less frequently, men and boys can still become victims.

A person may be more prone to violence for a variety of reasons, including not understanding their legal rights, being unemployed, having no social support, and being in a precarious financial condition. Moreover, patriarchal society, which regards males as the head of the household and anticipates that they will resist any act of disgrace Honor-based violence This often include extramarital affairs as well as flirtation, turning down an arranged marriage, having sex before getting married, and even being sexually assaulted. Any real or perceived transgression of a woman's family, community, or religion's sexual norms is seen as a source of contempt or shame. can bring shame on the household or community. To improve their reputation within the family and in society, the family members plan to murder the woman.

There are several factors that can increase an individual's likelihood of using violence, including ignorance of their legal rights, unemployment, a lack of social support system, and uncertain financial circumstances. Moreover, patriarchal society, which regards males as the head of the household and presumes they won't act in an unworthy manner According to estimates from the World Health Organization (WHO) in 2012, more than 5,000 people are killed each year in the name of honor globally. Studies show that common methods for Burning, stabbing, throwing stones, burning, and strangling are examples of honor crimes. The World Health Organization (WHO) estimated in 2012 that over 5,000 individuals are assassinated annually throughout the world in the sake of honor. Studies reveal that prevalent techniques for honor crimes include burning, stabbing, throwing stones, burning, and strangling. forcing her to throw herself out of a window or ingest poison. Guns, axes, and sharp items are among the weapons that are used occasionally. There are many "honor based" societies, especially in the Eastern Mediterranean Region (EMR), where the concept of honor is highly valued. As a result, many crimes have been perpetrated in the name of honor. The significance these cultures place on women's general social and sexual behaviour helps to explain the HK phenomena in these communities. Due to the strong importance placed on families and social networks in these cultures, HK is a collective decision made by a family or group council. (Heydari et al., 2021) It is driven by particular cultural norms about what makes for honorable behaviour rather than by personal preferences or decisions. Honor killings eventually need to be validated by the community in order to be considered legal. The HK rate fluctuates but is consistently dangerously high in the EMR member countries. As a result, the authors of this research want to elucidate honor killing in the EMR and its legal implications. Additionally, they intend to discuss the social facets of this particular region and elaborate on possible explanations for the elevated occurrence recorded in the EMR. The frequency of honor crimes in the countries that comprise this region and the attitudes of those populations toward Hong Kong are also examined in this study.

THE PHENOMENON OF HONOR KILLING

One of the most horrible and egregious crimes against women is honor killing (Gill, 2006). It is defined as the killing of a woman or girl for reasons connected to her sexual orientation by her own family (father, mother, siblings, uncles, grandparents, etc.) or, less frequently, by other members of the community (Siddiqui, 2005). Divergent opinions about what constitutes appropriate and inappropriate sexual behaviour can be found in communities and occasionally even within families.. In general, this includes flirting, declining an arranged marriage, having sex before being married, and even experiencing sexual assault in addition to having extra-marital affairs. A woman's actual or purported breaking of the sexual norms of her family, society, or religion is viewed as a sign of disdain or disgrace. and disgrace the family or neighbourhood. The family members intend to kill the woman in order to clear their name in the family or society. (Abu-Lughod, 2011)

Honor killings in Lebanon

Virginity is still a sensitive and divisive subject in Lebanon. One of the main things that make women valuable and honorable is their fear of losing their "hymen mystique" before marriage. Hymen repair surgeries have grown prevalent in Lebanon due to patriarchal social standards that perceive a woman as a sinner regardless of the reason for her loss of virginity. Hymens have three purposes: they are honorable, physiological, and social. This study explained the prevalence of hymenoplasty, as well as its causes, problems, and outcomes, as well as its link to women, in light of the dearth of research and literature on the subject. and bringing shame upon the family or community. Honor killings are a common occurrence in Lebanon, where numerous women have perished in the sake of upholding family honor. There are many different causes behind these homicides, but frequently they have to do with a woman's perceived infractions against the standards and beliefs of her community. These offenses might include everything from having a boyfriend to dressing immodestly to having sex before marriage. (KAFA, 2006)

In Lebanon, virginity is still a touchy and contentious topic. Women's dread of losing their "hymen mystique" before marriage is a key component of their value and honor. According to the patriarchal societal standards in Lebanon, a woman who has lost her virginity, regardless of the cause, is a sinner and is not entitled to existential rights. It attempted to investigate, from a structural feminist standpoint, the relationship between hymenoplasty and gender-based violence against women in Lebanon. To analyze the data, women's rights advocates used grounded theory. The results showed that ensuring bleeding during the wedding is the primary goal of hymen restoration. It makes them comply with the boundaries established by society rather than questioning and resisting it. The study ends with suggestions and potential ways to combat GBV. Enacting laws that protect women, removing the stigma associated with non-virginity, educating both genders about their rights and the value of their bodies, and bringing sexual education into schools are all necessary steps toward achieving gender equality and giving women the power to resist practices that violate their rights. Barbaric honor killings continue to be practiced in many regions of the world, including Lebanon. Honor killing is a cruel custom that frequently claims the lives of defenseless people. Honor killings are committed to preserve the family's honor or reputation, which might be damaged by deeds deemed disgraceful, including a woman having an affair, getting married before her time, or defying her family's wishes. Women in Lebanon are frequently the victims of honor killings because the populace believes that a man's honor and family reputation are related to a woman's virginity. This is particularly true when the women are suspected of having an affair with a male. (Gorar, 2021)

Furthermore, men are viewed differently in society when they participate in sexual activities. For example, patriarchates believe that men have sex needs and that it is normal for them to have sex before marriage because a man's virginity never affects anyone's honor or reputation. This demonstrates how honor has always been connected to a woman's virginity in order to prevent women from participating in society on an equal footing with men. In fact, it was discovered that the concept of honor served mainly to constrain and regulate the choices made by women. The dignity of the family is prioritized over the rights and welfare of its individual members under the patriarchal worldview. Women are considered as the property in this situation. make sure they don't embarrass or dishonor their family. In many Lebanese communities, this mentality is strongly embedded, and challenging it can be challenging. (Kulczycki & Windle, 2011) Honor killing is a notion that has become somewhat commonplace, serving as a reminder that we still live in a sexist nation that rewards men for killing women rather than penalizing them.

Honor killings are a common occurrence in Lebanon, where numerous women have perished in the sake of upholding family honor. There are many different causes behind these homicides, but frequently they have to do with a woman's perceived infractions against the standards and beliefs of her community. These offenses can include everything from dressing immodestly to possessing a dating someone or having sex before marriage. Honor killing is illegal in Lebanon, yet it's nonetheless a common practice throughout the nation, especially in the countryside. The Lebanese government has made some efforts to stop the practice, but they have not made much headway because they fear being assassinated by their own family. Indeed, the absence of strong legal protection for women is a major reason in the incidence of honor killings in Lebanon. Honor killings are prohibited, but because the legal system frequently discriminates against women, those who commit these crimes sometimes escape punishment by arguing that what they did was necessary to uphold the honor of their family. Additionally, a lot of women are afraid to disclose domestic abuse situations. violence or abuse to the authorities out of concern for societal disapproval or retaliation. (Heydari et al., 2021)

Human Rights Watch (Human Rights watch, 2016) Middle East women's rights (Chesler, 2010) researcher Nadya Khalife said, "Other Arab countries should follow Lebanon's example and abolish laws that provide excuses for murder and violence." "We applaud this action and hope that the parliament of Lebanon will now amend other laws that discriminate based on gender."

Some regions of the Middle East and North Africa, such as Iraq, Kuwait, Syria, Yemen, and the Occupied Palestinian Territories, have laws that offer lighter punishments for crimes involving honor. Judges frequently apply article 17 of the Egyptian penal code, which permits reduced punishments under "certain circumstances," to instances involving honor crimes. Within Jordan, February 20, 1999 The Lebanese Penal Code's Article 562 provided an exemption from penalty for offenses referred to as "honor crimes." Male characters like husbands, dads, and brothers commit honor crimes when they witness a female relative, like a sister, mother, or wife, do an adulterous or illegal behaviour. (Hasisi & Bernstein, 2019) sexual relations. These offenses may also be directed towards the male spouse involved in the aforementioned sexual activity. The male offenders were spared punishment for committing these offenses in both instances. This article was perceived as being in conflict with Lebanon's adoption of the Universal Declaration of Human Rights. In the end, the article was changed to permit a lighter penalty.

Article 562-CRPC

Article 562 of the Criminal Code, which lessened the punishment for those who claimed to have killed or maimed their wife, daughter, or other relative in order to preserve the family's "honor," was repealed by parliament on August 4, 2011. It is said that honor crimes are not common in Lebanon. A research conducted between 1999 and 2007 by the group KAFA (Enough Violence and Exploitation) listed 66 documented honor crimes. However, Human Rights Watch stated that Article 562 "persisted in the idea that the state approved of such violent crimes when a family's honor was supposedly damaged by a woman who is thought to be "misbehaving. "her roughly ten times in Chouifet, just like a lot of other women in Lebanon. Zeinab endured a significant deal of misogyny in her lifetime, but her family's and society's actions upon her,

Article-17 IPC

In their comments on the news, some people choose to defend the killer, Hassan Moussa Zaiter, by claiming that he suffers from mental health problems, and blame Zeinab for cheating on him. This demonstrates how misogynists will never stop blaming women for being abused and for standing up for men even when they commit crimes. Furthermore, the victim's brother made the decision to upload a video in which he declared his pride in the criminal Hassan for killing Zeinab, viewing the femicide as an honor killing necessary to restore the family's honor. Even if the 21st century is upon us, we are still able to Witness murderers who commit femicides who receive acclaim instead of humiliation and punishment.

Zeinab's murder was not the first to be deemed socially acceptable due to the fact that it was classified as a "honor killing." Similarly, Manal Assi's case gained attention in 2020 after the Murderer Harfoush committed the atrocity against his wife while also killing nine other individuals. Unfortunately, comments such as "What did the wife do to anger her husband?" are frequently left under social media posts about such cases, asking pointless questions that serve to legitimize the femicides.

Every month, a murder case is heard in Lebanon, where it has become routine. This alarming development is concerning and necessitates the adoption of stronger legislation, more awareness-raising initiatives, and more victim support service accessibility. NGOs have been assigned the task, but the state has not responded appropriately or provided the required funding to solve the problem, placing countless women at risk of abuse and violence. Politicians, who have been lying for years about how critical the economic crisis is, nevertheless believe that women are less significant and should be protected with significant efforts and reforms. However, recent events have demonstrated that huge choices, such as relocating the nation's whole time zone, can be made with the mere presence of two powerful politicians at a single meeting.

WOMEN IN LEBANON

Human Rights Watch claims that the Lebanese government is failing to uphold its legal duties to safeguard women from abuse and to end discrimination against them. Trans women, female sex workers, migrants, and those seeking asylum have all been subjected to systemic brutality, including rape, in Lebanese detention facilities. Women employed under the Kafala system as migrant labourers have suffered abuse and contempt from their employers due to a lack of labour standards, especially after the COVID-19 pandemic, the August 2019 financial crisis, as well as the Beirut port explosion in August 2020. The UN Human Rights Council received recommendations from The Universal Periodical Review (UPR) of Lebanon on January 18, 2021, with the goal of enhancing human rights laws and defenses in Lebanon. Given that the nation's most recent review occurred in 2015, Amnesty International stated the Lebanese government should bow to international pressure and address basic concerns With relation to the economic, social, and civic rights of women. During the UPR Working Group meeting, 47 states made proposals that included decriminalizing defamation, doing away with the practice of powerful people using torture and getting away with it, and the Kafala system and bolstering people's freedoms to protest, assemble, and use their right to free speech..

LEGAL FRAMEWORK

Gender inequality in Lebanese society is reinforced in large part by the legal system, especially by its personal status regulations and civil laws. The legal system in Lebanon is modeled after The Egyptian legal system and the French Civil Code, and it maintains the equal treatment of all residents. This is expressed in the Lebanese Constitution of 1926 in Articles 7 and 12, which provide that every person has same rights in employment, politics, and civil society. But particularly with regards to women's rights, this is not the truth. and the ongoing discrimination against them in society. The two main areas of law in Lebanon are personal status and civil laws; Gender inequality is primarily the result of the former. Articles 9 and 10 of the Constitution guarantee religious community members the freedom to adhere to their own rules regarding personal status.as they relate to their beliefs. Therefore, personal status laws—which cover all family-related matters like Religious courts uphold marriage, divorce, and inheritance. As a result, officially recognized religious organizations in Lebanon are empowered to enact and uphold their own unique set of circumstances regulations, separate and apart from the government. These rules frequently perpetuate the idea that women are less valuable than males, portraying them as citizens of a lower class with less more autonomy in their own lives than males These codes are often influenced by religious and cultural ideas. When women get married, this gets worse.In the majority of these religious establishments, the husband serves as the head of the household and its spokesman, seeing the wife and himself as one. Consequently, women who marry are seen as an extension of their husbands and virtually forfeit the majority of their civic rights. Numerous rules from various religious sects in Lebanon provide as evidence of this, giving the husband greater authority over marital matters like divorce and child custody.

Single Mother

Premarital sex and single motherhood are still frowned upon by a significant section of Lebanese culture, and numerous instances of Families in Lebanon have blacklisted Lebanese women for becoming pregnant before being married. Some have even gone so far as to murder their sister or daughter on the grounds that they had sex before marriage, referring to this as a "honor crime".

Workforce

The majority of women in Lebanon under 25 who responded to a survey 75% of respondents to a survey by the Institute for Women's Policy Research (IWPR) and the International Foundation for Electoral Systems (IFES) stated a wish to at least attend college or university. According to reports, business administration (15%), hard sciences (11%) and art and design (10%) are the top study areas for women under 25 Though most women say they aim to work in the future, just 37% of women actually work, compared to 78% of men. The majority of the time, or 58% of the time, women give for not working their housekeeping responsibilities.

Gender Roles

In Lebanon, socialization inside the family throughout childhood shapes gender roles at a young age. According to gender norms and ideals in society, girls are trained to be gentle and obedient, while guys are encouraged to be aggressive and domineering. In the Arab world, this is particularly true. The expectation placed on women from an early age is that they will marry, have children, raise them, and take care of household chores while their husband works to support the family. Consequently, some Because it goes against the social quo, women may feel under pressure to ignore their own goals and careers. They may even encounter barriers in the workplace due to the antiquated belief that women belong in the home as caregivers. (Hasisi & Bernstein, 2019) Married women are sometimes chastised by their partners or families for not wishing to stay at home with the kids and are expected to prioritize their responsibilities at home. This generates a disparity in power between men and women, with men holding more authority, which affects how society views and treats women both at home and in public (BBC, 2014). Nonetheless, as awareness of The marginalization of women in Lebanon and gender equality grows, so does this attitude. In an effort to alter deeply ingrained societal expectations, more women are placing a higher priority on their education and jobs than traditional gender roles.

Religious And Legal Status

In Lebanon, there are fifteen distinct personal status laws that govern personal affairs including marriage and inheritance. The legal status of the Druze, Shi'a, Sunni, and Maronite Christian parties was created the French mandate system along sectarian lines; as a result, these parties "compete to preserve narrow sectarian interests, not those of a unified Lebanon." There are at least fifteen personal status laws in Lebanon, which govern family problems due to the country's wide number of legally recognized religions. As a result, the legal protections available to Lebanese women differ based on their religion. In Muslim households, polygamy is permitted and marriage can begin as soon as a child reaches puberty. Muslim women are allowed to wed Jewish or Christian males. For instance, a Muslim woman may be married to a Lebanese Catholic man, provided that the couple baptizes their children. If not, the pair could choose to foreign civil marriage that is officially recognized by being able to be listed at any embassy of Lebanon. In actuality, this is a really well-liked option, with Cyprus typically being the preferred location.

Despite the inclusion of "equality in rights and obligations between all citizens without distinction or preference" in the Lebanese constitution, some laws still contain discriminatory clauses against women. This is because Lebanese women's citizenship is restricted by personal status restrictions. to the personal status of their fathers and husbands. The legal sectarian affiliation of males determines their personal standing. For instance, Lebanese women are unable to confer their nationality on a non-Lebanese spouse or offspring.

Feminism and Activism

Women who take part in political associations frequently face shame from society. For instance, many of the female members of the Palestinian resistance organization reside in camps in Lebanon. These ladies "frequently sleep away from home and attend political meetings at night." For doing so, many have been referred to as prostitutes. However, they have not wavered in their belief that family comes before country. Awareness of violence against women in Lebanon has grown thanks to local and regional efforts. Unfortunately, there are inadequate government rules regarding this, and efforts to enact new legislation that would shield women from abuse have encountered opposition. Spousal rape is not recognized by Lebanon's legal system and attempts to include it in the legislation have run afoul of Lebanese clergy. Every year, eight to eleven spouse killings and rapes are reported in the media.

To end domestic abuse of women, including spousal rape, A proposed Law to Safeguard Women from Family Violence was suggested in 2010. Due to the protests of religious conservatives, this measure was repeatedly changed over the course of its time trapped in Parliament. The section of the statute that listed marital rape as a criminal was removed as part of the amendment suggestions. A law against sexual harassment was passed by the Lebanese parliament. in December 2020, with potential jail sentences of up to four years for anyone who commit the offense.

CONCLUSION

In conclusion, underreporting of HKs persists and results in the loss of several innocent lives under false pretenses. Honor crimes are a serious problem that require serious attention, particularly in areas with low socioeconomic level and in nations with patriarchal societies. Due to the fact that these crimes are frequently justified and that the laws of many EMR countries can be lax in this regard, this research unequivocally highlights how important this matter is and how urgently legislation action is required. The lack of strong regulations has exacerbated the patriarchal hierarchy and impacted women's sense of protection and security. To close the gaps in the literature, further study on the subject of HK is also required. Additionally, The lack of strong regulations has exacerbated the patriarchal hierarchy and impacted women's sense of protection and security. To close the gaps in the literature, further study on the subject of HK is also required. Furthermore, because patriarchal dominance against women is believed to have a somewhat subjective moral justification in many Eastern Mediterranean societies, there is a greater need for willingness to change the unjust patriarchal infrastructure of these societies and end patriarchal dominance practices.

REFERENCES

Abu-Lughod, L. (2011). Seductions of the 'honor crime'. *Differences: A Journal of Feminist Cultural Studies*, 22(1), 17–63. DOI: 10.1215/10407391-1218238

AlQahtani, S., Almutairi, D., BinAqeel, E. A., Almutairi, R. A., Al-Qahtani, R. D., & Menezes, R. G. (2022). Honour Killings in the Eastern Mediterranean Region: A Narrative Review. *Health Care*, 11(1), 74. Advance online publication. DOI: 10.3390/healthcare11010074 PMID: 36611534

BBC. (2014, May 29). Why Do Families Kill Their Daughters? *BBC News*.

Chesler, P. (2010, Spring). Worldwide Trends in Honor Killing. *Middle East Quarterly*, 17, 3–11.

Conanghan, C. (1998): *Tort Litigation in the context of Intra- Familial Abuse in The Modern Law Review.* Vol 61

Glazer, I. M., & Ras, W. A. (1994). On aggression, human rights, and hegemonic discourse: The case of a murder for family honor in Israel. *Sex Roles*, 30, 269–288.

Gorar, M. (2021). Female sexual autonomy, virginity, and honour-based violence with special focus on the UK. *Journal of International Women's Studies*, 22(5), 5.

Hasisi, B., & Bernstein, D. (2019). Echoes of domestic silence: Mechanisms of concealment in cases of family honour killings in mandat Palestine. *Middle Eastern Studies*, 55(1), 60–73. DOI: 10.1080/00263206.2018.1485659

Heydari, A., Teymoori, A., & Trappes, R. (2021). Honor killing as a dark side of modernity: Prevalence, common discourses, and a critical view. *Social Sciences Information. Information Sur les Sciences Sociales*, 60(1), 86–106. DOI: 10.1177/0539018421994777

Human Rights watch. (2016). *Report on Lebanon: Reform Rape Laws.*

KAFA (2006). *Minutes of Regional Meeting on Legislation for Protection against Domestic Violence. Khater A.F (2006). Like Pure Gold: Sexuality and Honor Amongst Lebanese Immigrants, 1819-1920.*

Kulczycki, A., & Windle, S. (2011). Honor killings in the Middle East and North Africa. *Violence Against Women*, 17(11), 1442–1464. DOI: 10.1177/1077801211434127 PMID: 22312039

Patel, S., & Gadit, A. (2008). Karo-kari: A form of honour killing in Pakistan. *Transcultural Psychiatry*, 45(4), 683–694. DOI: 10.1177/1363461508100790 PMID: 19091732

Walters, G. D. (2001). The Relationship between masculinity, femininity, and criminal thinking in male and female offenders. *Sex Roles*, 45(9), 677–689. DOI: 10.1023/A:1014819926761

Chapter 10
Honor-Related Crimes in Egypt

Harshita Singh
Amity University, Noida, India

Deeksha Pandey
GLA University, Mathura, India

ABSTRACT

In Egypt, honor-related crimes constitute a complex and deeply rooted societal issue, reflecting a convergence of cultural norms, patriarchal structures, and legal ambiguities. These crimes predominantly target women perceived to have brought shame upon their families through alleged moral transgressions, such as premarital sex, extramarital affairs, or even suspicion thereof. The concept of family honor intertwines with societal expectations of female chastity and obedience, often enforced through rigid social codes and religious interpretations. Despite legislative reforms aimed at protecting women's rights, including amendments to penal codes, the implementation remains inconsistent, influenced by familial and community pressures, as well as perceptions of shame and dishonor.

Honor-related crimes represent a complex and deeply rooted societal issue with significant implications for individuals, families, and communities. This chapter explores the landscape of honor-related crimes in Egypt, shedding light on the cultural, social, and legal dimensions that contribute to the perpetuation of such acts. Drawing on a combination of scholarly research, legal analysis, and case studies, this chapter aims to provide a nuanced understanding of the factors driving honor-related crimes in Egypt. The study delves into the historical context, examining the cultural and traditional norms that have shaped perceptions of honor in Egyptian society. It explores the role of gender dynamics, family structures, and patriarchal

DOI: 10.4018/979-8-3693-7240-1.ch010

Copyright © 2025, IGI Global. Copying or distributing in print or electronic forms without written permission of IGI Global is prohibited.

traditions in influencing attitudes towards honor, often resulting in the justification of violence against individuals, especially women, perceived to have violated societal expectations.

Honor-related crimes in Egypt have been a significant concern, though comprehensive statistics can be challenging to obtain. Reports indicate that such crimes, which often involve violence against women perceived to have dishonoured the family, are notably prevalent. For instance, the Egyptian National Council for Women has highlighted that honor-based violence includes assaults, forced marriages, and even murders, primarily targeting women and girls. Despite efforts to combat these issues, cultural and legal obstacles persist, complicating the accurate measurement and reporting of these crimes. The actual figures might be underreported due to stigma, fear of retaliation, and inadequate legal protections.

The legal framework surrounding honor-related crimes in Egypt is also scrutinized, assessing the adequacy and enforcement of existing laws and regulations. The chapter discusses challenges in the legal system, such as gaps in legislation, insufficient protection for victims, and societal attitudes that may hinder effective prosecution and prevention. Moreover, the chapter highlights the impact of technological advancements and globalization on changing societal norms, potentially challenging traditional views on honor. It explores the role of education and awareness campaigns in challenging ingrained beliefs and fostering a more inclusive and egalitarian society.

RESEARCH METHODOLOGY

A qualitative research approach to studying honor-related crimes in Egypt involves examining the cultural, social, and legal contexts that contribute to these practices. This research could include conducting in-depth interviews with survivors, community members, and activists to understand personal experiences and perspectives on honor-related violence. Focus groups with diverse stakeholders, such as religious leaders, social workers, and legal experts, can reveal varying beliefs and attitudes about honor and gender roles. Additionally, participant observation within affected communities can provide insights into the everyday social dynamics and cultural norms that perpetuate these crimes. Analysing court cases and media reports allows researchers to explore how honor-related crimes are framed and addressed within legal and public discourses. This multi-method qualitative approach provides a comprehensive understanding of the factors that sustain honor-related violence in Egypt, highlighting the need for targeted interventions and policy reforms.

KEY TERMS

Key terms for a chapter on honor-related crimes in Egypt should include "honor-based violence," which refers to acts of violence committed to protect or defend the honor of a family, often targeting women and girls (Abdelmonem & Galal, 2019). Another important term is "gender-based violence," which highlights how these crimes are deeply rooted in gender inequality and societal norms (Ahmed, 2020). "Cultural relativism" is also a key concept, as it relates to the understanding of how cultural beliefs and practices influence perceptions and justifications of honor-related crimes (Youssef & Farag, 2021). Lastly, "legal framework" and "human rights" are essential terms to explore the legal responses and human rights implications associated with these crimes (Ibrahim & Soliman, 2018).

LITERATURE REVIEW

A literature review on honor-related crimes in Egypt reveals a complex interplay of cultural, social, and legal factors that sustain these practices. Studies indicate that honor crimes are often justified by traditional notions of family honor, which heavily emphasize female chastity and obedience (Sholkamy, Hania. 2002) Research also highlights the role of patriarchal structures and gender norms in legitimizing violence against women, often as a means of controlling their Behavior and maintaining male authority (Kandiyoti, D. 1991). The legal system in Egypt is often criticized for its leniency towards perpetrators, with some laws offering reduced sentences for those who commit crimes in the name of honor (UN Women. 2019). Furthermore, societal attitudes and the stigma surrounding victims of honor crimes contribute to a culture of silence, making it difficult for survivors to seek justice or support (Amer, M. 2016) Overall, the literature underscores the need for comprehensive legal reforms, increased awareness, and cultural change to address and prevent honor-related violence in Egypt.

Future Research Directions

Future research on honor-related crimes in Egypt should focus on a multidimensional approach that includes sociocultural, legal, and psychological perspectives. One key area of exploration is the impact of societal norms and gender roles on the perpetuation of honor-based violence, as well as the effectiveness of current legal frameworks in addressing these crimes (El-Sayed & Hammami, 2022). Additionally, research should investigate the psychological motivations and pressures faced by perpetrators, as well as the support systems available for victims.

Exploring community-based interventions and educational programs could also provide insights into preventative measures and the promotion of gender equality (Kamal & Mostafa, 2021).

INTRODUCTION

Historically, honor-related crimes have been intertwined with cultural and traditional norms that prioritize family reputation over individual rights, particularly those of women. In Egypt, these norms are deeply embedded in the social fabric, where honor is often linked to the Behavior of female family members. Women who are perceived to have violated societal expectations, whether through relationships, behaviour, or even rumours, may face severe repercussions, including violence and murder (El-Nadeem Centre for Rehabilitation of Victims of Violence, 2018). Such acts are frequently justified under the guise of preserving family honor, reflecting a patriarchal value system that subjugates women's autonomy and rights.

Gender dynamics and family structures play a critical role in the perpetuation of honor-related crimes. Patriarchal traditions in Egypt reinforce male authority over female family members, creating a power imbalance that facilitates control and violence. Men are often seen as the protectors of family honor, with the responsibility to punish perceived transgressions to restore the family's reputation (UN Women, 2017). This dynamic not only victimizes women but also perpetuates a cycle of violence and control that is difficult to break.

Legal frameworks in Egypt have historically been insufficient in addressing honor-related crimes. Although there have been some reforms, significant gaps remain in legislation and its enforcement. The Egyptian Penal Code, for instance, contains provisions that can be interpreted to justify lenient sentences for honor crimes, reflecting societal attitudes that condone such violence (Human Rights Watch, 2021). Victims of honor-related crimes often face barriers in seeking justice, including societal pressure to remain silent, fear of retribution, and lack of effective legal support.

Technological advancements and globalization are gradually influencing societal norms, potentially challenging traditional views on honor. The spread of information through social media and other digital platforms is raising awareness about gender equality and human rights, providing a counter-narrative to traditional beliefs. This shift is particularly evident among younger generations, who are increasingly questioning patriarchal norms and advocating for change (Amnesty International, 2022).

Education and awareness campaigns are crucial in addressing the root causes of honor-related crimes. Initiatives that promote gender equality, human rights, and the negative impacts of honor-based violence can help shift societal perceptions.

Educational programs targeting schools, community centers, and media outlets are essential in fostering a more inclusive and egalitarian society. Empowering women through education and economic opportunities is also vital in reducing their vulnerability to such crimes (National Council for Women, 2019).

Furthermore, community-based approaches involving local leaders, religious figures, and activists can create a supportive environment for change. These initiatives can promote dialogue about the value of women and the importance of their rights, gradually shifting societal perceptions. Establishing support networks and safe spaces for women at risk of honor-related violence can provide immediate assistance and long-term protection. This includes creating shelters and hotlines staffed by trained professionals who can offer psychological support, legal advice, and other necessary services (UN Women, 2020).

Media plays a powerful role in shaping public opinion and should be leveraged to combat honor-related crimes. Media campaigns that highlight the stories of survivors, educate the public about the legal and moral implications of honor crimes, and promote positive role models can help to challenge stereotypes and stigmatization. Training journalists to report on these issues sensitively and accurately is crucial in ensuring that media coverage contributes to awareness and change rather than reinforcing harmful norms (UN Women, 2023).

International cooperation and support can enhance national efforts to combat honor-related crimes. Partnerships with international organizations can provide technical assistance, funding, and best practice models. Egypt can benefit from participating in global networks that address violence against women, enabling the exchange of knowledge and strategies. Additionally, international pressure and advocacy can encourage the Egyptian government to prioritize this issue and adhere to international human rights standards (Human Rights Watch, 2021).

In conclusion, addressing honor-related crimes in Egypt requires a holistic approach that combines legal reforms, educational initiatives, social interventions, media engagement, international cooperation, and robust monitoring and evaluation mechanisms. By tackling the issue from multiple angles and involving all sectors of society, it is possible to create a cultural shift that condemns honor-based violence and upholds the rights and dignity of all individuals. This multifaceted strategy not only addresses the immediate needs of victims but also fosters long-term societal change, paving the way for a future where honor crimes are eradicated and gender equality is a reality.

HISTORICAL CONTEXT OF HONOR IN EGYPT: A COMPREHENSIVE ANALYSIS

The historical context of honor in Egypt is deeply embedded in its rich cultural and societal evolution. Honor in Egyptian society is intricately linked to traditional values, family reputation, and societal expectations. Understanding the historical development of the concept of honor provides significant insights into the complexities that shape contemporary attitudes and practices related to honor in Egyptian society.

Ancient Egyptian traditions laid the groundwork for many of the cultural norms that influence current perceptions of honor. In ancient Egypt, family reputation and social standing were highly valued. Individuals were expected to uphold the virtues associated with their social class and lineage, and adherence to societal norms was considered crucial for maintaining honor (Tyldesley, 2000). The societal fabric of ancient Egypt placed immense importance on familial duty, respect for elders, and upholding family reputation. This early cultural foundation established a persistent value system that equated personal honor with family honor, a principle that continued to influence Egyptian society through subsequent eras.

The spread of Islam in the 7th century significantly shaped Egyptian cultural and societal norms. Islamic values emphasize family cohesion, modesty, and morality. In this context, honor became closely associated with adherence to religious principles and the preservation of family dignity (Abu-Lughod, 2013). Islamic teachings reinforced the importance of honor, particularly in relation to female modesty and moral conduct. The integration of these values into the societal framework fostered a collective sense of honor where individual actions reflected on the family and community as a whole. This period also saw the codification of these values into legal and social norms, further entrenching the concept of honor in Egyptian society.

During the Ottoman and later colonial eras, Egypt experienced significant changes in governance and socio-political structures. The Ottoman Empire's influence introduced new legal systems and administrative structures, which coexisted with traditional values (Tucker, 1998). Despite the administrative changes, the importance of familial honor remained a steadfast cultural element. The Ottoman period reinforced patriarchal norms, emphasizing male authority over female family members and their role in safeguarding family honor. Even as new governance structures were established, these traditional values persisted, demonstrating the resilience of cultural norms related to honor.

The British occupation of Egypt in the 19th and early 20th centuries brought about profound cultural and social changes. Efforts towards modernization influenced urban centers, introducing new ideas and practices, including increased interactions with Western cultural norms (Cole, 1993). However, in rural areas and among conservative communities, traditional values continued to dominate perceptions of honor. The dichotomy between urban and rural experiences during this period highlighted the tension between modernization and traditional values. Urban centres began to adopt more liberal views on gender roles and family honor, while rural areas remained deeply rooted in traditional practices.

Following Egypt's independence in 1952, the country entered a period of significant political and social change. Modernization and urbanization efforts intensified, leading to a more pronounced clash between traditional values and the influences of a more secular and globalized world (Hatem, 1994). The dynamics of honor adapted to this changing socio-political landscape. While some segments of society began to challenge traditional norms, advocating for gender equality and individual rights, others held steadfast to conventional notions of honor. This period also saw efforts to reform personal status laws, aiming to balance traditional values with modern legal frameworks. However, the tension between preserving honor and embracing modernization continued to shape societal attitudes.

In contemporary Egypt, the historical context of honor remains deeply intertwined with complex socio-cultural dynamics. Honor is often linked to family reputation, female modesty, and adherence to societal expectations. The struggle between preserving traditional values and adapting to modernity is evident in ongoing debates and practices related to honor (Abouelnaga, 2016). Modern influences, including global human rights frameworks and local feminist movements, increasingly challenge traditional notions of honor. These movements advocate for women's rights and gender equality, seeking to dismantle the cultural and legal structures that perpetuate honor-based violence.

Technological advancements and globalization have also played significant roles in shaping contemporary perceptions of honor. The proliferation of digital media and global communication channels has exposed Egyptian society to diverse cultural norms and values. Social media platforms, in particular, have become spaces where traditional views on honor are questioned and debated. Younger generations, more connected to global networks, are increasingly advocating for a redefinition of honor that aligns with principles of individual autonomy and gender equality (Amnesty International, 2022). This generational shift reflects a broader trend towards questioning and potentially transforming long-held cultural norms.

Educational initiatives and awareness campaigns are crucial in addressing the root causes of honor-related violence and promoting a more inclusive understanding of honor. Programs that emphasize gender equality, human rights, and the negative impacts of honor-based violence can help shift societal perceptions. Schools, community centres, and media outlets play essential roles in fostering a more egalitarian society. Empowering women through education and economic opportunities is vital in reducing their vulnerability to honor-based violence (National Council for Women, 2019). These efforts contribute to creating an environment where honor is no longer used as a justification for violence but is redefined to include respect for individual rights and dignity.

Community-based approaches involving local leaders, religious figures, and activists are also essential in creating a supportive environment for change. These initiatives promote dialogue about the value of women and the importance of their rights, gradually shifting societal perceptions. Establishing support networks and safe spaces for women at risk of honor-related violence provides immediate assistance and long-term protection. This includes creating shelters and hotlines staffed by trained professionals who can offer psychological support, legal advice, and other necessary services (UN Women, 2020). These measures are crucial in providing comprehensive support to victims and promoting a culture of protection and respect.

In conclusion, the historical context of honor in Egypt reveals a complex interplay of cultural, religious, and socio-political influences. From ancient traditions to contemporary dynamics, the concept of honor has evolved, reflecting broader societal changes. Addressing honor-related issues in Egypt requires a multifaceted approach that includes legal reforms, educational initiatives, social interventions, and community engagement. By understanding the historical roots and contemporary manifestations of honor, stakeholders can develop strategies that promote gender equality, protect individual rights, and foster a more inclusive society. The evolution of human rights discourse and legal frameworks continues to play a crucial role in addressing and combating honor crimes globally.

SCOPE AND PREVALENCE OF HONOR RELATED CRIMES IN EGYPT

In Egypt, honor-related crimes constitute a significant but often underreported aspect of the country's social fabric. Rooted deeply in cultural and traditional norms, these crimes encompass a range of acts aimed at preserving perceived family honor, often at the expense of individual rights and freedoms, particularly those of women (Abdelgalil, Elsahn, & Mostafa, 2018). While comprehensive statistical data on honor crimes in Egypt is scarce due to the clandestine nature of many incidents and cultural barriers to reporting, available studies and anecdotal evidence suggest that they remain a persistent issue (Abdelgalil, Elsahn, & Mostafa, 2018).

Honor-related crimes in Egypt take various forms, including but not limited to honor killings, forced marriages, female genital mutilation (FGM), and domestic violence (Abdelgalil, Elsahn, & Mostafa, 2018). These crimes are frequently perpetrated against women and girls who are perceived to have transgressed social norms regarding modesty, chastity, or obedience to familial expectations (Abdelgalil, Elsahn, & Mostafa, 2018). The perpetrators of such acts are often close relatives or community members acting to enforce perceived codes of honor or uphold family reputation (Abdelgalil, Elsahn, & Mostafa, 2018).

Despite legal provisions aimed at protecting individuals from violence and discrimination, enforcement remains a challenge due to factors such as societal acceptance of honor-based violence, entrenched patriarchal attitudes, and the perception of family honor as sacrosanct (Abdelgalil, Elsahn, & Mostafa, 2018). Moreover, victims often face significant barriers to seeking justice or assistance, including fear of reprisal, lack of access to support services, and societal pressure to remain silent about familial matters (Abdelgalil, Elsahn, & Mostafa, 2018).

The prevalence of honor-related crimes in Egypt reflects broader issues of gender inequality, social control, and the intersections of culture, religion, and tradition (Abdelgalil, Elsahn, & Mostafa, 2018). Addressing this complex phenomenon requires a multifaceted approach encompassing legal reform, education, advocacy, and community engagement (Abdelgalil, Elsahn, & Mostafa, 2018). Efforts to combat honor-based violence must prioritize the protection of victims, the empowerment of marginalized individuals, and the challenging of discriminatory norms and practices within Egyptian society (Abdelgalil, Elsahn, & Mostafa, 2018).

International Perspectives and Comparative Analysis

International perspectives and comparative analyses on honor-related crimes provide valuable insights into understanding the complexities of this issue in Egypt and beyond. While cultural, legal, and social contexts vary across countries, similarities in the manifestations and underlying factors of honor violence highlight the need for global cooperation and exchange of best practices to address this pervasive problem.

In many countries, including Egypt, honor-related crimes are deeply entrenched in societal norms and traditions, often perpetuated by patriarchal structures and gender inequalities (Ahmad, Klasen, & Vollmer, 2017). However, the extent and forms of honor violence may differ based on cultural and religious interpretations, legal frameworks, and socioeconomic conditions. For example, while honor killings are prevalent in some regions, other forms of honor-based violence such as forced marriages and female genital mutilation (FGM) may be more common in others (Yüksel-Kutanoglu & Acar, 2019). Understanding these variations is crucial for developing targeted interventions and policies tailored to specific contexts.

Comparative analyses of legal responses to honor-related crimes reveal significant disparities in legislative frameworks and enforcement mechanisms across countries. While some nations have enacted comprehensive laws criminalizing honor violence and providing support services for victims, others lack specific legislation or face challenges in implementation due to cultural resistance and inadequate resources (Yüksel-Kutanoglu & Acar, 2019). Egypt, for instance, has made progress in enacting laws to address honor crimes, but gaps remain in enforcement and protection of victims (Abdelgalil, Elsahn, & Mostafa, 2018). By examining the strengths and weaknesses of different legal approaches, policymakers can identify strategies for enhancing legal protections and promoting accountability.

Moreover, international perspectives offer valuable lessons on the role of education, advocacy, and community engagement in challenging harmful norms and promoting gender equality. Initiatives such as awareness campaigns, school curricula revisions, and community-based interventions have shown promise in raising awareness about honor violence, empowering survivors, and mobilizing communities to take a stand against such practices (Ahmad, Klasen, & Vollmer, 2017). Collaborative efforts between government agencies, civil society organizations, and religious leaders have been instrumental in fostering social change and promoting alternative notions of honor based on respect for human rights and dignity.

At the same time, comparative analyses highlight the importance of context-specific approaches that acknowledge the intersecting factors of gender, class, ethnicity, and religion in shaping experiences of honor violence. Strategies that recognize and address these intersecting forms of oppression are essential for ensuring inclusive and effective interventions that meet the diverse needs of individuals and communities (Yüksel-Kutanoglu & Acar, 2019). By centring the voices and experiences of marginalized groups, policymakers can develop policies and programs that are sensitive to cultural nuances while upholding universal human rights standards.

In conclusion, international perspectives and comparative analyses play a critical role in advancing our understanding of honor-related crimes and informing evidence-based interventions to combat this global phenomenon. By examining similarities and differences across countries, policymakers can identify promising practices, address gaps in legal and social responses, and work towards creating a world where every individual is free from violence and discrimination.

The Role of Media and Advocacy in Addressing Honor-Related Crimes in Egypt

The role of media and advocacy in addressing honor-related crimes in Egypt is multifaceted and crucial for raising awareness, changing societal attitudes, and influencing policy. The media serves as a powerful tool in shaping public opinion and can either perpetuate harmful stereotypes or act as a catalyst for change. Advocacy groups, on the other hand, work tirelessly to provide support to victims, push for legal reforms, and challenge the societal norms that underpin honor-related violence. Together, media and advocacy efforts are essential in the fight against honor-related crimes in Egypt.

Media's Role in Shaping Public Perception

Media in Egypt, including television, newspapers, radio, and social media, plays a pivotal role in shaping public perceptions of honor-related crimes. Historically, media portrayal of such crimes has often been sensationalized, focusing on the violence and tragedy without delving into the underlying cultural and societal issues. This type of coverage can reinforce harmful stereotypes and stigmatize victims, making it harder for them to come forward (UN Women, 2017). However, more recently, there has been a shift towards more responsible journalism that aims to educate the public and foster empathy towards victims.

One significant aspect of media's role is raising awareness about the prevalence and severity of honor-related crimes. By reporting on these incidents, the media brings them into the public eye, challenging the notion that they are rare or culturally acceptable (Abu-Lughod, 2013). Investigative journalism has been particularly effective in uncovering the stories behind the headlines, revealing the social and familial pressures that lead to such violence. Documentaries and special reports often provide a platform for survivors to share their experiences, humanizing the issue and encouraging societal reflection and change.

Advocacy and Legal Reforms

Advocacy groups in Egypt are at the forefront of the fight against honor-related crimes, working to support victims, influence public policy, and change societal attitudes. These organizations engage in a range of activities, from providing direct support services to victims, such as legal aid and counselling, to campaigning for legislative reforms that protect women's rights (National Council for Women, 2019). By documenting cases and providing statistical evidence, advocacy groups create a compelling argument for the need for stronger protections and more stringent enforcement of existing laws.

Legal advocacy focuses on closing the gaps in legislation that allow honor-related crimes to persist. For example, some legal provisions in the Egyptian Penal Code can be interpreted to justify lenient sentences for perpetrators of honor crimes, reflecting societal attitudes that condone such violence (Human Rights Watch, 2021). Advocacy groups work to highlight these inconsistencies and push for reforms that ensure perpetrators are held accountable and victims receive the justice they deserve. Additionally, these groups often engage in strategic litigation, taking landmark cases to court to set legal precedents that benefit all victims.

Educational Campaigns and Community Engagement

Both media and advocacy groups utilize educational campaigns to challenge ingrained beliefs and foster a more inclusive and egalitarian society. These campaigns often target specific demographics, such as young people or rural communities, where traditional views on honor and gender roles may be more entrenched (Amnesty International, 2022). Through workshops, seminars, and public service announcements, these initiatives aim to change perceptions about gender and honor, promoting respect for women's rights and equality.

Community engagement is another critical aspect of these efforts. Advocacy groups often collaborate with local leaders, religious figures, and community organizations to create a supportive environment for change. By involving respected figures in the community, these campaigns can gain greater acceptance and influence more people. For example, religious leaders can play a crucial role in interpreting religious texts in a way that promotes gender equality and condemns violence (Abouelnaga, 2016).

Social Media and Digital Platforms

The advent of social media and digital platforms has transformed the landscape of media and advocacy. These platforms provide a space for survivors to share their stories, for activists to mobilize support, and for campaigns to reach a broader audience (Amnesty International, 2022). Hashtag campaigns, viral videos, and online petitions have become powerful tools in raising awareness and applying pressure on authorities to take action against honor-related crimes.

Social media also facilitates networking and collaboration among advocacy groups, allowing them to share resources, strategies, and support. It provides a platform for global solidarity, where international organizations can lend their voice and support to local efforts in Egypt. This interconnectedness enhances the impact of advocacy work and creates a unified front against honor-related violence.

Case Studies and Success Stories

Several case studies highlight the impact of media and advocacy on honor-related crimes in Egypt. For instance, the case of Souad Hosny, a prominent Egyptian actress whose death was initially ruled as suicide, was later scrutinized by investigative journalists and advocacy groups. Their persistent efforts led to a reopening of the case and a broader discussion about the pressures and violence faced by women in the public eye (El-Nadeem Center for Rehabilitation of Victims of Violence, 2018).

This case exemplifies how media and advocacy can work together to challenge official narratives and seek justice.

Another notable example is the campaign against female genital mutilation (FGM), which is closely tied to notions of honor and purity. Advocacy groups have utilized media campaigns, educational programs, and community engagement to combat FGM, resulting in significant legal reforms and a decrease in prevalence rates (UNICEF, 2020). This success demonstrates the potential of coordinated efforts to bring about cultural and legal change.

Challenges and Future Directions

Despite these successes, challenges remain. Media coverage can still be biased, sensationalist, or superficial, and there is a need for more in-depth, sensitive reporting that respects victims' dignity and privacy (UN Women, 2017). Advocacy groups often face resistance from conservative elements in society, limited funding, and legal obstacles. There is also a need for greater collaboration between media and advocacy groups to ensure that efforts are aligned and mutually reinforcing.

Future directions should focus on strengthening these collaborations, ensuring that media coverage supports advocacy efforts and that advocacy groups utilize media effectively. Training journalists to report on honor-related crimes with sensitivity and accuracy is crucial, as is continuing to leverage social media and digital platforms for awareness and mobilization. Moreover, engaging men and boys in these efforts is essential, as changing male attitudes and behaviours is critical to addressing the root causes of honor-related violence (UN Women, 2020).

In conclusion, the role of media and advocacy in addressing honor-related crimes in Egypt is vital. Through raising awareness, influencing public opinion, and advocating for legal reforms, these efforts work towards dismantling the cultural and societal structures that perpetuate honor-related violence. By continuing to innovate and collaborate, media and advocacy groups can create a more just and equitable society where honor is no longer used to justify violence and discrimination.

FUTURE PERSPECTIVES OF HONOR RELATED CRIMES IN EGYPT

The future perspectives of honor-related crimes in Egypt present a complex landscape shaped by evolving social, cultural, legal, and economic factors. While progress has been made in raising awareness and implementing legal reforms to address honor violence, significant challenges persist, and new dynamics may emerge in the years ahead.

One potential future trend is the impact of changing gender dynamics and women's empowerment initiatives on perceptions of honor and violence in Egyptian society. Increasing education and economic opportunities for women, along with advocacy efforts promoting gender equality, may challenge traditional patriarchal norms and reduce the prevalence of honor-related crimes (Abdelgalil, Elsahn, & Mostafa, 2018). However, resistance to gender equality measures and backlash against women's rights advancements could also fuel tensions and contribute to a backlash against women's autonomy, potentially leading to an increase in honor violence incidents (Yüksel-Kaptanoğlu & Acar, 2019).

Another future consideration is the role of technology and social media in shaping attitudes and behaviours related to honor violence. While social media platforms can serve as tools for raising awareness, facilitating support networks, and amplifying the voices of survivors, they can also be used to perpetuate harmful stereotypes, incite violence, and intimidate victims (Ahmad, Klasen, & Vollmer, 2017). As digital communication continues to play an increasingly central role in Egyptian society, understanding the implications of online spaces for honor-related crimes prevention and intervention will be essential.

Furthermore, the intersectionality of honor violence with other forms of discrimination, such as class, ethnicity, religion, and sexual orientation, will likely influence future dynamics. Marginalized groups, including LGBTQ+ individuals, religious minorities, and low-income communities, may face heightened risks of honor violence due to intersecting forms of oppression and discrimination (Yüksel-Kaptanoğlu & Acar, 2019). Efforts to address honor-related crimes must therefore adopt an intersectional approach that acknowledges and addresses these intersecting vulnerabilities.

In terms of legal and policy responses, the future trajectory of honor-related crimes in Egypt will depend on the government's commitment to enforcing existing laws, strengthening protections for victims, and promoting accountability for perpetrators. Continued collaboration between government agencies, civil society organizations, and international partners will be crucial for implementing comprehensive strategies that address the root causes of honor violence and support survivors (Abdelgalil, Elsahn, & Mostafa, 2018). Moreover, efforts to address honor violence must be integrated into broader initiatives aimed at promoting gender equality, human rights, and social justice in Egypt.

In conclusion, the future perspectives of honor-related crimes in Egypt are shaped by a complex interplay of social, cultural, legal, and technological factors. While progress has been made in raising awareness and implementing legal reforms, significant challenges remain, and new dynamics may emerge in the years ahead.

By adopting a holistic and intersectional approach, policymakers, advocates, and community members can work together to prevent honor violence, support survivors, and create a society where every individual can live with dignity and without fear. Looking ahead, the future of honor crimes is likely to be shaped by ongoing social, legal, and cultural shifts.

SOCIETAL ATTITUDES AND PERCEPTIONS

Societal impacts on honor-related crimes in Egypt encompass a wide range of consequences that affect individuals, families, communities, and the broader social fabric. These impacts are deeply intertwined with cultural norms, gender dynamics, legal frameworks, and socioeconomic factors, shaping both the perpetration of honor violence and the responses to it within Egyptian society.

One significant societal impact of honor-related crimes in Egypt is the perpetuation of gender inequality and the reinforcement of patriarchal norms. The enforcement of perceived codes of honor often targets women and girls, restricting their autonomy, mobility, and agency (Abdelgalil, Elsahn, & Mostafa, 2018). This perpetuates a cycle of violence and control, where women's bodies and behaviours are policed to uphold family honor, reinforcing traditional gender roles and power dynamics.

Moreover, honor-related crimes contribute to the normalization of violence and the erosion of trust within communities. The silence and complicity surrounding these crimes, fuelled by societal acceptance and fear of stigma, create a culture of impunity where perpetrators go unpunished (Ahmad, Klasen, & Vollmer, 2017). This normalization of violence not only perpetuates harm but also undermines efforts to promote human rights, dignity, and justice within Egyptian society.

Honor-related crimes also have profound psychological and emotional impacts on survivors, families, and communities. Victims of honor violence often experience trauma, shame, and isolation, compounded by the lack of support services and societal stigma (Abdelgalil, Elsahn, & Mostafa, 2018). Families may face social ostracization and economic hardships as a result of being associated with dishonor, leading to further marginalization and vulnerability (Ahmad, Klasen, & Vollmer, 2017). These psychological and social repercussions can have long-lasting effects on individuals and communities, perpetuating cycles of violence and perpetuating intergenerational trauma.

Furthermore, honor-related crimes undermine the rule of law and erode trust in the justice system. The lack of effective legal enforcement, coupled with cultural justifications for honor violence, undermines victims' access to justice and perpetuates impunity for perpetrators (Yüksel-Kaptanoğlu & Acar, 2019). This weakens the social contract between citizens and the state, fostering a sense of mistrust and disillusionment with institutions tasked with protecting human rights and upholding the rule of law.

In conclusion, societal impacts on honor-related crimes in Egypt are multifaceted and pervasive, shaping individual experiences, community dynamics, and the broader social fabric. Addressing these impacts requires a comprehensive approach that addresses the root causes of honor violence, challenges harmful cultural norms, strengthens legal protections for victims, and promotes gender equality and social justice within Egyptian society.

CONCLUSION

Honor-related crimes in Egypt remain a deeply entrenched issue, reflecting complex socio-cultural dynamics and patriarchal structures. These crimes, often involving violence against women perceived to have tarnished family honor, persist due to a combination of cultural, legal, and institutional factors. Despite some progress, including legal reforms and increased awareness campaigns, the enforcement of laws and protection for victims remain inadequate. To effectively address this issue, it is crucial to implement multifaceted strategies that involve legal, educational, and social interventions. Firstly, legal reforms must be robust and comprehensive. Current laws should be amended to ensure stricter penalties for perpetrators of honor crimes and to close loopholes that allow for reduced sentences based on cultural justifications. For instance, the Egyptian Penal Code's provisions on "honor defenses" should be critically revised. Furthermore, the legal system needs to be more accessible and supportive for victims, providing them with protection and ensuring that they are not re-victimized during the legal process (UN Women, 2017).

Educational initiatives play a vital role in challenging and changing the deep-seated cultural norms that underpin honor-related crimes. These initiatives should target multiple levels of society, including schools, community centres, and media outlets. Education programs should promote gender equality, human rights, and the detrimental impacts of honor-based violence. Empowering women through education and economic opportunities is also essential in reducing their vulnerability to such crimes. Additionally, engaging men and boys in these educational efforts can help to reshape harmful masculine norms and promote more egalitarian attitudes (El-Nadeem Center for Rehabilitation of Victims of Violence, 2018).

Social interventions are equally important. Community-based approaches that involve local leaders, religious figures, and activists can create a supportive environment for change. Initiatives that promote dialogue within communities about the value of women and the importance of their rights can gradually shift societal perceptions. Moreover, establishing support networks and safe spaces for women who are at risk of honor-related violence can provide immediate assistance and long-term protection. This involves creating shelters and hotlines staffed by trained professionals who can offer psychological support, legal advice, and other necessary services (National Council for Women, 2019).

Media plays a powerful role in shaping public opinion and should be leveraged to combat honor-related crimes. Media campaigns that highlight the stories of survivors, educate the public about the legal and moral implications of honor crimes, and promote positive role models can help to challenge stereotypes and stigmatization. Furthermore, training journalists to report on these issues sensitively and accurately is crucial in ensuring that media coverage contributes to awareness and change rather than reinforcing harmful norms (UN Women, 2020).

International cooperation and support can enhance national efforts to combat honor-related crimes. Partnerships with international organizations can provide technical assistance, funding, and best practice models. Egypt can also benefit from participating in global networks that address violence against women, enabling the exchange of knowledge and strategies. Additionally, international pressure and advocacy can encourage the Egyptian government to prioritize this issue and adhere to international human rights standards (Human Rights Watch, 2021).

Monitoring and evaluation mechanisms are essential to assess the effectiveness of interventions and policies addressing honor-related crimes. Establishing a national database to track incidents of honor crimes, their outcomes, and the effectiveness of various interventions can provide valuable data for continuous improvement. Regular reporting and transparency in the handling of these cases can also build public trust and accountability (Amnesty International, 2022).

In conclusion, addressing honor-related crimes in Egypt requires a holistic approach that combines legal reforms, educational initiatives, social interventions, media engagement, international cooperation, and robust monitoring and evaluation mechanisms. By tackling the issue from multiple angles and involving all sectors of society, it is possible to create a cultural shift that condemns honor-based violence and upholds the rights and dignity of all individuals. This multifaceted strategy not only addresses the immediate needs of victims but also fosters long-term societal change, paving the way for a future where honor crimes are eradicated and gender equality is a reality (UN Women, 2023).

REFERENCES

Abdel-Latif, O., & Vandeginste, S. (2011). Honour Killings and Violence against Women in Egypt. *International Journal of Humanities and Social Science*, 1(4), 59–67.

Abdelmonem, A. (2015). "Dynamics of Honor Killings in Egypt." (Doctoral dissertation, University of Central Lancashire).

Ahmed, S. (2020). *Gender-Based Violence in Egypt: Causes and Consequences.* Gender and Society Review.

Altorki, S. (1986). *Women in Saudi Arabia: Ideology and Behavior among the Elite.* Columbia University Press. DOI: 10.7312/alto94660

Amer, M. (2016). "Violence against Women in Egypt: Examining Honor Killings and the Role of Police in Facilitating and Preventing Such Crimes." (Doctoral dissertation, George Mason University).

Baghat, H. (2015). Honour Killings in Egypt: A Legal Perspective. *Egyptian Journal of Legal Studies*, 25(2), 150–168.

Ibrahim, H., & Soliman, N. (2018). *Legal Framework and Human Rights in Egypt.* Law and Human Rights Journal.

Kamal, N., & Mostafa, R. (2021). *Legal and Psychological Dimensions of Honor Crimes in Egypt.* Egyptian Law Review.

Kandiyoti, D. (1991). *Women, Islam, and the State.* Temple University Press. DOI: 10.1007/978-1-349-21178-4

Sholkamy, H. (2002). Patriarchy, Power, and the Politics of Gender in Modernising Egypt. *Gender and Development*, 10(1), 22–30.

Women, U. N. (2019). *Exploring Masculinities: Men.* Women, and Gender Relations in the Middle East and North Africa.

. Youssef, A., & Farag, H. (2021). *Cultural Relativism and Honor Crimes in Egypt.* Journal of Cultural Studies.

Chapter 11
Demystifying the Culture and Causes of Honor Killings in Canada

Abhishek Kumar
Integral University, Lucknow, India

Aniruddh Atul Garg
GLA University, Mathura, India

ABSTRACT

The chapter aims to unfold the mishaps of honor killings in the Canadian context comprising its key causes, and issues leading to honor-based offenses against the women in the family. Although, honor killings in Canada are rare to notice, but are prevalent majorly due to immigrant communities. The chapter also demystifies the case studies which witnessed honor killings in Canada. The Shafia case which is one of the landmark cases of the honor killing in Kingston, Canada led to the painful demise of three daughters and the first wife of Mohd. Shafia. Furthermore, it also explores the Canadian media reports on honor killing and how they create a biased view regarding the incidents surrounding these crimes in the public domain. In conclusion, several ways are highlighted upon which the Canadian government should act in order to diminish the prevalence of honor-based violence throughout Canada such as introducing effective immigration policies and making aware the youth of the laws concerning gender equality, freedom, and fairness.

Honor killings in Canada have been rare but still its incidents are prevalent. The cases and data of such honor crimes remain limited in Canada but they may generally lie under the broader homicide statistics with regards to domestic violence and cultural violence. However, it is observed that around thirteen or fifteen honor

DOI: 10.4018/979-8-3693-7240-1.ch011

Copyright © 2025, IGI Global. Copying or distributing in print or electronic forms without written permission of IGI Global is prohibited.

killings have been witnessed since 2002 in Canada (Aujla & Gill, n.d.). In 2021, the homicides increased to the rate of 2.06 per 100,000 people which denotes a 3% rise compared to 2020 (David & Jaffray, n.d.). In Canada, 27% of victims who belong to Indigenous communities faced violence during 2022 including homicide (Infographic: Homicide in Canada, 2022, 2023). Around 874 homicides were reported in 2022 in Canada which increased to 8% in comparison to 2021, resulting in a rate of 2.25 homicides per 100,000 population (Infographic: Homicide in Canada, 2022, 2023). The causes for this rising rate mainly remain the lack of proper support service from the authorities to help the victims and strict control over the autonomy of women. Deviation from strict cultural beliefs or norms by the female members of the family also resulted in increased no. of honor killing cases in Canada.

RESEARCH METHODOLOGY

The research methodology for this chapter employs a qualitative approach in order to understand the culture and causes of honor killings in Canada, including the intersection of immigration and gender-based violence. Some high-profile cases such as the Shafia Case, the murder of Jaswinder Kaur Sidhu, and the Aqsa Parvez murder case were explored to analyze the factors liable behind the honor killings in Canada within the immigrant communities. The research also involves the quantitative approach by utilizing multiple data collection methods including case studies, media reports, government publications to gather statistical data on reported cases of honor killings, legal documents, and scholarly works pertaining to the honor crimes in Canada. These sources provide the perspective on how honor killings are committed, reported, and addressed in Canada. They also show that it is frequently the case for someone to be the victim of abuse and torture when a community believes that they have violated cultural norms and values. Reports from the Royal Canadian Mounted Police, judicial decisions, and the Canadian Charter of Rights and Freedoms emphasized the legal framework for the treatment of honor killings in Canada. The scholarly work alongside the intersection of culture and immigration also outlined the challenges faced by immigrant women in Canada. Therefore, this methodological approach adds to a more nuanced understanding of the issue in Canada's multicultural society by demystifying the social, legal, and cultural perspectives.

KEY WORDS

Core terms include "Culture", "Causes", "Honor Killing", referring to the violent acts committed against the female members of the family to preserve its honor, especially in immigrant communities within Canada. Broader themes like "Gender Discrimination", "Patriarchy", "Conservative approach" contextualize the issue. Legal and Policy-related terms like "Canadian Bill of Rights, "Canadian Charter of Rights and Freedom", "Bill S-7: Zero Tolerance for Barbaric Cultural Practices Act", "Immigration Policy" connect to practical application. Analytical Perspectives like "Impact drawn to Canadian Society by Honor Killing", "Comparative Analysis" allow for exploring the complexities of honor killings across different cultural and legal contexts. "Shafia Case" is a landmark case of honor killing which is used throughout the chapter to portray the dynamics of honor-based violence in Canada.

Selecting the right journals and carefully conducting the inclusion/exclusion and article research is essential for a Research Paper on Demystifying the Culture and Causes of Honor Killings in Canada. The journal selection process focused on publications specializing in Honor Killings in Canada, Canadian Laws addressing Honor Killings, and How Canadian Media quote Honor Killings. The author opted for journals like *International Research Journal of Social Sciences, JOURNAL OF LAW AND CRIMINAL JUSTICE, International Journal of Child, Youth and Family Studies, SAGE Open* which align with the subject matter and provide a platform for scholarly discussions on these topics.

Inclusion criteria emphasized relevance, ensuring that only articles directly addressing the honor killings, the Status of Honor Killings in Canada, Factors responsible behind Honor-based violence from a Canadian perspective, and the associated Case Studies are considered. Peer-reviewed articles and government reports formed the core of our research to maintain academic rigor.

Exclusion criteria filtered out articles with only tangential relevance to the topic. Conducted article research using academic databases like JSTOR and Google Scholar is crucial, employing targeted keywords such as "Honor Killings in Canada", "Canadian Media Reports", "Immigration Communities" to identify the most pertinent studies for our paper.

LITERATURE REVIEW

Muhammad, A. A. has pointed out that honor-based crimes have existed since ancient Roman times. Shier, A., & Shor, E. have emphasized that Honor-based crimes are often committed due to cultural and ethnic backgrounds by mentioning the differences between South Asian/Muslim and Western values. Gill, J. K. has noticed that there is no universal definition of honor killing. Honor killing could be the premeditated murder of preadolescent, adolescent, or adult women by one or more male members of the family to preserve their honor. The study by Corinne L. Mason explained how the media covered the 2009 "Kingston Mills Murder" case and how it was labeled as an "honor killing" through a cultural lens. The author pointed out the interpretations used by different feminist and gender experts on these crimes to the media, often framing them as a "result of a clash of civilizations." It is also argued by the author that Western feminists need to rethink how they talk about different cultures to build stronger communities to tackle patriarchal violence. Singh, D., & Bhandari observed that new progressive ideas contaminate the cultural plurality. Whenever people (especially women) who with certain new liberal thoughts are often ostracized and may also face subsequent violence by their families. Aujla, W., & Gill, A. K. deeply examine the prevalence of honor killings in the diverse and multicultural society of Canada. The writers laid the importance on gender by highlighting honor killing as a result of real or perceived violations of family honor. Korteweg, A. C. has noted that apart from culture, honor-based violence lies under gender-based violence which affects all societies. Temowo_Adeniyi_Olasunkanmi (1). (n.d.). This article talks the honor killing in Canada. Various sources of oppression and their intersections need to be contemplated to find the meaning of honor killing. Honor Killings in Canada: A Way Towards Prevention. (2018, March 9). This article focused on the study of Canadian laws, including the section of the Criminal code on preventing incidents of honor killing.

FUTURE RESEARCH DIRECTIONS

The research is an attempt by the authors to provide a comprehensive analysis of the prevalence of honor killings in the Canadian context, emphasizing the role of immigrant communities and the cultural conflict behind the outbreak of honor-based violence against the female members of the family. The unique perspective distinguishes the research from the other studies as it not only covers the criminal aspects of honor killing but also signifies the societal and cultural dimensions that are often overlooked. The research closely examines the key themes including the culture and causes of honor killing, in-depth study of high-profile cases like the Shafia Case, and its aftermath. The research also mentions the Canadian legal frameworks addressing honor killings and the portrayal of such crimes in media reports.

To facilitate future research, numerous directions are recommended. Comparative analysis of honor killing could be done in Canada with the Asian and European counterparts to offer insights into varying legal and social responses. Furthermore, the research could be conducted to reflect the implications of immigration policies on the prevalence and reporting of honor-based crimes within immigrant communities to diminish the status of honor killing cases. The increasing role of education within immigrant communities could be analyzed to enhance the notion of gender equality, individualism, etc. The research showcases the landmark cases of honor killings like the Shafia Case but still lacks in providing how cultural integration policies could aid in the downfall of honor killing incidents.

STATUS OF HONOR KILLING IN CANADA

In the branch of criminology, we used to observe certain kinds of crimes committed all across the globe. There are various forms of crime including White-collar crimes, Cyber Crime, Violent Crimes, etc. The violent crimes have already been described through the term 'Violent' which decodes violence being prevalent in such crimes, usually against women. The violent crimes could be seen in the form of domestic violence, kidnapping, rape, murder, etc. The most essential component that constitutes such crimes as violent is the intentional harm using the physical means being caused by men to women. However, a problem emerges when honor killings are often isolated from the comprehensive terminology of violent crimes against women, especially the indigenous women in the Canadian boundary. The honor killing in Canada is rare to happen, but its probability gets uplifted due to immigrant communities. In Canada, honor killing refers to the act of violence committed against a family member (usually a woman) by their own family members (usually men) in order to restore their community's or family's honor or prestige around the society. The commencement of honor-based violence is driven centrally by the traditional, cultural, or religious reasons of the immigrant communities, mostly Muslims who aren't able to accommodate the Canadian values or laws of equality/gender neutrality. It is also said that the serious offense of honor killing is premeditated where the perpetrators or the family members not only decide the nature of the punishment but also determine the way the crime has to be committed (Aujla & Gill, n.d.). Honor crimes in Canada are often recognized as a foreign problem because these are majorly elevated by the immigrant communities which results in cultural and religious differences. In Canada, honor killing is being perplexed with domestic violence or patriarchal homicide. Some groups believe that since honor crimes are premeditated or pre-planned with a determined strategy, they should not fall under the ambit of all outbreaks of violence that happen against women. Some scholars say that honor killing must come under the broad term of violence against women which would also benefit the indigenous women as the government will strive to frame the policies addressing the violence against women (not particularly inclining to honor killing). The concept behind honor-based violence must not remain to stick to specific cultures or religions (Aujla & Gill, n.d.). This would result in vanishing the focus from the other imperative causes of honor killing such as the patriarchal structure that narrows its scope due to the failure of not including all the women victims regardless of their social status. Papp, an acknowledged researcher lays his special emphasis on the incidents of Honor Killing where she states that the honor-based violence in Canada includes victims who are generally the South-Asians and Muslim Women ('Honour' Killing and Violence_ Theory, Policy and Practice -- Aisha K_ Gill, Carolyn Strange, Karl Roberts (Eds_) -- 1, 2014 -- Palgrave Macmillan UK -- 9781137289568 -- 207796db8522f584c644dbaccc, n.d.). Moreover, she also recommends various anti-immigration policies and gender equality laws to weaken the trend of Honor Killings in Canada. The non-corporative nature of immigrant communities with the Canadian laws of equality and gender neutrality boosts the notion of the patriarchal structure of a family. This does not deem fit to ensure individualism in a society where the women derive from their individual decisions giving rise to their individual status. Thus, the notions of equality, rationality, and freedom should be the addition to children's education in Canada to shape their ideology favoring individualism. This initiative will strengthen the children of Canada with respect to their humanitarian rights demoting the patriarchy. The Canadian media often used to sensationalize honor killings especially those involving immigrant communities contributing to the biased and negative stereotypes (Gill, 2022). In other words, the prevalence of honor crimes taking place in Canada got pushed due to immigration which depicts women as victims of the violence being committed by their male family members to preserve their family honor. These crimes used to commence against the women due to their acts which seem to dishonor their family. It includes matters mostly linked to the victim's sexuality or behavior.

FACTORS LIABLE IN CANADA BEHIND HONOR KILLINGS

The significant cause which promotes the prevalence of honor crimes in Canada is immigrant communities based on distinguished cultures, norms, and religions. Cultural practices and religion differing from one community to another often produce numerous honor killings in Canada during which family commits violent acts in response to the woman's actions which are assumed to dishonor their community. However, this should not be viewed as the sole cause behind the honor-based violence against women. The patriarchal family structure where the men's decisions are viewed as chief to the family often results in dominating their will. Section 1 of the Canadian Bill of Rights talks about both the clauses based on non-discrimination and "equality before the law" (Canadian Bill of Rights, section 1). Section 15 of the Canadian Charter of Rights and Freedoms outlines the right to equal protection and equal benefit of the law without any discrimination (Canadian Charter of Rights and Freedom, section 15). According to Section 28, there must be no gender-based discrimination in the application of the rights and freedoms protected by the Charter (Canadian Charter of Rights and Freedom, section 28). Section 28 is often cited as a companion section with section 15 in cases alleged to raise gender discrimination issues (Guide to the Canadian Charter of Rights and Freedoms, n.d.). In Vriend v. Alberta, the trial judge held that discrimination on the basis of gender infringes section 15 of the Canadian Charter of Rights and Freedoms (Vriend v. Alberta, 1998). However, the major challenge emerges when the struggle arises with the lack of concern of immigrant communities for these Canadian laws of equality and gender neutrality. Honor Killings in Canada tend to get multiplied because such immigrant communities only keep the concern limited to their traditional practices and conservative approach. They refuse to respect concepts such as equality before the law, and non-discrimination outlining the importance of gender neutrality which results in sparking honor-based crimes. The victim's non-acceptance of the traditional norms in the Shafia case to adopt the Western approach led to the commencement of honor killing causing their painful death. This case reflected the defeat of 'individualism and humanitarian rights' where the victim's independent decision didn't get consideration in the family (Singh & Bhandari, 2021). Love marriages taking place in Canada often get noticed and held liable for maximizing the occurrence of Honor killings as many women who belong to the immigrant communities (in Canada) want to get married in the Western way. This further compels the family members to plan the honor crime against them or even by hiring a professional criminal. Jaswinder Kaur "Jassi" Sidhu was an Indo-Canadian who rejected to marry a rich man due to love marriage but her family who was a Sikh community residing in Canada refused her to marry the man of her choice, thus leading to honor-based violence (Singh & Bhandari, 2021). Lack of support from the authorities also contributes to honor crime against women in Canada where they aren't able to seek the assistance of officials exercising under the administration probably due to language barriers, lack of humanitarian rights offering them protection, or the Canadian laws restricting the inequality and discrimination based on sex and social status. Insufficient awareness of women relating to the laws based on their interests often withdraws their trust from the administration to acknowledge their serious problem (Honor-based violence). As a consequence of the same, they need to witness the pressure generated by their family to uphold their honor. Moreover, the fear of social stigma often creates excessive pressure on families to adhere to their cultural practices stringently. This transforms families even more strict, especially in matters where their culture or religion plays a pivotal role in deriving their honor. Youths (usually women) are targeted by the male members of the family due to social stigma. Because they had a common belief that their behavior or sexuality had an immense role in signifying their honor.

UNVEILING THE CASE STUDIES OF HONOR KILLING IN CANADA

Honor Killings in Canada are rare in figures, but they are not completely absent. Anna Korteweg (2012) noted that honor killings are comparatively rare in Canada (10 to 15 cases in a decade, as compared to the 60 women killed per year by partners or ex-partners) (Razack, 2021) Such gendered violence often becomes prevalent in Canada due to the context of immigration. Therefore, Honor-based violence is noticed as a cultural phenomenon that belongs to the 'old world and has no link with the West which also includes Canadian society and is often practiced by primitive immigrant people (Temowo_Adeniyi_Olasunkanmi (1), n.d.). The Shafia Case in Canada is the landmark case of Honor Killing which was committed due to immigration. It leads to the demise of four female members of the Shafia family.

The Shafia Case

Mohammed Shafia was born in a middle-class family in Kabul, Afghanistan. He left his education during his seventh class and got engaged in managing the family business. His determination and hard work made him enter the rich class where he was earning a decent amount. Eventually, he got married to his first wife Rona Muhammad Omar. She was the daughter of a retired colonel of the Afghanistan Army. They were successfully married in 1979, leading a good life. Subsequently, when Shafia realized that Rona was incapable of bearing a child, entered India for her treatment. The doctors in India told Shafia that Rona could not become pregnant. This changed the attitude of Shafia's family which it holds towards Rona. Mohd. Shafia being influenced by his family finally decided to do a second marriage. In fact, Rona backed Shafia in the course of his second marriage. In 1989, Shafia tied the knot with his second wife Tooba Mohammad Yahya. Some months later, Tooba became pregnant and gave birth to her first daughter, Zainab. She also gave birth to her son, Hamed, and one more daughter named Sahar. At the time, when Shafia, Rona, Tooba, and their children were completely settled being a family, the war commencing in different regions of Afghanistan also badly affected Kabul and subsequently weakened the economic status of Mohd. Shafia. The worsened condition of Shafia and his family compelled them to live in Pakistan. Shafia managed to meet the basic needs of the family. He ultimately transferred to the UAE in search of work. Shafia in UAE recovered his position when he associated with the import and export activities, and constructed the royal business of the luxurious cars exported from America to UAE, thus selling them in return for huge profits. Shafia still had a wish to obtain citizenship in UAE, but the government neglected him for the same. He tried to claim the citizenship of New Zealand, and Australia but remained unsuccessful. In 2007, the Government of Canada also launched its scheme which talked about the allocation of Canadian Citizenship to foreigners if they initiate an investment of 4000 dollars within Canada. Shafia, impressed with the Canadian policy, arrived there and did the needful. Finally, he received citizenship in Canada and prepared his family to move to Canada. As per the terms and conditions of the Canadian scheme, men with more than one spouse were not permitted to hold citizenship. But Shafia through his strategy insisted Roma not to join him, Tooba, and the children for the journey to Canada. He ensured his first wife, Roma that she would shortly be called to live in Canada. Shafia along with Tooba and his children arrived in Montreal and remained successful in claiming Canadian Citizenship. Shafia, being a rich person admitted his children to the well-reputed schools of Canada. Later, Roma was also called by Shafia to Canada by confirming her as his housemate in the application to secure the visa.

The daughters of the Mohd. Shafia was largely influenced by the Canadian Western Culture, refusing to adopt the culture of Afghanistan. Shafia and Tooba were largely dissatisfied with their daughter's inappropriate clothing (Aujla & Gill, n.d.). Zainab fell in love with a Pakistani boy, which was strongly opposed by her family except Roma. Roma always believed that her children should govern their lives by their own independent decisions. She undoubtedly supported her children's autonomy. Shafia's reaction to Zainab's affair with a Pakistani boy created many harsh restrictions where she was not allowed to go outside the house including her school to pursue her education. Shafia and his son Hamed also abused and slapped Zainab and her younger sister Seher when they were found with their boyfriends. Zainab's age was around 19 years, she wanted to lead her life based on her decisions, so she expressed her wish to marry her boyfriend, but it was opposed by her family. Being frustrated by the acts of the children leading to the disregard of the Afghan Culture, Shafia plans to kill Zainab (19 years), Sahar, 17 years), and Geeti (13 years) and his first wife Rona Amir Mohammad aged 50 years. In June 2009, Tooba's husband, Mohammad Shafia, and their son, Hamed, somehow managed to get three of her daughters and Shafia's other wife inside a car. They used another car to push the vehicle into a canal in Kingston, Ont (Shafia murders: Mother 'discovered freedom' behind bars, changed story, filed for divorce, 2019). This resulted in the deaths of four female members of the Shafia family. Shafia and Tooba who originally belonged to Afghanistan initially made their statement to the police that those four female members of the family disappeared during the family's return journey from a trip to Niagara Falls (Shafia murders: Mother 'discovered freedom' behind bars, changed story, filed for divorce, 2019). In Hamed Mohammad Shafia v. Her Majesty the Queen, Mohd. Shafia, Hamed Shafia, and Tooba Yahya were found guilty and therefore convicted due to the first-degree murder of three daughters and first wife, Roma. The Crown argued that Hamed and his parents had committed the brutal honor killing of their three daughters and Roma Amir Mohammad. Hamed's fresh evidence contending that he was a minor i.e. 17 years old during the commencement of the offense, also refused to admit by the Court of Appeal (Hamed Mohammad Shafia v. Her Majesty the Queen, n.d.).

Jaswinder Kaur Sidhu Case

Jaswinder Kaur Sidhu was the daughter of Multi-Millionaire Blueburry orchard owners in British Columbia, Canada who visited her mother's village, Kaonke Khosa, and fell in love with Sukhwinder Singh Sidhu (Mithu). Mithu belongs to a poor family who used to drive an auto-rickshaw. Both met each other in 1994 on 'bhoond' (a wasp-shaped auto rickshaw) (Murderous honour, undying love: The tale of Jassi and Mithu from Canada to Punjab, 2017). Their frequent meetings constructed their relationship deeper in love. Since Sukhwinder Singh belongs to the lower caste, Jasssi knew that her family would not accept their marriage. In 1999, Jassi decided to secretly marry Mithu in a Gurudwara. The hidden news of their secret marriage unfortunately went into the ears of Jassi's family. Her family forced her to return to Canada immediately. Jassi in Canada witnessed her parents' strong dissatisfaction and unacceptability towards the marriage done with Sidhu without their consent. Constant struggles were made by the family to manipulate Jassi into divorcing Mithu, but she stuck to her decision to continue her married life. Her family had finally realized that Jassi would not leave Mithu's acquaintance in any case. She was being mocked by her parents has accepted her marriage. As a result, Jassi was given several documents related to her husband, Mithu. She made her signatures on all the papers presented by her mother. But it was quite astonishing that Jassi also made her sign one of the documents which says that "Jaswinder Kaur wants to annul her marriage with Mithu" and "She was forced by her husband to do a love marriage in India." Its consequence was drawn when Mithu was finally arrested by the Punjab Police. When Jassi came to know about his husband's arrest in India, she contacted the Indian officials to ensure them that the information was falsely prescribed in that document. No response from the Indian Police drew her attention to the Royal Canadian Mounted Police for help and thus flew to India in 2000 for the acquittal of Mithu (Indo-Canadian honour killing: Jassi Sidhu's mother, uncle may walk out free, 2021). She presented her arguments before the officials to support him. During the same year, her mother and maternal uncle decided to hire professional hitmen to attack Jassi and Mithu. The hitmen attacked the couple when they both were riding on the scooter. The four killers brutally killed Mithu and his wife. Jassi was yelling all around seeking help for her husband. Furthermore, Jassi was brought to the farmhouse by the hitmen where she told her mother to expose her to the police (Indo-Canadian honour killing: Jassi Sidhu's mother, uncle may walk out free, 2021). Her mother had instructed the killers to also kill Jassi which marked the death or honor killing of the Indo-Canadian girl. Jaswinder's family believed she had offended their patriarchal values and violated the concept of caste honor in a socially unacceptable way, dishonoring the whole family (Aujla & Gill, n.d.). Jassi's dead body was found the next day morning. All four killers were arrested by the police officers. On September 7, 2017, the Supreme Court of Canada also in its final verdict ordered to extradite those two accused to face the charges (Shafia murders: Mother 'discovered freedom' behind bars, changed story, filed for divorce, 2019).

Aqsa Parvez Murder Case

Aqsa Parvez was 11 years old and originally belonged to Pakistan and later shifted to Canada. She remained unsatisfied with her family especially his father, Muhammad Parvez, and brother, Waqas Parvez who used to restrict her from practicing Western styles. They were hugely dissatisfied with the Aqsa's inappropriate clothing pattern. Aqsa's brutal treatment being done by her father was perpetually pressuring her to leave the home. Aqsa wanted to live her life in her stand-alone decisions supporting the Western ways of Canada. Aqsa's omission of the Hijab from her clothing was one of the leading causes that triggered her father and brother to commit unfair treatment in the house. She also communicated such disputes to her social groups at school for a speedy solution (Korteweg, n.d.). To address Aqsa's issue, the social groups of the school managed her to settle in a Shelter but afterward, she decided to return home. Even though Aqsa has returned home after living in the shelter, there was no variation in the beliefs of her family. Thus, putting pressure on Aqsa to improve her dress code following their community or culture. As Muhammed Parwaz and Waqas Parwaz were not stopping to traumatize Aqsa, so she again decided to end up living with her family. She was residing in her friend's house whose family was also hailed from Pakistan. Since she was continuing her life in the friend's house, the Aqsa family was perpetually striving to return their daughter home. Surprisingly, her father was ready to accommodate Aqsa's personal choices demanding personal freedom, allowing her to wear whatever she wanted to wear. But she knew that her father would surely disagree with her Western way of living a life. One fine morning when Aqsa was standing in wait for a bus, her brother, Waqas Parvez arrived there and therefore killed her collectively with the father, Muhammed Parvez (Korteweg, n.d.). This marked the death of Aqsa Parven by her father and brother in 2007. The victim's father believed that her daughter's action was badly insulting him in the community, thus depicting the fact that *"A father cannot control her daughter or Aqsa."* It was said that Mr. Parvez had taken an oath on the Quran that he would kill Aqsa if she did not return home. However, religious scholars do not approve that the Quran does not permit one to commit such a crime. They were even saying that it was not a case of honor killing but of domestic violence. After killing Aqsa, her father immediately called 911 where he confessed that he had murdered her daughter. Both were held guilty on account of second-degree murder and were sentenced to life in prison without any parole (Korteweg, n.d.). Aqsa's sister, Irim also played an immense role in the murder as she used to leak all the activities to Mr. Parvez and his son that the victim used to do in her surroundings.

Amandeep Atwal Murder Case

In this case, Rajender Singh Atwal (father of Amandeep Atwal) pleaded guilty to second-degree murder in July 2003, stabbing her teenage daughter (NRI Rajinder Atwal convicted for murder of his daughter Amandeep, n.d.). Amandeep Atwal was seventeen years old when she fell in love with her boyfriend, Todd in Canada. Their relationship was not revealed to her family. But her parents came to know that Amandeep used to love Todd when they both met with an accident. Amandeep had decided to spend time with Todd McIsaac in Prince George's. But she was asked by her father to accompany her family on vacation for two weeks to B.C. New Minister. Eventually, Rajender Singh Atwal further offered the couple to drop them to Prince George. In due course, Mr. Atwal pulled the car and stabbed her daughter approximately 17 times leading to her cruel death and took her to the hospital where he stated to the staff that the victim had committed suicide (Korteweg, n.d.). The case study denotes that the victim's father was not ready to accept Todd (Amandeep's boyfriend) due to traditional and religious parameters. Amandeep was not allowed to live her life with Todd because her family did not want to face the dishonor within their community. When the victim's family finally realized that their daughter would not leave her boyfriend in any scenario, it resulted in her honor killing. Initially, Rajender Singh Atwal represented his interest in Amandeep to live with Todd, but it was unluckily a false interest. Thus, it may be noted that in most cases of honor killings, the family especially the father and brother primarily draw their approval to adjust to the victim's choices and clothing, but they are actually tricking them into the trap of honor killing.

Amandeep Kaur Dhillon Murder Case

This case is related to honor killing of Amandeep Kaur Dhillon who was killed by her 48-year-old Indo-Canadian father-in-law in June 2010 (Muhammad & Canada. Department of Justice. Family, n.d.). Kamikar Singh Dhillon (father-in-law) who murdered her 22-year-old daughter-in-law told the Court that she was disgracing the honor of their family by not adopting her husband, Mr. Dhillon. She originally belonged to Isru Village near Ludhiana and moved to Canada in 2005 after marrying Dhillon's son (Punjab man gets lifer for honour killing in Canada, n.d.). When the father-in-law came to know that her daughter-in-law had an extra-marital affair, he decided to kill Amandeep Kaur due to the non-tolerance of dishonor of the family. Therefore, she was murdered by Kamikar Singh Dhillon. Her dead body was discovered inside the bathroom of the grocery store. Initially, when the police reached the spot after the murder, Dhillon tried to mislead them by telling them his daughter-in-law had been kidnapped by five masked black men (Punjab man gets lifer for honour killing in Canada, n.d.). But during the course of the investigation, it had already been proven that the victim's father-in-law was involved in killing her. The Court of Law pronouncing its final verdict held Kamiker Singh Dhillon guilty of the first-degree murder as he had done continuous stabbing of the victim to commit the murder. Hence, he was sentenced to life imprisonment with no parole for 15 years (Muhammad & Canada. Department of Justice. Family, n.d.).

Murder of Khatera Sadiqi & Feroz Mangal

In 2009, Hasibullah Sadiqi pleaded guilty by the Court of Law to the first-degree murder of his fiancé, Feroz Mangal, and sister, Khatera Sadiqi. It was said that Khatera Sidiqi wanted to marry a boy who belonged to 'Mangal'. She knew that her family especially the father would not accept their marriage. But she married him without the prior permission of her father who was estranged (Honour killings in Ottawa, 2012). When her brother, Hasibullah found her sister married to a boy outside of his community immensely experienced the family's dishonor or insult. He was purely dissatisfied with her sister's marriage as it was done without the involvement of the victim's father. Therefore, he decided to kill her sister to preserve the honor of the family. It was May 2009 when he killed the victims in the Elmvale Mall parking lot late (Honour killings in Ottawa, 2012).

Aysar Abbas Murder Case

In this case, a man named Adi Abdul Humaid was convicted of the first-degree murder of her wife, Aysar Abbas in 1999 in Ottawa, Canada. The husband of Aysar Abbas had stabbed her multiple times, especially in the neck. Later, Adi Abdul Humaid appealed before the Supreme Court of Canada where he contended before the court that her wife had provoked him to kill her as she was having an extra-marital affair with another man. He further told the honorable court that Islamic beliefs also consider female infidelity a very serious offense (Muhammad & Canada. Department of Justice. Family, n.d.). The Supreme Court of Canada interpreted that an individual cannot commit murder or any other heinous crime simply on the basis of the justification of cultural beliefs as Adi Abdul Humaid did. The court ruled that Abdul would be convicted of first-degree murder as he infringed the Canadian laws which are uniform to all of its citizens. Thus, the Supreme Court of Canada finally supported the gender-equality laws of Canada in front of Humaid's plea of cultural beliefs.

Kanwaljeet Kaur Nahar Murder Case

This case also marked the honor killing of Kanwaljeet Kaur Nahar by her husband. In 2001, Mr. Nahar killed her wife by stabbing her very badly (Muhammad & Canada. Department of Justice. Family, n.d.). According to Mr. Nahar, her wife used to smoke, consume alcohol, and engage with other men which was not tolerated in the Sikh community. Moreover, it was said by Mr. Nahar that he also made force on the victim by observing his community, leading to her painful death. Nahar claimed that his wife had once more rejected his pleas, saying, "You can't stop me." Nahar stated in his trial that "I felt like I was blind, and my brain went numb." He stabbed her while she was experiencing this "blindness." (Honour killing toll at least 15 in Canada in past two decades, 2015).

Tabassum v. Canada, 2009 FC 1185

A lady from Pakistan was scared as her family assumed that her acts were leading to the dishonor of the family. The family was extremely dissatisfied with her act of touching another man's hair in the course of her employment. When she was talking to a man belonging to Canada was also misunderstood by her family that she had contact with another man which is not apt for the honor of the family. She knew if her return to Pakistan was made, she would be killed in the honor killing. As a result, the lady demanded security from the pre-removal risk assessment (PRRA) officer, but he neglected her to offer help (Muhammad & Canada. Department of Justice.

Family, n.d.). The decision of the same was opposed by the Court of Law. As per the objective country evidence, the Government of Pakistan is not able to control honor killings, and domestic abuse is hardly protected by their police officials as they consider such acts as family problems (Tabassum v. Canada, 2018). According to the 2007 United States Department of State Country Reports on Human Rights Practices for Pakistan, honor killings are still an issue, with women being the main victims. Local human rights organizations documented between 1200 and 1500 cases throughout the course of the year and most certainly, many more went unreported (Tabassum v. Canada, 2018).

I.F.X. (Re) [2000] CDD No. 166

The 24-year-old Roman Catholic, Arab-Israeli girl was forced by her family to marry her first cousin at the age of 14 years. Eventually, she started dating the Canadian immigrant when her husband left her. She started feeling her family the fear of honor killing during her pregnancy and therefore she was granted refugee protection as the panel has analysed that her husband was very violent and cruel to her (Muhammad & Canada. Department of Justice. Family, n.d).

IMPACT DRAWN TO THE CANADIAN SOCIETY BY HONOR KILLING

Honor Killing in Canada deeply impacted Canadian society, especially after high-profile cases such as the Shafia case. This generated more awareness in society regarding such crimes. More efforts have been drawn to prevent such crimes by imposing certain reforms in legal and social services. Police faced numerous challenges dealing with these honor-based crimes. There are many cases of honor killing that remain underreported as the immigrant communities can't report them to the police due to some grounds such as linguistic barriers, immigration concerns, etc which often pose difficulty for them in handling those crimes and one of the major reasons is that such crimes often happen within the family which makes it difficult to identify the offender (Honour-based violence Complex issue needs greater awareness, 2016). Several discussions were also led by the Government to address the issue of whether to impose new laws against honor-based crimes or whether they should continue to be counted under domestic violence. The Shafia case, 2009 also made different agencies such as the global policing community think to act more strictly in preventing these serious issues (Honour-based violence Complex issue needs greater awareness, 2016). Furthermore, the cases of honor killing started getting showcased subsequently by the Canadian media and various newspapers such as Kingston Whig-Standard, Montreal Gazette, etc. Though, the honor killing in Canada is unknown, but it remains the serious issue as it witnessed as it is evident from recent cases like Kanwaljeet Kaur Nahar Murder Case, 2001, Shafia Case, 2009, etc.

How does Canadian media quote the Honor Killing

The Shafia case which led to the demise of four females of the family did not initially gain the media's attention. Subsequently, when the husband, Mohd. Shafia, his second wife, Tooba Yahya, and their son, Hamid Shafia were successfully arrested by the Kingston police, the case started to get showcased by the Canadian Media where various articles about the same got published in the *Kingston Whig-Standard* and *Montreal Gazette* regarding the Kingston Mills Murder (Corinne L, n.d.). The media while portraying such sorts of crime often failed to consider, how they emerged. In case, if there is the presence of Immigrant communities results in such honor-based violence, the media many times often find the Muslim communities responsible for depicting such honor killings are the outcomes of their family crises evolving by the acts of their daughter leading to the shame of their honor (Shier & Shor, 2016). The media does not consider what the leading cause is behind such serious honor killings. The Media's inappropriate interpretation of honor-based offenses often develops the wrong assumption in people's minds related to such offenses. Mohd. Shafia got hugely trolled by the print media when his arrest was done by the Kingston police (Corinne L, n.d.). In Canada, honor killings are often rare to witness, but it cannot be believed that there was no count of the same before the advent of immigrant communities. When such offenses are committed by people apart from the immigrant communities in Canada, the media is unsuccessful in unfolding the social or cultural reasons behind the honor-based crimes. They probably state that it was due to the psychological state of the preparator which triggered him to commit the murder of the victim constituting honor killing (Shier & Shor, 2016). When Canada notices honor killings where there is an intervention of the immigrant communities, the media tends to denote it was the cultural factors and the patriarchy which contributed to the painful demise of the victim (Shier & Shor, 2016). This often accounts for the biased view of the media with respect to honor killing. Thus, the media should aim to represent authentic information ranging from the reason that led to the outbreak of such crimes against women to every factor that created the conflict between the victim (woman) and the other family members. It also disturbs the statistics of the particular crime covering its figures, causes, and other parameters. The insufficient and molded picturization of honor killing cases by the media involving Canada develops wrong conceptions across the globe about some particular communities. It is not a fact, that honor killings are mostly done in Muslim communities as there is also a certain number of Islamic scholars who oppose the prevalence of honor killings (Shier & Shor, 2016). Media in Western countries tries to showcase that it is the different immigrant communities, especially from the Middle East or South Asia that follow the Muslim traditions (Shier & Shor, 2016). The so-called honor Killing which took place in the Shafia family leading to the deaths of three daughters and first wife got huge attention in the Canadian media where many articles were published in the newspapers. The term "honor killing" circulated pervasively, often without a definition or description, and rarely with an explanation of its immediate use to describe the murders in news media coverage (Corinne L, n.d.). Sometimes, it was said that communities authorize such crimes, but this is false. It is not necessarily true that communities always approve the honor-based crimes, but it is mostly represented by the media while displaying any case of honor killing. Thus, the media must solely focus on providing authentic details regarding any case to ensure better transparency and honesty with the public at large. It would also ensure the good trust of the people in the media for any news based on any domain.

Examining how Current Laws Address Honor Killing in Canada?

After the witness of high-profile cases of honor killing including the Shafia Case in Canada, the debate continued on whether there is a need to impose new laws particularly based on honor-based crimes or not. The Conservative cabinet minister Rona Ambrose proposed his statement to keep a separate charge for honor killing in the Criminal Code but the same was denied by the Justice Department (Canadian justice system has the tools deal with 'Honour killings': study, 2012). Although, honor killings in Canada are rare to notice but are also not completely absent. So, there was no specialized law made for these crimes but they are still indirectly covered under Part VIII of the Criminal Code which includes the assault and homicide laws, and thus offenses that may be committed by family members against the victims of honor crimes are prosecuted under these sections (Honour Killings in Canada: A Way Towards Prevention, 2018). Section 264(1) of the Criminal Code talks about assault which includes any bodily harm, to burn, destroy or damage real or personal property; or to kill, poison, or injure an animal or bird that is the property of any person. In the Amandeep Atwal Murder Case, Mr. Atwal stabbed her daughter 17 times which led to her painful death, and therefore he pleaded guilty to second-degree murder. Though there is no specific law made for the prevention of honor killing but there is a section based on homicide under section 222(1) of the Criminal Code. It punishes the person who directly or even indirectly caused the death. It is also clearly mentioned under Section 222(5)(c) that a person commits a culpable homicide if he performs such an act that results in the death of the victim. Likewise, Mohd. Shafia and his son in June 2009 also did this by making four females of the

Shafia family manage to settle in a separate car and used another car to push the vehicle into a canal in Kingston, Ont which led to their sad demise.

In order to address the violence against women and Children in Canada, Bill S-7: An Act to amend the Immigration and Refugee Protection Act, the Civil Marriage Act and the Criminal Code was introduced in the Senate in November 2014. It was also known as the Zero Tolerance for Barbaric Cultural Practices Act. This step from the Government of Canada gives freedom to the people of Canada or the people who want to settle in Canada to not to deprived of their human rights due to Cultural traditions (Bill S-7-Zero Tolerance for Barbaric Cultural Practices Act CANADIAN BAR ASSOCIATION CRIMINAL JUSTICE AND IMMIGRATION LAW SECTIONS, CHILDREN'S LAW COMMITTEE AND SEXUAL ORIENTATION AND GENDER IDENTITY CONFERENCE, 2015). It opposes the prevalence of forced marriages where the girls are compelled to marry the partner without their will. This remained a very significant amendment that worked to uplift the individuality of the girls residing in Canada by respecting their rights and freedom. Bill S-7 also made the celebrations, aid, or participation in marriages illegal where either party is unwilling to do the same or is below 16 years of age (Béchard et al., n.d.). Moreover, it made the immigration policy more strengthening by making women inadmissible to Canada who are/will practice polygamy with another man who is/will be physically present in the Canadian territory (Bill S-7-Zero Tolerance for Barbaric Cultural Practices Act CANADIAN BAR ASSOCIATION CRIMINAL JUSTICE AND IMMIGRATION LAW SECTIONS, CHILDREN'S LAW COMMITTEE AND SEXUAL ORIENTATION AND GENDER IDENTITY CONFERENCE, 2015).

Comparative Analysis of Honor Killing in Asia, Europe & Canada

Honor Killing in Asia, particularly in India happened majorly all over the country but especially in the states of Rajasthan, Haryana, and Western Uttar Pradesh. Studies reveal that patriarchal societies are one of the leading causes behind the outbreak of honor killings in India. Such patriarchal features of societies often suppress the will of female members of the family and they can't able to marry the person of their choice. Honor Killings in India even happen in the marriages of the same *gotra* (Clan) which again reflects the patriarchy within the society (Deol, 2014). The Khap panchayats in Haryana, India also restrict the couple from getting married in case their mother or grandmother has the the same *gotra* (clan). Therefore, the basic cause behind the counts of honor-based violence in India is due to complex socio-cultural patterns (Deol, 2014). This often poses challenges in various Inter-Caste and even Inter-Religion marriages in India. In Pakistan, there are also many factors such as poverty, lack of education, culture, customs, etc which lead to honor killing (Khaskheli et al., 2018). The honor killings in Pakistan are also the result of the good social pressure out of which the five girls in Kohistan (Pakistan) were also murdered (Singh & Bhandari, 2021). The Aurat Foundation which is an Islamabad-based women's organization stated that multiple women have been murdered in the marriage (Singh & Bhandari, 2021). This indicates that there is a prevalence of honor-based crimes in Pakistan. The status of Honor crimes in Europe occurs mainly in the Immigrant and ethnic minority communities and such crimes used to be detected as 'honor crimes' if they are reported. According to some sources, there are 25% of ordinary unreported crimes but 75% of honor crimes go unreported in the Netherlands (Prpic, 2015). The meeting in Hague in 2004 regarding the increasing honor killings in Europe made law enforcement officers from the U.K. begin reopening the old cases to know if certain murders were actually honor murders (Chesler, n.d.). In Canada too, honor killings though are rare to notice but they happen in immigrant communities of different cultures, norms, and religions. The Shafia Case, Aysar Abbas Murder Case (in Ottawa), etc are some of the high-profile cases of honor killing that made such honor crimes more serious in Canada, leading to the execution of more preventive actions and more awareness regarding the same.

CONCLUSION

Honor Killings in Canada are not purely absent but rare. It is through in-depth research and findings, we get to reveal that the immigration factor majorly plays a role in observing such honor crimes. Thus, the Canadian government must frame more immigration policies for the effective prevention of honor-based violence which is usually committed against women. In Shafia case, Mohd Shafia along with his children and second wife, Tooba had settled in Canada but later on, he was also successful in calling her first wife which was opposed to the Canadian Scheme. The strict immigration policies by the Canadian government would result in the preservation of the collective interest of women to safeguard their dignity and freedom in Canada. The subject of Canadian laws especially which are concerned about gender equality, freedom, rationality, etc, must be taught to the Canadian youth to protect their individual interest in the family or community. Moreover, the education of Canada should also focus on inculcating the basic knowledge related to the crimes which are most prone to students including honor killings. Even little awareness among the young children in Canada and other Western countries (most importantly, the young girls) would back them in examining the same. On the other side, Canadian media must also emphasize delivering the correct news regarding honor killings ignoring the biased character. Relatively few of the articles aggressively contested the inadequacies of Canadian societal structures in offering suitable assistance to women in violent situations (Gill, 2022). The Canadian government must be more stringent in describing the punishment against honor killings which should create fear in the minds of people who are planning to commit the honor killing. Some women victims often hesitate to seek support from the officials of the administration which should be avoided to acknowledge their serious problem. Proper research and data collection should be performed qualitatively to discover the causes and issues behind the counts of honor-based violence against women. This would further magnify the scope for effective policy formulation to tackle honor killing. Open discussions among the people should also be encouraged to unfold the factors responsible for creating the honor killings in Canada.

REFERENCES

Aujla, W., & Gill, A. K. (n.d.). All rights reserved. Under a creative commons Attribution-Noncommercial-Share Alike 2.5 India License Criminal Justice Sciences (IJCJS). *In Official Journal of the South Asian Society of Criminology and Victimology* (Vol. 9, Issue 1).

Béchard, J., Elgersma, S., & Nicol, J. (n.d.). Bill S-7: *An Act to amend the Immigration and Refugee Protection Act, the Civil Marriage Act and the Criminal Code and to make consequential amendments to other Acts.*

Bill S-7-Zero Tolerance for Barbaric Cultural Practices Act. (2015). *Canadian Bar Association Criminal Justice and Immigration Law Sections, Children's Law Committee and Sexual Orientation and Gender Identity Conference.* www.cba.org

Canadian Bill of Rights, section 1

Canadian Charter of Rights and Freedom, section 15

Canadian Charter of Rights and Freedom, section 28

Canadian justice system has the tools deal with 'Honour killings': study. (2012, January 24). National Post. https://nationalpost.com/news/canada/canadian-justice-system-has-the-tools-deal-with-honour-killings-study-says

Chesler, P. (n.d.). *Worldwide Trends in Honor Killings.*

Corinne, L. (n.d.). *The "Kingston Mills Murder" and the Construction of "Honour Killings" in Canadian News Media.* www.msvu.ca/atlantis

David, J.-D., & Jaffray, B. (n.d.). Homicide in Canada, 2021. www.statcan.gc.ca

Deol, S. S. (2014). Honour Killings in India: A Study of the Punjab State. In *International Research* []. www.isca.me]. *Journal of Social Sciences*, 3(6).

Gill, J. K. (2022). Problematizing "Honour Crimes" within the Canadian Context: A Postcolonial Feminist Analysis of Popular Media and Political Discourses. *In Societies* (Vol. 12, Issue 2). MDPI. https://doi.org/DOI: 10.3390/soc12020062

Guide to the Canadian Charter of Rights and Freedoms. (n.d.). Government of Canada. https://www.canada.ca/en/canadian-heritage/services/how-rights-protected/guide-canadian-charter-rights-freedoms.html#a2j4

Hamed Mohammad Shafia v. Her Majesty the Queen. (n.d.). Supreme Court of Canada. https://www.scc-csc.ca/case-dossier/info/sum-som-eng.aspx?cas=37387

Honour-based violence Complex issue needs greater awareness. (2016, October 3). Royal Canadian Mounted Police. https://www.rcmp-grc.gc.ca/en/gazette/honour-based-violence

'Honour' Killing and Violence_ Theory, Policy and Practice -- Aisha K_ Gill, Carolyn Strange, Karl Roberts (eds_) -- 1, 2014 -- Palgrave Macmillan UK -- 9781137289568 -- 207796db8522f584c644dbaccc. (n.d.).

Honour killing toll at least 15 in Canada in past two decades. (2015, December 22). Canadian Content Forums. https://forums.canadiancontent.net/threads/honor-killing-toll-at-least-15-in-canada-in-past-two-decades.140054/

Honour Killings in Canada: A Way Towards Prevention. (2018, March 9). https://www.linkedin.com/pulse/honour-killings-canada-way-towards-prevention-shireen-ali?utm_source=share&utm_medium=member_android&utm_campaign=share_via

Honour killings in Ottawa. (2012, January 30). Ottawa Sun. https://ottawasun.com/2012/01/30/furey-on-shafia-verdict

Indo-Canadian honour killing: Jassi Sidhu's mother, uncle may walk out free. (2021, December 27). The Canadian Bazar. https://www.thecanadianbazaar.com/jassi-sidhu-honor-killing-her-mother-uncle-may-go-scot-free/

Infographic: Homicide in Canada, 2022. (2023, November 29). Statistics Canada. https://www150.statcan.gc.ca/n1/pub/11-627-m/11-627-m2023058-eng.htm

Khaskheli, M. B., Saleem, H. A. R., Bibi, S., & Gsell Mapa, J. (2018). Comparative Analysis of Honor Killing Phenomena in China and Pakistan. *Journal of Law and Criminal Justice*, 6(2). Advance online publication. DOI: 10.15640/jlcj.v6n2a2

Korteweg, A. C. (n.d.). *Understanding Honour Killing and Honour-Related Violence in the Immigration Context: Implications for the Legal Profession and Beyond.* https://www.proquest.com/docview/1018564902/abstract/568DE891A2C4199PQ/1

Montreal Gazette. (2019, December 13). *Shafia murders: Mother 'discovered freedom' behind bars, changed story, filed for divorce.* https://montrealgazette.com/news/the-shafia-murders-mother-convicted-of-killing-daughters-finds-freedom-behind-bars

Muhammad, A. A., & Canada. Department of Justice. Family, C. and Y. S. (n.d.). *Preliminary examination of so-called "honour killings" in Canada.*

Murderous honour, undying love: The tale of Jassi and Mithu from Canada to Punjab. (2017, September 17). Hindustan Times. https://www.hindustantimes.com/punjab/when-jassi-met-mithu-and-love-met-honour/story-SJTNaYvsAmieRqkEJwnDPJ.html

NRI Internet.com. (n.d.). *Rajinder Atwal convicted for murder of his daughter Amandeep.* https://www.nriinternet.com/NRI_Murdered/CANADA/BC/2004/Amandeep_Atwal_Murder/1_0803.htm

Prpic, M. (2015). *Briefing European Parliamentary Research Service.*

Punjab man gets lifer for honour killing in Canada. (n.d.). The Tribune. https://m.tribuneindia.com/2010/20100606/main4.htm

Razack, S. H. (2021). Should feminists stop talking about culture in the context of violence against muslim women? The case of "honour killing.". *International Journal of Child, Youth & Family Studies*, 12(1), 31–48. DOI: 10.18357/ijcyfs121202120082

Shier, A., & Shor, E. (2016). "Shades of Foreign Evil": "Honor Killings" and "Family Murders" in the Canadian Press. *Violence Against Women*, 22(10), 1163–1188. DOI: 10.1177/1077801215621176 PMID: 26712236

Singh, D., & Bhandari, D. S. (2021). Legacy of Honor and Violence: An Analysis of Factors Responsible for Honor Killings in Afghanistan, Canada, India, and Pakistan as Discussed in Selected Documentaries on Real Cases. *SAGE Open*, 11(2). Advance online publication. DOI: 10.1177/21582440211022323

Tabassum v. Canada. (2018, January 29). Max Berger Professional Law Corporation. https://www.maxberger.ca/immigration-cases/pre-removal-risk-assessment-prra/tabassum-v-canada/

Temowo_Adeniyi_Olasunkanmi (1). (n.d.).

Vriend v. Alberta, [1998] 1 S.C.R. 493

Chapter 12
Legacy of Silence:
Exploring Honour Killings in the Tapestry of Jewish and Medieval European History

Pradeep Kumar
Vivekanada College of Law, Aligarh, India

Anushka Bhaskar
Amity University, Noida, India

ABSTRACT

In "Legacy of Silence," we embark on a profound exploration of the grim phenomenon of honour killings, particularly as it intertwines with the intricate historical fabrics of Jewish and Medieval European societies. This chapter seeks to shed light on a topic often shrouded in obscurity and misunderstanding, drawing connections between past traditions and the remnants of these practices in contemporary societies. By delving into the historical contexts of Jewish and Medieval European (Brundage & James A, 1987) cultures, we aim to uncover the roots, manifestations, and enduring impacts of honour killings in these societies. This exploration is not only a journey through time but also a critical examination of the cultural, religious, and social underpinnings that have perpetuated such acts of violence.

RESEARCH METHODOLOGY

This chapter employs a qualitative research methodology to explore the complex issue of honour killings within Jewish and Medieval European contexts, as well as their broader implications in contemporary societies. A combination of primary

DOI: 10.4018/979-8-3693-7240-1.ch012

Copyright © 2025, IGI Global. Copying or distributing in print or electronic forms without written permission of IGI Global is prohibited.

and secondary sources was used to develop a comprehensive understanding of the subject. Data was collected from various sources, including historical archives, library records, newspapers, magazines, interviews with historians, legal experts, and activists, and online databases. Primary data was gathered through interviews and surveys with individuals possessing expertise in the areas of history, law, human rights, and cultural studies. These perspectives provided valuable insights into the historical and cultural factors influencing honour killings. Secondary sources, such as scholarly articles, books, and reports from human rights organizations, were used to support the research findings and contextualize the historical roots of honour killings. The methodology was designed to minimize bias by carefully considering participant characteristics such as ethnicity, gender, and age. Furthermore, the research adopted a human rights framework, focusing on honour killings as a violation of the right to life with dignity.

KEY TERMS

"Honour Killing" (Assistant Professor R.K & S. Assistant Professor, 2019) central to the chapter, this term refers to the practice of murder committed by family members to restore or protect family honour, linking historical and contemporary instances of this violence. "Historical Context of Honour Killings" (Rana Husseini, n.d.,2021) this term examines the historical settings in Jewish and Medieval European societies where honour killings occurred, providing a backdrop for understanding their evolution and impact. "Jewish Legal Traditions"(Askhistorians, 2013) refers to the specific legal and cultural norms within Jewish communities that influenced honour and familial control practices. "Medieval European Norms" (Spierenburg, 2008) focuses on the societal and legal norms of Medieval Europe that shaped attitudes towards honour and violence, including feudal and religious influences. "Gender-Based Violence" (Amt,2013) highlights the broader category of violence, including honour killings, that is inflicted based on gender, providing a framework for understanding its prevalence and impact. "Social Norms and Honour" (Cohen, D.,1998) explores the rigid societal expectations and cultural norms surrounding honour in historical contexts, and how these norms perpetuated acts of violence. "Human Rights"(Assembly, 2003) examines how honour killings constitute a violation of fundamental human rights, including the right to life and dignity, linking historical practices with modern human rights concerns.

LITERATURE REVIEW

This chapter dwells into various perspectives on honour killings across different regions are explored to understand their historical and cultural roots. (Alka Tomer, n.d) links domestic violence to honour-based killings in South Asia, illustrating how patriarchal traditions justify such acts to enforce societal norms around female behaviour. (Anahid Devartanian Kulwicki, 2002) highlights honour crimes in the Arab world, emphasizing the precedence of family honour over individual rights and the need for reform. (Bhanbhro et al.,2013) examine Karo Kari in Sindh, Pakistan, revealing its deep cultural roots and how honour killings are used to restore familial honour. (Gill, 2006) discusses how patriarchal violence under the guise of honour reflects rigid cultural frameworks prioritizing family honour over women's rights. (Goldberg, 2010) explores the intertwining of honour, politics, and law in Imperial Germany, demonstrating how societal structures enforced honour-related violence. (Rana Husseini, n.d.) traces the persistence of honour crimes through history, showing how cultural and social justifications continue to underpin such violence.

Ultimately, this body of literature underscores the necessity for a comprehensive approach to addressing honour-based violence on a global scale. It reveals how the historical and cultural contexts of Medieval Europe, Jewish societies, and various Indian perspectives have shaped and perpetuated these practices. This analysis highlights the importance of understanding the multifaceted roots of honour-based violence to understand it across different cultural and historical landscapes.

FUTURE RESEARCH DIRECTIONS

This research has illuminated the connection between honour killings and the infringement of the right to life with dignity, stressing the importance of addressing this issue from a human rights perspective. Despite numerous judicial calls for legislative action and growing awareness, honour killings continue due to a lack of political will and inadequate public support (Puneet Kaur Grewal, 2012). Future research should prioritize comparative analyses of how different jurisdictions handle honour killings, assessing both historical and contemporary legal frameworks to identify effective legislative practices and gaps (Lama Abu-Odeh, 1997; Kumar Rana & Prasad Mishra, n.d.). Additionally, exploring the intersection of honour killings with broader gender-based violence could enhance understanding of how entrenched gender norms and patriarchal structures perpetuate these crimes (Gill, 2006).

Further investigation into historical contexts, particularly in Jewish and Medieval European societies, could provide insights into how cultural norms and societal expectations around honour have evolved and influenced violence (Brundage &

James A, 1987; Baskin, 2006). Additionally, a closer examination of the role of social and political influences in perpetuating honour-based violence would be beneficial (Nirenberg, 2002). These avenues of research are essential for developing more nuanced and effective approaches to combating honour killings, ultimately contributing to stronger legislative and social frameworks aimed at protecting human rights and dignity.

INTRODUCTION: DEFINING VARIOUS PARAMETERS OF HONOUR KILLINGS

Honour killings, a form of violence primarily against women, continue to challenge societies across the globe. Rooted in deeply entrenched cultural, societal, and sometimes religious beliefs, these acts are often committed by family members with the pretext of protecting or regaining family honour.

By definition Honour killing refers to the act of murder committed by family members against individuals, usually women, whom they perceive to have compromised family honour through perceived transgressions, as dictated by stringent cultural or societal norms (Kumar Rana & Prasad Mishra, n.d).

The complexity of honour killings (Assistant Professor R.K & S. Assistant Professor, 2019) lies not just in their violent nature but in the intricate web of factors that underlie these incidents. At the core of honour killings lie rigid societal norms and expectations regarding gender roles and behaviour, particularly relating to female sexuality and autonomy. These norms are often ingrained in the community's cultural and social fabric, passed down through generations, making them resistant to change. There are various parameters which somehow differs from each other based on the geographical position, below some perspectives are mentioned on how honour killings are understood in various parts of the world:

These killings are not confined to any one region but are a global affliction, with incidents reported across diverse cultures and continents, transcending geographic boundaries.

- **South Asia (including countries like Pakistan** (Bhanbhro et al., 2013), **India, Bangladesh):** In these regions, honour killings are often linked to deeply entrenched cultural norms and traditional views on family honour. Actions perceived as bringing shame can include refusing an arranged marriage. (Krishnan, 2005), having relationships outside of marriage, or even being a victim of rape. The motivation behind these killings is typically to restore family honour supposedly lost through the victim's behaviour.

- **Middle Eastern Countries:** In some Middle Eastern societies, honour killings are associated with conservative interpretations of Islam (Anahid Devartanian Kulwicki, 2002), although no religion explicitly condones such acts. Similar to South Asia, the perceived transgressions can range from premarital relationships to violations of modesty norms. These killings are sometimes tacitly tolerated or inadequately punished due to prevailing social and cultural attitudes.
- **Western Countries (Europe, North America):** In the Western context, honour killings are often viewed through the lens of immigrant communities upholding traditional practices from their countries of origin (Helba et al., 2015) . In these regions, such acts are typically treated as severe criminal offenses, and there's a greater emphasis on protecting human rights and ensuring gender equality. However, there can be challenges in addressing these crimes due to cultural sensitivities and the need for cultural competence among law enforcement.
- **Latin America:** While not commonly labelled as honour killings, there are instances in Latin America where violence against women, sometimes leading to murder, is excused or mitigated on the grounds of preserving family honour. This is often intertwined with machismo culture, where male dominance and control over female family members are prevalent.
- **Africa:** In some African cultures, honour killings may occur, although they are often not labelled as such. These acts might be linked to broader issues of gender-based violence and societal norms regarding female behaviour and sexuality. In some communities, practices like female genital mutilation and forced marriages are related to notions of honour and purity.
- **International Human Rights Perspective:** From a global human rights viewpoint, honour killings are considered a serious violation of fundamental human rights (Assembly, 2003), including the right to life, freedom from torture, and gender equality. International organizations and treaties, like the United Nations (UNITED NATIONS E Economic and Social Council, n.d.), actively work to combat such practices through advocacy, legal reform, and support for victims.

As we already know that Honour killings, a term shrouded in the tragic tapestry of cultural, religious, and social dogma, represent a grievous violation of human rights, predominantly targeting the sanctity of women's lives. These acts, often cloaked in the guise of preserving familial integrity, are a stark manifestation of deep-seated gender inequalities and archaic societal constructs. But there is more to it which will be covered further in the chapter, but a Summarized approach is give as under:

Cultural Ethos and Social Mores: At the heart of honour killings lie entrenched cultural (Irshad Altheimer, 2012) and social norms, venerating family honour as a paramount virtue. These norms often propagate stringent behavioural codes, particularly emphasizing the chastity, fidelity, and overall conduct of women.

The Catalyst of Dishonour: These killings are precipitated by actions perceived as sullying the family's name. Such actions span a spectrum, from the refusal of an arranged marriage to the pursuit of a taboo relationship, attire deemed inappropriate, or the harrowing circumstance of being a victim of sexual assault.

Complicity of Kin and Community: Distinct from other forms of homicide, honours often involve a collective consensus, with multiple family members orchestrating or executing the act, at times with veiled approval from the wider community specifically the masculine (Lavaque-Manty, 2006) approval from the society. They mostly remain in a Veil of Silence and Underreporting which talks about significant number of honour killings remain shrouded in secrecy, misreported as accidents or suicides, driven by the stigma attached and the fear of familial retribution.

A Lens of Human Rights: Viewed through the prism of human rights (Heydari et al., 2021), these killings are a blatant affront to fundamental human entitlements, including the inalienable right to life, freedom from violence, and the pursuit of gender parity.

Psychological Reverberations: The ramifications of honour killings extend beyond the physical realm, casting long shadows on the psychological (Cohen, 1998) well-being of family members, particularly the younger generation, and rippling through the communal conscience.

Addressing the phenomenon of honour killings requires a nuanced and multi-dimensional approach, acknowledging and challenging the deep-rooted beliefs and practices that perpetuate this practice. It is a journey towards cultural reformation, legal accountability, and the unwavering upholding of human dignity.

HISTORICAL CONTEXT: HONOUR KILLINGS IN MEDIEVAL EUROPE

In the tapestry of medieval European (Spierenburg, 2008) history, the phenomenon akin to what is contemporarily termed as 'honour killings' emerges as a complex and multifaceted narrative, intricately woven with the threads of societal ethos, patriarchal dominion, and the sanctity of familial repute. This era, characterized by its feudal mores and a stringent hierarchical structure, placed an extraordinary emphasis on the concept of honour – not merely as a personal virtue but as an indelible mark of one's lineage and familial stature, particularly within the echelons of nobility. The perpetrators, often male family members, believed that the restoration of honour required severe punitive measures.

This was a time of superstition and fear, where accusations of moral transgressions led to brutal reprisals, creating an atmosphere of terror. It was not formally recognized or systematically recorded, did occur in medieval Europe, influenced a lot by interplay of social, cultural, and legal factors. The canvas of medieval Europe, however, was not monochromatic in its approach to such matters. During the medieval (Amt,2013) period, which spans roughly from the 5th to the late 15th century, European societies were predominantly feudal and highly stratified. Women were often the subjects of these honour-based acts, largely due to the patriarchal nature of society and the emphasis on female chastity and fidelity as cornerstones of family honour. The notion of a woman's purity being tied to family reputation led to situations where men felt compelled to act violently to 'cleanse' or restore lost honour, sometimes resulting in what would today be recognized as honour killings.

These acts were not uniformly condoned or legally sanctioned across medieval Europe. Legal and moral attitudes varied significantly between regions, and over time, influenced by local customs, religious doctrines, and the gradual development of legal systems. However, this era's approach to honour and its defence, though bearing semblances to modern-day honour killings, must be interpreted through the prism of historical contextuality. The medieval mindset, undergirded by its own unique set of societal norms and legal frameworks, differs markedly from contemporary perspectives. The term 'honour killing', a product of modern lexicon, requires a nuanced understanding and cautious application when retrofitted into the medieval societal fabric, lest we oversimplify the intricate and varied tapestry of historical human behaviour and social norms. In delving deeper into the historical tapestry of honour dynamics in medieval Europe, one must acknowledge the influence of chivalric codes and feudal structures.

The chivalric (M. Girouard, 1981) code, which reached its zenith in the High Middle Ages, imposed a set of ideals on the nobility, emphasizing virtues such as courage, loyalty, and honour. Paradoxically, this code, while promoting ideals of protection for women, could also contribute to a culture of hyper-masculinity and a skewed interpretation of honour that justified violence in the name of defending one's reputation. Furthermore, the intricate interplay of religious doctrines and societal norms significantly shaped perceptions of honour and morality.

The Catholic Church, as a dominant moral authority, often wielded its influence on either condemn or justify acts of honour-based violence. Ecclesiastical doctrines condemning murder clashed with the societal expectations placed on individuals to safeguard family honour. The tension between secular and ecclesiastical authorities added layers of complexity to the moral and legal landscape. For instance, in certain parts of medieval Europe, especially within Germanic (Goldberg, 2010) cultures, the notion of 'wergild' or 'man price' was practiced. This was a system where compensation could be paid to the family of a murder victim as a form of restitution, and the value varied depending on the social status of the victim. In cases of honour-related violence, such practices could potentially influence the outcome for the perpetrator.

Legal systems during this era were diverse and lacked the standardized structures we recognize today. Feudal law, customary law, and ecclesiastical law coexisted, each contributing its own nuances to the acceptance or condemnation of honour killings. The absence of a centralized legal authority meant that justice was often dispensed at the local level, reflecting the peculiarities of regional cultures and traditions. Moreover, in some medieval societies, the concept of a 'trial by ordeal' or 'trial by combat' could be employed in cases where honour was at stake. These trials, though not specifically designed for honour-related disputes, reflected a societal belief in divine intervention in the judicial (Long-Term Historical Trends in Violent Crime, 2003) process and could indirectly impact cases involving honour.

Additionally, economic considerations played a role in shaping attitudes toward honour. Marriages were often strategic alliances between families, and any perceived stain on a woman's reputation could have far-reaching consequences for the entire lineage. The economic and social ramifications of a damaged reputation could incentivize extreme measures to restore honour, reinforcing the patriarchal control over familial honour.

While the prevalence of honour killings during this period remains challenging to quantify due to the scarcity of comprehensive historical records, the diverse and evolving nature of medieval European societies ensured that attitudes toward honour, morality, and violence exhibited a rich tapestry of regional variations and ideological influences. Exploring this intricate historical context sheds light on the complexity of human behaviour and societal norms during the medieval epoch.

JEWISH HISTORICAL PERSPECTIVES AND PRECEDENTS ON HONOUR AND VIOLENCE

Jewish (Baskin, 2006) historical perspectives and precedents on honour killing and violence are deeply rooted in Jewish law and ethics, which are primarily derived from the Torah, Talmud, and later rabbinical writings. In Jewish tradition, human life is considered sacred, and the preservation of life is of paramount importance. This perspective is encapsulated in the principle of "Pikuach Nefesh," which prioritizes saving a life over virtually all other commandments. In the context of honour killing – the murder of a family member, typically a female, who is perceived to have brought shame or dishonour upon the family – Jewish law is unequivocally opposed. Such acts are considered murder, which is strictly prohibited by the Torah.

The commandment "You shall not murder" is a fundamental precept in Judaism. There is no allowance in Jewish law that permits killing a person for reasons related to honour or family shame. The Talmud, a central text in Judaism that elaborates on the Torah's teachings, emphasizes the value of human dignity and the importance of preserving life. It also contains extensive discussions about the sanctity of life and the severe prohibition against shedding innocent blood. This perspective leaves no room for justifying honour killings or similar acts of violence. In historical practice, Jewish (Nirenberg, 2002) communities have generally adhered to these teachings. While there have been periods of violence in Jewish history, such as during conflicts or persecutions, these incidents are not associated with the concept of honour killings as understood in some other cultural contexts. Jewish law and ethics promote peaceful resolution of conflicts, respect for human life, and dignity for all individuals.

However, there are several negative points to consider in relation to how certain factors could have contributed to incidents that might be construed as honour killings, particularly in historical contexts where Jewish communities were influenced by surrounding non-Jewish cultures or where internal communal dynamics might have played a role:

Impact of Surrounding Cultures: In some historical periods, Jewish communities were situated within cultures where honour killings were more accepted. There's a risk that these external cultural norms could influence the behaviour of individuals within the Jewish community, leading to actions that are inconsistent with Jewish values.

Misinterpretation or Misapplication of Religious Principles: In some cases, religious principles were misinterpreted or misapplied to justify wrongful acts. For example, an extreme and misguided interpretation of concepts related to family honour and shame might lead to actions that are contrary to the fundamental teachings of Judaism.

Community Pressures and Isolation: Talks about the desire to handle matters internally within the community, partly due to the concept of Mesirah, could sometimes lead to a lack of transparency and accountability. This might result in inadequate responses to domestic or community conflicts, potentially escalating situations that could have been resolved peacefully.

Ultimately, in summary, while the core teachings of Judaism are clear in their opposition to honour killings, the historical context in which Jewish communities existed could sometimes lead to situations where communal pressures and the interplay of external cultural influences might result in behaviours that deviated from these teachings. However, such instances were not a reflection of Jewish law or ethics, but rather of the complex realities of living as minority communities under varying conditions throughout history.

COMPARATIVE ANALYSIS: JEWISH AND MEDIEVAL EUROPEAN CONTEXTS

Although honour killings in medieval Europe and Jewish history share common themes of communal honour, patriarchal structures, and severe consequences for perceived transgressions, there are notable differences in the religious and legal frameworks that governed these acts. The role of religious interpretation, communal governance, and social status influenced the nature and execution of honour killings in these distinct cultural contexts.

Table 1. Medieval Europe v. Jewish history

MEDIEVAL EUROPE	JEWISH HISTORY
Feudal systems and superstition based	Religious and communal influences based

In a comparative analysis between Jewish and Medieval European contexts regarding honour killings and violence, several key differences and similarities emerge, influenced by political, regional and social factors (Lama Abu-Odeh, 1997). Medieval Europe was characterized by a feudal system and a societal structure deeply influenced by Christian doctrine and local (Gill, 2006) customs. Honour played a significant role in medieval society, often intertwined with notions of nobility, family reputation, and chivalry. In this context, violence as a response to perceived dishonour was not uncommon, and in some cases, was even codified in practices like duelling or in the concept of "blood honour. The Church's view on such matters could differ, sometimes critical, at other times implicitly accepting, or even promoting certain types of violence under explicit circumstances.

In contrast, Jewish communities in Medieval Europe operated under a different set of religious and ethical guidelines, rooted in Jewish law (Halacha). The sanctity of life is a paramount value in Judaism, and the preservation of life overrides all other commandments. Honour killings, or any form of murder, are strictly prohibited. Jewish communities often had their own judicial systems (Beth Din) and community structures, which focused on resolving disputes through legal and ethical frameworks based on the Torah and Talmud. This often-placed Jewish communities at odds with the surrounding Christian society, particularly in matters of law and ethics.

A significant similarity between the two contexts is the influence of surrounding culture and societal norms. While Jewish law is explicit in its condemnation of murder and violence, Jewish communities in medieval Europe did not exist in isolation and could be influenced by the broader Christian and feudal culture in which they lived. This could lead to instances where the behaviour of individuals within Jewish communities reflected broader societal norms rather than Jewish law.

However, a key difference lies in the theological and legal foundations regarding the value of life and the concept of honour. While medieval Christian Europe often had a complex and sometimes contradictory stance towards violence and honour, Jewish (Askhistorians, 2013) law maintained a consistent message of the sanctity of life and the prohibition of murder, regardless of the motive.

In conclusion, while both Jewish and medieval European societies dealt with the concepts of honour and violence, their approaches were shaped by distinct religious and cultural paradigms. Medieval Europe's sometimes permissive attitude towards violence in the context of honour contrasts with Jewish law's unambiguous condemnation of such acts, reflecting a fundamental divergence in how these two societies conceptualized honour, justice, and the value of human life.

LEGAL ECHOES: HOW FEUDAL, CUSTOMARY, AND RELIGIOUS LAWS PERPETUATE PATRIARCHY AND FAVOURITISM:

Feudal law in Medieval Europe was characterized by a rigid hierarchical system that concentrated power in the hands of landowners and monarchs, reinforcing patriarchal values (Brundage, 1987). This legal framework was designed to uphold the authority of feudal lords and preserve the established social order, often to the detriment of women's rights. The laws inherently favoured male authority and largely excluded women from legal and economic rights, reflecting and perpetuating gender-based inequalities.

Customary law, prevalent in medieval European and Indian contexts, was based on long-standing community practices and traditions that institutionalized gender biases (Bhanbhro et al., 2013). These laws often upheld patriarchal structures by limiting women's rights in areas such as marriage, property ownership, and familial authority. The favouring of male heirs and the control exerted by male family members over female relatives exemplified how customary laws entrenched favouritism and reinforced patriarchal norms (Kumar Rana & Prasad Mishra, n.d.).

Religious laws significantly influenced the legal and social norms in both medieval European and Jewish societies, often reinforcing patriarchal values (Baskin, 2006; Brundage, 1987). In Medieval Europe, Christian doctrine heavily influenced legal practices, embedding gender biases into societal norms (Brundage, 1987). Similarly, religious laws in Jewish communities reflected patriarchal values that controlled aspects of women's lives, including their roles within the family and society (Baskin, 2006). These religious frameworks institutionalized gender discrimination and favouritism, deeply embedding these biases into legal and societal structures.

So, in a nutshell, the legal systems of feudal law, customary law, and religious law have historically reinforced patriarchy and favouritism by embedding gender biases into their frameworks. Feudal law, with its concentration of power in male landowners and monarchs, supported a hierarchical structure that perpetuated male dominance both legally and socially. Customary law, reflecting deeply ingrained societal norms, often institutionalized gender biases by favouring male authority in family and property matters, further entrenching patriarchal control (Kumar Rana & Prasad Mishra, n.d.). Religious laws across various cultures, including those in medieval Christian and Jewish contexts, also played a significant role. These laws enshrined patriarchal values, restricting women's rights and reinforcing their subordinate status within both religious and societal structures (Baskin, 2006; Nirenberg, 2002). By codifying these biases, these legal systems ensured that male privilege and dominance were maintained, resulting in systemic favouritism that marginalized women's roles and rights (Gill, 2006).

THE PSYCHOLOGICAL TOLL OF HONOUR KILLINGS ON INDIVIDUALS AND COMMUNITIES:

The psychological impact of honour killings extends deeply into the lives of individuals and the fabric of communities. For individuals, the trauma inflicted by honour killings is profound. Victims' families, who are often left behind, suffer from intense emotional distress, including symptoms of post-traumatic stress disorder (PTSD), depression, and anxiety. The grief of losing a loved one to such violence can be overwhelming, and survivors of honour-based violence may struggle with a persistent sense of fear, shame, and betrayal, compounded by societal stigma and isolation (Bhanbhro et al., 2013). Communities affected by honour killings face significant psychological challenges as well. These acts of violence create an atmosphere of fear and silence, stifling open dialogue and reinforcing harmful stereotypes. The acceptance of such violence within a community can normalize aggression and undermine efforts to promote gender equality and human rights. This normalization can perpetuate a cycle of violence and contribute to a pervasive sense of insecurity and injustice among community members (Gill, 2006; Heydari, Teymoori, & Trappes, 2021). The collective psychological impact includes a diminished sense of safety and a compromised social fabric, impeding progress towards more inclusive and supportive community dynamics.

AN EXPOSITION OF SYMBOLIC INSTANCES: DISSECTING CASE STUDIES AND HISTORICAL NARRATIVES

To further understand the dynamics of honour and violence in Jewish and medieval European contexts, we will examining specific case studies and historical narratives (Rana Husseini, n.d.) that can be illustrative. These instances offer a more nuanced view of how theoretical principles were applied or interpreted in real-life situations.

MEDIEVAL EUROPE

The Case of Abelard and Heloise (12th Century)

The tragic story of Abelard and Heloise, two lovers from medieval France, illustrates the societal repercussions of forbidden love. Abelard, a philosopher, and Heloise, his student, had a secret romantic relationship that led to Heloise's uncle having Abelard castrated in an act of vengeance. This act, driven by the preservation of family honour, exemplifies the extreme measures taken to uphold societal (A Revised Strain Theory of D Elinquency*, 2024) norms in medieval Europe.

Feuds and Vendettas in Italy

In medieval Italy, honour killings were often a part of larger feuds and vendettas between families or clans. These conflicts, often sparked by an affront to honour, could escalate into cycles of revenge killings that spanned generations. The concept of vendetta, deeply rooted in the medieval Italian honour culture, led to numerous cases of targeted killings in the name of family honour.

The Code of Chivalry and Honour-Related Violence

The chivalric code prevalent in medieval Europe often led to violent confrontations and acts of honour-related violence(Lonnie Athens, 2005). Disputes over matters of honour, such as perceived slights, insults, or challenges to one's reputation, frequently resulted in duels or other forms of violence intended to restore honour. The code of chivalry, while promoting ideals of bravery and honour, also contributed to a culture of violence in the pursuit of maintaining one's reputation.

Witch Hunts and Heresy Trials

These events reflect how notions of honour and purity were intertwined with violence. The Church and secular authorities often sanctioned severe punishments, including death, for those accused of heresy or witchcraft, partly to remove the perceived stain on communal or religious honour.

JEWISH COMMUNITIES

The Tragic Tale of Lea and Marozia (10th Century)

In the Jewish community of medieval Italy, the story of Lea and Marozia is a poignant example of honour killings. Lea, a young Jewish woman, was discovered to be in a clandestine relationship with a man from a rival family. Fearing the dishonour this relationship would bring upon their family, Lea's relatives orchestrated her murder, viewing it as a necessary sacrifice to uphold their family's honour and reputation within the community.

The Rhineland Massacres during the First Crusade (11th Century)

During the First Crusade, Jewish communities in the Rhineland faced widespread persecution and violence. Faced with the imminent threat of forced conversion or death at the hands of crusaders, some families chose to carry out mass killings of their own members, viewing it as a way to prevent the dishonour and suffering that would result from falling into the hands of their persecutors. These case studies and narratives highlight the complexities and varied applications of principles surrounding honour and violence in both Jewish and medieval European contexts. They underscore the divergence in how these societies conceptualized and responded to matters of honour, especially when it conflicted with ethical or legal standards.

Witch-Hunts and Honour Killings: Legal Alchemy in Society's Norms

"Witch-Hunts (Malcolm Gaskill, 2008) and Honour Killings: Legal Alchemy in Society's Norms" encapsulates the idea of how two distinct, yet eerily similar phenomena have historically manipulated legal and societal norms to justify extreme acts of violence, primarily against women. The term "Legal Alchemy" here implies a transformation or manipulation of the law and societal norms to validate actions that, under normal circumstances, would be considered reprehensible. This theme highlights the malleability of legal and ethical standards when influenced by deep-seated cultural, religious, or social beliefs.

WITCH-HUNTS: A DARK CHAPTER IN LEGAL HISTORY

Legal Justification for Superstition: Witch-hunts represented a period where superstition and fear were codified into law. The infamous "Malleus Maleficarum, 1487" a legal and theological document, played a pivotal role in legitimizing the witch-hunts in Europe, blurring the line between law, religion (Kelkar, G., & Nathan, D. 2020), and superstition.

State and Church Sanction: The involvement of both church and state authorities in the prosecution and execution of alleged witches shows how societal fears and religious beliefs can distort legal frameworks. Witch trials often lacked basic legal fairness, relying on torture and hearsay as evidence.

Societal Control: The witch-hunts were not just about punishing individuals; they were about maintaining a societal order. By targeting those perceived as deviant or threatening, these legal proceedings reinforced a rigid social and religious structure.

Both Of These Dark Titles Have Some Shared Characteristics Which Are As Follows

Targeting Women: Both witch-hunts and honour killings disproportionately affected women (Sarah Ahmed, 2019). In witch-hunts, women were often stereotyped as more susceptible to witchcraft and morally weaker, making them primary targets. In honour killings, women are typically victims due to perceived violations of cultural or sexual norms, with their behaviour seen as directly impacting family honour.

Enforcement of Social Norms: Both practices served to enforce strict societal norms. Witch-hunts were a means to control deviations from religious orthodoxy and societal expectations, often targeting those seen as outsiders or non-conformists. Honor killings are similarly used to enforce strict cultural and moral codes, particularly around issues of female chastity, marital fidelity, and family reputation.

Fear and Control: A common thread in both phenomena is the role of fear - fear of the unknown and supernatural in the case of witch-hunts, and fear of social disgrace or dishonour in honour killings. Both were used as tools to exert control over communities and individuals, particularly in regulating women's roles and behaviours.

Community and Authority Involvement: Both witch-hunts and honour killings often involved community complicity or even active participation. In witch-hunts, accusations could come from neighbours or community members, while in honour killings, the community or extended family might endorse or even demand the act. Additionally, both practices historically had some level of institutional support – whether from the Church and state in the case of witch-hunts or cultural and legal systems in the case of honour killings.

Justification of Violence: In both cases, extreme violence was justified under the prevailing moral and societal frameworks. Witch-hunts were justified through religious and moral panic, while honour killings have been justified as a defence of family and community honour.

THE "LEGAL ALCHEMY"

Here it serves as a stark reminder of the importance of grounding legal and ethical standards in principles of universal human rights, fairness, and justice, rather than mutable societal norms.

here are some laws governing Witch-hunting vary significantly around the world, including in India. Overview:

In India

Specific State Laws: India (NYAYA DEEP National Legal Services Authority, 2014) doesn't have a centralized national law specifically against Witch hunting. However, several states have enacted their own laws. For example:

Jharkhand: The Prevention of Witch (Daain) Practices Act, 2001.
Bihar: The Prevention of Witch (Daain) Practices Act, 1999.
Rajasthan: The Rajasthan Prevention of Witch-Hunting Act, 2015.
Assam: The Assam Witch Hunting Act, 2015. (For Prohibition, Prevention and Protection)
Provisions: These laws typically include provisions against identifying women as witches, imposing penalties for witch hunts, and measures to protect victims. They also provide for legal and medical aid to victims and contain provisions for their rehabilitation.
Indian Penal Code (IPC): In the absence of specific witch-hunting laws in some states, perpetrators can still be prosecuted under various sections of the IPC, including those pertaining to murder, assault, and intimidation.

In Europe

Similarly in Europe, The Witchcraft Act of 1541 was a significant piece of legislation in England concerning witchcraft and magic. This act was one of several such laws enacted during the Tudor period, reflecting the evolving attitudes and governmental approaches to witchcraft in England. This act was a pivotal law in the history of witchcraft legislation in England, marking a shift towards more severe penalization of alleged witchcraft practices and reflecting the changing religious and social landscape of the time.

CONCLUSION & CONTEMPORARY INSIGHTS: REFLECTION ON THE LEGACY OF SILENCE & UNVEILING MODERN UNDERSTANDINGS IN A NEW ERA

In the conclusion this chapter, is the examination of the historical legacy of honour killings in both Jewish and medieval European contexts is synthesized, highlighting essential insights and implications for contemporary society. This reflective summary underscores the criticality of comprehending this legacy to effectively address current issues pertaining to honour (Alka Tomer, n.d.) and violence. The legacy of witch-hunts and honour killings, and the historical silence surrounding these practices, offer profound insights into ongoing understandings of justice, human rights, and social norms. As we reflect on these aspects of our past, we gain a clearer perspective on how far society has come and the challenges that still lie ahead. Efforts to prevent and combat honour killings in India and globally have encompassed legislative reforms, women's rights advocacy, and community engagement. Grassroots organizations, governmental bodies, and international collaborations have worked tirelessly to dismantle the structures that perpetuate the notion (Kumar Rana & Prasad Mishra, n.d.) of honour at the expense of human. lives.

Table 2. Legislative reforms v. women's right advocacy

LEGISLATIVE REFORMS	WOMEN'S RIGHT ADVOCACY
Advocacy for legal changes to protect vulnerable individuals.	Empowering women and challenging patriarchal norms.

Ultimately, this study inspires optimism, showing that through increased awareness, cultural sensitivity, and a commitment to gender equality and justice, societies can continue to evolve and create safer, more respectful environments for all individuals. This historical insight provides a foundation for ongoing efforts to combat honour-based violence, emphasizing the importance of education, legal protection, and community engagement.

REFERENCES

A Revised Strain Theory of D elinquency*. (2024). https://academic.oup.com/sf/article/64/1/151/2231554

Abu-Odeh, L. (1997). Comparatively speaking: The honor of the East and the passion of the West. Utah L. Rev., 287.

Advance Praise. (n.d.).

Ahmed, S. (2019). The Honor Killing of Qandeel Baloch: Visibility Through Social Media and Its Repercussions. In BOOKWomen's Journey to Empowerment in the 21st Century: A Transnational Feminist Analysis of Women's Lives in Modern Times Women's Journey to Empowerment in the 21st Century: A Transnational Feminist Analysis of Women's Lives in Modern Times (pp. 135–146).

Altheimer, I. (2013). Cultural processes and homicide across nations. *International Journal of Offender Therapy and Comparative Criminology*, 57(7), 842–863.

Amt, E. (n.d.). Women's Lives in Medieval Europe.

Askhistorians, R. (2013). Jewish Historical Perspectives and Precedents on Honor Killing and Violence.

Assembly, G. (2003). Resolution adopted by the General Assembly.

Athens, L. (2005). Violent Encounters: Violent Engagements, Skirmishes, and Tiffs, 34 J. Contemp. Seton Hall University, 34(6).

Baskin, J. R. (2006). Pious and Rebellious: Jewish Women in Medieval Europe. By Avraham Grossman. Trans. Jonathan Chipman (Hanover, NH: Brandeis University Press, 2004. xv plus 329 pp. $29.95). *Journal of Social History*, 40(1), 281–283. DOI: 10.1353/jsh.2006.0069

Bhanbhro, S., Wassan, M. R., Sindh, J., Muhbat, P., Shah, A., Ashfaq, P., Talpur, A., & Wassan, A. A. (2013). Karo Kari-the murder of honour in Sindh Pakistan: an ethnographic study. In *International Journal of Asian Social Science* (Issue 3). http://www.aessweb.com/journal-detail.php?id=5007

Brundage, J. A. (2009). *Law, sex, and Christian society in medieval Europe*. University of Chicago Press.

Cohen, D. (1998). Culture, Social Organization, and Patterns of Violence. *Journal of Personality and Social Psychology*, 75(2), 408–419. DOI: 10.1037/0022-3514.75.2.408 PMID: 9731316

Gaskill, M. (2008). *Witchcraft and Evidence in Early Modern England*. University of East Anglia. DOI: 10.1093/pastj/gtm048

Gill, A. (2006). Patriarchal Violence in the Name of "Honour." In International Journal of Criminal Justice Sciences (Vol. 1, Issue 1).

Girouard, M. (1981). *A return to Camelot. The Wilson Quarterly* (1976-), 5(4), 178-189.

Goldberg, A. (Ann E.). (2010). *Honor, politics and the law in imperial Germany, 1871-1914*. Cambridge University Press.

Helba, C., Bernstein, M., Leonard, M., & Bauer, E. (2015). The author(s) shown below used Federal funds provided by the U.S. Department of Justice and prepared the following final report: Document Title: Report on Exploratory Study into Honor Violence Measurement Methods.

Heydari, A., Teymoori, A., & Trappes, R. (2021). Honor killing as a dark side of modernity: Prevalence, common discourses, and a critical view. *Social Sciences Information. Information Sur les Sciences Sociales*, 60(1), 86–106. DOI: 10.1177/0539018421994777

Husseini, R. (n.d.). Murdered women: A history of 'honour' crimes. Al Jazeera. https://www.aljazeera.com/features/2021/8/1/murdered-women-a-history-of-honour-crimes

Krishnan, S. (2005). Do structural inequalities contribute to marital violence? Ethnographic evidence from rural South India. *Violence Against Women*, 11(6), 759–775. DOI: 10.1177/1077801205276078 PMID: 16043570

Kulwicki, A. D. (2002). The practice of honor crimes: A glimpse of domestic violence in the Arab world. *Issues in Mental Health Nursing*, 23(1), 77–87.

Kumar Rana, D., & Prasad Mishra, B. (n.d.). Honour Killings-A gross violation of Human rights & Its Challenges. www.ijhssi.org

Lavaque-Manty, M. (2006). Forthcoming in Political Theory.

Long-Term Historical Trends in Violent Crime. (2003).

Nirenberg, D. (2002). Conversion, Sex, and Segregation: Jews and Christians in Medieval Spain. *The American Historical Review*, 107(4), 1065–1093. DOI: 10.1086/532664

Nyaya Deep. (2014). National Legal Services Authority. www.nalsa.gov.in

R. K., & K. K. (2019). Honour killing and women: human right's view. In *International Journal of Creative Research Thoughts*, (Vol. 7). www.ijcrt.org

Spierenburg, P. C. (2008). A history of murder: Personal violence in Europe from the Middle Ages to the present. *Polity*.

Tomer, A. (n.d.). *Domestic Violence And Honour Based Killing, Int'l Multidisciplinary Res*. E-J. Indian Scholar.Co.

United Nations. (n.d.). E Economic and Social Council

Chapter 13
Comparative Analysis of Various Factors of Honor Killing in India and European Countries

Anurag Sharma
Vivekananda College of Law, Aligarh, India

Salini Sharma
GLA University, Mathura, India

ABSTRACT

"Honor killings are the darkest manifestation of a society's fear of change and the loss of patriarchal control." Indeed, such killings are not crimes of honor, rather crime of horror. Protecting honor can never be the justification of murdering someone. Its supporters try to justify as are the sole method to restore honor & reputation of the family. This argument is contradictory in itself as how could honor be restored when there will be stain of being murderer on the family following such killing? In fact, the hidden motive behind these killing is nothing but to establish dominance and suppressing the voice of anyone who tries to free oneself from such shackles of patriarchy and orthodox practices. There are various factors behind such killings which vary from region to region. These factors include social, educational, economic, cultural, regional, religious believes, patriarchal norms etc. In this chapter, factors behind honor killings in India vis-à-vis European countries, i.e., France, Germany, Italy, Netherlands, Norway, Russia and Sweden have been examined carefully.

DOI: 10.4018/979-8-3693-7240-1.ch013

Copyright © 2025, IGI Global. Copying or distributing in print or electronic forms without written permission of IGI Global is prohibited.

INTRODUCTION

Honor killing is a sensitive & debatable topic throughout the world. Many societies and nations try to avoid the discussion on this heated issue as it is somehow connected with cultural, traditional & customary values. However, an examination of honor killings reveals that they are driven more by the irrational and self-proclaimed aspirations of individuals and groups than by custom, practices, or sharia rules. The practice stems from and is fueled by the influence of rumors, defamation, and public perception. Whether the act of assault is committed in a public or private setting, it is classified by international law as gender-based killings, or the deliberate killing of women for no other reason than that they are women. The Special Rapporteur's report on violence against women states that the number of women killed for gender-related reasons has risen dramatically throughout the world. These killings were described as a severe instance of violence against females, frequently the result of ongoing, overlooked incident of domestic abuse. According to UNFPA, as much as 5000 women and girls are subjected to honor killing yearly on global level, and almost one-third of those are from Pakistan and India. According to NCRB's report(2020), the no. of honor killings reported in India was 25 each in 2019 and 2020, and 33 in 2021. According to statistical data, there are no. of cases in Europe like 5 in Belgium, 12 in Germany, 10-12 in Great Britain and 11-14 in Netherlands in the recent dozen years.(Sadowa, K., 2015) The goal of this kind of violence is to create and maintain gender-based tiered social relationships. It exacerbates the disparity experienced by socially vulnerable groups—in this example, bias based on gender. (Antonova, 2018) Additionally, another main reason for such honor-based crimes is that the sexuality of women is considered to be the honor of the household, hence, males of the family should protect it. This thinking existed even before Judaism, Islam or Christianity came into existence. (Firat et al., 2016) So, it can be inferred that religion is not the sole reason behind such thinking but it still contributes to such honor-based killings. There are several factors behind honor killings which vary from country to country. It includes patriarchal norms, cultural & religious believes, mindsets of people in a particular region etc.

RESEARCH METHODOLOGY

The aim of this chapter is to gain an understanding of various factors of honor killing in India and European countries and also to find out the difference between the same. For the research purpose, qualitative method of research has been adopted. International journals, research articles, reports from government ministries, research paper & reports from international organizations, surveys, interviews etc.

has been referred to for the research purpose. The reason behind choosing qualitative method is that the sources are rather trustworthy and all sorts of factors whether social, cultural, conservative or gender-related, could be found out and hence, could be explained and elaborated. The research indicate that men, women and LGBTQ community are all its victims. However, it is to be pointed that women and LGBTQ community are mostly its victim in comparison to male victims. From the research, it could be concluded that religion does not play that much role in such killings which is contrary to the popular belief. According to the research conducted, patriarchy and conservative beliefs are the major factors behind such killings.

KEY TERMS

Core term include "Honor killing" (Firat et al., 2016) and "patriarchy" (Singhal, 2014) highlighting the fact that due to male dominance over women over the years has contributed significantly in such killings. The term "sexual purity" (Honour Related Violence within a Global Perspective: Mitigation and Prevention in Europe, 2004) and "masculinity" (Social and Legal Actions to Combat Honor Related Abuse Center for Sustainable Communities Development KUN Centre for Equality and Diversity, 2021) are inter-linked as loss of sexual impurity by a female family member is considered as lack of masculinity on the part of her male family members. "Inter-caste relationships" (Poddar, 2020) is seen as a threat to patriarchal norms and beliefs and a challenge to male dominance and hence, are not supported by the patriarchal society. Rather, "forced marriages" (Poddar, 2020) take place so as to prevent inter-caste relations and marriages and denial of the same lead to such killings. In some countries, the term "rape puzzle" (Eck, 2003) is popular. It refers to killing the romantic partner of the female family member and disguising it as a murder of the rapist of the female member who is in fact her lover.

LITERATURE REVIEW

The crime of honor is a form of inhumane discrimination against women and girls.(Jamuna K.V., 2022) It is a cultural crime where family members, often men, murder relatives to reclaim perceived family honor. (Singhal, 2014) Unfortunately, it is seen as a method of social control within a framework of a strong honor system. (Poddar, 2020) Honor killings violate women's rights to life and autonomy. (Firat et al., 2016) Cultural representations, such as operas and films, illustrate the societal implications of honor and violence against women. (De Cristofaro, 2018) Such killings are prevalent issue in Indian society due to medieval perceptions and caste divisions. (Suresh Kumar, 2023)

FUTURE RESEARCH DIRECTIONS

This research aims to find out the underlying factors behind honor killing in India and European countries. As there is lack of specific data on honor killing due to non-reporting and it not being recognized as a specific crime in almost all countries, this chapter emphasis on recognizing it as a specifying it as a distinct crime so as to set a deterrent in the minds of the perpetrators against such killings. The author has conducted a detailed analysis of factors like patriarchy, conservative beliefs and lack of governmental role in controlling such killings. (Kumar Rana & Prasad Mishra, 2013) This chapter discusses how male dominance led to killing of women, how maintaining sexual purity before marriage is seen as an honor and its violation as a disgrace to the family honor and how controlling conduct, especially sexual and social, of the female family members is considered as a sign of masculinity. (Social and Legal Actions to Combat Honor Related Abuse Center for Sustainable Communities Development KUN Centre for Equality and Diversity, 2021) This chapter highlights that loss of virginity by a woman before marriage is seen as an immoral act and it is deemed that a man who cannot control the sexual behaviour of his female family members is not masculine. (Honour Related Violence within a Global Perspective: Mitigation and Prevention in Europe, 2004) Moreover, the author lays emphasis on the fact that honor killing is seen as a heroic act, rather than as a crime by the perpetrators and the society which is a matter of serious concern. This chapter further highlights the imminent need to educate people about human rights and encourage reporting of such crimes. It also discusses factors like following modern way of dressing, wanting to go to college for further studies, even interaction with a man who is not a family member, divorce due to domestic violence & getting re-married to other person etc. as these factors are not talked about that much. Though the factors have been mentioned thoroughly, however the chapter is subjected to certain limitation as it does not mention the steps which has been taken to reduce these killings. Hence, future research could include the study of these steps and also the role of education & international organizations and NGOs in minimizing such killings.

HONOR KILLING IN INDIA

The concept of honor has been firmly embedded in family, community, and society traditions and behaviors since ancient times. Because they are considered to have the ability to influence the way men and women, but mainly women, view honor, males are considered the protectors of family honor. A woman's behaviors and demeanor have an impact on the entire family. It is said that she will be the family's symbol; hence, the integrity of the family as a whole is based on the woman's chastity. Men ought to monitor women's behavior and be in charge of reining in their sexuality. It is believed that men can be shown to be dominant when they behave brutally against women. It has been observed that in every society, women represent the values of honor and reputation in the home, community, and religion. When women or girls are believed to have behaved in a way that violates the family's code of honor or in a morally improper way, it will be considered that they have brought dishonor to the family and community. Therefore, efforts are made to restore the family and community's honor as well as to uphold the customary family practices which may result in family members murdering their daughter, wife, and son. Indian society has been facing the hot issue of honor killing. It has brought disgrace to Indian society because women are victims of this societal evil as well as men, making it a heinous crime. It is often not possible for girls to go freely outside of their homes. Female students have to head straight home and spend the remainder of the day indoors after finishing their classes, working, or attending college. Furthermore, it is common for girls to be denied access to all educational possibilities only because of their gender. Thus, it is also possible to draw a link between honor killings and forced marriages. In India, it has long been customary to choose the future husband for the daughters of the house. (Suresh Kumar, 2023) Therefore, when there is a denial of getting married according to the family's choice or urge to get married to the person whom he/she has chosen himself/herself, especially of another caste or religion or of the same village, the outcome could be the honor killing of such person. It shows that even in the 21st century, a large number of people do not have the freedom to get married or to choose one's partner according to one's wishes.

Factors of Honor Killing in India

1) Caste – It is popularly believed that inter-caste marriages or relationships are mainly the reason for honor killing. Instead, relationships within castes, are also associated with caste-related honor killings. A marriage or romantic relationship between people of the same gotra is considered incestuous because both of them share a common ancestor. Therefore, one could contend that the documented occurrences of honor killings in India in the twenty-first century

indicate that these crimes are carried out to preserve the sacredness of the same caste as well as gotra in addition to putting a stop to relationships with people outside of one's group.

2) Religion - In opposition to general belief, it seems that religion has little influence over the cases of honor killings. More precisely, only 2.67% of instances in North India were driven by religion, compared to an even lower rate of 1.61% in the country's lower half. Stated differently, there were five similar incidents in North India and only one in the Southern and Central regions. Contrary to common opinion, these statistics show that religion ranks sixth lowest (in terms of percentages) in both the Northern and Southern/Central Indian states, suggesting that it is not one of the lowest driving factors for honor killings. Furthermore, the prevailing opinion that links honor killings to specific religions, particularly Islam, is refuted by the absence of religious elements in the honor system. (Poddar, 2020)

3) Patriarchy - The foundation of all male-female relationships is the concept of patriarchy. Regardless of age, a female is always under guardianship. She is supervised by her father when she is unmarried. When she marries, her spouse becomes her guardian; after his passing, irrespective of the fact that she is a minor or a major, she is under the guardianship of his family until she marries again. In reality, a widow or an unmarried girl cannot exercise her right to choose her counterpart in a marriage arrangement. Unlike single women, widows can refuse remarriage, however, they can only get married as long as the male members of their marital family approve of the union. The male's influence over a woman, regardless of her age or status—married, single, or widowed—never wavers due to the pervasiveness of patriarchy. Her spouse and her son are now in a position of responsibility, replacing her father and brother. (Singhal, 2014)

4) Mindset: The mentality of the populace is a significant contributing factor to honor killing. Some people aren't ready for their kids to have romantic relationship with anyone before marriage, let alone relationship & wed outside of their caste and religion.

5) Social norms–
   a) Having a conversation with an unidentified or unrelated male is prohibited & punishable in many societies.
   b) Consensual extramarital relationships: In India, these relationships are a contributing factor to honor killings. Violence occurs within the family when a married individual has a relationship with someone other than their spouse. Thus, it is also regarded as a contributing factor to honor killing in India.

    c) Being a victim of sexual assault: It has been observed that in India, being a survivor of sexual assault can also result in such killing. The family believes that she has damaged the reputation of the family in the public domain.

    d) One more cause for honor killing is to pursue a divorce or to refuse to wed the man recommended by one's family or romantic relations before marriage.

    e) Participating in lesbian and homosexual partnerships or having pre-marital or extra-marital intercourse has also been linked to honor killing in the nation.

6) Illiteracy - The rise in crime in society is mostly attributed to illiteracy as people are unaware of their as well as other people's rights. (Jamuna K.V., 2022) They can't differentiate between right and wrong, whether morally or legally and keep on blindly following the conservative practices and patriarchal norms. Sir Francis Bacon has rightly said, "Knowledge is power." Since, the people who haven't received any education and hence, don't have any knowledge cannot challenge such horrible crimes even if they are against it, and those who are not against it, keep on thinking that they are justified in doing such crimes and that what they are doing is not a crime. They are unable to comprehend its highly negative consequences on other people's life.

7) Khap Panchayats - Members of a specific caste make up the so-called "Khap Panchayats," which decide and order the majority of honor killings. Frequently, these Panchayats support the entrenched practice of honor killings or other crimes against young men and women from diverse castes and religious backgrounds who aspire to marry or have already been married. There are claims that close relatives or other third parties have resorted to harsh measures against the alleged offending pair, including unjust detention, continuous intimidation & assault; mental or physical, inflicting severe physical injury, and even killing them. Likewise, the decisions & directions given by Khap Panchayats such as social boycotts along with other penalties that impact the concerned couple, their families, and even a part of the local population are frequently encountered.

8) Inadequate Governmental Measures - The main reason why there is a rise in honor killings is that ruling political parties & governments have been unable to get their grip on rural areas. In addition, incapability and corruption in administration are yet another reason for unreported or unsolved honor killing cases. Furthermore, the pendency of cases in the legal system makes people lose faith in the judiciary which results in compromises which in turn leads to non-reporting of cases. As a result, this practice persists even though it ought to have been discontinued a long time ago. (Kumar Rana & Prasad Mishra, 2013)

HONOR KILLING IN EUROPEAN COUNTRIES

As mentioned earlier, one of the especially hazardous and unsettling methods of controlling women's conduct is honor killing. It is a global practice that dates back thousands of years, with populations from Asia, the Middle East, and European nations being the main practitioners, though they are not the only ones. According to estimates from the UN Population Fund, 5,000 women are murdered every year under the pretext of honor. This may be an understatement and the true prevalence is probably greater due to unregistered instances. According to certain statistics, the number of honor killings has been on the rise recently. From 1989 to 2009, the global number of honor killings that have been reported has increased significantly. Rather than a rise in the actual number of incidents, this reported increase could be the result of increased reporting, news coverage, and registration of such cases. It's challenging to estimate how common honor killing is because so many incidents are unregistered. Therefore, it is essential to address the crime and its causes due to the high prevalence of honor killing. Numerous initiatives have been made to reduce the incidence of honor killings, such as the initiatives of international organizations like the CEDAW and WHO, human rights lawyers and activists, NGOs, legal reformation, and even movies. Even though raising public awareness through these actions has been vital, the frequency of honor killings remains disturbingly high.(Heydari et al., 2021) In the next pages, factors responsible for honor killing has been discussed.

France

In some communities, if girls show a particular conduct not in align with the conservative beliefs, they are subjected to harassment. Such conduct includes wearing make-up, signs of wanting to be self-dependent, going out except to school. They are expected to take care of their family and return to home as soon as school ends. Those who do not do that are referred to as 'whores.' In addition, since it is believed that men are superior to women, hence, they took out their frustration and anger on them, verbally or physically. Moreover, since chastity is so valued, many females undergo surgery to repair their hymns, and some parents seek a gynecologist to attest to their virginity. Many girls are prohibited from stepping out at all, or they prevent themselves, due to the two-edged threat of becoming targets or jeopardizing their esteem. There have been instances where a guy killed his ex-wife because she chose to start a new life and have a child with another man following their divorce. The killer got everyone's support who claimed that "it was her fault." The majority of honor killings take place in nations where women are primarily seen as the family's public face. The various kinds of patriarchal tyranny are our enemies. The following are examples of crimes committed in the name of honor: violence against women; abuse, oppression, and exclusion of girls and women as a means of preserving or regaining family honor etc. (Honour Related Violence within a Global Perspective: Mitigation and Prevention in Europe, 2004)

Germany

There have been many cases of honor killings in Germany. Family members in Berlin have assassinated Muslim women for conveying disgrace. In one such instance, a brother murdered her sister for behaving like a German woman and for leaving the man she had been compelled to tie the knot with. Here, immigrants account for the majority of honor killing victims. (Xavier, 2015) The disputed work Die Fremde Braut Kelek by Necla Kelek was published at the same time as Hatun Sürücü's assassination by her brother. This work and several other publications depicted Muslim immigrants in Germany as perpetrating specific types of violence based on gender and criticized Islam as being a regressive faith that mistreats women. The murder of Hatun Sürücü and the book by Necla Kelek sparked heated discussions in the press about honor killing and the unequal treatment of men and women by Turkish immigrants. Immigrant values or not accepting German values is also said to be a factor behind honor killings. (Yurdakul & Korteweg, 2013)

Italy

The concept of honor is a bit different in Italy. Northern part of Italy emphasis more on individualistic honor and dignity rather on collectivistic honor of the community. Hence, gender roles are quite liberal. However, cases of honor killing still exist in some societies. For instance, a person in Italy wounded his sibling eighteen times because the family's disgrace had been caused by his homosexuality. (Xavier, 2015) In addition, the ability of the patriarch, i.e., the head male member, to manage the conduct of members is correlated with the status of a family. Women, particularly, those who are thought to lack discipline, need to be monitored to make sure they don't lose their virginity or jeopardize their marital fidelity. These need to be safeguarded since their metaphorical worth is comparable to that of real estate or homes. In the end, the honor killing projection ignores the customary limitations placed on women by men: marital limitations for wives, and potential restraints for daughters. It is considered that there is an apparent relationship between the concepts of moral and physical integrity. Thus, the only way the husband, whose wife's adultery has disgraced him, can redeem himself in the eyes of the public is by resorting to violence. The only action that demonstrates the strength he has in protecting his 'territory' from rival males is that one. (De Cristofaro, 2018) In case of a daughter who is still unmarried and has been in relationship with someone, then, the father has to restore the family's honor by killing her and the man who has violated her honor.

Netherlands

In the Netherlands, honor killing is a rather unknown term.

There was no name for it until Ane Nauta created it in 1978 with the Dutch word 'eerwraak' which means honor retaliation. It is mentioned in Dutch jurisprudence but not in the official vocabulary. Since 'blood revenge' is a more common term, we occasionally come across it in media and even court documents when honor killing is actually the intended outcome. On the other hand, blood revenge is the term used to describe a murder that takes place as a result of another murder, in which a family kills a member of the offender's family in order to exact retribution for the death of one of its members. Conversely, honor killing is the 'first murder.'

Kressel cites two motives for why honor killings target female blood relatives. First of all, it is simpler to kill the girl than to deal with the murder of the man as it would only become an internal family issue. Second, it discourages other women in the family from acting in a way that jeopardizes their namus, i.e., their chastity, making them reconsider. The sole means of stopping other daughters from pursuing their sister's career path is, therefore, the second justification. Since no blood relative will avenge the daughter, after all, she was murdered by her own blood relatives, killing the daughter will not result in a blood feud, making it less consequential than killing the male involved. Here, the Tekin case serves as a frightening illustration. Another daughter informed the police that she was also surprised by what occurred the night before, after Tekin killed the guy who had violated her dignity. She said that her dad had consistently held her sister accountable for everything. Never once did he swear to do the man anything. Had he murdered her sister, she could have accepted it and not been as upset. She was the one who, after all, embarrassed their family. However, she would now always be terrified of that man's family and would apprehend for them to get revenge on her family. However, a family may choose to accuse a daughter of being raped rather than acknowledge that she is in a relationship. This means that rather than the young woman, the family has to assassinate her lover, the "rapist." This is occasionally described as a "rape puzzle" in magazines. Women can, likewise, utilize this justification too. They may excuse themselves by claiming they were sexually assaulted when their immoral behavior is exposed. The husband or other close members of the family frequently know what exactly occurred, but they uphold this version of events to justify the honor violator's death. Many families are probably incapable of murdering a female member because of emotions. It would also not be economically advantageous for them to suffer the loss of a female, especially a wife. (Eck, 2003)

Norway

In Norway, in order to restore family honor, honor-related violence involves a range of punishments. From forced marriage and murder to social isolation, the word refers to a wide range of violent crimes with differing levels of severity. Even while the physical penalties could appear more severe and conspicuous to onlookers, it is important to realize and acknowledge the possibility that the person being punished could end up alone or rejected. Forced marriage, harsh social control, physical violence, honor killings, and being sent abroad - either to marry or be made to attend school against one's will—have received the majority of attention in Norway. The concept of sexual purity is linked to the honor of women and girls. This primarily refers to remaining a virgin when getting married. However, there are several other purity-related conventions that influence women's day-to-day life, such as acting and dressing decently, refraining from socializing with people of the opposite sex, taking care of others, and doing domestic responsibilities and caregiving. It is expected of men to protect women's honor, provide for them, and make decisions on their behalf. In this system, roles can differ for men and boys. They may be involved in forced marriages, violence, or control as offenders or victims. In an effort to protect the group's honor, they may also be expected or coerced into using violence, controlling others, or participating in forced marriages. Stated differently, boys and men are held accountable for upholding the group's honor. As long as they adhere to the traditional gender norms set forth by their families, boys and men typically have greater independence than women and girls. If boys don't live up to the traditional roles of masculinity, they may face the same consequences as girls. Here, girls are especially prone to this kind of assault because of cultural conventions that associate family reputation with their sexual conduct. Intense patriarchal and collective beliefs tend to prevail in families where this kind of violence happens. The same applies to violence perpetrated to keep one's honor intact in the future. Honor-related violence also includes compelled marital unions, constraints on liberty, etc. The result of violence related to honor is honor killing. Close family relatives are usually the ones that start honor-related violence. The offender tends to be a family member. Men and women both possess honor, but standards of what constitutes honor and disgrace are typically categorized based on gender. The concept of sexual purity is linked to the honor of females. This primarily refers to remaining a virgin before the wedding. However, other purity-related norms affect women's day-to-day lives. These include way of clothing and acting appropriately, abstaining from social interactions with people of another gender, and taking care of the home and taking care of children. It is expected of men to take care of women, make choices for them, and protect their dignity. (Social and Legal Actions to Combat Honor Related Abuse Center for Sustainable Communities Development KUN Centre for Equality and Diversity, 2021)

Russia

These homicides did occur here in the past, according to the experts inquired, but they were not referred to as 'honor killings', in actually, they had no specific term anyhow. Each community possessed its own set of adats or rules, that prescribed penalties for being unfaithful, adulterous, or immoral. The severity of their punishments varied; not all of these situations resulted in death. People of one's family, group, and society still have a shared duty according to traditional Caucasian civilization. Here, personhood is not independent. An individual is becoming more and more integrated into social institutions. In these communities, women's autonomy is far less than men's. A woman lives mostly alone in her environment, governed by the rest of society and customs that dictate every aspect of her life. Because of this, the idea of 'women's honor' which includes women's crucial participation in upholding their modesty and the reputation of the family is ingrained in the thoughts of the inhabitants of the North Caucasus. Executing someone as retribution for breaking customary practices, as a purifying ritual, getting rid of disgrace, resentment, and impunity, or as a means of preventing dishonor from tarnishing the family, and using murder as a warning to deter future acts of defiance by women, as a tactic to control their conduct and as a show of force, are some of the reasons for honor killing in North Caucasus of Russia where the population is majorly Muslim. Some other factors that contribute to these killings are society's opposition to dehumanization and identity deprivation, gender standards based on patriarchy, shared persona: absence of independent personality, household reliance, and structure. (Antonova, 2018)

Sweden

Honor killings are not new to Sweden or to say Sweden has not been remained untouched from this horrible crime. There are different believes, norms and other factors which lead to the commission of these crimes. The dignity of girl is not sole reason behind her killing by her family. In some instances, it has been seen that challenging the patriarchal norms in whatsoever, way, be it a desire to go to school or to get a job, could lead to homicide. In its societies, some individuals believed that honor killing was a custom where women were expected to be subservient to men and to bear children. Another reason is cultural sensitivity, under which there is a type of prejudice that permits the sacrifice of women from ethnic communities.

In a tragic instance, a girl was assassinated in the name of dignity for two separate factors: she was seeing a Swedish man, and she had decided to further her studies. Unfortunately, for those of us who are familiar with the background of honor in many nations such as Turkey, Iran, Iraq, Jordan, and so on, honor killing is not a novel kind of violence against women. However, the majority of ethnic Swedes found this to be a horrific and unusual experience. How could a parent kill his own daughter and still have his friends and family defend him? The nation was stunned once more before the discussion began. It may be argued that there wasn't a lot of awareness & information regarding honor killings. The shame and worry of being seen as racist and intolerable toward immigrants were the second issue. Political leaders, the press, and activists were fearful of aggravating the situation & cautious not to give reasons for discrimination to the racist groups and parties. (Honour Related Violence within a Global Perspective: Mitigation and Prevention in Europe, 2004) Hence, they are afraid to address this issue as it could do more bad than good in their view because if they address it, other people from different countries, international NGOs & welfare organizations would start criticizing the government & it would also negatively impact the so-called good image and in turn, economy of the country to some extent. It could also lead to internal conflict within the country and among the various communities, including immigrants.

COMPARATIVE ANALYSIS OF FACTORS IN INDIA VIS-À-VIS EUROPEAN COUNTRIES

In India, inter-caste marriages or relationships, the male's influence over a woman, regardless of her age or status—married, single, or widowed are mainly the reason for honor killing. In addition, Khap Panchayats, social norms like having a conversation with an unidentified or unrelated male, consensual extramarital relationships, lesbian and homosexual partnerships etc. are seen as unethical or immoral acts and hence, these contribute to such killings.

While in European countries going against conservative beliefs like if girls show a particular conduct not in align with the conservative beliefs, they are subjected to harassment. Such conduct includes wearing make-up, signs of wanting to be self-dependent, going out except to school etc. are the main factors behind such killings. So, social norms and patriarchy play significant role in such killings in India while on other hand, culture, immigration and conservative beliefs are the major factors behind honor killing in European Countries. However, going against patriarchal norms, losing virginity before marriage, being in relationship with a person from different community and lack of governmental role in punishing the perpetrators strictly are common factors both in India and European Countries. It is concerning that despite significant rise in such killings, governments have failed to make strict laws to punish the criminals. The fact that honor killing has not been recognized in almost all the countries as a specific crime despite being an inhumane crime depicts how unserious and unbothered the governments are about this issue. Most of these killings go either non-reported or disguised as other crime such as suicide and even death due to medical conditions in several cases. It is significant to address these killings as hiding the head in the sand, like an ostrich won't solve the problem and moreover, would increase the audacity of the perpetrators.

Suggestion

As honor killing is a social evil and affects society at large negatively, therefore, there is immense need to educate people about its impact, how to report it, how to escape it, how to save someone from its claws and to make them aware about human rights. It is the duty of government as well as moral obligation of NGOs and other organizations working for welfare of people to let people know about the horrific consequences of such killings. Government should also work toward providing better education to more and more people as illiteracy is also one of the factors behind honor killings.

CONCLUSION

Honor Killing is a concerning issue on a global level. Many countries have guidelines on how to address situations of Honor-based violence. In light of this, avoidance, safeguarding, and empowerment are the most effective approaches to address these offenses. Raising attention regarding safety, security forces, and other pertinent state agencies coupled with research on the root causes and consequences of crimes committed against women, can help us develop efficient solutions. International agreements could facilitate the necessary efficient tracking and evaluation. In addition to developing several organizations that might offer survivors refuge, help lines, and health care, judicial and emotional support, the criminal justice system must guarantee the safety of women. Educating and including women in making resolutions is the last stage of women's empowerment. They should have their role when it comes to peace and security on a global, state, and domestic scale. (Rekha Verma, 2023) It is argued that the motive behind making rules & regulations against such killings is undermining traditional values and beliefs. However, opposing the conventional belief systems prevalent in India is a very different matter. Here, the matter of concern is that the number of innocent lives lost in the name of these cultural beliefs, however, is perplexing. It stunts human brain development and makes the mind confine itself to the fantasy world it has built. Government intervention is badly needed. Honor killings must end, and the government must impose severe penalties. Every ruling rendered by these panchayats in the countryside ought to be completely outlawed. For numerous innocent lives, these decisions have proven to be lethal. (Singhal, 2014) To resolve this situation, everyone needs to get engaged and take accountability for their part. This is a societal issue rather than one exclusive to women. It's also a straightforward human rights issue. Collaborating with other nations on these matters, both inside and beyond the European Union, would also be a significant step. (Honour Related Violence within a Global Perspective: Mitigation and Prevention in Europe, 2004)

REFERENCES

Antonova, Y. A. (2018). *Killed by gossip "Honor killings" of women in the North Caucasus Report on the results of a qualitative study in the republics of Dagestan, Ingushetia and Chechnya (Russian Federation)*. https://www.srji.org/upload/iblock/52c/fgm_dagestan_2016_eng_final_edited_2017.pdf

De Cristofaro, E. (2018). *The crime of honor: an Italian story*. In Historia et ius(Vol. 14 Issue 1). www.historiaetius.eu

Firat, S., Iltas, Y., & Gulmen, M. K. (2016). *Honor Killing a Cultural Issue: Global or Regional?* E-Journal Law (Vol. 2, Issue 1). https://www.ohchr.org/en/professionalinterest/pages/ccpr.aspx

Heydari, A., Teymoori, A., & Trappes, R. (2021). Honor killing as a dark side of modernity: Prevalence, common discourses, and a critical view. *Social Sciences Information. Information Sur les Sciences Sociales*, 60(1), 86–106. DOI: 10.1177/0539018421994777

Honour Related Violence within a Global Perspective: Mitigation and Prevention in Europe. (2004). Stockholm.

Jamuna, K. V. (2022). A Study on Etiology of Honour Killing in India: A Critical Analysis. In *Peer Reviewed and Refereed Journal* (Issue 5). http://ijmer.in.doi./2022/11.05.57

Kumar Rana, D., & Prasad Mishra, B. (2013). *Honour Killings-A gross violation of Human rights & Its Challenges*. In International Journal of Humanities and Social Science Invention (Vol. 2 Issue 6) www.ijhssi.org

Poddar, A. (2020). *Reprehensible Behaviour: The Social Meaning Behind Honour Killings in India*. In Department of Sociology. Brown University

Rekha Verma, D. (2023). Psycho-socio facets of honour killing. In *Russian Law Journal: Vol. XI*.

Sadowa, K. (2015). Honour Killings in Europe as an effect of migration process: Perspective for Poland. *International Letters of Social and Humanistic Sciences*, 58, 83–90. . DOI: 10.18052/www.scipress.com/ILSHS.58.83

Singhal, V. K. (2014). *Honour Killing in India: An Assessment*. SSRN Electronic Journal. https://ssrn.com/abstract=2406031 DOI: 10.2139/ssrn.2406031

Social and legal actions to combat honor related abuse Centre for Sustainable Communities Development KUN centre for equality and diversity (2021).

Suresh Kumar, M. (2023). Honor Killing and Its Causes in Indian Panorama. In *International Journal of Research in Engineering and Science,* (Vol. 11). www.ijres.org

van Eck, C. (2003). *Purified by Blood: Honour Killings amongst Turks in the Netherlands.* Amsterdam University Press.

Sreedevi Xavier, M. (2015). *Honor Killings: A Global Concern.* In Indian Journal of Research (Vol. 4 Issue 3)

Yurdakul, G., & Korteweg, A. C. (2013). Gender equality and immigrant integration: Honor killing and forced marriage debates in the Netherlands, Germany, and Britain. *Women's Studies International Forum*, 41, 204–214. DOI: 10.1016/j.wsif.2013.07.011

Chapter 14
A Critical Study of Honor-Related Violence in Germany

Madhulika Mishra
GLA University, Mathura, India

Shweta Singh
https://orcid.org/0009-0001-7127-264X
GLA University, Mathura, India

ABSTRACT

This chapter delves into the multifaceted issue of honor-related violence in Germany, examining the responsibilities of families, the state, and civic entities in preventing such crimes. It begins by defining honor-related violence, emphasizing that it is a significant social problem that predominantly affects women and often stems from patriarchal notions of family honor. The chapter scrutinizes the concept of "honor killing," exploring whether Islamic teachings support or condemn this practice. It elucidates that while some perpetrators may claim religious justification, mainstream Islamic theology and scholars overwhelmingly reject honor killings as un-Islamic and contrary to the principles of justice and compassion. By investigating the root causes, the chapter identifies factors such as patriarchal cultural norms, social pressures, and the struggle to maintain traditional values within a Western context as key drivers of honor-related violence.

The role of the state is critically examined, focusing on the legal framework, law enforcement practices, and social services designed to protect potential victims and prosecute offenders. The effectiveness of these measures is assessed, highlighting both successes and areas needing improvement. The chapter underscores the

DOI: 10.4018/979-8-3693-7240-1.ch014

significance of civic participation, arguing that community-based interventions, awareness campaigns, and support networks are essential in preventing honor-related crimes. It points to successful initiatives where local communities, NGOs, and social workers collaborate to provide education, support, and protection to at-risk individuals. Additionally, it addresses the challenge of forced marriages, presenting them as a form of honor-related abuse that necessitates comprehensive legal and social strategies to combat.

The dynamics within Muslim immigrant families are explored, noting that gender discrimination often stems from deeply ingrained cultural traditions rather than religious doctrines. The chapter contrasts families that rigidly adhere to these traditions with those that integrate more fluidly into German society, highlighting the diversity within the Muslim community. It acknowledges the tension between preserving cultural identity and adhering to Germanic values, proposing that a nuanced approach is necessary to bridge these differences. Finally, the chapter provides a detailed analysis of the German civil code, specifically the legal provisions that address honor-related violence. It outlines the punitive measures for perpetrators, illustrating how the legal system seeks to deter such crimes and deliver justice for victims.

The chapter concludes by advocating for a multi-pronged approach that combines legal action, social support, and community engagement to effectively combat honor-related violence. By integrating perspectives from law, sociology, and theology, this comprehensive analysis offers a deeper understanding of the complexities surrounding honor-related crimes in Germany and proposes actionable solutions to protect vulnerable individuals and foster a more inclusive society. The chapter's holistic approach underscores the importance of addressing both the symptoms and the root causes of honor-related violence, advocating for a collaborative effort among families, the state, and civic society to create lasting change. In order to guarantee that the values of justice, equality, and human rights are respected and to provide a more secure and fair environment for everyone, regardless of their cultural or religious background, it asks for constant communication, education, and reform. By doing this critical analysis, the chapter hopes to add to the larger conversation about honor-related violence by providing information that will help shape practice, policy, and future studies in this important field.

Honor killings in Germany are not highly prevalent, but they remain a serious issue, particularly within certain immigrant communities. The data on such crimes are often underreported and may be categorized within broader domestic violence or cultural violence statistics. According to research, there have been approximately 70 honor killings reported in Germany between 1996 and 2005, indicating an ongoing concern (Kaya, n.d.). In 2023, it was reported that the rate of violent crimes, including those related to forced marriages and honor-based violence, has seen an increase, with an estimated 1.5 cases per 100,000 people related to cultural violence (German Federal Police Report, 2023).

The immigrant population in Germany has also been affected significantly, with reports indicating that 60% of honor-based violence cases involve families of Turkish or Kurdish origin (Özlem, n.d.). Additionally, in 2022, there were over 150 cases of forced marriages reported, with 80% of the victims being women under the age of 25 (Federal Ministry for Family Affairs, 2023). The rise in these crimes is often attributed to strict adherence to traditional cultural norms, control over women's autonomy, and the lack of effective integration policies. These factors, combined with insufficient legal protections and support services, contribute to the persistence of honor killings and related violence in Germany.

RESEARCH METHODOLOGY

The purpose of this chapter is to gain an understanding of honour killings. To achieve this, a comprehensive research methodology was employed, involving the collection of data from various sources such as records from libraries, newspapers, magazines, interviews, surveys, and online platforms (Korteweg & Yurdakul, 2010a). The research approach was primarily qualitative, focusing on understanding the complexities surrounding honour killings through both primary and secondary data. Qualitative methods were chosen to explore the perceptions and beliefs associated with honour killings. The study considered important demographic factors such as ethnicity, age, and gender of participants to ensure that the analysis was not biased. This approach helped in understanding whether honour killings are perceived as socio-political, cultural, or religious phenomena [Yurdakul, G., & Yükleyen]. Through the collected data, it was found that honour killings are not condoned by any religion but are instead driven by cultural norms and values. The research revealed that when individuals are perceived to have violated these norms, they are often subjected to violence. The study also highlighted that honour killings are not confined to any particular region but occur globally, indicating that this is an issue with significant human rights implications.

KEY WORDS

Core Terms include "Honor Killing," "Forced Marriage," (Korteweg & Yurdakul, 2010a)) and "Violence," which allude to acts frequently performed to maintain imagined family honor, particularly in immigrant populations. Religion and Cultural Contexts such as "Islam," "Cultural Practices" (Korteweg & Yurdakul, 2010a),and the role of "Islamic Teachings" are critical in understanding the context and rationale for these activities. Broader themes such as "Gender Equality," "Human Rights," and "Social Change" place the issue in a global and societal context, emphasizing the hardships of women and the impact of patriarchal norms. Legal and Policy-related the engagement of the "German Government" (Crenshaw, 1991),its stance on "Immigrants," and the "Legal Responsibility" it carries are all related to the practical application of legislation aimed to fight these concerns. The role of "State Responsibility" in guaranteeing "Protection," "Prevention," and "Prosecution" is critical in combating these crimes and assisting victims. Analytical perspectives, such as the impact of "Integration" on immigrant populations, the "Role of Family and Community" (Dr. Sana, 2019), and how these influence incidences of honor-based violence, enable a more in-depth examination of the complexity involved. The connection between "Media" representation and public perception, as well as how these situations are portrayed, has a considerable impact on society attitudes. A research paper on Decoding Honor Killings and Forced Marriages in Immigrant Communities in Germany requires careful journal selection and consideration during the inclusion/exclusion process. The selection method highlighted journals specializing in issues such as "Honor Killings," "Gender Discrimination," and "Immigrant Integration in Germany." Journals such as the International Journal of Law, Crime, and Justice, Gender & Society, and Journal of Ethnic and Migration Studies were chosen based on their subject matter relevance and scholarly contribution to these issues.

LITERATURE REVIEW

Brenninkmeijer, N. highlights how honor-related violence in the Netherlands is influenced by cultural and social dynamics, calling for culturally specific interventions [Brenninkmeijer, N.]. Crenshaw, K.emphasizes the concept of intersectionality, illustrating how honor-based violence intersects with race, gender, and cultural identity, compounding the vulnerabilities of women [Crenshaw, K.]. Janssen, J.discusses the challenges in identifying honor-related violence within broader domestic violence statistics, stressing the need for accurate data collection [Janssen, J.]. Korteweg, A. C., & Yurdakul, G. explore how honor-based violence is framed in public discourse, particularly in relation to immigrant communities in Europe, and the role of legal frameworks in addressing these crimes [Korteweg, A. C., & Yurdakul, G.]. Statham, P., et al. examine how Islamic communities in Europe negotiate cultural practices in secular societies, providing insights into the socio-political context of honor-based violence [Statham, P.]. Yurdakul, G., & Yükleyen, A. focus on the integration of Muslim immigrants in Germany, highlighting the relationship between religion, culture, and honor-based violence [Yurdakul, G., & Yükleyen]. Dr. Sana, analyzes the portrayal of honor-based violence in literature, discussing how cultural narratives shape societal attitudes towards these practices (Dr. Sana, 2019).

FUTURE RESEARCH DIRECTIONS

This chapter primarily focuses on important components to improve knowledge of honor killings, but it also provides room for additional investigation into criminological and psychological aspects that may offer a more complete picture of the problem. Despite significant constraints, such as the authors' inability to understand certain pertinent German works, they endeavoured to utilize the accessible materials. Even though it was difficult to include those sources directly, the chapter's major goal is still to offer insightful information. Future study could further deepen the analysis by incorporating more insights from German texts, as made possible by the prominent focus on Germany. A more thorough methodological approach will be used in subsequent research to close the gaps in this chapter. In order to monitor changes in patriarchal norms within immigrant groups, this will involve longitudinal studies and a comparative legal analysis of the laws of European nations pertaining to honour-related violence (Janssen, n.d.). Qualitative case studies that incorporate interviews with survivors and support groups will enhance our comprehension of the social and cultural elements that propel honor killings (Dr. Sana, 2019). Media content analysis will look at how honour killings are depicted in the media and how it affects public perception. Surveys and interviews will also be used to assess the success of education and awareness programs (Korteweg & Yurdakul, 2010b). In conclusion, by examining prosecution rates, sentencing patterns, and recidivism in addition to conducting interviews with legal experts and law enforcement personnel, policy evaluation will concentrate on the efficacy of legislative reforms and law enforcement tactics. This comprehensive method will offer a deep comprehension of violence connected to honor and guide future preventative measures.

INTRODUCTION

Honor killing and marriage by force were brought to the attention of German lawmakers by the 2003 and 2004 campaigns of Terre des Femmes, a women's non-governmental organization, and a report titled Life Situation, Safety, and Well-being of Females in the Federal Republic of Germany. Renate Schmidt, the federal minister of family, senior, female, and youth (Bundesministerium für Familie, Senioren, Frauen und Jugend 2004)1, was affiliated with the Social Democratic Party and represented the SPD. The campaign and the study made a clear connection between forced marriage and acts of honor killing and violence related to honor. But neither the press nor the parliament gave much attention to either topic, and defining governmental duty halted at publishing of this report. Hatun Aynur Sürücü, 23, was brutally murdered by her brother in 2005, which accelerated an open discussion of the role played by the German government in preventing honour killings in Germany as well as family violence in Muslim immigrant communities. As stated in newspapers, this was Berlin's sixth murder of the type in a single year. The debatable book Die Fremde Braut (The Foreign Bride, 2005(Korteweg & Yurdakul, 2010a)) by Turkish-German sociologist Necla Kelek was published at the same time as Hatun Sürücü's Murder Foreign Bride. This book, in addition to several other media outlets, accused German-born Muslims of certain kinds of gender-based abuse. Numerous media discussions on honour killing and the uneven mistreatment of women by Turkish immigrants were sparked by the killing of Hatun Sürücü and Necla Kelek's book. Certain types of gendered violence were being perpetrated by Muslim immigrants in Germany, according to this book and several other writings. Following the 2005 media exposés on forced marriage and honour killing, a national dialogue on these topics was initiated by the federal parliament as well as the state legislatures of Berlin and Baden-Württemberg Land level parliaments. Even though honor killing was covered by newspapers as a distinct topic, politicians preferred to attribute honor allied vehemence to forcible wedlock or at least to the issue. As a result, they put forth proposals to prolong the immigration permits of individuals living in foreign forced marriages and to raise the marriage age meant for spouses(Korteweg & Yurdakul, 2010b)uses from nations such as Turkey (a resident visa generally expires six months after leaving Germany). The CDU's (Christian Democratic Union) lack of support for the residency permit extension caused it to fall apart, and neither the plan that selectively raised the marriage age was authorized nor was it declared unconstitutional. The coalition government of the CDU and Social Democrats (SPD, Sozial Demokratische Partei Deutschlands/Social Democratic Party) has since passed more legislation to wrestle with forcible wedlock and, consequently, bodily destruction associated with it. The aforementioned initiatives include forcing brides to be (and men to marry) to study German overseas before obtaining an entrance visa and making coerced marriage a crime. Nevertheless, an exhaustive strategy to deal with forced marriage and honor-related violence has yet to emerge from these extremely divisive laws and policy initiatives. Even if lawmakers and decision-makers from all political stripes agree that marriages by force and other ways to commit violence against immigrants, particularly Muslims, are necessary to end, the formulation of policies is nevertheless reluctant and prickly(Korteweg & Yurdakul, 2010a).

At least two women were slain in Germany in 2009, and it is assumed that the reason for these deaths was to defame their families.

Who specifically were the victims?

Mizgin B., an 18-year-old resident of Harsewinkel, near Götersloh, became a victim on January 1. Born in Germany, this woman of Kurdish descent married her cousin Önder B. in Turkey when she was seventeen years old. Due to the fact that the marriage appeared to have been arranged under the Mizgin declined to meet her spouse in front of her family. Consequently, in October 2008, he entered Germany illegally. Before moving into his wife's family's home, he was residing in Dortmund. After leaving Mizgin's friends' New Year's Eve celebration, the couple committed criminal act. Envious of his wife, Önder used a knife to caress her body and drove over her person. In order to get him arrested, he then called the police.

The second fatality occurred on March 2, 2009, and was Gülsüm S., a 20-year-old from Rees, close to Krefeld. When Gülsüm's family applied for asylum in 1995, they fled southeast Turkey and travelled to Germany as a small child. Gülsüm had moved out of the asylum accommodations and was living in an apartment in Rees with her brother and sister approximately a year before she passed away. Bild, a popular daily, claimed that because Gülsüm had a partner in Germany, her family had forced her into an unwelcome marriage in Turkey. It was Gülsüm who fell pregnant in November 2008. She went to an Amsterdam hospital to undergo an abortion five months into her pregnancy, most likely out of dread. Not long later, she was killed. These two specific instances serve as a partial representation of the widespread kinds of honor killings that are prevalent in German culture today. Even while these incidents—mostly committed by Turkish citizens living in Deutschland and German Turks—have gained more attention recently, it is still unclear whether and how Islam is related to this problem.

IS HONOR KILLINGS A CONCEPT IN ISLAM?

Recently a question on honor killings was addressed to Islamic scholars: "What is the position of Islam on honor killings? Does Islam truly believe in honor killings? Since women make up the majority of the victims, does Islam actually command the murdering of women for reasons of honor?"

The answer is to find in a fatwa5 from Jun 17, 2002:

"Wa`alykum As-Salaamu Warahmatullahi Wabarakaatuh."

"God's kindness and blessings, as well as peace, be upon you."

In the name of the Most Gracious and Merciful Allah. Allah is the only one deserving of praise and gratitude; may His Messenger have peace and happiness. We are grateful for your inquiry, dear sister in Islam, as it shows how committed you are to learning the real meaning of the religion. May Allah keep us all on the straight path and bless your efforts in pursuing knowledge.

Islam forbids the violation of life and fervently defends its sanctity. According to what Allah says in the Qur'an, "He who willfully kills a believer will spend eternity in Hell as his punishment." Allah has prepared a harsh retribution for him, is enraged with him, and has cursed him. (An-Nisa: 93).

The Prophet Muhammad, peace and blessings be upon him, is reported by Abdullah ibn Masud, may Allah be pleased with him, to have said, "A Muslim's blood can only be legally shed in three cases: a married person who commits adultery, a life for a life, and someone who abandons their religion and the community." (Sources: Muslim and Al-Bukhari)"

In the fatwa issued on June 17, 2002, Islamic scholars addressed the issue of honor killings within the context of Islamic teachings. Here's a summary of the main points typically covered in such fatwas regarding honor killings:

1. Prohibition of Unlawful Killing: Islam firmly prohibits killing someone, regardless of the reason for doing so. The value of human life is emphasized in several Quranic passages and Hadiths, which are the sayings of the Prophet Muhammad. This is because Islam holds that human life is sacred.
    2. No Foundation in Islamic Law: Sharia law does not support honor killings. Islamic teachings have no idea that supports murdering someone in order to preserve or restore family honor. Islamic law does not condone acts of violence against women or any other person on the grounds of supposed transgressions of honor.
    3. Justice and Accountability: Islam places a strong emphasis on these two concepts. Islamic law mandates that all forms of retaliation or punishment follow the correct legal and judicial procedures. It is extremely unlawful for someone to take the law into their own hands and commit murder.
    4. Rights and Dignity of Women: Islamic law accords women the right and dignity to live their lives. It is against Islamic beliefs to mistreat, abuse, or kill women without cause. Due process and legal protection are rights that belong to women.

    5. Religious Teachings vs. Cultural Practices: Rather than being derived from religious doctrine, many customs connected to honor killings are rooted in tribal or cultural traditions. It's critical to distinguish between Islamic teachings and cultural practices.

For those who steer clear of skepticism "honor killing" is not a phenomenon in Islam. That's according to Sheikh Ahmad Kutty, a scholar of Islam and prominent professor at the Islamic Institute of Toronto in Toronto, Ontario, Canada. Islam respects every soul and forbids any sin against it. It forbids anyone from enforcing the law themselves and enforcing justice since doing so would result in anarchy and lawlessness. Islam forbids these kinds of killings as a result. First and foremost, a legally binding decision rendered by a recognized court is required to authorize killing. People in and of themselves are not qualified to make decisions or judge issues.

In essence, the fatwa likely emphasizes that honor killings are not sanctioned by Islam and that such acts are condemned as unlawful and unjust. Islam promotes the protection of life, the rule of law, and the dignity and rights of all individuals, including women.

ROLE OF FAMILIES AND COMMUNITIES IN PREVENTING HONOR KILLINGS

Honor killings can be avoided in large part through the involvement of families and communities. To stop honor killings, it is critical to advance human rights and gender equality in families and communities. Communities and families can work together to stop honor killings by:

1) Questioning established norms- Gender norms that restrict women's possibilities can be actively questioned and challenged by communities and families in order to advance gender equality. This entails promoting equal rights and establishing welcoming conditions that inspire women to pursue higher education and careers (Kumar, 2013). Scholarships, mentorship, and career training should be given, and media representation, neighbourhood dialogues, and inclusive education should be employed to promote cultural changes. Furthermore, misconceptions can be dispelled by public campaigns and role models, and family dynamics should support equal opportunity and treatment for boys and girls. By doing this, it will be possible to foster an environment of equality and respect for one another, which will empower people of all genders.

2) Growing consciousness- Communities and families can organize educational activities including seminars, workshops, and community gatherings to help raise awareness about the harmful effects of honor killings. These incidents can offer accurate data, firsthand accounts, and professional insights into the terrible effects of honor killings on people and society. These projects aim to dispel myths, promote empathy, and draw attention to the moral and legal ramifications of such acts by providing forums for open discussion. These initiatives can be

strengthened by working together with law enforcement, NGOs, and municipal authorities to provide a thorough approach to prevention and education. Communities can develop a greater awareness of the risks connected to honor killings and strive toward ending this practice by working together to achieve these goals.

3) Assisting Women-Women who are at risk of honor killings can benefit greatly from the support of their families and communities, which might include safe havens, financial aid, and legal advice. By creating safe houses or shelters, we can guarantee that these women have safe places to live that are out of direct danger. By assisting them in becoming independent and stable, financial support lessens their dependency on possibly violent family members. Legal representation and advice are crucial in assisting individuals in understanding their legal rights and the judicial system, as well as in ensuring their safety and justice. Counseling can also provide them with the emotional and psychological support they need to deal with trauma and create a strong support system that both protects and empowers them. Families and communities can play a critical role in shielding women from honor-based violence by pooling their resources together. (Dr. Sana, 2019)

4) Reporting incidents- In order to ensure accountability and stop such crimes in the future, communities and families play a crucial role in reporting honor killing instances to the appropriate authorities. Community members can be given the confidence to take action without fear of reprisal by making them aware of their legal responsibilities and the significance of reporting crimes of this nature. More persons may come forward if anonymous and confidential reporting channels are established. To ensure that reports are taken seriously and handled quickly, it is essential to foster trust between the community and law enforcement. Community support networks can offer advocacy and protection to individuals who come forward, and highlighting successful prosecutions of offenders can function as a disincentive and show that justice is possible.

STATE RESPONSIBILITY

Germany bears the same responsibility as any other state for maintaining international law and averting breaches of human rights. Honor killings are viewed as human rights violations and are strongly denounced by the global community. Claims in the press that honor killing originates from a desire to be more German encouraged lawmakers to emphasize immigrant integration in general rather than the particulars of violence related to honor. To the members of different parties, this point of view of congressional oversight, as it related to assimilating immigrants, changed. Correspondingly certain political players, the state must safeguard "German values" and a relatively homogeneous community. For instance, according to several officials of CDU, Muslims live in separate metropolitan areas called Parallelgesellschaften, rare interactions with Germans, in addition to enforcing their particular traditions & regulations that went contrary to the general welfare of German society, notably about female equality.(Statham et al., 2005) Nicolas Zimmer, the CDU Fraction's president in the Berlin Parliament in 2005, made the following claim: "The concept of a "multicultural society" was a failure. It promoted the split of cultural groups based on moral principles and the establishment of parallel societies. This results in the "honor killing," which is the most destructive kind of self-justice.". It follows that the people already regarded as Germans are the focus of state duty. The state's role in immigrants is to either embrace them (turn them into Germans) or to keep them out of the nation entirely. Significant claims were those made by politicians from the ruling party, precisely the CDU, which cited honor-related violence to support wider integration programs. The CDU member of the Federal Parliament, Michaella Noll, for instance, contended that: "We intend to give newly arrived spouses in Germany the freedom to live their own lives since this will give them the best chance of merging. But communication is the only thing that makes this attainable. Speaking German is crucial for me in terms of protecting victims, in my opinion. In what other way might a young lady about to accept an arranged marriage be able to protect herself in this situation? She won't be able to alert others to her emergency and request assistance unless she has this fundamental understanding. If not, it won't function. In years to come, this is a precaution, in my opinion, to keep girls from becoming foreign new wives." The minimal social rights given to victims of such violence are demonstrated by Noll's statements. It is difficult to argue against the benefits that the young lady in Noll's instance would gain from learning German, but language proficiency on its own would not be adequate. However, in the lack of rules establishing broad programming in shelters addressing such concerns, it is unclear if this young lady would get support in her situation of being shackled into marriage. The ability to contact the police is only a limited social right; it is also unclear if front-line workers, including the police, would be able to assist her if they lacked specialized training and comprehension of the intricacies surrounding forced marriage and violence related to honor. (Crenshaw, 1991)

The Dutch definition of state responsibility is the duty to protect those who are vulnerable and weak against violence using efforts to promote social change at the community level and safeguard them from damage directly by providing resources like shelters and prosecuting offenders.(Brenninkmeijer, n.d.) But in Germany, the primary focus is on prosecution, protection is restricted, and prevention is not talked about. For instance, the parliament of Baden-Württemberg, which was governed by the Christian Socialist Union until 2011, defined the issue of honour murders in connection with forcible wedlock, presented data demonstrating its importance, and devised practical solutions by creating the Sachkomission, an advisory commission and introducing the Zwangsheirat-Bekämpfungsgesetz, a law against forced marriage, to the Bundestag in 2004. This intervention may serve as the cornerstone of a comprehensive state strategy to address violence related to honor. On the other hand, an attorney and expert on legal issues such as forcible wedlock and murder by honour Regina Kalthegener claims that the main goal of Baden- www Württemberg's proposals to the Bundestag is to punish the criminals severely while offering the victims as little protection as possible. This intervention may serve as the cornerstone of a comprehensive state strategy to address violence related to honour. On the other hand, an attorney and an authority on lawful matters like forced unions and the murder of honor. According to Regina Kalthegener. Baden-Württemberg's recommendations to the Bundestag are primarily focused on punishing the offenders severely while providing minimal protection to the victims. (Korteweg & Yurdakul, 2010b)

The left presents a third interpretation of state responsibility. Rather than criticizing and segregating Muslim communities, they believe that the state's primary duty should be to treat all of its inhabitants equally. Die Linke member of the federal parliament Sevim Dağdelen nude it quite evident that she considered the CDU/SPD federal coalition government's actions to be purposeful obstructionisan. She contended in the forced marriage debate in parliament, "We all can acknowledge that marriage under duress is a form of violence, but as this disagreement demonstrates, the Union [CDU] has used it not only to divert attention from the social and multicultural measures of previous governments but additionally to stigmatize immigrants alongside Muslim ancestry and portray them as disadvantaged and regressive."(Korteweg & Yurdakul, 2010a)

She went on to say that it is now challenging to safeguard the women who are victims of this type of assault because of the "finger-pointing." Lastly, she accused the ruling coalition of the CDU and SPD of acting more like negligent state officials by using women's plight to stop immigration rather than forcing them into marriage. In an attempt to transform Muslims and Turks into German citizens, the CDU-SPD partnership, which was in power throughout these talks, finally coalesced around the issue of forced marriage and other acts of violence related to honor.(Yurdakul & Yükleyen, 2009) The debates on violence related to honor at the federal level focused more on women who were either new to Germany or were in the process of entering it than on German citizens or long-term residents who were victims of this kind of violence. Furthermore, the new regulations mandate that spouses study German before traveling to Germany and increase the number of hours they must spend in required language classes after arriving. Coalition politicians contended that both policies would increase the level of independence amongst spouses.

Nonetheless, these laws also act as barriers to immigration, making it more challenging for people to come here. Furthermore, the CDU/SPD alliance proposed raising the marriage age for some immigrant communities. Immigration would once more be hampered by this, despite the CDU/SPD's claim that this was an effort to guarantee that couples make educated choices regarding their marriages. The unconstitutionality of this motion caused it to fail. Whether they are implemented or just suggested, all of these immigration and integration regulations assume that a woman or other dependent person is immature and may become a victim of a Turkish immigrant family living in Germany. Their complete political engagement in German society is hindered by such assumptions that deny Muslim women agency & instead portray them as victims of their communities. Certain Turkish citizens in Deutschland made an effort to challenge the ideas of government accountability that formed the basis of the ruling parties' policy answers, and they opposed the mistreatment of immigrants that resulted from these designations as unknowns. For instance, Giyasettin Sayan, a German-Kurdish member of Die Linke, the German Left party, stated in the Berlin Parliament that immigrants were to be seen as constituents of German society. She mentioned that "The claim that the family has not been able to integrate into German society places the issue outside of our community. Beyond the specific examples, this leads to potentially harmful conclusions: The issue will be resolved once individuals depart. However, the true causes are found in our culture, and they may be resolved there."(Korteweg & Yurdakul, 2010a) This strategy stood in juxtaposition to the CDU's and presented immigrants as complete members of German society.

CIVIC PARTICIPATION

An additional alternate discourse was offered by Safter Çinar, the Türkische Bund Berlin-Brandenburg's spokeswoman. Through the introduction of the human rights rhetoric as a shared ideal that both German and immigrant values should abide by, Çinar sought to ease the friction between "us" and "them": "We contend that mistreatment of women, compelled marriage, and honor killings are incompatible with our religion. However, the majority community must also at last give up talking about German ideals that immigrants must adapt to. German or Turkish values are irrelevant in this situation. It has to do with fundamental human rights."(Janssen, n.d.)In order to highlight Turkish immigrants' right to be recognized as full members of German society, representatives of immigrant civil society organizations like Çinar organized the human rights discourse.

He used transnational rhetoric to make the case that collective actors ought to organize around a social issue rather than ethnic group membership in the lack of a clear definition of social rights. Collective actors can discover political chances to collaborate with state authorities in this fashion. There's some evidence that the German Bundestag is listening to civil society organizations. For instance, the main women's group in Germany that campaigns against honor killing and forced marriage is called Terre des Femmes. It is mentioned during legislative discussions as an organization to work with for fruitful collaboration. Agisra e.V. in Cologne, Rosa wohnprojekt and Yasemin in Stuttgart, BIG Intervention center, and Papatya in Berlin are among the other groups named.(14/208, n.d.)

As a result of the introduction of an online consultation program, additionally, Papatya has ties to other women's centers. For instance, according to the Abgeordnetenhaus Berlin, Drucksache 16/21 and 22 November 2007, Recently, several training facilities for males who assault women were constructed. We are unsure, though, if these facilities also instruct men who expressly coerce their relatives into marriage by threatening to kill them for reasons of honor. Several members of the parliament have taken up these organizations' calls for greater financial support to safeguard women's shelters, pointing out that these facilities receive far less funding than they should (Bundestag 08.11.2005, Drucksache 16/61). In particular, since 2000, the amount of money provided to the Baden Württemberg Parliament for roughly the same number of women and children in need of safeguarding has dropped significantly.(Landtag von Baden-Württemberg, n.d.) (In Baden Württemberg, about 4000 women and children each year) It is evident from this that civil society organizations—especially those led by women—have some sway over the discursive constructions of state accountability, even if these interpretations do not prevail over others. In addition, considering the significant financial cuts in the field of services for violence against women, the actions of women's organizations highlight the lack of institutional and material support for resolving honor-related violence in Germany.

STATE RESPONSIBILITY VERSUS CIVIC PARTICIPATION

In light of the press and political discussions that we have assessed, we have arrived at three conclusions: Firstly, political actors have put forward identical proposals for dealing with honor killings at the level of the land at a federal magnitude. They described accountability of the country in different forms, nonetheless more in abused rights of humans & accompanied with "Deutschland beliefs." Because of party conflicts, the federal parliament was unable to approve any regulations, particularly concerning the residence legislation. No real progress has been made on the important motions by the opposition parties that advocate for stronger victim protection as opposed to harsher punishment for the offenders. Therefore, the entirety of state duty for addressing violence against immigrant women is not included in definitions of state accountability. Secondly, cooperation with civil society organizations is another aspect of institutional responsibility for the state that seems to be limited in Deutschland due to fiscal concerns and the dearth of connections. Land-level parliaments make an effort to collaborate with non-governmental organizations (NGOs) in the fight against the prevention of honor killings; however, the NGOs' financial support appears to be insufficient and even declining, even though the figure of women and children who require safety is not going to change. Given the severity of the problem, there is relatively little financial support available to help the victims, such as by offering safer housing. Furthermore, the provincial police stations continue to offer little victim protection.

Lastly, there's a big connection between civic engagement and state responsibility. Honor killing was a problem that the German state authorities were supposed to address, but it was mixed up with immigration integration discussions and used as an excuse for restrictive immigration integration laws, like raising the age at which partners can marry and when they lead leave Germany (a plan that the Bundestag rejected because it was against the law of constitution) and requiring language and integration classes to prevent compelled marriages. Representatives have noted that these reforms may hinder immigrants' collective civic engagement, but they haven't offered a strong case for how they would safeguard victims.(14/208, n.d.)

PUNISHMENT UNDER THE GERMAN CRIMINAL CODE FOR HONOR KILLINGS

Honor killings have not yet been given their section in the German Criminal Code. primarily two provisions for which the perpetrators were prosecuted:

Section 211 of the German Criminal Code, Murder under Particularly Severe Circumstantial Evidence, stipulates that "(1) Anyone found guilty of murder under the terms of this clause faces a life sentence in prison. (2) Under this section, a person is considered a murderer if they kill someone for fun, for sex, out of greed or other low motivations, covertly or brutally, or by ways that endanger the public, or if they do it to enable or conceal another crime."

Section 212 of the German Criminal Code, Murder, under Special aggravating circumstances, stipulates that "(1) Anyone found guilty of murder under section 211 and not already serving a minimum of five years in jail will be found guilty of the crime. (2) Life imprisonment is the punishment for really serious crimes."

REFERENCES

Brenninkmeijer, N. (n.d.). *Eergerelateerd Geweld in Nederland.*

Crenshaw, K. (1991). Stanford Law Review Mapping the Margins: Intersectionality, Identity Politics, and Violence against Women of. In *Source*[). *Stanford Law Review*, 43(6), https://about.jstor.org/terms. DOI: 10.2307/1229039

Sana. (2019). The dishonorable honor crimes in literature. *International Journal of English Language, Literature and Translation Studies* (1st ed., Vol. 6).

Janssen, J. (n.d.). *Deelrapport 2-Analyse-van-mogelijke-eerzaken.* https://www.researchgate.net/publication/336564295

Korteweg, A. C., & Yurdakul, G. (2010). *Palais des Nations, 1211 Geneva 10, Switzerland. UNRISD welcomes such applications.*

Kumar, R. K. (2013). Honour Killing: Challenges Indian Judicial System. *International Journal of Creative Research Thoughts*, 11(4).

Landtag von Baden-Württemberg. (n.d.). www.landtag-bw.de/Dokumente

Statham, P., Koopmans, R., Giugni, M., & Passy, F. (2005). Resilient or adaptable Islam?: Multiculturalism, religion and migrants' claims-making for group demands in Britain, the Netherlands and France. *Ethnicities*, 5(4), 427–459. DOI: 10.1177/1468796805058092

Yurdakul, G., & Yükleyen, A. (2009). Islam, conflict, and integration: Turkish religious associations in Germany. *Turkish Studies*, 10(2), 217–231. DOI: 10.1080/14683840902864010

Chapter 15
Shattered Honor:
Understanding and Addressing Honor-Related Crimes in the Netherlands and India

Pratibha Singh
Karnataka State Law University, Hubli, India

Sahil Gupta
https://orcid.org/0009-0008-4841-1577
Amity University, Noida, India

ABSTRACT

Honor killings motivated by false ideas of communal honor remain a tragically pervasive social problem in a variety of cultural contexts. This chapter examines honor killings in India and the Netherlands, two countries that have different legal systems, social structures, and cultural backgrounds yet are united in their opposition to this horrible behavior. The research employs a multifaceted method to investigate the historical and contemporary elements that have shaped honor killings in each nation. It investigates how cultural norms, gender inequality, and patriarchy contribute to this violence. This chapter examines the existing legislative frameworks and enforcement measures aimed at curbing honor killings, emphasizing the advantages and disadvantages of each in the given situations. In the end, the goal of this comparative research is to pinpoint possible best practices and practical approaches to stop and end honor killings.

DOI: 10.4018/979-8-3693-7240-1.ch015

INTRODUCTION

Honor killings refer to the killing of a family member by another family member for bringing dishonor to the family by going against the family norms, tradition, or culture. On a global platform, both India and the Netherlands appear largely different in their functioning, population, and socio-economic criteria. But both nations suffer through this secretive murder practice in the name of family respect and cultural continuance. This chapter tends to prepare a comparative analysis between the two nations, understanding the factors responsible for the commission of honor killings. Through this chapter, the aim is not to compare the pain or suffering but to connect the dots for understanding the reasoning and status of honor killing crime in both these nations.

Despite the differences in functioning, economy, or legal frameworks, there are a few common threads that bind the narratives of honor killings in India and the Netherlands. Patriarchy can be seen as a foundation in both these societies, whereby women are believed to be subordinate to men, and this creates a justifiable ground for violence against women, be it in India through arranged marriages or be it in the Netherlands through restrictive cultural norms. In both societies, misinterpretation of tradition is a root cause to justify violence. From caste hierarchies and specific interpretations of religion in India to cultural clashes with immigrant communities, all contribute to the act of violence.

Amidst the similarities, it becomes crucial to also acknowledge the different problems shaping the honor killing realities in each of these nations. The triggers for the commission of honor killings differ in both these nations. In India, the socio-cultural landscape is affected by inter-caste relationships, defying arranged marriages, or choosing distinct career practices that do not align with the family's culture. In the Netherlands, the cultural clashes of immigrants against the Dutch values and controlling family dynamics lead to the triggering of violence. The Netherlands though not one hundred percent immune to these issues but relatively, holds a stronger stand against societal attitudes toward honor killings.

Honor killings must be stopped with a multidimensional strategy that takes into account the contextual subtleties as well as the common threads. Important first efforts include education and awareness campaigns that question prevailing ideas about gender roles, confront damaging interpretations of religion and tradition, and advance gender equality. Breaking the cycle of violence also requires empowering women via economic independence, safe spaces, and access to healthcare and education. Strengthening legal frameworks with strong sanctions for abusers and effective protection for victims is crucial. Breaking the taboo around gender-based violence and promoting open dialogues and awareness campaigns with religious leaders, community leaders, and civil society organizations can help transform attitudes.

Recognizing the cross-border shadow of honor killings, India and the Netherlands may have a fruitful conversation, sharing experiences and working together to devise practical solutions. This is not just a comparative study; rather, it is a call to action and a journey that we can all take together to create a future free from the violence and fear that stem from "honor" killings.

STATISTICAL DATA

India witnesses a significant number of honor killings annually, with some estimates suggesting hundreds of cases reported each year. According to reports, states like Uttar Pradesh, Haryana, and Punjab account for a majority of these incidents due to deeply entrenched caste-based and patriarchal norms (Smita Satapathy, 2023). A study found that about 70-80% of honor killings in India involve inter-caste relationships or marriages that defy societal expectations (Singhal, n.d.). Rural areas see a higher incidence of honor killings, with a significant portion of victims being women aged 15-30 years (Grewal, 2013).

The conviction rate for honor killings in India remains low, estimated at less than 30% in many regions, due to social pressures, witness intimidation, and insufficient evidence (Dhull, 2017). The Indian Penal Code, under sections like Sec-302, handles murder cases including honor killings, but specific legal provisions targeting honor-related crimes are still lacking, making precise legal statistics difficult to compile (Dhull, 2017). Data from various reports indicate that despite the presence of laws like the Dowry Prohibition Act and the Domestic Violence Act, enforcement is inconsistent, with many cases either under-reported or dismissed due to lack of evidence (Dhull, 2017).

While the overall rate of honor killings in the Netherlands is lower compared to countries like India, the country has seen an increase in such cases, particularly among immigrant communities. Reports indicate that about 80% of honor-related violence cases in the Netherlands involve immigrants from Turkish and Moroccan backgrounds (Yurdakul & Korteweg, 2020). The Dutch government has recorded an average of 10-15 cases of honor-related violence annually, with a notable proportion leading to fatal outcomes (Yurdakul & Korteweg, 2020).

The Dutch legal system categorizes honor killings as aggravated murder, with Article 289 of the Dutch Penal Code providing for a maximum of life imprisonment. However, the complexity of prosecuting these cases, particularly within immigrant communities, often results in lower conviction rates compared to other types of murder (Yurdakul & Korteweg, 2013a). Statistics show that honor-related cases in the Netherlands often involve extensive legal proceedings due to cultural considerations, with cases sometimes taking years to resolve (Eck, 2003a).

RESEARCH METHODOLOGY

The research methodology employed in this study on honor killings in India and the Netherlands is designed to provide a comprehensive, comparative analysis of the phenomenon, integrating multiple perspectives and data sources. The methodological approach encompasses qualitative and comparative research methods, allowing for a deep understanding of the cultural, legal, and social factors that underpin honor-related crimes in these two countries.

1. **Research Design:** This study utilizes a comparative research design to explore the similarities and differences in the occurrence, social contexts, and legal responses to honor killings in India and the Netherlands. The comparative framework is essential in highlighting how varying cultural, legal, and societal structures influence the manifestation and mitigation of honor-related crimes in different contexts.
2. Data Collection:
   a. Primary Sources:

   - **Legislative Texts and Legal Documents:** The study closely examines key legal documents, including the Indian Penal Code (IPC), the Dowry Prohibition Act of 1961, the Domestic Violence Act of 2005, and Article 289 of the Dutch Penal Code. These sources are critical for understanding the legal frameworks within which honor killings are addressed in each country (Dhull, 2017; Yurdakul & Korteweg, 2013a).
   - **NGO Reports and Case Studies:** The research incorporates data from reports and case studies provided by NGOs active in combating honor killings, such as Dhanak of Humanity and Shakti Vahini in India, and Fier and Movisie in the Netherlands. These reports provide insights into the ground-level realities of honor killings and the effectiveness of interventions by civil society (Verkoren & van Leeuwen, 2013).

   b. Secondary Sources:

   - **Academic Literature:** A thorough review of academic literature, including journal articles, books, and conference papers, is conducted to establish the theoretical foundation of the research. Key sources include works by Smita Satapathy (2023) on the cultural and legal aspects of honor killings in India and Yurdakul &

Korteweg (2020) on the social dynamics of honor killings within immigrant communities in the Netherlands.
- **Government and International Reports:** The study also draws on reports from international organizations such as the United Nations, as well as government publications from both India and the Netherlands. These reports provide statistical data, policy analysis, and recommendations relevant to the study.

3. Data Analysis
   a. **Thematic Analysis:** A thematic analysis is employed to identify and explore recurring themes across the collected data. These themes include patriarchy, cultural norms, gender-based violence, and legal responses. The thematic analysis allows for a nuanced understanding of how these factors contribute to the prevalence and perpetuation of honor killings in both India and the Netherlands.
   b. **Comparative Analysis:** The comparative aspect of the research involves juxtaposing the social, legal, and cultural factors influencing honor killings in India and the Netherlands. This analysis is crucial for identifying best practices, challenges, and gaps in the current approaches to addressing honor-related violence in both contexts.
   c. **Case Study Analysis:** Detailed case studies of specific honor killings in both India and the Netherlands are analyzed to illustrate the real-world application of legal frameworks and the impact of cultural norms. These case studies are drawn from NGO reports and media coverage, providing concrete examples of the phenomenon under study.
4. **Ethical Considerations:** Given the sensitive nature of honor killings, the research methodology incorporates stringent ethical guidelines. The study ensures confidentiality and anonymity for all individuals and families involved in the case studies. Additionally, the research adheres to ethical standards in handling data from NGOs and other organizations, ensuring that all information is used responsibly and with respect to the dignity of the victims and survivors.
5. **Limitations:** The research acknowledges certain limitations, including the challenges of accessing reliable data on honor killings due to underreporting and the clandestine nature of these crimes, particularly in India. Additionally, the study recognizes the difficulty in drawing direct comparisons between two countries with vastly different cultural and legal systems. These limitations are mitigated through the use of diverse data sources and the triangulation of findings.

KEY TERMS

Core terms like, "Honor Killing" i.e., Central to the discussion, this term connects directly with the phenomenon being examined across different cultural and legal landscapes. Broader themes like "Patriarchy" & Cultural Norms" reflects crucial concept that underpins the societal structures facilitating honor-related crimes, particularly in India and these are significant in understanding how different societies justify or combat honor killings. Terms like "Gender-Based Violence" contextualizes honor killings within the spectrum of violence against women. The legal and policy-related terms including "International Human Rights Law", "Legal Frameworks" or "Policy Implementation" are key in understanding honor killings with practical and legal point of view. Analytical Perspectives like "Comparative Analysis" and "Intersectionality" enables the exploration of how honor killings are approached in India and the Netherlands, offering insights into different cultural and legal contexts.

In line with Verkoren & van Leeuwen (2013) and Grewal, I. (2013), we used these keywords to select relevant articles from multiple sources, for example, 'Springer, JSTOR, Sage, Scopus, IJSSHR, Web of Science, Taylor & Francis, Google Scholar and Google Books.

Selecting the right journals and carefully conducting inclusion/exclusion and article research is essential for a Research Paper on Honor Killings. The journal selection process focussed on publications specializing in human rights, gender studies, international law, and related interdisciplinary fields. Inclusion criteria emphasized on relevance, ensuring that only articles directly addressing honor killings, or associated legal and cultural issues like International Human Rights are considered. Recent publications, preferably within the last decade, were prioritized which led to incorporation of current perspectives and data. Peer-reviewed articles and government and recognised NGOs reports formed the core of our research to maintain academic rigor.

Exclusion criteria filtered out non-academic sources, such as blogs or opinion pieces, and articles with only tangential relevance to the topic. Conducted article research using academic databases like JSTOR, PubMed, and Google Scholar is crucial, employing targeted keywords such as "Honor Killing,"," "Gender-Based Violence," and "Human Rights Law" to identify the most pertinent studies for our paper. Non-Peer Reviewed research articles were excluded for better research and coverage of relevant topics. Similarly, non-credible online sources and news articles were excluded to avoid any discrepancies.

LITERATURE REVIEW

Honor killings are a pervasive issue rooted in the complex interplay of cultural, social, and legal factors. The phenomenon, while globally recognized, manifests differently across various regions, reflecting distinct cultural norms, societal structures, and legal frameworks. This literature review synthesizes existing research on honor killings, focusing particularly on the contexts of India and the Netherlands, as explored in the comparative study "Shattered Honor: Understanding and Addressing Honor-Related Crimes in Netherlands and India." Honor killings are typically defined as the murder of a family member, usually female, who is perceived to have brought dishonor to the family by violating cultural or societal norms. In India, these acts are deeply intertwined with the caste system, patriarchy, and traditional practices that uphold rigid social hierarchies (Smita Satapathy, 2023). The Indian context highlights how caste and arranged marriages often serve as triggers for such crimes, with societal pressure and the preservation of family honor being paramount (Grewal, 2013).

In contrast, honor killings in the Netherlands are more frequently associated with immigrant communities where traditional values from countries of origin clash with the progressive and egalitarian norms of Dutch society (Yurdakul & Korteweg, 2020). Here, the concept of honor is often linked to maintaining control within family structures, especially concerning women's autonomy. The Netherlands, despite its strong legal framework promoting gender equality, faces challenges in addressing honor killings due to cultural sensitivities and the secrecy surrounding these crimes (Eck, 2003a).

The legal responses to honor killings in India and the Netherlands differ significantly due to their distinct legal traditions. India's legal system, rooted in a mix of codified laws and customary practices, addresses honor killings primarily through general criminal statutes like the Indian Penal Code (IPC), which includes provisions for murder (Sec-302) and other relevant acts such as the Dowry Prohibition Act of 1961 and the Domestic Violence Act of 2005 (Dhull, 2017). However, these laws often fall short due to social pressures, witness intimidation, and inadequate enforcement, leading to low conviction rates (Dhull, 2017). In contrast, the Dutch legal system, grounded in individual rights and gender equality, addresses honor killings through its penal code, with specific provisions for murder under aggravating circumstances (Yurdakul & Korteweg, 2013a). The Netherlands also implements comprehensive programs like the Integrale Aanpak Huiselijk Geweld (Integral Approach to Domestic Violence), which integrates legal measures with public awareness and victim support services (Yurdakul & Korteweg, 2013a). Despite these measures, the prosecution of honor killings in the Netherlands remains challenging due to cultural considerations and the need for more targeted interventions within immigrant communities.

The social structures in India and the Netherlands significantly influence the prevalence and response to honor killings. In India, the deeply ingrained caste system, patriarchal dominance, and emphasis on family honor create an environment where such crimes are more likely to occur and less likely to be reported or prosecuted (Singhal, n.d.). The extended family structure and communal living further complicate efforts to address these crimes, as social cohesion often outweighs individual rights (Smita Satapathy, 2023). In the Netherlands, while the society is generally more individualistic and egalitarian, honor killings predominantly occur within immigrant communities that maintain strong ties to traditional values (Yurdakul & Korteweg, 2020). The Dutch approach to social integration and gender equality has made strides in reducing the incidence of honor killings, but cultural clashes and the persistence of patriarchal norms within these communities continue to pose significant challenges (Yurdakul & Korteweg, 2020).

NGOs play a critical role in combating honor killings in both India and the Netherlands. In India, organizations like Dhanak of Humanity and Shakti Vahini provide essential services such as safe shelters, legal aid, and psychological support to victims, while also advocating for stronger legal protections and societal change (Verkoren & van Leeuwen, 2013). These NGOs work within communities to challenge harmful traditions and promote human rights, often facing significant resistance from conservative segments of society (Verkoren & van Leeuwen, 2013). Similarly, in the Netherlands, NGOs like Fier and Movisie are at the forefront of providing support to victims, raising awareness, and influencing policy reforms (Verkoren & van Leeuwen, 2013). These organizations focus on both immediate intervention and long-term societal change by engaging with immigrant communities and training professionals to better recognize and respond to honor-based violence (Verkoren & van Leeuwen, 2013). Despite their successes, NGOs in both countries face ongoing challenges, including resource limitations, cultural resistance, and the complexities of navigating deeply entrenched social norms.

The comparative study of honor killings in India and the Netherlands offers valuable insights into the interplay between cultural norms, legal frameworks, and social structures in addressing this issue. While both countries face unique challenges, the common threads of patriarchal control, gender-based violence, and the misinterpretation of tradition underscore the global nature of honor killings (Yurdakul & Korteweg, 2020). Future research should continue to explore these intersections, focusing on the effectiveness of legal reforms, the role of NGOs, and the impact of cultural integration on reducing the prevalence of honor killings.

FUTURE RESEARCH DIRECTIONS

This chapter employs several key parameters to systematically analyze and compare honor killings in India and the Netherlands, two culturally distinct countries. By focusing on cultural norms and social structures, the chapter examines how these foundational elements shape behaviors and justifications for honor killings. In India, the caste system, patriarchal dominance, and traditional family values are highlighted as key factors perpetuating honor killings. Conversely, the analysis in the Netherlands centers on cultural clashes within immigrant communities, where traditional values conflict with Dutch societal norms. This comparative analysis helps contextualize these crimes within the broader societal fabric, shedding light on the root causes and resistance to change in each country.

Another critical parameter is the examination of legal frameworks and policy implementation related to honor killings. The chapter analyzes the Indian Penal Code (IPC) and the Dutch Penal Code to assess the effectiveness of these laws in prosecuting perpetrators and protecting victims. By comparing the legal approaches of India and the Netherlands, the author identifies strengths and weaknesses in both systems, offering insights into potential legal reforms. The role of NGOs in combating honor killings is also explored. The chapter examines how organizations like Dhanak of Humanity in India and Fier in the Netherlands support victims, raise awareness, and advocate for policy changes. NGOs are crucial in bridging the gap between legal frameworks and social realities, often leading grassroots efforts for societal change. Gender dynamics and the influence of patriarchy are further analyzed to understand the power structures that perpetuate honor killings. Despite cultural differences, both India and the Netherlands are affected by patriarchal norms that place women in subordinate roles. This focus on gender dynamics highlights the gendered nature of honor killings and underscores the need for gender-sensitive approaches to address the issue.

What sets this chapter apart is its comparative approach, contrasting honor killings in two countries with vastly different cultural and legal landscapes. While other works might focus on a single cultural or national context, this chapter provides a broader perspective by examining how the phenomenon manifests and is addressed in both India and the Netherlands (Yurdakul & Korteweg, 2020; Smita Satapathy, 2023). It emphasizes the intersectionality of various factors, such as caste, religion, gender, and immigrant status, in understanding honor killings, moving beyond simplistic analyses (Grewal, 2013; Yurdakul & Korteweg, 2020). By integrating social, legal, and grassroots perspectives, the chapter offers a holistic and nuanced analysis of honor killings, suggesting that solutions must be multifaceted, involving legal reform, social change, and grassroots activism (Verkoren & van Leeuwen, 2013).

The exploration of honor killings in India and the Netherlands provides a critical foundation for understanding the cultural, legal, and social dynamics that sustain this form of violence, but the persistence of honor-related crimes across diverse contexts indicates a need for further research (Eck, 2003a; Singhal, n.d.). Future studies should delve into the intersectionality of factors like caste, religion, socioeconomic status, and gender, exploring how these elements create unique vulnerabilities in different communities (Smita Satapathy, 2023; Yurdakul & Korteweg, 2020). Comparative legal studies are also necessary to evaluate how various countries, especially those adhering to international conventions like CEDAW, address honor killings, identifying best practices for legal reform (Dhull, 2017; Yurdakul & Korteweg, 2013a). The impact of international organizations, such as the UN and the EU, on combating honor killings should be examined, focusing on how global campaigns influence local practices and law enforcement (Verkoren & van Leeuwen, 2013).

Additionally, research on cultural sensitivity in legal and social interventions is crucial to balance respect for cultural diversity with the protection of human rights (Yurdakul & Korteweg, 2020). Longitudinal studies are needed to assess the long-term effectiveness of interventions, such as legal reforms and NGO initiatives, in changing attitudes and reducing honor-related violence (Verkoren & van Leeuwen, 2013; Fier, 2013). Investigating evolving gender dynamics, including the role of men in both perpetuating and combating honor killings, will provide insights into how shifting norms influence these crimes (Grewal, 2013). Furthermore, studies on the psychological and social support available to survivors are essential for understanding and improving their long-term outcomes, while research on media representation will help gauge how public perceptions of honor killings are shaped and how media can aid in prevention (Smita Satapathy, 2023). By pursuing these research directions, scholars and practitioners can enhance global efforts to eradicate honor killings and develop more effective, culturally sensitive strategies to protect human rights (Yurdakul & Korteweg, 2020).

DEFINING HONOR KILLINGS W.R.T NETHERLANDS

Honor Killings is a tragic practice whereby family members take the toll of another member's life for bringing dishonor to the family, or for transcending the cultural norms and native practices of the family. While this complex issue can be seen taking place globally, the Netherlands has also been grappled with Honor killings with unique issues or characteristics in comparison to the other parts of the globe. This dishonor can root out from various acts like premarital relationships, pursuing education or a career against a family member's will, choosing a life partner outside the family's consent, etc.(Al-Rawhi, n.d.)

Talking about a particular definition for honor killings, one cannot find a precise or particular one, but some of the common key elements of honor killing definition are **motivation by perceived dishonor** (i.e., the whole act is committed on the belief that the victim or his actions have brought shame or dishonor to the name of family), **perpetrated by family members** (killing has been committed by blood relations like father, brother, uncle) and **justified by traditions** (i.e., the act is justified by family members for upholding traditional values or protecting family reputation). (Korteweg et al., 2009a)

While the rate of honor killing is not too prevalent in the concerned country i.e., the Netherlands in comparison to other countries concern is the rising of cases over the years, majorly involving immigrant communities, specifically immigrant families with strong traditions, that contradicts the Dutch legal norms. Majorly, cases having Dutch-Moroccan & Dutch-Turkish communities have highlighted the persistence of patriarchal structures and traditional beliefs that can fuel such violence. The Dutch legal systems recognize honor killings as a form of murder with aggravating circumstances but successfully prosecuting these types of cases can be challenging due to family pressure, cultural sensitivities, and the secretive nature of crimes.(Eck, 2003a)

COMPLEXITIES RELATED TO HONOR KILLINGS W.R.T INDIA & NETHERLANDS

India and the Netherlands, two countries apart by great distances and thousands of years in history, have quite different social structures. Recognizing the patterns in which these tapestries are embroidered as well as the threads they are composed of is essential to understanding them. This paper delves into this complex analogy, elucidating the historical, cultural, and economic factors that have influenced these divergent social environments. The primary distinction is found in the underlying structures. India's intricate and age-old caste system is a major pillar of its social structure. Even though it was formally abolished in 1950, social mobility, marriage, and career choices are still greatly impacted by this hierarchical web.

There are thousands of sub-castes within the four primary castes of Brahmins, Kshatriyas, Vaishyas, and Shudras. These castes determine social status and frequently limit prospects. Caste is still a strong influence, especially in rural areas, even though industrialization has caused some boundaries to become hazier. The Netherlands, in sharp contrast, has an egalitarian and individualistic society. Though historical class distinctions persisted, particularly between the landed gentry and the working class, post-war social and economic changes have weaved a society with extraordinary social mobility. One's place in the fabric is established by their merit and accomplishments, not by inherited traits. This emphasis on equality extends to gender relations, where the Netherlands routinely ranks among the top countries in the world for gender equality.

These social canvases are also painted in distinctive hues by religion. Hinduism, Islam, Christianity, Sikhism, and Buddhism all cohabit in India, a country known for its robust religious pluralism, but there are occasionally conflicts between them. Caste and religious identity are entwined, thus complicating the social structure. Conversely, the Netherlands has seen a drop in religious observance as secularism has taken center stage. Although there are still faith communities, they have less of an impact on society at large. Another contrasting theme is economic structures. India is a country that is developing quickly and is facing severe income inequality. Much of the population is still impoverished despite tremendous economic progress, especially in rural areas.(Singhal, n.d.)

On the other hand, the Netherlands has a healthy middle class and welfare system, which leads to a more equitable distribution of wealth. The idea of social mobility and individual autonomy in Dutch society is bolstered by this economic stability. Divergent patterns can also be seen in family structures. Indian families have always been extended and patriarchal, placing a high value on communal life and filial piety. The idea of the family is still fundamental to Indian social identity, even though modernity has resulted in a shift towards nuclear households, particularly in metropolitan areas. In contrast, Dutch households tend to be smaller and more individualistic, with younger children obtaining independence.(Yurdakul & Korteweg, 2020)

Different images are painted by education, which is a crucial thread in determining a country's future. Even while India has made great progress in increasing access to education, there are still quality issues, especially for underprivileged groups. On the other hand, the Netherlands has a highly developed educational system that places a high value on quality and accessibility, which helps to explain its highly trained labor force and robust social safety net. These different social tapestries are not static. The Netherlands and India are both in transition as they deal with the effects of globalization, shifting demography, and advances in technology. India is engaged in a continuous battle to guarantee inclusive growth and eliminate the disparities maintained by the caste system. The Netherlands faces the challenge of preserving its robust social safety net in the face of growing economic strain and cultural diversity.

Thus, a fascinating study of difference may be found when comparing the social structures of India and the Netherlands. All countries provide different perspectives on the intricate relationship between history, culture, and economics in forming social structures, ranging from the deeply ingrained hierarchical systems of India to the egalitarian fabric of the Netherlands. Knowing these countries' unique social fabrics can help us create inclusive and egalitarian societies as they negotiate the changing 21st-century terrain. In the end, both tapestries—despite their dissimilar designs—share a common goal: to create a world in which our own choices—rather than the hues of our birth—determine our opportunities and levels of fulfillment. Now, let's discuss comparatively social structures, legal frameworks, and motivations- for the commission of honor killing crimes in India and the Netherlands.

SOCIAL STRUCTURES

The India and Netherlands celebrate different cultural liberties, but the interplay between the social structure and the commission of honor killing crime becomes a crucial factor to be referred to. The different approaches of both these nations towards gender roles, family, and concepts of honor, impacts the existence and complexities of honor killing in different ways. On one hand, India, a country fully loaded with cultural and community values, supports family essence and encourages a hierarchical structure. In today's time, though the caste system, patriarchal dominance, and repressive approaches have been officially struck down but still prevail in society. (Smita Satapathy, 2023)

In this 21st century too, the independent approaches to selecting life partners are assumed to be a sin. Sons of the family are believed, to be the custodians of the family's honor while the honor is related to females' chastity and obedience which is used as a strong reasoning or justification by perpetrators of the honor killing crime. Lack of education, conservative societal pressure, and the approach of arranged marriage are some of the roots contributing to the end of the independence of free will. Due to the structure and prevalence of such practices, perpetrators get a green flag for committing honor killing crimes in India. (Grewal, I. 2013)

While in the Netherlands, the Dutch society presents a more equitable yet compromiser view. The free individual approach is preferred over family or community pressures. This egalitarian landscape gives birth to the concept of gender equality i.e., enshrined in law and promotes the socio-economic development of society. the native citizens regardless of their gender i.e., male or female are free to choose their life partner, lifestyle, and careers. This egalitarian approach makes the Netherlands relatively less prone to honor killing crime. However, the social structures are not too easy to define, despite the Netherlands' progressive setting, it is not immune to gender discrimination & related crimes whereas India being a developing nation, is shifting towards achieving equal rights for women.

LEGAL FRAMEWORKS

Killing for bringing dishonor to the family is a barbaric practice, while it gets influenced by cultural contexts, legal frameworks are a counter-stopping mechanism. The legal framework in India regarding honor killing is not direct but is connected through various dots. The major criminal act i.e., the *Indian Penal Code (IPC)* provides sections like *Sec-302* which deals with murder. To address this problem, a more specific focus acts like the *Dowry Prohibition Act, of 1961* criminalizes giving or taking of dowry (one of the common triggers for honor killings), or the *Domestic Violence Act, of 2005* protects women against violence from family members. Despite these acts, the rate of conviction for honor killing crimes stays low due to social pressure, witness intimidation, inadequate police investigations, or lack of evidence due to intimidation commission.(Dhull, 2017)

While the Netherlands has a contrasting approach to dealing with honor killings. The Dutch legal system & Constitution are rooted in the principles of individual rights and gender equality. *Article 289* of the **Dutch Penal Code** provides a maximum of lifetime imprisonment for the commission of murder including honor killing commission. The Netherlands has also adopted programs like Integrale Aanpak Huiselijk Geweld (Integral Approach to Domestic Violence) program of 1998 to implement strategies, legal measures, and awareness programs related thereto. The Dutch Legal system aims to prioritize the victim's safety while taking action against the perpetrator through law. The Dutch courts consider the cultural background of the perpetrator as a contributing factor but not a justification for the commission of a crime.(Yurdakul & Korteweg, 2013a)

On exploring further, both legal systems reveal that India's legal system is a blend of codified laws and customary practices while the Netherlands is strictly adhered to a codified basis. The Netherlands has a general criminal code and human rights framework whereas India has enacted specific laws like the Dowry Prohibition Act. While both legal systems share condemnation of honor killings, maximum punishment and provisions with special emphasis on victim protection are in common. (Korteweg et al., 2009b)

MOTIVATION

Honor killing is deeply rooted in socio-cultural beliefs, thus, making direct comparisons in motivation across both countries is not reasonable. Both India & Netherlands have a unique history, religious aspects, and societal factors contributing to the commission of honor killings. In India, honor killing is intertwined with approaches of patriarchal society, caste-based hierarchy (not legal, but still prevails in rural areas), etc. The motivation in India is fuelled by a variety of factors including caste and community pressure, patriarchal control, and misinterpretation of traditions or religious texts. The scenario in the Netherlands is the opposite i.e., the commission of honor killings occurs within the immigrant communities.(Janssen & Reed, n.d.)

In cases of conflict between the cultural norms of an immigrant community and the Dutch values (Independence, gender equality), there attracts a catch of violence leading to honor killings. Or other motivations for honor killings in the Netherlands can include the controlling behaviors of family members or a misplaced sense of honor. But the similar factors, evident in both countries are gender-based violence, misinterpretation of tradition and religion, and maintaining family control.(Eck, 2003b) (Yurdakul & Korteweg, 2013b)

CONTRIBUTIONS OF NON-GOVERNMENTAL ORGANIZATIONS IN COMBATING HONOR-RELATED CRIMES IN THE NETHERLANDS

Non-governmental organizations (NGOs) and civil society play a crucial role in combating honor-related crimes in the Netherlands by providing essential support to victims, raising awareness, and advocating for policy changes. NGOs such as *Fier* and *Movisie* are at the forefront, offering immediate assistance through safe shelters, legal aid, and psychological support. These organizations create safe spaces for victims, enabling them to escape violent situations and access the resources needed for long-term rehabilitation. A key aspect of the NGOs' efforts is raising awareness about honor-related crimes. They conduct educational programs and workshops targeting both the general public and specific communities. These initiatives help demystify cultural justifications for such crimes and promote human rights and individual autonomy over traditional notions of honor. By fostering a broader understanding of the issue, NGOs help to shift societal attitudes and reduce the stigma faced by victims.

In addition to public education, NGOs focus on training professionals such as social workers, and educators, who are likely to encounter honor-related crimes in their work. These training programs equip professionals with the knowledge and tools needed to identify and respond effectively to cases of honor-based violence. Enhancing the capacity of these frontline workers is crucial for improving the overall societal response to such crimes. Policy advocacy is another vital component of NGOs' work. They engage with government bodies to influence legislative and policy reforms, ensuring that the legal framework addresses the complexities of honor-related crimes. This includes advocating for stricter laws, better enforcement mechanisms, and comprehensive support systems for victims. Through persistent advocacy efforts, NGOs aim to create a legal environment that provides adequate protection and justice for victims.(Verkoren & van Leeuwen, 2013)

Understanding that honor-related crimes are deeply rooted in cultural beliefs, NGOs also engage directly with communities where these crimes are prevalent. By fostering dialogue within these communities, they challenge and change harmful traditions and beliefs that perpetuate honor-based violence. This grassroots approach is essential for creating lasting cultural change and preventing future crimes. While there have been significant successes, such as increased reporting of honor-related crimes and better protection for victims, challenges remain. Resistance from conservative segments of society and the need for more resources to support comprehensive intervention programs are ongoing issues. Despite these challenges, the multifaceted approach of NGOs and civil society in the Netherlands is crucial in the fight against honor-related crimes, helping to foster a society that upholds the dignity and rights of all individuals.

CONTRIBUTIONS OF NON-GOVERNMENTAL ORGANIZATIONS IN COMBATING HONOR-RELATED CRIMES IN INDIA

Non-governmental organizations (NGOs) and civil society in India play a pivotal role in combating honor-related crimes through various initiatives aimed at supporting victims, raising awareness, and influencing policy changes. NGOs such as **Dhanak of Humanity** and **Shakti Vahini** provide critical support to victims by offering safe shelters, legal assistance, and psychological counseling. These organizations ensure that victims have a refuge from violence and the resources necessary for their rehabilitation and reintegration into society. A significant part of the NGOs' work involves raising awareness about honor-related crimes, which often go underreported due to societal stigma and fear of retribution. Educational programs and community outreach initiatives are conducted to enlighten the public about the severe implications of such crimes and to promote the principles of human rights and individual freedoms over traditional and patriarchal notions of honor. These efforts aim to foster a societal shift in attitudes, reducing the stigma and encouraging more victims to come forward.

Training and capacity building for professionals who might encounter honor-related crimes, such as police officers, social workers, and healthcare providers, are crucial components of the NGOs' strategy. By equipping these frontline workers with the knowledge and skills to identify and respond to honor-based violence effectively, NGOs enhance the overall capacity of the system to support victims and bring perpetrators to justice. Policy advocacy is another critical area where NGOs in India make substantial contributions. They engage with government bodies and policymakers to advocate for stronger legal frameworks and enforcement mechanisms that adequately address the complexities of honor-related crimes. This includes pushing for more stringent laws, improved protective measures for victims, and comprehensive support systems to ensure justice and safety.

Community engagement is essential in the context of honor-related crimes, which are often deeply entrenched in cultural and familial norms. NGOs work within communities to challenge and change harmful traditions and beliefs that justify honor-based violence. Through dialogues, workshops, and grassroots campaigns, these organizations aim to transform societal norms and prevent future occurrences of such crimes. Despite notable successes, including heightened awareness and better victim protection, challenges persist. These include resistance from conservative sections of society, the prevalence of deeply ingrained patriarchal values, and a lack of resources to support expansive intervention programs. Nonetheless, the efforts of NGOs and civil society in India are indispensable in the fight against honor-related crimes, contributing significantly to the protection of human rights and the promotion of a more just and equitable society.

SUCCESS STORIES AND CHALLENGES FACED BY NGOS

Following are few exemplary success stories of NGO's w.r.t honor killings in relation to both countries, India & Netherlands:

Dhanak of Humanity: This NGO has been instrumental in rescuing and supporting interfaith and intercaste couples who face threats of honor killings. They provide safe houses, legal aid, and counseling. Their advocacy has led to increased awareness and changes in local police practices, ensuring better protection for at-risk couples.

Shakti Vahini: This organization has successfully intervened in numerous cases of honor-based violence, saving lives and providing ongoing support to victims. Their work has brought significant media attention to the issue, increasing public awareness and putting pressure on authorities to act.

Fier: This organization operates shelters and provides comprehensive support services for victims of honor-related violence. Their successful interventions have helped many victims escape dangerous situations and start new lives. Fier also collaborates with law enforcement to improve response strategies.

AWARE Foundation: By focusing on education and awareness, AWARE has contributed to significant cultural shifts within communities. They have conducted successful outreach programs that engage with community leaders, resulting in decreased instances of honor-based violence.

These are few of the NGOs which highlight a brighter future and strength of today's union to combat heinous crimes like honor killings. But the NGOs and civil society's faces a lot of challenges and hurdles which restricts their functioning against honor killings:

One of the foremost challenges faced by NGOs and civil society in both India and the Netherlands is dealing with deeply entrenched cultural norms and patriarchal values that justify and perpetuate honor killings. In India, traditional notions of family honor, caste, and community often override individual rights, making it difficult to challenge and change harmful beliefs. Similarly, in the Netherlands, honor-related violence within certain immigrant communities is often rooted in cultural practices and values imported from their countries of origin. Addressing these deeply ingrained beliefs requires a nuanced, culturally sensitive approach that can be difficult to implement effectively.

NGOs often encounter significant resistance from the very communities they aim to help. In India, families and communities may actively oppose interventions, viewing them as threats to their honor and cultural practices. This resistance can manifest in various ways, from non-cooperation to direct threats against NGO workers. In the Netherlands, while the legal and social frameworks are generally more supportive, resistance from within immigrant communities can still pose significant barriers. Convincing these communities to accept and support anti-honor killing initiatives often requires persistent effort and strategic engagement.

Resource limitations are a significant hurdle for NGOs in both countries. Many organizations operate with limited funding, which restricts their ability to provide comprehensive support to victims, including safe housing, legal aid, and psychological counseling. In India, the sheer scale of the problem, coupled with widespread poverty and socio-economic challenges, exacerbates the issue. In the Netherlands, while the scale may be smaller, the need for specialized services that cater to the unique cultural and psychological needs of victims requires substantial funding, which is not always readily available.

Despite existing legal frameworks to combat honor killings, enforcement remains inconsistent. In India, corruption, lack of training, and insensitivity among police and judiciary officials can undermine efforts to protect victims and prosecute perpetrators effectively. Legal proceedings are often slow and can be influenced by local power dynamics. In the Netherlands, although the legal system is generally more robust, gaps remain in the effective identification and prosecution of honor-related crimes. Victims may also fear retribution or social ostracism, deterring them from seeking legal recourse.

A lack of awareness about honor killings and the resources available to combat them is a pervasive issue. In India, many victims and their families are unaware of their rights or the support services available to them. This lack of awareness extends to the general public and even some professionals who might encounter these cases. In the Netherlands, victims within immigrant communities may not report honor-related violence due to fear of social consequences or mistrust of authorities. Enhancing awareness and encouraging reporting through targeted outreach and education campaigns is a significant challenge.

Balancing cultural sensitivity with the imperative to protect victims and uphold human rights is a complex task. NGOs must navigate cultural dynamics carefully to avoid alienating the communities they aim to help. In both countries, this requires a deep understanding of cultural contexts and the ability to build trust within these communities. However, achieving this balance can be challenging, especially when cultural practices directly conflict with human rights principles.

Thus, NGOs and civil societies in India and the Netherlands face multifaceted challenges in their efforts to combat honor killings. These include deep-rooted cultural norms, community resistance, resource constraints, legal and institutional barriers, lack of awareness and reporting, and the need for cultural sensitivity. Addressing these challenges requires a comprehensive, multi-pronged approach that combines advocacy, support services, community engagement, and policy reform.

WAYS TO COMBAT HONOR KILLINGS

India and the Netherlands both confront particular difficulties in the fight against honor killings, but they may both significantly improve the safety of those who are most vulnerable if they address common core reasons and customize solutions for their particular situations. Here are a few potential approaches:

- **Comprehensive laws:** By tackling honor killings expressly, both nations can strengthen their legal frameworks, resulting in more severe penalties and precise definitions.
- **Investigate and prosecute cases quickly:** Setting up specialized courts or processes can help victims receive justice more quickly and discourage possible offenders.
- **Witness protection:** Securing convictions depends on protecting witnesses by providing relocation facilities and anonymity programs.
- **Education and awareness campaigns:** It is crucial to educate the public and law enforcement about the illegality and terrible effects of honor killings.
- **Community outreach initiatives:** Talking with key people in vulnerable areas, such as religious leaders and elders, can promote discussion and dismantle harmful customs.

- **Assistance for victims and their families:** Offering safe havens, therapy, legal representation, and job prospects enables victims to start over and end the cycle of abuse.
- **Encouraging gender parity:** Undermining patriarchal customs and advocating for women's equal rights and opportunities is essential to breaking the power imbalances that give rise to honor killings.
- **Caste and social hierarchies:** By addressing systematic discrimination and advancing inclusivity, inflexible social institutions that frequently serve as justifications for honor killings are less powerful.
- **Encouraging cultural sensitivity:** Understanding and bridging cultural gaps can be achieved by valuing individual autonomy and universal human rights while respecting cultural backgrounds.
- **Cross-cultural cooperation:** Exchanging best practices and knowledge between the Netherlands and India can bolster global efforts and offer insightful information for addressing the problem on a global scale.
- **Funding research and data collection:** By comprehending the subtleties of honor killings in various settings, policies, and interventions can be developed that are more successful.
- **Working together with NGOs and civil society groups:** Making the most of grassroots organizations' experience and network helps improve community involvement and survivor assistance.

CONCLUSION

As we reach the culmination of this chapter, we are confronted with a stark reality that shakes us to our core: honor killings, a savage blemish on the human race, are not confined to a single corner of the world but spread their insidious influence across various cultural terrains. India and the Netherlands, despite their apparent divergence in culture, find themselves bound by a sorrowful thread - the merciless extinguishing of lives under the guise of a distorted concept of familial or communal "honor". Through our thorough examination, we have unraveled the intricate web of motivations and circumstances that drive the abhorrent act of honor killings. In both societies, the oppressive dominance of patriarchy looms heavy, reducing women to mere pawns in a game of social manipulation, where their personal choices and independence are deemed insignificant when compared to the preservation of family "honor." The distortion and misinterpretation of long-held traditions and religious beliefs further tighten the grip, offering a distorted rationale for the perpetration of violence. In India, the rigid social hierarchies dictated by caste systems and specific interpretations of religion serve as fuel for this destructive fire. Meanwhile, in the

Netherlands, clashes of cultures and misguided notions of honor within immigrant communities can serve as catalysts for igniting these flames. In both situations, the daunting presence of community disapproval and social disgrace casts a heavy shadow. Families, constrained by apprehension and the expectation to fit in, might silently approve or even commit acts of violence against their daughters and sisters. This sets off a harmful cycle of oppression, magnifying the voices of those responsible and muting the pleas of the victims.

As we delve deeper into these narratives, we can observe that although they are connected in some ways, they also reveal unique patterns. The reasons behind honor killings vary depending on the cultural context. In India, going against arranged marriages, crossing caste boundaries, and even making choices about clothing can be seen as violations deserving of the most severe consequences. On the other hand, in the Netherlands, clashes between cultures, controlling family dynamics, and misunderstandings about honor due to assimilation challenges can serve as triggers for brutal reactions. The social and legal scenarios related to gender-based violence exhibit disparities as well. In India, there are hurdles in terms of broad societal approval of honor killings, along with a less comprehensive legal structure. On the other hand, even though the Netherlands is not completely impervious to these problems, it possesses a more formidable legal system and generally fosters a more discerning societal perspective towards honor killings.

A multifaceted approach is necessary to untangle this yarn and weave a future without the stain of honor killings. The first step in dismantling the scaffolding of patriarchy is through education and awareness programs that challenge traditional gender roles, address harmful interpretations of religion and tradition, and promote gender equality. To break the cycle of violence and give women the tools to rewrite their narratives, they must be empowered through economic independence, access to education and healthcare, and safe spaces.

It is important to have strong legal frameworks with severe punishments for perpetrators and effective protection for victims. This requires not only robust legislation but also effective implementation and cultural shifts that prioritize safety and justice for women. Open dialogues with community leaders, religious figures, and civil society organizations as well as awareness campaigns can foster attitudinal change and break the silence surrounding gender-based violence. This active engagement can dismantle the walls of stigma and create a culture of support and empathy.

REFERENCES

Al-Rawhi, S. (n.d.). Honour-based killings: conceptual framework. *South East Asia Journal of Contemporary Business, Economics and Law, 11*(4). https://www.du.edu/intl/humanrights/violencepkstn.pdf

Dhull, K. (2017). Impact Factor: RJIF 5.12 www.educationjournal.org Volume 2; Issue 6. In *International Journal of Advanced Educational Research*. www.educationjournal.org

Janssen, J. H. L. J., & Reed, B. (n.d.). *Focus on honour : an exploration of cases of honour-related violence for police officers and other professionals.*

Korteweg, A. C., Janssen, J., Timmer, W., Ouchan, K., Dogan, C., Bakker, H., Gortworst, J., Van Groesen, S., Dekker, A.-F., Metin, S., Simsek, J., Clijnk, A., & Van Der Zee, R. (2009a). *Understanding Honour Killing and Honour-Related Violence in the Immigration Context: Implications for the Legal Profession and Beyond.* http://vorige.nrc.nl/article1855988.ece

Singhal, V. K. (n.d.). *Honour Killing in India : An Assessment.* https://ssrn.com/abstract=2406031 DOI: 10.2139/ssrn.2406031

Smita Satapathy, D. R. (2023). Honour Killing as a Crime in India. *International Journal of Law Management & Humanities*, 6. Advance online publication. DOI: 10.10000/IJLMH.114514

van Eck, C. (2003a). *Purified by blood : honour killings amongst Turks in the Netherlands.* Amsterdam University Press.

Verkoren, W., & van Leeuwen, M. (2013). Civil Society in Peacebuilding: Global Discourse, Local Reality. *International Peacekeeping*, 20(2), 159–172. DOI: 10.1080/13533312.2013.791560

Yurdakul, G., & Korteweg, A. C. (2013). Gender equality and immigrant integration: Honor killing and forced marriage debates in the Netherlands, Germany, and Britain. *Women's Studies International Forum*, 41, 204–214. DOI: 10.1016/j.wsif.2013.07.011

Yurdakul, G., & Korteweg, A. C. (2020). State responsibility and differential inclusion: Addressing honor-based violence in the netherlands and germany. *Social Politics*, 27(2), 187–211. DOI: 10.1093/sp/jxz004

Chapter 16
Honor Killing:
A Socio-Legal Analysis With Special Reference to Haryana, India

Jae-Seung Lee
College of Liberal Arts and Applied Science, Miami University, USA

Punya Singh
GLA University, Mathura, India

ABSTRACT

The research was carried out using a detailed study of the case, content evaluation techniques, and an observational-analytical framework. According to the report, honor-based crime arises when parents are intolerant of their daughters' premarital relationships and marital choices, particularly when these decisions involve marriages between different castes or religions. The study also notes that a significant proportion of killings based on honor are carried out as crimes of passion sparked by unexpected incitement when the girls' families discover the couples in precarious conditions. It has been observed that the traditional beliefs of a culture dominated by males prevent girls from forming connections before marriage or from selecting the men they wish to wed. Honor killings are a common practice with social and cultural context legality due to the society's support and poor enforcement of the law. Thus, despite enacting strict rules and harsh penalties to address the issue, The chapter will deal with the above problems with special reference to Haryana, India.

The report identifies five primary reasons why honor killings occur in Haryana. The primary cause of 47 incidents is inter-caste affairs, whereas relationships between girls and boys from the same gotra (same lineage and clan) account for 17% of

DOI: 10.4018/979-8-3693-7240-1.ch016

Copyright © 2025, IGI Global. Copying or distributing in print or electronic forms without written permission of IGI Global is prohibited.

cases when honor killings occur. Once more, 17% of cases involve the girl's family members being merely obnoxious and intolerant of her relationship with any boy, regardless of his caste, religion, or social status. In an additional 13% of cases, honor killings are motivated by a girl's affair with a boy from the same area. Additionally, 6% of cases involve the prohibition of interreligious or intersect relationships to the point where, if they do occur, they end up being the catalyst for honor killings. It is a well-established fact that much as in other regions of India, intercaste marriage is strictly prohibited in Haryana, especially among the state's rural population and the Jat community in particular. In the State, social stratification based on caste and gotra is prevalent and inflexible. For ages, the endogamic ties between castes and gotras have been supported by the caste and gotra-based Khaps (Caste Councils). In these stories, when the girls and boys form relationships across caste lines and want to get married, their requests are denied, and when the couples defy these bigoted social norms, they are brutally killed. Similarly, tight restrictions exist on intimate relationships and marriages between members of the same gotra.

METHODOLOGY

The primary goal of the research is to perform a thorough examination of the many aspects and characteristics of honor killings in Haryana, India. This research was carried out using a combination of analytical and observational methodologies. With the main emphasis on India, a historical-analytical method has been used to accurately observe the theory, its very nature, and the occurrence of honor killings globally. The recorded approach to case studies as well as the evaluation method was used to conduct the main portion of the study. Individuals associated with the two sides (the family members of the murdered girls and boys) are unwilling to reveal anything to any person, especially someone who is unimportant and unfamiliar, because honor killing is evidently a delicate, discriminatory, and introverted matter related to the honor and societal position of those in concern. As a result, the recorded scenario approach and content analysis method have been used to familiarise oneself with the most thorough analysis. By giving researchers suitable accessibility to the instances of honor killings that occurred within a particular period, the method is used to enhance the research. As a result, attention has been given to one hundred incidents of murder for the honor that happened in the geographic region of Haryana between 2005 and 2013 and were reported by The Tribune (an English daily newspaper).

KEY TERMS

Fundamental terms include "Honor Killing" and "Haryana", directly links the honor based crimes with special reference to Haryana, India. Broader themes like "Gender-Based violence"(Baxi P., 2006), "Khap Panchayats"(Kumar A., 2006), "Jat Community"(Wasti T.H., 2010), and "Patriarchal Ideology"(Ali Y., 2008) contextualize the issue. The strong adherence to traditional values and practices i.e. "Socio-cultural norms"(Welchman L.& Hossain S., 2005), "Inter-caste and Inter-religious Marriages"(Vishwanath J., 2011) and "Caste System"(Brandon J., & Hafez S., 2008) contributes to the prevalence of honor based violence. Research perspectives like "Observational-Analytical Framework"(Bernard S., 2013) have been used to study honor killings, focusing on specific cases in Haryana.

Notable references include Baxi, Rai, & Ali's (2006) work on "Crimes of Honour" in India, which provides a comparative legal perspective, and Wasti's (2010) examination of the evolution of honor killing laws in South Asia. These sources offer insights into the socio-legal frameworks and cultural practices that perpetuate honor crimes, making them essential for understanding the specificities of Haryana's social fabric. Additionally, the Law Commission of India's Report on preventing interference in matrimonial alliances highlights the legal challenges in combating such crimes. These references were pivotal in grounding the study within a broader socio-legal context.

Relevance was a key component of the inclusion criteria, which made sure that only papers that directly addressed honor based violence in Haryana, or related legal and cultural issues and norms are taken into account. Current viewpoints and data were included as a result of prioritizing recent articles, ideally those that were published within the last ten years. The foundation of our research, in order to uphold academic rigor, consisted of government and recognized NGOs reports as well as peer-reviewed literature.

Articles with minimal relation to the subject matter and non-academic sources such as blogs and opinion pieces were eliminated using exclusion criteria. To find the most relevant papers for our study, we must do article research using scholarly databases like JSTOR, PubMed, and Google Scholar. Targeted keywords like "Honor Killing," "Patriarchy,", "Jat Community", "Gender-Based Violence," and "Khap Panchayat" should be used. To improve research and coverage of pertinent themes, non-peer-reviewed research publications were eliminated. News items and unreliable internet sources were also eliminated to prevent inconsistencies.

LITERATURE REVIEW

The primary driver behind honor killings is the preservation of family honor, which is often tied to the control of female sexuality and behavior. Patriarchal traditions imply that a family's dignity lies in the conduct of its female members in many societies where honor killings take place. Family honor is threatened by any departure from traditional gender roles, including selecting a spouse, filing for divorce, and having extramarital or before-marriage affairs (Gill, 2009). The National Crime Records Bureau in India records numerous honor killings each year; however, because of societal stigma and legal loopholes, the actual number may be understated (Chesler, 2010). Honor killings can also be more common depending on one's socioeconomic standing. Poverty and illiteracy can sometimes make upholding traditional values—which might include honor-based violence—even more extreme. Reliance on male family members for financial support may also keep women from fleeing violent relationships or seeking safety (Perry, 2012).In certain countries, honor killings are ingrained in the culture. Honor is frequently linked to social status, prestige in the family, and purity. In these kinds of communities, society is crucial in upholding these standards, and to maintain harmony within the community, honor-based violence is occasionally encouraged (Abu-Lughod, 2011).Certain cultures use misconstrued cultural customs and religious beliefs as justifications for honor killings. It is important to remember, nevertheless, that no significant religion expressly supports honor killings. Rather than religious teachings, these acts are frequently the consequence of deeply ingrained cultural norms (Chesler, 2010). Honor killings affect victims, relatives, and society's psychological health in addition to the acute demise of life. Those who survive attempted honor killings frequently deal with trauma, rejection from society, and ongoing threats. Additionally, the acceptance of honor-based violence feeds an environment based on dread and control, limiting the liberties and rights of women (Gill & Brah, 2014).

RESEARCH GAP

This chapter highlights the unique context of Haryana, where honor killings are intricately linked to caste and religious norms, and contrasts with broader global studies by focusing on this specific region. The chapter employs a comprehensive approach, utilizing case studies, content evaluation techniques, and an observational-analytical framework to investigate honor killings, with a focus on Haryana, India. The research examines how honor-based crimes are triggered by familial intolerance towards premarital relationships and marriages outside caste or religion, often resulting in passionate, impulsive violence by family members or hired perpetrators.

The study highlights that traditional, male-dominated cultures in Haryana enforce strict norms that limit women's autonomy in forming relationships, creating a fertile ground for honor killings.

The chapter stands out by emphasizing recent data and employing a rigorous methodology that includes analyzing one hundred cases reported in a certain time frame. This approach is distinct from other studies due to its focused geographical scope and detailed case examination, providing a nuanced understanding of how deeply ingrained societal attitudes and legal inadequacies perpetuate these crimes. By contrast, other research may offer broader overviews or lack specific, recent case data, potentially missing the contemporary dynamics of honor-based violence in Haryana.

The chapter reveals the deeply entrenched cultural and social factors driving these heinous crimes. It highlights that honor killings are predominantly influenced by the region's semi-tribal and patriarchal structures, particularly within Jat communities. Key parameters used in the study include the geographical distribution of crimes, the demographic profiles of victims (age and gender), and the socio-cultural dynamics influencing honor-based violence. The analysis shows a stark prevalence of such crimes in Jat-dominated areas, with a notable bias against women. The chapter underscores the urgent need for both legal reform and cultural change to address these entrenched practices and protect women's rights in the face of enduring patriarchal values.

INTRODUCTION

Humans are both socially and mentally integrated into society. The guy acknowledges and accepts societal standards as legitimate ethical requirements rather than as inevitable social constraints. It makes sense that societal and cultural norms have a strong influence on a man's mental makeup. Through socialisation of the cultural and social environments in which he lives, the concepts of virtue and vice, holy and filthy, ethical and unethical, acceptable and restricted, honor and dishonor, are ingrained in a man's thinking. In terms of his sociocultural beliefs, man interprets the social behaviour, position, and roles that apply to him and other people. Every community has several social behaviours deemed inappropriate and, if carried out, recognised as disrespectful and defiant based on the social standing and roles of different community members. The penalties in these situations differ from community to community, depending on the type and severity of the disobedience and dishonor. The practice known as "honor killings" results from the socio-psychic environment of ordinary communities, wherein likely acts, especially those of females, are acknowledged to bring dishonor to their loved ones and neighbourhoods, and the lost honor is compensated by killing the offending individuals.

Concept and Dimensions of Honor Killings

The practice of honor killing is widespread throughout the world(Welchman & Hossain, 2005) and has been documented in numerous nations, including the country of Bangladesh, Algeria, Brazil, Ecuador, Morocco, Israel, Ethiopia, Somalia, Uganda, the Balkans, Sweden, Holland, Germany, Italy, Yemen, India, and many more(Ali, 2008). The Population Fund of the UN estimates that as many as five thousand females are killed annually in what is known as "honor killings" by families across the globe (UNIFEM, 2007).

Honor killing is described as "the intentional prearranged homicide, usually of a woman, carried out at the direction of the woman's family, prompted by the belief that the woman has disgraced the family" in the Oxford Dictionary of Law Enforcement .Honor killings are crimes of assault, typically homicide, perpetrated by masculine family members upon female members of the family, who are viewed to have inflicted disgrace upon the family," according to the organization Human Rights Watch (2004). For several reasons, such as declining to get married in an arranged marriage, experiencing sexual harassment, filing for divorce—even from a violent husband—or (supposedly) engaging in adultery, a woman may become the prey of her family. A mere idea that a woman has done anything to "dishonor" her entire family might set off an assault.

According to the Law Commission of India (The Law Commission of India, 2012), the terms "honor killings" and "honor crimes" are utilized indiscriminately as shorthand to refer to instances of assault and abuse inflicted upon new couples who are planning to get married or who have already tied the knot contrary to the will of their families or their community. They are not as appropriate and true phrases as they are utilized more as catchphrases.

Additionally, scholars view the issue of honor killings as a result of other factors. Multiple research efforts have identified the main factors, which include: inter-caste or interreligious marriages; contradiction to male-female relationships before and after marriage; and restrictions on women's ability to choose their spouses. While exposing the reasons for honor killings, Haile describes them as a custom in which masculine gender blood relatives murder a female relative who is thought to have compromised the honor of the family. If a woman engages in discussion with a not-related male, consents to illicit sexual activity, is raped, or declines to wed a family-approved candidate, she may be committing honor killing. If there is even the slightest indication that the lady has committed any of the aforementioned offenses, this action may be taken. According to Kumar(Kumar, 2012), a female family member faces a high risk of cruel and inhumane loss of life if she opts for marriage in opposition to the will of her parents, engages in extramarital or premarital relationships, gets married within her social class, exterior her social strata, or with an intimate relative from another caste because she believes that doing so has brought shame to her loved ones, social group, or society.

Honor killings are more precisely defined by the experts as gender-specific crimes. According to Bernard, women's varied behaviors, such as disobeying the suggested clothing code, dating men who are not associated with her, or challenging their dad or siblings, might make honor crimes worse (Bernard, 2013). Nonetheless, behaviors that increase the likelihood of honor killing include the girl engaging in extramarital or premarital sexual activities, irrespective of whether she consented to or not. One ought not to regard murders based on honor as an independent occurrence. When closely examined, it is the most detrimental element among several facets of honor-based violence. Coerced unions, spousal abuse, and ultimately honor killings are examples of honor-based atrocities(Brandon & Hafez, 2008). When girls agree to marry beyond their caste or religion, they are forced into weddings with members of their chosen households. Domestic abuse towards girls who refuse to be coerced into weddings results from their refusal to marry. There is a clear increase in the probability of murders based on honor if the females decide to run out or marry someone of their selection.

HONOR KILLINGS IN INDIA

Since ancient times, honor-based assault, and especially the tradition of killings based on honor, have existed in India (Ali, 2008). The states of Haryana, Punjab, Rajasthan, and Western Uttar Pradesh are the ones wherein these occurrences happen more often; however, cases have been reported in practically every portion of India (Vishwanath et al., 2011). There is no trustworthy information accessible from any government or nongovernmental organization regarding the severity of the events. Nonetheless, research carried out by many civil society groups indicates that the nation of India is among the most severely impacted countries. According to estimates, reported murders for honor in India result in the deaths of about one thousand people annually, both male and female. Due to its intricate social and cultural customs, India has a variety of reasons why honor killings occur there. Numerous academics reveal that the primary cause of honor killings in India is the higher castes' hostility towards girls in inter-caste marriages or premarital relationships. In the northern regions of India, especially in the state of Haryana, marriages into the same gotra—that is, the same lineage, clan, or descendants—have been identified as contributing factors to honor killings. In addition to these inter or intra-caste dynamics, inter-religious marriages have been identified as an independent variable in cases where parents murder children they love in an attempt to regain their lost honor (Baxi et al., 2006).

The societal embrace of honor-based brutality, including honor killings, is a clear reality in all the societies where these practices are common. In India, the majority of honor killings takes place in an extremely male-dominated communities that are also known as "honor-based" communities, such as the Jat-Sikhs of Punjab, the Jats of Haryana, and the Rajputs of Rajasthan. In the patriarchal systems of the past, succession is patrilineal. Furthermore, the fundamental social, financial, and political unit is a family or kinship rather than the individual. Consequently, it is possible to see that in all such societies, the function of neighbors, elders, and community councils—such as KhapPanchayats in Haryana—is to patronize honor killings and shield those who carry them out. Unexpectedly, these established conservative communities reject the government's and the legal system's efforts to stop honor killings, viewing them as an unwelcome intrusion on their social and cultural customs and family structures. In addition to sociocultural sponsorship, legal clemency has played a significant role in the establishment of honor killings in India. In addition to strengthening this socio-cultural norm, a century-old legal tradition that the British supported throughout their control over India and which treated such murders leniently also turned this norm into an avenue for legal recourse (Wasti, 2010).This norm of society was treated leniently under the Penal Code of 1860, Section 300, Exception I, on the grounds of grave and sudden provocation. "Culpable homicide is not murder if the perpetrator, while devoid of the ability of self-control by grave and sudden provocation, results in the loss of life of the individual who imparted the incitement or induced the loss of life of any other person by mistake or accident," states Exception 1 of Section 300 of the Penal Code of 1860. The British Government's first law commission, which was formed in 1835–1837, focused on the problem of killings for honor while creating India's penal code. In light of the severe and unexpected provocation, they gave the matter some thought and came to a favorable conclusion. They sympathized with the men whose honor was betrayed if a person engaged in sexual activity with their spouse or sister, without delving too deeply into the specifics and definitions of honor. According to Section 295 of the 1837 draft of the Indian Penal Code, "if a male finds somebody having a sexual relationship with his spouse, child, or sister and murders the individual, or women, or either, such an act should not be classified as murder, but should be demoted to manslaughter only. The men who framed the Indian Penal Code saw honor killings as a widespread crime in which men kill other men for having an extramarital affair with their spouses or children, rather than as a socio-religious problem unique to a few groups living in a specific region or culture on the Indian subcontinent.

CONSTITUTIONAL AND LEGISLATIVE PROVISIONS IN INDIA

Articles 14, 15 (1) & (3), 17, 18, 19, and 21 of the Indian Constitution are also violated by honor killings. All people, regardless of nationality, are guaranteed their constitutional right to life and liberty by Article 21 of the Indian Constitution's chapter on fundamental rights. The apex court of India has ruled in several pertinent cases that the stipulations found in the present legal framework are adequate to safeguard a variety of human rights, which include the right to life. According to the seminal rulings establishing the right to life, this encompasses not only the right to a dignified (*Francis vs. Union Territory*, 1981) existence but also the right to livelihood (*Chandrabahan vs. Union of India*,1983), health (*Vincent vs. Union of India*, 1987), education (*Mohini vs. State of Karnataka*,1992), and so on. Nevertheless, the judgement-based explanations do not specifically encompass that. Though it is indicated that the right to live with respect supports the right to get married to the girl or boy of one's choice, the inferences made possible by rulings do not specifically include that right. According to the Indian Penal Code, honor killings are severe offences that involve murder.

The IPC addresses culpable homicide that is not equivalent to murder in Sections 299 and 301, whilst Section 300 tackles murder. Honor killing is tantamount to homicide and murder when those targeted are killed since it is believed that they have brought shame to the family. The IPC's Section 302 provides for possible punishments for offenders. Under Section 302 of the IPC, relatives and community members may face prosecution for organizing, inciting, or fabricating murder or assassinations as well as for illegally harboring the perpetrators. The IPC has several pertinent sections, including section 302, which permits the criminal investigation of both community members and relatives. According to section 34 of the IPC, homicides committed by four or fewer people, which includes close family members, are crimes under section 302 of the IPC; however, if five or more individuals are involved, community members may face accusations of murder under section 145 of the Criminal Procedure Code. In addition, under sections 120(b) and 202 of the IPC, community members who are believed to be guilty of willfully hiding information regarding the preparation and/or carrying out a murder may be prosecuted under the provisions of section 302 of the IPC.

RESULTS

Assaults on honor occur often in several places, including Haryana. The semi-tribal and male-dominated social systems that characterise the state's cultural and social life include the majority of people living in remote regions and working in agricultural fields, as well as the state's adherence to societal traditional values and conformity to culture despite the state's swift economy and infrastructure growth. Honor-based crimes and murders of honor aren't unusual in the area. Upon careful examination of the cultural and social mentality of the majority of groups, particularly those who belong to martial groups (mostly Jats), it becomes evident that the concept of "honor" has great importance in some of these societies. The word "honor" is very important in the state of Haryana, where it is seen as an essential part of social and cultural norms. The notion of honor and pride-based homicides of women has several dimensions in this community. Another factor is that it is deemed an affront to the honor of masculine members of the family when a woman is abused sexually, humiliated, taunted, or mistreated by another man. It probably encourages hostility towards the accused as well, which may result in his murder. The third part addresses cases in which a husband believes that a wife's illicit activities with another man constitute a violation of his honor. When a female shows her readiness to marry the boy of her choice and/or develops improper affections for any boy before marriage, this is another type of honor-related crime that also results in honor killings. The girl's paternal relatives view her before marriage, love, or intimate relationships as an affront to their honor and will not put up with it. It is understood that the girl will damage the family's honor even if she is ready to get married to the man of her choice. When the girl has an affair and is even ready to tie the knot with a boy from a lower social stratum or belief system, the scenario becomes extremely problematic. There are clear chances that the girl may experience honor-based assault, which typically ends with the girl, the guy, or both of them being killed. This specific type of honor killing in the region of Haryana is the focus of the current study. As was already noted, there are many societal parallels between Punjab and Haryana. Among the most concerning issues in Haryana is the issue of honor murders. As a result of its fast industrialization and agricultural productivity, Haryana has been regarded as being one of the most industrialised regions. In terms of the societal attitude and social behaviour of the rural people, Haryana has similarities to Punjab in that it nevertheless reflects the characteristics of a tribe or semi-tribal territory. The practice of honor murders in the state of Haryana is frequently caused by opposition to love weddings and, in particular, by prejudice against unions between members of different castes and religions. This section of the research is dedicated to looking at many angles of the honor homicide instances that have occurred in Haryana. Analysing the number of murders for honor in different parts of the province is the first problem. There are clear chances that the girl may experience honor-based assault, which typically ends with the girl, the teenage boy, or both of them being killed. This is the focus of the current study. As was already noted, there are many sociological parallels between Punjab and Haryana. Arguably the most concerning trouble in Haryana is the issue of murders of honor. As a result of its fast industrialization and agricultural growth, Haryana has been regarded as one of the most advanced states. In terms of the societal attitude and societal actions of rural people, Haryana yet has similarities to Punjab in that it nevertheless reflects the beliefs of a tribal territory. The practice of honor killings in the province is frequently caused by opposition to love marriages and, in particular, by hostility against relationships between members of different castes and religions. This section of the research is concerned with looking at many angles of the honor murder instances that have occurred in Haryana. Analysing the number of honor killings in different parts of the province is the first problem.

SEVERITY OF THE INCIDENTS ACROSS DIFFERENT REGIONS

It is not possible to find an official, solid division of the geographic area based on social and cultural factors in Haryana. As a result, all of Haryana's districts have been geographically divided into three regions—the Jat-dominated area, the Yadav-dominated area, and the area with mixed population—based on the density of inhabitants and the overwhelming majority of specific groups in each area. This has allowed for the methodical revelation of the shifts in the severity of events in each region. The area with a predominantly Jat population consists of ten regions (the Sirsa region, Fatehabad, Hisar, Bhiwani, Jind, Rohtak, Sonipat, Karnal, Panipat, Kaithal); the area with a predominantly Yadav group consists of a total of four districts (Narnauli, Mahendragarh, Rewari, Jhajjar); and the geographical area with a mixed population consists of four districts (Panchkula, Ambala, Yamunanagar, Kurukshetra). The analysis shows that only in the Jat-dominated area do seventy-four of these crimes occur. The area concentrated by the Yadav community experiences twenty-three percent of the events, while the zone with a mixed population experiences just three percent of the incidences.

The statistics clearly show concern that over two-thirds of these heinous instances occur in the region where Jats make up the majority population and where they dominate the socio-cultural, socio-economic, and socio-political domains. It proves that the practice of carrying out crimes against honor is widespread among Jats in Haryana, striking similarities with Punjab. It makes sense that the Jats of Punjab and Haryana share comparable racial, ethnic, and genetic heritage. Their ethnic-racial patterns' tribal and patriarchal tendencies, along with an excessive sense of honor-related possessiveness, make them more likely to commit crimes against honor. Although there are Yadav tendencies towards crimes against honor as well, these are significantly less common in comparison to Jats. It makes sense that the Jats identify as the most dominant class within the class system and associate their past with different royal dynasties. As a result, they have a custom of being resentful of their kids' marriages, particularly those involving girls, and of individuals or families who are purportedly from the lower castes and socioeconomic classes. Although the Yadavs recognize them as members of the Yadav dynasty, they do not enjoy the position of being the most affluent class in the Indian regions and cultures in which they live, especially in Haryana. As a result, they are somewhat more accepting of marriages between different castes and religions.

PROPORTION OF THE KILLINGS OF GIRLS AND BOYS

Honor-based crimes also show up to be greater gender-based crimes in Haryana than they do in society at large. The girl individually dies in fifty-two percent of instances, whereas the teenage boy individually is murdered in ten percent of instances, according to the examination of the hundred sampling instances. In thirty-eight percent of instances, the adolescent boy and girl die together.

It proves that ninety percent of these types of events involve the murder of girls. In addition, it is an offence committed against women exclusively, yet in forty-eight percent of cases, the young man who is associated with the girl also gets killed. One thing that stands out in this situation is the fact that the girls occasionally get killed. Their paramours are killed in ten percent of circumstances, but the girls' families spare them. After closely examining the cases, it was found that almost all of this, 10% of situations involve the girl's passionate affair (especially one that is inter-caste, inter-religious, or within her similar gotra) coming to the attention of relatives and that no separation or secret, unapproved wedding occurs. In these situations, the girl's relatives encourage, caution, and warn her to end her contact with the men. If the connection persists, the woman's family decides to kill the offending male and compel the daughter to marry a man of their selection to put an end to it. Most of the occurrences whereby solely the girl gets murdered entail family members choosing to end the dispute by killing the girl out of the cold when they discover the girl is still having an illicit affair with the man. In these situations, the relatives believe that by killing the girl in private, they will be able to hide her connection with any male and protect the family's honor. Additionally, cases, where the couple elopes or marries one another in defiance of the female family's protests and cautions, constitute those in which both are killed. When a woman's family members catch the couple in a precarious situation, both of them are also killed.

AGE VARIABLES OF GIRLS KILLED FOR HONOR

Two age groupings—14–19 and 20–25—have been considered to determine the most likely ages of the girls murdered in Haryana for honor. These age ranges were established by taking note of the lowest and highest ages of the girls who were slaughtered in Haryana for their honor. Analysis of the collection of cases reveals that the females who are killed for honor in Haryana must be at least 14 years old. However, the upper age limit has been determined to be 25 years old. Girls between the ages of 14 and 19 make up 46% of those slain for honor, and girls between the ages of 20 and 25 make up fifty-four percent of those who died.

Most of the dead girls, who were between the ages of 14 and 19, weren't murdered as they declined to wed the male of their own accord despite the wishes of their relatives. However, they are easily eliminated when their connection to the men is discovered. According to the report, even girls between the ages of 14 and 19 who are mentally and physically wrapping up their youth are not forgiven by their own families. Because of the inevitable mental shifts that occur around this phase, the females in this age category get physically or psychologically attached to the men. Nonetheless, in Haryana, where a large number of rural people continue the practice of marriage between children and where the political, economic, and socially wealthy individuals of the area support and condone this custom, teenage girls aren't considered as mentally undeveloped but rather as beneath them, subservient, and unimportant family members who are typically executed for seeking connections with men. The majority of girls in the 20–25 age range are killed by family members when they marry, elope, or vehemently persist in getting the men of their choosing despite the wishes of their families.

AGE VARIABLES OF BOYS KILLED FOR HONOR

Three categories of ages have been created using the age parameters of the males who passed away: 17–19 years old, 20–25 years old, and 26–30 years old. After looking through 100 sample instances, it was found that the lowest age for boys and men slain by relatives of girls and women in heinous crime incidents was 17 years old, while the highest age at which they died was 30 years old. Out of all the incidents of boys being killed, 20% fall into the 17–19 age range; concerning 65% fall into the 20–25 age group, with the rest 15% falling into the 26–30 category. In Haryana, there is profound distaste for partnerships between men and women. Earlier research revealed that girls between the ages of 14 and 19 are slain in forty-six percent of instances. The age distribution of boys killed in these types of instances shows that in five out of every six cases, a girl's family relatives have killed a teenage boy between the ages of 17 and 19. The lads in the same age bracket who passed away were the ones who forged connections with the girls in the 14–19 age range. It confirms that in the state of Haryana, the close bonds that boys form with ladies, their fellow students at educational institutions, and their friends in their neighborhood or village.

CONCLUSION

The study concludes that honor crimes have been carried out in Haryana, primarily in the areas where the Jat population is the majority in terms of population size as well as the economic, social, and political realms. Although women are disproportionately affected by the issue of crimes against honor, it is not just a problem that affects women. Notably, teenagers between the ages of 14 and 19 make up 40% of the girls who are killed for honor, while teenagers between the ages of 20 and 25 make up the remaining 60%. Furthermore, almost all of the men killed for honor are between the ages of 20 and 25; yet 20% of dead men were teenagers between the ages of 17 and 19. The dads along with siblings of the girls are directly involved in nearly each of the incidents. One noteworthy problem is that moms are directly involved in three percent of heinous crime instances. Moreover, it has been discovered that the state frequently sees an immediate role of maternal and possibly paternal uncles in the assassination of girls. It is also discovered that relatives and friends were involved in the girls' killings. Based on the research, it can be concluded that such crimes are more socially and familial acceptable and supported in Haryana. The participation of contract murderers has only been noted in a very small number of cases. It proves that the people of Haryana deal with honor killing occurrences quite severely, carrying out the murders with bare hands. Additionally, marriages between members of the same social group or belief leads to honor-based assault; however, the severity, scope, and parameters of these causes—such as escapes, illegal secret weddings, and the sudden revelation of intimate relationships—further exacerbate the issue and leads to the killings of girls, boys, or couples. Over twenty-five percent of honor murders are done as crimes of desires sparked by unexpected incitement, in which the girls' family participants find themselves in compromising circumstances with their paramour(s). When considering the issue within the socio-historical framework, it becomes clear that the issue is more than just a gender-based issue resulting from violence against women or a class-specific trend brought about by disputes within Haryana's caste hierarchy. An oversimplified understanding of the causes of killings for honor would be to see them solely as a kind of assault against women or possibly a product of caste selfishness. The issue should be noted in order to understand the precise reasons behind the horror of murders for honor. Understanding the precise reasons behind the horror of honor killings requires observing and analyzing the issue from a socio-historical angle. The study reveals that the Jat community in Haryana is primarily responsible for honor killings. Like many other ethnic-racial groupings in India's northern region, the Jats are part of a socioeconomic stratum that has stayed tribal for millennia. While many Indian ethno-racial communities have become more or less urbanized and literate in response to the trend of mental and social advancement, the Jats, who are predominantly rural and largely illiterate, continue to adhere to their semi-tribal ethno-community-based social and cultural system of values.

It also seems from this angle that the reasons for the community's support of honor killings can be seen. The Haryanvi people's allegiance and credibility, particularly that of the Jats, towards their community-based system of values and group wealthy individuals (khap panchayats) as opposed to state law can be seen as a reflection of the state's late progress in social, psychological, and legal-political modernization. Once more, the predominant characteristics of a belief system based on ethnic group are authoritarianism and intra-caste marriage relationships. Therefore, the acceptance of social class, society and gender-specific inclusiveness as components of the cultural and social process is still pending. Women have been marginalized to a subservient position in their society for millennia as men have dominated the family, social, economic, and political spheres. Women have been marginalized to a subservient position in their society for millennia as men have dominated the family, economic, social, and political spheres. As a result, because this is a socially and culturally tribal country, intra-caste marriages are still common, and choosing a mate is mostly a family and community decision instead of a personal choice. For generations, women have been relegated to a subservient position in their society while men have controlled the house, the financial system, and the realms of politics and society. Due to this, choosing a partner is primarily a family and social decision instead of one that is personal, and in this socially and culturally tribal country, intra-caste marriages are still common. However, in recent years, both the government and civil society have grown more worried as a result of the rise of feminist movements, media investigation, and India's shift from a firmly male-dominated to an egalitarian society as well as from an old-fashioned bias society to one that is legal and rational. However, the socially and culturally tribal tribes continue pursuing the wicked act of honor killings as a recognized and even prized socio-cultural trend because they have not been affected by the procedure of social, mental, legal, or political modernization. The study also raises the alarming statistic that over 25 per cent of killings for honor in Haryana occur as a result of abrupt instigation in which the pair is seen by a girl's family member or members in hazardous settings. It is not sufficient to consider this particular trend in honor killings as a crime committed in a moment of intense emotion or as a societal or gender-based occurrence. Instead, it is better to analyze it as a psychological tendency that men have been instilled with through their cultural and social system of values and that they find deeply offensive. Rather, it is better to analyze it as a mental feeling that men are instilled with via a cultural and social value system, making them incredibly intolerant of the sexual paths taken by the women who are connected their way via any kind of relationship with men who are not familiar to them. It is therefore imperative to swiftly alter the thinking of prejudiced male communities to become receptive to their girls' choices for the union, particularly about among castes and inter-religious marriages, in addition to enacting strict regulations and harsh punishments. However, changing the socio-cultural psychology of people who are far more possessive and loyal within their cultural and social norms than the community, country, and court is a difficult assignment for citizens, the governing body, and the court system.

REFERENCES

Abu-Lughod, L. (2011). Honor and the Sentiments of Loss in the Global Discourse on Muslim Women. In *Violence and Belonging: The Quest for Identity in Post-Colonial Africa* (pp. 16–37). Routledge.

AIR. (1981). *Francis vs. Union Territory*, SC 746

AIR. (1983). *Chandrabahan vs. Union of India*, SC 803

AIR. (1987). *Vincent vs. Union of India*, SC 990

AIR. (1992). *Mohini vs. State of Karnataka*, SC 1858

Ali, Y. (2008). *Honor, the State, and Its Implications: an Examination of Honor Killing in Jordan and the Efforts of Local Activists*.

Baxi, P., Rai, S. M., & Ali, S. S. (2006). Legacies of common law: "Crimes of honour" in India and Pakistan. *Third World Quarterly*, 27(7), 1239–1253. DOI: 10.1080/01436590600933404

Bernard, S. (2013). Combating Honour Crimes in Europe. (SURGIR Foundation Publication 9) Geneva

Brandon, J., & Hafez, S. (2008). *Crimes of the Community: Honour-Based Violence in the UK*.

Chesler, P. (2010). Worldwide Trends in Honor Killings. *Middle East Quarterly*.

Gill, A. (2009). Honor Killings and the Quest for Justice in Black and Minority Ethnic Communities in the UK. *Criminal Justice Matters*, 75(1), 28–30.

Kumar, A. (2012). Public Policy Imperatives for Curbing Honour Killings in India. *Journal of Politics & Governance*, 1(1), 36–40.

Perry, A. (2012). *Honor Killings in Pakistan: An Everyday Matter*. TIME Magazine.

The Law Commission of India, Prevention of Interference with the Freedom of Matrimonial Alliances. (2012, August). (in the name of Honour and Tradition): A Suggested Legal Framework, Report No. 242, Government of India.

The Oxford Dictionary of Law Enforcement. (2007). *Honour Killing*. Oxford University Press.

UNIFEM. (2007). *Fact and Figures on Harmful Traditional Practices*. UNIFEM Publication.

Vishwanath, J., Srinivas, &, & Palakonda, C. C. (2011). Patriarchal Ideology of Honour and Honour Crimes in India. *International Journal of Criminal Justice Sciences*, 6(2), 386–395.

Wasti, T. H. (2010). The Law on Honour Killing: A British Innovation in the Criminal Law of the Indian Subcontinent and its Subsequent Metamorphosis under Pakistan Penal Code. *South Asian Studies*, 25(2), 261–311.

Welchman, L., & Hossain, S. (2005). 'Honour', rights and wrongs. *"Honor": Crimes, Paradigms and Violence against. Women*, 1–21.

Chapter 17
Study of Judgments in India

Chunyre Kim
Saint Joseph's University, USA

Mohmmad Shoaib
GLA University, Mathura, India

ABSTRACT

The praiseworthy peculiarity killings in India have been a longstanding issue, well established in friendly, social, and familial elements. Honor killings, frequently executed against people who oppose customary cultural standards in regard to rank, religion, or between position relationships, certainly stand out both locally and universally. These demonstrations of viciousness, serious for the sake of protecting family honor or station virtue, have brought up basic issues about equity, common liberties, and law and order in India. This exposition looks at the advancement of legal perspectives and approaches towards honor killings in India, breaking down eminent decisions that have molded lawful talk and affected cultural discernment. By diving into the legitimate standards, points of reference, and cultural ramifications of these decisions, this paper looks to give a far-reaching comprehension of the legal reaction to respect killings in India and the continuous mission for equity and responsibility even with settled in social practices.

STATISTICAL DATA

While precise data on honor killings in India can be challenging to obtain due to underreporting, available statistics indicate a significant number of cases. According to the National Crime Records Bureau (NCRB), the number of reported honor kill-

DOI: 10.4018/979-8-3693-7240-1.ch017

Copyright © 2025, IGI Global. Copying or distributing in print or electronic forms without written permission of IGI Global is prohibited.

ings has fluctuated over the years. While there has been a decline in recent years, the issue remains a serious concern in certain regions of India. (*Global Human Rights Club: Arizona State University*)

In 2019, NCRB reported 24 cases categorized explicitly as honour killings, though experts suggest the actual numbers could be higher due to underreporting and misclassification. The conviction rate for honour killings remains low, often attributed to inadequate evidence, lack of witness protection, and social stigma. Until 2014, the Indian government did not keep an extensive record of honor killings. Originally to this, these types of fatalities were often considered to be suicides or homicides because there were no laws specifically targeting honor-based violence. In the period between 2014 and 2016, the Indian Supreme Court recorded 288 instances of honor murders. But according to information gathered by the non-governmental group Evidence, from 2012 to 2017, there were 187 incidents in Tamil Nadu alone. (*Honor Killing In India: An Analysis On Indian Statutes: K.Vikas*)

The Indian Population Statistics poll (IPSS) launched a poll in Delhi in the second quarter of 2007 and found that there were about 655 occurrences of honor murders reported in India. In juxtaposition with Haryana, where the percentage reached as high as 35%, Uttar Pradesh was responsible for 25% of these instances, according to the survey data. In the northwest of India, honor killings made up approximately forty per cent of the total. Two North Indian states that are well-known for honor killings have been highlighted and analyzed in this study due to their high honor killing rates. It indicates that the northwest portions of India are responsible for approximately forty per cent of all honor killings. (*The Modern Face of Honor Killing: Factors, Legal Issues, and Policy Recommendations 2010Author(s): Vitoshka, Diana Y*)

DATABASE SELECTION AND ARTICLE RESEARCH

In the above Journal there have been various Studies which have been done "Oxford Human rights Journal", "Survey of Times of India on Honour Killing", "Indian journal of criminology", "Feminist Legal Studies", "Economic and Political Weekly", Articles were also taken from "Legal services India" and "IP Blog post Leaders" under the Criteria that they were on the study of Honour killing in India. Case studies were also taken like "Romesh thappar vs State of Madras", "Manoj Babli case Judgment", "Shakti Vahini vs The union of India", "The Nirupamma Pathak case", smt Lakshmi Kacchawa vs State of Rajasthan" and the "Rajasthan Prohibition Act", "Murder References of 2010 and 2007", "National Crime Bureau Reports", "Indian Population Statistics Poll" .

KEY TERMS:

Honour Killing, Patriarchal Social Structure Violation of Human Rights, Caste and Community Pressures, Manoj Babli Case 2007(*Murder References No. 2, 2010*) stands as a merciless and grievous sign of the well-established social wrongs that plague India. **The Nirupama Pathak Case** which was of major concern regarding honour killing in India, the case revolved around the rank and age challenges and their related stereotypes. **Shakti Vahini vs. Union of India (Shakti Vahini vs Union of India, 2018)** is on well-known issue of Honor killings. **Khap Panchayat (Smt. Laxmi Kachhwaha vs. The state of Rajasthan (1999))**, "National Crime Bureau Reports", "Indian Population Statistics Poll", "Times Of India Article on Honor killing in Haryana, State of Uttar Pradesh Vs Krishna Master (2010), Sec 141, 143, 503 and 506 IPC, Indian Penal Code, 1860, Section 151 CrPC, Code of Criminal Procedure, 1973

LITERATURE REVIEW

The Chapter provides a comprehensive analysis of the issue of honor killings within the Indian legal and cultural context. It examines the evolution of judicial perspectives and approaches toward honour killings in India, analysing key judgments that have shaped legal discourse and influenced social perceptions. Honor killings in India are acts of violence, usually murder, committed by family members against a relative, primarily women, who are perceived to have brought dishonor to the family. These acts are often justified as necessary to protect the family's honor and social standing. The document highlights the deep-rooted cultural and social elements that contribute to the persistence of honor killings in India. Traditional cultural norms, caste-based discrimination, and patriarchal societal structures are significant contributors to these crimes. Honor killings are a severe violation of human rights, especially the right to life and personal autonomy. The document underscores the blatant disregard for individual freedoms and the right to choose one's partner, which these killings represent. It highlights the ongoing struggle to align traditional values with modern legal and human rights principles. The Chapter presents several case studies, including the *Manoj-Babli case (2007)* and the *Nirupama Pathak case (2010)*, illustrating the complexities of judicial proceedings in honor killing cases. It explores the difficulties faced by the judiciary in effectively prosecuting honor killings and the need for stronger legal frameworks and faster trials to deter such crimes. *Shakti Vahini v. Union of India (2018)* a significant Supreme Court ruling that directed state governments and police departments to create a comprehensive framework to combat honor killings. The case underscored the need for legal and social reforms to address this issue effectively. Efforts to address honor killings often meet resistance from those who view these practices as integral to their cultural or religious identity. The document addresses the challenge of balancing respect for cultural traditions with the need to uphold human rights.

FUTURE RESEARCH DIRECTIONS

This research is an attempt by the authors condemning honor-based violence, they view this wrong as a grave violation of human rights and highlight ingrained patriarchy leading to such violence against females. Future research on honor killings should focus on several key areas to enhance understanding and inform policy development. First, an in-depth analysis of judicial reforms and legal provisions is necessary to assess their effectiveness in combating honor killings, including the implementation and impact of state-specific laws and Supreme Court directives. Additionally, more research is needed on the sociocultural dynamics that sustain honor killings, particularly the roles of caste, community pressures, and patriarchal norms, as understanding these factors could help develop targeted interventions to prevent such violence. Another area for future studies is the evaluation of awareness campaigns and educational programs to determine their effectiveness in changing societal attitudes toward honor killings, both in rural and urban contexts, and their role in empowering individuals to make autonomous choices. Research should also examine the role of law enforcement agencies in addressing honor killings, including the challenges they face in investigating and prosecuting these crimes, and explore potential reforms to enhance police accountability and responsiveness. Further studies are needed to analyze media representation of honor killings and its impact on public perception and policy formulation, as understanding how media coverage influences societal attitudes and legal responses could promote more responsible reporting. Comparative studies could provide valuable insights by analyzing honor killings in India alongside similar practices in other countries, highlighting different legal, social, and cultural approaches to addressing the issue and identifying best practices for policy development. (*Global Human Rights Club: Arizona State University*)Additionally, future research should focus on the effectiveness of support systems for victims of honor killings, including legal aid, safe shelters, and rehabilitation programs, exploring the challenges faced by these systems and suggesting improvements. Lastly, longitudinal studies tracking changes in societal attitudes and the prevalence of honor killings over time would provide critical insights into the progress made and highlight areas requiring further attention. The Indian government has undertaken several judicial reforms to combat honor killings. The Supreme Court has directed law enforcement agencies to take prompt action in cases involving honor killings and to ensure the protection of victims and their families. The court has also stressed the importance of conducting swift investigations and expedited trials for these cases. In addition, the government has introduced legislation to impose stricter penalties on those guilty of honor killings, including the death penalty in certain situations. Efforts have also been made to increase public awareness about the issue through educational campaigns and to provide support services for victims and their families. These reforms are aimed at fostering a more just and equitable society where women's rights are safeguarded, and honor killings are no longer accepted.

INTRODUCTION

"The death of women for presumed disobedience from sexual norms established by society" is the term defined as honour killing. Extreme forms of violence towards women committed in the notion that an honour code has been broken, bringing perceived shame upon the family, are defined as honour killings. Furthermore, women may endure the shame of stereotypical masculine abuses of their "honour" in sexual relations and might be killed for bearing children as a result of rape and incest. Suspicion of sexual deviance, such as extramarital pregnancy or adulterous behaviours, is also considered a sufficient reason for punishing a woman. What makes "honour killings" particularly tragic is the potential for widening involvement beyond the immediate perpetrator. Not only spouses or partners, but also family members like mothers, brothers, uncles, and cousins can become complicit or even active participants in these crimes. This highlights the deeply ingrained social and community pressures that contribute to these acts of violence.

Honor killings in India are a deeply troubling issue that reflect the clash between traditional values and modern legal and human rights principles. The act of honour killing involves the murder of a family member, usually a woman, who is perceived to have brought shame or dishonour to the family, often due to relationships, marriage choices, or perceived sexual behaviour that defies traditional norms.

COMMUNITY CONCERNS REGARDING HONOR KILLINGS IN INDIA:

1. **Violation of Human Rights:**
    o Honor killings are a severe violation of human rights, particularly the right to life. Communities are increasingly concerned about the blatant

disregard for individual autonomy and the freedom to choose one's partner.
2. **Patriarchal Social Structure:**
    o   Many communities are entrenched in patriarchal structures where family honor is often linked to the control of women's bodies and choices. There is concern over the persistence of these outdated norms that devalue women's lives.
3. **Failure of Law Enforcement:**
    o   Despite legal provisions against honour killings, there is widespread concern over the inadequate response from law enforcement. Families often go unpunished due to societal support, police apathy, or even complicity. Honor killings are still widespread, but they are not explicitly covered by any national laws. The Law Commission of India recommended a law in 2012 designed to tackle the problem of honour murders from occurring, but it was never implemented. The only distinctive law that specifically addresses honour killings in the entire country at current time is the **Rajasthan Prohibition of Interference with the Freedom of Matrimonial Alliances in the Name of Honour and Tradition Bill of 2019**. The statute stipulates that honour killings carry a death or life sentence in jail and lists other consequences that make it illegal to jeopardize a couple's rights or cause them to be tormented in any manner whatsoever. (Oxford Human Rights Hub: Addressing "Honour Killings In India")
4. **Caste and Community Pressures:**
    o   Honor killings are often linked to inter-caste or inter-religious marriages, with communities exerting pressure to conform to caste or community boundaries. This reinforces discriminatory practices and exacerbates social divisions. As in the recent case in Rajkot in a village of Gir Somnath district family members killed one of their own for having the extra marital affair with his sister-in-law however the family members were against to lodge the complaint of the murder or even divulge the circumstances in which the man was butchered to the administration of that district. The local public administration finally come to an end of the Investigation that the family members have done Honour Killing and arrested 5 members of the family who were the culprits of the case. (Murder Reference of Honour killing: Times of India)
5. **Lack of Education and Awareness:**
    o   A lack of education and awareness in rural and even some urban areas contribute to the perpetuation of honor killings. Communities are con-

cerned about the need for greater education on human rights and the legal consequences of such actions.

6. **Social Stigma and Fear:**
    o   Victims of honor killings, or those at risk, often face social stigma and fear of reprisal, making it difficult for them to seek help. Communities are concerned about the need for better support systems and protection for potential victims.
7. **Judicial Challenges:**
    o   The judicial system faces challenges in prosecuting honor killings effectively. There are concerns about the need for stronger legal frameworks, faster trials, and harsher punishments to deter such crimes.
8. **Role of Media:**
    o   While media has played a role in bringing attention to honor killings, there are concerns about sensationalism and the potential for reinforcing harmful stereotypes. There is a call for more responsible reporting and focus on solutions(*Romesh Thapper v. State of Madras AIR 1950SC 124*)
9. **Efforts for Social Reform:**
    o   Community leaders, activists, and NGOs are working towards social reform by advocating for gender equality, promoting inter-caste marriages, and challenging patriarchal norms. These efforts are seen as essential in changing the mindset that leads to honor killings.
10. **Cultural Resistance to Change:**
    o   Efforts to address honor killings often meet with resistance from those who see these practices as integral to cultural or religious identity. There is concern over how to balance respect for cultural traditions with the need to uphold human rights.

ONGOING EFFORTS AND THE WAY FORWARD:

- **Legal Measures:** Strengthening and enforcing laws against honor killings, including specific legal provisions, is essential.
- **Awareness Campaigns:** Increased awareness and education campaigns can help change societal attitudes and empower individuals to make their own choices.
- **Community Engagement:** Engaging with communities to challenge patriarchal norms and promote gender equality is crucial.

- **Support for Victims:** Providing support services for those at risk of honor killings, including safe shelters and legal aid, is important.
- **Media Responsibility:** Media should focus on highlighting positive stories of change and the impact of legal and social reforms.

The following cases which were of great concern regarding honour killing judgment in India are:

Manoj Babli Case 2007

The Manoj-Babli honor killing instance of 2007 (*Murder Reference No. 2, 2010*) stands as a merciless and grievous sign of the well-established social wrongs that plague India. It is an account of two youthful lives snuffed out for the sake of a twisted feeling of custom and rank pride. Manoj Banwala and Babli had a place with similar town in Haryana, a state in North India known for its man centrist cultural standards and the commonness of khap panchayats, position-based gatherings that frequently use gigantic power, especially in rustic regions. Regardless of having a place with the equivalent 'gotra' (family), a social no locally, Manoj and Babli became hopelessly enamored and chosen to wed in 2007.

Confronting the Rage of Tradition

Their association was met with savage resistance from Babli's family, especially her granddad, Gangaraj, a strong khap pioneer. The panchayat considered their marriage a demonstration of disobedience against their social request and a stain on their local area's honor. They brought the couple and forced them to revoke their marriage, undermining desperate results if they denied.

A Merciless Finish to a Dream

Resolute by the dangers, Manoj and Babli wouldn't surrender. Their insubordination fixed their lamentable destiny. On June 14, 2007, Babli's sibling, Suresh, constrained her to consume pesticide under the full concentrations' eyes of other relatives. In the meantime, Manoj was overwhelmed and choked to death with a noose. Their bodies were then unloaded in a channel to conceal the proof. The police at first battled to gain ground because of the family's impact and the code of quietness in the town. Notwithstanding, persevering endeavors by Manoj's mom and supported media pressure gradually worked on the mass of quietness. In the end, Babli's sibling, Suresh, alongside other relatives, was captured.

A Milestone Verdict

The preliminary that followed was firmly watched across India. In a milestone decision in 2010, the Punjab and Haryana High Court condemned Ganga raj and four others blamed to death, denoting the initial occasion when culprits of an honor killing in India dealt with such a cruel repercussion. The excess blamed got life sentences. (*Times Of India Article on Honor killing in Haryana*)

Past the Verdict

While the decision brought a similarity to equity for Manoj and Babli, it likewise started a warmed discussion about honor killings and the job of khap panchayats (*State of Uttar Pradesh Vs Krishna Master*) in Indian culture. The case featured the requirement for stricter regulations, social changes, and mindfulness missions to battle these savage practices.

A Tradition of Hope

The Manoj-Babli case remains a powerful image of the battle against honor killings. It fills in as a sign of the overwhelming results of visually impaired adherence to old practices and the significance of individual decision and opportunity. While the scars of their misfortune run profound, their story likewise lights a glint of expectation for a future where love and opportunity win over bias and persecution.

Further Focus to Consider

* The effect of the Manoj-Babli case on ensuing legitimate improvements in India, including the Criminal Regulation (Change) Act, 2013, which explicitly perceives honor killing as a particular offence.
* The continuous difficulties in destroying honor killings, including the job of destitution, absence of schooling, and the impact of standing and local area pressures.
* The significance of enabling ladies and elevating orientation uniformity to battle well established man centric practices.

The case was critical not just for a fair consequence given to Manoj and Babli yet additionally for igniting a more extensive discussion about honor killings in India. It incited conversations on the critical requirement for lawful and cultural changes to kill the well-established biases that lead to such demonstrations of viciousness. Be that as it may, in spite of legitimate mediations and decisions like the one in the

Manoj-Babli case, honor killings keep on being a diligent issue in certain pieces of India. Endeavors to battle these practices include a blend of legitimate changes, social mindfulness missions, and local area commitment to challenge imbued convictions and biases. The disastrous story of Manoj and Babli stays an unmistakable sign of the intricacies encompassing issues of honor, love, and cultural assumptions in many regions of the planet.

The Nirupama Pathak Case

In the second case, **The Nirupama Pathak Case** which was of major concern regarding honor killing in India, the case revolved around the rank and age challenges and their related stereotypes. The Nirupama Pathak case is a disastrous and profoundly upsetting story that unfurled in 2010, featuring the terrible truth of honor killings and the diligence of backward normal practices in present day India. Nirupama Pathak, a youthful and aggressive writer from Jharkhand, was fiercely killed supposedly by her own relatives for the sake of safeguarding family honor. This case shook the country as well as exposed the intricacies encompassing station, honor, and orientation in Indian culture. Nirupama, a brilliant and decided lady, was seeking after her fantasies about turning into a fruitful writer. Nonetheless, her desires conflicted with the profoundly dug-in standing order common locally. Naturally introduced to a Brahmin family, Nirupama became hopelessly enamoured with a man from a lower station, Priyabhanshu Ranjan, during her school years. Their relationship tested the unbending station limits and cultural standards, prompting energetic resistance from Nirupama's loved ones. As their relationship extended, Nirupama and Priyabhanshu chose to wed against the desires of Nirupama's loved ones. Be that as it may, their arrangements were met with savage opposition from her moderate relatives, who eagerly went against the between station association. In April 2010, Nirupama was found dead under secretive conditions in her family home in Koderma, Jharkhand. Starting reports recommended self-destruction, yet ensuing examinations uncovered proof of treachery.

The Nirupama Pathak case accumulated broad media consideration, revealing insight into the unavoidable issue of honor killings in India. It uncovered the severe results looked by people who set out to challenge age-old accepted practices and rank biases. The case additionally highlighted the distinct truth of orientation disparity and the absence of organization stood to ladies in man centric social orders. As the examination unfurled, stunning subtleties arose, ensnaring Nirupama's own relatives in her homicide. It was claimed that Nirupama's mom, Sudha Pathak, and maternal granddad, Babulal Pathak, assumed a focal part in organizing her killing. They allegedly contrived to take out Nirupama to safeguard the family's honor and maintain their position pride.

The rationale behind Nirupama's homicide was established in the old-fashioned faith in standing immaculateness and the conservation of family honor at any expense. Her family's eager resistance to her relationship with a man from a lower standing encapsulated the firmly established bias and segregation pervasive in Indian culture. The case uncovered the severe reality looked by incalculable people who try to challenge these backward standards. Despite beginning endeavors to conceal the wrongdoing and depict Nirupama's demise as a self-destruction, reality in the long run became known. The Focal Department of Examination (CBI) assumed control over the case and sent off an intensive examination concerning the conditions encompassing Nirupama's demise. The proof revealed by the CBI highlighted unfairness and ensnared a few individuals from Nirupama's family in her homicide.

In October 2011, the CBI recorded charges against Nirupama's mom, Sudha Pathak, and maternal granddad, Babulal Pathak, alongside three others, including her cousin and an auntie. They were accused of homicide, criminal connivance, and obliteration of proof. The preliminary procedures brought to the front the chilling subtleties of Nirupama's last minutes and the cutthroat idea of her killing. The Nirupama Pathak case started an inescapable shock and provoked calls for equity and change. It reignited the discussion on honor killings and highlighted the earnest requirement for authoritative and cultural mediation to battle this egregious practice. The case filled in as a reminder for Indian culture, constraining individuals to defy the well-established biases and treacheries that keep on tormenting the country. The judicial procedures encompassing Nirupama's homicide were delayed for quite a long time, further featuring the difficulties faced by survivors of honor killings in looking for equity. Despite overpowering proof against the blamed, the wheels of equity moved gradually, delaying the anguish for Nirupama's family and friends and family. Nonetheless, the case filled in as a point of reference for considering culprits of honor killings responsible and sending major areas of strength for the belief that such violations wouldn't go on without serious consequences.

Eventually, the Nirupama Pathak case fills in as a dreary sign of the brutal real factors looked at by people who set out to oppose cultural standards and seek after adoration and opportunity. It is a lamentable demonstration of the getting-through battle for fairness, equity, and pride in a public tormented by position-based separation and male-centric mistreatment. Nirupama's less than ideal demise might have quieted her voice; however, her story keeps on repeating uproariously, requesting equity and starting a development for change.

During the court procedures, a few key perceptions were made:

1. Murder Allegations: The court charged Nirupama's mom, Sudha Pathak, with murder, alongside other relatives who were engaged in her killing, to assert that they. The indictment contended that Nirupama was killed in light of the fact that her family opposed her relationship with a man from a lower station.
2. Intention: The indictment introduced proof recommending that Nirupama's family was roused by thoughts of honor and standing virtue, driving them to carry out the wrongdoing to safeguard their family's standing.
3. Witness Declarations: Witnesses, including neighbors and colleagues, gave declarations supporting the indictment's case, specifying occasions of pressure inside Nirupama's family in regard to her relationship and pregnancy.
4. Scientific Proof: Criminological proof, including DNA examination and post-mortem reports, assumed a critical part in laying out the reason for Nirupama's demise and discrediting the underlying cases of self-destruction.
5. Social Ramifications: The case featured more extensive issues connected with standing based segregation, honor killings, and cultural standards in India. It started discussions and conversations about the requirement for lawful changes and social change to successfully address such wrongdoings.

At last, the court's perceptions highlighted the requirement for equity and responsibility in instances of honor killings, accentuating the significance of maintaining individual freedoms and battling backward friendly mentalities.

Shakti Vahini v. Union of India [2018]

The case law of Shakti Vahini vs. Union of India (Shakti Vahini vs Union of India, 2018) is well known. In this case, the Supreme Court of the country gave the state government and the police department instructions to create an intricate system that will assist society in reducing the issue of honor killings. The petitioners in this case, the Shakti Vahini organisation, were tasked with investigating the murders that were occurring in Western UP, Punjab, and Haryana. They produced a startling statistics study indicating that honor killing instances had increased dramatically in these specific localities. Article 32 of the Indian Constitution was the basis for the petition's filing. To tackle this problem, the federal and state governments have to work together. Even though it was limited to a handful of regions of India, this issue was having an impact on the entire nation. Consequently, it was determined that the law commission should suggest a measure called "The Prohibition of Interference with the Freedom of Matrimonial Alliance Bill" to address this issue. Following that, several additional states also responded to the petition, indicating that they were willing to address this matter.

By consequence of a decision dated 22/12/2009, the petitioner's organization was granted authorization by the National Commission for Women to conduct a study on honour murders in western Uttar Pradesh and Haryana. According to the report, there is a rise in the number of individuals who choose not to get married because they are frightened, especially in Punjab, Uttar Pradesh, and Haryana. 288 occurrences of honour murders were documented in total, according to National Crime Records Bureau (NCRB) records for the years 2014, 2015, and 2016. There were 28 of these instances in 2014, 251 in 2015, and 77 in 2016. The petitioner requested orders from the parties who responded, which comprised the federal and state governments, in accordance with the Indian Constitution. The goal of these orders was to put preventative measures in place against crimes such as honour murders and other comparable offenses. The petitioner also asked to produce state and federal action plans with the objective of reducing and managing these kinds of crimes. In addition, government agencies requested the establishment of cells to ensure the security and welfare of couples. The petitioner also requested a writ of mandamus to compel state governments to commence prosecutions in each honour killing case and to take necessary measures to change the social mindset that contributes to such murderous acts.

As stated in the petition, it is determined that the following behaviors or causes are related to honour crimes:

1. virginity loss outside of marriage
2. pregnancy before marriage
3. The act of adultery
4. Having connections that are not authorized
5. opposing arranged unions.
6. submitting a divorce request
7. requesting child custody following a divorce
8. Leaving the married or family residence without authorization
9. generating rumors or disagreement in the neighborhoods
10. Rape victimization

Issues Involved

The following are the points brought up in the Union of India v. Shakti Vahini case.

1. Who has the right to carry out the custom of honour killing—a married couple's family members or an individual?
2. Can modern Indian laws effectively curb the influence of traditional elements, particularly in areas overseen by non-official bodies such as Khap Panchayats?
3. Is the Khap Panchayat's ruling on honour killing cases legitimate, particularly in light of the lack of official government recognition?
4. Is the Indian government doing enough to safeguard the freedom to effectively select a life partner?
5. Does the Indian Constitution's Article 21 provide the right to life and personal liberty, including the freedom to select the life partner of one's choosing? If this right is restricted, may it be deemed a violation of that person's human rights?

Traditional community councils with questionable influence

- **Informal groups:** Khap Panchayats are unofficial gatherings of elders within specific communities, mainly in northern India. They hold no legal authority but wield significant social power.
- **Community focus:** They address internal social issues like education, dowries, and customs, typically focusing on upholding traditional norms.
- **Distinction from official bodies:** Unlike democratically elected Panchayats, Khaps have no government ties and operate outside legal frameworks.

Social influence with a dark side

- **Powerful sway:** Despite lacking legal sanction, Khap Panchayats can exert immense pressure within their communities due to entrenched patriarchal norms and fear of social exclusion.
- **Human rights concerns:** Their pronouncements often violate individual rights, especially for women and minorities. Examples include banning inter-caste marriages, dictating dress codes, and even condoning honor killings.
- **Lack of accountability:** Their non-democratic structure and unofficial status makes them difficult to hold accountable for decisions or injustices committed.

Complexities and efforts to address them

- **Debated role:** Opinions differ on the role of Khap Panchayats. Some see them as maintaining social order, while others highlight their harmful practices.

- **Challenges and change:** Legal measures, awareness campaigns, and women's empowerment initiatives aim to tackle human rights violations and promote individual freedom within these communities.

HOSTILITY OF THE PETITIONER

In accordance with the petitioner, states like Delhi, Haryana, Punjab, Jharkhand, and Uttar Pradesh have a higher incidence of honour killings than do the states in the south. It has been observed that during the past three years, there have been over 300 incidents of honour crimes in these states. The oppressive methods of certain core organizations that saw themselves as the law makers, along with social pressure and inhumane treatment, still create terror in the hearts of their victims and force them to either commit suicide or endure hardship at the hands of these groups. These core organizations constitute basically parallel law enforcement bodies that are identified themselves, quasi-judicial, and not legally recognized. They are primarily made up of male members who have ties to the members of the same. The religion and caste system, which are frequently brought together to address issues that concern members of the community, these organizations, which go by the name "Panchayat," have the authority to implement punishment for crimes, order a social boycott, or order the murder of an individual by a mob. A lady or a man who chooses a life partner wholly against the expectations of the community is viewed as dishonourable and subsequently unintentionally summons death at the hands of the harsh general prescription. The petition argues that senior males from a caste or lineage make up the parallel law enforcement body and meet regularly to discuss matters that affect the group. *(IpLeaders: Honour killings in India and need for urgent reforms and new laws)*

HOSTILITY OF THE RESPONDENTS

Several have contended that honor killings come under the definition of murder (Sec 300 of the IPC, 1860), 1860, and are thus subject to Section 302 penalties. Since the Indian Constitution places a premium on state authority over the police and public order, the states are mostly responsible for addressing honor murders. The Central Government has additionally suggested amending the Indian Penal Code (IPC) or enacting the legislation to mark the issue of honor killing and related problems.

To address the issue of "honor killing," the Law Commission of India's report suggested adopting a measure named **"The Prohibition of Interference with the Freedom of Matrimonial Alliances Bill."**[1] In addition, the Union of India states that because the 242nd report of the Law Commission of India is encompassed by the Indian Constitution's contemporaneous list, consultation with the governments of the States and Union Territories ("22 States, UTs Support Bill to Prevent ' Honour Killing,'" 2014) is required before a policy decision can be made on the topic.

NCT OF DELHI

There has been a filing of the counter-affidavit on behalf of the NCT of Delhi. The affidavit claims that the Delhi Police Department fails to keep separate files for incidents of "honour killing." On the contrary, it is said that at the time the affidavit was submitted, 11 occurrences had been recorded. There is no need to set up a particular cell in each police district; as a substitute, it is recommended that instances of this nature be submitted to the Delhi Police's special cell for major offenses concerning internal security, which is currently in operation. It has been emphasized that the Delhi Police has made field personnel more cognizant of this, enabling the issues to be handled with the necessary tact and consideration.

THE STATE OF UTTAR PRADESH

The State of Uttar Pradesh filed two affidavits that stated that the state's primary obligation is to uphold the fundamental rights outlined and guaranteed by the Indian Constitution. In addition, it was stated that even though there isn't any apparent legislation in place to control and outlaw "honour killing," enforcement personnel are still using the law as it is to take effective action. Giving recommendations along with suggestions to law enforcement agents is one of these approaches. The State of Uttar Pradesh also made it known that there were no cases of "honour killing" from January 2010 to December 2012. Despite this, police stations are being instructed to monitor the operations and undertakings of khap panchayats.

THE STATE OF BIHAR

Honour killing is an atrocious act that breaches individuals' fundamental rights, as acknowledged by the State of Bihar in an affidavit. Although there are almost no instances of any honour killing in the state, Bihar has recorded five cases that may be considered honour killings. Additionally, it was said that the state has implemented several reform initiatives for the empowerment and elevation of women and that ongoing attempts are being made to raise public awareness. It was also mentioned that the state of Bihar has launched an initiative called the "National Saving Certificate," which offers a cash incentive of Rs. 25,000 to any woman who marries outside her caste to secure her financial independence.

MARRIAGE UNDER LAWS IN INDIA

Hindu Marriage Act of 1955

An adherent of Buddhism, Sikhism, Jainism, or Hinduism can get married as a convert to one of the above-stated faiths and register their marriage. (Hindu Marriage Act, 1955). This legislation regards marriage as a sacrament rather than a legally binding agreement.

Special Marriage Act of 1954

Regardless of religion, any individual can marry anyone in accordance with the 1954 Special Marriage Act. The legislation in question acknowledges marriage as a legal contract; a sacred or religious ceremony is not an obligation to complete the relationship.

Right to Marry under the Indian Constitution

Two individuals who consent to getting married is not a violation that anyone has the authority to punish. The Constitution's Articles 19 and 21 both acknowledge this. The permission of one's ancestry, locality, or clan is not a requirement for an alliance between two adults. The right to life includes the right to marriage, as stated in Article 21 of the Indian Constitution. Therefore, no law or clause in the constitution prevents or deems inter-caste or inter-religious marriages to be illegal.

Supreme Court's Judgement

The Supreme Court made it clear that children's fundamental rights come first, even when they clash with traditional notions of family or community "honour." This means individuals, regardless of their gender, have a right to choose their own life partner without needing approval from their family, community, or clan. This right is protected by the Constitution's Articles 19 and 21, which guarantee freedom of choice and personal liberty. In short, love and individual choice trump outdated notions of collective honour. The Supreme Court has officially defined a "khap panchayat" as any gathering, formal or informal, whose purpose is to condemn marriages not banned by law. This includes proposed marriages and those deemed "shameful" for violating caste or community customs. The court further instructed state governments to identify areas reporting khap panchayat activities or honour killings actively within the past five years.

1. Khap panchayats: Now legally defined as any group aiming to denounce legal marriages based on community norms.
2. Focus: Targeting marriages deemed "embarrassing" or violating caste/community traditions.
3. Action by states: Required to identify areas with khap panchayat activities or honor killings in the past five years.

This definition and directive highlight the court's stance against khap panchayats' interference in individual choices and its attempt to curb honour killings associated with such practices.

To foster greater understanding among law enforcement entities, the Indian government's Home Department must take charge while working alongside state governments. To tackle such kinds of violence while adhering to the fundamental principles of equal treatment and the rule of law, everybody concerned must take responsibility and come up with preventative measures. There must be an institutional structure in place that coordinates the activities of everyone with an interest. To bring down such violence, the federal government and various state governments ought to concentrate on educating law enforcement authorities to advocate social change and awareness.

REMEDIAL STEPS ISSUED BY THE SUPREME COURT

1. Even with police efforts, if local authorities discover a Khap Panchayat targeting an inter-caste or religious marriage, swift action is mandatory. This includes filing a First Information Report (FIR) under specific Indian Penal Code sections (141, 143, 503 read with 506) to address threats and harassment. This ensures immediate legal response to protect the couple and family from potential harm.
2. If a Khap Panchayat targets a couple or family in an inter-cast or any religious marriage, immediate legal action is crucial. Filing an FIR under relevant sections (Sec 141, 143, 503 and 506 IPC, 1860) ensures swift investigation and protection from threats and harassment. Notification of the FIR must reach the Superintendent or Deputy Superintendent of Police to prioritize the case. Urgent security measures like relocation to a safe house within the district or elsewhere are mandatory, considering the couple's safety concerns. To facilitate

this, state governments should establish safe houses at district headquarters, supervised by the District Magistrate and Superintendent of Police. These safe heavens provide immediate refuge for couples facing Khap Panchayat threats and ensure their safety while legal action progresses.
3. This comprehensive approach emphasizes the importance of swift legal response, immediate protection for vulnerable families, and readily accessible safe heavens to combat the harmful influence of Khap Panchayats on individual freedom and inter-cast or any religious marriages.
4. Protecting inter-caste couples from Khap Panchayat threats requires a robust response system. An Additional Superintendent of Police will investigate complaints or information about threats to such relationships. If the threats are deemed valid and serious, a report will be submitted to the Superintendent of Police. The Superintendent of Police will then instruct the Deputy Superintendent of Police to register an FIR against those threatening the couple. Additionally, section 151 of the Criminal Procedure Code (Sec 151, CrPC) may be invoked to prevent potential violence. The Deputy Superintendent of Police will closely monitor the investigation, ensuring all participants are involved. This includes Khap Panchayat members, who could face charges of conspiracy or aiding and abetting if their involvement is proven.

Key features of this system:

- Swift initial investigation: The Additional Superintendent of Police ensures prompt action on complaints.
- Escalation based on severity: The Superintendent of Police decides on FIR registration and possible preventive measures.
- Close monitoring: The Deputy Superintendent of Police oversees the investigation and holds participants accountable.
- Potential charges for Khap Panchayat involvement: This deters interference and promotes accountability.

5. This system aims to protect inter-caste couples by responding quickly and decisively to threats, investigating thoroughly, and holding perpetrators accountable. This discourages Khap Panchayat interference and ensures the safety and rights of couples choosing inter-caste marriages.
6. The Supreme Court swiftly addressed honour killings, implementing measures and amending existing ones. To prioritize individual and couple safety, they outlined specific requirements. Additionally, the Delhi Commission for Women (DCW) intervened, seeking protection for victims and challenging the application of guidelines established in the Shakti Vahini case

This multi-pronged approach demonstrates a proactive effort to tackle this serious issue.

Key Points

- Supreme Court implemented and amended measures.
- Specific safety requirements for individuals and couples established.
- DCW intervened for victim protection and challenged existing guidelines.

CONCLUSION

The finality of decisions in honour killing cases in India frequently accentuates the significance of equity, responsibility, and the assurance of individual freedoms. Courts ordinarily feature the need to address backward cultural perspectives, rank-based separation, and thoughts of honor that lead to such appalling violations. The decisions highlight the basics for lawful changes to battle honor killings successfully and to guarantee that culprits are considered responsible for their activities. Additionally, decisions stress the meaning of maintaining the standards of correspondence, nobility, and regard for individual decisions, paying little mind to rank, religion, or orientation. At last, the end of decisions in honor killing cases in India fills in as a source of inspiration for cultural change, upholding a more comprehensive and just society where everyone's freedoms are shielded.

Moreover, no individual, whether a family member or member of a Khap Panchayat, has the right to receive punishment for such reprehensible acts. It is imperative that any illegal activity be promptly reported, regardless of the perpetrator's age. Failure to report such crimes will only serve to perpetuate them. It is the responsibility of every citizen to uphold the law, and any punishment must be administered through the legal system, which exists for this purpose. A key takeaway from the court's ruling in this case is not only the issuance of directives to eradicate the concept and practice of honour killings but also the initiation of a significant step towards abolishing this widespread social phenomenon (*Smt. Laxmi Kachhwaha vs. The state of Rajasthan (1999)*).

It is still a conviction in society that wives, daughters, and sisters of males will always be underneath them. Having said that, the man or woman in a Hindu marriage is often chosen after taking into account a number of factors, including caste, community, gotra, etc. Although there is no constitutional penalty for this, the current scenario is quite different because of the honor killing that is occurring. The Indian Constitution's Article 21 is squarely in conflict with the idea of honor killing. Since Article 21 is a fundamental right, it is appropriate that this matter be given the highest attention. honor killing is a behaviour that is utterly repulsive. A person cannot murder another person to uphold family values or pride. The murder of a person does not have any good impact on society and is a heinous crime in the eyes of the law and in the view of the laws that are regulatory in India.

REFERENCES

22 States, UTs support bill to prevent ' Honour Killing". (2014, December). The Economic Times.

AIR. (1950). *Romesh Thapper v. State of Madras*, SC 124

Code of Criminal Procedure. (1973). Section 151 CrPC,

Global Human Rights Club: Arizona State University

HMA. (1955). Hindu Marriage Act, 1955

Honor Killing In India: An Analysis On Indian Statutes: K.Vikas

Indian Penal Code. (1860). Sec 141, 143, 503 and 506 IPC,

Indian Penal Code. (1860). Section 300 of IPC,

Indian Population Statistics Poll

Ip Leaders: Honour killings in India and need for urgent reforms and new laws

Murder Reference of Honour killing: Times of India

No. M. R. 2 of 2010 Appeal no,479-DB of 2010 and Criminal revision No.2173 of 2010 In The High Court Of Punjab & Haryana, Chandigarh. http://nlrd.org/wp-content/uploads/2012/01/Manoj-andBabli.pdf

Oxford Human Rights Hub: Addressing "Honour Killings in India"

Shakti Vahini vs Union of India (2018). 7 SCC 192

Smt. Laxmi Kachhwaha vs. The state of Rajasthan (1999).

State of Uttar Pradesh Vs Krishna Master (2010).

The Rajasthan Prohibition of Interference with the Freedom of Matrimonial Alliances in the Name of Honour and Tradition Bill of 2019

Times Of India Article on Honor killing in Haryana

Vitoshka, D. Y. (2010). The Modern Face of Honor Killing: Factors, Legal Issues, and Policy Recommendations.

Yadav, B. (2019). Khap Panchayats: Stealing Freedom? *Journal of Legal studies and Research*, Volume 2(Issue 2).

Chapter 18
Honor Killing AD REM With Special Reference to Religious Dogmatism in India

Tarun Pratap Yadav
https://orcid.org/0009-0005-4262-0683
GLA University, Mathura, India

Shanu Singh
https://orcid.org/0009-0009-4095-9519
GLA University, Mathura, India

ABSTRACT

Chapter covers Honor Killing from the prism of religious dogmatism, intersection of culture and religion and case studies. Further legal provisions, penalties, protective measures, solutions and a way forward have also been highlighted in the chapter. According to Hindu religion, marrying or having intimacy with a member of a different caste and religion is strictly forbidden. Although Islam does not categorically countersign killing female family members, some honor killing entail contention of adultery, which are indictable by death under Islamic law. The preservation of women's virginity and "sexual compelling" are considered to be the burden of male relatives like her father, brother and then her husband. However, a women can intend for murder for a variety of discernment, that includes refusing to enter into an arranged marriage or divorce or separation. They think that women have acted in manner that could damage her family's notoriety. Amusingly, female relatives usually contend the killing and help set them up. All the above have been substantially elaborated in the chapter.

DOI: 10.4018/979-8-3693-7240-1.ch018

INTRODUCTION

Honor killing is a heinous act that has persistently plagued Indian society, fuelled by deep-seated religious dogmatism. It is a form of violence directed towards individuals, typically women, who are perceived to have brought shame or dishonor to their families or communities. This chapter aims to explore the phenomenon of honor killings in India, with a specific focus on the role of religious dogmatism in perpetuating this practice of violence. In India, honor killing is considered both an offence under Indian penal code 309 and an insult to religious beliefs. Honor killings are not limited to a particular religion, but rather occur across various cultures and societies worldwide. However, in the Indian context, religious dogmatism plays a prominent role in justifying and perpetuating honor killings. Religious dogmatism in India is deeply entrenched in societal norms and practices, which places a strong emphasis on preserving the so-called "honor" of the family and community, often at the expense of individual rights and freedoms. This chapter will examine the historical and cultural roots of religious dogmatism in India and how it contributes to the prevalence of honor killings. The chapter will also discuss the ways in which religious dogmatism influences social attitudes and perceptions towards honor killings, shaping patriarchal power structures and reinforcing gender inequality. (Kanchan et al., 2016) Furthermore, this chapter will critically analyse the role of religious texts, such as the Manu smriti in Hinduism and certain interpretations of Sharia law in Islam, in perpetuating patriarchal norms and justifying violence against women in the name of honor. Additionally, this chapter will examine the ways in which religious leaders and institutions contribute to the perpetuation of honor killings through their teachings and ideologies. This chapter will also explore the impact of socio-economic factors on honor killings in India, as poverty and lack of education often exacerbate existing patriarchal norms and religious dogmatism, leading to a higher prevalence of honor killings. Moreover, this chapter will shed light on the role of state institutions and legal frameworks in addressing honor killings in India. It will critically analyse the effectiveness and limitations of existing laws and policies in combating this practice, while also examining the role of government initiatives and grassroots movements in challenging religious dogmatism and promoting gender equality. Finally, this chapter will conclude by highlighting the importance of addressing religious dogmatism as a root cause for honor killings in India. The chapter will argue that religious dogmatism perpetuates patriarchal power structures and contributes to the prevalence of honor killings in India. In her work on honor killings in American and Indian media, Inderpal Grewal asserts that "a broad array of technologies of governance have come into existence in response to honor killings". These technologies of governance not only involve legal measures and law enforcement, but also encompass social and cultural interventions aimed at challenging and changing patriarchal norms rooted in religious dogmatism.(Olwan, 2013). Therefore, in order to effectively combat honor killings and promote gender equality, it is crucial to address religious dogmatism and its influence on social attitudes and behaviours towards women.

As evidenced by Korte Weg and Yurdakul, in the scientific literature there is a huge debate about the role of religion in the genesis of honor killings.(Caffaro et al., 2014). In particular, the issue of the debate is whether honor killings can be accounted for more by the Islamic religion or by the oppressive practices related to the undisputed authority of the patriarch which puts the woman in a subordinated position within the family, as well as within society. This debate raises important questions about the intersectionality of religious beliefs, patriarchal power dynamics, and the subordination of women within both family and societal structures. To further understand the complexities of honor killings in India, it is essential to analyse the deep-seated patriarchy that underlies these acts, as well as the ways in which religious dogmatism reinforces and perpetuates this patriarchal power.

KEY TERMS

The nuts and bolts of the term Includes "Honor Killing" and "Religious Dogmatism" directly linking the subject matter to the chapter's framework. Broader themes like "Domestic Abuse"(Kanchan et al., 2016) & "Offence Against Women"(Singh & Bhandari, 2021) contextualize the issue. Analytical perspectives like "Violence"(Vitoshka, 2010), "Societal Factors"(Hosseini & C, 2015), "Family's Honor"(Dr. Sana, 2019) & "Marital Life"(King, 2013) allow for exploring the complexities upon "Intersection Of Culture And Religion" of Honor Killing across different Cultural and legal context.

Supervisor, (Caffaro et al., 2014),(Olwan, 2013) we used these keywords to select relevant articles from multiple online sources, for example, 'Library of Congress, Research Gate, Google Books, Springer, JSTOR, Sage, IJSSHR, Scopus, Web of Science, Taylor & Francis and Google Scholar'.

An Honor Killings Research Paper and Religious Dogmatism requires careful consideration of inclusion/exclusion and article research, as well as the selection of appropriate publications. Publications with an emphasis on international law, gender studies, human rights, and related interdisciplinary topics were chosen for publishing in the journal selection process.

In order to create a longer shortlist of research papers that are appropriate for this Chapter, we established inclusion and exclusion criteria. Studies where "experience" has been examined as a variable or a concept in the context of ecotourism met our inclusion criteria. Studies have to be published in English, and they can only be published in journals that have an impact factor of 1.0 or above in Journal Citation Reports and peer-reviewed papers, or they have to be B graded or higher on the Journal Quality list.

RESEARCH GAP

This chapter is different from others as it focuses on the theme of honor killing. Furthermore, future research directions should aim to explore the intersections of honor killings with various socio-economic factors, including education levels, economic independence, and the role of non-governmental organizations in advocacy and prevention efforts. Additionally, future studies could investigate the ways in which effective legal frameworks, alongside community awareness programmes, can contribute to a paradigm shift in social attitudes towards honor-based violence, thus fostering an environment that discourages such practices and promotes gender equality instead (Barat, D., 2015). Furthermore, the potential impact of religious dogmatism in shaping perceptions of honor within diverse communities warrants thorough examination, as it could provide crucial insights into the mechanisms that perpetuate these violent practices and hinder progress toward gender equality and justice for victims of honor-based crimes. Moreover, understanding the intricate relationship between religious dogmatism and honor killings may reveal how certain interpretations of religious texts can be manipulated to justify acts of violence against individuals perceived to have brought dishonor upon their families, thereby necessitating a critical examination of religious doctrines and their influence on cultural norms.

THE HISTORICAL CONTEXT OF HONOR KILLING IN INDIA

The historical context of honor killing in India is deeply intertwined with the socio-cultural fabric of the nation. Throughout history, India has grappled with complex social hierarchies, deeply rooted patriarchal structures, and religious dogmatism, all of which have contributed to the prevalence of honor killings. The concept of honor, often linked to family reputation and communal standing, has been a pervasive ideology in Indian society and has been used to control and subjugate women. In traditional Indian society, the notion of honor is deeply entrenched in religious teachings and texts. For instance, within Hinduism, the Manu smriti, an ancient legal text, includes codes and principles that perpetuate the subordination of women and endorse the idea of women as property, thereby fostering an environment where honor killings are justified as a means of upholding these traditional beliefs. Similarly, certain interpretations of Sharia law in Islam have been used to justify honor killings, further highlighting the intersection of religious dogmatism and gender-based violence.(Vesvikar & Agarwal, 2022)

Moreover, the historical economic and educational disparities in India have contributed to the perpetuation of honor killings. Poverty and lack of education have reinforced existing patriarchal norms, making women more vulnerable to violence and discrimination. The intersection of religious dogmatism, patriarchal norms, and socio-economic factors has created a complex web within which honor killings thrive. State institutions and legal frameworks have played a crucial role in addressing honor killings in India. The effectiveness and limitations of existing laws and policies have been a subject of intense scrutiny, as they form the backbone of the societal response to this issue.(Singh & Bhandari, 2021) Furthermore, government initiatives and grassroots movements have emerged as significant players in challenging religious dogmatism and promoting gender equality. These efforts have been instrumental in challenging deeply ingrained patriarchal norms and religious dogmatism that perpetuate honor killings.

To fully comprehend the phenomenon of honor killings in India, it is essential to delve into the intricate interplay between religious dogmatism, societal norms, and historical contexts. Only by understanding these multidimensional factors can comprehensive measures be devised to effectively combat this pervasive form of gender-based violence. Despite the recognition of the role played by underlying social norms in honor killings in South Asia, research about socioeconomic individual or household-level risk factors, motivations and patterns is limited.(D'Lima et al., 2020). This chapter aims to address these gaps through a content analysis that elucidates key motivations, perpetrators, and victims of honor killings in recent years in Pakistan and India. One of the key motivations for honor killings in India is the desire for preservation of family or communal honor. This motivation is deeply rooted in cultural and social norms that place a high value on family honor and reputation. Religious dogmatism, particularly within the context of certain conservative interpretations of Islam and Hinduism, exacerbates the problem by perpetuating patriarchal norms and justifying violence against women who are perceived to have violated societal norms.(Vesvikar & Agarwal, 2022) Additionally, societal changes brought about by factors such as urbanization, globalization, and economic development have also played a role in shaping the dynamics of honor killings in India. Religious dogmatism in India has historically played a significant role in shaping societal attitudes towards honor killings. It is important to note that while honor killings can occur in any religious community, the association with Islam has been heavily emphasized in media and academic discourse. This emphasis has led to a heated debate regarding the role of religion in honor killings. Some argue that honor killings are primarily a result of oppressive practices related to the undisputed authority of patriarchal figures, which place women in subordinate positions within the family and society.

RELIGIOUS DOGMATISM AND ITS ROLE IN HONOR KILLINGS

Honor killings in India are deeply rooted in the historical and cultural context, and to truly understand the prevalence of this practice, it is crucial to examine the role of religious dogmatism. Religious dogmatism in India has played a significant role in justifying and perpetuating honor killings, particularly through the lens of societal norms that place a strong emphasis on preserving family and community "honor."(King, 2013). The influence of religious texts, such as the Manu smriti in Hinduism, and certain interpretations of Sharia law in Islam, has contributed to the perpetuation of patriarchal norms and the subjugation of women. These texts have been used to validate the idea of women as property and have fostered an environment where honor killings are seen as a means to uphold traditional beliefs.

Moreover, religious leaders and institutions have contributed to the perpetuation of honor killings through their teachings and ideologies. Their influence on social attitudes and perceptions towards honor killings has reinforced gender inequality and patriarchal power structures in Indian society. Furthermore, the impact of socio-economic factors on honor killings in India cannot be overlooked. Poverty and lack of education exacerbate existing patriarchal norms and religious dogmatism, making women more vulnerable to violence and discrimination. The intersection of religious dogmatism, patriarchal norms, and socio-economic factors has created a complex environment where honor killings thrive.

In the midst of this complex web of influences, state institutions and legal frameworks have played a critical role in addressing honor killings in India. The effectiveness and limitations of existing laws and policies have been under scrutiny, as they form the backbone of the societal response to this issue. Additionally, government initiatives and grassroots movements have emerged as significant players in challenging religious dogmatism and promoting gender equality. These efforts have been instrumental in challenging deeply ingrained patriarchal norms and religious dogmatism that perpetuate honor killings. To comprehensively address the issue of honor killings in India, it is imperative to acknowledge and understand the multidimensional factors at play.(Newme, 2018) By examining the historical and cultural roots, the role of religious dogmatism, and the impact of socio-economic factors, we can devise comprehensive measures to combat this pervasive form of gender-based violence. The prevalence of honor killings in India is not solely a consequence of religious dogmatism, but rather, a complex interplay of various factors including historical, societal, economic, and religious influences. It is imperative to acknowledge that while religious dogmatism plays a significant role in justifying and perpetuating honor killings, societal norms and historical context also contribute to the prevalence of this practice.

Historically, India has grappled with complex social hierarchies, deeply rooted patriarchal structures, and the notion of honor deeply entrenched in religious teachings, as mentioned earlier. Moreover, the economic and educational disparities in India have further amplified the vulnerability of women to violence and discrimination. These factors have created a fertile ground within which honor killings continue to thrive. State institutions and legal frameworks play a crucial role in addressing honor killings in India. The effectiveness and limitations of existing laws and policies have been a subject of intense scrutiny, as they form the backbone of the societal response to this issue. Furthermore, government initiatives and grassroots movements have emerged as significant players in challenging religious dogmatism and promoting gender equality, as mentioned previously. These efforts have been instrumental in challenging deeply ingrained patriarchal norms and religious dogmatism that perpetuate honor killings.

To fully comprehend the phenomenon of honor killings in India, it is essential to delve into the intricate interplay between religious dogmatism, societal norms, historical contexts, and the impact of socio-economic factors.(Newme, 2018) Only by understanding these multidimensional factors can comprehensive measures be devised to effectively combat this pervasive form of gender-based violence. In light of the complex interplay of various factors contributing to honor killings in India, it is necessary to adopt a multifaceted approach that addresses the social, economic, and religious dimensions of this issue. By acknowledging the historical, cultural, and socio-economic complexities surrounding honor killings, comprehensive measures can be implemented to combat this deeply entrenched form of gender-based violence.

THE INTERSECTION OF CULTURE, RELIGION AND HONOR KILLINGS

The prevalence of honor killings in India is deeply intertwined with the intersection of culture, religion, and the societal perception of honor. Culture and tradition play a significant role in shaping attitudes towards women and perpetuating the practice of honor killings. The cultural emphasis on family honor and the subjugation of women has created an environment where honor killings are rationalized and even glorified as a means of upholding these traditional beliefs. Aggression that transcends the limits of an individual's autonomy and identity is referred to as violence.(Rao Mamta, 2018). "Domestic violence" refers to signs of personal or familiar battering in relation to an idealized family unit that operates in a private, isolated, and suitably concealed manner from the general public.(King, 2013). Domestic violence frequently takes the shape of more subdued verbal, physical, or psychological abuse than violence found in other contexts.(Dr. Sana, 2019)

Religion, as a powerful social institution, has historically influenced and reinforced patriarchal norms, often at the expense of women's rights and freedoms. The interpretation of religious scriptures, such as the Manu smriti in Hinduism and certain interpretations of Sharia law in Islam, has been instrumental in justifying the subjugation of women and the practice of honor killings. The institutionalization of these interpretations within religious communities has further perpetuated gender inequality and served as a catalyst for honor-based violence.

Moreover, the notion of honor, deeply embedded in cultural and religious narratives, has contributed to the normalization of violence against women, particularly in the name of preserving family or communal honor. The social construction of honor as a communal asset, predominantly tied to the actions and behaviours of women, has created a conducive environment for the perpetuation of honor killings. To fully address the multifaceted nature of honor killings, it is essential to acknowledge the intricate interplay between culture, religion, and societal attitudes towards honor. These interconnected factors not only shape the prevalence of honor killings but also contribute to the perpetuation of gender inequality and the subjugation of women in Indian society.

By delving into the complex dynamics of culture, religion, and honor, comprehensive measures can be developed to dismantle the deeply ingrained patriarchal norms and religious dogmatism that perpetuate honor killings in India. Efforts to challenge these societal constructs and promote gender equality are pivotal in addressing the root causes of honor-based violence and fostering a more equitable and just society. This interconnectedness of culture, religion, and societal attitudes towards honor provides a critical lens through which the prevalence of honor killings in India can be understood. It underscores the intricate web of influences that perpetuate this form of gender-based violence, emphasizing the need for a comprehensive approach that addresses the underlying cultural and religious narratives that justify and sustain honor killings.(Vitoshka, 2010)

The intersection of culture, religion, and honor killings in India reflects the entrenchment of deeply ingrained patriarchal norms and the historical subjugation of women. The cultural emphasis on family honor often places the burden of upholding this honor squarely on women, leading to their increased vulnerability to violence and discrimination. Moreover, religious interpretations that reinforce the subordination of women have further entrenched this societal dynamic, creating an environment where honor killings are rationalized within the framework of religious and cultural norms.

In addressing honor killings in India, it is crucial to recognize the historical and cultural roots that have shaped the prevailing attitudes towards honor, particularly as it pertains to women. The deeply entrenched patriarchal structures and the commodification of women's honor intersect with religious teachings, perpetuating a system that sanctions violence against women in the name of preserving familial and communal honor. Moreover, this complex interplay of culture, religion, and societal attitudes towards honor underscores the need for comprehensive measures that challenge existing power structures and promote gender equality. By unpacking the deeply entrenched cultural and religious narratives that perpetuate honor killings, efforts can be directed towards dismantling patriarchal norms and fostering a more equitable and just society in India.(Kaushal, 2020)

In delving into the multifaceted nature of honor killings and their intersection with culture, religion, and societal attitudes, it becomes evident that the prevalence of honor killings cannot be attributed to a single factor. Rather, it is the culmination of historical, cultural, religious, and societal influences that create an environment where violence against women is rationalized and perpetuated. Only by acknowledging and addressing these interconnected influences can effective strategies be devised to combat honor killings and promote gender equality in Indian society.

CASE STUDIES OF HONOR KILLINGS IN INDIA

Case 1: The Nirbhaya Case

In December 2012, the brutal gang-rape and murder of a young woman in Delhi sent shockwaves throughout India and sparked widespread protests demanding justice and an end to gender-based violence. This case, commonly known as the Nirbhaya Case, highlighted both the prevalence of violence against women in India and the systemic failures in addressing such crimes. Despite the attention and outrage generated by the case, it is important to note that the issue of honor killings was not directly involved in this particular incident. (Wikipedia Contributors, 2024)

Case 2: The Manoj-Babli Case

In 2007, the Manoj-Babli case brought national attention to the issue of honor killings in India. Manoj and Babli, a young couple from different castes, fell in love and eloped against the wishes of their families. Tragically, their decision to marry resulted in their brutal murder by Babli's own family in what is widely regarded as an honor killing. The case gained widespread media coverage and sparked a national conversation on honor killings, caste-based discrimination, and the need for legal reforms to protect individuals from such atrocities.(Wikipedia contributors, 2024)

Case 3: The Qandeel Baloch Case

In 2016, Pakistani social media star Qandeel Baloch was murdered by her own brother in what is often referred to as an honor killing motivated by a desire to protect the family's honor. These case studies serve as a stark reminder of the devastating consequences of honor killings and highlight the urgent need for action to address this issue in India.(Qandeel-Baloch-Case-Judgement, n.d.)

Case 4: In 2014, when a father discovered his eighteen-year-old daughter, Sarita Devi, with her lover, Dinesh Kumar, in Naurankhera Village, Sonipat District, Haryana, he killed her. They are from different castes and were both undergraduate students at Gohana College. The girl's grandfather and father were taken into custody.(Kejriwal, n.d.)

Case 5: In the Rohtak District of Haryana's Kansala village, a villager killed his 32-year-old sister Murti Devi in 2014 because she had an extramarital affair with a relative. The woman was married and had two kids when she moved in with her husband's relative out of love. Her brother was infuriated and shot her as a result. Her sibling was falsely accused of murder.

Case 6: Bhavna Yadav, a student at Delhi University, was assassinated in 2014 by her parents for having secretly wed a man from a different caste. Bhavna Yadav, a resident of south west Delhi, was reportedly battered, strangled, and her body thrown into a car. The car was then taken to Alwar, Rajasthan, the home of her parents, where it was quickly burned. The victim's mother stays at home while her father deals in real estate. There were also claims that a maternal uncle took part in the crime.

As per the latest data from the National Crime Records Bureau (NCRB), the number of honour killings reported in India was 25 each in 2019 and 2020, and 33 in 2021.

Honor killings, as evidenced by the case studies, underscore the prevalence of violence against women and the distinct societal ideologies that perpetuate such acts. These cases exemplify the alarming consequences of rigid caste structures, patriarchal norms, and the commodification of women's honor within the sociocultural fabric of India and its neighbouring countries.

LEGAL PERSPECTIVES AND PENALTIES ON HONOR KILLINGS IN INDIA

The legal perspective on honor killings in India brings to light the urgent need for comprehensive reforms to address the complex web of cultural, religious, and societal factors that perpetuate this form of gender-based violence. As the case studies of Nirbhaya, Manoj-Babli, and Qandeel Baloch illustrate, honor killings are deeply rooted in patriarchal norms and cultural ideologies, necessitating a nuanced legal approach to combat this pervasive issue.

Efforts to address honor killings from a legal standpoint must encompass multifaceted measures that hold perpetrators accountable while also challenging the entrenched power structures that enable such violence. While existing legal frameworks provide a foundation for prosecuting individuals involved in honor killings, it is imperative to recognize the limitations and inadequacies within the legal system that hinder effective justice for the victims. Moreover, legal reforms should not only focus on punitive measures but also prioritize preventive strategies that target the root causes of honor-based violence. This entails combating discriminatory cultural and religious narratives that uphold the notion of family honor as contingent on women's behaviour and relationships. By promoting gender-sensitive legal provisions and educational initiatives, the legal system can play a pivotal role in challenging societal attitudes towards honor and fostering a culture of gender equality and respect for women's rights.(Kumar, 2013)

In addition to legislative changes, collaborations between legal authorities, women's rights organizations, and community leaders are essential for creating a holistic approach to combat honor killings. This collaborative effort can involve the development of culturally relevant interventions, community-based support services for at-risk individuals, and awareness campaigns that challenge regressive norms surrounding honor and gender roles. Furthermore, international human rights standards must inform the legal discourse on honor killings, emphasizing the imperative to address such crimes as a fundamental violation of women's rights. By contextualizing honor killings within the framework of domestic violence and discrimination, legal perspectives can effectively dismantle the cultural and religious justifications that perpetuate this form of gender-based violence.

Penalties Under The Indian Penal Code, 1862 (IPC)

What the Indian Penal Code's actual penalties are:

- Anyone found guilty of murder or culpable homicide that does not amount to murder is punished under **Sections 299–304**. The murder penalty consists of a fine, life in prison, or death. Non-murder culpable homicide carries a life sentence or a maximum 10-year sentence in prison, as well as a fine.
- **Section 307:** Threats to kill are punishable by up to ten years in prison and a fine. If someone is hurt, they may receive a life sentence in prison.
- **Section 308:** Penalties for attempting to commit culpable homicide include up to three years in jail, a fine, or both. If it results in harm, the offender faces a maximum 7-year jail sentence, a fine, or both.
- Penalties apply to anybody who participates in a criminal conspiracy under **Sections 120A and 120B.**
- People who aid and abet homicides, including murder and culpable homicide, are punished under **Sections 107–116.**
- **Sections 34 and 35:** Criminal offenses committed by multiple people in service of a common goal are punished.

In conclusion, the legal perspective on honor killings in India demands a comprehensive and nuanced approach that goes beyond punitive measures to address the deep-rooted cultural, religious, and societal factors that sustain this form of violence. As illustrated by the case studies and the broader societal context, combatting honor killings necessitates a concerted effort to challenge patriarchal norms and promote gender equality within legal frameworks and broader societal narratives. (Chaturvedi Parul, 2021)

PREVENTIVE MEASURES AND SOLUTIONS

Preventing honor killings requires a multi-faceted approach that addresses the entrenched cultural, religious, and societal factors contributing to this form of gender-based violence. While legal reforms are crucial, complementary preventive measures and solutions are equally imperative in creating meaningful change.

One of the fundamental strategies in preventing honor killings is the implementation of educational initiatives and public awareness campaigns aimed at challenging regressive norms and beliefs surrounding honor and gender roles. These campaigns should target both urban and rural communities, engaging with diverse age groups to promote a culture of gender equality and respect for women's rights. By fostering critical thinking and deconstructing harmful beliefs, education can serve as a powerful tool in combating the root causes of honor-based violence.

Empowering women and at-risk individuals through access to support services is pivotal in preventing honor killings. Community-based support networks, counselling services, and shelters for women facing threats of honor-based violence can provide vital resources for those in vulnerable situations. Additionally, economic empowerment programs and skill-building initiatives can offer alternative pathways for women to assert their autonomy and independence, reducing their susceptibility to honor-based violence. Alongside the importance of legal reforms, advocacy efforts to implement and enforce gender-sensitive legislation are critical in preventing honor killings. Advocates and legal experts can work to ensure that laws explicitly prohibit discrimination and violence against women, holding perpetrators of honor-based violence accountable. Furthermore, legal professionals can advocate for the recognition of cultural and religious justifications as invalid defences in cases of honor killings, emphasizing the overarching principles of human rights and gender equality.(Hosseini & C, 2015)

Engaging with community leaders, religious authorities, and grassroots organizations is essential in shifting societal attitudes and norms that perpetuate honor killings. Dialogues that address the intersections of culture, religion, and gender-based violence can facilitate constructive conversations aimed at challenging harmful practices and promoting inclusive perspectives on honor and family dynamics. By fostering community-driven initiatives and interventions, stakeholders can collectively work towards dismantling patriarchal structures that condone honor-based violence. International cooperation and advocacy are integral in the global effort to eliminate honor killings. By partnering with international human rights organizations, governments can leverage cross-border resources, expertise, and advocacy platforms to address honor-based violence as a universal concern. This collaboration can also facilitate the sharing of best practices, research, and strategies for preventing honor killings, enriching the collective effort to combat gender-based violence on a global scale(Kumar, 2013)

In summary, the prevention of honor killings necessitates a comprehensive approach that encompasses educational initiatives, empowerment programs, legal advocacy, community engagement, and international collaboration. By addressing the interconnected cultural, religious, and societal factors that perpetuate honor-based violence, these preventive measures and solutions can contribute to the creation of a more equitable and just society, free from the pernicious influence of patriarchal norms and gender-based violence.

CONCLUSION: PROGRESS AND FUTURE DIRECTIONS AGAINST HONOR KILLINGS

In conclusion, the multifaceted approach to preventing honor killings outlined in this chapter encompasses educational initiatives, empowerment programs, legal advocacy, community engagement, and international collaboration. By addressing the interconnected cultural, religious, and societal factors that perpetuate honor-based violence, these preventive measures and solutions can contribute to the creation of a more equitable and just society, free from the pernicious influence of patriarchal norms and gender-based violence.

Taking a more holistic approach to tackling honor killings is crucial in challenging the deeply ingrained patriarchal structures and regressive norms that sustain this form of violence. While legal reforms are essential, complementary efforts focused on education, empowerment, and community engagement are equally imperative in effecting meaningful and lasting change.(rai, 2023)

Moving forward, sustained commitment to these preventive measures, as well as international collaboration and advocacy, will be integral in the global effort to eliminate honor killings and combat gender-based violence universally. It is through collective and concerted action that societies can work towards achieving a more just and equitable future for all individuals, free from the constraints of harmful cultural and religious practices. In this chapter the authors have effectively highlighted the multi-faceted approach to preventing honor killings, emphasizing the interconnected cultural, religious, and societal factors that perpetuate this form of violence. The comprehensive strategies that have been presented, from educational initiatives to legal advocacy and international collaboration, reflect a holistic understanding of the complexities involved in combatting honor killings. The multifaceted approach shown in the chapter has described is crucial in challenging the deeply ingrained patriarchal structures and regressive norms that sustain this form of violence.(rai, 2023) By emphasizing that legal reforms should be complemented by efforts focused on education, empowerment, and community engagement, the chapter has underscored the importance of addressing the root causes of honor-based violence. Author's emphasis on sustained commitment to preventive measures, as well as international collaboration and advocacy, resonates with the need for a collective and concerted action to address honor killings and combat gender-based violence universally. It is through this comprehensive approach that societies can work towards achieving a more just and equitable future for all individuals, free from the constraints of harmful cultural and religious practices. The conclusion effectively summarizes the need for a nuanced and comprehensive approach to tackle honor killings, reflecting an understanding of the necessity to go beyond punitive measures and address the underlying cultural, religious, and societal factors that sustain this form of violence.

REFERENCES

Caffaro, F., Ferraris, F., & Schmidt, S. (2014). Gender Differences in the Perception of Honour Killing in Individualist Versus Collectivistic Cultures: Comparison Between Italy and Turkey. *Sex Roles*, 71(9–10), 296–318. DOI: 10.1007/s11199-014-0413-5

D'Lima, T., Solotaroff, J. L., & Pande, R. P. (2020). For the Sake of Family and Tradition: Honour Killings in India and Pakistan. *ANTYAJAA: Indian Journal of Women and Social Change*, 5(1), 22–39. DOI: 10.1177/2455632719880852

Hosseini, S., & C, B. (2015). Study on Honor Killing as a Crime in India-Cause and Solutions. *International Journal of Preventive Medicine*, 2.

Kanchan, T., Tandon, A., & Krishan, K. (2016). Honor Killing: Where Pride Defeats Reason. *Science and Engineering Ethics*, 22(6), 1861–1862. DOI: 10.1007/s11948-015-9694-5 PMID: 26293131

Kaushal, K. (2020). No Honour in Honour Killing: Comparative Analysis of Indian Traditional Social Structure vis-à-vis Gender Violence. *ANTYAJAA: Indian Journal of Women and Social Change*, 5(1), 52–69. DOI: 10.1177/2455632719880870

Kejriwal, N. (2018). Honour Killing in North India. Pro Bono India, 01.

King, A. (2013). Mohammad Mazher Idriss and Tahir Abbas (eds.), Honour, Violence, Women and Islam, (Abingdon: Routledge-Cavendish, 2010) ISBN 978-0-415-56542-4, 248 pp. *Religion and Human Rights*, 8(1), 93–99. DOI: 10.1163/18710328-12341245

Kumar, R. K. (2013). Honour Killing: Challenges Indian Judicial System. *International Journal of Creative Research Thoughts*, 11(4).

Mamta, R. (2018). *Law relating to Women & Children* (4th ed., Vol. 1). Eastern Book Company.

Newme, W. (2018). Honour Killings in India. *Journal of Emerging Technologies and Innovative Research*, 5(9), 333–338.

Olwan, D. M. (2013). Gendered Violence, Cultural Otherness, and Honour Crimes in Canadian National Logics. *Canadian Journal of Sociology*, 38(4), 533–556. DOI: 10.29173/cjs21196

Parul, C. (2021). Honour killings in India and need for urgent reforms and new laws. *IPleaders*.

Rai, G. (2023). Comparative Analysis on Honour Killing Prevalent in India and Sweden. SSRN *Electronic Journal*. DOI: 10.2139/ssrn.4520199

Sana. (2019). The dishonorable honor crimes in literature. *International Journal of English Language, Literature and Translation Studies*, (1st ed., Vol. 6).

Singh, D., & Bhandari, D. S. (2021). Legacy of Honor and Violence: An Analysis of Factors Responsible for Honor Killings in Afghanistan, Canada, India, and Pakistan as Discussed in Selected Documentaries on Real Cases. *SAGE Open*, 11(2), 215824402110223. DOI: 10.1177/21582440211022323

Vesvikar, M., & Agarwal, M. (2022). Honour killing in India. *Perspectives in Social Work*, 31(1), 48–62.

Vitoshka, D. Y. (2010). The Modern Face of Honor Killing: Factors, Legal Issues, and Policy Recommendations. *Berkeley Undergraduate Journal*, 22(2). Advance online publication. DOI: 10.5070/B3222007673

Wikipedia Contributors. (2024). 2012 Delhi gang rape and murder. In *Wikipedia, The Free Encyclopedia*. Wikipedia, The Free Encyclopedia.

Wikipedia contributors. (2024). Manoj–Babli honour killing case. In *Wikipedia, The Free Encyclopedia*. Wikipedia, The Free Encyclopedia.

Chapter 19
Honour Killing Among Women in India:
A Scoping Review

Divya Raghunath Iyengar
https://orcid.org/0009-0009-0498-352X
O.P. Jindal Global University, India

Soumya T. Varghese
https://orcid.org/0000-0002-7124-6898
O.P. Jindal Global University, India

ABSTRACT

Honor killing is a form of homicide where an individual becomes a victim if s/he engages in any act, unacceptable to the norms of the society. As per the data reported by National Crime Records Bureau (NCRB), crime rate with respect to honor killing has seen a rise in the last few years. Women are more likely to become victims because they are assumed to bear the weight of protecting the family honor and any deviance from the family's protocol is considered to affect the prestige of the family. Recent research has also found individuals belonging to LGBTQ community to also be a victim of honor killing. Given this backdrop, the current research reviews the literature regarding honor killing with the objective of understanding why women are more prone to be victims of honor killing. Further it aims to trace the role of technology, social and cultural aspects of honor killing. Research will aid in contributing to literature by identifying gaps in policy and human rights interventions to facilitate better implementation and advocacy regarding honor killing and help reduce crime in India.

DOI: 10.4018/979-8-3693-7240-1.ch019

INTRODUCTION

The shocking evidence regarding the victimization and perpetration of honor killing speaks volume about the disproportionate way it affects the women community across several countries spread across the globe. As per the recent statistics reported by NCRB (National Crime Records Bureau), honor killings in India were reported to be 25 in number, consecutively in the years, 2019 and 2020. In 2021, the number of honor killing deaths surged to around 33 in 2021. These statistics are mere figures that are officially reported owing to the reality that the cases might be more than those that are officially reported figures (Sripad, 2023). News reports also suggest that around 251 cases of honor killing were recorded in 2015 (Al Jazeera, 2016). Honor killing, also known as shame killing, is a form of homicide where often, women are the victims and are murdered under the name of protecting honor (Maryada) of the family. If the woman refuses an arranged marriage, the members decide to kill her to protect the honor of the family as she is assumed to endanger the honor of the family (Chesler & Bloom, 2012, pp. 43-52). Women in Pakistan are killed when they are found to elope with men, engage in adultery or even share their photographs or videos of themselves online (Mehsud et. al., 2023). Reports also suggest that one-fifth of the honor killings or 1000 of the averagely 5000 killings in the world are seen to take place in Pakistan, like that of India (Janjua, 2022). Victims of honor killing are seen to be adolescent girls aged between 14 years and 60% of the victims falling in the age range of 20-25 years. Additionally, boys in the age group of 20-25 years, with 20% of them falling in the age bracket of 17-19 years are victims of honor killing, especially in the state of Haryana, India where Jats constitute majority of the population (Dublish & Khan, 2021). Findings also suggest that Muslims and other migrants from South Asia or Middle East become victims of honor killing due to associated factors such as culture, shame, honor and religion (Shier & Shor, 2016). Not only do women get victimized against the crime, but there are other cases where sometimes, even LGBTQ community or homosexual couples may become victims of honor killing, when they reveal their sexual identity to their family members (Bhadra, 2019; Pathak & Rai, 2019). Perpetrators justify the crime by stating that it was carried out to restore the dignity of the family as women are considered to be the primary bearers of honor in the family while immoral character, inter-caste or inter-religious involvement pollute the honor upheld by the family (Chesler & Bloom, 2012, pp. 43-52). Perpetrators of crime who have a criminal mindset are found to have a positive perspective towards honor killing, refuting the myth that such killers are not ordinary and that these honor killings are justified under the purview of culture, traditions, rage, social pressure, etc. (Rahim, 2017). Additionally, since there is a dearth of laws, police officers bracket the cases of honor killing under the broad category of 'murder' and do not investigate them in detail which leads to such cases being documented as newspaper headlines very often (Al Jazeera, 2016). Social norms play an important role in upholding the quality and this quality is maintained through purification, also depriving women educational opportunities, dressing constraints imposed on women through education and job prospects. In cases where property feuds are lesser and where emphasis on setting up families and marriage alliances are lower, killings for the sake of honor are lesser (Thrasher & Handfield, 2017).

From a cultural perspective, though it is witnessed that honor killing is more common in Islam, religious texts like Quran do not justify such acts of crime (Korteweg & Yurdakul, 2010). Sociological factors, such as poverty, lower socio-economic status, modernization, etc., play an important role in the increasing incidence of honor killing among Arab females, and it does not relate to any particular cultural practice such as Arab community or Islamic traditions (Dayan, 2019). Not only are such practices common in Arab countries, culturally prevalent practices in India such as dowry also play a crucial role in encouraging the practice of honor killing (Kaur & Byard 2020). Socio-economically, any deviance from the social norms might affect the possibility of the woman getting married in a good family (Korteweg & Yurdakul, 2010). In Haryana, a state in India, honor is defined very differently. When a woman is assaulted sexually or physically by a man, outside of the family, he could face death as a consequence due to the fact that the family's honor is threatened. If a woman is married and has an extra-marital affair, then the husband's honor is thought to be threatened (Dublish & Khan, 2021). Additionally, by killing the daughter of the house as a punishment for breaching the honor of the family, it apparently increases the possibility of the cousins to get married and this leads to lesser chances of the woman and her family to get compensated for the loss of her life (Thrasher & Handfield, 2017). With the advent of technology, there are cases in India where women have been burnt alive by the men in the family as they chose to marry someone from another culture or caste. With the advent of technology and cell phones, women's rights and dignity are threatened as people might click obscene pictures and circulate them on social media and such applications (D'Lima et. al., 2020). Thus, honor killing is not a crime that is just limited to the four walls of the house. It has extended to be a form of crime having social, technological and cultural impact on the larger society, especially the vulnerable women. To understand the reason for provocation of perpetrating honor killing, a test is deemed necessary, incorporating objective and subjective factors. Objective factors include answering if a reasonable person would have committed the same action as that of the perpetrator.

Thus, reasons and consequences of engaging in honor killing could be social, political or economical in nature. Given the context and the increasing crime rate in the name of honor killing and varied aspects that are quoted as reasons of engaging in the same, it becomes essential to delve deeper into understanding the cultural, social and technological factors that compel an individual to become perpetrators or victims of honor killing. A scoping review is a precursor to a systematic review that aids in identifying gaps in literature and pave way for more in-depth research in that particular area that requires due attention (Munn et. al., 2018). As honor killing is a growing cause of societal concern and with limited literature in the Indian context, a scoping review is conducted to understand the extent of literature available and the gaps that instigate further research.

AIM AND OBJECTIVES

Aim

The current review aims to understand the reasons for women to be prone to become victims of honor killing, further trying to understand the role of social, cultural and technological factors that compel an individual to be a victim or perpetrator of the crime conducted for safeguarding honor.

Objectives

The objectives are as follows

1. To understand the role of women as victims of honor killing by the family members
2. To understand the social, cultural and technological factors that compel an individual to be victims of honor killing

Research Questions

a) Why are women more often killed in the name of safeguarding honor in the family?
b) What are the social, technological and cultural factors that propel an individual to be victims of honor killing?

Method

The current scoping review was conducted by following the framework propounded by Arksey and O'Mayley, which includes six steps. a) Identifying the research question, b) Identifying relevant studies, c) Selecting studies to be included in the review, d) Charting the data, e) Collating, summarizing and reporting the results and lastly f) Consulting stakeholders in the field (Mak & Thomas, 2022).

Search Strategy

Using the recent articles available on Google Scholar, the authors came forth with a few keywords that were used to search for articles to answer the research questions raised. These keywords included "honor killing, India, women, marriage, technology and social media". Only journal articles were retrieved from the SCOPUS database, published in English language between the years 2017 to 2024. Book chapters, newsletters published in other languages, not pertaining to the years mentioned, were excluded from the study. A thorough review at different levels was carried out. At the beginning, a title filter was done where titles that did not seem to answer the research questions were excluded from the study. Following the title filter, an abstract filter was carried out wherein articles were reviewed based on the abstract for screening out. Finally, through the full paper review, the entire article was studied for screening out those which did not appear to meet the research objectives. Figure 1.1 depicts the PRISMA diagram with the number of finally collated articles.

Procedure

Firstly, after the finalization of the research questions and objectives. articles were downloaded from the SCOPUS database. Duplicates were screened and removed. Further, based on title, abstract and full paper review, articles were shortlisted for the analysis. Using thematic analysis by Braun and Clarke (2006), themes were retrieved and were analyzed. Table 1.2 provides a comprehensive picture of a brief summary of the articles.

Results

After the search was conducted on SCOPUS, 21 articles were identified in the process. Books and book chapters were removed from the analysis. So, 17 articles were shortlisted for the study. Duplicates were removed from a manual screening process and 16 articles were shortlisted for the study. Screening for the remaining articles were conducted at three levels, namely, the title, abstract and full paper review wherein 5 articles were screened out as they did not seem to answer the objectives of the study. Finally, 11 articles were shortlisted for the analysis. After the selection of the studies, full-text PDF files of those studies were downloaded for further analysis, through the Library support, provided by the University to which the authors are affiliated. This process is depicted through the PRISMA model in Figure 1. Through a thematic approach by Braun and Clarke (2006), the articles were classified into border themes such as Social factors, Cultural factors and technological factors that contribute to engagement in honor killing. Table 1.

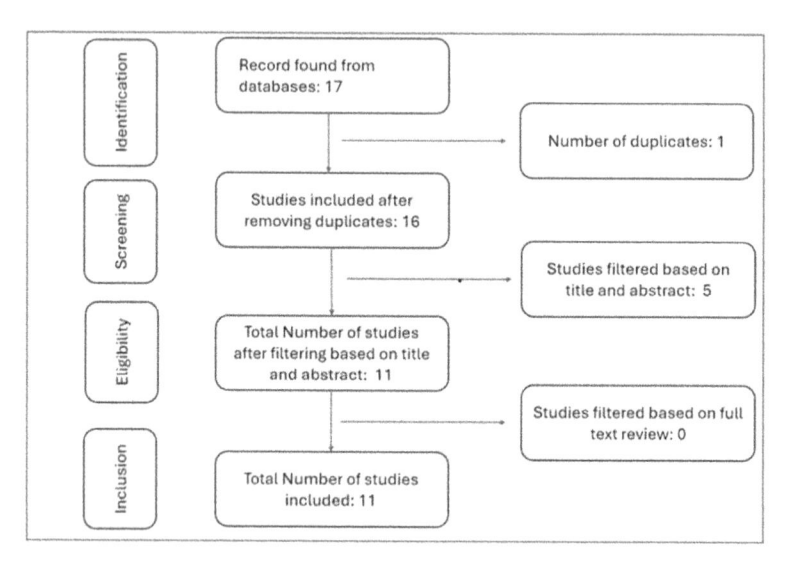

Figure 1. PRISMA model

```
Identification:   Record found from databases: 17
                      │
                      ├──────────────► Number of duplicates: 1
                      ▼
Screening:        Studies included after removing duplicates: 16
                      │
                      ├──────────────► Studies filtered based on title and abstract: 5
                      ▼
Eligibility:      Total Number of studies after filtering based on title and abstract: 11
                      │
                      ├──────────────► Studies filtered based on full text review: 0
                      ▼
Inclusion:        Total Number of studies included: 11
```

Table 1. Summary of articles

Author	Year	Geographical location	Sample	Results	Recommendations and future directions
Ashok G & Rupavath R	2022	India		The practice of endogamy is forced upon individuals. Caste based norms are enforced when it comes to a friendship between a male and a female. Evidence show that caste based division is still prevalent especially in Southern India	It is essential to Dalit movements to check for how discrimination happens based on sub-castes in the socio-political areas of life
Kalyani V, Arumugam T & Kumar S	2022	India	Indian (Kollywood) movies depicting violence against women	The atrocities that women from lower castes include caste discrimination, slavery, honor killings, oppression, witness fights by the other caste females etc. Women in India have to stand for their rights to get justice and punishment for the perpetrators of such atrocities	Expanding the effectiveness of such films is required for the betterment of the society
Singh. R., Hurley, D., Singh D	2016	Northern India	65 students studying in university and colleges in India	Looking through the lens of Heise's theory of Violence Against Women, it was seen that violence against women was impacted by several levels inclusive of ecological level, cultural level, social level and the individual level	
Chetty & Alathu	2019	India		Role of social media in expression of hate emotions and the need to control it to control honor based violence. Cultural, social and individual factors as equally responsible facets involved in honor killing	With the fast growing pace of digitization in the community, it becomes essential to educate individuals through online honor and hate based content streaming, alongwith using the knowledge diligently

continued on following page

383

Table 1. Continued

Author	Year	Geographical location	Sample	Results	Recommendations and future directions
Narzary. P., Ladusingh L	2019	India	Data from India Human Development Survey. Interviewing women 15 years and older	Inter-caste marriage is still frowned upon and not encouraged, which compels even educated women to look for partners in the same caste in spite of advancements in technology, westernization and such developments.	Efforts towards encouraging inter-caste marriage is crucial to reduce the biased notion towards casteism. A larger study towards inter-caste marriage is also necessary
Pathak, M., Rai.,S.	2019	India		Honor killing is more prominent where the society is a male-dominated one and the villages where Khap Pnachanyats are predominant such as in states of Uttar Pradesh and Haryana. Further, areas where caste division is explicitly done and laws are not effective, cases of honor killing may seem more. The article outlines various triggers of honor killing inclusive of love marriage, adultery, inter-caste marriage, women who seek divorce, inappropriate clothing, rape survivors and homo-sexuality	Need for special laws and provisions under CrPC or IPC wherein honor killing is considered as a criminal offense, wherein families might consider to kill an individual, in majority cases, a woman if they engage in acts that is considered to cause dishonor to the family
Singh, A.	2020	India		Women's reproductive capacity makes her responsible for upholding the honor in the family. When she chooses her own partner, she is considered to pollute herself and her community. Pakistan has brought in legal interventions to curb honor killings and in this light, it becomes essential for India to also frame similar laws	

continued on following page

Table 1. Continued

Author	Year	Geographical location	Sample	Results	Recommendations and future directions
Singh, D & Bhandari, D	2021	India, Pakistan, Afganistan, Canada	Documentaries in these countries related to honor killing	Nations that believe in equal rights for everyone, occasionally do encounter instances of honor crime. In spite of being liberal, nations might stick on to the rigid norms and rules established. Though laws mention the right to freedom of individuals and safeguarding rights, some may not agree to such laws just to preserve family honor. It becomes difficult to find witnesses against honor killing and thus, such crimes may witness a delay in punishment	Honor related violence thrives due to the lack of evidence, delays in legal punishment.
Zinck. P	2019	India	Indian movies	Indian movies such as those released as Bollywood, Kollywood and Lollywood choose to screen movies that depict politically sensitive movies, such as that of thriller and gangster ones. Patriarchy and a need for the women to be rescued and be supported by a man is clearly depicted by Bollywood movies, failing to represent issues such as rape, genocide, honor killing etc.	Expansion of Genres in Bollywood to incorporate other prevalent social issues such as Genocide, Rape, Honor Killing etc. is required especially through the new generation of artists and NRI directors who have less radicalized approach towards such themes.

continued on following page

Table 1. Continued

Author	Year	Geographical location	Sample	Results	Recommendations and future directions
Shroff. S.	2021		Case study from Pakistan	Being a feminist scholar, the author defines honor as a type of radicalized property and creation of wealth. The value placed on women depends on the honor that they receive. Taking the case study of a Pakistani media star who was murdered, the author comments on honor killing as a form of hertropatriarchy where she mentions the crime being committed as a part of property rather than a crime of culture. She further talks of the lens through which a woman's body is looked at which is radicalised and sexualized	

continued on following page

Table 1. Continued

Author	Year	Geographical location	Sample	Results	Recommendations and future directions
Sen. A., Kaur. R., Zabiliute E.	2019	India		The authors mention about various types of violence that women encounter which includes rape, discrimination, honor killing, sex-related murders etc. Women become victims of sexual violence and it is often referred in the context of caste, religion, honor and respect. With rape cases being heard in Delhi and Mumbai, it is seen that men are not able to, any longer, protect the ambitious women. Sexual violence is seen as an urban phenomena because there is a rise in sexual encounters even in the intimate areas of the urban setup. Furthermore, there are changes in the central and peripheral areas of the cities, social capital and the economies. Other major component includes communities divided based on religion, caste and class, not staying peacefully	

SOCIAL FACTORS AFFECTING HONOR KILLING

Caste Based Division

In India, division on the basis of caste is a social issue and from the lens of Micheal Foucault's theoretical framework of biopolitics, the practice of endogamy was analyzed in India. Women's sexuality, sexual activity and freedom plays a crucial role in preserving the honor in the society with an emphasis on practicing endogamy wherein the choice of bride or groom is from the same caste which the either belongs to (Ashok & Rupavath, 2022). Marriage being considered as one of the social institutions, in India, marrying out of caste is not still looked upon from a favorable lens despite modernization and other technological advances (Narzary & Ladusingh, 2019, Pathank & Rai, 2019). Marriage, as an informal institution, is often intertwined with rigid societal structures of power dynamics and caste identity. In this regard, though it may be very empowering for educated women, especially to choose their mates, they may prefer getting acquainted and forming a partnership with males from the same caste than going into an inter-caste marriage (Narzary & Ladusingh, 2019). Modernization and urbanization have shifted marriage dynamics, and increasingly, individuals choose partners based on compatibility rather than social identities. However, resistance and anguish toward inter-caste marriages remain prevalent and often serve as themes in films. Social constructs of honor killing as a crime against women are also showcased through films such as "Jai Bhim," "Madha Yannai Kooitam" that showcase how women from lower castes have to fight back the indirect discrimination in the Southern areas of India.

Fight Against the Traditional Norms

Women have to fight back the traditional social norms and have to raise their opinions regarding the consequence of violence that the perpetrators should face (Kalyani & Kumar, 2022). Ingrained in the social factors, some individual factors such as lower self-confidence, isolation, psychological trauma and may require mental health support to get their lives back on track (Chetty & Alathur, 2019).

Urbanization

With urbanization and changes in the social setup, women are experiencing sexual violence more often especially in urban cities such as Delhi and Mumbai due to various factors such as differences in caste, religion, honor and respect (Sen et. al., 2019). Cities like Delhi and Mumbai witness a rise in rape cases making sexual violence, an urban phenomenon because there of the rise in sexual encounters even in the intimate areas of the urban setup (Sen et. al., 2019). It was further witnessed that honor killings were found to be on the rise from the time Telengana was formed as a new state as the state firmly relied on the hegemonic practices exerted by the caste system (Ashok & Rupavath, 2022). Furthermore, there are changes in the central and peripheral areas of the cities, social capital and the economies, division of communities on religion, caste and class etc. disrupting the peaceful atmosphere (Sen et. al., 2019).

TECHNOLOGICAL FACTORS AFFECTING HONOR KILLING

Social Media

Social media, news reports, literature reviews are sources that people access to get themselves updates about the world outside. With the advent of social media, communicating, connecting and networking have become easy, along with individuals actively posting their pictures and selfies on social networking sites like Instagram and Facebook (Fox & Rooney, 2015). Fear, anger, disgust, sadness are some of the emotions that are expressed showcasing hatred through social media and online public platforms. The control of explicit expression of such explicit negative emotions could be one way of curbing honor-based violence (Chetty & Alathur, 2019). Social media, digital rights, privacy and freedom of expression further complicates the aspects centered around honor killing (Shroff, 2021). In essence, it is arguable that honor killings are deeply rooted in heteropatriarchal structures. These acts uphold the idea that a woman's body and behavior are considered property, subject to male acknowledgment, praise, and control.

Movie Depictions

Analysis of depiction of honor crime in movies across India, Pakistan, Afghanistan and Canada have shown the rigidity in terms of adhering to the gender roles prescribed by the society. It further showcases how some people may be of a liberal mindset and be more accepting while on the other hand some may still hold on to the rigid norms set just to retain the honor in the society and family (Singh & Bhandari, 2021). Contrastingly, though movies become a platform for entertainment and raising awareness on several issues, not all films or directors choose to represent the latter part in the society through movies. Bollywood films often mirror societal norms and cultural attitudes. Unfortunately, this portrayal has perpetuated gender inequality and reinforced traditional roles. The perspectives on power dynamics depicted in films often unknowingly reinforce conservative attitudes, portraying women as vulnerable, dependent, and weak. It is observed that Bollywood movies show resistance to screen movies that depict gendered based violence and choose to release movies that portray terrorist attacks, religious differences and so on (Zinck, 2019). Bollywood reflects through its movies, a conservative attitude with predominantly male viewers, portraying women to be at a mercy of the men and a very hypersexualized depiction of their bodies (Zinck, 2019).

CULTURAL FACTORS AFFECTING HONOR KILLING

Cultural Boundaries

Looking through the lens of Heise's theory of Violence Against Women, it was seen that violence against women was impacted by several levels inclusive of ecological level, cultural level, social level and the individual level (Singh et. al., 2016). Cultural leaders have set boundaries which, when threatened by the women fold, leads to them being victims of honor killing by the family as women are considered to bear the honor in the family (Pathak & Rai, 2019). Women have gained momentum as they have started to speak for themselves and that is seen even in the rural parts of Northern India as well, starting to form their own political identity, achieving justice and equality (Singh et. al., 2016). Culturally, one way of preserving honor in the family is presumed to be through killing of the family member who deviates from the norms of the general family functioning, such as one of the reasons being marrying against the will of family members (Chetty & Alathur, 2019; Pathak & Rai, 2019). Honor killings are a multi-faceted horror, intertwining notions of honor, pride, and the perceived right to be granted honor. These acts of violence stem from cultural norms and patriarchal systems, where a woman's actions are seen as reflective of her family's honor. Culture plays a valid role in this context as the system of values, rules and symbols are varied across cultures. The nature of any relationship must be understood within the context of culture, and this understanding is particularly evident in the concept of long-lasting relationships or marriages. The primary purpose of marriage in India is to carry forward the lineage and the standpoint between modern values and traditional notions, is a point where honor killings lie, where individuals have disregarded the norms related to matrimony (Singh, 2020).

The Rural-Urban Divide and Heteropatriarchy

People living in rural areas appear to be more conservative than those living in the urban areas due to their conservative mindsets and when women get into conflict with the traditional norms, it is said to be an influence of the Western cultures

(Singh, 2020). Taking the case study of a Pakistani media star who was murdered, the author comments on honor killing as a form of heteropatriarchy where she mentions the crime being committed as a part of property rather than a crime of culture. She further mentions the radicalized and sexualized lens of looking at a woman's body (Shroff, 2021). This incident adds to the growing prevalence of honor killings and honor-based violence. Tragically, it involves perceived violations of cultural norms or family honor. Heteropatriarchy is a system where male dominance and heterosexuality intersect, reinforcing traditional and conservative gender roles that emphasize male authority and control over women. It will be an ongoing struggle to fight against honor killings to demand societal change and legal accountability.

DISCUSSION

Through the review, it becomes visible that social factors such as caste-based division, urbanization, traditional norms, technological factors such as movie depictions, social media and cultural factors contribute towards being victimized against honor killing. Taking a revolutionary standpoint, social media and movie releases can serve in ways to bring about awareness and change in the approach that contributes to being victimized against honor killing (Zinck. 2019; Singh & Bhandari, 2021). Despite implementation of stricter governmental laws, reported instances of violence against women have remained the same implying that simply changing the norms and laws may not bring about a change in front of the deeply entrenched cultural traditions, demographic values and individual experiences (Singh et. al., 2016). Contrastingly, some other studies have mentioned that education, incorporating inter-caste education, change in legal procedures and human rights interventions will bring about a change in such casteist ideologies (Narzary and Ladusingh, 2019; Singh & Bhandari, 2021). In order to control killings that are honor based, it has to be treated like an issue nationally spread across with the need to design appropriate policy interventions (Chetty & Alathur, 2019). Humans decide the punishment for another fellow human being to be a death penalty just because they do not want to be embarrassed or humiliated on their deviance from the socially set norms by them (Pathak & Rai, 2019). With Pakistan implementing laws related to curb honor killing, it is essential for India to also learn and implement laws to reduce such crimes (Singh, 2020). Movies, especially those outside directed and released by NRIs, become a good channel for raising awareness related to the ongoing atrocities and crimes in the neighborhood (Zinck, 2019; Singh & Bhandari, 2021). Sadly, Bollywood pictures in India have not been able to adequately capture and screen gender-based violence. NRI directors have not been restrictive in their approach, having a similar perspective such as that of the new generation of artists who are able to appropriately capture crimes such that that of rape, prostitution, honor killing etc (Zinck, 2019).

IMPLICATION

Findings have suggested that it is very difficult to strike a balance between the traditional obligations and a person's independence in the patriarchal society and to attain a significant balance, it is necessary to firstly change one's attitude towards marriage (Jeyasanthi et. al., 2014). One of the ways to tackle honor killing is to address it at its roots by understanding the meaning of violence and how this differs from homicides, serial killing, passion crimes etc. Further, dysfunctional cultural beliefs that enforce individuals to engage in such actions have to be demystified as marriage related choices of an individual should be respected and develop acceptance towards inter-caste or inter-religion mate selection (Parasar et. al., 2016). Effective human rights interventions have to be created that help women who are the victims of honor killing along with taking the broader social and political perspective; women's basic human rights should be prioritized over the traditionally functioning patriarchal practices that may cause any kind of harm (Metoo & Mirza, 2007). Education is one of the strongest ways to train an individual's mind right from the beginning such that schools can incorporate training programs to have an open-minded approach towards inter-caste killings and using appropriate solutions to problems instead of resorting to violence related behaviors (Jeyasanthi et. al., 2014). Implementing stricter as well as clearer law and order to prevent honor killing is one of the biggest changes that needs to be brought about. Media portrayals and awareness regarding the redefinition of honor and healthy ways to retain it in the family becomes a need for the hour (Grewal, 2013). Thus, it is important to identify why women are more prone to be victims of honor killing and the role of such explicit crimes that compel an individual to be a part of such crimes. At the grassroot level, the term 'honor' should be changed because the authors suggest that there is nothing honorable behind such crime. Politics and such disgusting crimes should never enter a family setup as it only worsens the situation by breaking the family (Jeyasanthi et. al., 2014). Further, trying to make a distinction between what is essential and what is strategized is necessary and to majorly understand which crime is categorized as 'honor killing' and which ones are done as a part of spousal or familial murder (Shier & Shor, 2016). Perpetrators generally mention that they had no choice, or it was not in their hands and that it might have been done because of self-defense, where killing was the only option which requires acquittal, and the lost honor can be restored through killing the other person (Dogan, 2016). There are cultural differences in how honor can be retained through more acceptable and tolerable ways, and this is the reason why there is a perspective shift in those people who have had family members, who have breached honor but have not resorted to killing as a means in spite of staying in environments where killings for honor have been committed (Dogan, 2016).

FUTURE RESEARCH DIRECTIONS

Future research needs to delve deeper into the casteist ideologies, dalit movements and other such social issues, pilfering into the perpetration and victimization of honor killing (Ashok & Rupavath, 2022), including inter-caste marriages (Narzary & Ladusingh, 2019). Directors and producers can be more creative and invest in movies that aid in creating awareness related to such issues of honor killing (Kalyani & Kumar, 2022), incorporating serious themes such as rape, genocide, honor killing etc (Zinck, 2019).

CONCLUSION

The review helps answer the research questions raised with regard to why women are more prone to being victims of honor killing and the social, technological and cultural factors involved in disrupting a marriage by killing the woman who is assumed to be a threat to the family's honor. Honor killing, a form of violence where the basic human rights of the victim are threatened and in cases where women are the victims, patriarchy may be a contributing factor. Women, particularly, are expected to behave, dress, aspire in a certain way and when she defies such notions, the resultant is her being a victim and eventually her death. Societally, it is believed that when a daughter of the family has deviant actions, she must be eliminated from the family, as otherwise, the entire family will face exclusion and ostracism, and no one will marry the daughters in the family (Chesler, 2015). Honor killing is no solution to the societally held fixtures and assumptions. It is essential to address the issue legally, socially, psychologically and taking a multi-dimensional perspective.

REFERENCES

Ashok, G., & Rupavath, R. (2022). The Biopolitics of Caste: Analysing the (Dis) honour Killings in South India. *Contemporary Voice of Dalit*, 2455328X2210766. https://doi.org/DOI: 10.1177/2455328X221076657

Bhadra, K. (2019, November 20). Parents threaten to kill gay couple, drive them out. *The Times of India*. https://timesofindia.indiatimes.com/city/kolkata/parents-threaten-to-kill-gay-couple-drive-them-out/articleshow/72150985.cms

Braun, V., & Clarke, V. (2006). Using thematic analysis in psychology. *Qualitative Research in Psychology*, 3(2), 77–101. DOI: 10.1191/1478088706qp063oa

Chesler, P. (2015). When women commit honor killings. *Middle East Quarterly*, 22(4). https://www.meforum.org/5477/when-women-commit-honor-killings

Chesler, P. (2019). Honour killings: Some observations. *Sociology International Journal*, 3(1), 1–10. DOI: 10.1177/2455632719880852

Chesler, P., & Bloom, N. (2012). Hindu vs. Muslim honor killings. *Middle East Quarterly*. Retrieved from https://www.meforum.org/3287/hindu-muslim-honor-killings

Chetty, N., & Alathur, S. (2019). Honour, hate and violence in social media: Insights from India. *International Journal of Web Based Communities*, 15(4), 315. DOI: 10.1504/IJWBC.2019.103189

D'Lima, T., Solotaroff, J. L., & Pande, R. P. (2020). For the Sake of Family and Tradition: Honour Killings in India and Pakistan. *ANTYAJAA: Indian Journal of Women and Social Change*, 5(1), 22–39. DOI: 10.1177/2455632719880852

Dayan, H. (2019). Female honor killing: The role of low socio-economic status and rapid modernization. *Journal of Interpersonal Violence*. Advance online publication. DOI: 10.1177/0886260519872984 PMID: 31524058

Doğan, R. (2016). The Dynamics of Honor Killings and the Perpetrators' Experiences. *Homicide Studies*, 20(1), 53–79. DOI: 10.1177/1088767914563389

Dublish, D., & Khan, Y. (2021). Impact of Honour Killings in Haryana, India. *Social Science Journal for Advanced Research*, 1(2), 33–40. DOI: 10.54741/ssjar.1.2.6

Faqir, F. (2001). Sexual double standards and honour crimes in Jordan: Community and women's perspectives. *Gender and Development*, 9(2), 49–58. DOI: 10.1177/2455632719880870

Fox, J., & Rooney, M. C. (2015). The Dark Triad and trait self-objectification as predictors of men's use and self-presentation behaviors on social networking sites. *Personality and Individual Differences*, 76, 161–165. DOI: 10.1016/j.paid.2014.12.017

Grewal, I. (2013). Outsourcing Patriarchy. *International Feminist Journal of Politics*, 15(1), 1–19. DOI: 10.1080/14616742.2012.755352

Janjua, H. (2022). The horror of honor killings. *Asia Democracy Chronicles*.

Jazeera, A. (2016, December 7). India sees huge spike in 'honour' killings. India. Retrieved from https://www.aljazeera.com/news/2016/12/india-sees-huge-spike-honour-killings161207153333597.html

Jeyasanthi, V., Mayileswari, S., & Abirami, R. (2014). Honour Killing: A National Outcry. *Journal for Bloomers Research*, 6(2), 917–942.

Kalyani, V., Arumugam, T., & Surya Kumar, M. (2022). Women in Oppressive Societies as Portrayed in Kollywood Movies. *American Journal of Economics and Sociology*, 81(1), 173–185. DOI: 10.1111/ajes.12450

Kaur, N., & Byard, R. W. (2020). Bride burning: A unique and ongoing form of gender-based violence. *Journal of Forensic and Legal Medicine*, 75, 102035. DOI: 10.1016/j.jflm.2020.102035 PMID: 32871350

Korteweg, A. C., & Yurdakul, G. (2010). Understanding honour killing and honour-related violence in the immigration context: Implications for the legal profession and beyond. Canadian Council of Muslim Women. https://cdhpi.ca/sites/cdhpi.ca/files/korteweg_cclr-understanding-honour-killing.pdf

Mak, S., & Thomas, A. (2022). Steps for Conducting a Scoping Review. *Journal of Graduate Medical Education*, 14(5), 565–567. DOI: 10.4300/JGME-D-22-00621.1 PMID: 36274762

Meetoo, V., & Mirza, H. S. (2007). There is nothing 'honourable' about honour killings: Gender, violence and the limits of multiculturalism. *Women's Studies International Forum*, 30(3), 187–200. DOI: 10.1016/j.wsif.2007.03.001

Mehsud, I., Khan, N., & Amirzada, M. (2023). *Death of Honor Killings Put Spotlight on 'Honor' Killings in Pakistan*. RadioFree Europe Radio Liberty.

Munn, Z., Peters, M. D. J., Stern, C., Tufanaru, C., McArthur, A., & Aromataris, E. (2018). Systematic review or scoping review? Guidance for authors when choosing between a systematic or scoping review approach. *BMC Medical Research Methodology*, 18(1), 143. DOI: 10.1186/s12874-018-0611-x PMID: 30453902

Narzary, P. K., & Ladusingh, L. (2019). Discovering the Saga of Inter-caste Marriage in India. *Journal of Asian and African Studies*, 54(4), 588–599. DOI: 10.1177/0021909619829896

Parasar, A., & Gopal, D. Saha and Baskar, Nisha, Honor Killings in India: A Study on the State of Uttar Pradesh (march 2016). International Journal of Recent Scientific Research (IJRSR), Volume: 7(3) March -2016, Available at SSRN: https://ssrn.com/abstract=4496100

Pathak, M. K., & Rai, S. (2019). Honour Killing: Gruesome Murder For The Sake of False Honour. *Journal of Punjab Academy of Forensic Medicine & Toxicology*, 19(2), 181. DOI: 10.5958/0974-083X.2020.00040.0

Rahim, S. (2017). Attitude toward honour killing among honor killers. *WU Journal of Social Sciences, 11*(1), 254-263. Retrieved from http://sbbwu.edu.pk/journal/WU_Journal_of_Social_Sciences_Summer_2017_Vol_11_No_1/23%20Attitude%20Toward%20Honour%20%20killing%20among%20honor%20killers.pdf

Sen, A., Kaur, R., & Zabiliūtė, E. (2020). (En)countering sexual violence in the Indian city. *Gender, Place and Culture*, 27(1), 1–12. DOI: 10.1080/0966369X.2019.1612856

Shier, A., & Shor, E. (2016) "Shades of foreign evil": "honour killings" and "family murders" in the Canadian press. Violence Against Women, 22 (10). pp. 1163-1188. ISSN 1077-8012

Shroff, S. (2021). Bold Women, Bad Assets: Honour, Property and Techno-Promiscuities. *Feminist Review*, 128(1), 62–78. DOI: 10.1177/01417789211016438

Singh, A. K. (2020). The Paradox Between Universalism of Human Rights and Relativism of Culture. *Journal of Southeast Asian Human Rights*, 4(1), 253. DOI: 10.19184/jseahr.v4i1.8597

Singh, D., & Bhandari, D. S. (2021). Legacy of Honor and Violence: An Analysis of Factors Responsible for Honor Killings in Afghanistan, Canada, India, and Pakistan as Discussed in Selected Documentaries on Real Cases. *SAGE Open*, 11(2). Advance online publication. DOI: 10.1177/21582440211022323

Singh, R. N., Hurley, D., & Singh, D. (2017). Towards identifying and ranking selected types of violence against women in North India. *International Journal of Comparative and Applied Criminal Justice*, 41(1–2), 19–29. DOI: 10.1080/01924036.2016.1212246

Sripad, A. M. (2023, September 4). Killing honour in the name of 'honour killings'. *The New Indian Express*. Retrieved from https://www.newindianexpress.com/states/karnataka/2023/Sep/04/killing-honour-in-the-name-of-honour-killings-2611437.html

Thrasher, J., & Handfield, T. (2017). Honor and Violence. *Human Nature (Hawthorne, N.Y.)*, 29(4), 371–389. DOI: 10.1007/s12110-018-9324-4 PMID: 30251000

Zinck, P. (2019). Disobedient bodies: Gendered violence in South Asian and desi film. *South Asian Popular Culture*, 17(3), 269–282. DOI: 10.1080/14746689.2019.1668590

Chapter 20
The Dark Face and Hidden Atrocity of Honor Killing Cases in Turkey

Praveen Kumar Mall
Teerthanker Mahaveer University, Moradabad, India

Shreyanshi Goyal
https://orcid.org/0009-0001-9787-5705
GLA University, Mathura, India

ABSTRACT

Several key research questions will be addressed in this chapter: 1. What is the Prevalence of Honor Killing in Turkey? 2. What are the cultural and societal factors that contribute to the prevalence of honor killings in Turkey? 3. What are the Prejudices and Misconceptions Associated with Honor Killing? 4. Exploring Gender Roles in Honor Killing Incidents in Turkey. 5. Laws and Punishments for Honor Killing in Turkey. 6. What is the Role of Community in Propagating Honor Killings? 7. Understanding the Impact of Honor Killings on Turkish Society. 8. Recommendations for Eradicating Honor Killings in Turkey. In order to address these research questions, the chapter will utilize a mixed-methods approach, combining qualitative interviews and analysis of existing literature on honor killings in Turkey. The findings from this research chapter will contribute to a deeper understanding of the social prejudice surrounding honor killings in Turkey and provide insights for developing targeted interventions and strategies to combat and eradicate this form of violence.

DOI: 10.4018/979-8-3693-7240-1.ch020

Honor killings, also known as honor-based abuse, are a complex and deeply entrenched issue that transcends cultural, ethnic, and religious boundaries. The term "Honor Killing" is often used to describe the violent acts committed against individuals, typically women, who are perceived to have brought shame or dishonor to their family or community. These acts of violence are often rooted in the traditional concept of honor, where the family or community's reputation is closely tied to the behaviour of its members, particularly its female members. In some instances, honor-based abuse escalates to the point of domestic homicides, commonly referred to as "Honor Killings". This grim phenomenon is not confined to a specific geographical location or cultural group, as it occurs worldwide.

Turkey, as a country with a diverse population and complex social dynamics, faces significant challenges in addressing honor killings. These challenges include deeply rooted cultural and religious beliefs, societal prejudice, and a lack of adequate legal measures and enforcement. To effectively address honor killings in Turkey, it is essential to recognize and understand the cultural and religious factors that contribute to their prevalence. It is important to approach the issue with cultural sensitivity and engage with community leaders, religious institutions, and civil society organizations to promote dialogue, education, and awareness. Moreover, efforts to combat honor killings in Turkey should also focus on providing support and resources for victims and their families. This can include safe shelters, counselling services, and financial assistance to help survivors rebuild their lives. Furthermore, it is crucial to involve men and boys in the efforts to address honor killings. This can be done through education programs that promote gender equality, challenge patriarchal norms, and encourage men to become allies in the fight against honor-based violence. In order to create lasting change, it is imperative to address the underlying social norms and attitudes that perpetuate honor killings in Turkey.

This chapter aims to explore the social prejudice that surrounds honor killings in Turkey. It will examine the intersection of patriarchal norms, colonial history, sectarian and ethnonational violence, and toxic masculinities that contribute to an environment conducive to honor killings in Turkey. Specifically, this chapter will draw from the aforementioned sources to analyse the attitudes and justifications for honor killings in Turkey. Building on the arguments made in the sources, the chapter will argue that honor killings in Turkey are unique and distinct from other honor-related homicides, both in terms of the concept of honor and the nature of the relationships between the perpetrators and victims.(Doğan, 2014). Furthermore, this chapter will discuss the role of cultural norms in perpetuating prejudices against women in Turkey, particularly in rural areas where traditional beliefs and values are deeply entrenched. Given the cultural and religious factors involved in honor killings, it is crucial to approach this issue with cultural sensitivity and engage with community leaders, religious institutions, and civil society organizations to promote dialogue, education, and awareness. By understanding the root causes of honor killings in Turkey, we can work towards dismantling social prejudice and creating a society where women are valued, respected, and protected from violence.

Objectives are as Follows:

1. Recognizing and comprehending the cultural and religious elements that contribute to the incidence of honor killings in Turkey is crucial for developing successful strategies to address the issue.
2. The purpose of this chapter is to examine the social bias that exists in Turkey regarding honor killings.
3. The views and explanations for honor killings in Turkey will be examined in this chapter, which will consult the previously stated sources.
4. The importance of cultural norms in sustaining discrimination against women in Turkey will be covered in this chapter, with a focus on rural areas where traditional values and beliefs are ingrained.

INTRODUCTION

Honor killing is a deeply ingrained issue in many societies, and the complex nature of the relationship between the defendants and the victims in Turkey sets it apart from other forms of honor-related homicides. The former Turkish Criminal Law once required a reduction in punishment for both male and female honor killers, reflecting a deeply rooted societal attitude towards honor killings. However, discussions surrounding honor killings often oversimplify the cultural dynamics at play, as they tend to dichotomize traditional versus modern perspectives. This oversimplification obscures important dynamics and cultural specificities that are crucial to understanding the root causes of honor killings in Turkey.

Furthermore, the available literature on honor killings often lacks a comprehensive analysis of the patterns, dynamics, and events that lead to such femicide cases. The voices of the perpetrators, who are crucial in understanding the entire picture and the dynamics behind these killings, have rarely been heard. This highlights the need for a more nuanced understanding of honor killing, especially in countries like Italy and Turkey, where family honor holds significant cultural value. The roles of patriarchy in shaping societal attitudes also plays a significant role in the history of both cultures, despite the different developments in social organization in the two countries in recent decades. Therefore, it is vital to conduct a thorough analysis of male and female perceptions of honor killings in Turkey and Italy, taking into account the attribution of victim and assailant responsibility, proposed punishment for the assailant, and evaluation of honor killing as a crime (Caffaro et al., 2014). By examining the societal motives embedded in the notion of honor, along with the gendered meanings of honor and the dynamics behind honor killings, we can gain a deeper understanding of the complexities of this issue. The cultural forces and traditions in Turkey have played a significant role in shaping attitudes towards honor killings, and it is crucial to consider the interplay between religious beliefs, rural population values, and cultural norms that contribute to prejudices against women.

Moreover, the analysis should not overlook the specificities of Kurdish cultural forces, especially in the context of immigrants in Sweden, as highlighted by Mikael Kurkiala. The study of the Turkish-Kurds immigrants in Sweden provides valuable insights into the underlying factors that contribute to honor killings, as demonstrated in the case of Fadime Sahindal. Understanding the cultural dimensions of honor killings is essential for crafting effective interventions and policies to address this deeply rooted issue. Also, Criminal laws in certain nations frequently allow for leniency in the sentencing of those found guilty of Honor crimes(Secretary-General, 2002). A person who commits a crime of Honor in Lebanon will be found guilty but may not go to jail. In Israel, a woman who murders another while having an illicit sexual relationship may be freed from prison after serving 10–12 years.(J. Ginat, 2006; Seedat et al., 2009). This punishment is unsatisfactory and far from being preventive. Turkey's eastern region is home to the nearly one-million-person city of Malatya. The eastern region of Turkey is where honor killings are most commonly found, and the cultural norms their support honor killings.

In the context of Italy and Turkey, where family honor is deeply ingrained in the culture, it is important to delve into the male and female perceptions of honor killings. Assessing the attribution of victim and assailant responsibility, proposed punishment for the assailant, and the evaluation of honor killing as a crime will shed light on the cultural and societal attitudes towards this issue. The influence of patriarchy, albeit in different degrees, has shaped the historical and contemporary perspectives on honor killings in both countries, underscoring the need for a nuanced analysis.

Moving forward, a comprehensive analysis that considers the cultural, religious, and societal factors contributing to honor killings will provide valuable insights for addressing this complex issue in a meaningful and impactful way.

KEY TERMS

The nucleus of the term includes "Honor Killing" and its "Dark Face" & "Hidden Atrocity". Broader themes like "Social Prejudice" (Doğan, 2014), "Honor-Based Abused" (Seedat et al., 2009) & "Religious Beliefs" (Sev'Er & Yurdakul, 2001) contextualize the issue. And the "Violence" (Xavier, 2015) & "Horrible Offence" (Gorar, 2020) happens "Against Women" (AlQahtani et al., 2022) because of "Caste System" (Eck van Clementine, 2003), "Marital Life" (Ginat, 2006) & "Patriarchal Society" (Kaya & Turan, 2018).

Supervisor, (Bethany, 2014), (Mammadova & Joamets, 2021) we used these keywords to select relevant articles from multiple online sources, for example, 'Library of Congress, Research Gate, Google Books, Springer, JSTOR, Sage, IJSSHR, Scopus, Web of Science, Taylor & Francis and Google Scholar'.

An Honor Killings Research Paper on its Dark Face and Hidden Atrocity requires careful consideration of inclusion/exclusion and article research, as well as the selection of appropriate publications. Publications with an emphasis on international law, gender studies, human rights, and related interdisciplinary topics were chosen for publishing in the journal selection process.

In order to further narrow down the research publications that are pertinent for this Chapter, we have established both inclusion and exclusion criteria. The following studies met our inclusion criteria: ones where "experience" was examined as a concept or a variable in the context of ecotourism; Research must be published in English and restricted to journal articles—that is, those having an impact factor of 1.0 or above in Journal Citation Reports and peer-reviewed papers, or those with a B grade or higher in the Journal Quality list.

LITERATURE REVIEW

Honor killings in Turkey have long been a subject of academic and public discourse, revealing a complex web of cultural, social, and legal factors that perpetuate this abhorrent practice. This Chapter aims to provide a comprehensive overview of the research on the dark face and hidden atrocity of honor killing cases in Turkey, exploring the root causes, societal attitudes, and the challenges in addressing this persistent issue.

The existing research on honor killings in Turkey highlights the intricate interplay between gender inequality, patriarchal structures, and the perpetuation of traditional cultural norms. Scholars have emphasized the need to dissociate honor killings from a particular religious belief system and instead locate them on a continuum of patriarchal patterns of violence against women (Sev'Er & Yurdakul, 2001). The concept of "culture conflict" has been explored, with studies examining the experiences of perpetrators and the circumstances that lead to these heinous crimes (Doğan, 2014).

One of the key findings from the literature is the notion that the revised Turkish Penal Code of 2004, which increased sentences for honor killing perpetrators and their family members, has led to a shift from honor killings to honor suicides, where females are encouraged to take their own lives to minimize the penalization (Bethany, 2014).

RESEARCH GAP

This chapter is different from others as it brings new insights to the issue of honor killings in Turkey, thereby expanding the discourse on the social prejudices that underpin these tragic events and highlighting the need for interdisciplinary methods to unravel the complexities of the social, cultural, religious, and economic factors at play. There has been few studies related to it but this is different as it brings new elements to the debate. This chapter is poised to offer a critical examination of the various elements contributing to honor killings, thus addressing a gap in the literature that has often overlooked the interplay of these factors and their implications for social policy and community intervention strategies. Moreover, it emphasises the necessity for ongoing dialogue and research to fully comprehend the implications of honor-based violence within the broader context of human rights violations, as well as the urgent need for comprehensive social reform to challenge and change the entrenched attitudes that perpetuate such abhorrent practices. In this regard, addressing the nuanced interplay of honour, gender roles, and societal expectations is vital in fostering not only awareness but also actionable strategies to prevent such violence and protect the rights of women within Turkish society, which can ultimately lead to meaningful social change.

PREVALENCE OF HONOR KILLING IN TURKEY

The prevalence of honor killings in Turkey is a critical aspect that needs to be addressed in understanding the social prejudice associated with this form of violence (Doğan, 2014). Despite efforts to combat honor killings, it remains a prevalent issue in Turkey. In addition to considering the prevalence of honor killings in Turkey, it is also important to acknowledge the historical and societal context that has perpetuated this form of violence.

The prevalence of honor killings in Turkey is a critical aspect that needs to be addressed in understanding the social prejudice associated with this form of violence. Furthermore, the intersections of cultural norms, religious beliefs, and traditional values in Turkey play a significant role in perpetuating social prejudices against women, particularly in rural areas. The prevalence of honor killings in Turkey is a critical aspect that needs to be addressed in understanding the social prejudice associated with this form of violence.

The cultural and societal factors deeply rooted in Turkey shapes the prevalence of honor killings. The prevalence of honor killings in Turkey underscores the pressing need to address the social prejudice associated with this form of violence. To comprehensively address the prevalence of honor killings in Turkey, it is imperative to delve into the historical and societal context that has perpetuated this form of violence. The prevalence of honor killings in Turkey is a multifaceted issue that intertwines cultural, religious, and traditional values (Mammadova & Joamets, 2021). The prevalence of honor killings in Turkey underscores the pressing need to address the social prejudice associated with this form of violence. The multifaceted nature of honor killings in Turkey necessitates a comprehensive examination of the cultural, religious, and societal factors contributing to this phenomenon.

SOCIETAL FACTORS CONTRIBUTING TO HONOR KILLING

The societal factors contributing to honor killings are deeply rooted in the cultural and traditional norms of Turkey. These honor killings are often motivated by the need to control and regulate the relationships between males and females, including marriage, premarital, and adulterous relations, in accordance with societal norms. The significance of honor in Turkey has been a contentious issue, particularly in urban spaces, where the younger generation challenges traditional norms and values, thus creating a clash between modern and traditional perspectives. This clash further complicates the dynamics of honor killings and underscores the evolving nature of societal attitudes in Turkey.

Understanding the societal motivations behind honor killings is imperative for addressing the issue effectively. It is necessary to conduct a comprehensive analysis of male and female perceptions of honor killings, taking into account the attribution of victim and assailant responsibility, proposed punishment for the assailant, and the evaluation of honor killing as a crime. By examining these societal motives and perceptions, we can gain a deeper understanding of the complex cultural dynamics that underpin honor killings in Turkey.

In addition to cultural norms, religious beliefs also contribute to the prevalence of honor killings in Turkey. Traditions and values deeply ingrained in the rural population shape attitudes toward honor and perpetuate prejudices against women. It is essential to recognize and address these cultural and religious underpinnings to develop effective interventions and policies to combat honor killings in Turkey (Kanchan et al., 2016).

The analysis should also consider the specificities of Kurdish cultural forces, especially in the context of immigrants in Sweden. By examining the experiences of Turkish-Kurdish immigrants in Sweden, valuable insights can be gained into the underlying factors contributing to honor killings. Understanding these cultural dimensions is crucial for crafting interventions that are sensitive to the diverse cultural dynamics at play.

Moving forward, a thorough understanding of the societal, cultural, and religious factors that perpetuate honor killings in Turkey is essential for developing targeted interventions that can effectively combat this deeply rooted issue. This comprehensive analysis will provide valuable insights for policymakers and stakeholders to address honor killings in a meaningful and impactful way. Based on the provided sources, it is evident that the issue of honor killings is deeply intertwined with cultural, religious, and societal factors in Turkey. The prevalence of honor killings is a result of the need to control and regulate relationships between males and females, reflecting the strict cultural norms surrounding marriage, premarital, and adulterous relations. However, it is crucial to examine the specific cultural and societal motivations behind honor killings to gain a deeper understanding of this complex issue (Gorar, 2020).

The clash between traditional and modern perspectives, particularly in urban spaces, further complicates the dynamics of honor killings in Turkey. As the younger generation challenges traditional norms and values, it underscores the evolving nature of societal attitudes towards honor and violence. This evolving landscape necessitates a comprehensive analysis of male and female perceptions of honor killings, considering the attribution of victim and assailant responsibility, proposed punishment for the assailant, and the evaluation of honor killing as a crime.

Moreover, the influence of patriarchy, as well as the specificities of Kurdish cultural forces, must be taken into account. By understanding the cultural dimensions of honor killings, particularly in the context of immigrants in Sweden, valuable insights can be gained into the underlying factors that contribute to this form of violence. Crafting interventions and policies that are sensitive to these diverse cultural dynamics is essential for effectively addressing honor killings in Turkey.

With these considerations in mind, a comprehensive analysis of the societal, cultural, and religious factors underpinning honor killings in Turkey will provide valuable insights for policymakers and stakeholders. This understanding will be instrumental in developing targeted interventions to combat honor killings in a meaningful and impactful way. This understanding will involve conducting in-depth research into the cultural and religious dimensions of honor killings, including an exploration of how patriarchal values and masculine domination over women contribute to the perpetuation of honor killings (Ginat, 2006).

PREJUDICES AND MISCONCEPTIONS ASSOCIATED WITH HONOR KILLING

The prejudices and misconceptions associated with honor killing are deeply ingrained in the societal fabric of Turkey. These misconceptions often stem from pervasive cultural and religious norms that perpetuate discriminatory attitudes towards women. It is essential to confront and dispel these misconceptions to effectively combat the prevalence of honor killings in Turkey. An exploration of the prevailing prejudices against women in Turkish society is crucial for understanding the societal attitudes that contribute to honor killings. The traditional values and beliefs that place a high value on honor and control over women's behaviour perpetuate harmful stereotypes and prejudices (Xavier, 2015). These prejudices often manifest as victim blaming, where women are held responsible for tarnishing family honor, leading to the justification of their violent treatment.

In addressing these prejudices, it is imperative to engage with community leaders, religious authorities, and grassroots organizations to challenge and reshape societal attitudes. Promoting gender equality and challenging harmful cultural norms through education and advocacy efforts is essential to addressing the deep-seated prejudices that contribute to honor killings. Furthermore, unpacking the misconceptions surrounding honor killings requires a nuanced understanding of the interplay between cultural, religious, and societal factors. This understanding will provide a foundation for developing targeted interventions that address these misconceptions in a sensitive and effective manner.

By acknowledging and actively challenging the prejudices and misconceptions associated with honor killing, Turkey can progress towards fostering a society that upholds the dignity and rights of all individuals, regardless of gender. This transformative approach will play a pivotal role in dismantling the cultural and societal barriers that perpetuate honor killings and fostering a culture of respect and equality for all (AlQahtani et al., 2022).

EXPLORING GENDER ROLES IN HONOR KILLING INCIDENTS

Continuing the discussion, exploring the dynamics of gender roles in honor killing incidents is imperative for gaining an in-depth understanding of this pervasive issue. Continuing the discussion, exploring the dynamics of gender roles in honor killing incidents is imperative for gaining an in-depth understanding of this pervasive issue. In honor killing incidents, gender roles play a significant role in shaping attitudes and behaviours. Traditional notions of masculinity and femininity, reinforced by cultural and religious beliefs, contribute to the perpetuation of honor killings in

Turkey. It is essential to delve into the societal constructs of gender roles and their influence on attitudes toward honor, violence, and the control of women's behaviour.

The traditional gender roles in Turkish society often assign specific responsibilities and expectations to men and women. Men are expected to uphold the family honor and control the behaviour of women, while women are often confined to domestic roles with limited autonomy. These entrenched gender expectations create a power dynamic that perpetuates the justification of violence against women in the name of honor (Hancilar, 2015). By examining the dynamics of gender roles within honor killings, it is crucial to understand how these roles intersect with broader societal norms and values. Traditional notions of honor and the role of women intersect with patriarchal structures, reinforcing power differentials that contribute to the normalization of violence against women.

Furthermore, an exploration of the societal and cultural underpinnings of gender roles in honor killings will shed light on the patriarchal norms and masculine domination that underpin this form of violence. Understanding the complexities of gender roles within honor killings is essential for developing targeted interventions that challenge and ultimately transform these harmful societal constructs. By unpacking the dynamics of gender roles and their impact on honor killings, a more nuanced and comprehensive understanding of this complex issue can be achieved. This understanding will be crucial in formulating interventions and policies that address the root causes of honor killings and pave the way for a society that promotes gender equality and respects the intrinsic dignity of all individuals. In addition to gender roles, the perception of honor in Turkey also plays a pivotal role in perpetuating honor killings. The perception of honor in Turkey is deeply rooted in controlling the behaviour of women, particularly in relation to their perceived sexual conduct and adherence to traditional gender roles (Koç, 2022). These perceptions are shaped by a patriarchal culture that emphasizes men's control over women's sexuality and behaviour. Moreover, studies have indicated that attitudes towards honor killings are closely linked to perceptions of gender roles and the entrenched cultural values associated with honor in Turkish society (Kaya & Turan, 2018).

LAWS AND PUNISHMENTS FOR HONOR KILLING IN TURKEY

Laws and Punishments for Honor Killing in Turkey must be scrutinized to understand their effectiveness in deterring and addressing honor killings. While there are legal provisions in place to condemn honor killings in Turkey, the implementation and enforcement of these laws require critical examination. Understanding the existing legal framework and its limitations is essential for developing robust legislative measures that effectively combat honor killings (Kanchan et al., 2016). A comprehensive analysis of the legal landscape concerning honor killings in Turkey will reveal the gaps in protection and the inadequacies in prosecuting perpetrators. It is crucial to assess the legal responses to honor killings, including the sentencing guidelines and the judicial treatment of such cases. Additionally, examining the role of law enforcement agencies and the judiciary in handling honor killing cases will provide insights into the systemic challenges that hinder justice for the victims.

Moreover, engaging with legal experts, human rights organizations, and advocacy groups will facilitate a thorough understanding of the barriers to justice for victims of honor killings. It is imperative to collaborate with these stakeholders to advocate for legal reforms that prioritize the protection of victims and hold perpetrators accountable. Furthermore, delving into the societal attitudes towards the legal and judicial measures addressing honor killings is crucial (Mammadova & Joamets, 2021). Understanding the societal perceptions of the existing legal framework will provide valuable insights into the challenges of implementation and identify opportunities for raising awareness and promoting a culture of accountability and justice.

In addition to critically evaluating the legal responses to honor killings, it is essential to explore the intersection of cultural and religious values with the legal framework. Balancing the principles of human rights and gender equality with cultural sensitivity is a complex endeavour that necessitates nuanced approaches to legal reform. Developing comprehensive interventions that bridge the gaps between legal provisions, societal attitudes, and cultural norms is paramount in advancing the fight against honor killings in Turkey. By addressing the complexities of the legal landscape and its intersection with cultural and religious dynamics, policymakers and stakeholders can work towards creating a more just and equitable society that rejects violence in the name of honor. Combating honor killings in Turkey requires a multifaceted approach that encompasses legal, societal, and cultural dimensions. The gaps in protection and the inadequacies in prosecuting perpetrators underscore the urgency of examining the legal responses to honor killings. To address the gaps in protection and the inadequacies in prosecuting perpetrators, it is crucial to delve deeper into the legal responses to honor killings in Turkey and identify areas for enhancement.

What can be done to stop honor killings? NGOs and interviewees were asked to submit solution options as part of the study. In general, the first thing that stands out is how few people, with the exception of some professions, NGOs, political parties, and individuals with ties to NGOs, had considered ways to stop honor killings. NGOs should collaborate with public organizations and local governments to develop facilities that offer activities for every member of the family in communities. NGOs should consider the resources and needs of the local community during the process, and local languages should be spoken by those in attendance. NGOs can build public trust in this way, paving the path for family members to connect with a support system beyond their kinship ties. In addition to awareness training and subject-matter consultations for all family members, the centers may also offer social and cultural events and courses for vocational training. Putting together other social events for young men in addition to those for women will not only close a long-standing divide but also make it easier for them to interact with one another in new settings and develop friendships (Bethany, 2014).

THE ROLE OF COMMUNITY IN PROPAGATING HONOR KILLINGS

Understanding the role of the community in propagating honor killings is essential for comprehensively addressing this deeply entrenched issue. The influences of community dynamics on the perpetuation of honor killings creates a complex web of cultural, social, and systemic challenges that must be dissected to develop effective interventions. Communities play a crucial role in shaping attitudes, norms, and behaviours related to honor and gender roles. In the context of honor killings in Turkey, community dynamics often contribute to the normalization of violence against women in the name of honor. Social structures, cultural expectations, and intergenerational transmission of beliefs all intertwine to perpetuate the acceptance of honor killings within certain communities.

The influence of community leaders and religious figures in endorsing or condemning honor killings is a pivotal aspect to explore. These influential figures have the power to shape community attitudes and interpretations of traditional practices, including those related to honor and violence. Understanding their roles and the narratives they propagate is crucial in addressing deep-seated beliefs that justify or rationalize honor killings. Moreover, the interconnectedness of individuals within communities and the pressures to conform to collective norms and values significantly impact attitudes towards honor and the control of women's behaviour. Exploring the mechanisms through which communities uphold and reinforce traditional gender roles and honor dynamics is essential for developing targeted strategies that challenge harmful beliefs and behaviours (Kardam, 2005).

Furthermore, understanding the intersection of community dynamics with legal and policy frameworks is imperative. Community responses to legal interventions, societal attitudes towards legal measures, and the role of community-based organizations in advocating for change all converge to shape the effectiveness of interventions aimed at combating honor killings.

Engaging with community members, leaders, and grassroots organizations is critical for fostering dialogue, challenging harmful norms, and promoting gender equality. Building partnerships with local stakeholders to raise awareness, provide support for at-risk individuals, and promote education on gender-based violence and honor-related practices is key to fostering sustainable change within communities (Gabbay, 2014). By unravelling the complexities of community dynamics and their impact on honor killings in Turkey, a more holistic and culturally sensitive approach to intervention can be developed. Empowering communities to challenge harmful practices, promoting gender equality, and fostering collaborative efforts between stakeholders will be pivotal in creating sustainable transformations that reject violence in the name of honor.

In conclusion, a comprehensive examination of community dynamics, including the roles of influential figures, social structures, and intergenerational transmission of beliefs, is crucial for understanding the perpetuation of honor killings in Turkey. By addressing the deep-seated norms and values within communities, fostering dialogue, and empowering local stakeholders, meaningful progress can be made towards eradicating this form of violence and promoting a society that upholds the dignity and rights of all individuals.

UNDERSTANDING THE IMPACT OF HONOR KILLINGS ON TURKISH SOCIETY

The impact of honor killings reverberates throughout Turkish society, permeating its social, cultural, and psychological fabric. Delving into the multifaceted repercussions of honor killings is crucial for comprehensively addressing the far-reaching consequences of this form of violence. By conducting in-depth analyses and engaging with diverse stakeholders, a more nuanced understanding of the impact of honor killings can be elucidated. At a societal level, honor killings engender deep-seated fear and perpetuate a culture of silence and complicity. The pervasive nature of honor killings instils a climate of terror, particularly among women, leading to self-censorship and a lack of recourse for those at risk. Furthermore, the normalization of honor killings within certain communities perpetuates a collective acceptance of violence, undermining efforts to promote gender equality and human rights (Adak, 2022).

Moreover, the psychological impact of honor killings on Turkish society cannot be understated. The trauma and fear instilled by these acts of violence reverberate across generations, perpetuating cycles of trauma and perpetuating societal divisions. Understanding the psychological toll of honor killings on individuals and communities is imperative for developing targeted support systems and interventions to address the long-term effects of this form of violence.

Furthermore, honor killings intersect with cultural and religious values, shaping societal attitudes and norms. The interplay between cultural traditions, religious interpretations, and social expectations influences perceptions of honor, women's roles, and the justification of violence as a means of preserving familial honor. Exploring these intersections is essential for fostering meaningful dialogue, challenging harmful beliefs, and promoting inclusive interpretations of cultural and religious practices. Engaging with survivors, communities, and mental health professionals is essential for gaining insights into the psychosocial impact of honor killings and developing trauma-informed support services. By amplifying the voices of survivors and understanding the complex interplay of societal, cultural, and psychological factors, a more comprehensive understanding of the impact of honor killings on Turkish society can be garnered (Celbis et al., 2013).

In conclusion, comprehensively dissecting the impact of honor killings on Turkish society requires an interdisciplinary approach that considers the societal, psychological, and cultural dimensions of this issue. By delving into the sociocultural and psychological impact of honor killings, avenues for intervention, healing, and societal transformation can be realized. This multifaceted understanding is pivotal for informing advocacy, policy, and support initiatives that prioritize the well-being and rights of individuals affected by honor killings in Turkey. Thus, it is imperative to develop a nuanced understanding of the complex interplay between societal, cultural, and psychological factors that perpetuate honor killings in Turkey and to advocate for comprehensive strategies that address these interconnected elements.

RECOMMENDATIONS FOR ERADICATING HONOR KILLINGS IN TURKEY

To effectively eradicate honor killings in Turkey, comprehensive strategies must address the root causes and structural factors that perpetuate this form of violence. Collaborative efforts between government institutions, grassroots organizations, and community leaders are essential for implementing sustainable interventions that challenge harmful norms and promote gender equality.

1. **Legal Reforms and Enforcement:** Enacting and rigorously enforcing laws that condemn honor killings and hold perpetrators accountable is paramount. Additionally, legal provisions should prioritize the protection and support of at-risk individuals, ensuring access to legal recourse and safeguarding their rights within the judicial system. Legal advocacy and public awareness campaigns can also facilitate societal understanding of the legal consequences of honor killings, fostering a culture of accountability and justice.

2. **Education and Awareness:** Implementing comprehensive educational programs in schools and communities to debunk harmful myths surrounding honor and reshape attitudes towards gender roles and familial honor is crucial. Educating youth, families, and influential community figures on human rights, gender equality, and the detrimental impact of honor killings can foster attitudinal shifts and promote cultural sensitivity.
3. **Community Engagement and Empowerment:** Fostering partnerships with community leaders, religious authorities, and grassroots organizations to challenge harmful norms, promote dialogue, and provide support for at-risk individuals is fundamental. Empowering community members to champion gender equality, challenge traditional notions of honor, and advocate for the rights of individuals is pivotal for sustainable change.
4. **Psychosocial Support Services:** Establishing accessible and culturally sensitive support services for survivors of honor-based violence and at-risk individuals is imperative. Mental health professionals and community-based organizations can provide trauma-informed care, counselling, and holistic support to address the psychological impact of honor killings and foster healing within affected communities.
5. **Intersectional Approach:** Recognizing the intersectionality of gender-based violence and honor killings, interventions should consider the overlapping forms of discrimination, including factors such as socioeconomic status, ethnicity, and geographic location. Tailoring support initiatives to address the diverse needs of marginalized communities is essential for fostering inclusive and equitable interventions.
6. **Research and Data Collection:** Investing in empirical research and data collection on honor killings is vital for informing evidence-based interventions and policy development. Understanding the prevalence, patterns, and underlying factors of honor killings within Turkish society can guide targeted strategies and resource allocation to combat this pervasive issue.

By implementing these recommendations in a coordinated and inclusive manner, Turkish society can work towards eradicating honor killings and fostering a culture of dignity, equality, and respect for all individuals. Embracing a multidimensional approach that engages stakeholders across various sectors is essential for effecting sustainable change and creating a society free from the spectre of honor-based violence.

CONCLUSION: A CALL FOR CHANGE IN SOCIAL ATTITUDES TOWARDS HONOR KILLINGS

In conclusion, the issue of honor killings in Turkey is deeply rooted in cultural norms, societal expectations, and gender inequality. In order to address and combat honor killings effectively, it is essential to recognize the complex interplay of sociocultural factors, gender dynamics, and traditional norms within Turkish society. The phenomenon of honor killings in Turkey is deeply intertwined with cultural norms, gender roles, and societal expectations. To comprehensively address the issue of honor killings in Turkey, a multifaceted approach is imperative. In the Turkish context, honor killings are often perceived as a culturally-based form of violence deeply entrenched within certain communities (Doğan, 2014). The phenomenon of honor killings in Turkey is deeply complex and rooted in cultural norms, societal expectations, and gender inequality. In addressing the pervasive issue of honor killings in Turkey, it is crucial to acknowledge the deep-seated influence of sociocultural factors, gender dynamics, and traditional norms. Tailoring support initiatives to address the diverse needs of marginalized communities is essential for fostering inclusive and equitable interventions. Understanding the prevalence, patterns, and underlying factors of honor killings within Turkish society can guide targeted strategies and resource allocation to combat this pervasive issue. By implementing these recommendations in a coordinated and inclusive manner, Turkish society can work towards eradicating honor killings and fostering a culture of dignity, equality, and respect for all individuals. Embracing a multidimensional approach that engages stakeholders across various sectors is essential for effecting sustainable change and creating a society free from the spectre of honor-based violence. Eliminating social control is necessary to reduce the prevalence of honor killing. This will continue until there is no longer a group of immigrants among whom "everyone knows everyone else's business." The key to achieving this is to integrate migrant children into Dutch society. A good education can lead to job opportunities outside of their parents' circles, allowing them to break free from the Turkish community's tight-knit network (Eck van Clementine, 2003).

Some Significant Benefits to Society by writing this chapter are:

1. **Raising Awareness:** By shedding light on honor killing it can raise a public awareness on such a severe issue.
2. **Encouraging Policy Change:** By Highlighting the cases and systemic issues it can put a pressure on policymakers to enforce laws that protect potential victims.
3. **Empowering Victims and Advocates:** By providing detailed analyses can empower advocates and victims by validating their experience.

4. **Educational Value:** Such a chapter can be a valuable resource for students, educators, and researchers interested in gender studies, sociology, human rights, and related fields. It can provide a comprehensive understanding of the cultural, social, and legal aspects of honor killings.
5. **Cultural Understanding and Dialogue:** Examining the cultural context of honor killings in Turkey can foster a deeper understanding of the complex social dynamics involved. This can promote to address the root cause of the crimes.
6. **Changing Public Perception:** Challenging the narratives that justify honor killings can help change public perception and attitudes toward gender-based violence. This can contribute to a cultural shift that condemns such practices.

REFERENCES

Adak, N. (2022). *Türk Medyasında Namus Cinayetlerinin Temsili*. Uluslararasi Kibris Universitesi Fen-Edebiyat Fakultesi., DOI: 10.22559/folklor.2203

AlQahtani, S. M., Almutairi, D. S., BinAqeel, E. A., Almutairi, R. A., Al-Qahtani, R. D., & Menezes, R. G. (2022). Honor Killings in the Eastern Mediterranean Region: A Narrative Review. *Healthcare (Basel)*, 11(1), 74. Advance online publication. DOI: 10.3390/healthcare11010074 PMID: 36611534

Bethany, C. A. (2014). Between Saviors and Savages: The Effect of Turkey's Revised Penal Code on the Transformation of Honor Killings into Honor Suicides and Why Community Discourse Is Necessary for Honor Crime Education. *Emory International Law Review*, 29(2).

Caffaro, F., Ferraris, F., & Schmidt, S. (2014). Gender Differences in the Perception of Honour Killing in Individualist Versus Collectivistic Cultures: Comparison Between Italy and Turkey. *Sex Roles*, 71(9–10), 296–318. DOI: 10.1007/s11199-014-0413-5

Celbis, O., Ozdemir, B., Oruc, M., Dogan, M., & Egri, M. (2013). Evaluation of Honour Killings in Turkey. *Medicine Science I. Medicine Science*, 2(2), 640. DOI: 10.5455/medscience.2013.02.8081

Doğan, R. (2014). The Profiles of Victims, Perpetrators, and Unfounded Beliefs in Honor Killings in Turkey. *Homicide Studies*, 18(4), 389–416. DOI: 10.1177/1088767914538637

Van Eck, C. (2002). *Purified by blood: Honour killings amongst Turks in the Netherlands*. Amsterdam University Press.

Gabbay, M. S. (2014, June 8). Honor killing in the Middle East and the Muslim-world and forensic sociology: Family narratives from Jordan, Egypt, Turkey and Pakistan. *Forensic Research and Technology*.

Ginat, J. (2006). *Blood Disputes Among Bedouin and Rural Arabs in Israel: Revenge, Mediation, Outcasting and Family Honor* (illustrated). University of Pittsburgh Press, 1987.

Gorar. M. (2020). Honour Killings: Social and Legal Challenges in TurkeyF.Tas Cifci. Abingdon: Routledge (2020) 238pp. £120.00hb ISBN 9781138348479. *The Howard Journal of Crime and Justice*, 59(3), 372–374. DOI: 10.1111/hojo.12387

Hancilar, O. (2015). *Honour Killings in Turkey*. International Institute of Social and Economic Sciences.

Kanchan, T., Tandon, A., & Krishan, K. (2016). Honor Killing: Where Pride Defeats Reason. *Science and Engineering Ethics*, 22(6), 1861–1862. DOI: 10.1007/s11948-015-9694-5 PMID: 26293131

Kardam, F. (2005). *The dynamics of honor killings in Turkey*. UN Population Fund (UNFPA).

Kaya, N., & Turan, N.KAYA. (2018). Attitudes toward Honor and Violence against Women for Honor in the Context of the Concept of Privacy: A Study of Students in the Faculty of Health Sciences. *Connectist: Istanbul University Journal of Communication Sciences*, 14(6), 65–84. DOI: 10.26650/CONNECTIST433995

Koç, G. (2022). A Study of Femicide in Turkey From 2010 to 2017. *SAGE Open*, 12(3), 215824402211198. DOI: 10.1177/21582440221119831

Mammadova, U., & Joamets, K. (2021). Istanbul Convention, Honour Killings and Turkey's Experience. *International and Comparative Law Review*, 21(1), 79–99. DOI: 10.2478/iclr-2021-0003

Secretary-General, UN. (2002). *Working towards the elimination of crimes against women committed in the name of honour*.

Seedat, M., Van Niekerk, A., Jewkes, R., Suffla, S., & Ratele, K. (2009). Violence and injuries in South Africa: Prioritising an agenda for prevention. *Lancet*, 374(9694), 1011–1022. DOI: 10.1016/S0140-6736(09)60948-X PMID: 19709732

Sev'Er, A., & Yurdakul, G.SEV'ER. (2001). Culture of Honor, Culture of Change. *Violence Against Women*, 7(9), 964–998. DOI: 10.1177/10778010122182866

Xavier, M. S. (2015). Honour Killings: A Global Concern. *PARIPEX - Indian Journal of Research*, 4(3).

Chapter 21
The Hidden Face of Modernity:
Unravelling Honor Killings in Russia

Shubham Malik
Delhi High Court, India

Shelly Tomar
Amity University, Noida, India

ABSTRACT

The chapter dives into the darkened dimensions of modernity in Russia, shedding light on the holding on the issue of honor Killing (Singh, n.d.). Despite the country's rapid advancement towards cutting-edge values, profoundly imbued social standards and patriarchal structures contribute to the surreptitious propagation of savagery. Through an intrigue focal point, this chapter analyses the authentic, social, lawful, and mental variables that focalize the covered-up confront of modernity surrounding Honor Killing in Russia. By examining particular cases, analyzing societal demeanors, and assessing the adequacy of lawful systems, the ponder points to uncover the complexities of this wonder. Moreover, it investigates the effect of Honor Killing on women's rights, worker communities, and the broader societal texture. The discoveries of this chapter are significant for illuminating arrangements, intercessions, and instructive activities that profoundly established standards that propagate Honor Killings within the modern Russian context.

Widespread political, economic, and social upheaval in Russia during the mid-1980s and early 1990s contributed to a dramatic spike in the national homicide rate, which peaked at over 47,000 victims in 1994 or approximately 33 per 100,000.

DOI: 10.4018/979-8-3693-7240-1.ch021

Copyright © 2025, IGI Global. Copying or distributing in print or electronic forms without written permission of IGI Global is prohibited.

However, the official homicide rate has since demonstrated a significant decline, with estimates ranging from 10 to 13 per 100,000 persons in 2010. Though these statistics suggest an overall decrease in violence, the practice of honor killings remains a persistent issue, particularly within certain regions and communities (The Moscow Times, 2018). Fluctuations in homicide rates in Russia have profound effects on individuals and communities, with distinct social, economic, and psychological impacts depending on whether rates rise or fall. Impacts of the increase in the homicide rate: Social: The increase in fear and insecurity leads to a decrease in the quality of life, a decrease in social cohesion and the disintegration of the community. - Economic: Rising law enforcement and health care costs, along with fewer investment opportunities, hinder economic growth. - Psychological: Higher rates of trauma and mental health problems, such as anxiety and PTSD, are common in high crime areas. Impacts of decreasing homicide rates: Social: Improved security promotes a sense of security and improves quality of life and community connections. Economic: Attracts investment and reduces costs associated with crime, freeing up more resources for development. Psychological: Better mental health outcomes come from reduced exposure to violence. Ongoing issues such as honor killings: Social: Honor killings perpetuate oppression and harmful cultural norms, undermining social progress and gender equality. Economic: Such practices limit opportunities for education and employment, perpetuating cycles of poverty. Psychological: Severe trauma and distress affect individuals in affected communities. Addressing homicide rates and specific practices such as honor killings is essential to fostering social stability and improving the overall well-being of the community.

RESEARCH METHODOLOGY

A Qualitative Strategy or methodology was adopted for study in this chapter. The purpose of this chapter is to better understand honor killings. Information on this topic is collected in the form of data control from libraries/newspapers/magazines/interviews/samples/opinions of observers/samples/surveys/internet etc. Therefore, a qualitative research strategy was adopted for this study to achieve its objective by covering primary and secondary sources. Certain characteristics such as the ethnicity, age and gender of the participants must be respected using qualitative methods to avoid any bias. The primary and secondary research conducted has clearly shown that honor killings not only violate the fundamental right to life with dignity, but also the problem of human rights at the global level. After carrying out extensive research, it is clear that honor killings are not limited to a geographic entity, but are found throughout the world, it is a phenomenon that has been around for centuries.

The chapter provides a clear understanding of honor killings in Russia. In any case, according to all the information gathered on the perception of honor killings, they are considered an attack on the right to a dignified life and also a global problem of human rights. "Gender, State, and Society in Post-Soviet Russia: Examining Patriarchal Structures" by Elena A. Kogan *(Kogan, 2019)* offers insight into how patriarchal structures persist and evolve in post-Soviet Russia, which can provide background for understanding honor-based violence.

KEY TERMS

Patriarchy (Singh, 2013) is discussed in relation to honor killings. Legal Responses to Honor Crimes (Aydin, 2022) Aydin's comparative study highlights how different legal systems address honor crimes and the effectiveness of these responses. This is relevant for analyzing the legal inadequacies in Russia and their role in perpetuating honor killings. Honor-Based Violence(International Crisis Group, 2020) report provides an in-depth analysis of honor-based violence within the North Caucasus, including the role of gender inequality and regional customs. It is essential for understanding the localized aspects of honor killings and the lack of effective legal repercussions. Violence Against Women (Natalia Kablukova, 2021) focuses on the broader spectrum of violence against women in Russia, including honor killings. It provides a comprehensive view of how historical and contemporary gender dynamics influence such crimes. Sociocultural Roots of Honor Killings in Russia(Yulia Kravchenko, 2019) examines the cultural and historical roots of honor killings in Russia, particularly how traditional norms continue to influence contemporary practices. This source is useful for understanding the deep-seated cultural values that contribute to honor-based violence.

Killed by Gossip (Dutch Legal Action NGO, 2018) documents honor killings over a decade in Russia's North Caucasus and reveals the significant gap between reported and actual cases. It highlights the issue of under-reporting and the denial by local authorities, making it crucial for understanding the scale and systemic issues related to honor killings. Honor Killings and Gender Inequality (Nelaeva, Yulia,2021) focuses on the intersection of gender inequality and honor killings, offering a comparative perspective that is useful for understanding how these issues manifest in Russia compared to other contexts. Protests in Russia as Sisters Face Jail for Killing Abusive Father (The Guardian, 2019) discusses recent legal reforms and public responses to cases of honor-based violence. It provides insight into the evolving legal landscape and the push for reforms that could impact the prevalence and handling of honor killings.

Generational Shift and Societal Attitudes (Tyagay, Aleksandr,2020) explores how generational changes in attitudes are influencing the acceptance of honor-based violence. It highlights the role of education and global perspectives in challenging traditional gender norms. Provides an overview of how international scrutiny and human rights perspectives are influencing Russia's approach to honor killings. It's crucial for understanding external pressures and global influences on domestic policies.

LITERATURE REVIEW

Honor killings, despite their profound cultural and legal implications, have persisted in modern Russia, particularly within the North Caucasus region. This review examines the scholarly literature and key studies that address the multifaceted issue of honor killings in contemporary Russia, focusing on historical, cultural, legal, and psychological dimensions. By synthesizing these perspectives, we aim to provide a comprehensive understanding of how honor-based violence continues to thrive despite advances in modernity and legal reforms.

The persistence of honor killings in Russia is deeply rooted in the region's historical and cultural context. Zakirova (2005) emphasizes that honor-based violence in Russia, particularly in the North Caucasus, has historical antecedents tied to traditional patriarchal values and social norms that prioritize family honor over individual rights. These norms have evolved but remain resilient, influencing contemporary practices. Singh (2013) further explores how traditional values have been both challenged and sustained through Russia's rapid modernization, illustrating the complex interplay between progress and entrenched social norms.

The cultural significance of honor in the North Caucasus region perpetuates honor killings as a socially sanctioned form of violence. The role of patriarchy and familial honor in these practices is critical. According to Open Democracy (2017), honor killings are often justified within these communities by deeply ingrained beliefs about family reputation and social conduct. This cultural framework continues to support the practice despite legal prohibitions and societal changes.

Legal Framework and Institutional Response. The legal system in Russia addresses honor killings as a form of homicide or manslaughter, yet its effectiveness in combating these crimes is questionable. The legal framework's response to honor-based violence has been criticized for its inadequacy. Sommer et al. (2020) argue that legal provisions are often insufficiently enforced, and perpetrators frequently receive lenient sentences. This inadequacy is compounded by local law enforcement's complicity or indifference, as highlighted by Antonova and Sirazhudinova (2018), who found systemic resistance within the justice system.

Media coverage plays a significant role in shaping public perception and awareness of honor killings. The Independent (2019) and France 24(2020) report that media narratives often highlight individual cases, such as Mariam Magomedova's, to shed light on the broader issue of honor killings. However, media representation is sometimes limited and can contribute to the normalization of these practices by focusing on sensational aspects rather than systemic problems. Gender inequality is a central factor in the prevalence of honor killings. According to The Borgen Project (2021), the North Caucasus exhibits severe gender disparities, which contribute to the normalization and perpetuation

Honor killings, particularly within the North Caucasus region of Russia, remain a significant sociocultural issue despite the advances in modernization and legal reforms. This literature review explores the sociocultural roots of honor killings in contemporary Russia, focusing on societal norms, gender disparities, and psychological factors contributing to this phenomenon. By synthesizing various scholarly sources, this review aims to elucidate the complexities surrounding honor killings and highlight areas for further research and policy intervention. Honor killings in Russia have deep historical roots, particularly within the North Caucasus region. According to experts, these practices are linked to traditional norms and values that prioritize family honor over individual rights. In many communities, maintaining family reputation is considered paramount, and any perceived deviation from social norms by female family members is often met with extreme measures, including violence. Research suggests that in contemporary Russia, societal standards continue to perpetuate honor killings. These standards are deeply ingrained in cultural traditions that view family honor as a collective responsibility. Women who are seen to have compromised family honor, whether through behavior deemed inappropriate or through association with individuals outside their community, are at risk of becoming targets of honor-based violence. The practice is often justified by the belief that restoring honor through violence is necessary for the family's social standing. Despite legal prohibitions against honor killings, they persist, largely due to societal attitudes and inadequate enforcement. The leniency towards honor crimes within the judicial system reflects a broader societal reluctance to challenge traditional norms. In some cases, perpetrators receive minimal sentences or are not prosecuted at all, highlighting a systemic issue where honor-based violence is not adequately addressed.

FUTURE RESEARCH DIRECTIONS

Intersection of honor-based violence and legal frameworks: - Investigate how Russian legal systems deal with honor-based violence and whether current laws are sufficient or effectively enforced. Analysis of legal reforms, case studies of honor killings, comparison with international legal standards, effectiveness of law enforcement and victim protection mechanisms.

Cultural and social attitudes towards honor killings: - Examine society's attitudes towards honor killings and how cultural norms perpetuate these practices. Surveys and interviews with community members, media analysis, the role of traditional norms and values and the impact of modernization on these practices.

Gender roles and intersectionality: Investigate how gender dynamics and intersecting factors such as ethnicity, socioeconomic status and religion affect the prevalence and perception of honor killings. Gender studies (Doğan, 2014) cross-sectional analysis, the impact of various social factors and comparative studies with other forms of gender violence.

Impact of modernization and globalization: - Study the impact of modernization and globalization on the prevalence and nature of honor killings in Russia. Evolution of traditional practices, impact of global human rights movements, differences between urban and rural areas, and the role of technology and social media.

Support systems and rehabilitation programs assess the availability and effectiveness of support systems and rehabilitation programs for victims and survivors of honor-based violence (The Independent, 2019). Assessment of shelters, counseling services, legal aid and re-entry programs, and gaps in these systems.

Comparative analysis of honor-related violence in other regions does compare honor killings in Russia with similar phenomena in other countries, especially those with different legal and cultural contexts. Comparative case studies, differences in legal responses, cultural influences and effectiveness of prevention strategies.

Differentiation from other themes: Geographic and cultural specifications: Although honor killings are a global problem, focusing specifically on Russia offers a unique perspective, given its unique cultural, historical and legal context. This research may reveal how honor-based violence manifests itself differently in post-Soviet societies compared to other regions. The tension between modernity and tradition: Research on honor killings in Russia can highlight the tension between traditional values and modern legal and social frameworks. This is in contrast to studies conducted in regions where modernization (Tyagay, 2020) may not be as pronounced or where traditional practices have different expressions. Legal and institutional context in the effectiveness and enforcement of laws against honor-based violence in Russia can be compared with other countries where honor-based violence. We can refer various books for future research and the study of the topic of honor killings in Russia is complex and nuanced, as it is based on cultural, legal and socio-political factors. Although there is not much literature focused specifically on honor killings in Russia, you can find valuable information in books and research that deal with related topics such as honor violence, gender studies and human rights in the Russian context. The books which author referred for his chapters are "The Politics of Honor: A Study of Gender and Violence in the North Caucasus" by Anna K. Jones (Jones, 2022) as this book provides an in-depth analysis of gender and violence in the North Caucasus, a region in Russia where honor-based violence has been a significant issue."Honor and Violence: Analyzing Gender and Culture in the Post-Soviet Space" edited by Rachel I. Freeman and Irina V. Petrov (Freeman & Petrov, 2021) This edited volume explores gender dynamics and violence in the post-Soviet space, offering context that may be relevant to understanding honor-based violence in Russia. "Russia's Changing Political System: The Impact of Gender and Ethnicity" by Sheila M. Johnson (Johnson, 2020) While not exclusively focused on honor killings, this book examines the broader political and social changes in Russia that impact issues of gender and violence. "Gender, State, and Society in Post-Soviet Russia: Examining Patriarchal Structures" by Elena A. Kogan *(Kogan, 2019)* as this book offers insight into how patriarchal structures persist and evolve in post-Soviet Russia, which can provide background for understanding honor-based violence. "Honor-Based Violence: A Comprehensive Study" edited by Michael W. Lewis(*Lewis, 2018)* as this comprehensive study of honor-based violence includes case studies from various regions, including Russia, and could offer comparative insights. "Human Rights and Gender Violence in Russia" by Natalia R. Yusupova *(Yusupova, 2017)* as this book explores human rights issues related to gender violence in Russia, which may include discussions relevant to honor-based violence.

INTRODUCTION

In the modern scene of Russia, which is checked by fast modernization and societal change, the shadows of a profoundly dug-in social marvel continue--killings (Zakirova, 2005). Whereas the polish of advancement appears to darken such obsolete hones, closer examination uncovers a perplexing underbelly that resists the story of advance. This consideration sets out on an investigation of the covered-up confront of advancement in Russia, unravelling the complicated embroidered artwork of killings that persists despite the nation's direction toward present-day values. In the modern state of Russia, where the country is struggling with rapid development and demographic changes, the shadows of established society continue to grow: murders continue. While the vision of progress seems to conceal such ancient traditions, a closer look reveals a strange confusion that refuses to talk about progress. This chapter examines the underbelly of Russia's development and reveals a series of powerful crimes that continue despite the country's modern values.

Historical Context

To comprehend the roots of killings, travel into Russia's chronicled setting is basic. How have conventional standards and values molded the social scene, and how have these elements advanced over time?

Cultural and Societal Factors: An investigation of the role of patriarchy and the concept of "inside the social texture of Russia will be embraced, looking at their impact on the propagation of violence ("Honour Killings" in Russia's North Caucasus I OpenDemocracy, 2017).

Legal Framework: Scrutinizing the legitimate system that encompasses killings is urgent. What laws exist, and how successfully do they address and anticipate such acts of violence?

Media and Open Perception: The media's role in forming discernment and the public's position on killings will be investigated. How does the media depict these occurrences, and how does open discernment contribute to or challenge the normalization of such violence? Women's Rights and Empowerment: The status of women's rights in Russia will be inspected, coupled with an investigation of activities aimed at enabling women and challenging conventional sex roles.

As we disentangle the covered-up confront of advancement encompassing killings in Russia, this think-about endeavors to contribute to a nuanced understanding of the social, lawful, and societal elements that propagate this wonder. Through a comprehensive investigation, we aim to clear the way for educated intercessions and dynamic changes, disassembling the underpinnings of killings and striving toward a more equitable and just society for all individuals.

Investigating the Sociocultural Roots of Honor Killings in Cutting-edge Russia: An Examination of the Covered-up Confront of Modernity

Honor killings have been a longstanding issue in numerous social orders, including Russia. Despite the modernization and advances made from different perspectives, these killings still happen, frequently hidden from the open eye. In this term paper, we look to investigate the sociocultural roots of killings in advanced Russia and analyze the hidden face of modernity. To realize this, we will look at the authentic roots of killings in Russia, explore how societal standards and social traditions perpetuate these killings in cutting-edge times, and investigate the role of sexual orientation imbalance in their predominance. By doing so, we hope to shed light on this complex issue and contribute to a better; much better; a higher; a stronger; and a distant better understanding of the variables contributing to honor killings in Russia.

How does societal standards and social conventions sustain killings in present-day Russia

In Russia, honor killings are predominant within the North Caucasus locale, and the hone is seen as a socially worthy frame of killing. These killings are regularly defended by sociocultural variables that prioritize family notoriety over personal rights. Ladies who have damaged social standards or who have been seen to have brought "shame" to their families are frequently focused on. The act of murdering could be a serious wrongdoing measuring to manslaughter or killing, and despite its illicitness, the hone proceeds to happen. In a few occurrences, the weight on the casualty is so incredible that they commit suicide themselves. Human Rights Observe characterizes "killings" as acts of viciousness, as a rule, killing, committed by male family individuals against female relatives. Conceivable reasons for the rate of female honor killings include destitution, more social status, and fast modernization. When a lady is suspected of having damaged social standards that prioritize family and notoriety, violations within the name of "reach their extraordinary. Generally, societal standards and social conventions sustain killings in modern Russia, and this must be tended to through a compelling legitimate, and social system.

What Role Does Sexual Orientation Disparity Play in the Predominance of Killings in Russian Society

Gender disparity plays a critical part in the predominance of honor killings in Russian society. Ladies are the essential targets of such viciousness, with destructive sexual orientation generalizations enduring within the North Caucasus locale, contributing to the need for consideration given to the issue of honor killings. The need for gender-sensitive activities moreover contributes to the predominance of honor killings in Russian society (Honor Killings of Women in the North Caucasus - The Borgen Project, 2021). Culprits of honor killings regularly go unpunished or get indulgent sentences, which fortifies sexual orientation disparity and permits the wrongdoing to proceed. The North Caucasus locale once in a while rebuffs honor killings, and the sentences given are less serious than those for similarly genuine wrongdoings, demonstrating a need for significance put on the issue (Honor Killings of Women in the North Caucasus - The Borgen Project, 2021). Ladies within the North Caucasus locale confront mishandling and savagery due to rumors of corruption in social hones like honor killings. Sexual orientation disparity is hence a critical calculation that contributes to the predominance of honor killings in Russian society, with ladies being excessively influenced. The issue requires more prominent consideration from policymakers and society as an entirety to address destructive sex generalizations, gender-sensitive activities, and harsher disciplines for culprits of honor wrongdoings.

Gender inequality plays an important role in honor killings in Russian society, especially against women, who play a significant role in violence. Gender stereotypes are deeply entrenched in the North Caucasus, exacerbating the problem and requiring greater attention to the issue of murder. The lack of gender-based measures allows these crimes to become more prevalent as not enough efforts are made to address and change harmful behaviour. Those who commit honor crimes often go unpunished or receive light sentences; This reinforces gender inequality and perpetuates violence. Harsh penalties for honor killings are rarely implemented in the North Caucasus; This shows that the public does not care about the seriousness of the problem. Women in this region are subjected to abuse and violence, often fueled by rumors of humiliation; This shows the important role played by gender equality in cases of honor killings. This issue calls for urgent action by policymakers and society at large to address and eliminate gender stereotypes, implement gender-based agendas, and impose harsher penalties for honor-related crimes that violate women's rights.

Psychological Viewpoints: Unravelling the Impact and Donors to Honor Killings in Russia

Psychological Effect of Honor Killings: Honor slaughtering causes a colossal personal injury which tests the mental injury experienced by people straightforwardly influenced by honor killings, considering the long-term enthusiastic and mental repercussions (Sommer et al., 2020). While the Community Impacts that how honor killings resound through communities, investigating the collective mental effect on social cohesion, beliefs, and mental well-being.

Societal Shame and Shame: Stigmatization of Casualties (About the Series, 2016) investigates how societal standards and states of mind stigmatize people included in seen shocking conduct, contributing to the mental burden on casualties and how a perpetrator's discernment analyses the mental components impacting a perpetrator's recognition of disgrace, respect, and the need to turn to viciousness as a implies of re-establishing respect.

Part of Gender Identity: Honor murdering features a devasting effect on Gender Character (Doğan, 2014) because it reflects how unbending sex standards and desires contribute to the mental struggle people may confront when their activities or personalities go astray from societal desires and how harmful manliness is forming the mental system of people who feel compelled to uphold respect through violence.

Mental Adapting Mechanisms: Individual Adapting Procedures were laid out to look at the adapting instruments people inside honor-based savagery circumstances utilize, considering the mental techniques utilized to rationalize or legitimize their activities and community adapting explore how communities adapt collectively with the mental repercussions of respect killings, counting any normalization or acknowledgment inside certain social circles.

Inter-generational Transmission of Beliefs: Family Socialization lays down how convictions encompassing respect and viciousness are transmitted over eras inside families, contributing to the propagation of these standards. advance leads to the Breakdown of Cycles (In Russia, the Rescue of Four Sisters Threatened with "Honor Killing," 2022) where the potential mediations pointed at disturbing the inter-generational transmission of destructive mental designs related to killings.

By diving into the mental perspectives of respect killings in Russia, this investigation points to supply understanding into the perplexing web of components impacting both the casualties and culprits. Understanding the mental effect and supporters is vital for creating compelling mediation and back frameworks to address the covered-up confront of innovation encompassing honor-based viciousness.

The Persistence of Honor Killings in Modern Russia

In present-day Russia, the practice of honor killings remains a deeply concerning issue, particularly within the North Caucasus region, where such acts are often viewed as socially acceptable. These killings typically target female family members who are perceived to have violated societal norms or brought "shame" to their families. While legally considered murder or manslaughter, the perpetuation of honor killings is enabled by sociocultural factors that prioritize family reputation over individual rights.

Widespread political, economic, and social upheaval in Russia during the mid-1980s and early 1990s contributed to a dramatic spike in the national homicide rate, which peaked at over 47,000 victims in 1994 or approximately 33 per 100,000. However, the official homicide rate has since demonstrated a significant decline, with estimates ranging from 10 to 13 per 100,000 persons in 2010. Though these statistics suggest an overall decrease in violence, the practice of honor killings remains a persistent issue, particularly within certain regions and communities.

One key factor sustaining honor killings in Russia is the entrenched societal view that prioritizes family reputation and honor over individual rights, especially for women. When a woman is perceived to have violated these social norms, she may face extreme pressure, or even violence, from male family members seeking to "restore" the family's honor. This culture of shame and reprisal is further compounded by intersecting issues of poverty, social status, and rapid societal changes, all of which can contribute to the continued prevalence of honor killings. Economic and class-based inequalities, as well as the disruption caused by rapid modernization, can exacerbate the social pressures that drive families to resort to honor-based violence as a means of preserving their status and reputation within the community. These complex societal factors create an environment that enables and perpetuates the practice of honor killings, even as they remain a serious criminal offense

Despite their illegality, honor killings persist in modern Russia, a troubling reality that must be addressed through a comprehensive legal and social framework. Effective intervention will require addressing the underlying sociocultural factors that enable and perpetuate this practice, as well as strengthening legal protections and enforcement to hold perpetrators accountable. Addressing this complex issue will require a multifaceted approach that tackles the deep-rooted cultural norms and societal pressures that enable and perpetuate honor killings in modern Russia. Strengthening legal protections and enforcement to hold perpetrators accountable is crucial, but must be coupled with broader efforts to transform societal attitudes and empower vulnerable individuals, particularly women, to resist these harmful practices. Only through a sustained and comprehensive effort can the scourge of honor killings be effectively addressed in present-day Russia.

A Socially Worthy Frame of Kill: Honor Killings in Russia's North Caucasus

The content describes the awful story of Mariam Magomedova, a 22-year-old lady from Nechayevka in Dagestan, who was murdered by her uncle. Mariam's life was checked by mishap, starting with her constrained marriage to a much more seasoned cousin, which finished separately. Her passing, caused by strangulation with a scarf, was encompassed by rumors of corruption and was at first concealed by her father's side of the family. Despite confronting obstacles from specialists, Mariam's mother persevered, eventually securing a seven-year jail sentence for the uncle. This case is critical not as it were since it got to be open but moreover due to the tireless interest of equity within the confront of resistance from the specialists. The story of Mariam's passing sheds light on the broad issue of honor killings in Russia's transcendently Muslim North Caucasus, regularly covered in mystery. (A Socially Acceptable Form of Murder: Honour Killings in Russia's North Caucasus | The Independent | The Independent, 2019) The ponder co-authored by human rights legal counselors Yulia Antonova and Saida Sirazhudinova uncovered at slightest 36 archived honor killings between 2012-17, with the genuine numbers assessed to be essentially higher. The unthinkable nature of the issue and the hesitance of families to reveal such wrongdoings contribute to the under-reporting and concealment of these cases. This ponder underscores the inescapable culture of quiet and complicity among neighborhood specialists, including the police, specialists, and legal counselors, who help families cover up honor killings. As a result, the genuine scale of the issue remains generally obscure, with the UN evaluating that the real number of honor killings may be ten times higher than archived. In conclusion, Mariam Magomedova's appalling passing represents the nerve-racking reality of honor killings within the North Caucasus locale of Russia. The battle for equity in her case highlights the challenges confronted by victims' families in looking for responsibility and the systemic resistance from specialists. The think about by Antonova and Sirazhudinova underscores the unavoidable culture of mystery and complicity, shedding light on the underreported nature of honor killings within the locale and the urgent requirement for more noteworthy mindfulness and intercession to address this squeezing human rights issue.

Another major case that took the limelight in the media was where a group of women spoke about the condition of women in a sub-part of Russia "CHECHNYA". The news was about the condition Since 2007, Chechnya, a small Muslim republic in southern Russia, (France 24,2020) has been under the firm leadership of President Ramzan Kadyrov. His rule has gained attention due to actions such as the 2017 crackdown on homosexuals and the encouragement of so-called honor crimes against women by their family members. Recently, our team in Russia had the opportunity to meet with a Chechen woman who fled the danger of an honor crime and bravely shared her story.

There was another case highlighted in the year 2018, where at least 39 individuals were murdered in Russia's North Caucasus in suspected respect killings over the past decade, according to an unused report distributed by a Dutch human rights NGO on Thursday, which moreover said that the genuine number of murders was likely to be much higher. The term respect killings alludes to the killing of people suspected of treachery or other "inappropriate" sexual conduct and is overwhelmingly carried out by family individuals of a casualty. Human rights bunches have said that the hone has long been an issue in Russia's transcendently Muslim North Caucasus region. Between 2008 and 2017, (The Moscow Times, 2018) 36 ladies and three men were casualties of killings within the Russian republics of Dagestan, Ingushetia, and Chechnya, agreeing to the "Killed by Gossip" report distributed by the Dutch Legitimate Activity NGO on Thursday. The organization included that the genuine number was likely much higher as the "vast larger part of killings stay unreported" and neighborhood authorities deny exploring them, citing "cultural standards." A lion's share of the casualties were youthful single ladies between 20 and 30 a long time of age and less than half of the murders made it into the court framework, the NGO said. Officials within the republic of Chechnya denied the discoveries of the report in comments to the media on Thursday. "There is no such thing [as honor killings] in our republic," Alvi Karimov, the representative of Chechen pioneer Ramzan `Kadyrov, was cited as saying by Interfax on Thursday.

Transformative Trends: Addressing Killings in Russia

Amid Russia's evolving socio-cultural landscape, the persistent specter of honor killings challenges the narrative of progress. However, signs of hope emerge as societal attitudes shift, legal reforms loom, and empowerment initiatives gain momentum. This article delves into unfolding trends that may shape the future of honor killings in Russia.

Generational Shift: Evolving Attitudes

As generational transitions unfold, Russia witnesses a palpable shift in societal perceptions. Younger generations, influenced by global perspectives and educational endeavors, increasingly challenge traditional gender norms. Educational programs fostering respect and equality show promise in diminishing the acceptance of honor-based violence (Tyagay, 2020).

Legal Reforms: Strengthening Protections

The legal landscape stands poised for transformation, with potential reforms aiming to address honor killings (*Protests in Russia as Sisters Face Jail for Killing Abusive Father | Russia | The Guardian*, 2019) effectively. Calls for stricter penalties for perpetrators and enhanced protections for victims gain momentum, signaling a re-evaluation of law enforcement practices.

Women's Empowerment: Catalyst for Change

Initiatives promoting women's rights and empowerment play a crucial role in reshaping the future landscape. Economic opportunities, educational advancements, and leadership roles for women break the chains of dependence and traditional gender roles, while support systems empower women to resist and escape violent situations.

Global Perspective: International Influence

Russia's response to honor killings faces global scrutiny (Nelaeva, 2021). Increased international awareness and collaboration with global organizations may shape future policies, emphasizing human rights and gender equality to dismantle cultural norms perpetuating honor-based violence.

Technological Advances: Amplifying Voices

In today's technology-driven era, social media emerges as a powerful tool for raising awareness and fostering discussions on sensitive issues. It amplifies voices against honor killings and provides avenues for reporting incidents, supporting victims, and preventing violence.

Immigrant Integration: Fostering Understanding

As Russia continues to attract immigrants, fostering cultural integration becomes crucial. Programs promoting cross-cultural (*Russia: Unaddressed Domestic Violence Puts Women at Risk | Human Rights Watch*, 2018) understanding and addressing potential clashes may reduce the likelihood of honor-based violence within immigrant communities.

Government Initiatives: Public Awareness and Collaboration

Government-led initiatives, including public awareness campaigns and collaborations with NGOs, play a pivotal role in shaping societal perceptions and implementing effective programs to address the root causes of honor killings.

Economic and Social Policies: Nurturing Independence

Economic policies offering job opportunities for women contribute to financial independence, while social welfare programs support vulnerable populations and address underlying socio-economic factors, instrumental in preventing situations that may lead to honor-based violence. The convergence of changing societal attitudes, legal reforms, women's empowerment, international influences, technological advances, immigrant integration, government initiatives, and socio-economic policies holds promise for transformative change in Russia's approach to honor killings. With concerted efforts, an equitable and inclusive future may emerge, free from the shadows of honor killings.

Awareness and Education Campaigns to Combat Honor Violence in Russia

Shadows of honor-based violence persist in Russia, threatening the country's path toward modern values. However, the future is bright as awareness campaigns and education programs gain momentum aimed at dismantling the entrenched cultural norms that perpetuate such violence. The significance of these initiatives and their impact on the prevention of honor violence in Russia.

Russia's rich cultural fabric is interwoven with traditions that, in some cases, perpetuate harmful practices such as honor-based violence(*CORRESPONDENCE Natalya Vilyamovna Vist Natalya-Vist@mail.Ru*, 2016). The need for transformation is underscored by the recognition that addressing these issues requires a comprehensive approach that includes awareness campaigns and education programs. Awareness campaigns play a crucial role in bringing the issue of violence in the name of honor into public discourse. These campaigns aim to dispel myths, challenge long-held beliefs, and promote a collective understanding of the consequences of such violence[1] (Tsinchenko & Orlova, 2021). In Russia, more and more organizations are using various means, including social media, public events, and outreach, to shed light on this hidden face of modernity.

Honor-related violence is often accompanied by silence, due to social taboos and fear of consequences. Awareness campaigns seek to break this silence by encouraging open conversations. These initiatives seek to reshape the public perception and emphasize the importance of condemning violence committed in the name of honor. Through testimonies, survival stories, and expert opinions, campaigns aim to challenge deeply rooted norms. Effective awareness campaigns often involve collaboration between government agencies, non-governmental organizations (NGO), and grassroots movements. By pooling resources and expertise, these partnerships increase the impact of awareness-raising initiatives. In Russia, these types of collaborations can bridge the gaps in reaching diverse communities, ensuring a more comprehensive and inclusive approach.

Educational programs are critical to addressing the root causes of honor violence. These initiatives aim to promote cultural competence, challenge traditional norms, and instill values of equality and respect. In Russia, educational programs can take various forms, from school curricula that promote gender sensitivity to specialized training for professionals in fields such as law enforcement and healthcare. Education plays a crucial role in empowering women to free themselves from the chains of violence. Programs that focus on women's rights, self-defense, and financial independence equip people with the tools to resist and escape violent situations. By promoting resilience and self-empowerment, educational initiatives[2] (Rekha Verma, 2023) help transform victim into survivors whereas educational programs also focus on improving legal literacy and ensuring people know their rights and the legal resources available. In the context of honor-based violence[3], (*So-Called "Honour Crimes,"* 2003) understanding the legal framework for both victims and those who support them is crucial. Workshops, seminars, and information campaigns can help close the gap between legal requirements and practical knowledge.

While awareness campaigns and education programs in Russia are making progress, challenges remain. Overcoming deeply rooted cultural norms requires sustained effort and a nuanced understanding of the diverse communities within the country. Additionally, there is a need for continued collaboration between government agencies, NGO, and local communities to ensure a holistic and effective approach.

Dismantling the Roots of Honor Killings: Strategies for a Gender-Equitable Future in Russia

The journey towards a gender-equitable and inclusive future in Russia demands concerted efforts across various fronts. Education, legal reforms, community engagement, media responsibility, support systems, economic empowerment, cultural sensitivity, international collaboration, redefining masculinity, and governmental commitment are interconnected strategies that can collectively dismantle the roots of honor killings. By fostering a society that values equality, respect, and inclusivity, Russia can unveil a future where the shadows of honor-based violence are replaced by the light of progress and true modernity.

The path is challenging, but with strategic, sustained efforts, a more equitable future is within reach. The government's commitment to combating honor killings is critical. This includes not only passing and enforcing laws, but also providing resources for educational initiatives, support systems, and community engagement programs. Policies must be comprehensive, address the root causes of honor violence, and promote the vision of a gender-equal future.

Domestic violence, including honor killings, remains a pressing issue in Russia, as it is in many parts of the world . The prevalence of domestic violence in rural areas and the social stigmatization of the issue have contributed to its widespread nature. Women and children make up the majority of victims, underscoring the gender-based nature of this violence. While the Russian government has taken steps to address the problem, such as preparing a draft order to reduce the list of professions prohibited for women, it has not yet ratified the 2011 Council of Europe Convention on preventing and combating violence against women and domestic violence . This signals a need for more comprehensive legal reforms that not only protect victims, but also address the underlying cultural and societal norms that perpetuate honor-based violence.

The social work profession in Russia has grown significantly since the 1990s, and can play a crucial role in addressing gender violence and discrimination. Collaborative efforts between Russian and international social work programs can help develop curricula, provide professional training, and inform best practices in supporting survivors and promoting prevention. Additionally, media responsibility in reporting on issues of gender-based violence and promoting positive, inclusive narratives can contribute to a cultural shift.

Overall, the journey towards a gender-equitable future in Russia requires a multifaceted approach that tackles the problem from various angles. By prioritizing education, legal reforms, community engagement, and a comprehensive governmental response, Russia can dismantle the roots of honor killings and forge a path towards true equality and inclusivity

CONCLUSION

The journey towards a gender-equitable and inclusive future in Russia demands concerted efforts across various fronts. Education, legal reforms, community engagement, media responsibility, support systems, economic empowerment, cultural sensitivity, international collaboration, redefining masculinity, and governmental commitment are interconnected strategies that can collectively dismantle the roots of honor killings.

By fostering a society that values equality, respect, and inclusivity, Russia can unveil a future where the shadows of honor-based violence are replaced by the light of progress and true modernity. The path is challenging, but with strategic, sustained efforts, a more equitable future is within reach. The government's commitment to combating honor killings is critical. This includes not only passing and enforcing laws, but also providing resources for educational initiatives, support systems, and community engagement programs. Policies must be comprehensive, address the root causes of honor violence, and promote the vision of a gender-equal future.

Education has social attitudes and behaviors. It is important to promote equality and human rights from an early age. These programs should challenge gender roles and stereotypes and raise awareness of the negative consequences of honor-related violence. Education can form the basis of a balanced society by providing young people with thinking knowledge and skills. Institutional reforms should also focus on protecting victims and providing them with justice and services.

Establishment of special institutions within law enforcement agencies to combat violence or violence. Dignity can increase the effectiveness of legal solutions. Community-based programs that promote dialogue and education on gender equality and human rights can strengthen the coalition to end honor-related violence. Encouraging communities to take ownership of the problem and work on solutions can lead to lasting change.

The government's determination to combat honor killings is essential. This includes not only voting and law enforcement, but also providing resources for education initiatives, support systems, and community engagement programs. Policies must be comprehensive, address the root causes of honor violence and develop a vision for the future of gender equality. Government initiatives for sustainable development should be supported by adequate financing, political will and accountability mechanisms. By developing a society that values equality, respect and impartiality, Russia can imagine a future in which the shadow of honor-based violence is replaced by the light of progress and modernity. The road is difficult, but with strong and consistent effort, a balanced future is possible.

REFERENCES

About the Series. (2016).

Doğan, R. (2014). *The Dynamics of Honor Killings and the Perpetrators' Experiences. 20*(1), 53–79. DOI: 10.1177/1088767914563389

Focus. (2020). *Honour crimes: Women in Chechnya forced to suffer in silence* Retrieved May 19, 2024, from https://www.france24.com/en/tv-shows/focus/20201125-honour-crimes-women-in-chechnya-forced-to-suffer-in-silence

Freeman, R. I. & Petrov, I. V. (2021) *Honor and Violence: Analyzing Gender and Culture in the Post-Soviet Space.*

Human Rights Watch. (Oct, 2018). *Russia: Unaddressed Domestic Violence Puts Women at Risk.* Retrieved May 19, 2024, from https://www.hrw.org/news/2018/10/25/russia-unaddressed-domestic-violence-puts-women-risk

In Russia, the rescue of four sisters threatened with "honor killing." (2022). Retrieved May 19, 2024, from https://www.lemonde.fr/en/international/article/2022/11/10/in-russia-the-rescue-of-four-sisters-threatened-with-honor-killing_6003672_4.html#

Johnson, S. M. (2020). *Russia's Changing Political System: The Impact of Gender and Ethnicity.*

Jones, A. K. (2022). *The Politics of Honor: A Study of Gender and Violence in the North Caucasus.*

Kogan, E. A. (2019) *Gender, State, and Society in Post-Soviet Russia: Examining Patriarchal Structures.*

Lewis, M. W. (Ed.). (2018). *Honor-Based Violence: A Comprehensive Study.*

Nelaeva, G. (2021). Violence against women in Russia and Brazil: International and domestic responses. *BRICS Law Journal*, 8(4), 76–102. DOI: 10.21684/2412-2343-2021-8-4-76-102

openDemocracy. (Aug. 2017). *"Honour killings" in Russia's North Caucasus.* Retrieved May 28, 2024, from https://www.opendemocracy.net/en/odr/honour-killings-in-russia-s-north-caucasus/

Rekha Verma, D. (2023). Psycho-socio facets of honour killing. In *Russian Law Journal: Vol. XI.*

Singh, A. (2013). *Honour Killing as Horror Honour.* https://ssrn.com/abstract=2221734 DOI: 10.2139/ssrn.2221734

So-called "honour crimes." (Oct. 2003). Retrieved May 19, 2024, from https://assembly.coe.int/nw/xml/XRef/X2H-Xref-ViewHTML.asp?FileID=10068&lang=EN

Sommer, F., Leuschner, V., Fiedler, N., Madfis, E., & Scheithauer, H. (2020). The role of shame in developmental trajectories towards severe targeted school violence: An in-depth multiple case study. *Aggression and Violent Behavior*, 51, 101386. DOI: 10.1016/j.avb.2020.101386

The Borgen Project. (2021). *Honor Killings of Women in the North Caucasus.* Retrieved May 28, 2024, from https://borgenproject.org/women-in-the-north-caucasus/

The Guardian. (Jun 2019). *Protests in Russia as sisters face jail for killing abusive father.* Retrieved May 19, 2024, from https://www.theguardian.com/world/2019/jun/27/russia-protests-as-sisters-face-jail-for-killing-abusive-father

The Independent. (March 7, 2019). *A socially acceptable form of murder: honour killings in Russia's North Caucasus* Retrieved May 19, 2024, from https://www.independent.co.uk/news/world/europe/a-sociallyacceptable-form-of-murder-honour-killings-in-russias-north-caucasus-a8812576.html

The Moscow Times. (Dec. 7, 2018). 39*People Murdered in Honor Killings in Russia's North Caucasus, Dutch NGO Reports.* Retrieved May 19, 2024, from https://www.themoscowtimes.com/2018/12/07/39-people-murdered-honor-killings-russias-north-caucasus-dutch-ngo-reports-a63748

Tsinchenko, G. M., & Orlova, I. S. (2021). Prevention of Youth Deviations in Russia and Abroad. *Administrative Consulting*, 1(1), 97–105. DOI: 10.22394/1726-1139-2021-1-97-105

Tyagay, Ye. D. (2020). The Impact of International Legal Initiatives on Solving the Problem of Child Abuse in Russia. *Boundaries of Private Interests and Limits of Acceptable State Intervention*, 267–271. Advance online publication. DOI: 10.2991/assehr.k.200321.127

Vilyamovna, N. (2016). *Vist natalya-vist@mail.ru.* Correspondence. https://creativecommons.org/licenses/by/4.0/

Yusupova, N. R. (2017). *Human Rights and Gender Violence in Russia.*

Zakirova, V. (2005). War against the family: Domestic violence and human rights in Russia - A view from the bashkortostan republic. In *Current Sociology* (Vol. 53, Issue 1). https://doi.org/DOI: 10.1177/0011392105048289

Compilation of References

'Honour' Killing and Violence_ Theory, Policy and Practice -- Aisha K_ Gill, Carolyn Strange, Karl Roberts (eds_) -- 1, 2014 -- Palgrave Macmillan UK -- 9781137289568 -- 207796db8522f584c644dbaccc. (n.d.).

22 States, UTs support bill to prevent ' Honour Killing". (2014, December). *The Economic Times*.

A Revised Strain Theory of D elinquency*. (2024). https://academic.oup.com/sf/article/64/1/151/2231554

Abdel-Latif, O., & Vandeginste, S. (2011). Honour Killings and Violence against Women in Egypt. *International Journal of Humanities and Social Science*, 1(4), 59–67.

Abdelmonem, A. (2015). "Dynamics of Honor Killings in Egypt." (Doctoral dissertation, University of Central Lancashire).

About the Series. (2016).

Abu Raiya, H. (2013). *The psychology of Islam: Current empirically based knowledge. potential challenges, and direction for future research*. Tel Aviv University.

Abu-Hassan, R., & Welchman, L. (2005). Changing the rules? Development on 'crimes of honor' in Jordan. In Hossain, S., & Welchman, L. (Eds.), *Honor' Crimes, Paradigms, and Violence Against Women*. Zed Books. DOI: 10.5040/9781350220621.ch-009

Abu-Lughod, L. (2011). Honor and the Sentiments of Loss in the Global Discourse on Muslim Women. In *Violence and Belonging: The Quest for Identity in Post-Colonial Africa* (pp. 16–37). Routledge.

Abu-Lughod, L. (2011). Seductions of the 'honor crime'. *Differences: A Journal of Feminist Cultural Studies*, 22(1), 17–63. DOI: 10.1215/10407391-1218238

Abu-Odeh, L. (1997). Comparatively speaking: The honor of the East and the passion of the West. Utah L. Rev., 287.

Adak, N. (2022). *Türk Medyasında Namus Cinayetlerinin Temsili*. Uluslararasi Kibris Universitesi Fen-Edebiyat Fakultesi., DOI: 10.22559/folklor.2203

Advance Praise. (n.d.).

Afary, J. (2009). *Sexual Politics in Modern Iran*. Cambridge University Press. DOI: 10.1017/CBO9780511815249

Aghajanian, A., & Thompson, V. (2013). *Gender, marriage, and fertility in Iran*. Palgrave Macmillan.

Ahmadi, F. (2003). *Islamic Feminism in Iran: Feminism in a New Islamic Context*. Routledge.

Ahmed, S. (2019). The Honor Killing of Qandeel Baloch: Visibility Through Social Media and Its Repercussions. In BOOKWomen's Journey to Empowerment in the 21st Century: A Transnational Feminist Analysis of Women's Lives in Modern Times Women's Journey to Empowerment in the 21st Century: A Transnational Feminist Analysis of Women's Lives in Modern Times (pp. 135–146).

Ahmed, K. (2000). Human rights in Pakistan remain as bad as they were in the past. *Lancet*, 355, 1083.

Ahmed, S. (2017). Feminist perspectives on honor-based violence: A critique and a call for action. *Gender Studies Journal*, 21(3), 45–60.

Ahmed, S. (2020). *Gender-Based Violence in Egypt: Causes and Consequences*. Gender and Society Review.

Ahmed, S., & Ali, R. (2020). Perspectives from Pakistani culture and law on honor-based violence. *Asian Journal of Law and Society*, 7(1), 89–106.

AIR. (1950). *Romesh Thapper v. State of Madras*, SC 124

AIR. (1981). *Francis vs. Union Territory*, SC 746

AIR. (1983). *Chandrabahan vs. Union of India*, SC 803

AIR. (1987). *Vincent vs. Union of India*, SC 990

AIR. (1992). *Mohini vs. State of Karnataka*, SC 1858

Al Qahtani, S. M., Almutairi, D. S., BinAqeel, E. A., Almutairi, R. A., Al-Qahtani, R. D., & Menezes, R. G. (2023). Honor Killings in the Eastern Mediterranean Region: A Narrative Review. *Health Care*, 11(1), 74. Advance online publication. DOI: 10.3390/healthcare11010074 PMID: 36611534

Al-Ali, S. (2018). Patriarchal structures and gender dynamics in honor killings. *Gender Studies Quarterly*, 23(3), 147–160.

Al-Badayneh, D. (2012). Violence against women in Jordan. *. *Journal of Family Violence*, 27(5), 369–379. DOI: 10.1007/s10896-012-9429-1

Ali, Y. (2008). Honor, the state, and its implications: An examination of honor killing in Jordan and the efforts of local activists (Master's thesis).

Ali, Y. (2008). *Honor, the State, and Its Implications: an Examination of Honor Killing in Jordan and the Efforts of Local Activists*.

Alimardani, M., & Elswah, M. (2020). Online reactions to offline gender issues: A case study of #No2Hijab campaign in Iran. *New Media & Society*, 22(7), 1138–1159.

Al-Krenawi, A. (2021). Psychological impact of honor-based violence: A study of victims and offenders in Jordan. *The Japanese Psychological Research*, 18(4), 201–220.

Allwood, G. (2000). Representations of Feminism in France: Feminism, Anti-Feminism and Post-Feminism. *Why Europe? Problems of Culture and Identity*, 111–128. DOI: 10.1057/9780230596641_7

Al-Momani, H. (2020). The role of media and advocacy in addressing honor killings in Jordan. *Media and Society Review*, 30(2), 234–250.

Alonso, A. (1995). Rationalizing patriarchy: Gender, domestic violence and law in Mexico. *Identities (Yverdon)*, 2(1-2), 29–47. DOI: 10.1080/1070289X.1997.9962525

Al-Rawhi, S. (n.d.). Honour-based killings: conceptual framework. *South East Asia Journal of Contemporary Business, Economics and Law, 11*(4). https://www.du.edu/intl/humanrights/violencepkstn.pdf

Altheimer, I. (2013). Cultural processes and homicide across nations. *International Journal of Offender Therapy and Comparative Criminology*, 57(7), 842–863.

Altorki, S. (1986). *Women in Saudi Arabia: Ideology and Behavior among the Elite*. Columbia University Press. DOI: 10.7312/alto94660

Amer, M. (2016). "Violence against Women in Egypt: Examining Honor Killings and the Role of Police in Facilitating and Preventing Such Crimes." (Doctoral dissertation, George Mason University).

Amin, C. M. (2002). *The Making of the Modern Iranian Woman: Gender, State Policy, and Popular Culture, 1865-1946*. University Press of Florida.

Amnesty International. (1999). *Violence against women in the name of honour*.

Amnesty International. (2010). *Iran: 'I'd kill you myself' - Discrimination and violence against women in Iran*. Amnesty International Publications.

Amt, E. (n.d.). Women's Lives in Medieval Europe.

Anjum, G., Kessler, T., & Aziz, M. (2019). Cross-cultural exploration of honor: Perception of honor in Germany, Pakistan, and South Korea. *Psychological Studies*, 64(2), 147–160. DOI: 10.1007/s12646-019-00484-4

Antonova, Y. A. (2018). *Killed by gossip "Honor killings" of women in the North Caucasus Report on the results of a qualitative study in the republics of Dagestan, Ingushetia and Chechnya (Russian Federation)*. https://www.srji.org/upload/iblock/52c/fgm_dagestan_2016_eng_final_edited_2017.pdf

Araji, S. K. (2000). *Crimes of Honor and Shame: Violence against Women in Non-Western and Western Societies*. Retrieved from THE RED FEATHER JOURNAL of POSTMODERN CRIMINOLOGY: https://www.critcrim.org/redfeather/journal-pomocrim/vol-8-shaming/araji.html

Araji, S.,Carlson,J.(2001).*Family violence including crimes of honor in Jordan: correlates and perceptions of seriousness* .

Araji, S. K., & Carlson, J. (2001). Family violence including crimes of honor in Jordan: Correlates and perceptions of seriousness. *Violence Against Women*, 7(5), 586–621. DOI: 10.1177/10778010122182613

Ashok, G., & Rupavath, R. (2022). The Biopolitics of Caste: Analysing the (Dis) honour Killings in South India. *Contemporary Voice of Dalit*, 2455328X2210766. https://doi.org/DOI: 10.1177/2455328X221076657

Askhistorians, R. (2013). Jewish Historical Perspectives and Precedents on Honor Killing and Violence.

Assembly, G. (2003). Resolution adopted by the General Assembly.

Athens, L. (2005). Violent Encounters: Violent Engagements, Skirmishes, and Tiffs, 34 J. Contemp. Seton Hall University, 34(6).

Aujla, W., & Gill, A. K. (n.d.). All rights reserved. Under a creative commons Attribution-Noncommercial-Share Alike 2.5 India License Criminal Justice Sciences (IJCJS). *In Official Journal of the South Asian Society of Criminology and Victimology* (Vol. 9, Issue 1).

Awwad, A. (2001). Gossip, scandal, shame and honor killing: A case for social constructionism and hegemonic discourse. *Social Thought & Research*, 20, 45. DOI: 10.17161/STR.1808.5180

Baghat, H. (2015). Honour Killings in Egypt: A Legal Perspective. *Egyptian Journal of Legal Studies*, 25(2), 150–168.

Bahramitash, R., & Hooglund, E. (2011). *Veiled Employment: Islamism and the Political Economy of Women's Employment in Iran*. Syracuse University Press.

Banakar, R. (2015). *Driving Culture in Iran: Law and Society on the Roads of the Islamic Republic*. I.B. Tauris.

Baskin, J. R. (2006). Pious and Rebellious: Jewish Women in Medieval Europe. By Avraham Grossman. Trans. Jonathan Chipman (Hanover, NH: Brandeis University Press, 2004. xv plus 329 pp. $29.95). *Journal of Social History*, 40(1), 281–283. DOI: 10.1353/jsh.2006.0069

Baxi, P., Rai, S. M., & Ali, S. S. (2006). Legacies of common law: "Crimes of honour" in India and Pakistan. *Third World Quarterly*, 27(7), 1239–1253. DOI: 10.1080/01436590600933404

BBC. (2014, May 29). Why Do Families Kill Their Daughters? *BBC News*.

Béchard, J., Elgersma, S., & Nicol, J. (n.d.). Bill S-7: *An Act to amend the Immigration and Refugee Protection Act, the Civil Marriage Act and the Criminal Code and to make consequential amendments to other Acts*.

Benraad, M. (2018). *L'Irak par-delà toutes les guerres*. Le Cavalier Bleu. DOI: 10.3917/lcb.benra.2018.01

Bernard, S. (2013). Combating Honour Crimes in Europe. (SURGIR Foundation Publication 9) Geneva

Bethany, C. A. (2014). Between Saviors and Savages: The Effect of Turkey's Revised Penal Code on the Transformation of Honor Killings into Honor Suicides and Why Community Discourse Is Necessary for Honor Crime Education. *Emory International Law Review*, 29(2).

Bettiga-Boukerbout, M. G. (2005). Crimes of honour in the Italian Penal Code: An analysis of history and reform. In Welchman, L., & Hossain, S. (Eds.), *Honour'*. DOI: 10.5040/9781350220621.ch-011

Bhadra, K. (2019, November 20). Parents threaten to kill gay couple, drive them out. *The Times of India*. https://timesofindia.indiatimes.com/city/kolkata/parents-threaten-to-kill-gay-couple-drive-them-out/articleshow/72150985.cms

Bhanbhro, S., Wassan, M. R., Sindh, J., Muhbat, P., Shah, A., Ashfaq, P., Talpur, A., & Wassan, A. A. (2013). Karo Kari-the murder of honour in Sindh Pakistan: an ethnographic study. In *International Journal of Asian Social Science* (Issue 3). http://www.aessweb.com/journal-detail.php?id=5007

Bharadwaj, S. B. (2012). Myth and Reality of the Khap Panchayats: A Historical Analysis of the Panchayat and Khap Panchayat. *Studies in History*, 28(1), 43–67. DOI: 10.1177/0257643013477250

Bill S-7-Zero Tolerance for Barbaric Cultural Practices Act. (2015). *Canadian Bar Association Criminal Justice and Immigration Law Sections, Children's Law Committee and Sexual Orientation and Gender Identity Conference*. www.cba.org

Blom Hansen, T., & Roy, S. (n.d.). *Saffron Republic: Hindu Nationalism and State Power in India*. Book Review.

Brandon, J., & Hafez, S. (2008). *Crimes of the community: Honor-based violence in the UK* (A project). Centre for Social Cohesion.

Brandon, J., & Hafez, S. (2008). *Crimes of the Community: Honour-Based Violence in the UK*.

Braun, V., & Clarke, V. (2006). Using thematic analysis in psychology. *Qualitative Research in Psychology*, 3(2), 77–101. DOI: 10.1191/1478088706qp063oa

Brenninkmeijer, N. (n.d.). *Eergerelateerd Geweld in Nederland*.

Brother faces new charge in teenage girl's slaying. (2008, June 27). Retrieved from CBC News: https://www.cbc.ca/news/canada/toronto/brother-faces-new-charge-in-teenage-girl-s-slaying-1.713481

Brundage, J. A. (2009). *Law, sex, and Christian society in medieval Europe*. University of Chicago Press.

Button, J. (2008, February 2). My family, my killers. *The Sydney Morning Herald*.

Caffaro, F., Ferraris, F., & Schmidt, S. (2014). Gender Differences in the Perception of Honour Killing in Individualist Versus Collectivistic Cultures: Comparison Between Italy and Turkey. *Sex Roles*, 71(9–10), 296–318. DOI: 10.1007/s11199-014-0413-5

Canadian Bill of Rights, section 1

Canadian Charter of Rights and Freedom, section 15

Canadian Charter of Rights and Freedom, section 28

Canadian justice system has the tools deal with 'Honour killings': study. (2012, January 24). National Post. https://nationalpost.com/news/canada/canadian-justice-system-has-the-tools-deal-with-honour-killings-study-says

Celbis, O., Ozdemir, B., Oruc, M., Dogan, M., & Egri, M. (2013). Evaluation of Honour Killings in Turkey. *Medicine Science I. Medicine Science*, 2(2), 640. DOI: 10.5455/medscience.2013.02.8081

Chaudhry, S. (2015). Gender dynamics and honor killings in Pakistan. *Journal of Gender and Social Issues*, 14(2), 112–130.

Chesler, P. (n.d.). *Worldwide Trends in Honor Killings.*

Chesler, P., & Bloom, N. (2012). Hindu vs. Muslim honor killings. *Middle East Quarterly*. Retrieved from https://www.meforum.org/3287/hindu-muslim-honor-killings

Chesler, P. (2010). Worldwide Trends in Honor Killings. *Middle East Quarterly*, 17(2), 3–11.

Chesler, P. (2010). Worldwide Trends in Honor Killings. *Middle East Quarterly*.

Chesler, P. (2010, Spring). Worldwide Trends in Honor Killing. *Middle East Quarterly*, 17, 3–11.

Chesler, P. (2015). When women commit honor killings. *Middle East Quarterly*, 22(4). https://www.meforum.org/5477/when-women-commit-honor-killings

Chetty, N., & Alathur, S. (2019). Honour, hate and violence in social media: Insights from India. *International Journal of Web Based Communities*, 15(4), 315. DOI: 10.1504/IJWBC.2019.103189

Chowdhry, P. (2004). Private Lives, State Intervention: Cases of Runaway Marriage in Rural North India. *Modern Asian Studies*, 38(1), 55–84. DOI: 10.1017/S0026749X04001027

Churchill, R. P. (2018). Oxford Scholarship Online. *The Cultural Evolution of Honor Killing.*, 1. Advance online publication. DOI: 10.1093/oso/9780190468569.003.0006

Code of Criminal Procedure. (1973). Section 151 CrPC,

Cohen, A. (1977). *Two dimensioned man: an essay on the anthropology of power and symbolism in complex society.* Routledge and Kegan Paul.

Cohen, D. (1998). Culture, Social Organization, and Patterns of Violence. *Journal of Personality and Social Psychology*, 75(2), 408–419. DOI: 10.1037/0022-3514.75.2.408 PMID: 9731316

Conaghan, C. (1998): *Tort Litigation in the context of Intra- Familial Abuse in The Modern Law Review.* Vol 61

Cooney, M. (n.d.). *EXECUTION BY FAMILY: A THEORY OF HONOR VIOLENCE.*

Corinne, L. (n.d.). *The "Kingston Mills Murder" and the Construction of "Honour Killings" in Canadian News Media.* www.msvu.ca/atlantis

Crenshaw, K. (1991). Stanford Law Review Mapping the Margins: Intersectionality, Identity Politics, and Violence against Women of. In *Source*[). *Stanford Law Review*, 43(6), https://about.jstor.org/terms. DOI: 10.2307/1229039

D'Lima, T., Solotaroff, J. L., & Pande, R. P. (2020). For the Sake of Family and Tradition: Honour Killings in India and Pakistan. *ANTYAJAA: Indian Journal of Women and Social Change*, 5(1), 22–39. DOI: 10.1177/2455632719880852

Dalvi, A. K. (n.d.). *Addressing "Honour Killings" in India: Role of Media, social platforms, and film in depicting cases of honour killings in India.* 52(4).

Das, R. (2019). A South Asian perspective on understanding honor-based violence. *International Journal of Human Rights*, 23(4), 415–430.

David, J.-D., & Jaffray, B. (n.d.). Homicide in Canada, 2021. www.statcan.gc.ca

Dayan, H. (2021). Female Honor Killing: The Role of Low Socio-Economic Status and Rapid Modernization. *Journal of Interpersonal Violence*, 36(19-20), NP10393–NP10410. DOI: 10.1177/0886260519872984 PMID: 31524058

De Cristofaro, E. (2018). *The crime of honor: an Italian story.* In Historia et ius(Vol. 14 Issue 1). www.historiaetius.eu

Deeyah. (2012, November 3). *Banaz: An 'honor' killing.* Retrieved from IKWRO: https://ikwro.org.uk/2012/11/03/banaz-an-honour-killing/

Deol, S. S. (2014). Honour Killings in India: A Study of the Punjab State. In *International Research* []. www.isca.me]. *Journal of Social Sciences*, 3(6).

Dessaux, N. (15 aout 2005). La lutte des femmes en Irak avant et depuis l'occupation, Courant Alternatif, 148. https://sisyphe.org/spip.php?article190

Dhull, K. (2017). Impact Factor: RJIF 5.12 www.educationjournal.org Volume 2; Issue 6. In *International Journal of Advanced Educational Research*. www.educationjournal.org

Doğan, R. (2014). The Profiles of Victims, Perpetrators, and Unfounded Beliefs in Honor Killings in Turkey. *Homicide Studies*, 18(4), 389–416. DOI: 10.1177/1088767914538637

Doğan, R. (2016). The Dynamics of Honor Killings and the Perpetrators' Experiences. *Homicide Studies*, 20(1), 53–79. DOI: 10.1177/1088767914563389

Dublish, D., & Khan, Y. (2021). Impact of Honour Killings in Haryana, India. *Social Science Journal for Advanced Research*, 1(2), 33–40. DOI: 10.54741/ssjar.1.2.6

Eid, J. A. (2020). *A Qualitative Study of the Impact of Domestic Violence by Male Relatives on Saudi Female Students in the United States* (Doctoral dissertation, Howard University).

El Muhtaseb, R. (2020). Gender-based violence and the law in Jordan: Legal reforms and cultural challenges. *International Journal of Middle East Studies*, 52(1), 45–63.

El Muhtaseb, R., & Husseini, R. (2009). *Murder in the name of honour: The true story of one woman's heroic fight against an unbelievable crime*. Oneworld Publications.

Elakkary, S., Franke, B., Shokri, D., Hartwig, S., Tsokos, M., & Puschel, K. (2014). Honor crimes: Review and proposed definition. *Forensic Science, Medicine, and Pathology*, 10(1), 76–82. DOI: 10.1007/s12024-013-9455-1 PMID: 23771767

Epstein, C. F. (2010). Death by gender. *Dissent*, 57(2), 54–57. DOI: 10.1353/dss.0.0143

Faqir, F. (2001). Intrafamily femicide in defence of honor: The case of Jordan. *. *Third World Quarterly*, 22(1), 65–82. DOI: 10.1080/713701138

Farhi, F. (2005). Women, The State, and Ideology in Iran. *The Muslim World*, 95(4), 479–510.

Fernandez, M. (2006). *Cultural beliefs and domestic violence*. New York Academy of Sciences. DOI: 10.1196/annals.1385.005

Firat, S., Iltas, Y., & Gulmen, M. K. (2016). *Honor Killing a Cultural Issue: Global or Regional?* E-Journal Law (Vol. 2, Issue 1). https://www.ohchr.org/en/professionalinterest/pages/ccpr.aspx

Focus. (2020). *Honour crimes: Women in Chechnya forced to suffer in silence* Retrieved May 19, 2024, from https://www.france24.com/en/tv-shows/focus/20201125-honour-crimes-women-in-chechnya-forced-to-suffer-in-silence

Fox, J., & Rooney, M. C. (2015). The Dark Triad and trait self-objectification as predictors of men's use and self-presentation behaviors on social networking sites. *Personality and Individual Differences*, 76, 161–165. DOI: 10.1016/j.paid.2014.12.017

Freeman, R. I. & Petrov, I. V. (2021) *Honor and Violence: Analyzing Gender and Culture in the Post-Soviet Space.*

Gabbay, M. S. (2014, June 8). Honor killing in the Middle East and the Muslim-world and forensic sociology: Family narratives from Jordan, Egypt, Turkey and Pakistan. *Forensic Research and Technology.*

Gah, S. (2003). *Karol Kari, Tor Tora, Siyahkari, Kala Kali.* Shirkat Gah.

Gale, N. (2003). *Violence against women: A normal or deviant behaviour.* Hameuchad Publishing House.

Gaskill, M. (2008). *Witchcraft and Evidence in Early Modern England.* University of East Anglia. DOI: 10.1093/pastj/gtm048

Gibbs, A., Said, N., Corboz, J., & Jewkes, R. (2019). Factors associated with 'honour killing' in Afghanistan and the occupied Palestinian Territories: Two cross-sectional studies. *PLoS One*, 14(8), e0219125. DOI: 10.1371/journal.pone.0219125 PMID: 31393873

Gill, A. (2006). Patriarchal Violence in the Name of "Honour." In International Journal of Criminal Justice Sciences (Vol. 1, Issue 1).

Gill, A. K. (2014). Introduction: 'Honour' and 'Honour'-Based Violence: Challenging Common Assumptions. *"Honour" Killing and Violence*, 1–23. DOI: 10.1057/9781137289568_1

Gill, J. K. (2022). Problematizing "Honour Crimes" within the Canadian Context: A Postcolonial Feminist Analysis of Popular Media and Political Discourses. *In Societies* (Vol. 12, Issue 2). MDPI. https://doi.org/DOI: 10.3390/soc12020062

Gill, A. (2009). Honor Killings and the Quest for Justice in Black and Minority Ethnic Communities in the UK. *Criminal Justice Matters*, 75(1), 28–30.

Gill, A. K. (2019). Social and cultural implications of 'honor'-based violence. In Reilly, N. (Ed.), *International Human Rights: Human Rights of Women*. Springer. DOI: 10.1007/978-981-10-8905-3_25

Ginat, J. (2006). *Blood Disputes Among Bedouin and Rural Arabs in Israel: Revenge, Mediation, Outcasting and Family Honor* (illustrated). University of Pittsburgh Press, 1987.

Ginat, J. *Bedouin Bisha'h Justice: ordeal by fire*. (2009). Brighton & Port-land: Sussex Academic Press.

Ginat, J., & Khazanov, A. (1998).*Changing nomads in a changing world* (eds). Sussex Academic Press, Brighton UK, p.149.

Ginat, J. (2000). *Blood revenge: outcasting mediation and family honor*. University Press.

Girouard, M. (1981). *A return to Camelot. The Wilson Quarterly* (1976-), 5(4), 178-189.

Glazer, I. M., & Ras, W. A. (1994). On aggression, human rights, and hegemonic discourse: The case of a murder for family honor in Israel. *Sex Roles*, 30, 269–288.

Global Human Rights Club: Arizona State University

Goldberg, A. (Ann E.). (2010). *Honor, politics and the law in imperial Germany, 1871-1914*. Cambridge University Press.

Goldstein, M. A. (2002). The biological roots of heat-of-passion crimes and honour killings. *Politics and the Life Sciences*, 21(2), 28–37. PMID: 16859346

Goodarzi, S. (2012). Honor killings and the quest for justice in Iran. *Iranian Studies*, 45(4), 535–556.

Gorar. M. (2020). Honour Killings: Social and Legal Challenges in TurkeyF.Tas Cifci. Abingdon: Routledge (2020) 238pp. £120.00hb ISBN 9781138348479. *The Howard Journal of Crime and Justice*, 59(3), 372–374. DOI: 10.1111/hojo.12387

Gorar, M. (2021). Female sexual autonomy, virginity, and honour-based violence with special focus on the UK. *Journal of International Women's Studies*, 22(5), 5.

Gregory, G., Fox, J., & Howard, B. (2020). Honour-based violence: Awareness and recognition. *Paediatrics and Child Health (Oxford)*, 30(11), 365–370. DOI: 10.1016/j.paed.2020.08.001

Grewal, I. (2013). Outsourcing Patriarchy. *International Feminist Journal of Politics*, 15(1), 1–19. DOI: 10.1080/14616742.2012.755352

Grzyb, M. A. (2016). An explanation of honour-related killings of women in Europe through Bourdieu's concept of symbolic violence and masculine domination. *Current Sociology*, 64(7), 1036–1053.

Guide to the Canadian Charter of Rights and Freedoms. (n.d.). Government of Canada. https://www.canada.ca/en/canadian-heritage/services/how-rights-protected/guide-canadian-charter-rights-freedoms.html#a2j4

Gul, A. (2014). Legal reforms and the struggle against honor killings in Pakistan. *Law & Society Review*, 48(4), 789–810.

Hamed Mohammad Shafia v. Her Majesty the Queen. (n.d.). Supreme Court of Canada. https://www.scc-csc.ca/case-dossier/info/sum-som-eng.aspx?cas=37387

Hancilar, O. (2015). *Honour Killings in Turkey*. International Institute of Social and Economic Sciences.

Hasisi, B., & Bernstein, D. (2019). Echoes of domestic silence: Mechanisms of concealment in cases of family honour killings in mandat Palestine. [CrossRef] [Google Scholar]. *Middle Eastern Studies*, 55(1), 60–73. DOI: 10.1080/00263206.2018.1485659

Hegland, M. E. (2009). Flagellation and Fundamentalism: (Trans)forming Meaning, Identity, and Gender through Pakistani Women's Rituals of Mourning. *American Ethnologist*, 32(3), 294–310.

Helba, C., Bernstein, M., Leonard, M., & Bauer, E. (2015). The author(s) shown below used Federal funds provided by the U.S. Department of Justice and prepared the following final report: Document Title: Report on Exploratory Study into Honor Violence Measurement Methods.

Heydari, A., Teymoori, A., & Trappes, R. (2021). Honor killing as a dark side of modernity: Prevalence, common discourses, and a critical view. *Social Sciences Information. Information Sur les Sciences Sociales*, 60(1), 86–106. DOI: 10.1177/0539018421994777

Hildebrandt, A. (2009, July 25). *Honour killings: domestic abuse by another name?* Retrieved from CBC News: https://www.cbc.ca/news/canada/honour-killings-domestic-abuse-by-another-name-1.792907

HMA. (1955). Hindu Marriage Act, 1955

Honor Killing In India: An Analysis On Indian Statutes: K.Vikas

Honour Honour Crimes and Violence against Women Preventing and Punishing Honour Crimes. (n.d.-a).

Honour Honour Crimes and Violence against Women Preventing and Punishing Honour Crimes. (n.d.-b).

Honour killing toll at least 15 in Canada in past two decades. (2015, December 22). Canadian Content Forums. https://forums.canadiancontent.net/threads/honor-killing-toll-at-least-15-in-canada-in-past-two-decades.140054/

Honour Killings in Canada: A Way Towards Prevention. (2018, March 9). https://www.linkedin.com/pulse/honour-killings-canada-way-towards-prevention-shireen-ali?utm_source=share&utm_medium=member_android&utm_campaign=share_via

Honour killings in Ottawa. (2012, January 30). Ottawa Sun. https://ottawasun.com/2012/01/30/furey-on-shafia-verdict

Honour Related Violence within a Global Perspective: Mitigation and Prevention in Europe. (2004). Stockholm.

Honour-based violence Complex issue needs greater awareness. (2016, October 3). Royal Canadian Mounted Police. https://www.rcmp-grc.gc.ca/en/gazette/honour-based-violence

Hoodfar, H. (1999). The Women's Movement in Iran: Women at the Crossroads of Secularization and Islamization. *The Middle East Journal*, 53(4), 453–473.

Hosseini, S., & C, B. (2015). Study on Honor Killing as a Crime in India-Cause and Solutions. *International Journal of Preventive Medicine*, 2.

Huang, X. (2023). Feminism in Diverse Conditions: Analyzing about Feminism on Social Media Platforms. *Communications in Humanities Research*, 20(1), 46–51. DOI: 10.54254/2753-7064/20/20231283

Huda, S., & Kamal, A. (2020). Development and Validation of Attitude Towards Honour Killing Scale. *2020, VOL. 35, NO. 2, 35*(35), 227–251. DOI: 10.33824/PJPR.2020.35.2.13

Huda, S., & Kamal, A. (2022). Assessing demographics-based differences in attitude toward honor killings. *Journal of Interpersonal Violence*, 37(5-6), NP3224–NP3241. DOI: 10.1177/0886260520927499 PMID: 32529938

Human Rights watch. (2016). *Report on Lebanon: Reform Rape Laws*.

Human Rights Watch. (2019). *Institutional responses to honor-based violence*.

Human Rights Watch. (Oct, 2018). *Russia: Unaddressed Domestic Violence Puts Women at Risk*. Retrieved May 19, 2024, from https://www.hrw.org/news/2018/10/25/russia-unaddressed-domestic-violence-puts-women-risk

Hussain, M. (2006). Take my riches, give me justice: A contextual analysis of Pakistan's honor crimes legislation. *Harvard Journal of Law & Gender*, 29, 223–246.

Hussain, M. (2018). Honor killings: A comparative study of Pakistan and other nations. *International Journal of Comparative Criminology*, 16(1), 55–72.

Husseini, R. (n.d.). Murdered women: A history of 'honour' crimes. Al Jazeera. https://www.aljazeera.com/features/2021/8/1/murdered-women-a-history-of-honour-crimes

Husseini, R. (2012). *Murder in the Name of Honour: The True Face of Honour Killing*. Women's Press.

Ibrahim, H., & Soliman, N. (2018). *Legal Framework and Human Rights in Egypt*. Law and Human Rights Journal.

In Russia, the rescue of four sisters threatened with "honor killing." (2022). Retrieved May 19, 2024, from https://www.lemonde.fr/en/international/article/2022/11/10/in-russia-the-rescue-of-four-sisters-threatened-with-honor-killing_6003672_4.html#

Indian Penal Code. (1860). Sec 141, 143, 503 and 506 IPC,

Indian Penal Code. (1860). Section 300 of IPC,

Indian Population Statistics Poll

Indo-Canadian honour killing: Jassi Sidhu's mother, uncle may walk out free. (2021, December 27). The Canadian Bazar. https://www.thecanadianbazaar.com/jassi-sidhu-honor-killing-her-mother-uncle-may-go-scot-free/

Infographic: Homicide in Canada, 2022. (2023, November 29). Statistics Canada. https://www150.statcan.gc.ca/n1/pub/11-627-m/11-627-m2023058-eng.htm

Ip Leaders: Honour killings in India and need for urgent reforms and new laws

Iqbal, M. (2006). *Honor killing and silence of justice system in Pakistan* (Master's thesis). Lund University, Centre for East and Southeast Asian Studies.

Jafri, A. H. (2008). In *honour killing: Dilemma, ritual, understanding*. Karachi, Pakistan: Oxford University Press.

Jakhar, S. (n.d.). *KHAP Panchayats: Changing Perspectives*. Retrieved August 1, 2024, from https://www.academia.edu/37068474/KHAP_PANCHAYATS_CHANGING_PERSPECTIVES

Jamuna, K. V. (2022). A Study on Etiology of Honour Killing in India: A Critical Analysis. In *Peer Reviewed and Refereed Journal* (Issue 5). http://ijmer.in.doi./2022/11.05.57

Janjua, H. (2022). The horror of honor killings. *Asia Democracy Chronicles*.

Janssen, J. (n.d.). *Deelrapport 2-Analyse-van-mogelijke-eerzaken*. https://www.researchgate.net/publication/336564295

Janssen, J. H. L. J., & Reed, B. (n.d.). *Focus on honour : an exploration of cases of honour-related violence for police officers and other professionals*.

Jazeera, A. (2016, December 7). India sees huge spike in 'honour' killings. India. Retrieved from https://www.aljazeera.com/news/2016/12/india-sees-huge-spike-honour-killings161207153333597.html

Jeyasanthi, V., Mayileswari, S., & Abirami, R. (2014). Honour Killing: A National Outcry. *Journal for Bloomers Research*, 6(2), 917–942.

Johnson, S. M. (2020). *Russia's Changing Political System: The Impact of Gender and Ethnicity*.

Jones, A. K. (2022). *The Politics of Honor: A Study of Gender and Violence in the North Caucasus*.

Juškevičiūtė, J., & Jakab, M. (n.d.). *Honour Killings: A Social and Legal Approach*. https://doi.org/DOI: 10.13165/PSPO-20-25-12

KAFA (2006). *Minutes of Regional Meeting on Legislation for Protection against Domestic Violence. Khater A.F (2006). Like Pure Gold: Sexuality and Honor Amongst Lebanese Immigrants, 1819-1920*.

Kalyani, V., Arumugam, T., & Surya Kumar, M. (2022). Women in Oppressive Societies as Portrayed in Kollywood Movies. *American Journal of Economics and Sociology*, 81(1), 173–185. DOI: 10.1111/ajes.12450

Kamal, N., & Mostafa, R. (2021). *Legal and Psychological Dimensions of Honor Crimes in Egypt*. Egyptian Law Review.

Kanchan, T., Tandon, A., & Krishan, K. (2016). Honor Killing: Where Pride Defeats Reason. *Science and Engineering Ethics*, 22(6), 1861–1862. DOI: 10.1007/s11948-015-9694-5 PMID: 26293131

Kandiyoti, D. (1991). *Women, Islam, and the State*. Temple University Press. DOI: 10.1007/978-1-349-21178-4

Kanwal, S. (2020). Honor killing: A case study of Pakistan. [JLSS]. *Journal of Law & Social Studies*, 3(1), 38–43. DOI: 10.52279/jlss.03.01.3843

Kardam, F. (2005). *The dynamics of honor killings in Turkey*. UN Population Fund (UNFPA).

Kaur, N., & Byard, R. W. (2020). Bride burning: A unique and ongoing form of gender-based violence. *Journal of Forensic and Legal Medicine*, 75, 102035. DOI: 10.1016/j.jflm.2020.102035 PMID: 32871350

Kaushal, K. (2020). No Honour in Honour Killing: Comparative Analysis of Indian Traditional Social Structure vis-à-vis Gender Violence. *ANTYAJAA: Indian Journal of Women and Social Change*, 5(1), 52–69. DOI: 10.1177/2455632719880870

Kaya, N., & Turan, N.KAYA. (2018). Attitudes toward Honor and Violence against Women for Honor in the Context of the Concept of Privacy: A Study of Students in the Faculty of Health Sciences. *Connectist: Istanbul University Journal of Communication Sciences*, 14(6), 65–84. DOI: 10.26650/CONNECTIST433995

Kejriwal, N. (2018). Honour Killing in North India. Pro Bono India, 01.

Kejriwal, -Neelam. (n.d.). *Honour Killing in North India*.

Kejriwal, -Neelam. (n.d.). *HONOUR KILLING IN NORTH INDIA*.

Khalid v. State of Pakistan, PLD 2017 SC 488.

Khalili, M. I. (2002). A comment on heat-of-passion crimes, honor killings, and Islam. *Politics and the Life Sciences*, 38–40.

Khan, A. (2004, July 23). Two killed in honor killing case in Sindh. *The Dawn News*.

Khan, A., & Hussain, R. (2006). Violence against women in Pakistan: Perceptions and experiences of domestic violence. *Asian Studies Review*, 32(2), 239–253. DOI: 10.1080/10357820802062181

Khan, F. (2016). Assessing the impact of legal reforms on honor killings in Pakistan. *Pakistan Law Journal*, 32(1), 34–50.

Khan, M., Shah, S., & Khan, F. (2018). An overview of the causes and effects of honor killing in Pakistan. *The Journal of Social Issues*, 14(2), 55–72.

Khan, Y. (n.d.). A Sociological Perspective of Honour Killing in India. *International Journal of Engineering and Management Research*. Advance online publication. DOI: 10.31033/ijemr.9.6.21

Khaskheli, M. B., Saleem, H. A. R., Bibi, S., & Gsell Mapa, J. (2018). Comparative Analysis of Honor Killing Phenomena in China and Pakistan. *Journal of Law and Criminal Justice*, 6(2). Advance online publication. DOI: 10.15640/jlcj.v6n2a2

Khazanov, A. (1981). *Comments, Currents Anthropol. Killing of Youtube star by her father causes outrage in Iraq* (2023, February 4). Aljazeera. https://www.aljazeera.com/news/2023/2/4/iraqis-outraged-after-father-kills-youtube-star-daughter

Kian, A. (2014). *Gender and Women's Studies in Iran: A Comparative Perspective*. Springer.

Kian, A. (1997). Modernization and Gender Regime in Iran. *Iranian Studies*, 30(3-4), 385–408.

Kiener, R. (2011). Honour killings: Can murders of women and girls be stopped? *Global Researcher*, 5(8), 185.

King, A. (2013). Mohammad Mazher Idriss and Tahir Abbas (eds.), Honour, Violence, Women and Islam, (Abingdon: Routledge-Cavendish, 2010) ISBN 978-0-415-56542-4, 248 pp. *Religion and Human Rights,* 8(1), 93–99. DOI: 10.1163/18710328-12341245

Koç, G. (2022). A Study of Femicide in Turkey From 2010 to 2017. *SAGE Open*, 12(3), 215824402211198. DOI: 10.1177/21582440221119831

Kogan, E. A. (2019) *Gender, State, and Society in Post-Soviet Russia: Examining Patriarchal Structures*.

Korteweg, A. C. (n.d.). *Understanding Honour Killing and Honour-Related Violence in the Immigration Context: Implications for the Legal Profession and Beyond*. https://www.proquest.com/docview/1018564902/abstract/568DE891A2C4199PQ/1

Korteweg, A. C., & Yurdakul, G. (2010). *Palais des Nations, 1211 Geneva 10, Switzerland. UNRISD welcomes such applications*.

Korteweg, A. C., & Yurdakul, G. (2010). Understanding honour killing and honour-related violence in the immigration context: Implications for the legal profession and beyond. Canadian Council of Muslim Women. https://cdhpi.ca/sites/cdhpi.ca/files/korteweg_cclr-understanding-honour-killing.pdf

Korteweg, A. C., Janssen, J., Timmer, W., Ouchan, K., Dogan, C., Bakker, H., Gortworst, J., Van Groesen, S., Dekker, A.-F., Metin, S., Simsek, J., Clijnk, A., & Van Der Zee, R. (2009a). *Understanding Honour Killing and Honour-Related Violence in the Immigration Context: Implications for the Legal Profession and Beyond*. http://vorige.nrc.nl/article1855988.ece

Kressel, G. M. (1992). Shame and gender. *Anthropological Quarterly*, 34–46.

Kressel, G., Bausani, A., Ginat, J., Joseph, R., Khazanov, A. M., Landau, S. F., Marx, E., & Shokeid, M. (1981). Sororicide/ filiacide: Homicide for family honor. *Current Anthropology*, 22(2), 141–158. DOI: 10.1086/202632

Krishnan, S. (2005). Do structural inequalities contribute to marital violence? Ethnographic evidence from rural South India. *Violence Against Women*, 11(6), 759–775. DOI: 10.1177/1077801205276078 PMID: 16043570

Kulczycki, A., & Windle, S. (2011). Honor killings in the Middle East and North Africa. *Violence Against Women*, 17(11), 1442–1464. DOI: 10.1177/1077801211434127 PMID: 22312039

Kulwicki, A. D. (2002). The practice of honor crimes: A glimpse of domestic violence in the Arab world. *Issues in Mental Health Nursing*, 23(1), 77–87.

Kumar Rana, D., & Prasad Mishra, B. (2013). *Honour Killings-A gross violation of Human rights & Its Challenges*. In International Journal of Humanities and Social Science Invention (Vol. 2 Issue 6) www.ijhssi.org

Kumar Rana, D., & Prasad Mishra, B. (n.d.). Honour Killings-A gross violation of Human rights & Its Challenges. www.ijhssi.org

Kumar, A. (2012). Public Policy Imperatives for Curbing Honour Killings in India. *Journal of Politics & Governance*, 1(1), 36–40.

Kumar, A. (2012). Public policy imperatives for curbing honour killings in India. *Journal of Politics and Governance*, 1(1), 36–40.

Kumar, N. (2013). Juidicial response towards KHAP panchayat. *JOURNAL OF GLOBAL RESEARCH & ANALYSIS*, 2(1), 114–117.

Kumar, R. K. (2013). Honour Killing: Challenges Indian Judicial System. *International Journal of Creative Research Thoughts*, 11(4).

Lakshmi, D. L. (2003, September 30). *After a Marriage for Love, a Death for 'Honor'*. Retrieved from The Washington Post: https://www.washingtonpost.com/archive/lifestyle/2003/10/01/after-a-marriage-for-love-a-death-for-honor/fb1b98fd-94e6-47d1-8f81-ce656c6b4e94/

Lama, A. (2010) *Honor Killings and the Construction of Gender in Arab Societies*.

Landtag von Baden-Württemberg. (n.d.). www.landtag-bw.de/Dokumente

Lari, M. Z. (2011). *Honour killings in Pakistan and compliance of law*. Legislative Watch Programme for Women's Empowerment.

Laura, B. (n.d.). *Feminism | Definition, History, Types, Waves, Examples, & Facts | Britannica*. Retrieved May 26, 2024, from https://www.britannica.com/topic/feminism

Lavaque-Manty, M. (2006). Forthcoming in Political Theory.

Lewis, M. W. (Ed.). (2018). *Honor-Based Violence: A Comprehensive Study*.

Long-Term Historical Trends in Violent Crime. (2003).

Lorenzi-Cioldi, F., & Kulich, C. (2015). *Sexism* (2nd ed.). International Encyclopedia of the Social & Behavioral Sciences., DOI: 10.1016/B978-0-08-097086-8.24089-0

Luebering, J. (2024, July 30). murder. Encyclopedia Britannica. https://www.britannica.com/topic/murder-crime

MacVeigh, T. (2012, September 22). *'They're following me': chilling words of girl who was 'honour killing' victim*. Retrieved from The Guardian: https://www.theguardian.com/world/2012/sep/22/banaz-mahmod-honour-killing

Madek, C. (2005). Killing dishonor: Effective eradication of honor killing. *Suffolk Transnational Law Review*, 29(1), 53.

Maffesoli, M. (1995). *The Time of the Tribes: The Decline of Individualism in Mass Society*. Sage.

Mahajan, A. (2020, September 5). *Comprehending Honour Killings in India*. Retrieved from Round Table India: https://www.roundtableindia.co.in/comprehending-honour-killings-in-india/

Mahmoudian, H., & Hosseini-Chavoshi, M. (2011). Revolution, war, and modernization: Population policy and fertility change in Iran. *Journal of Population Research*, 28(3), 247–266.

Mak, S., & Thomas, A. (2022). Steps for Conducting a Scoping Review. *Journal of Graduate Medical Education*, 14(5), 565–567. DOI: 10.4300/JGME-D-22-00621.1 PMID: 36274762

Mammadova, U., & Joamets, K. (2021). Istanbul Convention, Honour Killings and Turkey's Experience. *International and Comparative Law Review, 21*(1), 79–99. DOI: 10.2478/iclr-2021-0003

Mamta, R. (2018). *Law relating to Women & Children* (4th ed., Vol. 1). Eastern Book Company.

Mansur, Y., Shteiwi, M., & Murad, N. (2009). The economic underpinnings of honor crimes in Jordan. Information and Research Centre, King Hussein Foundation, Jordan.

Martins, A. (2022). Feminism, Leadership, and Social Media. *International Journal of Social Media and Online Communities*, 14(2), 1–18. DOI: 10.4018/IJSMOC.308288

Marwick, M. (1965). *Sorcery in its social setting*. Humanities Press.

Matabangsa, J. (2011). Honor Killings in the Middle East: Cultural Practice or Human Rights Violation? In Ahmed, A. (Ed.), *Human Rights in the Arab World* (pp. 122–145). University of Pennsylvania Press.

Mayell, H. (2002). Thousands of women killed for family honor. *National Geographic News*, 12, 15.

McLaren, M. A. (2019). *Women's Activism, Feminism, and Social Justice*. Women's Activism, Feminism, and Social Justice., DOI: 10.1093/oso/9780190947705.001.0001

Meetoo, V., & Mirza, H. (2007). There is nothing honourable about honour killings: Gender, violence and the limits of multiculturalism. *Women's Studies International Forum*, 30(3), 187–200. DOI: 10.1016/j.wsif.2007.03.001

Mehsud, I., Khan, N., & Amirzada, M. (2023). *Death of Honor Killings Put Spotlight on 'Honor' Killings in Pakistan*. RadioFree Europe Radio Liberty.

Mir-Hosseini, Z. (2002). *Marriage on Trial: Islamic Family Law in Iran and Morocco*. I.B. Tauris.

Mishra, A. (n.d.). *HONOUR KILLINGS: THE LAW IT IS AND THE LAW IT OUGHT TO BE*. https://www.hrw.org/press/2001/04/un

Mitchell, B. (2010, June 16). *'I killed my daughter... with my hands'*. Retrieved from Toronto Star: https://www.thestar.com/news/crime/i-killed-my-daughter-with-my-hands/article_cec7714d-78fd-5212-a430-1b3dc7de47ec.html

Montreal Gazette. (2019, December 13). *Shafia murders: Mother 'discovered freedom' behind bars, changed story, filed for divorce*.https://montrealgazette.com/news/the-shafia-murders-mother-convicted-of-killing-daughters-finds-freedom-behind-bars

Moosavi, L. (2015). The Crises of Masculinity and Unveiling the Real in Iranian Cinema: A Gendered Analysis of A Separation. *Middle East Journal of Culture and Communication*, 8(3), 260–276.

Mostafa, S., & Ramin, M. (9 February 2022). *United States. Iranian husband beheads teenage wife, authorities say, shocking the country*. CNN. https://amp.cnn.com/cnn/2022/02/09/middleeast/iran-teenage-wife-beheaded-intl/index.html

Muhammad, A. A., & Canada. Department of Justice. Family, C. and Y. S. (n.d.). *Preliminary examination of so-called "honour killings" in Canada*.

Muhammad, N., Ahmed, M. M. M., Abdullah, A., Omer, F., & Shah, N. H. (2012). Honor killing in Pakistan: An Islamic perspective. *Asian Social Science*, 8(10), 180. DOI: 10.5539/ass.v8n10p180

Munn, Z., Peters, M. D. J., Stern, C., Tufanaru, C., McArthur, A., & Aromataris, E. (2018). Systematic review or scoping review? Guidance for authors when choosing between a systematic or scoping review approach. *BMC Medical Research Methodology*, 18(1), 143. DOI: 10.1186/s12874-018-0611-x PMID: 30453902

Murder Reference of Honour killing: Times of India

Murderous honour, undying love: The tale of Jassi and Mithu from Canada to Punjab. (2017, September 17). Hindustan Times. https://www.hindustantimes.com/punjab/when-jassi-met-mithu-and-love-met-honour/story-SJTNaYvsAmieRqkEJwnDPJ.html

Najmabadi, A. (2005). *Women with Mustaches and Men without Beards: Gender and Sexual Anxieties of Iranian Modernity*. University of California Press. DOI: 10.1525/9780520931381

Narzary, P. K., & Ladusingh, L. (2019). Discovering the Saga of Inter-caste Marriage in India. *Journal of Asian and African Studies*, 54(4), 588–599. DOI: 10.1177/0021909619829896

Nasrullah, M., Haqqi, S., & Cummings, K. J. (2009). The epidemiological patterns of honour killing of women in Pakistan. *European Journal of Public Health*, 19(2), 193–197. DOI: 10.1093/eurpub/ckp021 PMID: 19286837

Nelaeva, G. (2021). Violence against women in Russia and Brazil: International and domestic responses. *BRICS Law Journal*, 8(4), 76–102. DOI: 10.21684/2412-2343-2021-8-4-76-102

Newme, W. (2018). Honour Killings in India. *Journal of Emerging Technologies and Innovative Research*, 5(9), 333–338.

Nimry, L. *Crimes of Honor in Jordan and the Arab World.* (2010). Retrived from https://www.c-we.org/eng/show.art.asp?aid=749

Nirenberg, D. (2002). Conversion, Sex, and Segregation: Jews and Christians in Medieval Spain. *The American Historical Review*, 107(4), 1065–1093. DOI: 10.1086/532664

No. M. R. 2 of 2010 Appeal no,479-DB of 2010 and Criminal revision No.2173 of 2010 In The High Court Of Punjab & Haryana, Chandigarh. http://nlrd.org/wp-content/uploads/2012/01/Manoj-andBabli.pdf

Nowak, A., Gelfand, M. J., Borkowski, W., Cohen, D., & Hernandez, I. (2015). The evolutionary basis of Honor cultures. *Psychological Science*, 27(1), 12–24. DOI: 10.1177/0956797615602860 PMID: 26607976

NRI Internet.com. (n.d.). *Rajinder Atwal convicted for murder of his daughter Amandeep.* https://www.nriinternet.com/NRI_Murdered/CANADA/BC/2004/Amandeep_Atwal_Murder/1_0803.htm

Nyaya Deep. (2014). National Legal Services Authority. www.nalsa.gov.in

Olwan, D. M. (2013). Gendered Violence, Cultural Otherness, and Honour Crimes in Canadian National Logics. *Canadian Journal of Sociology*, 38(4), 533–556. DOI: 10.29173/cjs21196

openDemocracy. (Aug. 2017). *"Honour killings" in Russia's North Caucasus.* Retrieved May 28, 2024, from https://www.opendemocracy.net/en/odr/honour-killings-in-russia-s-north-caucasus/

Osanloo, A. (2009). *The Politics of Women's Rights in Iran.* Princeton University Press. DOI: 10.1515/9781400833160

Oxford Human Rights Hub: Addressing "Honour Killings in India"

Parasar, A., & Gopal, D. Saha and Baskar, Nisha, Honor Killings in India: A Study on the State of Uttar Pradesh (march 2016). International Journal of Recent Scientific Research (IJRSR), Volume: 7(3) March -2016, Available at SSRN: https://ssrn.com/abstract=4496100

Parul, C. (2021). Honour killings in India and need for urgent reforms and new laws. *IPleaders*.

Patel, V. (n.d.). *Smart Cities have to be Safe Cities Prof. Vibhuti Patel.* https://www.researchgate.net/publication/291514771

Patel, S., & Gadit, A. (2008). Karo-kari: A form of honour killing in Pakistan. *Transcultural Psychiatry*, 45(4), 683–694. DOI: 10.1177/1363461508100790 PMID: 19091732

Pathak, M. K., & Rai, S. (2019). Honour Killing: Gruesome Murder For The Sake of False Honour. *Journal of Punjab Academy of Forensic Medicine & Toxicology*, 19(2), 181. DOI: 10.5958/0974-083X.2020.00040.0

pdf-honour-killing-in-india_compress. (n.d.).

Perry, A. (2012). *Honor Killings in Pakistan: An Everyday Matter.* TIME Magazine.

Pina-López, E. (2014). The Role of Honor and Patriarchy in the Perpetuation of Honor-Based Violence. *Violence Against Women*, 20(1), 24–41.

Pirnia, B., Pirnia, F., & Pirnia, K. (2020). Honour killings and violence against women in Iran during the COVID-19 pandemic. *The Lancet. Psychiatry*, 7(10), e60. DOI: 10.1016/S2215-0366(20)30359-X PMID: 32949522

Plant, R. (2006). Honor killings and the asylum gender gap. *Journal of Transnational Law & Policy*, 15(2).

Poddar, A. (2020). *Reprehensible Behaviour: The Social Meaning Behind Honour Killings in India*.

Poddar, A. (2020). *Reprehensible Behaviour: The Social Meaning Behind Honour Killings in India*. In Department of Sociology. Brown University

Prpic, M. (2015). *Briefing European Parliamentary Research Service*.

Punjab man gets lifer for honour killing in Canada. (n.d.). The Tribune. https://m.tribuneindia.com/2010/20100606/main4.htm

Qur'an: The Meaning of the Glorious Qur'an (1979). Text and explanatory translation by Marmaduke Pickthall (Karachi-Lahore-Rawalpindi: Taj Company, p.2-4, 1979.

R. K., & K. K. (2019). Honour killing and women: human right's view. In *International Journal of Creative Research Thoughts*, (Vol. 7). www.ijcrt.org

Rabinowitz, D. (1995). *The twisting journey for the rescue of brown women*. Hebrew: Teorya Uvikoret.

Rahim, S. (2017). Attitude toward honour killing among honor killers. *WU Journal of Social Sciences, 11*(1), 254-263. Retrieved from http://sbbwu.edu.pk/journal/WU_Journal_of_Social_Sciences_Summer_2017_Vol_11_No_1/23%20Attitude%20Toward%20Honour%20%20killing%20among%20honor%20killers.pdf

Rai, G. (2023). Comparative Analysis on Honour Killing Prevalent in India and Sweden. SSRN *Electronic Journal*. DOI: 10.2139/ssrn.4520199

Ravishankar, S. (2017, December 15). Six men sentenced to death in India for Dalit "honour" killing. https://www.theguardian.com/global-development/2017/dec/15/six-men-sentenced-to-death-india-dalit-honour-killing

Ray, U. (1999). *'Idealizing Motherhood': The Brahmanical discourse on women in Ancient India (circa 500 BCE-300 CE)*. University of London, School of Oriental and African Studies.

Razack, S. H. (2021). Should feminists stop talking about culture in the context of violence against muslim women? The case of "honour killing.". *International Journal of Child, Youth & Family Studies*, 12(1), 31–48. DOI: 10.18357/ijcyfs121202120082

Rehman, A. (2020). International responses to honor killings in Pakistan: A critical analysis. *Human Rights Quarterly*, 42(2), 300–318.

Rekha Verma, D. (2023). Psycho-socio facets of honour killing. In *Russian Law Journal: Vol. XI*.

Roberts, K. A., Campbell, G., & Lloyd, G. (2013). Honor-based violence: Policing and prevention. *Honor-Based Violence: Policing and Prevention*, 1–197. DOI: 10.1201/b16114

Roberts, J. (2022). Comparative analysis of honor-based violence: Jordan and the Middle East. *International Journal of Comparative Studies*, 15(1), 102–118.

Ruggi, S. (1998). *Commodifying Honor in Female Sexuality*. Retrieved from Middle East Report 206: https://merip.org/1998/06/commodifying-honor-in-female-sexuality/

Ruggi, S. *Commodifying Honor in Female Sexuality: Honor Killings in Palestine* (2008). Retrieved from https://www.merip.org/mer/mer206/ruggi.htm

Sadowa, K. (2015). Honour Killings in Europe as an effect of migration process: Perspective for Poland. *International Letters of Social and Humanistic Sciences*, 58, 83–90. . DOI: 10.18052/www.scipress.com/ILSHS.58.83

Sana. (2019). The dishonorable honor crimes in literature. *International Journal of English Language, Literature and Translation Studies* (1st ed., Vol. 6).

Sana. (2019). The dishonorable honor crimes in literature. *International Journal of English Language, Literature and Translation Studies*, (1st ed., Vol. 6).

Sanchez-Ruiz, M. J., El Ahmad, P., Karam, M., & Saliba, M. A. (2021). Rape myth acceptance in Lebanon: The role of sexual assault experience/familiarity, sexism, honor beliefs, and the Dark Triad. *Personality and Individual Differences*, 170, 110403. DOI: 10.1016/j.paid.2020.110403

Secretary-General, UN. (2002). *Working towards the elimination of crimes against women committed in the name of honour*.

Seedat, M., Van Niekerk, A., Jewkes, R., Suffla, S., & Ratele, K. (2009). Violence and injuries in South Africa: Prioritising an agenda for prevention. *Lancet*, 374(9694), 1011–1022. DOI: 10.1016/S0140-6736(09)60948-X PMID: 19709732

Sen, A., Kaur, R., & Zabiliūtė, E. (2020). (En)countering sexual violence in the Indian city. *Gender, Place and Culture*, 27(1), 1–12. DOI: 10.1080/0966369X.2019.1612856

Sen, P. (2005). Crimes of honour, value and meaning. In Welchman, L., & Hossain, S. (Eds.), *Honour': Crimes, Paradigms, and Violence Against Women* (pp. 47–63). Zed Book. DOI: 10.5040/9781350220621.ch-002

Sev'Er, A., & Yurdakul, G.SEV'ER. (2001). Culture of Honor, Culture of Change. *Violence Against Women*, 7(9), 964–998. DOI: 10.1177/10778010122182866

Shaheed, F. (2013). Class and honor: Socioeconomic factors in honor killings in Pakistan. *South Asian Studies Review*, 19(1), 77–95.

Shahid, A., Awan, M. H., & Rana, F. A. (2024). Honour Killings in Pakistan: Legal Perspectives and Reforms. *Qlantic Journal of Social Sciences*, 5(1), 134–140. DOI: 10.55737/qjss.547319279

Shakti Vahini vs Union of India (2018). 7 SCC 192

Shier, A., & Shor, E. (2016) "Shades of foreign evil": "honour killings" and "family murders" in the Canadian press. Violence Against Women, 22 (10). pp. 1163-1188. ISSN 1077-8012

Shier, A., & Shor, E. (2016). "Shades of Foreign Evil": "Honor Killings" and "Family Murders" in the Canadian Press. *Violence Against Women*, 22(10), 1163–1188. DOI: 10.1177/1077801215621176 PMID: 26712236

Shirazi, F. (2010). *Muslim Women in War and Crisis: Representation and Reality*. University of Texas Press.

Sholkamy, H. (2002). Patriarchy, Power, and the Politics of Gender in Modernising Egypt. *Gender and Development*, 10(1), 22–30.

Shoro, S. (n.d.). *The real stories behind honour killing*.

Shripad, A. M. (2024). *Gender-Based Violence: A Contemporary Analysis*. Routledge.

Shroff, S. (2021). Bold Women, Bad Assets: Honour, Property and Techno-Promiscuities. *Feminist Review*, 128(1), 62–78. DOI: 10.1177/01417789211016438

Shteiwi, M. Y., Murad, N., & Mansur, Y. (2009). The economic underpinnings of honor crimes in Jordan. Information and Research Centre, King Hussein Foundation, Jordan.

Siddiqui, M. (2010). Cultural norms and honor-based violence in Pakistan. *Journal of Southeast Asian Studies*, 22(4), 120–135.

Singh, A. (2013). *Honour Killing as Horror Honour.* https://ssrn.com/abstract=2221734 DOI: 10.2139/ssrn.2221734

Singh, R. N., & Dailey, J. D. "honor killing". Encyclopedia Britannica, 27 Aug. 2023, https://www.britannica.com/topic/honor-killing. Accessed 1 September 2024.

Singh, A. K. (2020). The Paradox Between Universalism of Human Rights and Relativism of Culture. *Journal of Southeast Asian Human Rights*, 4(1), 253. DOI: 10.19184/jseahr.v4i1.8597

Singhal, V. K. (2014). *Honour Killing in India: An Assessment.* SSRN Electronic Journal. https://ssrn.com/abstract=2406031 DOI: 10.2139/ssrn.2406031

Singh, D., & Bhandari, D. S. (2021). Legacy of Honor and Violence: An Analysis of Factors Responsible for Honor Killings in Afghanistan, Canada, India, and Pakistan as Discussed in Selected Documentaries on Real Cases. *SAGE Open*, 11(2). Advance online publication. DOI: 10.1177/21582440211022323

Singh, R. N., Hurley, D., & Singh, D. (2017). Towards identifying and ranking selected types of violence against women in North India. *International Journal of Comparative and Applied Criminal Justice*, 41(1–2), 19–29. DOI: 10.1080/01924036.2016.1212246

Smita Satapathy, D. R. (2023). Honour Killing as a Crime in India. *International Journal of Law Management & Humanities*, 6. Advance online publication. DOI: 10.10000/IJLMH.114514

Smith, A. (2004). Murder in Jerba: Honour, shame and hospitality among Maltese in Ottoman Tunisia. *History and Anthropology*, 15(2), 107–132. DOI: 10.1080/0275720041000168994

Smt. Laxmi Kachhwaha vs. The state of Rajasthan (1999).

Sneha, S., Sarathi, S., Kumar, P. S., Rajesh, R., & Jagdish Kamal, C. U. (2020). Perspective on the immorality of Honor Killings-A review article. *Medico-Legal Update*, 20(1), 68–71. DOI: 10.37506/v20/i1/2020/mlu/194296

So-called "honour crimes." (Oct. 2003). Retrieved May 19, 2024, from https://assembly.coe.int/nw/xml/XRef/X2H-Xref-ViewHTML.asp?FileID=10068&lang=EN

Social and legal actions to combat honor related abuse Centre for Sustainable Communities Development KUN centre for equality and diversity (2021).

Sohail Akbar Warraich. (2005). 'Honor Killings' and the law in Pakistan. In Welchmann, L., & Hossain, S. (Eds.), *Honour': Crimes, Paradigms, and Violence against Women* (pp. 84–97). Zed Books.

Solotaroff, J. L., Pande, R. (Rohini P.), & World Bank. (n.d.). *Violence against women and girls: lessons from South Asia*.

Sommer, F., Leuschner, V., Fiedler, N., Madfis, E., & Scheithauer, H. (2020). The role of shame in developmental trajectories towards severe targeted school violence: An in-depth multiple case study. *Aggression and Violent Behavior*, 51, 101386. DOI: 10.1016/j.avb.2020.101386

Sonbol, A. (2003). *Women of Jordan: Islam, labour and the law*. Syracuse University Press.

Spierenburg, P. C. (2008). A history of murder: Personal violence in Europe from the Middle Ages to the present. *Polity*.

Sreedevi Xavier, M. (2015). *Honor Killings: A Global Concern*. In Indian Journal of Research (Vol. 4 Issue 3)

Sripad, A. M. (2023, September 4). Killing honour in the name of 'honour killings'. *The New Indian Express*. Retrieved from https://www.newindianexpress.com/states/karnataka/2023/Sep/04/killing-honour-in-the-name-of-honour-killings-2611437.html

Srivastava, K., Chaudhury, S., Bhat, P., & Sahu, S. (2017). Misogyny, feminism, and sexual harassment. *Industrial Psychiatry Journal*, 26(2), 111. DOI: 10.4103/ipj.ipj_32_18 PMID: 30089955

State of Uttar Pradesh Vs Krishna Master (2010).

Statham, P., Koopmans, R., Giugni, M., & Passy, F. (2005). Resilient or adaptable Islam?: Multiculturalism, religion and migrants' claims-making for group demands in Britain, the Netherlands and France. *Ethnicities*, 5(4), 427–459. DOI: 10.1177/1468796805058092

Suresh Kumar, M. (2023). Honor Killing and Its Causes in Indian Panorama. In *International Journal of Research in Engineering and Science,* (Vol. 11). www.ijres.org

Tabassum v. Canada. (2018, January 29). Max Berger Professional Law Corporation. https://www.maxberger.ca/immigration-cases/pre-removal-risk-assessment-prra/tabassum-v-canada/

Temowo_Adeniyi_Olasunkanmi (1). (n.d.).

The Borgen Project. (2021). *Honor Killings of Women in the North Caucasus.* Retrieved May 28, 2024, from https://borgenproject.org/women-in-the-north-caucasus/

The Guardian. (Jun 2019). *Protests in Russia as sisters face jail for killing abusive father.* Retrieved May 19, 2024, from https://www.theguardian.com/world/2019/jun/27/russia-protests-as-sisters-face-jail-for-killing-abusive-father

The Independent. (March 7, 2019). *A socially acceptable form of murder: honour killings in Russia's North Caucasus* Retrieved May 19, 2024, from https://www.independent.co.uk/news/world/europe/a-sociallyacceptable-form-of-murder-honour-killings-in-russias-north-caucasus-a8812576.html

The Law Commission of India, Prevention of Interference with the Freedom of Matrimonial Alliances. (2012, August). (in the name of Honour and Tradition): A Suggested Legal Framework, Report No. 242, Government of India.

The Moscow Times. (Dec. 7, 2018). 39*People Murdered in Honor Killings in Russia's North Caucasus, Dutch NGO Reports.* Retrieved May 19, 2024, from https://www.themoscowtimes.com/2018/12/07/39-people-murdered-honor-killings-russias-north-caucasus-dutch-ngo-reports-a63748

The Oxford Dictionary of Law Enforcement. (2007). *Honour Killing.* Oxford University Press.

The Rajasthan Prohibition of Interference with the Freedom of Matrimonial Alliances in the Name of Honour and Tradition Bill of 2019

The State v. Muhammad Siddique & Another, (2011). Islamabad High Court, Islamabad, Capital Sentence Reference No. 02-T of 2011.

Thrasher, J., & Handfield, T. (2017). Honor and Violence. *Human Nature (Hawthorne, N.Y.),* 29(4), 371–389. DOI: 10.1007/s12110-018-9324-4 PMID: 30251000

Times Of India Article on Honor killing in Haryana

Tomer, A. (n.d.). *Domestic Violence And Honour Based Killing, Int'l Multidisciplinary Res.* E-J. Indian Scholar.Co.

Tsinchenko, G. M., & Orlova, I. S. (2021). Prevention of Youth Deviations in Russia and Abroad. *Administrative Consulting,* 1(1), 97–105. DOI: 10.22394/1726-1139-2021-1-97-105

Tunick, M. (2004). Can culture excuse crime? Evaluating the inability thesis. Punishment & Society, 6(2), 201-217.

Tyagay, Ye. D. (2020). The Impact of International Legal Initiatives on Solving the Problem of Child Abuse in Russia. *Boundaries of Private Interests and Limits of Acceptable State Intervention*, 267–271. Advance online publication. DOI: 10.2991/assehr.k.200321.127

UNIFEM. (2007). *Fact and Figures on Harmful Traditional Practices*. UNIFEM Publication.

United Nations. (n.d.). E Economic and Social Council

Valentine, G., Jackson, L., & Mayblin, L. (2014). Ways of seeing: Sexism the forgotten prejudice? *Gender, Place and Culture*, 21(4), 401–414. DOI: 10.1080/0966369X.2014.913007

Van Eck, C. (2002). *Purified by blood: Honour killings amongst Turks in the Netherlands*. Amsterdam University Press.

van Eck, C. (2003). *Purified by Blood: Honour Killings amongst Turks in the Netherlands*. Amsterdam University Press.

van Eck, C. (2003a). *Purified by blood : honour killings amongst Turks in the Netherlands*. Amsterdam University Press.

Vaughan, D. (n.d.). *Mass Murder*. Retrieved from Britannica: https://www.britannica.com/topic/mass-murder

Verkoren, W., & van Leeuwen, M. (2013). Civil Society in Peacebuilding: Global Discourse, Local Reality. *International Peacekeeping*, 20(2), 159–172. DOI: 10.1080/13533312.2013.791560

Verot, M. P. (2023). *Une femme est victime de féminicide chaque jours en Turquie*. RadioFrance. Retrived from https://www.radiofrance.fr/franceinter/une-femme-est-victime-de-feminicide-chaque-jour-en-turquie-7721900

Versus, M. A. (1996). *The State PLD*.

Vesvikar, M., & Agarwal, M. (2022). Honour killing in India. *Perspectives in Social Work*, 31(1), 48–62.

Vilyamovna, N. (2016). *Vist natalya-vist@mail.ru*. Correspondence. https://creativecommons.org/licenses/by/4.0/

Vishwanath, J., Srinivas, &, & Palakonda, C. C. (2011). Patriarchal Ideology of Honour and Honour Crimes in India. *International Journal of Criminal Justice Sciences*, 6(2), 386–395.

Vishwanath, J., & Palakonda, S. C. (2011). Patriarchal ideology of honour and honour crimes in India. *International Journal of Criminal Justice Sciences*, 6(1).

Vitoshka, D. Y. (2010). The Modern Face of Honor Killing: Factors, Legal Issues, and Policy Recommendations.

Vitoshka, D. Y. (2010). The Modern Face of Honor Killing: Factors, Legal Issues, and Policy Recommendations. *Berkeley Undergraduate Journal*, 22(2). Advance online publication. DOI: 10.5070/B3222007673

Vriend v. Alberta, [1998] 1 S.C.R. 493

Walters, G. D. (2001). The Relationship between masculinity, femininity, and criminal thinking in male and female offenders. *Sex Roles*, 45(9), 677–689. DOI: 10.1023/A:1014819926761

Wasti, T. H. (2010). The Law on Honour Killing: A British Innovation in the Criminal Law of the Indian Subcontinent and its Subsequent Metamorphosis under Pakistan Penal Code. *South Asian Studies*, 25(2), 261–311.

Welchman, L., & Hossain, S. (2005). 'Honour', rights and wrongs. *"Honor": Crimes, Paradigms and Violence against. Women*, 1–21.

Welchman, L., & Hossain, S. (2005). Introduction: Honour, rights and wrongs. In Welchman, L., & Hossain, S. (Eds.), *Honour: Crimes, paradigms, and violence against women* (pp. xi–xiv). Zed Books. DOI: 10.5040/9781350220621.0006

What Does (and Does Not) Affect Crime in India? (n.d.).

Wikipedia Contributors. (2024). 2012 Delhi gang rape and murder. In *Wikipedia, The Free Encyclopedia*. Wikipedia, The Free Encyclopedia.

Wikipedia contributors. (2024). Manoj–Babli honour killing case. In *Wikipedia, The Free Encyclopedia*. Wikipedia, The Free Encyclopedia.

Women, U. N. (2019). *Exploring Masculinities: Men*. Women, and Gender Relations in the Middle East and North Africa.

Wynn, L. L. (2021). 7. "Honor Killing": On Anthropological Writing in an International Political Economy of Representations. *Love, Sex, and Desire in Modern Egypt*, 137–155. https://doi.org/DOI: 10.7560/317044-008/XML

Xavier, M. S. (2015). Honour Killings: A Global Concern. *PARIPEX - Indian Journal of Research, 4*(3).

Yadav, B. (2019). Khap Panchayats: Stealing Freedom? *Journal of Legal studies and Research*, Volume 2(Issue 2).

Yadav, R. S., Singh, R., Aggarwal, V., Semwal, M., Kumar Dy Director, R., Singh Associate Professor, V., Assistant Professor, V., Sharma Associate Professor, K. K., Assistant Professor, R., & Lal Dhanda Principal, R. (n.d.). *Editorial Board*.

Yurdakul, G., & Korteweg, A. C. (2013). Gender equality and immigrant integration: Honor killing and forced marriage debates in the Netherlands, Germany, and Britain. *Women's Studies International Forum*, 41, 204–214. DOI: 10.1016/j.wsif.2013.07.011

Yurdakul, G., & Korteweg, A. C. (2020). State responsibility and differential inclusion: Addressing honor-based violence in the netherlands and germany. *Social Politics*, 27(2), 187–211. DOI: 10.1093/sp/jxz004

Yurdakul, G., & Yükleyen, A. (2009). Islam, conflict, and integration: Turkish religious associations in Germany. *Turkish Studies*, 10(2), 217–231. DOI: 10.1080/14683840902864010

Yusupova, N. R. (2017). *Human Rights and Gender Violence in Russia*.

Zafar, F., & Ali, R. (2020). Understanding the Causes of Honor Killing: An Exploratory Study in South Punjab, Pakistan. In *Pakistan Journal of Social Sciences (PJSS)* (Vol. 40, Issue 2).

Zafar, F. (2020). Contribution of fiscal decentralization to economic growth: Evidence from Pakistan. [PJSS]. *Pakistan Journal of Social Sciences*, 40(2), 937–947.

Zakirova, V. (2005). War against the family: Domestic violence and human rights in Russia - A view from the bashkortostan republic. In *Current Sociology* (Vol. 53, Issue 1). https://doi.org/DOI: 10.1177/0011392105048289

Zawati, H. (2012). Hidden Deaths of Libyan Rape Survivors: Rape Casualties Should Be Considered Wounded Combatants Rather Than Mere Victims of Sexual Violence. SSRN *Products & Services*.

Zinck, P. (2019). Disobedient bodies: Gendered violence in South Asian and desi film. *South Asian Popular Culture*, 17(3), 269–282. DOI: 10.1080/14746689.2019.1668590

About the Contributors

Somesh Dhamjia A well-known name in the fraternity of Human Capital, Prof. (Dr.) Somesh Dhamija is associated with Institute of Legal Studies & Research, GLA University, Mathura, India in the capacity of Dean. He has a judicious blend of corporate exposure along with academic acclaim spanning over a period of more than three decades. Along with this, he has proven his mettle as an accomplished Trainer vis-à-vis various facets of Leadership. With a strong research profile, he has various authored and edited books, proceedings and journals. He attended International Leadership Program at Central European University, Budapest, Hungary sponsored by European Environmental Agency and Asia-Pacific Leadership Program at Tongji University, Shanghai, China, sponsored by the United Nations. He has been bestowed with "Asia Pacific Regional Champion 2020 Award for Teaching Excellence" by the Chartered Institute of Management Accountants, UK and "Exemplary Academic Leader of 2020 Award" by the Centre for Education Growth and Research (CEGR), New Delhi.

Tarun Pratap Yadav is Assistant Professor, Institute of Legal Studies and Research, GLA University, Mathura, India. He is Doctorate from CCS University, Meerut, India. He has an academic and industry experience of 10 Years. He had previously worked at Amity University, Noida, GGS Indraprastha University, Delhi etc. His area is specialization is Legal History, Constitutional Law & Business Law. He has publications /paper presentations/participations in many International and National Seminars. He is Life time member of Indian History Congress, U.P History Congress, Rajasthan History Congress, Income Tax Appellate Tribunal (ITAT), New Delhi etc. He is a die-hard fan of Real Madrid.

Jae Seung Lee is Assistant Professor in Department of Justice and Community Studies College of Liberal Arts & Applied Science, Miami University, USA. He completed his Ph.D from Department of Criminal Justice and Criminology, College of Criminal Justice, Sam Houstan State University. Huntsville, TX. He has many peer reviewed research papers and Manuscripts to his name. He has taught various courses like Introduction to Criminal Justice, Introduction to Policing, The Criminal Court, Correctional System and Practises, Perspectives in Crime, Criminal Justice Research Methods, Juvenile Justice etc.

Harshita Singh is the Assistant Professor of Law in Amity Law School, Amity University Noida(U.P). She is doctorate from Mewar University, Chittorgarh, India. She is an ardent academician and an editor at Journal of Law and Public Policy. Dr. Singh has published many books and contributed various research papers and chapters. She is a lifetime member of prestigious International Journals like Asian Resonance and Periodic Review. She has an assortment of paper presentation to her credit. Her areas of specialization include Constitutional Law, Labour Law, Women and Criminal Law.

Myunghoon Roh is an Assistant Professor in the Department of Criminal Justice and Criminology at Salve Regina University, Rhode Island, USA. He is Doctorate of Philosophy in Criminology and Justice Policy Northeastern University, Boston, Massachusetts, USA. He is comparative criminologist testing contemporary criminology theories on juvenile delinquency. Dr. Roh has published various research papers on several peer-reviewed journal, including Violence & Victims, BMC Public Health, etc. His areas of research specialization include Criminology Theory, Juvenile Delinquency, Comparative Research in Criminology, and Human Microbiome.

***

Aarya Arora is currently pursuing a combined Bachelor of Commerce and Bachelor of Laws (B. Com LLB) degree, currently in her second year of studies. Born and raised in India, she has demonstrated a strong academic commitment and passion for the fields of commerce and law. Through out her academic journey, Aarya Arora has shown exemplary dedication to both disciplines. She excels in studies, combining a deep understanding of commerce with a keen interest in legal principles and practices. Aarya Arora actively participates in moot courts, research paper writings, internships, legal awareness camps etc. Beyond academics, Aarya Arora is known for management skills, which includes coordinating and volunteering any event. Looking forward, Aarya Arora is driven by her aspirations to a Judicial Magistrate, leveraging her combined knowledge of commerce and law. She resides in India and continue to explore her academic and personal interests, balancing her studies with her diverse passions. Through her journey as a B. Com LLB student, Aarya Arora embodies good communication skills, analytical skills, legal aptitude making her a valued member of her academic community and poised for future success in the fields of commerce and law.

Aishna Arora is a legal scholar at GLA University, Mathura, India . She is passionate about justice and advocacy from an early age . Her keen interest in the legal world makes her stand apart . Proactive participation in law school activities like Moot courts and MUNs enhances her honing oral advocacy skills . She remains occupied by actively serving as a legal intern for advocates and law firms. Outside the realm of law she has great management skills with a creative mind

Siddhi Baranwal is a dedicated undergraduate student currently pursuing her Bachelor's degree in Business Administration and Bachelor of Laws (BALLB). Born with a passion for justice and a keen interest in the intricacies of law, Siddhi aspires to become a judge to uphold fairness and ensure justice in society. Beyond her academic pursuits, Siddhi is deeply involved in research, particularly focusing on areas that intersect law and social justice. Her commitment to understanding complex legal issues and contributing to scholarly discourse reflects her dedication to making a positive impact through the legal profession. In her leisure time, Siddhi finds solace in music, where she enjoys listening to a diverse range of genres that inspire and energize her. This passion for music not only provides a creative outlet but also enhances her ability to approach challenges with a balanced perspective.

Nishi Kant Bibhu is an assistant professor of Law at Bennett University (The Times Group). He has pursued PhD and M.Phil in Corporate Laws. He completed LL.M (corporate Laws) from NLU Jodhpur and B.A LL.B from CNLU, Patna. Having an academic experience of eight years, he has made a major impact on legal scholarship and practice. He is an associate member of the International Society for Development and Sustainability (ISDS) in Japan as well as member of the Centre for Competition Law & Economics (CCLE) in Bengaluru. Dr. Bibhu has been a resource person for various universities and organisations and has several publications on his name in esteemed national and international journals. He is also the guest editor for Journal of Capital Market & Securities Law & Journal of Corporate Governance and International Business Law STM Journals, A division of Consortium e Learning Network Pvt Ltd. Noida. His research areas include Competition Law, Investment & Securities Law, Mergers & acquisitions, Insolvency Laws and Company Law.

Tapan Kumar Chandola is a Professor and Dean in Law, at ICFAI University, Dehradun, India. He did his LL.D(DOCTOR OF LAWS), from Lucknow University, India. All his higher education got completed from University of Allahabad, India and MJP Rohilkhand University Bareilly, India. His experience in academics is of more than 19 years and industrial experience is of 06.2 years which constitutes a rich experience of 24 years in total. His publications of research papers and articles are in Scopus indexed journals, Thompson Reuters and many international and national reputed journals including book chapters which are more than fifty in numbers. He has to his credit, as an author, four books. He has successfully supervised many Ph.Ds' under his supervision and currently good number of PhD scholars are pursuing their Ph.D. under him. Regularly he gets invitations to participate as an external expert for the award of research degrees from Universities across pan- India. Also, to his credit is dissertations, approximately hundred in numbers, which got completed under his supervision of LL.M students. He has handled many research projects sponsored by Goverment of India,, ICPR, ICSSR etc. He is editor and advisor in many reputed national and international Journals of various National and State Universities and Publication Houses. His field of expertise is in Cyber laws, Corporate Laws, Administrative Laws, Trade Laws, Labour Laws, Taxation Laws. His primary research domain is in Cyber Laws, Corporate laws, IPR, Environmental laws, Trade laws and Constitutional Laws.

Aniruddh Atul Garg is a student of law at GLA University, Mathura, India. From a young age, he thirsted to learn something new that backs him to guide his life. Studying law has not only deepened his analytical skills but also deepened the understanding of justice. It made him explore various intricacies of the legal system. Apart from the academic pursuits, he has an immense interest in reading different non-fictional books which perpetually inspires him to extend his horizons and add fresh perspectives. He is also passionate about doing content creation via different social media platforms to share the ideas, creativity, and journey with new people. This helps him to connect with them for the improved networking skills. Exploring new places is also what fascinates him as it provides something new to learn for developing the personality. Writing various research papers, blogs, and chapters based on various branches of law broadens his legal knowledge and fulfills the interest in legal research.

Radhika Goswami: A Brief Biography Name: Radhika Goswami Education: Undergraduate in B.A LL.B (HONS) Career Aspiration: Aspiring Judge Interests: Research Radhika Goswami is an ambitious and dedicated undergraduate student pursuing a B.A LL.B (HONS) degree. With a passion for law and justice, Radhika has set her sights on becoming a judge in the future. Her academic journey is marked by a strong commitment to excellence and a keen interest in understanding the complexities of the legal system. Beyond her aspirations in the judiciary, Radhika is deeply drawn to the field of research. She finds immense satisfaction in exploring new ideas, analyzing legal precedents, and contributing to the development of knowledge within her field. Her interest in research not only enhances her academic pursuits but also equips her with the skills and insights necessary to excel in her future career as a judge.

Shreyanshi Goyal is student at Institute of Legal Studies and Research, GLA University, India. At GLA University, she is an active member and Discipline Vice-Head of the university's Expositio Club. She has contributed to various research publications, like her paper on the "Guarding The Children From Deadly Implication Of The Digital Era" published in IJEMH and Conference Abstract Publication in 'Souvenir' of Banaras Hindu University, Varanasi, India on the title 'Evolution Of Legal Education'. She aims to specialize further in Criminal Law and aspire to join the Indian Judicial Services.

Sahil Gupta Law Student Amity Law School, Noida Amity University Uttar Pradesh (India) He is a detailed scholar with distinguished research, drafting, organization and leadership skills along with the propensity to effectively prioritize simultaneous responsibilities within time limits. With regard to his practicum experience, he has interned under Supreme Court, High Court advocates, non-governmental organizations, corporate firms and public-private research blogs. He has got research papers published in International & National journals. Also, his chapters are published in various books. He is member of Tribal associated Forum to serve for different tribal groups across India. With regard to his experience in holding position of responsibilities, he has been class representative and has also served as student editor for various books, and journals. Add to this, he has been convener to various successful academic and extra-curricular events at his university.

Chunrye Kim, an associate professor in the Department of Sociology and Criminal Justice at Saint Joseph's University, specializes in studying various aspects of violence within intimate relationships, such as intimate partner violence, stalking, and violence against women. She also examines the policies related to these issues, particularly community-based intervention policies. Kim takes an interdisciplinary approach to her research agenda, conducting numerous studies that align with her research interests. Her work has been published in reputable peer-reviewed journals, including Trauma, Violence, and Abuse, Journal of Interpersonal Violence, Child Abuse and Neglect, and Journal of Family Violence. Additionally, she has a wide range of research interests that extend to contemporary social problems, such as mass shootings, abortion, and the social stigma surrounding victimization disclosure.

Nupur Kulshrestha is a post-graduate(LL.M.) with specialisation in Cyber & Data Privacy Law from GLA University, Mathura. She has Pursued B.A.LL.B(2015-2020) from Swami Vivekananda Subharti University, Meerut and she backed gold medal in the course. She has pursued her High School from Sacred Heart Convent Hr. Sec. School, Mathura in the year 2013 and Intermediate from Kanha Makhan Public School, Mathura in the year 2015. She has participated in various moot court competitions at both inter-college and intra-college level and further served as a mentor too in one of the inter moot court competition. She has attended various conferences/seminars/workshops at both national and international level and has organised various competitions at college level.

Pradeep Kumar is currently working as a Assistant Professor in Vivekananda College of Law, Aligarh & also working as a guest faculty in Non-Collegiate women's Education Board (NCWEB), Delhi University and School of Learning (SOL), Delhi University. As an experienced teacher he had participated in a number of seminars and workshops. His research interests are Dalit politics, Other Backward class politics and also minority issues. He had published several Articles / Research papers in various reputed National and internal Journals. As a freelance writer, he frequently contributes to various newspapers and magazines.

Sudhir Kumar is Professor and Head of School of Legal Studies, Babu Banarasi Das University Lucknow, India. He has academic experience of 17 years in the field of law, specializing in Constitutional Law and Criminal.In Administration, Dr. Kumar has extensive background in managing academic programs, curriculum development, and student affairs. Dr. Kumar has authored 35 research publications, including a significant publication in Scopus Indexed Journals. He has contributed to 5 book chapters, demonstrating expertise and contribution to legal scholarship. Dr. Kumar has successfully supervised 11 Ph.D students to completion, contributing to the advancement of legal education and research. He has a deep knowledge and experience in legal studies, with a focus on Legal Research Methodology, Law and Justice.

Nupur Kumari is working as an Assistant Professor in School of Law, Bennett University; Greater Noida. Having qualified UGC NET examination, she is currently pursuing PhD in law from Chanakya National Law University Patna. She has completed her LLM in International Human Rights Laws from the prestigious National Law School of India University, Bangalore. She has her specialization in the areas of Human Rights Laws and International Refugee Laws.

Shubham Malik is a distinguished legal professional specializing in Intellectual Property Rights. He completed his B.B.A. LL.B (Hons.) from Amity University, Noida, where he developed a robust foundation in legal principles and specialized in the intricacies of intellectual property law. Currently registered under the Bar Council of Delhi, Advocate Shubham Malik is practising law with Advocate Amit Sahni, where he has been instrumental in handling a diverse range of legal cases, particularly those involving intellectual property disputes. His dedication and expertise have earned him a reputable position within the legal community. In addition to his legal practice, Advocate Shubham Malik is actively engaged in the political arena. He serves as the Media Head of the Bharatiya Janata Yuva Morcha (BJYM) for Delhi. His role in BJYM underscores his commitment to public service and his ability to effectively communicate and represent the youth's perspective in political discourse. Advocate Shubham Malik's dual involvement in law and politics highlights his dynamic personality and his dedication to contributing positively to society. His career is marked by a blend of legal acumen and active civic engagement, positioning him as a notable figure in both fields.

Praveen Kumar Mall is working as Head of Department in Faculty of Juridical Science, Rama University, Kanpur. He is the author of book Hindu Law of Divorce. He has been awarded Doctorate Degree for his thesis in the area of "Critical Study of the concept of divorce under Hindu Law: A Socio-Legal Study from the Department of Law, University of Lucknow. Dr. Praveen has contributed immensely in formulation and introduction of B.A.LL.B., B.B.A.LL.B., B.Com. LL.B. and LL.M.. programmes of several Universities. Having long teaching and administrative experience, Dr. Praveen, besides contributing research articles in reputed law journals has also participated in several National and International conferences, seminars and workshops. He has also been very active in organizing Conference and Legal Literacy Camps, and has also adjudged various Moot Court Competitions. His areas of interest are Law of Contract, Family Law and Law of Criminal Procedure.

Abhijit Mishra is currently working as Assistant Professor in School of Law, Bennett University (The Times Group), Greater Noida, India. He has done his Masters and Ph.D. from Dr. Ram Manohar Lohiya, National Law University, Lucknow, India. He has co-authored one book and five research papers.

Madhulika Mishra is currently working as Assistant Professor of Law in Institute of Legal Studies and Research, GLA University, India She has done her Ph.D from Dr. Ram Manohar Lohiya National Law University, Lucknow, India and completed her Masters from Gujarat National Law Unuversity, Gandhinagar, India. She published more than eight research papers to her name and has contributed chapters in three books.

Garima Rajput is a dedicated and driven law student currently pursuing her Bachelor of Arts and Bachelor of Legislative Law (BA.LLB) degree at the prestigious GLA University in Mathura, India. She hails from Aligarh, Uttar Pradesh where she has completed her intermediate studies from Aligarh Muslim University, Aligarh. Her commitment to legal education extends beyond her personal pursuits. She has been an active member of the university's legal aid clinic. Her ambitions are driven by a desire to contribute to the ever-evolving landscape of law and justice. Her unwavering dedication, coupled with her intellect and compassionate nature, position her as a promising future legal professional poised to make a significant impact in her chosen field.

Anurag Sharma is currently working as a professor / principal in Vivekananda College of Law, Aligarh, India. He has experience of teaching law for more than 22 years and industry experience of 2 years at Delhi High Court. He has completed his LLM from Aligarh Muslim University, Aligarh, India and qualified UGC-NET in 2001. He had served lecturer in National Institute of Law, Faridabad (presently known as Institute of Law & Research) for nearly seven years and also served as professor in JIMS Greater Noida(affiliated to I.P. University, Delhi). He had been the examiner of various judicial exams like Punjab Judicial Services, Haryana Judicial Services Exams and also paper setter of Haryana Judicial Service. Apart from that he had been the examiner of Dr. B.R. Ambedkar University, Agra. He has published several articles in various reputed National and Internationals Journals.

Salini Sharma is a B.A. LL.B.(H.) student of Institute of Legal Studies and Research, GLA University, Mathura(U.P.), India. Her main area of interest is Human Rights Law and Criminal law. She has a keen interest in research writing and is an active speaker. She has also participated in various debate competitions, conferences, seminars and workshops at national level. She is a good orator and has excellent communication skills.

Mohmmad Shoaib is an undergraduate pursuing B.A LL.B (H) from GLA University. I want to go for higher studies abroad ChatGPT Mohammad Shoaib is currently an undergraduate student at GLA University, pursuing a B.A LL.B (Hons) degree. Born with a passion for law and justice, Shoaib has dedicated himself to academic excellence and personal growth throughout his educational journey. With a keen interest in international law and a desire to broaden his horizons, Shoaib aspires to pursue higher studies abroad. His ambition is fueled by a deep-seated commitment to understanding diverse legal systems and contributing positively to global legal frameworks. Outside of academics, Shoaib actively participates in extracurricular activities, enhancing his leadership skills and fostering a well-rounded personality. He believes in the power of education to transform societies and hopes to leverage his knowledge and skills gained abroad to make a meaningful impact in the field of law upon his return. As he continues his undergraduate studies, Shoaib remains focused on achieving academic milestones and preparing diligently for the challenges and opportunities that lie ahead in his pursuit of higher education abroad

Abhishek Kumar's expertise bridges academia and real-world application seamlessly. Dr. Kumar's extensive research publications serve as a testament to his dedication and depth of knowledge in the legal field. His unique blend of theoretical understanding and practical insights makes him a valuable asset in combating cyber threats and educating others about legal implications in the digital realm. His contributions to academia and beyond are invaluable in shaping the future of cyber law and security.

Indra Kumar Singh serves as an Assistant Professor and Program Coordinator at the Institute of Legal Studies & Research, GLA University, Mathura, U.P. He holds a Ph.D. in Law from Shri Ramswaroop Memorial University, Lucknow, focusing on the impact of biodiversity laws in Gorakhpur. Dr. Singh is a distinguished academic with qualifications including UGC-NET, M.Phil., LL.M., and LL.B. His professional journey spans multiple institutions, including Shri Ram Swaroop Memorial University and Dr. Ram Manohar Lohiya National Law University, where he held roles such as Research Assistant and Assistant Proctor. Dr. Singh has contributed extensively to legal academia, supervising Ph.D. and LL.M. students, and publishing numerous research papers and book chapters on diverse legal topics like intellectual property rights, cyber law, and humanitarian law. He has presented papers at various national and international conferences and organized significant seminars and workshops. Dr. Singh has also been a guest lecturer and resource person at several universities and served as an external examiner and paper setter. His extracurricular achievements include representing Uttar Pradesh in national baseball championships and leading the Lucknow University Softball team. With a passion for continual learning and development, Dr. Singh is committed to contributing to the field of legal education and research.

Narendra Singh is a dedicated student of law currently pursuing his B.A. LL.B degree at GLA University. Born with a passion for justice and a desire to make a positive impact in society, Narendra has seamlessly integrated his academic pursuits with his commitment to social work. As a student, Narendra excels academically, demonstrating a keen interest in understanding the intricacies of legal principles and their practical applications. His coursework at GLA University has equipped him with a solid foundation in law, preparing him to address complex legal challenges with competence and diligence. Beyond academics, Narendra is actively involved in social work, where his leadership qualities shine through. He serves as the President of the Legal Aid Committee, a role that reflects his deep-seated belief in providing legal assistance to those in need. Under his leadership, the committee has undertaken numerous initiatives aimed at promoting access to justice for marginalized communities and individuals facing socio-economic challenges. Narendra's passion for social justice extends beyond his university campus. He actively participates in community outreach programs, legal awareness campaigns, and pro-bono legal clinics, demonstrating his commitment to empowering individuals through legal education and advocacy. His efforts have not only enriched his own understanding of legal practice but have also made a tangible difference in the lives of many.

Pratibha Singh LL. B, LL.M Assistant Professor B.M.S. College of Law, Bengaluru, Karnataka, (India) She has completed her LL. B. from CCS University, Meerut and LL.M in IPR (Intellectual Property Rights) from RML National Law University, Lucknow. She has qualified UGC National Eligibility Test (NET) for Asst. Professor of Law. She is currently pursuing her Ph.D. from CMR University, Bengaluru on the topic "Implication of Intellectual Property Rights Regime on Agricultural Biodiversity: A study with reference to India". She has worked as Teaching Associate at RML National Law University, Lucknow, as Assistant Professor in Oxford Law College, Bengaluru and Bangalore Institute of Legal Studies, Bengaluru. Currently working as Assistant Professor in B.M.S. College of Law Bengaluru, Karnataka. She has presented a number of papers in State, National Seminars and published papers in various Journals. Her areas of interest include IPR, Family Law, Transfer of Property and Law of Torts.

Punya Singh is a fourth-year law student at the Institute of Legal Studies and Research, GLA University, Mathura, U.P., India. She is pursuing the course of B.Com.L.L.B(H) with a keen interest in the legal arena, spanning from criminal law and constitutional law to extracurricular activities including booting and research-related work. She has authored manuscripts in peer-reviewed books and always tries to strive hard with sheer dedication.

Shanu Singh is student at Institute of Legal Studies and Research, GLA University, India. At GLA University, He is Discipline Head in Expositio Club & also he is an active member of the university's Juris Club . He has contributed to various research publications, like Conference Abstract Publication in 'Souvenir' of Banaras Hindu University, Varanasi, India on the title 'Evolution Of Legal Education' and Also participated in Various MUNs and Won the Best Deligate Award at Amity University, Noida & High Commodation at GLA University, Mathura and ICFAI University, Dehradun. He aims to specialize further in Criminal Law and aspire to join the Indian Judicial Services.

Shweta Singh is a dedicated student at the Institute of Legal and Research Studies, GLA University, India, where she is pursuing a Bachelor of Commerce and Bachelor of Laws (BCom LLB) degree. With a keen interest in legal research, she is committed to exploring various aspects of law and contributing to the field through her studies and research endeavors.

Shelly Tomar is a dedicated law student currently pursuing a Bachelor of Arts and Bachelor of Laws (BALLB) with Honors from Amity University. Specializing in Business Law, she also harbors a keen interest in Criminal Law. Throughout her academic journey, Shelly has gained practical experience by working with various advocates, government institutions, and non-governmental organizations (NGOs). Her commitment to the legal field is further demonstrated by her role as a student editor for a law journal, where she contributes to the academic and professional discourse in law. Shelly's diverse experiences and dedication to both Business and Criminal Law make her a promising future legal professional.

Soumya Thankam Varghese is an Assistant Professor at the Jindal Institute of Behavioural Sciences (JIBS), O. P. Jindal Global University. With three years of dedicated experience in teaching and research, she brings a wealth of knowledge and passion to her work. Dr. Varghese specializes in neuropedagogy, academic performance, and disability studies, exploring innovative ways to enhance learning and support diverse student needs. Her commitment to advancing education and understanding in these fields makes her a valuable asset to the academic community.

Tanuj Vashistha is a student of B.A.LL.B (Hons) at institute of legal studies and research, GLA University, Mathura, INDIA. His Interests align with criminal, environmental, international and arbitration law. Mr. Vashistha is committed to contributing to the field of legal education and research.

Index

A

Adultery 4, 8, 9, 102, 118, 126, 162, 165, 173, 269, 286, 324, 349, 359, 378, 384
Arab society 9, 71, 72, 74, 75, 78, 82, 84, 87, 89, 90, 93, 94, 96, 182
assault 5, 8, 11, 79, 97, 104, 109, 131, 164, 173, 182, 186, 231, 244, 254, 262, 267, 271, 290, 292, 324, 325, 328, 332
Autonomy 23, 24, 46, 52, 55, 57, 85, 88, 114, 141, 142, 144, 149, 152, 183, 190, 194, 200, 203, 210, 211, 216, 223, 242, 263, 272, 281, 303, 308, 311, 316, 323, 339, 342, 365, 371, 408

B

Bedouin 72, 74, 82, 83, 84, 85, 91, 416

C

Caste System 16, 24, 303, 304, 305, 307, 308, 309, 321, 351, 389, 403
CEDAW 268, 306
Civil Society Organizations 64, 150, 153, 206, 210, 292, 293, 298, 317, 400, 401
Comparative Analysis 179, 205, 217, 218, 232, 236, 248, 261, 273, 298, 300, 301, 302, 305, 374, 375, 424
confront of advancement 425, 426
Critical Analysis 135, 140, 181, 182, 276, 280
Cultural attitudes 56, 81, 88, 89, 160, 243, 389
Cultural Norms 7, 26, 38, 39, 43, 55, 56, 57, 61, 62, 64, 65, 66, 87, 90, 112, 113, 114, 115, 116, 117, 121, 124, 125, 128, 135, 138, 145, 149, 158, 160, 163, 175, 185, 197, 198, 202, 203, 211, 212, 216, 240, 241, 242, 247, 279, 281, 297, 298, 301, 302, 303, 304, 305, 306, 311, 314, 315, 321, 322, 323, 328, 339, 362, 366, 390, 391, 400, 401, 402, 403, 404, 405, 406, 407, 409, 414, 420, 424, 430, 432, 433, 435
Cultural Practices 4, 11, 13, 54, 61, 85, 114, 117, 130, 139, 140, 147, 148, 152, 217, 220, 221, 232, 235, 281, 282, 286, 314, 315, 321
cultural ramifications 337
cultural sensitivity 255, 272, 306, 315, 316, 400, 409, 413, 435, 436

D

Dishonor 1, 8, 9, 10, 13, 57, 61, 127, 134, 172, 184, 187, 197, 211, 220, 226, 227, 228, 265, 272, 298, 303, 306, 307, 310, 323, 324, 339, 360, 362, 384, 400
domestic abuse 10, 19, 105, 132, 173, 188, 192, 229, 262, 325, 361
Dutch-Moroccan 307
Dutch-Turkish 307

E

Educational Activities 287
Equality 11, 14, 26, 41, 42, 44, 46, 51, 55, 56, 57, 59, 60, 62, 63, 64, 66, 75, 76, 85, 86, 90, 96, 129, 145, 149, 150, 151, 152, 153, 166, 176, 187, 191, 192, 200, 201, 203, 204, 206, 208, 210, 212, 213, 215, 219, 220, 221, 228, 233, 243, 250, 255, 263, 264, 272, 276, 277, 280, 282, 287, 289, 298, 303, 304, 308, 309, 310, 311, 317, 318, 343, 360, 361, 362, 363, 364, 365, 366, 367, 369, 370, 371, 390, 400, 407, 408, 409, 410, 411, 412, 413, 414, 420, 428, 432, 434, 435, 436, 437

F

Family Dynamics 287, 298, 317, 371
Family Honor 2, 3, 4, 5, 6, 10, 12, 14, 42, 46, 48, 51, 52, 53, 55, 57, 60, 61, 63, 64, 66, 72, 73, 74, 79, 80, 82, 87, 91, 93, 94, 101, 104, 107, 109, 114, 116,

117, 118, 134, 138, 141, 146, 152, 159, 160, 166, 182, 186, 187, 194, 197, 199, 200, 202, 203, 204, 205, 211, 212, 218, 220, 240, 241, 242, 243, 244, 245, 247, 251, 253, 263, 264, 265, 269, 271, 279, 281, 286, 303, 304, 314, 322, 337, 342, 346, 347, 363, 365, 366, 369, 377, 385, 391, 401, 402, 407, 408, 416, 422, 423

Female chastity 119, 181, 197, 199, 245, 253

Feminism 41, 42, 43, 44, 45, 46, 47, 50, 51, 58, 59, 60, 62, 63, 66, 67, 68, 69, 71, 75, 77, 79, 139, 140, 154, 192

Forced Marriages 8, 55, 117, 141, 198, 204, 205, 232, 243, 263, 265, 271, 280, 281, 282, 284

G

Gender-based violence 57, 59, 78, 111, 114, 135, 139, 140, 141, 143, 148, 149, 152, 159, 174, 176, 178, 187, 199, 214, 216, 218, 240, 241, 243, 298, 301, 302, 304, 311, 317, 321, 363, 364, 365, 366, 367, 369, 370, 371, 372, 391, 395, 411, 413, 415, 436

Gender Discrimination 41, 42, 51, 55, 175, 217, 221, 249, 280, 282, 309

Gender Equality 26, 42, 44, 51, 55, 56, 57, 59, 60, 62, 63, 66, 76, 85, 86, 96, 145, 150, 151, 152, 153, 166, 176, 187, 191, 200, 201, 203, 204, 206, 208, 210, 212, 213, 215, 219, 220, 233, 243, 250, 255, 277, 282, 287, 298, 303, 304, 308, 309, 310, 311, 317, 318, 343, 360, 361, 362, 363, 364, 365, 366, 367, 369, 370, 371, 400, 407, 408, 409, 410, 411, 412, 413, 420, 428, 432, 436, 437

gender stereotypes 86, 101, 428

Gender Violence 113, 159, 374, 424, 425, 435, 439

H

hate crime 24, 30

Honor-Based Abused 402

honor killings 1, 2, 3, 4, 5, 6, 7, 8, 9, 10, 11, 12, 13, 14, 16, 17, 18, 21, 30, 32, 37, 38, 41, 42, 43, 44, 45, 46, 47, 48, 49, 51, 52, 53, 54, 55, 56, 57, 58, 61, 62, 63, 64, 65, 66, 67, 71, 72, 73, 75, 81, 84, 86, 91, 92, 93, 94, 95, 96, 98, 101, 106, 107, 108, 109, 110, 111, 112, 113, 114, 115, 116, 117, 118, 119, 120, 121, 122, 123, 124, 125, 126, 127, 128, 129, 130, 131, 133, 134, 135, 137, 138, 139, 140, 141, 142, 143, 144, 145, 146, 147, 148, 149, 150, 151, 152, 153, 154, 155, 157, 158, 159, 160, 161, 162, 163, 165, 168, 173, 175, 176, 178, 179, 181, 182, 183, 184, 185, 186, 187, 188, 194, 204, 205, 214, 215, 216, 217, 218, 219, 220, 221, 222, 226, 229, 230, 231, 232, 233, 234, 235, 237, 253, 261, 262, 263, 265, 266, 267, 268, 269, 270, 271, 272, 273, 274, 275, 276, 277, 279, 280, 281, 282, 283, 285, 286, 287, 288, 291, 292, 293, 297, 298, 299, 300, 301, 302, 303, 304, 305, 306, 307, 310, 311, 313, 314, 315, 316, 317, 319, 320, 321, 322, 323, 324, 325, 326, 327, 328, 329, 333, 335, 337, 338, 339, 340, 341, 342, 343, 344, 345, 346, 347, 348, 350, 351, 354, 356, 360, 361, 362, 363, 364, 365, 366, 367, 368, 369, 370, 371, 372, 375, 378, 383, 384, 389, 390, 391, 394, 395, 396, 399, 400, 401, 402, 403, 404, 405, 406, 407, 408, 409, 410, 411, 412, 413, 414, 415, 416, 417, 419, 420, 421, 422, 423, 424, 425, 426, 427, 428, 429, 430, 431, 432, 433, 435, 436, 438, 439

Horrible Offence 403

Human Rights 2, 7, 8, 17, 26, 27, 29, 39, 43, 45, 46, 47, 49, 55, 56, 57, 61, 62, 63, 64, 65, 66, 90, 94, 98, 104, 105, 106, 111, 112, 113, 115, 118, 119, 133, 134, 135, 138, 139, 140, 141, 143, 144, 145, 149, 150, 151, 152,

155, 158, 159, 160, 175, 176, 178, 179, 181, 182, 188, 189, 190, 194, 199, 200, 201, 203, 204, 206, 207, 210, 211, 212, 213, 214, 229, 232, 240, 241, 242, 243, 244, 250, 254, 255, 258, 264, 268, 274, 275, 276, 280, 281, 282, 287, 288, 291, 292, 302, 304, 306, 310, 311, 312, 313, 315, 316, 324, 327, 338, 339, 340, 341, 342, 343, 350, 351, 358, 361, 369, 371, 374, 377, 391, 392, 393, 396, 403, 404, 409, 411, 413, 415, 420, 421, 422, 424, 425, 427, 430, 431, 432, 433, 436, 438, 439

I

Immigrant communities 37, 39, 49, 65, 215, 216, 217, 218, 219, 220, 221, 229, 230, 231, 233, 243, 280, 282, 284, 291, 298, 299, 301, 303, 304, 305, 307, 311, 314, 315, 317, 433
Immigrant Integration 277, 282, 288, 318, 433
Immigrants 194, 269, 273, 282, 284, 289, 290, 291, 293, 298, 299, 402, 405, 406, 414, 433
Integrity 113, 114, 137, 243, 265, 269
Intersection of Culture and Religion 359, 361

K

Karo-Kari 109, 117, 124, 195
khap panchayat 16, 33, 68, 321, 339, 350, 353, 354, 355, 356

L

Legal Reforms 26, 27, 37, 40, 41, 42, 49, 56, 57, 61, 63, 66, 77, 78, 85, 89, 90, 112, 133, 134, 150, 152, 153, 159, 175, 176, 178, 199, 201, 204, 206, 207, 209, 210, 212, 213, 304, 305, 306, 368, 369, 370, 371, 372, 409, 412, 421, 422, 423, 424, 432, 433, 435, 436
Legal System 7, 27, 88, 105, 130, 137, 142, 143, 149, 150, 152, 159, 164, 166, 188, 190, 192, 198, 199, 212, 267, 280, 299, 303, 310, 314, 317, 326, 356, 369, 422

M

Marital Life 361, 403
masculine abuses 341

O

Offence Against Women 361

P

Patriarchal norms 41, 42, 48, 55, 57, 58, 66, 139, 147, 149, 151, 152, 159, 200, 202, 210, 211, 249, 255, 261, 262, 263, 267, 272, 273, 282, 283, 299, 304, 305, 340, 343, 350, 360, 361, 363, 364, 365, 366, 367, 368, 369, 370, 371, 372, 400, 408
Patriarchal Society 94, 99, 100, 101, 104, 182, 184, 185, 263, 310, 392, 403
Patriarchal values 87, 115, 116, 152, 225, 249, 250, 313, 314, 323, 406, 422

R

Religious Beliefs 15, 40, 48, 57, 129, 145, 149, 242, 253, 316, 322, 360, 361, 400, 402, 404, 405, 407
Reporting Incidents 150, 288, 433

S

Safe Havens 175, 288, 316
sexual orientation 45, 46, 47, 60, 73, 79, 186, 210, 232, 235, 426, 427
Shakti vahini 300, 304, 312, 313, 338, 339, 348, 349, 355, 358
Sheikhs 71, 72, 83, 84
social media 3, 27, 37, 40, 41, 42, 49, 50, 55, 56, 58, 65, 68, 69, 72, 86, 98, 104, 116, 125, 142, 158, 161, 189, 200, 203, 207, 208, 209, 210, 257, 368, 379,

381, 383, 389, 391, 394, 424, 433, 434
Social Prejudice 28, 399, 400, 401, 402, 404, 405
Social stigma 31, 159, 221, 222, 338, 343
Societal Factors 14, 310, 361, 369, 370, 371, 372, 373, 399, 402, 405, 406, 407, 426, 430
State Responsibility 282, 288, 289, 290, 292, 293, 318
Stigma 4, 6, 11, 31, 90, 101, 150, 159, 187, 198, 199, 211, 221, 222, 244, 250, 311, 312, 317, 322, 338, 343

T

Taboo 11, 72, 78, 103, 244, 298

V

Victim 3, 5, 6, 7, 8, 10, 11, 12, 13, 14, 16, 17, 20, 40, 73, 78, 79, 82, 90, 93, 96, 100, 101, 104, 107, 117, 121, 123, 141, 142, 144, 145, 150, 164, 165, 166, 168, 169, 170, 171, 172, 173, 174, 175, 176, 184, 189, 216, 220, 221, 226, 227, 228, 230, 231, 242, 244, 246, 263, 267, 285, 291, 293, 303, 307, 310, 313, 356, 368, 377, 380, 393, 402, 405, 406, 407, 424, 434
Victim blaming 90, 407
violence 3, 4, 5, 6, 7, 8, 9, 12, 15, 19, 20, 21, 24, 26, 27, 37, 39, 40, 42, 43, 45, 46, 48, 49, 51, 52, 55, 56, 57, 58, 59, 61, 62, 65, 66, 67, 68, 69, 71, 72, 74, 78, 80, 81, 84, 85, 86, 89, 91, 93, 94, 95, 96, 97, 101, 104, 105, 108, 109, 110, 111, 112, 113, 114, 115, 116, 117, 119, 120, 121, 122, 124, 130, 131, 133, 134, 135, 137, 138, 139, 140, 141, 142, 143, 145, 146, 148, 149, 150, 151, 152, 153, 154, 158, 159, 160, 161, 163, 165, 173, 174, 175, 176, 178, 179, 181, 182, 183, 184, 185, 187, 188, 189, 192, 194, 198, 199, 200, 201, 203, 204, 205, 206, 207, 208, 209, 210, 211, 212, 213, 214, 215, 216, 217, 218, 219, 220, 221, 222, 226, 229, 230, 232, 233, 234, 236, 237, 239, 240, 241, 242, 243, 244, 245, 246, 247, 248, 249, 250, 251, 252, 254, 255, 256, 257, 258, 259, 262, 263, 264, 266, 269, 271, 273, 274, 275, 276, 279, 280, 281, 282, 283, 284, 286, 288, 289, 290, 292, 293, 295, 297, 298, 299, 300, 301, 302, 303, 304, 306, 307, 310, 311, 312, 313, 314, 315, 316, 317, 318, 321, 322, 323, 325, 332, 335, 336, 338, 339, 340, 341, 354, 355, 360, 361, 362, 363, 364, 365, 366, 367, 368, 369, 370, 371, 372, 373, 374, 375, 383, 385, 387, 388, 389, 390, 391, 392, 393, 394, 395, 396, 397, 399, 400, 401, 403, 404, 405, 406, 408, 409, 410, 411, 412, 413, 414, 415, 417, 420, 421, 422, 423, 424, 425, 426, 428, 429, 430, 432, 433, 434, 435, 436, 437, 438, 439

W

WHO 97, 185, 268
Women Rights 52
women's honor 271, 272, 367, 368